Sacred Realism

For Carol
Con un fuerte abrazo)
Noël

NOËL VALIS

Sacred Realism

RELIGION AND THE IMAGINATION
IN MODERN SPANISH
NARRATIVE

Yale University Press
New Haven &
London

Published with assistance from the foundation established in memory of
Amasa Stone Mather of the Class of 1907, Yale College.

Set in Sabon type by Keystone Typesetting, Inc.
Printed in the United States of America by Sheridan Books, Ann Arbor, Michigan.

Library of Congress Cataloging-in-Publication Data
Valis, Noël Maureen, 1945–
   Sacred realism : religion and the imagination in modern Spanish narrative /
Noël Valis.
      p. cm.
   Includes bibliographical references and index.
   ISBN 978-0-300-15234-0 (alk. paper)
      1. Spanish fiction—History and criticism. 2. Religion in literature. 3. Faith in
literature. 4. Realism in literature. 5. Religion and literature—Spain—History.
I. Title.
   PQ6140.R4V35 2010
   863.009'3823—dc22
   2009033261

A catalogue record for this book is available from the British Library.

This paper meets therequirements of ANSI/NISO Z39.48–1992
(Permanence of Paper).

10 9 8 7 6 5 4 3 2 1

For my brother Greg, always there for me

Contents

Acknowledgments   ix

Introduction   1

1. The Relics of Faith   57

2. The Philanthropic Embrace   93

3. The Confessional Body   151

4. The Politics of Martyrdom   195

Epilogue   238

Notes   247

Bibliography   297

Index   341

Acknowledgments

My most grateful thanks go to Cal Walker and my family, Monroe Hafter, David Gies, René Prieto, Carol Maier, Susan Kirkpatrick, Gustavo Pérez Firmat, Rolena Adorno, Phillip Deacon, Wilda Anderson, Milad Doueihi, Sebastiaan Faber, Mary Vásquez, Enrique Serrano Asenjo, Joan Ramon Resina, Lisa Surwillo, Michael Predmore, Luis Fernández Cifuentes, José M. del Pino, Annabel Martín, Txetxu Aguado, Paula Sprague, Virginia Santos-Rivero, Janet Pérez, Genaro Pérez, John Beusterien, Carmen Pereira-Muro, Gridley McKim-Smith, Israel Rolón Barada, Curt Wasson, Evelyn Scaramella, Larry Kenney, and, especially, Roberto González Echevarría. Some of you helped me to understand more clearly my project in both its earlier and later phases; some of you helped me locate or identify difficult-to-find sources or information; and then there are those who have just been there for me, in tough times.

This book benefited greatly from the generous fellowship support awarded me by the John Simon Guggenheim Foundation and the National Endowment for the Humanities and from the steady encouragement of Yale University and the Department of Spanish and Portuguese. I also gained much from the spirited discussions with colleagues at Stanford University, Dartmouth College, Harvard University, Reed College, the University of Oregon, Texas Tech University, and Bryn Mawr College, where parts of this book were first given as talks; and from thoughtful exchanges with students in classes at Johns Hopkins University and Yale University, as we worked our way through several of the texts studied here.

Part of chapter 4, now revised and much expanded, first appeared in my article "Aspects of an Improper Birth: Clarín's *La Regenta*," in *New Hispanisms: Literature, Culture, Theory,* ed. Mark Millington and Paul Julian Smith (Ottawa: Dovehouse, 1994).

Introduction

A few years before the novelist Leopoldo Alas (Clarín) wrote his realist masterpiece *La Regenta* (The judge's wife) (1884–85), he talked about the pain and loss he felt after his childhood faith was shaken by liberal conviction:

> Of myself I can say to you that while I believed in God, simply because, because *something ineffable* flowed through my heart, I was religious, sincere . . . but intermittent. Then came those hours of [spiritual] dryness of which a mystic saint speaks in which neither prayer nor faith is enough to make water spring from a rock . . . if I fixed upon as the substance of [my] vertigo the idea of God, the torment was horrible. Is there a God? Or isn't there? I asked myself, and as my heart in such agony said nothing to me, and *the proofs of the existence of God* are commonplaces, *topics* of logic . . . [of] a barren intellectualism, there was no way to escape that arid, sterile pain.[1]

Alas's lived sense of inner vertigo, his radical doubt, is symptomatic of a larger religious crisis that shaped how modern life in the nineteenth century was experienced in Spain and throughout much of Western culture. His anguish was not expressed simply as something personal but extended outward in his writings to include Restoration society as a deeply conflicted site of competing secular and spiritual authorities. Religious belief, viewed as a set of accepted external practices, was in reality unsettled and fractured from within, subject to the same questioning to which Alas submitted his heart and mind.

That Spanish Catholicism, once a rallying cry to national unity and identity, should be seen not as a solution but as a problem for the individual and for society is one of the defining features of emerging modernity in Spain since the late eighteenth century. Until the advent of the Second Republic in 1931, Spain was a confessional state. Much of its population were still practicing Roman Catholics, though, by the early twentieth century, signs of secularization, a de-Christianized working class, and growing anticlericalism had appeared. Indeed, during much of the period under study, from the late eighteenth to the mid-twentieth century, Spain was indisputably Catholic. But questions persistently arose as to how Catholic it really was, and what defined a Catholic. To what extent did Spaniards really believe and understand their faith in a divisive world in which politics often shaped religion? Could you be Catholic and liberal at the same time? Could you be Catholic and a believer in progress? Conversely, could you be Catholic and ignore social and economic distress? In short, could you be Catholic in the modern world?

Stating the problem this way implies that religion and modernity are fundamentally incompatible. This position, which typically sees religion as a pre-modern vestige destined to wither away under the modern state, is not one I share. While the enormous pressures of modern worldly life undoubtedly put faith to the test, I expect most believers would say that it has always been hard to practice one's faith, no matter the times. In a sermon delivered while Britain was at war, a sermon that never fails to move me, a lapsed Catholic, the Anglican C. S. Lewis spoke of "the weight of glory," by which he was referring to the Christian aspiration to be loved by God, in 2 Corinthians 4:17. He saw that desire as an ache, a longing to be let in, for "the door on which we have been knocking all our lives [to] open at last" and thence to glory as luminosity. In a word, Lewis understood such longing as universal, as a need that no measure of modern civilization could destroy, but also as something intrinsically difficult to experience in a world that is pure estrangement: "The sense that in this universe we are treated as strangers, the longing to be acknowledged, to meet with some response, to bridge some chasm that yawns between us and reality, is part of our inconsolable secret. . . . We can be left utterly and absolutely *outside*—repelled, exiled, estranged, finally and unspeakably ignored. On the other hand, we can be called in, welcomed, received, acknowledged. We walk every day on the razor edge between these two incredible possibilities."[2]

Clarín expressed the same condition metaphorically as one of orphanhood in *La Regenta*. Despite the richly detailed social and religious network that his protagonist Ana Ozores inhabits, she is fundamentally estranged. In the end, she is literally and symbolically left alone, "utterly and absolutely *outside*" everything that matters to her, most especially her religion. Alas's contemporary Benito Pérez Galdós, on the other hand, attaches his characters to the social fabric of their lives in *Fortunata y Jacinta*. Moreover, he makes that attachment an act of communion comparable to a kind of Eucharistic narrative, which is precisely the conclusion Lewis is leading us toward. He asks his listeners to think of their neighbors' weight of glory, too, for "next to the Blessed Sacrament itself, your neighbour is the holiest object presented to your senses." "There are no *ordinary* people," he says, a statement to which a novelist like Galdós could easily subscribe. In a pared-down, nontheological argument, Emmanuel Levinas draws a similar conclusion: that "being-for-the-other" or "responsibility for the neighbor" who is a stranger is holiness.[3]

In juxtaposing moderns like Lewis and Levinas — not to mention Galdós and Clarín — we see that there is something basic that pertains to all of them: the enduring religious underpinnings of the ties of sociality and hence the moral sense that is attached to being in the world with others. The realist novel has always understood this. *Don Quijote*, the first modern novel, underscores that neighborliness through the fumbling but well-intentioned efforts of a Christian knight determined to reinvent and better not only himself but the world as well. This task, created of human frailty and optimism, is "a very humble, Christian position, and Cervantes was a profoundly Christian writer."[4] Cervantes's irony necessarily tempers any divine workings in his fiction but does not allow us to dismiss the ethical foundation upon which it is built.

[margin note: Unamuno would argue with this, in Mi confesion pp. 43-44]

Nineteenth-century realist novels are unquestionably the children of Cervantes. But the world had changed, and so had novel writing. What had not changed was the ground on which the novel rested: the uniquely social worlds in which human beings either made room for each other or did not. The relation between self and community, the very understanding of community, continued to drive fiction. Most important, that overriding social concern, which secularizes the novel form — indeed makes it the premier artistic expression of the secular — possesses an inner structure which is inherently ethical. First, such concern posits the necessary connectedness and mutual care of humankind (even, or especially, when it is lacking) and, second, it imagines that community into fictional existence, by believing and making us as readers believe in it. In speaking about how the Judeo-Christian God is present in scriptures, Elaine Scarry maintains that "belief is the act of imagining. It is what the act of imagining is called when the object created is credited with more reality (and all that is entailed in greater 'realness,' more power, more authority) than oneself."[5] This theory, which goes back to Ludwig Feuerbach and others in seeing God as an expression of the human imagination, is not, in the strict sense, a theory of the novel. It does permit us, however, to see that there is a relation between religious belief and other kinds of belief, or perhaps even a common source for them, that encourages a quasi-religious belief in the fictional creation of alternative worlds. When novelists convince us through the skillful persuasiveness of words that places like Yonville or Vetusta or Middlemarch exist in our minds, is it simply the willing suspension of disbelief? or does some other thing come into play, a willingness to believe, to activate the imagination by casting it into an unreal realm that now seems real?

Kristeva's "need"?

No doubt belief in God and belief in imaginary worlds are two different things, especially for the believer for whom God is real and novels are not (at least not in the same sense). We do not, after all, really believe in fictional worlds the way one might believe in the divinity. Rather, we believe that they *can* exist and that they have something true to say to us about the way we live now (or have lived, which is actualized through reading). It is helpful here to recall what Marcus Borg has to say about such distinctions with regard to religious belief: "For most modern Christians, believing means believing a set of claims, a set of statements: believing that God exists. . . . But prior to about the year 1600, the verb 'believe' had a very different meaning within Christianity as well as in popular usage. It did not mean believing statements to be true; the object of the verb 'believe' was always a person, not a statement. This is the difference between *believing that* and *believing in.* To believe *in* a person is quite different from believing *that* a series of statements about the person are true. In premodern English, believing meant *believing in* and thus a relationship of trust, loyalty, and love. Most simply, to believe meant to belove."[6] While it is perilous to make claims of transcendence about fiction, there is no doubt that modern novels often dance right on the edge between *believing in* and *believing that.* Don Quixote believes in his chivalric quest and in the enchanted Dulcinea. This, he takes on faith. But when he believes that windmills are giants, that statement cannot be taken on faith and must be tested.

Fiducia (trust) and *fidelitas* (faithfulness) inform belief in.[7] Believing that a statement is true turns faith into something verifiable (or not), a change in mindset characteristic of the Enlightenment and of which Cervantes's book is a harbinger. These distinctions in understanding how religious belief is lived bear some resemblance, though no exact equivalence, to how fiction is experienced by characters and, to varying degrees, by readers. In this sense, they point to a particular relation that fiction has with reality, with the world, by straddling the gap between belief in and belief that.

In the modern novel after Cervantes, belief that has prevailed far more than belief in, reflecting the fault line of uncertainty that has only deepened since the Enlightenment. Confidence in religious belief has eroded, though, arguably, belief itself has not. The novel as an alternative secular site of community (or its absence) has provided an ideal imaginary space in which to reconstruct belief in something, while simultaneously acknowledging how belief itself can provoke more questions than answers, shaking the ground of its very existence. The novel seems to take sustenance from a mental structure that is at once uniquely moral and unstable.

What happens when belief systems in crisis and arising out of a particular historic circumstance commingle with the novel? What is the relation, then, between fiction and faith? This book examines how a reenvisioned Catholicism, alternately accepted and contested, in an unsettling period of both secularization and religious revival, plays a fundamental imaginative-moral role in key texts of modern Spanish narrative from the late eighteenth to the mid-twentieth century, creating a special form of sacred realism. Imaginative by shaping new narrative structures and perspectives; moral by prompting these texts to focus on ethical-religious issues of belief and social concern. It is commonplace to see Spain as the cradle of sixteenth- and seventeenth-century Counter-Reformation religiosity, in which Catholic and Spanish became synonymous. It is also commonplace to see Spanish Catholicism, once a vibrant imaginative-moral force in literature and the arts, as spent and largely dead in the nineteenth and twentieth centuries, as, in a word, a vestige, irrelevant to modernity and to modern artifacts like the novel. This view, which remains for the most part unexamined among literary critics, is not mine.

While historians have been busy investigating the complexities of modern Spanish Catholicism, the picture in literary studies during the past twenty years or so is rather different.[8] Up to the 1970s roughly, the theme of religion in modern Spanish literature was a stock item, gradually fading away as structuralist and poststructuralist approaches held sway. Beginning in the 1990s especially, under the somewhat belated and dismal impact of Michel Foucault, religion was perceived mostly as repressive, as an instrument of power.[9] As an institution the Church was undeniably powerful. By espousing this reductive view, however, critics have ignored in turn the question of faith and belief, the relation between religion and identity, or between religion and community, and above all the influence of religion on structures of the imagination in narrative.

In critiquing the limitations of Foucauldianism, as I do in later chapters, I mean to suggest that posthumanist and poststructuralist approaches like Foucauldianism do not appear well equipped to deal with issues like religion precisely because they see everything, including religion, as purely secular or secularized. How can such an approach even begin to understand the intricate question of belief or things of the spirit, if the relation and distinction between the profane and the sacred are swept away by the inability or refusal to recognize the religious domain? Belief constitutes the human as an entity of imaginative, fully sentient being, capable of feeling and conceiving the neighbor as oneself, which makes possible faith in ourselves. The modern novel is a privileged form for expressing that philanthropic embrace, particularly within the religiously infused, humanitarian sensibility that developed in the eighteenth century and flourished in the nineteenth. The Foucauldian view that philanthropy is little more than a middle-class policing tool to control the lower classes cannot account for the spiritual impulses from which eighteenth- and nineteenth-century philanthropy arose. Significantly, it cannot account for the kind of largehearted imagination that occupies the core of the philanthropic embrace and, by extension, the fictional exploration of the sacred ground upon which the social bond rests.

Novelists like Galdós and Clarín in the nineteenth century and Ramón Sender in the twentieth were capacious in their rendering of the human spirit, whether that spirit soared or plummeted to the depths of despair. Anything less mansioned in our reading of them will not do justice to these works. I hope that by reexamining the relation between belief and the novel readers will come away with a fuller understanding of this literature. We can do so only by getting past the academy's own contemporary prejudices, often unconsciously maintained, I suspect, against the significance of religious thought and feeling.

The field of modern Spanish literature is not alone in holding such views. I was struck by how often I ran across the same issue in different areas of study. In reading modernist novelists like Henry James and Marcel Proust, Pericles Lewis argues "for the continuing significance of institutionalized religion for a variety of agnostic or atheistic modern authors." Such an approach requires a shift in thinking, from regarding the novel as purely secular to something else, something in which "a sense of the sacred persists in . . . apparently godless novels." In other words, this shift must confront the dominant master narrative found in many disciplines: the theory of secularization, which has been so persuasive in explaining the decline of religion in modern society. Unfortunately it also suggests that "religion is not important in the modern world," a conclusion that tends to shut down inquiry prematurely.[10]

Typically, most current-day secular readings of literature and other cultural texts tend to bracket religious concerns off from nonreligious ones. Yet in the case of nineteenth-century British literature there was no insistence "on rigid boundaries between the sacred and secular [which] demarcate[s] religious space in a narrow and misleading manner." Religion wasn't just a theme or an isolated aspect of the social fabric; it permeated "every area of life, from family to politics, sport to work, church architecture to philanthropy."[11] The same can be said of Spain in that period.

Because religion was and continues to be so pervasive as both an institutional presence and an individual experience, it is not surprising that the sacred should persist in texts readers think of as uniquely secular. Indeed, the book as sacred has deep roots in the Judeo-Christian scriptural tradition, illustrated literally with the red lettering of titles and capitals in medieval manuscripts to recall the spilt blood of martyrs. The marvelous book of nature itself partook of the divine, as the theologian Luis de Granada was fond of pointing out. The task of the philologist, for whom "the text is always, in some way, sacred," went hand in hand with Christian humanism's passion for holy writings, bent on "releasing a power inherent in the texts they revered." This was the salvational power to transform individuals. The ultimately "ineffable and uncommunicable" nature of such writings has since carried over to nonscriptural texts in the guise of heightened aesthetic experience. Under the postrevolutionary influence of Enlightenment faith in humanity, the Romantic poet as seer assumed a new spiritual authority. Catholic writers like François-René de Chateaubriand defended sacred texts, creating an aesthetic of nature and a theology of sentiment. Chateaubriand's *Génie du christianisme* (1802) emerged out of revolutionary chaos and the debris of temples. Out of sacred ruins he aimed to rebuild the edifice of Christianity, his own version of a sacred text.[12]

Within literary studies, however, there is no consensus on how to understand the sacred (nor should there be), perhaps in part because "a chronicle of the relations between literature and religion, at least in the West, constitutes a history of spiritual displacements."[13] In this view, literature gradually becomes either a substitute for religion or a consolation for its absence. The Romantics and their offspring the Symbolists, among others, can be seen as having secularized religion or, alternatively, as having sacralized literature (see Paul Bénichou). What they didn't do was separate the two.

Under the sign of the Enlightenment, however, religion is not simply deracinated; it is frequently dismissed as primitive, irrational, prone to violence, conservative if not reactionary, and, in its aesthetic forms, inferior to profane art. Much of Voltaire's *Dictionnaire philosophique* (1764) is devoted not to philosophy, but to punching holes in religion, even as his dictionary entries reveal to what extent philosophy and political thought are bound to religious premises. The enduring pervasiveness of this negative view in the academy is hard to ignore, leaving aside legitimate criticism of such serious matters as church abuses, historical blindness, and the violence of fanaticism. The art historian Sally Promey finds similar reductive preconceptions in her field: "In twentieth-century scholarship, the marginalization of religion has been reinforced by prevalent modernist intellectual assumptions concerning religion's restriction of creative individuality, its responsibility for an inferior aesthetic or taste culture, and its presumed universal proclivity toward conservative, sectarian, and ideological obsessions."[14]

One need only read Debora Silverman's study of the sacred found in the modernist artists Vincent van Gogh and Paul Gauguin to understand how much people gain by reconsidering the force of religion in the realm of the imagination. Her reenvisioning of their work illuminates how differing religious traditions shaped both. For van Gogh it was the evangelical sanctification of labor and Christ's social activism; for Gauguin, the French Catholic revivalism represented by Bishop Félix-Antoine-Philibert Dupanloup, which led the painter to the "martyrdom in, and of, the psyche." The larger point Silverman makes is the "need to reemphasize the critical role of religion in the development of modernism, to bring religion back into the story of artists' mentalities and formations" rather than "to oversecularize the avant-garde."[15]

"To bring religion back into the story" is also my aim, which means taking religion seriously. It is impossible to speak of modernity and secularization and of secular forms like fiction without talking about religion. Even the terms we use lead back to a religious source. The medieval *saeculum* referred to a post-lapsarian time of sinfulness. "Secular" referred to clergy not living in a religious community or not bound by monastic vows; and "secularization" to "the expropriation of church property by the state." Likewise, the words "lay" and "laity" (French *laïque* and *laïcité*) applied originally to "the non-sacerdotal part of a religious confession." Being in and of the world invariably conjures up its sacred twin.[16]

In the case of modern Spain, the role of religion in society and culture has often been viewed solely as contentious, an obstacle standing in the road toward modernity. Similar tensions between church and state, secular and nonsecular thinking appeared in other parts of nineteenth-century Europe (see Étienne Fouilloux). Otto von Bismarck's efforts to control Catholicism as a political force in Germany (*Kulturkampf*), the religious–lay struggle over schooling in Belgium, the clash between the Kingdom of Italy and the Papal States, and the anticlerical measures of the French Third Republic readily come to mind. Religious–secular conflict in Spain lasted well into the twentieth century, which resulted in the separation of Church and State and anticlerical legislation during the Second Republic (1931–36) and erupted in a bloodbath of priest killings in the first months of the civil war. Under the dictatorship of Francisco Franco, Catholicism was nationalized, eagerly embraced by adherents, and force-fed to the rest, effectively politicizing and thus secularizing religion through the abuse of power. Disaffection toward religion after Franco's death and in the transition to democracy should come as no surprise.

Indifference toward and dislike of religion can thus be found in current-day Spanish intellectual and academic circles, as in those of the United States, though the reasons for such attitudes lie in very different historical and cultural circumstances.[17] There is much need to reexamine religion from a more distanced and open perspective, to see it not simply as disabling but also as enabling, historically and imaginatively. Literary critics of modern Spanish literature, for example, have tended to view Spanish Catholicism and Catholic writers as a monolithic block of political conservatism and immobility, with the implicit understanding that religious thought and feeling in general reduce the possibilities of imaginative literature. The works of traditionalist-minded authors like Fernán Caballero and José María de Pereda are cited as models for a nostalgic, rural Catholicism. By contrast, those of politically liberal writers, such as Clarín and Galdós, are seen as either anticlerical or secular and tolerant.

The limitations of this view should be apparent: it allows little room for other, less restrictive, nonpolarizing considerations and fails to consider Catholicism as a living, historical thing. Implied is a split between the secular and the religious. A liberal writer is seen as progressive and secular, in a word, modern; a conservative is not. The defining difference is religion or, more bluntly, the politicization of religion. On the one hand, Catholic writers — Pereda, Father Luis Coloma, and Fernán Caballero — were undeniably conservative. Their writings, while still of much interest, have overall not withstood the passage of time, though one suspects any deficiencies lie less in the political and more in the aesthetic realm. But conversely, writers like Clarín, Galdós, and Sender were not at all irreligious or simply critical of religion and little else. Indeed, one could argue that a conservative streak runs through many liberal writers, in that they return repeatedly to a sacred ground of sociability and the possibility of individual redemption. In other words, the crudeness of this model does not allow for writers who were modern and liberal-minded to be drawn toward religious experience precisely because modernity and religion are largely seen as opposed to each other.[18]

The point is not to deny the historical clash between religion and secularizing modernity but to disclose what the oppositional model masks: the degree to which both are intertwined, the one embedded in the other, mutually defining one another in periods of change and crisis. Spanish Catholicism had developed historically through national and imperial design. As the empire weakened and at last vanished in the nineteenth century and as modest signs of modernity appeared, the role of faith needed to be redefined. Faith, in Spain as elsewhere, was and is a matter of individual conscience, but it had also been felt collectively as an affirmation of national identity. By the late eighteenth century faith and identity had begun to turn problematic. A singular note not much seen since the brief flowering of sixteenth-century Erasmianism and visible, for example, in José Cadalso's *Noches lúgubres* (Mournful nights) (written ca. 1774) is the experiencing of faith as an intimately lived crisis which affects not only an individual's understanding of self in society but the very form literature takes. Critics have assumed that changes and innovations in literary form since the late eighteenth century are signs of modernity in Spanish literature. Not considered, however, is the possibility that modernity may not be the sole fulcrum moving literature in new directions. In other words, modernity, so closely linked to secularization, might be expressed and understood in narrative through a crisis of faith, in which a struggle over belief in occupies the same space as belief that. These are not separate phenomena but interrelated in a society, culture, and literature still deeply permeated with religious feeling. As in nineteenth-century British literature, "there is a continual slippage between the sacred and the secular."[19] It is the intricate relation between faith, modernity, and the fashioning of modern Spanish narrative that has not been addressed.

Three historical periods in particular, along with the fiction produced in them, highlight how a religious view of things is part and parcel of the secularizing forces of modernity in Spain: the late eighteenth and early nineteenth centuries reaching into the 1840s; the Bourbon Restoration (1875–1902); and the Second Republic, followed by civil war (1936–39). I want to outline the narrative and historic arc of my study before I draw out more fully the concepts being discussed, the historical-religious backdrop, and the status of the Spanish novel during the period in question.

By the late eighteenth century, Enlightenment values had made some inroads into the intellectual minority's understanding of faith. Most of the population, however, remained religious and the institution of the Church strong if somewhat complacent.[20] A vaguely humanitarian desire to infuse more authentic, evangelical feeling into spiritual experience and religious practice began to develop. An increased beneficence and an emphasis on making the clergy more useful to society signaled change. After Napoleon's armies attacked Spain in 1808, a national legislative body, the Cortes, assembled in Cádiz (1810–12), marking the first modern liberal intrusion into the traditional autonomy of the Church. The Cortes instituted political and social changes such as the declaration of national sovereignty and the elimination of landed seigneurial rights. It also abolished the Inquisition, which brought greater freedom of thought while reconfirming Spain as a confessional state. An anticlerical press sprang up, goading the traditionalists to respond. Muzzled under Ferdinand VII, anticlericalism grew in words and actions during the triennium of liberal governance (1820–23). By the time the first Carlist War, a struggle of dynastic-religious character, broke out in 1833 a pattern had emerged, one that lasted well into the twentieth century: anticlericalism and clericalism were locked together in mutual provocation. In the late 1830s and 1840s, progressive democrats and early socialist utopian thinkers were appealing to a religiously inspired humanitarianism to remedy social ills. Mid-century also brought a Catholic Revival of devotional and charitable practices. A similar movement occurred in the 1870s and 1880s even as another Carlist war erupted, the relation between Church and State was being hotly debated in parliament, ultramontanists were equating liberalism to sin, and anticlericalism became entrenched.

The critical role of faith in society reached a bloody climax during the Spanish Civil War, when the religious question divided families and social classes politically but also exploded in violence with the killing of nearly seven thousand clergy. This event was one of the most horrific incidences of lethal anticlericalism in modern European history. The religious crisis in these three periods marks how conflictive the process of modernity was in Spanish society, which was increasingly defined by the greater visibility of class identities and demands in contrast to national and spiritual ones. What role did this continuing crisis play in creating the modern forms of fiction in Spain?

Late eighteenth-century works like Cadalso's *Noches lúgubres*, Pablo de Olavide's *El evangelio en triunfo* (The gospel triumphant), and Luis Gutiérrez's *Cornelia Bororquia o la víctima de la Inquisición* (Cornelia Bororquia, or the victim of the Inquisition) suggest that one of the pathways to modern Spanish narrative (though certainly not the only one) lay in a religiously inspired humanitarianism, a response to a changing historical context and worsening social-economic circumstances for the disadvantaged. In Cadalso's text, one of the most intriguing and interpretively resistant works of the period, the disconsolate, wellborn protagonist Tediato endeavors to exhume his beloved's dead body because he cannot accept the fact of her death. At the same time, he cannot believe in her resurrection. His inner crisis is expressed through tense dialogue form in this hybrid narrative. Even more significant is the way he imagines his beloved's dead body as a sacred relic, so that her body ends up incarnating vestiges of a traditional belief system. Ultimately, however, he reaches an impasse, in which neither Catholic belief nor the Enlightenment values of rational thought allow him to let go of the lost love-object. Instead, he redirects that desire into a humanitarian impulse intent on saving others, specifically the laboring poor symbolized in the character of the gravedigger Lorenzo. A similar humanitarian drive inspires Olavide and Gutiérrez. Their texts, like Cadalso's, attempt to resurrect or save, through means that are both secular and spiritual, those marginalized persons and social classes who are invisible, symbolically dead to society.

This religious-philanthropic gesture, still grounded in an Enlightenment faith in humanity, can be linked to the fictional worlds of nineteenth-century novels like Wenceslao Ayguals de Izco's *María, la hija de un jornalero* (María, the laborer's daughter) and Galdós's *Fortunata y Jacinta*. These texts underscore how deeply the social question is embedded in the religious question. Echoing the social romanticism made popular by Eugène Sue, George Sand, and Victor Hugo, *María*, published in 1845–46, prepared the ground for later realists by reimagining through the humanitarian lens of a privileged viewer or narrator the lower orders mired in urban poverty and social inequities. Setting his book in the midst of the first Carlist War, Ayguals, a republican democrat and fervent anti-Carlist, used the novel as a platform not simply to vent his hatred of the ultratraditionalist Carlists but also to propose a vision of community, evangelically conceived. This vision was to be a counter to what he considered the threatened loss of communitas under the Carlists. Fueled by the religion of politics in a period of crisis, *María* is also about the politics of religion.[21]

The novelist turned philanthropist, which Olavide intuited and Ayguals de Izco introduced into Spanish narrative, reaches its apex in Galdós's realist masterpiece *Fortunata y Jacinta* (1886–87), produced during the Restoration period. Unlike Cadalso's *Noches lúgubres*, Galdós's novel arises less from individual spiritual anguish than from a humanitarian embrace of his fictional world. The Catholic charity activist Guillermina Pacheco highlights both the positive and questionable aspects of redemptive realism; the vision of communitas presented here is already noticeable in the works of religiously inspired social reformers like Joseph-Marie de Gérando and Concepción Arenal. Guillermina's efforts reflect a burgeoning Catholic Revival based on renewed devotionalism and good works. This movement attempted, with varying degrees of success given its inadequate understanding of modern economic forces, to address the pressing social question of urban poverty and social injustice. The bonds of sociality are generated through a beautifully conceived Eucharistic narrative of communion welded to social-religious philanthropy. A secularized adaptation of Catholic philanthropy and communion provides the imaginative structure that can address both the internal and external worlds of Galdós's characters. This helps to explain how the working-class Fortunata is able to experience Guillermina's persona "inside [herself], as if she had swallowed her or taken her like a Communion wafer."[22] Likewise it also illuminates the ways in which Galdós endeavors to bridge the separation between the rich and the poor. By contrast with Ayguals, however, he harbors no illusions of the novel as a transcendent vehicle of social deliverance. The social world of *Fortunata y Jacinta* is deeply flawed, individual lives troubled, and redemption uncertain.

There is far less consolation in Alas's powerful novel *La Regenta*, written in the same period as Galdós's work. Often read as a narrative of adultery, the real driving force of *La Regenta* arises from a vision of the world as socially fractured, lacking communitas, and profoundly unredeemed. Like Ana Ozores (the titular Regenta), in whom a psychic split issues from an unfounded accusation of carnal sin during childhood, the social body of the fictional provincial city Vetusta has suffered a deep wound to its collective moral spirit. Fittingly, the principal imaginative structure followed is confessional, in which the ragged edges of hidden psychic and social realities are to be revealed under the aegis of the proper authority, whether priestly or narrative. The question of authority was of key importance to a liberal like Clarín. His worldview, on the one hand, conflicted with the authority of the Church and, on the other, pointed to the classic problem of nineteenth-century liberal Catholics: harmonizing freedom with authority.

Religion is divisive in *La Regenta* in two major ways. At the collective level, the institution of the Church is heavily politicized through ecclesiastical intrigue as the clergy jockey for position within the local hierarchy. Religion is also experienced differently according to social class, politics, and gender. Devotional habits are identified as a middle- and upper-class practice, while the working classes appear alienated from the Church. Politically liberal characters like Pompeyo Guimarán and Don Álvaro (the local Don Juan) are either atheist or religiously indifferent. Women attend Mass, make confession, and participate in pious and charitable activities more than men. At the psychic, emotional level, religion is alternately a consolation and a torment for Ana Ozores, as mystical impulses swerve between spiritual dryness and hysterical frenzy, intensifying the inner, guilt-ridden split of her persona.

By metaphorically linking the wound of original sin with the Regenta's suspect family origins, Clarín grounds the novel in a religious imagination, which is in turn socially driven. Because religion is presented as a problem rather than a solution in *La Regenta*, readers often see the novel as anticlerical. Not considered is the degree to which Alas's critique also makes a strong case in favor of religion as an emotional and imaginative structure fundamental to both individual and society. At the same time — and this goes to the heart of his critique — there is a clear lack of consensus as to what actually constitutes religion. Reflecting this difficulty, he once suggested "grafting liberal Spain onto Catholic Spain." This idea was a hybrid solution that neither in historical reality nor in a fictional universe appeared to be possible.[23]

The politicization of religion characteristic of nineteenth-century Spanish society and literature is another way of expressing a religious crisis that eventually exploded during the first months of the civil war in 1936. The religious imagination shapes the war writings of Republicans and Nationalists, or Francoists, alike. Franco supporters sacralized their cause, calling it a crusade and those who sacrificed themselves for it martyrs. Imagery of martyrdom and holy war also informed the vision of the other side. The six-volume series of novelized memoirs called *La revolución de los patibularios* (The gallows men revolution [1940]), by the popular journalist José María Carretero (El Caballero Audaz), is representative of the Francoist side. One volume is titled *Nosotros los mártires* (We martyrs) and another, *¡Arriba los espectros!* (Long live our ghosts!), illuminating the intertwined themes of martyred blood and resurrection that drive the narrative implacably forward through all six volumes. Indeed, Carretero apparently planned only five volumes but seemed unable to stop himself from writing the sixth, as though his fevered pen could not staunch all that blood. Like Ayguals de Izco's narrative, this one moves between the religion of politics and the politics of religion. Carretero's series blurs political and religious belief systems in the same way the Franco regime of National Catholicism successfully did for decades afterward.[24]

Martyrdom and resurrection also structure one of the great works to issue from the Republican side of the conflict: Sender's *Réquiem por un campesino español* (*Requiem for a Spanish Peasant*) (1953). The martyred peasant Paco dies for the Republic and is emotionally resurrected one year later through the guilty conscience (and veiled confession) of the priest Mosén Millán, who betrayed him to the *falangistas*, or fascists, and through the acolyte's popular ballad about Paco. The politics of martyrdom that shapes Sender's compact narrative stunningly demonstrates "the centrality of religion to popular consciousness and political action, the distinctive ways that religion provides ordinary people with resources for creative interpretations of and action in history," as Anna Peterson observes in another context. She was referring to the ways in which progressive Catholics breathed new life into the idea of martyrdom during the Salvadoran civil war of the late 1970s and 1980s. The murders of ordinary people by death squads were seen "as chapters in sacred history." They embodied an *imitatio Christi*, as a "victory over death only through death."[25] While Sender's narrative is necessarily a secular one, filled with irony, a religious imagination gives Paco's death its ultimate meaning, even as faith in humankind is put to the test.

In all these works, the experiencing of faith and the practice of religion as a lived crisis are deeply connected to the difficulties and problems of nascent modernity in the larger social body. This crisis is richly dramatized in texts by liberal and radical writers, hence my decision to center discussion on them (while including the extreme rightist Carretero) rather than on conservative writers like Pereda or Coloma whose faith is not in question. (This does not mean religious tension and the issue of modernity are absent from their works, a subject worthy of further study.) In Cadalso and Galdós a religious philanthropic drive both disguises and rechannels the spiritual, while attempting to reduce class distinctions and social misery. In Alas and Sender anguish and guilt have fractured faith, revealing how religious belief and identity had become a divisive issue. By contrast, in Carretero religious belief cracks violently in two under the weight of wartime politics and reasserts itself as an exclusive national identity. Reflecting a conflict-ridden past that will not go away, the narratives of Sender and Carretero are especially noteworthy as undying political and ideological wars of the dead, expressed through martyrdom and resurrection.

Deeply rooted in historical circumstances, all these novels suggest that the shape of fiction, especially realism, may depend less on generic conventions, though these certainly play a role, than on a response to a secularizing world. The presence of imaginative structures in the form of the Eucharist or communion, confession, martyrdom, and resurrection as a vehicle of realism reinforces the degree to which religion is wrapped up in, is an indissoluble part of, that secularizing world. In a word, religion is part of the modern. The religious lens through which the world is viewed in these novels makes modern reality not only meaningful but readable as something modern, in part because such imaginative structures are generally, if at times only implicitly, recognizable (a convention, in that sense) and in large part because they incarnate traces of the sacred. They imbue the profane with meanings that surpass or belie the presumed ordinariness of the world.

By bringing religion back into the story, my aim is both restorative and gently, if paradoxically, revisionist, in returning to a tradition, namely, religion, that critics have tended to ignore. Left out of the understanding of modern Spanish fiction is something so basic that its absence creates a gaping hole, making it difficult for critics to explain why these novels matter or why people should bother to read them. Novels that matter should make a difference to readers' lives — the best should set the faded heart to pounding and the dulled mind on fire. To recuperate the religious imagination is to probe more deeply into the sources of the creative mind and to restore the distinctive role faith plays in art. A fundamental question needs to be asked: how does the relation between diverse forms of belief figure in the writing and reading of modern narrative? There is no single explanation of what goes into the creation of a novel or into the development of a genre, and not every novel displays the features of those under study. This line of inquiry posits a strong link between religion as a crisis of modernity and the changing shape of the modern Spanish novel, a link between faith and realism. A fresh look at religion as an imaginative-moral force not only reimagines what these texts mean but firmly connects them with social and moral issues as fundamental and inescapable as belief itself.

One of the difficulties in discussing faith and realism together is what one means by such terms. I neither hope to nor wish to have the final word on concepts like religion, the sacred, the imagination, or realism, but it is worthwhile to situate them usefully, while retaining the idea of not severing the bonds between the secular and the sacred. James Thrower's book on the classical theories of religion classifies them as either religious or naturalistic. The first refers to religion as revelation, as experience, and as philosophy; the second, to religion as human construct, as primitive error, and as psychological or social construct.

Catholicism is an example of a revealed religion; that is, it is the result "of an act or a series of acts of divine revelation." There is a logical connection between revealed religion and religious experience, "for that which a tradition claims as a revelation was, at some point in time, some particular persons' . . . religious experience."[26] Religion as feeling has been expressed in multiple ways, notably through mystical states. That feeling was also embodied in the sacred or holy, which Rudolf Otto called the numinous. This is a category that is impossible to define but that is at once subjective and real, just as belief is equally nonrational and rational. The numinous is an ineffable *mysterium tremendum*, evoking dread and awe, especially in Catholicism's "singular power . . . [and its] forms of worship and sacramental symbolism."[27] Another type of theory turns religion into philosophy, especially during the Enlightenment period and afterward, in an attempt to align it with reason (Immanuel Kant's moral law) or with history (G. W. F. Hegel).

Naturalistic theories of religion have been around since at least the ancient Greeks and Romans. As a human construct, religion was seen to be useful in controlling morality and human behavior in general. Eighteenth-century thinkers embraced the notion as applicable to their social inferiors, while dismissing Judeo-Christian religion as infected by pagan superstition.[28] The nineteenth-century anthropologists Edward Tylor and James Frazer later popularized the closely related view of religion as primitive error.

Religion as a human invention took on new coloration, defining, for example, "the essence of Christianity" for Feuerbach in 1841: "Religion being identical with the distinctive characteristic of man, is then identical with self-consciousness — with the consciousness which man has of his nature." Friedrich Nietzsche saw Christianity as a harmful and imaginary product of weakness, doomed to disappear, though the impending loss seems to have given him little comfort. A godless universe was a plunging "infinite nothing," cold and black as night. His most heated statements appear in *The Antichrist* (1888): "At the bottom of Christianity is the rancor of the sick, instinct directed *against* the healthy, *against* health itself." For Sigmund Freud religion was a man-made illusion, a form of wish fulfillment that flies in the face of reality, its teachings "neurotic relics." Faithful to his positivist heritage, he rejected as unconvincing the attempt to justify belief as a practical fiction; and could not fathom how an intelligent person might "accept uncritically ... the absurdities [of] religious doctrines," a viewpoint often shared, if unstated, by the academy. (Freud's critique does not explain how intelligent persons like Dante, C. S. Lewis, Graham Greene, Georges Bernanos, and Jacques Maritain were also believers.) Like Karl Marx, he compared "the effect of religious consolation . . . to that of a narcotic." Marx argued in 1844 it was an oppressive illusion: "The abolition of religion, as the illusory happiness of the people, is the demand for their real happiness." "Man makes religion," he wrote, "religion does not make man." (This point is the bedrock for Christopher Hitchens and others.) And, in a functional though not materialist approach, Émile Durkheim conflated religion with worship of the clan: "If religion has given birth to all that is essential in society, it is because the idea of society is the soul of religion."[29]

The theories of religion that Thrower synthesizes, and from which among many others I have drawn these examples, demonstrate how little unanimity there is concerning the nature of religion. Seen from a larger perspective, however, he says, "the big divide . . . is between those who see religion as a genuine response to a transcendent 'Other' and those who do not and who seek, therefore, to explain religion as a wholly human construct." This divide bears some resemblance to the realism/antirealism debate in current philosophy of religion studies: "Religious realism, in brief, is the view that there is a transcendent divine reality independent of human thought."[30] Thus Feuerbach, who equated the essence of Christianity with the essence of humanity, and Nietzsche, who declared God dead, were nonrealists (see Jack Verheyden).

If the divine is but a figment of the human imagination, what of the rest of the world? For a religious realist, the very structure of the universe is at stake. Christianity is not alone in being a transformative religion, in which salvation figures foremost. Absent the divine, John Hick writes, "we must face the grim fact that the marvelous human spiritual potential will only be fulfilled to the very fragmentary extent that it is in fact fulfilled in this world."[31] A theory of religion without a transcendent divine reality, from this perspective, seems almost a contradiction, cutting away at the very foundation of belief.

Religion, however one regards it, provides an explanation of the universe, by giving it a shape through a set of beliefs. In that sense, it is a cultural system, and beliefs are a template. More important, the sense of the sacred creates a world. Christianity, like other religions, is also a way of life, to which the faithful adhere as individuals and as part of a larger community, meaning that it "is already institutional in the earliest of its documents" and in its very constitution.[32]

Taken as a cultural system, religion is a construct. Spiritual belief, however, is not a matter of theory for believers, but of religious feeling and practices that incarnate belief. It can be legitimately argued that a belief system is just as much a construct as the various theories of religion noted above. Yet there is always an irreducible element to religious belief that cannot be theorized or rationalized. At least part of this element is contained in the numinous, or the holy, powerfully embodied in such forms as Catholic worship. In this regard, "the sacredness of an object was not caused by rational thinking. Therefore the end of that sacredness could not be caused only by rational thinking."[33]

The nonrational component of religion is drawn from a deep emotional and imaginative wellspring that senses itself to be attached to something larger than the self, beyond the self. This component is generally expressed in human, natural language because it is the only way it can be said. We see it in mystical writings and in the phenomenon of speaking in tongues, or glossolalia. This experience is what Clarín referred to in attempting to reconnect with the faith of his childhood: "I pray in my own way, with what I feel, with what I remember of my childhood . . . with what the music of the organ and the chanting of the choir say to my soul, their words do not reach my ear, though I tremble inside with their melody . . . my spirit speaks within, a kind of glossolalia which must resemble that of the early Christians, still untutored in the concrete affirmations of dogma but filled with ineffable emotion."[34] Clarín's feeling of numinosity is a form of poetry that arises out of belief. Lewis said, "Theology is . . . poetry to me because I believe in it; I do not believe it because it is poetry."[35]

Lewis and Clarín are both talking about a kind of religious imagination the source of which is difficult, if not impossible, to pin down. Lewis observes that "a believed idea *feels* different from an idea that is not believed." It possesses "a special sort of imaginative enjoyment." The belief informing this special imagination obviously differs from the aesthetic disengagement from belief, for "it seeks to create an aura of utter actuality. It is this sense of the 'really real' upon which the religious perspective rests." I am not convinced, however, that religious belief and fictional belief are as far apart as most accounts like this one assume. At the very least, many novels appear to depend upon the imaginative structures of belief to convince readers of their fictional reality. This alone suggests a symbiotic relation between religion and literature, as Giles

Gunn argues.[36] One could say that such novels work on the delicate premise that belief in illusory worlds is predicated on a belief that something might be real.

Gunn also maintains that one of the purposes of literature and works of art in general "is to help us know what we feel about these [religious] paradigms, and feel what we know, by illuminating the implications of what they conceal as well as disclose."[37] Literature can tell us if belief systems fail us or die or need replacing. This view, despite its sensitivity to the presence of the sacred, runs perilously close to a functional one. In the social sciences, religion becomes the instrument for understanding the social and the cultural; and in some cases, for molding a discipline. Such thinkers tend to functionalize the transcendent. But to write a novel is to transcend the functional.

If novelists reenact or imaginatively recreate religious structures, there must be something deeply appealing aesthetically and emotionally in those structures, even when the historic institutions of religion appear flawed or troubled. In responding to the crisis of modernity in its religious form, writers like Clarín, Galdós, and Sender also reshaped it through the secular genre of the modern novel. That crisis ultimately had to do with belief, at both the individual and collective levels, as the institution of the Catholic Church in Spain and its membership, like most of Western Europe, were subjected increasingly to the challenges and diverse pressures of secularization. Had that belief system been of so little value or consequence, it appears doubtful these novelists would have pursued its sacred forms so tenaciously. There appears to be at least some shared territory between the special religious imagination to which Lewis alludes and the literary or artistic imagination. If faith is a "sustained imagining," so too is the novel, albeit a belief system of a different nature. Miguel de Unamuno simply observed, "To believe is to create."[38]

I do not think, however, one can really define the religious imagination present in these and other novels, partly because that imagination can take many forms, partly because it participates in the ineffable character of the transcendent without being equal to it, and partly because one simply cannot understand its nature except through a lesser language of metaphor and symbol, the same language system to which fiction belongs. There have been some attempts to establish a Catholic imagination. Notably, Andrew Greeley explores with sensitivity what he describes as the enchanted world of Catholicism, a world in which "the objects, events, and persons of daily life are revelations of grace. . . . This special Catholic imagination . . . sees created reality as a 'sacrament,' that is, a revelation of the presence of God." The material, visible world thus becomes the "container of the invisible."[39]

The "sacraments of sensibility" are above all manifested through metaphor.

Eleanor Heartney convincingly argues for seeing the sacramental presence of the Incarnation in the body imagery of Catholic (and former Catholic) postmodern artists like Andy Warhol, Robert Mapplethorpe, and Andrés Serrano. Their conflictive, ambivalent relation with religion coexists with a religious sensibility. Like Greeley, Heartney relies on an oppositional, Puritan-inspired Protestant imagination bereft of metaphor and the human body to make her case for a special Catholic imagination.[40] This dualistic approach oversimplifies, however, the complex relation between art and religion and reinforces religious and aesthetic stereotyping: "Christian scripture is itself a fundamentally metaphoric medium of expression, communication, and interpretation."[41] It is for these reasons I refer to religion and the imagination and to diverse forms of a religious imagination rather than to a single Catholic imagination. I do not discard, however, the sacramental presence or the role of historical Catholicism in literature. It is especially important to make these distinctions in discussing the writings of authors like Clarín and Sender, whose religious views are unorthodox and whose works are produced in a world that is distinctly disenchanted.

Greeley is on firmer ground in noting that "the origins and raw power of religion are at the imaginative (that is, experiential and narrative) level both for the individual and for the tradition." "The Church," he says later, "shaped faith by shaping imaginations." Historically, however, the Church often distrusted the imagination. Throughout medieval Western Christendom moving into the Renaissance and later, the imagination was beheld as troubling, for it was both marvelous and deceptive. Faith, warned Giovan Francesco Pico della Mirandola, can be "ruined by false imagination." Uncontrolled and carried away by emotion, the imagination could lead the faithful astray or to disorder, as the Jesuit Luis de la Puente notes "of thoughts and the imagination, which are disordered, whether from injurious or vain things, or inappropriate for the occasion, or overly emphasized." Like the Jesuit founder Ignatius of Loyola, whom he follows here, he is most interested in a special form of religious imagination that is regulated through the examination of conscience prior to confession and, more broadly, through the primary aim of salvation. Thus de la Puente finds it perfectly appropriate to make use of the imaginative faculties in order to "imagine one's soul within the body, like a criminal in prison, with a chain around the neck, with leg irons around the ankles and manacles on the hands."[42] The chains are sins linked together, the leg irons and manacles passions and vicious habits. The penitent is to concentrate the mind on the long and multiple succession of sinfulness in the literally solid image of chains, with the aim of purging one kind of imagination through another. The influential Loyolan model has "shaped faith by shaping imaginations," but it has also shaped literature, as I suggest later, providing an aesthetic-emotional vehicle of the psyche for novels like Clarín's *La Regenta* and, to a lesser extent, Sender's *Réquiem.*

Clerics and other spokesmen for society's moral values traditionally viewed narrative fabrications such as the romances of chivalry either as pernicious instruments of an excessive imagination, purveyors of untruth, or a waste of time. Some were more ambivalent and attempted to build an aesthetic defense of fiction by reconciling the marvelous and the verisimilar, as does the Canon of Toledo in *Don Quijote.* Many of the harsher moralistic views of imaginative writing, not just in Spain but elsewhere in Europe, go back to Plato's critique of poets as mere image makers "whose images are far removed from the truth." In this vein, the Christian humanist Juan Luis Vives proscribes a broad array of fictions from the *Celestina* and *Cárcel de amor (Prison of Love)* to the romances of chivalry, finding them especially injurious to the corruptible nature of young ladies. The Augustinian theologian Pedro Malón de Chaide judged the pastoral novel equally offensive, though overall the highly popular romances of chivalry were the primary target of hostile criticism from a host of clergymen and others. Barry Ife surmises that the romances may have stood for imaginative literature in general in these attacks. He also suggests that "in Spain, opposition to literature seems to form part of a general Catholic opposition to the ideals of *pietas litterata*, to the promotion of scripture in the vernacular, and the consequent elimination of the clergy's role as exegetes of the Word and intermediaries between man and God. The unacceptable directness and the individualist nature of literary experience inevitably smacked of a Protestant frame of mind." There may very well be some truth to his observation, for how else to explain why so many clergy and moralists were so vehemently opposed to a form of writing they otherwise considered frivolous and a waste of time? Still, it does not necessarily explain why a good many Erasmian humanists also objected to romances of chivalry. Or did such objections reveal "a serious and deeply-felt anxiety about the effects of fictional literature in general on the reading public"?[43]

Moral strictures against imaginative writing, conjoined to a sense of unease with the faculty of the imagination, moreover, persisted, appearing well after the Renaissance and baroque periods. The inventive, fecund character of the imagination, regularly conflated with the notion of fantasy, was a matter of some concern in the eighteenth century. Juan Pablo Forner deplored a diminishing capacity of the faculty in Spaniards: "Where is that prodigious fecundity of the imagination that, surpassing the limits of that which is advisable, like a river overflowing its banks, made poetry more poetic than expected?" The Jesuit José Francisco de Isla, who mocked overripe, empty, neobaroque flights of fancy in sacred oratory, nonetheless felt compelled to defend his own imaginative faculty in his popular satire *Fray Gerundio de Campazas*. If Plato, René Descartes, and Bernard de Fontenelle could create imaginary worlds, he wrote, "what reason, divine or human, prevents my imagination from amusing itself in fabricating a plump, preening, and lively little friar . . . ? [Is their] imagination somehow . . . more privileged than mine, however poor and sinful?" Cadalso, however, considered the phantoms of the imagination to be "monsters produced by fantasy filled with sadness: human fantasy, fecund only in chimeras, illusions and objects of terror!" In that vein, the Benedictine *ilustrado*, or Enlightenment thinker, Benito Jerónimo Feijoo observed in 1753, "There are no small number of persons who by night believe they've seen specters, or ghosts, although reason dictates to most that they are no more than deceptive appearances."[44]

Remarking upon the emotional effects of novels, plays, and fanciful stories in readers and spectators, Feijoo wrote, "But those who read or hear these fabulous narrations, don't they know what they are? . . . Don't they also know that only real events, and certainly not make-believe ones, deserve to move our feelings? . . . What is this but an exercise of tyrannical power, a confessed *Despotism of the Imaginative Faculty*, a violent intrusion of the latter upon the rights of understanding, a usurpation that the inferior faculty exercises over the privileges of the superior one?"[45]

Here, the traditional position regarding the untruth and moral peril of imaginative literature is inserted in an Enlightenment critique of the irrational as an infringement upon the rights of reason, couched in political language. Feijoo found especially troubling the perceived inclination of women to privilege the imagination over reason. This propensity was readily observed, he said, in the false visions and voices pious ladies claimed to have seen and heard after reading about the lives of saints. This view could still be found at the end of the nineteenth century and beginning of the early twentieth. A training manual from 1896 for female elementary school teachers recommends the exact sciences as an antidote to excessive flights of fancy in young girls, while encouraging the restrained use of the imagination in writing exercises.[46]

In 1905, the bishop of Jaca reframed the attack on imaginative literature, the naturalist novel (then completely out of fashion) being his special target of opportunity, by exploiting the psycho-physiological language of the very works he deplored: "The reading of novels can end up violently altering the regular functioning of the nerves, producing the profoundest cerebral disturbances. . . . It is not uncommon that women indulging in these unsettling readings suffer from hysterical attacks, have nightmares, and at the slightest indication burst into nervous tears." He goes on to list other consequences of reading novels, injurious to both men and women, which include "night terrors, hallucinations, vertigo, fainting, unreal forebodings, and puerile fears." In sum, "the abuse of the imagination produces the wasting of the brain's cells."[47]

There was evidently a market for this kind of book. One of the more popular ones was Father Pablo Ladrón de Guevara's *Novelistas malos y buenos* (1910), which catalogues and harshly judges thousands of writers. I have a well-thumbed fourth edition from 1933. Ayguals de Izco's *María, la hija de un jornalero*, for example, is dealt with summarily: "Immoral, dishonest, socialist, with other wicked ideas. Abominable slandering of the friars. It is vile [*infame*]." The most damning reason not to read novels is left for the last page and comes from the Jesuit R. V. Ugarte: " 'I defy you to give me a single person, young or old, man or woman, a reader of bad or good novels, who reading them frequently, possesses an ounce of true piety.' "[48] Under the Franco regime of National Catholicism and stifling censorship, books of this sort were still being published. *Lecturas buenas y malas a la luz del dogma y de la moral* (Good and bad readings in the light of dogma and morality), by the Jesuit Garmendia de Otaola, appeared in 1949 and incorporates and expands upon Ladrón de Guevara's catalogue.

Even a clergyman novelist like the Jesuit Luis Coloma, best known for his cutting satire of the aristocracy in *Pequeñeces* (Bagatelles) (1890), came down hard on novels of any sort. Well-intentioned narratives, he wrote in 1884, lead readers astray by sentimentalizing religion. They produce merely aesthetic effects and pleasing impressions. In general, "the novel . . . exalts . . . the imagination of the inexperienced reader . . . and forges in his fantasy an ideal, beautiful world . . . : from this comes early disillusionment, the discontent with practical life."[49]

It is startling to think that Coloma's observations appeared at the very same time as novels like *La Regenta* and *Fortunata y Jacinta*. These fictions stressed, though not to the exclusion of the ideal, precisely what the clergyman found lacking in most novels: "that arid thing called the prose of life, which depoeticizes all dreams." By contrast, Coloma's own stories seem insipid and overly moralizing, bent on avoiding the pitfalls of fantasy through a reliance on what he calls "historical facts."[50] On the surface, the Jesuit novelist appears more a realist than the realists themselves. In truth his distrust of the imagination (and of the novel) places him in an untenable position, one in which he is forced to defend fiction as something it is not: history. Like other church moralists, he is a regulator of the imaginative faculty.

Ironically, whatever the religious imagination is in modern Spanish fiction, it is not generally the imagination that most religious figures like Coloma envisioned. Traditional attacks on the misuse of the imagination betray a territorial anxiety. One senses that the Church and its representatives were losing ground, not simply as the sole arbiters in the moral realm of conscience and as the retainers of the sacred but as guardians of the imagination. Such criticisms also arose in reaction to particular historical-cultural circumstances. Thus their arguments reflected the language and mental frame of the period, as, for example, in the Enlightenment charge that the imagination was an assault on reason. In the sixteenth and seventeenth centuries, Erasmianism and Protestantism were the two most obvious spiritual and ideological challenges to the faith. By the nineteenth century, churchmen were battling liberalism, socialism, and free thought. It wasn't simply that these later secular challenges were perceived as anti-Catholic or antireligious; they also had a hold on the imagination, drawing people's minds and hearts away from the things that truly mattered in the eyes of the Church.

Novels were in the same secular category. In its most extreme ultramontane form, the argument against novels was analogous to the argument against liberalism and other presumed political heresies. Pius IX's *Syllabus of Errors*, issued in 1864, condemned liberalism as well as a host of other propositions such as pantheism, indifferentism, socialism, and secularism. The question became, could a liberal be Catholic? The most conservative did not think so. A liberal was worse "than being a blasphemer, thief, adulterer or murderer."[51] A liberal Catholic or a Catholic liberal was a contradiction in terms. For the clergyman Félix Sardá y Salvany liberalism was a sin, as the title of his book *El liberalismo es pecado* (1884) makes clear.

The thinking about novels and novel reading was part of the same mental universe in these circles. The parallel question was, could a reader of novels still be considered devout? Evidently not, according to Father Ugarte, who merely stated more openly what other clergy expressed through rational, aesthetic, or moral critiques. Novels like *La Regenta* and *Fortunata y Jacinta* can be seen as mixing the sacred and the profane, two categories normally intended to be kept apart in belief systems.[52] A double charge was laid against the novel form. First, the novel was accused of treating the sacred in a profane manner (hence Coloma's critique of fiction for equating religion to an aesthetic effect). Second, it was seen as propagating immorality. Novels distracted readers from more transcendent concerns. They opened up the private universes of individuals to hitherto unexamined but, in the eyes of the Church, dangerous issues and feelings, for example, the hysterical states, a euphemism for heightened sexual awareness, against which Antolín López Peláez fulminated.

The novel was like liberalism itself, for presumably suggesting a "freedom of thought with no limitation whatsoever politically, morally or religiously."[53] The thing connecting liberalism and the modern novel, in this view, is the open-ended character of the imagination. The novel, in particular the realist novel, operates ideally with creative autonomy, encumbered with few formal restrictions, an abyss of imaginative possibilities appealing to the emotions and earthly interests of readers.

Clarín made the connection between literature (especially the novel), liberalism, and the imagination in an essay titled "El libre examen y nuestra literatura presente" (Free thought and our present-day literature) (1881). Without referring explicitly to the imagination, he suggested, perhaps somewhat optimistically, that Spanish literature since the liberal September Revolution of 1868 had freed itself from fanaticism and dullness of spirit, under "liberal influence, expansive, noble, profound, spontaneous." The highly popular Galdós above all incarnates that liberating *élan vital*, he says: "his novels have not only had an impact on free-thinking students and members of athenaeums and clubs, but have penetrated the sanctuary of the home, where the nourishment of the spirit used to be books of devotion and profane books filled with a hypocritical or tedious conventional morality, without grandeur or beauty." By stark contrast, Ladrón de Guevara called Galdós a priest-hater and a "defender of revolutionary, irreligious ideas" who cunningly undermines Catholicism's hold on believers.[54] Like Clarín, the more intransigent members of the Church understood that fiction was competing for the imaginations of churchgoers.

The success of such intemperate attacks as those of López Peláez and Ladrón de Guevara can be measured by the effect they had upon the writing of fiction, which is to say, relatively little, to judge from the thousands of novels published during the period. Still, no novelist could simply ignore these critics, whose heated commentaries were generally meant to provoke a response in the same way as those of their anticlerical enemies. There is very little here of that enchanted world of the Catholic imagination, but rather an intensifying politicization of religion, which played out not only in the press and pulpit, but also in the pages of fiction and the homes of readers. Nineteenth-century clerical hostility toward the novel and the imagination tells us much about the changing position of religion in a secularizing world and about the relation between religious crisis and a key secular form, the novel.

This brings me back to the historical-religious context in which fiction was produced. The personal, noninstitutional experience of religion expressed in novels cannot be separated from the historical institutional role of the Church or from the tenets of its belief system, especially when both institution and doctrines are being questioned. Whatever is felt is felt in history. To speak of spiritual feeling or the sense of the sacred without situating them in their concrete circumstances turns both into abstract entities, contradicting not only the dense reality of fiction but the embedded quality of the spiritual and sacred in religious practice. Thus, all the texts under discussion here at once reveal an unresolved pattern of conflict and convergence with religion. They also indicate that religion as both system and feeling and secularization as symptomatic of modernity must be understood together as part of the same dynamic. There is, in other words, no theory of religion in these novels, as useful as it is to understand religion in the various ways noted above. In one sense, such theories help one to see how religion as a construct might be incorporated into another construct, that of the novel. They also highlight that the ground upon which such theories are built is rocky and unstable, historically positioned and responding to changing historical circumstance. Émile Durkheim's brilliant reconstruction of archaic religion in 1912, for example, issues in part from his perception of present-day spiritual malaise: "If we find a little difficulty to-day in imagining what [the] feasts and ceremonies of the future could consist in, it is because we are going through a stage of transition and moral mediocrity. The great things of the past which filled our fathers with enthusiasm do not excite the same ardour in us . . . but as yet there is nothing to replace them . . . the old gods are growing old or already dead, and others are not yet born."[55]

Novels, historically grounded in general, are rarely built on theory alone. Famously, Émile Zola's theory of naturalist fiction arose after the fact. Novels are more like the lived experience of religion, in this sense, arising as a practice first; in turn, fiction, until fairly recently at least, historically reflected the practice and beliefs of religion. One can scarcely understand the importance of social politics and mutual tolerance in Elizabeth Gaskell's *North and South* (1855) without considering her Unitarian religious beliefs; or the underlying significance of transgression in a *fin de siècle* decadent text like Joris-Karl Huysmans's *À rebours* (*Against Nature*) (1884) without recognizing that the author's interest in Catholicism predates his actual conversion; or Unamuno's *San Manuel Bueno, mártir* (*Saint Manuel Bueno, Martyr*) (1933) and nearly all his other writings without acknowledging that his religion of uncertainty points not to disbelief but to spiritual struggle as the deepening of the human wellspring. In "Mi religión" (1907), Unamuno wrote, "My religion is to seek the truth in life and the life in truth, but knowing I will not find them while I live; my religion is to struggle incessantly, tirelessly, with mystery; my religion is to struggle with God from the break of dawn until the fall of night."[56]

Unamuno's fractured faith recalls the earlier case of Alas's spiritual predicament, as Unamuno himself was well aware, but it also points to a series of crises of religion in Spain, from roughly the late eighteenth century to the civil war in 1936. Indeed, the word "crisis" begins to assume a privileged place in the political-religious vocabulary of the period. I do not mean to imply, however, that the Church in the sixteenth and seventeenth centuries was a monolithic force capable of subjecting everyone to its views or of seamlessly accomplishing its mission in every sphere. Religious belief was by no means uniform in early modern Spain. Neither forced conversions of the Jews and Muslims in Spain nor evangelization in the New World always went smoothly, as revolts, persecutions, expulsions, and Inquisition records testify. There were other spiritual cracks as well. Erasmianism and like-minded reform movements, which were later accused of being too close to Protestantism, called for a less ritualized, more inner-directed faith. The Church itself undertook a massive, post-Tridentine Christianization of the populace, often ill tutored in Catholic doctrine and practice. It sought improvement of the ecclesiastical estate, plagued with lax morality, ignorance, and secularism. By the early seventeenth century, stressed by demographic and economic crisis, the rapid growth of the clerical profession was seen as being complicit in the crisis. The clericalization of Spanish society drew much contemporary criticism for fostering idleness and creating a great fiscal burden. At the same time the strong sense of national and personal identity established through membership in the Church — a "chosen people" complex forged historically through the medieval *Reconquista* and imperial-spiritual expansion and distinct from other peoples — did not diminish. As Helen Rawlings points out, "The need to secure one's place in heaven by one's actions on earth . . . led to a heavy investment . . . in the least productive sector of society."[57]

The Spanish Church, its power and privileges tied to absolute monarchy, survived undiminished into the eighteenth century, a period that historians generally agree was one of the most devout. The earlier crusade mentality of the Reconquest, the Christianizing mission abroad, the intense religiosity and model of sainthood epitomized in Ignacio de Loyola, Teresa de Jesús, and Juan de la Cruz may have been largely a thing of the past. Yet traditional religion was by no means dead. Popular evangelizing missions, favored especially by the Jesuits and the Capuchins, served to renew religious fervor, educate the masses in Church doctrine, and spread such devotions as those of the Stations of the Cross and the Sacred Heart. Preachers like Pedro de Calatayud, Antonio Garcés, and Diego José de Cádiz defended "the traditional assumptions of Spain's Christian, overwhelmingly agrarian, and hierarchical society."[58] Fearing the signs of modernity they perceived in the crown's promotion of trade, industry, and commerce, the missionaries also gained the enmity of the enlightened minority.

More private devotional practices, coming from France especially and inspired by the works of Saint Francis de Sales (1567–1622) and Saint Alphonsus Liguori (1696–1787), emphasized the individual's relation with God and salvation. Like de Sales, Liguori recommended mental prayer as necessary to salvation, disposing "the heart to the practice of virtues": "By the contemplation of the divine goodness, the great love which God has borne him . . . man is inflamed with love, his heart is softened, and made obedient to the divine inspirations."[59]

As an institution, the Church, under the control of the Bourbon monarchy, was prosperous, sustained through considerable though fragmented landholdings. It was not, however, well organized either internally or geographically. The authority of bishops over dioceses and religious orders was frequently challenged; and bishops did not speak to each other. In contrast to the hierarchy, the parish clergy was inadequately educated, often weak in religious commitment, as Isla demonstrated in *Fray Gerundio de Campazas* (1758–70). Both the secular and the regular clergy were, moreover, poorly distributed, clustered in the north and northeast and in urban centers. This continuation of an earlier trend would also characterize the next two centuries, profoundly affecting religious practice as a matter of geography.[60] Increasingly, Enlightenment reformers (including some churchmen) and a regalist State saw the religious orders as unproductive, focused on contemplation rather than on good works, whether spiritual or material, such as education and charity. A socially active order like the Sisters of Charity, for example, encountered resistance to its work in the 1780s. The quality, effectiveness, and usefulness of the ecclesiastical estate left much to be desired.

The Church did not neglect social problems like poverty but dealt with it traditionally, through the sacred duty of almsgiving and the distribution of food and clothing. The poor were regarded as representatives of Christ. As William Callahan observes, "Hospitals and other charitable institutions operated under ecclesiastical auspices, but religious personnel rarely worked directly with the unfortunate."[61] Without the material and spiritual help of the Church, however, most of the poor would have been in even worse shape than they already were.

Agrarian failures, natural disasters, depressed wages, and chronic unemployment in an unevenly and only partially developed economy magnified social-economic distress among the laboring classes. Beggars, vagabonds, and other down-and-outers proliferated in the streets. During the second half of the eighteenth century projects to ameliorate the problem by reforming poor relief were proposed. These included periodic sweeps to clear towns of beggars, the discouraging of indiscriminate charity, and the founding of *hospicios* to confine the poor and of neighborhood relief associations in Madrid. There were precedents for these reforms, most notably the Christian humanist Juan Luis Vives's set of recommendations from 1526 for the secular authorities to identify, register, and, if necessary, confine the disadvantaged while putting them to work. His proposal relied on church charity only secondarily. Vives's plan, which was addressed to the city council and senate of Bruges, where he resided, exerted some influence in northern Europe but not apparently in Spain, where reform projects of the sixteenth and seventeenth centuries were hotly debated.[62]

An enlightened government and elite saw the social-economic crisis as both a civil and an ecclesiastical problem in the eighteenth century. Vives was not alone in viewing the masses of poor folk as a threat to social stability, hence the obligation of the State to improve their condition. At the same time, he brings up the Christian commitment to one's neighbor by returning to the Gospel as the spiritual-ethical foundation of faith: "In another era when the life of Christ was still vital, all believers cast their wealth at the feet of the Apostles to be distributed by them to everyone according to need. . . . However, as the ardor for the blood of Christ increasingly abated . . . , the Church began to copy the world and to rival it in pomp, pride, and luxury. . . . If only the Spirit of God would touch them and recall to their minds whence they had received it, who had given it, and for what reason! If only they would remember that out of the substance of the poor they had become powerful!"[63]

Vives goes on to say that bishops, with their large incomes, "should follow the example of Paul, to be absolutely perfect in charity . . . placing themselves on the same level with all men in order to help them." The significance of the Erasmian Vives's words would have been cuttingly clear to his readers in Spain. His evangelical message of perfect charity also resonated with late eighteenth-century ilustrados like Gaspar Melchor de Jovellanos, Juan Meléndez Valdés, Olavide, and Gutiérrez, who sought an inner faith filled with the original teachings and practice of the Gospel.[64] There was, in Jean Sarrailh's words, "a crisis of religious conscience" in such men, whose dissatisfaction with the spiritual complacency and wealth of the Church was transparent.[65]

Social-economic woes like poverty and mendicity were also a religious problem. First, the Church, historically (and naturally), had assumed charity as part of its mission. And second, the eighteenth-century elite, driven by both Enlightenment rationalism and religious concern, perceived that that mission left much to be desired. It neither addressed the problem rationally and practically nor kept faith with the message of the Gospel. For example, the impatience Meléndez Valdés reveals in 1802 with the customary and to his mind inadequate view of the poor as sacred also discloses the effort required to reconcile traditional Catholic belief with an increasingly secular mind: "The maxims that speak of *the poor person [as] a living image of the Redeemer; God [loving] poverty; the poor man of Christ; poor, but honest,* applied to begging through ignorance or unthinking charity, foment begging, they canonize it and produce in society the most fatal consequences. . . . Know that Christianity not only recommends labor as a remedy against the seductive temptations of idleness, but rigorously requires it as punishment for our corrupted nature. Know that begging is a plague of society that degrades and destroys it. . . . Know that we are obliged to distribute alms with discretion and knowledge, if we want to offer them according to reason and the Gospel."[66]

The attempt to shape faith to the dictates of reason and reason to evangelical feeling also appears in the literature of the period, expressing at the same time the intertwined nature of the social question with the religious question. Consider, for example, the reform-minded Olavide's *El evangelio en triunfo*, the fourth and final volume of which is dedicated to the protagonist's Enlightenment project to improve the miserable lot of villagers on his estate. The first three volumes are taken up with the protagonist Philosopher's spiritual crisis and eventual conversion. His philanthropic embrace of the poor, however, results from his working through of a religious crisis, albeit imperfectly, in which he ultimately brackets his unresolved spiritual doubts and presents the village improvement plan as a kind of narrative proof of belief.

The quandary of reconciling faith with reason is symptomatic of a larger crisis of belief in the Enlightenment, a crisis Ernst Cassirer illuminates with characteristic lucidity: "The more insufficient one finds previous religious answers to basic questions of knowledge and morality, the more intensive and passionate become these questions themselves. The controversy from now on is no longer concerned with particular religious dogmas and their interpretation, but with the nature of religious certainty; it no longer deals with what is merely believed but with the nature, tendency, and function of belief as such. Thus . . . the fundamental objective is not the dissolution of religion but its 'transcendental' justification and foundation."[67]

The fundamental problem of belief shapes two other texts to be analyzed more closely in chapter 1, Cadalso's *Noches lúgubres* and Gutiérrez's *Cornelia Bororquia*. Despair rips Cadalso's protagonist apart as he faces the inescapable fact of his beloved's physical death. Without the hope of resurrection, there is no religious consolation. The attempt to sacralize the beloved's body, to regain that " 'transcendental' justification and foundation," fails. While the precise nature of Cadalso's and his protagonist's belief system eludes us, its eventual embodiment in saving the laboring poor bespeaks not only the need to believe in something, but the need to create something in which to believe.

This too lies at the heart of Gutiérrez's narration of the Inquisition. Here, the problem of belief is developed through the issue of religious tolerance, a matter of central importance to the Enlightenment in general. In the same manner the texts of Olavide and Cadalso link the social-economic welfare of the poor to its religious source, this one firmly positions tolerance upon an evangelical foundation: "*The man of Christ* should be sweet, humble and charitable; there is never any justification for mistreating his brother. When I say brother, don't think that I am excluding those individuals from other creeds, no matter the faith . . . because God tells me that all men are my brothers."[68] In other words, tolerance is the eighteenth-century manifestation of treating one's neighbor as holy and at the same time a way to shore up belief when, as Gutiérrez's novel shows, trust in religious institutions no longer exists. Unsurprisingly the work landed on the Holy Office's Index of Prohibited Books. In the final pages, tellingly, faith in humanity cannot fully replace the consolations of religion, as Vargas, emotionally and spiritually battered, tries to come to grips with his beloved Cornelia's death at the hands of the Inquisition.

By the 1790s, it was not just the intellectual minority but the Church itself that was beginning to feel the ground rumbling beneath its feet, especially in the aftershocks of the French Revolution. In addition, the royal favorite Manuel de Godoy, under the reign of Charles IV (1788–1808), further expanded State control over the Church, and this included replacing recalcitrant hierarchy like Francisco Antonio Cardinal de Lorenzana of Toledo, among the small group of enlightened ecclesiastics, with more compliant figures. War with France in 1793 and later with England in 1796 required huge expenditures, for which the Church was heavily taxed. In 1798 a fiscal crisis of the State led to the auctioning of Church properties devoted to charitable undertakings. Within two years "the traditional system of charity was in crisis."[69]

The next several years shattered the traditional relation between Church and State and ultimately affected the standing of the Church within Spanish society. It has been said that "loss of faith in enlightened despotism . . . was the real revolution of the late eighteenth century."[70] Dissatisfaction with Godoy's influence, the impact of the French Revolution, and the exigencies of war contributed to this crucial change of attitude, which inevitably affected the intellectual minority's view of the Church, so closely allied to the throne. While government at first attempted to silence news of the cataclysm in France, French propaganda and the experiences of émigrés began to filter in. The execution of Louis XVI and the Terror of '93 marked a turning point. Traditionalists rushed to translate even more works of French Catholic apologists and attacked revolutionary ideas from the pulpit and the printing press, waging holy war through the rhetoric of crusade.[71] At the same time, enlightened efforts by laymen and clergy to reduce the power of the Inquisition, to simplify and interiorize religious life, and to reform the ecclesiastical estate met with resistance from the traditionalists, who saw the proof of the pudding in the French Revolution. In a word, the "struggle [over church reform] epitomized the waxing conflict between partisans of old and new ideas."[72]

The Napoleonic invasion of Spain in 1808 exposed the problem of religious and political divisiveness among the elite, as the convening of the Cortes at Cádiz made painfully clear in the wrangling over Church–State relations and over the future of the religious orders and of the Inquisition. Espousing religious tolerance in 1792, José Marchena and others had called for the revival of the medieval Cortes, an idea that was to bear liberal fruit in the turmoil of war and occupation. The war itself brought chaos and privation to the Church. When the French occupied monasteries and suppressed religious orders, monks and friars spread the message of resistance, becoming warriors in a new crusade against the godless invaders.[73] Ninety-seven secular clergymen participated in the Cortes, some of the most ardently messianic among them burning to transform a nation perceived as tainted by the Enlightenment's moral corruption and spiritual laxity, to create a new political theocracy.

Both liberals and traditionalists at the Cortes were aware that the moment was a watershed in Spanish history. One publication fashioned itself as "the Annals in which the memorable events of the present crisis are recorded, of which the historian may make use." At the same time, an endemic sense of crisis becomes a defining quality of experience from 1808 on, one characterized by feelings of anxiety and uncertainty. Nothing ever seemed definitively settled: as Mariano José de Larra observed, "The crisis is still with us."[74] The Cortes passed a liberal Constitution, but Ferdinand VII brushed it aside in 1814. Liberals prevailed again from 1820 to 1823, and this time, with the help of foreign troops, Ferdinand reestablished his power. Upon his death in 1833 a dynastic conflict arose between two branches of Spanish Bourbons — Ferdinand's ultra-Catholic, traditionalist brother Charles versus the late king's daughter Isabel, whom liberals supported. This first Carlist War (1833–40) was also religious in nature, pointing once more to how deeply entwined the political-social and the religious questions were.

The nature of such fractiousness led one commentator to call nineteenth-century Spanish history "one long war of religion: belligerent Catholicism against belligerent liberalism." While the statement suffers from oversimplification, it highlights the larger problem, felt throughout Western Europe, of reconciling religion with secular systems of thought like liberalism.[75] This defining issue heavily marks the conflictive history of nineteenth-and much of twentieth-century Spanish history. Under liberalism, religion is bracketed; more important, it is no longer the supreme authority governing men and institutions. The struggle over competing authorities was played out repeatedly in Catholic Spain, with no side really winning the big prize until, perhaps,

Franco. Even here however, religious conformity was forced upon the losing side in an effort to turn back the clock of history.

It is tempting to see historical development as a continuous, inevitable turn toward secularism, but the process of secularization was never completed in Spain (nor, I suspect, in very many other cultures). Religion and religious feeling persisted not simply because the Church was politically powerful but because most people, including those who styled themselves liberals, were still believers and still moved in a landscape permeated with the sacred.[76] Even something as mundane as a reading primer presents its lessons in a moral-religious context, as, for example, in Vicente Naharro's *Método práctico de enseñar á leer* (Practical method to teach reading) (1815?), reprinted throughout the century. The first word to be learned is "soul" ("al-ma") and the last paragraph is a brief prayer asking God's grace "to receive this study as part of my penitence, so that my knowledge be free of error and vanity."[77] The edition I consulted is from 1856 and advertises not only Naharro's textbooks but Jerónimo de Ripalda's *Catechism* as being available at several Madrid bookstores. Naharro (1750–1823) was persecuted for his liberal views. Another of his textbooks, a handwriting manual from 1820, was censored and its publication held up for two years until the liberal triennium of 1820–23. He dedicated the book to parliament, placing his work under "the protection of the Cortes," meaning the Constitution, and alluded to himself as Citizen Naharro.[78]

Naharro is literally and figuratively a textbook example, showing, first, how Catholicism regularly and without remark permeated even the most prosaic spaces of daily life; and, second, how many liberals held religious convictions and considered themselves Catholic. This does not mean Catholics found it easy to be liberal in nineteenth-century Spain, as Naharro's difficulties suggest. Well before the appearance of the *Syllabus* in 1864, Church spokesmen looked with suspicion and hostility upon liberal views, which they saw as issuing from the Enlightenment's presumed libertine mindset. (Subsequent events — the liberal Constitution and triennium, the struggles between theocratic Carlists and liberals, the weakening of the Church's economic and social base — all these things, in their eyes, confirmed their suspicions.) More problematic to liberal Catholics was the critical matter of harmonizing liberty and the modern world with religion. In his translator's preface (1836) to Félicité de Lamennais's *Paroles d'un croyant* (*Words of a Believer*) (1834), Larra specifically addressed that problem. He argued that those who oppose the notion of progress and human perfectibility "blaspheme against Providence . . . because they assume that Providence has made of our hearts a struggle between belief and reality. To bring us into the world for that would have been a farce."[79] How could God make justice unrealizable in the world, he asks? But he also faults liberals for not fully embracing religion, thus turning it to their advantage, the way Protestantism did by separating Church and State and thereby ultimately guaranteeing liberty and religion as a matter of individual conscience. These, he concludes, are his principles: "Pure religion, the source of moral life, and religion . . . accompanied by tolerance and freedom of conscience; civil liberty; complete equality before the law and equality [of opportunity] . . . and absolute freedom of written thought. This is the translator's profession of faith."[80]

By Larra's time, the Church had turned defensively conservative, and there were few liberal or reform-minded clergymen. One can imagine how poorly received his words were in such circles. The sixteen-year-old Leopoldo Alas, on the other hand, was thrilled to read both the preface and text in the summer of 1868: "I have just read them and my soul has been profoundly affected. . . . Religion and justice, these are the foundations of earthly happiness. . . . To seek the temporal happiness of our fellow men is the most beautiful gift we can give our Maker in order to attain our own eternal happiness. . . . [W]ho will deny me that progress is beloved of God, because it strives to present to Him children worthy of his divine love? . . . [I]s God the author of happiness, or is it progress? God, I respond, is the author. He has presented it to us as within reach, and it is up to us to reach it."[81]

Yvan Lissorgues is right in claiming that here is the core of Alas's subsequent beliefs, but I would add, here also is the source of his torment, echoing Larra's. For nothing in their lives or works suggests that either Larra or Alas was able to submerge or assuage feelings of despair and debilitating uncertainty. Less than a year after translating Lamennais, Larra killed himself.[82] And Alas suffered periods of spiritual dryness that no amount of reasoning could dispel.

Larra's preface appeared in the midst of the first Carlist War, with a Church in disarray, many of whose clergy were allied with the Carlists. The ecclesiastical estate had already taken a battering in the liberal triennium. As Callahan observes, "It was not until the second liberal regime that hostility against the Church spread so extensively that it assumed broader significance." The liberal government voted to suppress most of the monasteries and began selling off Church properties. Royalist revolts, supported by many churchmen, lit a tinderbox among the more radical elements of society. For the first time in the modern period a violent, popular anticlericalism, though modest in scale and generally urban, showed its face, destroying property and attacking clergy, crying, "Death to the friars" in the streets.[83] During the next ten years, 1823–33, with Ferdinand VII firmly restored to his former power, the Church recovered for the most part and was now vehemently committed to crushing liberalism in Spain.

This turn of events set the stage for the crucial period after Ferdinand's death, 1833–43, which signaled the end of the old regime Church and the intensification of a conflict between Church and State that was still not fully settled well into the twentieth century. In 1833 the conflict was not between Catholics and anti-Catholics, since few Spaniards of the time identified themselves as anti-Catholics. For liberals, who ran the gamut from moderate to radical, it was a matter of redefining the role of the Church to make it more responsive and useful to a changing society. Spain remained a confessional State, but even as Larra was preparing his translation of Lamennais's *Paroles* the head of government, Juan Álvarez Mendizábal, was dismantling most of the regular clergy and disentailing ecclesiastical properties. Liberals like Mendizábal, Larra, and Ayguals de Izco strongly opposed Church privilege and wealth, but even more fundamentally the theocratic ideology underpinning its power.

The period is remarkable for the heavy blow dealt to the organization and social-economic well-being of the Church in Spain. Even more striking is the apparent sifting downward of the elites' attitudes and frustrations with respect to the institution and its clergymen into popular venues already deeply affected by turbulent social-political conditions. The single most dramatic episode came with the *matanza de los frailes* on 17 July 1834. *Madrileño* mobs from the lower classes and the popular urban militia wrecked ecclesiastical properties and killed seventy-eight Jesuits, Franciscans, Dominicans, and Mercedarians. This event was recreated in the fiction of Ayguals de Izco, Galdós, and Pío Baroja. Whether the mayhem was unplanned or part of a radical conspiracy is hard to say. Callahan argues convincingly that "the truth may lie somewhere between."[84] Though nothing in the nineteenth century would match the horrendous anticlerical bloodletting in the first months of the Spanish Civil War, this first outburst marks the degree to which the social-spiritual bonds between Church and community had been tested and found wanting.

The difficulties and sufferings of the Church in a chaotic and violent period, coupled with the political hardening of both the clerical and the liberal sides, certainly added up to a religious crisis never before seen in Spain. The Church apologist Cardinal Nicholas Wiseman, who had family connections in Spain, personally surveyed the situation in 1845. "Can anything be more lamentable," he wrote, "than the accumulation of ruins which encumber the fairest cities of that country, in consequence of the sale, and either destruction or dilapidation, of conventual buildings? It gives to streets and public squares the appearance of a place tumbling down in decay, or just delivered from a siege." He sees Spain as "just emerging from a succession of political convulsions, in which religion has been awfully shaken," weakening peoples' faith.[85]

Nonetheless, Wiseman, who figured prominently in the English Catholic

Revival, was optimistic, for he was also witness to a reflowering of devotion as the Church in Spain began to recuperate in the 1840s. Thus, for example, the exposition of the Blessed Eucharist continues without interruption for the forty hours' prayer: "Yet it is only by the charity of the people that the expenses of this worship can be defrayed."[86] Whether the cardinal's hopes were wishful thinking or truly reflective of a collective return to faith is impossible to say. But his eagerness to reestablish the sense of *communitas,* the critical role the Church played in people's lives in the midst of devastation is worthy of remark.

Wiseman's essay is thoughtful and informative, but one expects that apologists would blame liberal governments and liberal ideology for the Church's present difficulties. This position, however, does not give the whole story, for it suggests that only traditionalists (that is, the faithful, in this view) suffered, that liberals alone were responsible for the crisis and, more important, did not experience the trauma of spiritual and social upheaval. That is not the case. Certainly both liberals (of all persuasions) and Carlists contributed to the worsening politicization of religion. Nonetheless, liberals were as deeply affected by the conflict as conservatives and traditionalists, even if they understood it differently. The Republican democrat Ayguals de Izco's *María, la hija de un jornalero*, which focuses on the period of the Carlist War but is a product of the 1840s, exploits the deadly mix of politics and religion, though it is not always clear how aware he is of his own voice aggravating the problem in the narrative. His book was no doubt the commercial enterprise of a shrewd marketer, as critics have often pointed out, but *María* would have been inconceivable without the Carlist War (an element that also distinguishes the novel from its major source of inspiration, Sue's *Les Mystères de Paris*).[87] Ayguals's anticlerical rage against the theocratic Carlists has nothing to do with opportunism and everything to do with religious crisis, a religious crisis that is inseparable from a social crisis. Indeed, the philanthropic impulse that drives his narrative forward, as we will see in chapter 1, stems from a liberal-inspired religious feeling, a desire to evangelize through social reform.

Ayguals is not alone here. Liberals in the period seem determined to rescue religion by rehumanizing it. It wasn't simply the bloodshed wrought in the name of religion, or the Church's near collapse and inability to fulfill its mission, or even its hostility toward liberalism that upset liberals. There was a larger malaise suggestive of deep peril in the very marrow of society and uncertainty of the soul, as liberals, following in the footsteps of the ilustrados, attempted to make religion modern, to make it part of the modern world. The violent response of the Carlist War brutally exposed how the two, religion and the modern world, were reshaping each other, like an eruption produced by the grinding clash of tectonic plates.

There were few atheists or even religiously lukewarm individuals among liberals in the 1830s and 1840s. But were there liberal Catholics? Could liberal Catholicism be said to exist in Spain? José Aranguren apparently didn't think so, declaring that "the total absence of a *liberal Catholicism* throughout the nineteenth century was fatal for Spain. Catholicism and modernity have had to be lived simultaneously, separately, quasi-contradictorily, by many Spaniards." He grudgingly admits there were "many liberals who were personally Catholic, but who did not act publicly as such." Miguel Artola echoed the sentiment: "Liberal Catholicism in Spain had no representative figure."[88]

While liberal clergy were in short supply and a liberal Catholic movement did not exist, statements like those above strike me as somewhat precipitate. What is one to make then of Larra, whom one of the premier historians of Spanish Catholicism calls an important figure of liberal Catholicism? How can one ignore the stream of liberal Catholic opinion another historian has documented in Barcelona newspapers and other publications of the 1830s and 1840s? Or Ayguals de Izco, who called Christ the "first Apostle of Democracy"? The father of the traditionalist Marcelino Menéndez Pelayo was a *progresista and* a Catholic. Carlists and moderate conservatives often accused liberals, especially the progressively inclined, of being irreligious, but what actually occurred was a rethinking of religion as fundamental to the life of the community. Children of the Enlightenment and readers of influential French liberal Catholics like Lamennais, early nineteenth-century Spanish liberals and progressives reinterpreted the evangelical origins of faith to fit the historical-political shape of events, to fit historical change. Thus many of them saw Christianity as liberal: "The Christian religion," said *El Guardia Nacional*, "even disregarding its divine character, and politically speaking, is the freest and first constitution of the world." The same paper claims that "the Christian religion is . . . the religion of humankind and joined to liberty."[89] Religious tolerance was a logical consequence.

In line with a more evangelical faith, liberal Catholics also linked religion to social philanthropy, especially at the local level. They sought to make religion more civic-minded within a vaguely defined movement of humanitarian democracy. The humanitarian impulse drew inspiration from the notion of "universal fraternity, the fraternity of Christ . . . the *humanity* announced by Christ, which includes all humankind," according to a columnist in *El Constitucional*. Universal fraternity also signified a utopian classless society to the most progressive elements of liberalism: "Christ came for all . . . before his arrival there were two kinds of men: that of master and slave. He made them disappear." Radical equality will throw "all classes together . . . rich and poor, the wise and the ignorant, the progressive and the reactionary, the democrat and the aristocrat."[90]

It is easy to see how such sentiments favor turning religion into the politics of democratic action, in which the truths of religion are revealed through society itself. Questions of transcendence and dogma melted into the background when met with the dual insistence on a simpler, evangelical faith and a nontheocratic State. The Italian republican Joseph Mazzini, who influenced and corresponded with Spanish democrats and progressives like the statesman Emilio Castelar (1832–99), wrote in 1835, "Politics deal with men *where* and *as* they are: they define their tendencies and regulate their actions in accordance with them. It is only religious thought that can transfigure both. Religious thought is the breath of life of Humanity: at once its life and soul, its spirit and its outward sign."[91] He advocated a "Humanitarian Faith" for Italian republicanism: "We fell as a political party: we must rise again as a religious party. The religious element is universal and immortal: it binds men together in a universal brotherhood. . . . Heralds of a new world, we must found a moral unity, the Catholicism of Humanity . . . we seek the new Gospel, of which [Jesus] left us, ere He died, the immortal hope, and of which the Christian Gospel is the germ, as *man* is the germ of HUMANITY."[92]

Emphasis on the here and now, on the social polis, suggested, however, that the immutable truths of the faith were subject to the laws of change. Consequently, what was important to Mazzini, Lamennais, and many liberal Catholics of this period was to act: "That which Christ did Humanity can do. . . . Believe, and act. Action is the Word of God: passive thought is but its shadow." The one great principle of authority, for Mazzini, was the Law of Progress, in which "every *social* revolution is essentially *religious*." Like Lamennais, he was alarmed by the rise of Carlism in Spain, which he saw as theocratic and resistant to social change. Addressing himself to the clergy, he wrote, "The world moves; progress is its law; the patriots are the faithful, the apostles of that law." The burning of Spanish convents, he said, referring to the events of 17 July 1834, is the result of such factious resistance, which "dissociates religion from the great humanitarian movement."[93]

Mazzini saw politics through the lens of religion because he believed that "the question which agitates the world is a religious question." The Carlist War, which pitted an ultramontane, counterrevolutionary movement against more liberalizing forces in Spain, laid bare both a dynastic quarrel and a religious conflict that shaped the social thinking of liberals and conservatives alike. Mazzini thought that "religious sentiment is declining day by day . . . amid the irritation born of barren party strife, under the evil influence of an odious and reactionary policy." At the same time politics was sacred: "The republican Party . . . is an essentially religious party. It has its faith, its doctrine, its martyrs from Spartacus onwards; and it must have doctrine inviolable, authority infallible, the martyr's spirit and call to self-sacrifice."[94] No less politicized, conservatives saw the same religious decline but considered the conversion of politics into religion anathema and a contributing factor in the decay of belief, by challenging the supremacy of Church authority and encouraging further secularization of the social body.

Spanish liberal Catholics treaded on perilous ground, uncertain if the spirit of reform might endanger the very faith they meant to revitalize. Moreover, they were accused throughout the century of being irreligious and spiritually indifferent. Castelar, who struggled to reconcile faith with liberalism, felt constrained in 1858 to defend the religious foundation of progressive thought: "Democracy is not contrary to Christianity, it is the social realization of Christianity." He went further, declaring that religion was not opposed to progress, that in fact "progress is our belief, our faith. Progress is . . . the faith of the nineteenth century."[95]

A response was not long in coming. In a probing critique from 1859, Juan Valera (1824–1905) objected to Castelar's conflating of progress and faith and to his use of religion for political purposes. Christianity, he argued, cannot be called *progresista*, at least not in the current, secular sense of the word (though *progresistas* can be Christian). Nor can one speak of the Christian religion as progressing without contradicting the already perfect being of the divine. Progress is a modern human creation: "To consider Christianity as progress is equivalent to saying it is a human invention." Valera is asking, what is the relation between Christianity and modernity? Is there one, in effect, if progress is modern and secular and the Christian faith is not? Furthermore, can the consequences of progress lead believers to "fall into the shadows"? What most provokes the future author of *Pepita Jiménez* is the partisan use to which religion is subjected: "There are those who have said that Christianity is liberal so that liberals will be Christians; and others, that it is absolutist, so that absolutists will be Christians."[96]

For Valera, politics and religion should not mix; he denies that Christianity "is a political and social doctrine." In sum, Castelar "may be at once a democrat, liberal, progressive, and fervent Catholic. . . . What I loathe is making . . . a dangerous synthesis or combination of all these doctrines, sustaining them, or having them originate in the holy doctrine of Our Lord Jesus Christ."[97]

In rejecting social Catholicism — Mazzini's humanitarian faith is specifically cited as an example — Valera did not throw modernity overboard, only what he judged to be the political perversion of religion. In so doing he ended up proposing a modest theory of secularization.[98] The religious disagreement between Valera and Castelar was also political. Valera inclined toward the *moderados*, and Castelar was a progressive democrat. Given that both of these men were liberal Catholics, a narrow definition of the phrase is probably a contradiction in terms. Moreover, to be a liberal Catholic in Catholic Spain was a complicated matter.

Valera is a case in point. Shortly after his essay appeared in book form, his nephew Salvador read it and evidently had a lot of questions. Here is the heart of his uncle's response: "I think that the most *impious* articles of the volume are those that shock you as too theological: the articles against Castelar. All those mysticisms and theology serve as nothing more than to strip the Catholic religion of all influence upon civilization and real human destiny, reducing it to an excellent thing for those who want to go straight to heaven. This is to diminish religion and convert it into something useless for everything great, active, and energetic in the life of nations, art, politics, science, and social economy. How do you expect that in Spain, without rendering me useless for everything and forever, I would have been able to say such things without veiling them with reticence and irony?"[99]

In a sensitive and nuanced essay, Francisco Pérez Gutiérrez tied himself in knots trying to decipher the meaning behind this letter.[100] The ambiguous wording does not allow one to penetrate its full significance, for Valera has turned his irony upon himself. I really could not express what I wanted to write clearly and openly, he seems to be saying, so I did the next best thing. The public expression of faith in Spain is inadequate, it is all "mysticisms and theology," but he can't say that; whereas religion itself possesses grandeur and energy. Here, it is as though the critique of Castelar's views were a pretext for a deeper dissatisfaction with the lived understanding of religion in mid-nineteenth-century Spain.

It is no wonder the label of hypocrite and smug pragmatist has stuck to poor Valera. Manuel Azaña was utterly dismissive of the novelist's religious sentiments: "He was not a believing Catholic, not even a Christian, but publicly he held to a liberal Catholicism."[101] This rather hasty assessment does not bear close scrutiny, given our inability to plumb the inner recesses of Valera's heart, a guarded castle compared to Clarín's openly expressed spiritual malaise. Was he instead "a skeptic always ready to believe, and a sincere, if not firm, believer always on the point of vacillating: always and at once, the two things together"?[102] Whatever the complexities of Valera's faith, his layered use of irony, a defining feature of his art, is a double-edged sword, always poised to wound its bearer, as the letter to his nephew suggests. In matters of belief, who is to judge where irony ends and doubt begins?

Certainly in his essay on Castelar, Valera does not hesitate to call himself "a man of little faith": "[yet] I desire and hope that faith [will] return to my soul." The spiritual desire found within Spanish liberalism did not diminish in the second half of the nineteenth century. In 1875 the future novelist Armando

Palacio Valdés thought the religious problem "the most striking of all things troubling present-day society." He was referring less to the institutional and political question of Church–State relations or to religion in society than to belief, in particular the appeal and vogue of rational faith since Kant.[103] Indeed, Francisco de P. Canalejas (1834–83) observed that there was "a hunger for the supernatural," especially among educated men impatient with the pace of modern life. He wrote, "We have torn orthodoxy from the bosom of present society. . . . [I]n religion, as in politics, to break with tradition is equivalent to burdening oneself with a painful, unsettling pilgrimage through the veritable labyrinth which the febrile spiritual activity of our century has created and in which it has incessantly entangled us. We need to take a manly, noble decision in this spiritual crisis."[104]

In espousing a rational faith, Canalejas was attempting to straddle the vexed line between liberal independence of reason and acceptance of spiritual transcendence, between modernity and tradition. He skirts the dicey issue of miracles by intimating that belief in miracles is not essential to the Christian religion. But he is also acutely aware of the ironies implicated in the exercise of liberty, saying, "It is the negation of God that man has the terrible faculty of formulating, a negation that continues to grow as a witness to human liberty, even as religion does its work, acts, and enlarges the spirit of men. . . . Atheism will always appear with greater intensity in the most religious periods, expressing the logical relation that links affirmation with negation."[105]

In 1874, when these words appeared, Spain was indeed in crisis mode. It was not simply the religious crisis of individual belief alluded to here, but a set of political-social conditions ushered in by the Revolution of 1868 that eventually tempered liberal enthusiasm for progress, confirming, in effect, that "revolutions pass, but the state of crisis persists."[106] Spaniards were once again embroiled in a Carlist War. They had worn out a foreign-born king (the dethroned Isabel II's replacement), torn through four presidents (including the conciliatory Castelar) during the short-lived First Republic, experienced destabilizing cantonalist revolts in the Levante and the south, and were fighting an insurrection in Cuba.

At the start of the Revolution of 1868, the Church endured anticlerical harassment, though no large-scale violence, by the revolutionary juntas set up in many towns. Political slogans and red revolutionary-style hats briefly stirred up church services. Reining in the juntas, the provisional government in Madrid also took steps to reduce the number of religious communities, including the expulsion of the Society of Jesus (for the fourth time in Spanish history), and to disallow the owning of property by the orders. Defenders of the Church and of religious unity were especially incensed, though, by the freedom of religion clause voted into the Constitution of 1869. They saw this clause as an attack upon the faith. The parliamentary debates over the issue had been fierce, and Church–State relations remained tense through tumultuous changes of government until the Bourbon Restoration of 1875.

In these circumstances, it is not surprising that a feeling of crisis, even of impending doom, dovetailing with an apocalyptic tradition of long standing, should have invaded Catholic circles, even though the difficulties the Church experienced between 1868 and 1874 were not as severe as the trauma of 1833–43. Thus, for example, in a little book with a long title — *El fin del mundo: Los tres días de tinieblas y la gran crisis social seguida del triunfo de la Iglesia* (The end of the world: the three days of darkness and the great social crisis followed by the triumph of the Church), by D.J.M.L. — prophecies ranging from those of St. Catherine of Siena and Savonarola to the revelations of Mélanie and Maximin, the two children who saw a vision of Mary at La Salette in France in 1846, predict the downfall of a modern, impious society. The crisis, one reads, will arrive with the era of steam and electricity, a period that has fed the wildest ambitions of republicans, socialists, communists, and internationalists (alluding to the First International) and issued in wars. People live in an "age of enlightenment . . . surrounded by darkness. It calls itself humanitarian, and invents all manner of ways to kill. . . . It calls itself philanthropic, loving the people, and it destroys all the elements that gave life to the proletarian classes."[107] This comment, which may be a reference to the radical Paris Commune of 1871 and ensuing bloodbath, underscores the negative connotations of revolutionary excess that more conservative Catholics attached to a humanitarian ethos identified as secular and therefore destructive of "the elements that gave life to the proletarian classes." What those elements might be is not clear, though possibly, the dual support system of religion and capital. The religious crisis that fills the pages of *El fin del mundo* with such alarm and dread is inseparable from a social-political crisis of equally terrifying dimensions.

The book, which was published in 1874, aimed for a certain timeliness. It cited, for example, from a pamphlet dated November 1871, *El desengaño del porvenir* (The disillusionment of the future) by Manuel Mos y Rosa, from another published communication of his from April 1872, and from a letter of Mélanie, now a nun, written in May 1872. It also includes the secrets of Mélanie of La Salette, which first appeared in 1871, though news of the apparition she saw in 1846 had reached Spain within months in pamphlets written in Spanish and Catalan.[108]

The copy from my library was published in Mexico, but the cultural-religious world contained in *El fin del mundo* is overwhelmingly west European. It refers to such events as the coming of the republic to France, Spain, and Italy, which suggests the first audience for this book, possibly even a translation enriched with Spanish allusions, was not Mexican. The array of religious and cultural references points to two related phenomena: a Catholic readership of European and, here, Hispanic reach that had common concerns and a publishing forum that connected national issues with international ones. Ultramontane thought, centered on Rome's authority, reveals the extent to which clergy and laity read broadly, that is, across national boundaries, translating and reprinting articles, pamphlets, and books from other national cultures.[109]

In other words, the feeling of religious crisis was not limited to Spain but was pervasive throughout an increasingly secularized Europe riding the whirlwind of social-economic change. France, to cite the premier example, had already experienced apocalypse at the end of the eighteenth century. End-of-the-world visions and predictions, in which the memory of the French Revolution and the Terror of '93 was ever present, constituted one response to a perceived crisis. Increased devotionalism from midcentury on, though sometimes inseparable from the apocalyptic tradition, was much more characteristic. After the Paris Commune, in which the archbishop of Paris and several clergy were executed, efforts to sacralize the nation redoubled. There was a surge in the promoting of devotions like the cult of the Sacred Heart, historically associated with the royalists and prophecies of the monarchy's restoration and now "the image of Catholic resistance to the scourge of Revolution." Plans to build the Basilica of Sacré-Coeur at Montmartre got an additional boost at this time.[110]

Catholic Spain too experienced a revival, at first modestly in the 1840s and 1850s, in part as disbanded ecclesiastics returned from France, bringing back devotional practices, books, and renewed fervor. But the major impetus to revival came after the Revolution of 1868 and with the Bourbon Restoration in 1875, when Church–State relations stabilized. Along with educational expansion, the greater visibility of religiosity, both individual and collective, became a hallmark of the Spanish Church in the seventies and eighties.

Here too the Sacred Heart of Jesus cult, promoted through lay associations, pilgrimages, and monuments, was especially noteworthy. *Mensajero del Corazón de Jesús* (The messenger of the Sacred Heart) (Bilbao, 1886–1931), a Jesuit publication, worked tirelessly to spread the Sacred Heart image everywhere, "not just to strengthen the piety of the faithful but to claim Catholic conservative influence over civic and political life."[111] Such efforts reached a high symbolic mark on 30 May 1919, when Alphonse XIII inaugurated the statue of the Sacred Heart of Jesus at Cerro de los Ángeles, on the outskirts of Madrid, seen as the geographical heart of Spain. (Formal dedication ceremonies for Sacré-Coeur in Montmartre took place a few months later on October 16.) When civil war broke out in July 1936, Republican militiamen took potshots at the monument (it was later blown up), as a symbol of Catholic triumphalism.[112] During the war Carlists and even Franco's Moroccan troops wore Sacred Heart badges called *detentes* as divine protection.

Symbols like the Sacred Heart monuments were not uniformly welcomed in the heavily politicized environment of late nineteenth- and early twentieth-century Spain.[113] Public religiosity like processions and pilgrimages provoked antipathy and even violence. To safeguard sacred images, seminary students in Oviedo armed themselves with sticks in religious processions. Organizers of religious acts also turned piety into politics. A Marian procession from Bilbao to the sanctuary-shrine of the Virgin of Begoña in 1889 was meant "solemnly to proclaim the rights of God and the social reign of the Heart of Jesus, in opposition to the diabolical centenary of 'the rights of man.' "[114]

Symbols identified with the history of Spain also aroused debate, like the proposed shrine at Covadonga, the cradle of the Reconquest, for which the bishop of Oviedo, Benito Sanz y Forés, had begun campaigning in 1872. Catholics saw Covadonga as part of the salvation history of the nation, but liberals wanted it to express the desire for freedom. Sanz y Forés's successor, Ramón Martínez Vigil, imagined Covadonga as the site of a modern Reconquest, saying, "There is no need to demonstrate that our century bears a marked similarity to the century of Pelayo . . . The Moors of our day don't brandish the scimitar . . . instead, they brandish the book, the pamphlet and the newspaper . . . in order to poison hearts and pervert the consciences of nations, to rip out their faith in Christ and their devotion to Most Holy Mary."[115] Catholics won the initial skirmish over secularists, but in the long run Covadonga failed to catch on as a symbol of national redemption, despite the Franco regime's efforts, regionalism and tourism having diminished its significance (see Carolyn Boyd).

The example of Covadonga does reveal, however, that, the international reach of Roman Catholicism notwithstanding, religion was rooted in national histories and cultures and sometimes, as in this case, in conflict. Memory sites do not always signify social cohesion.[116] Most important, religion in the late nineteenth and early twentieth centuries was often polarizing, as Clarín in *La Regenta* illustrates, mordantly dissecting the politics of religion, on the one hand, and painfully probing the anguish of belief, on the other. He brilliantly weaves together the ways in which personal belief and religious politics sometimes become mutually implicated. For example, the secondary character Santos Barinaga, a seller of religious artifacts, is financially ruined by his priestly competitor Fermín de Pas and eventually loses his faith.

The entanglement of faith and politics is exemplified above all in his protagonist Ana Ozores. Ana's deeply felt spiritual life is simultaneously her own
and not her own, as the directed use of confession, historically central to
resacramentalizing Restoration society, becomes instrumental in making and
unmaking her persona. In this sense, she embodies the Catholic Revival in
Spain, the desire to reclaim faith through individualized devotional practices
under carefully controlled, institutional conditions. Even her emotional identification with Saint Teresa de Jesús, which appears like a spontaneous outpouring of her soul, needs to be seen against the religious boosterism and
politicization of the saint in the 1870s and 1880s. This was another example
of the Catholic Revival, which encouraged female piety. Santa Teresa was
enthusiastically promoted through the activities and publications of Father
Enrique de Ossó (1840–96), founder of the journal *Santa Teresa de Jesús*
(1872–96), the Asociación de Hijas de María Inmaculada y Santa Teresa de
Jesús (1873), which had over 120,000 members by 1882, and the religious
(non-Carmelite) order the Compañía de Santa Teresa de Jesús (1876). In 1877
he organized the first national pilgrimage to the birthplace and burial site of
Santa Teresa. De Ossó also created the Hermandad Teresiana Universal, one
of the first mass movements in modern religious history. His manual *El cuarto
de hora de oración, según las enseñanzas de la seráfica doctora Santa Teresa de
Jesús* (The fifteen-minute prayer, according to the teachings of the seraphic
doctor Saint Teresa de Jesús) (1874), had gone through fifty-two editions by
1977 and was used by countless numbers of young women in Spain.[117] As
preparations for the tricentennial of the saint in 1882 got underway, de Ossó
withdrew from the tribute in protest over what he regarded as the excessive
presence of civilian or secular participation. The celebration, filled with the
same fervent and somewhat saccharine adoration favored by de Ossó and the
Catholic Revival in general, had also become heatedly politicized. Ultraconservative political-religious groups of *integristas* accused the more accommodating Unión Católica, aligned with the government, of manipulating the
tricentennial commission for their own ends.[118] Traditionalists also disliked
intensely the participation of liberals and nonclergy politicians like Práxedes
Sagasta and Francisco Silvela and poets like Gaspar Núñez de Arce, in the
commission. In the end, Saint Teresa's iconic status was assured. Clarín, meanwhile, followed all these developments closely.[119]

Endemic political-religious squabbling and manipulation in the public
arena of Spanish history or in the pages of *La Regenta* signal not so much a
Foucauldian panopticon of power relations as an ongoing set of unresolved
issues in which the Catholic Revival, while fervently sincere as a devotional
movement, was caught up. A response to a perceived social-spiritual crisis, the

revival, which saw the crisis as a consequence of the modern world and of secularism, was inevitably politicized and was thus as much a part of the modern world as the forces to which it was opposed. Indeed, the movers behind the revival and the Church in general made shrewd use of modern methods of communication and activism through the press, mass mobilization, and voluntary associations.[120]

The politics of religion played a major part in defining the Restoration period. Tradition-minded Catholics believed, as one clergyman put it in 1890, that " 'the religious crisis, the principal cause of the social crisis, has in Catholicism its most effective remedy.' "[121] The modern world needed to be molded to religion. The problem was, in this sense, theological. For liberals like Alas, however, the religious question was at the heart of the social question because religion had failed to come to grips with the modern world. Thus, two major issues during the Restoration, religious freedom and social-economic reform, were connected to the larger picture of Spain's emerging modernity.

Constitutional debate over Church–State relations was intense in 1876. Article 11 was approved ultimately as a compromise. It reconfirmed Roman Catholicism as the religion of the State and proclaimed religious tolerance but disallowed public displays of religion other than Catholicism. The proponents of both religious unity and religious freedom (established in the Constitution of 1869) were left dissatisfied with this solution, but the liberal conservative and major architect of the Restoration's political system, Antonio Cánovas del Castillo, argued for passage of the article: "In the article under debate . . . religious unity is not blocked, religious intolerance is not blocked, because that unity and intolerance, for better or worse, have been broken and blocked for some time. The Government maintains that it is not possible to consider this question in isolation, separating it from the examination and impartial judgment of the intellectual situation and the moral situation of the modern world."[122]

In many ways, Cánovas was a pragmatist. He understood that things had changed, that the alliance of throne and altar, indeed Church authority itself, no longer possessed the same near-universal symbolic and emotional drawing power it once had. Article 11 maintained the façade of the old order but left the back door to alternative views ajar. It was representative of a social-political system that operated on different levels, one visible (parliament on paper) and one hidden (shared power through backstairs electoral manipulation), reluctantly acknowledging the more fluid, surface realities of modern life while buttressing the cracked underground pillars of religious and political authority. Recreated through plot, behavior, and language in *La Regenta*, the system encouraged duplicity and concealment, along with the pressure to reveal secrets, under the granting of authority, hence the imaginative structure of confession informing Clarín's novel. What the system was less capable of dealing with was the challenge of disorder erupting periodically to the surface of Restoration society. Its unsettling disclosure, whether psychic or social in nature, underscored the unresolved strains between freedom and authority. This nervous push-and-pull movement is also narratively present in *La Regenta* and is indicative not only of Alas's ambivalent attitude toward both freedom and authority, but also of the religious framework of sin and redemption in which this tension and disorder are understood. On the one hand, Alas advocated freedoms of all kinds. On the other, he appeared unable and even at times unwilling to free himself or his novel from deeply entrenched structures of authority.

For liberals like Galdós and Clarín, the reigning institutions were also simply not up to the task. The Church's attempts to address the social question bedeviling Restoration Spain were, by all accounts, woefully wanting, despite the inspiration of Leo XIII's encyclical of 1891, *Rerum Novarum,* and the establishment of Catholic workers' circles and mutual assistance groups in the waning years of the century. Government also dragged its feet. There were private initiatives, often with State backing or supervision, most notably the networks of beneficence that flourished in the period. This philanthropic impulse, associated with the Catholic Revival and still working on the laudable if inadequate premise of charity, is richly embodied in Galdós's *Fortunata y Jacinta.* The famously complex, intertwined, reciprocal relationship of his characters is also modeled on the social hierarchy of clientelism, which was basic to the structure of the religiously inspired philanthropic enterprise. In her comings and goings, Guillermina Pacheco, a fictional portrait of the charity activist Ernestina Manuel de Villena, links rich and poor even as she underscores class distinctions. Deeply religious, the aristocratic Ernestina incarnated a new lay Catholic activism among women and, like her contemporary Concepción Arenal, adopted a modern approach to fundraising through the press and private initiatives. In *Fortunata y Jacinta* the physical presence of well-to-do women caring for the poor in their homes underlines the degree to which *caritas* was considered a domestic virtue.[123] The title "Spiritual Naturalism" given chapter 6, part 3, captures the social-religious humanitarian ethos of the entire novel as a vision of flawed *communitas.* By contrast, the unredeemed world of *La Regenta* is the same vision gone dark.

Galdós was under no illusion that beneficence alone could solve the problems of deprivation, unemployment, and insufficient education among the working classes. By the 1880s and 1890s such issues were being debated and discussed in forums like the Commission for Social Reform established in

1884 and were of great interest to writers like Galdós and Alas. In late 1882, Clarín began a series of investigative reports for *El Día* on labor unrest and anarchism in Andalusia. These pieces show him to be deeply sympathetic toward rural working-class misery but unreceptive of radical ideologies and the use of violence. In the last months of his life, in 1901, he went to see the Gijón strike for himself and ended up mediating between labor and capital.[124] In Galdós's case, his first stint as a liberal deputy in the Spanish Parliament from 1886 to 1890 left few traces, but he was reelected as a Republican in 1907 and 1914 and gave impassioned speeches on behalf of the working classes.[125] The social question for Galdós, Clarín, and indeed most nineteenth-century commentators was inherently an economic one as well.

By the turn of the century, both Alas and Galdós had moved further left-ward politically, in a period of increasing political factionalism over reform of the religious orders, class strife, and anticlerical agitation (which had been mostly dormant since 1868), amid much talk of regeneration after the debacle of the Spanish-American War in 1898. In 1901, there were anticlerical riots, spurred on in part by Galdós's play *Electra*, which was sharply critical of the Church. Animosity against the clergy was also directed toward the Catholic Revival's efforts to resacralize Spanish society, even as large numbers of French religious, fleeing the secularization brought on by the passage of new laws, crossed the border into Spain. Anarchists in Spain (and elsewhere) turned violent, assassinating politicians, bombing buildings, and burning convents. They were held largely responsible for the Barcelona Tragic Week in 1909, which was marked by anticlerical destructiveness and antimilitarist protest.[126] Lower-class resentment of the clergy, especially the orders, simmered in the early twentieth century. An English observer wrote in 1910, the year the ultimately ineffectual padlock law (Ley del Candado) was passed to control the numbers of religious communities, "The crucial question to-day in Spain is the religious question. Not the belief or disbelief of the people in their religion, but the relations of the Church—i.e., that of the priests and, far more, of the Religious Orders—to the nation."[127] In *Spain from Within*, a book bearing little resemblance to the stereotypical guidebook views of Spain then favored, Rafael Shaw commented on working-class hostility toward the clergy: "For years past I have noticed that no member of the working classes salutes a priest or friar in the streets. Day after day . . . I never saw an artisan greet a priest or friar, or vice versa. . . . The priests kept their eyes bent on the ground, one hand grasping the skirts and the other pressed on the breast, a typical attitude, which is jeered at by the poor as 'canting.' The workmen kept their eyes fixed on the work on which they were engaged."[128]

Working-class alienation from religion goes in hand in hand with the clergy's inability to connect with the workers.[129] But Shaw also insists that "the mass of the people are untouched by modern skepticism, and are deeply and sincerely religious." He singles out the mental attitude of worshipers toward religious images, which he finds "intricate and difficult to disentangle," saying that "the prayers offered before these images are in most cases addressed, not to the Person represented, but to the image itself." This intimate, emotional relationship is not new and extends to other religious traditions as well, in which "likenesses [are] not merely likenesses but [are] their subjects."[130] Sacred images, like relics, were a direct conduit to the divine. Certainly Galdós understood this relationship when he imagined, with ironic sympathy, an inebriated Mauricia la Dura speaking directly to the Host. Similarly, Sender transformed Paco's presence, his martyred body, into a relic in *Réquiem por un campesino español*. Shaw indirectly reminds us that in an age of secularization the persistence of the divine is not an anomaly but a reality for believers. And while he distinguishes between the problems of belief and the social, institutional role of the Church, historical circumstances affirm that in reality these two things are deeply interrelated. How can working-class hostility toward the clergy be separated from the question of belief?

By the time the Second Republic was declared in April 1931, many leftward-leaning middle-class and working-class Spaniards had turned away from the Church, which had become closely identified with the dictatorship of Miguel Primo de Rivera (1923–30). Republican anticlerical measures, in turn, mobilized Catholics, as both sides racheted up the rhetoric. Manuel Azaña, then–minister of war and cofounder of the political party Acción Republicana, inflamed Catholic sentiment when he declared, "Spain has ceased to be Catholic."

Azaña's statement needs to be read within the context of the speech he gave on 13 October 1931 in parliament advocating, among other things, separation of Church and State, dissolution of the Society of Jesus, and the elimination of Catholic education (all would be voted in). There were three fundamental problems in Spain today, he said: "The problem of the local autonomies, the social problem in its most urgent and acute form, which is the reform of property, and the present so-called religious problem, which is strictly speaking the implantation of a secular State." For Azaña, the religious problem was a political one, the only "authentic religious problem" a matter of individual conscience. Allowing that there were millions of believers in Spain, he argued that Catholicism had ceased to be a vibrant and creative force in the national culture, hence his observation in the same speech that "Spain has ceased to be Catholic."[131]

Azaña's move to make the religious problem go away by converting it into a uniquely political issue—his fervent desire for the complete secularization of the State — should not blind one to the role belief, or, perhaps better said here, loss of belief, plays in his formulation of the issue. The future head of government had no use for the Church or for its representatives, especially the religious orders, whose deleterious influence over young minds he decried, reflecting his own unhappy experiences under Augustinian tutelage.[132] Such comments were greeted with great applause in parliament.

Azaña simply brushed away the belief of millions of Spanish Catholics by relegating faith to a position of irrelevance in the cultural life of the country. To say that Catholicism no longer served to unify and define national identity was one thing; to privatize religion was another, for that divorced belief from its public practice, undercutting Azaña's claim that the religious problem was purely political. It *was* political, but also religious. In this sense, Durkheim was right to stress that "the idea of society is the soul of religion," producing a malaise when belief systems are in crisis. Azaña seemingly wanted to replace that soul with the secular State itself. Hence, for example, his scornful dismissal of applying the Gospel to politics. Echoing Valera, whose work he admired, he said, "The most monstrous deformation of the figure of Jesus is to present him as a propagandist for democracy or as a reader of Michelet and Castelar, or, who's to say, a precursor of the Agrarian Law."[133]

The strict separation of politics and religion Azaña advocated brought about the very opposite effect during the Second Republic and the civil war, in part because such advocacy was already politicized.[134] Secularization mobilized Catholics to get politically involved, which provoked in turn more extreme anticlerical reaction. Church burnings and prophetic visions of world's end occupy the same violent landscape of catastrophe in 1930s Spain. Azaña was not responsible for the apocalyptic character of the war, but his confrontational laicism was symptomatic of a prevailing mindset in which intolerance of other views was widespread on both sides.

Demonizing the enemy also went hand in hand with sacralizing one's dead: the very language welds religion to politics, signaling that each term served to explicate the other and in other cases to substitute one for the other.[135] Carretero, for example, ends the first part of *Declaración de guerra* (Declaration of war) with the burial of a Nationalist "protomartyr," the assassinated rightist José Calvo Sotelo. He opens the second part with a chapter titled "Resurrection," which alludes to the imminent end of the war and Franco's victory in 1939. Seeking a hidden manuscript he feverishly wrote in July 1936, Carretero returns to his home, only to find it has been vandalized and pillaged. These pages, yellowed and mildewed, which are the first part of the book just read, have now become sacred relics, he says. They embody the memory of the protomartyr; and they are ruins among the ruins. They speak in the midst of devastation, in the same way Carretero in part 1 has Calvo Sotelo speak of faith among the charred remains of the Villarrobledo parish church. Just as historically the politician's murder became the flash point for the Nationalist uprising, so he serves here as the mythic spark for El Caballero Audaz's enflamed narrative to burn and slash through the already desecrated landscape of civil war.

Sender's tightly constructed *Réquiem por un campesino español*, with its explosive climax, appears to inhabit a radically different universe from Carretero's overheated rhetoric. And yet both narratives essentially begin with a post-factum assassination. Paco's death has already happened, the purpose of the narrative being to resurrect his life through memory. *Réquiem* literally begins in the consecrated space of the village church but symbolically converts the entire story into sacred ground. The same narrative turn motivates Carretero, albeit his writer's ego often gets in the way. Most significant, by beginning with a murder remembered, both texts reenact wars of the dead. It is not simply the war or the array of issues leading to the war that is refought; it is also the dead who are brought back to live and die once more, continually restored with successive readings.

The desire to resurrect the dead links these narratives to the realm of the transcendent, much as Corinthians 1:13 speaks to the fundamental point that if "there be no resurrection of the dead, then is Christ not risen." Was this what Sender meant by creating a Christ figure in the peasant Paco? Or Carretero, in the martyred Calvo Sotelo? Do these stories represent the secularization of religion or a turning back to religion? Is it politics or is it religion that fuels such narrative wars of the dead? Can we speak of one without the other? Carretero's savior is a politician, and his martyrdom is a declaration of war. Sender's peasant-hero recalls Azaña's mocking allusion to the figure of Jesus "as a propagandist for democracy or as a reader of Michelet and Castelar, or, who's to say, a precursor of the Agrarian Law." One cannot, however, dismiss the novelist's characterization of his protagonist as merely ironic: his secular hero is far too infused with the language of transcendence, drawn from both Catholic sources and the rich political tradition of progressive and anarchist thought.[136] Negating the spiritual meaning of *Réquiem* effaces its social-political import. In other words, whatever Sender's personal belief, belief as a structure of significance makes his novel meaningful.

Such is the historical-religious context in which these works, from Cadalso's *Noches lúgubres* to Ayguals de Izco's *María*, from Alas's *La Regenta* and Galdós's *Fortunata y Jacinta* to Carretero's *Revolución* and Sender's *Réquiem*, were produced. All of them participate in a form of sacred realism, but, immersed as they are in history, they are *not* sacred texts. The presence of the sacred in novels of a period of increasing secularization, from the late eighteenth century to the mid-twentieth, suggests that Georg Lukács's view of the genre may need to be revised or at least reconsidered. "The novel," he wrote, "is the epic of a world that has been abandoned by God." But he went on to say, "Irony, with intuitive double vision, can see where God is to be found in a world abandoned by God."[137]

Lukács began writing *The Theory of the Novel* in 1914 at the start of the Great War. Three years later, in a resonant vein, Max Weber delivered his wartime lecture "Science as a Vocation," saying, "Our age is characterized by rationalization and intellectualization, and above all, by the disenchantment of the world. Its resulting fate is that precisely the ultimate and most sublime values have withdrawn from public life. . . . It is no accident that our greatest art is intimate rather than monumental."[138]

In an age "alien to God," the divine has retired from public view.[139] Less absolute in his judgment than Lukács, Weber points to a way back into the transcendent, through forms of the intimate, to which the novel belongs. But even Lukács is unable to let go entirely of the notion of God, clutching at irony in the novel as the ultimate recognition of the divine through its very loss. God may have abandoned the world, but not the novel. The crisis in belief, both individual and collective, that has shaped the modern history of Spain since the late eighteenth century has also shaped the changing form of the novel, precisely where it resides, in the passageway between belief in and belief that. In other words, the enchantment of which Greeley speaks so eloquently to characterize the Catholic imagination sometimes hides within the very recesses of disenchantment. Belief in something is so powerful that even denied it may erupt into belief that something is or may be true. At the heart of disillusionment lies an illusion. Disenchantment is a ruse in the modern novel, a lure to make one reconsider the uses of enchantment in reimagining the world. One has to believe in something, to imagine it, in order to believe that something is or may be true, even if it isn't. Here is the secret of Don Quijote's success, not his failure. Thus even in a novel that has often been called a model narrative of romantic disillusionment, *La Regenta*, the unredeemed world Alas creates is not the same as a disenchanted one, for a fallen world is always aching for reenchantment, for the powers of imagining.[140]

Realism in the novel, at least in the Western, Judeo-Christian tradition, in some ways comes to us already inscribed in the sacred. Long ago Erich Auerbach pointed out that the break with classical theory's segregation of comic and tragic styles appears in "the story of Christ, with its ruthless mixture of everyday reality and the highest and most sublime tragedy." He argued that figural realism characterized premodern literature. By that he meant that earthly events, while understood as here and now, anticipated the heavenly kingdom, which signified "a oneness within the divine plan, of which all occurrences are parts and reflections."[141] Underlying this notion is the belief in divine reality, corresponding to the category of religious realism in contemporary philosophy of religion studies.

Modern realism, however, is predicated on uncertainty. The sense of community based on belief now has a deep fault line running through it, the scarred traces of desacralization.[142] Viewed this way, realism is what it is because it is in crisis. Marshall Brown notes that "realism developed into a central issue in mid-[nineteenth] century precisely because the conception of reality had become increasingly problematic."[143] Signs of the problem are already evident in Cervantes's fiction and in the picaresque. The fundamental ambiguity of the *Lazarillo de Tormes,* for example, resides to a significant degree in whether we still see traces of the sacred in the protagonist's character and actions. The name and persona of the *pícaro* Lázaro are associated, however ironically, to the two different biblical stories of Lazarus (those of the beggar and the dead man), to Saint Lazarus patron saint of lepers and the figure of the leper, and to the *sanctus pauper* as the charitable nexus to salvation. His hungry adoration—and consumption—of the bread rolls is transparently modeled on the sacrament of Holy Communion. If Lázaro has no sacred aura by the end, this narrative turn leads one critic to state that "the abandonment of the Christian ideal of charity is precisely what is at stake in the novel."[144] But what is also at stake is the novel itself as a secular form predicated on sacred values.

How early readers regarded Lázaro we don't know. As a poor person, perhaps he was not taken "seriously as a human being."[145] The poor as symbolic of sacred charity were not individualized; yet it is Lázaro's persona that attracts readers today. We do take him seriously. But does his textual, if not psychological, complexity arise from secularizing him or from valuing his flawed humanity as something special, marked through his liminality? Can we truly separate the secular from the sacred in the *Lazarillo de Tormes*? The irresolvable quality, the narrative ambiguity of the text, does not permit readers to do so.

The pícaro was certainly not seen as a sympathetic object deserving of humanitarian reform, someone to be reintegrated into the community in the way that writers like Cadalso, Olavide, Ayguals de Izco, and Galdós envisioned embracing the marginalized.[146] The liminal nature of his social category, which poses him on the border between the secular and the sacred, hints at a communal dilemma, an inability to incorporate this figure (and the larger sign of the poor that he represents) into a social structure that was also religious. Lázaro's predicament is social and economic in nature, but his debasement cannot be overcome simply by social or economic means. He is also abject because he represents the inability to keep apart the sacred and the profane. He is a threat to the sacred because he keeps dipping into it, literally consuming its symbolic representations, spreading the sacred into inappropriate zones. Religion is not by any means a residual effect here: it paradoxically defines how readers see the pícaro, namely, as a profane figure.[147] In this sense the sacred makes him real, bordering on the "really real" that Clifford Geertz finds in the religious perspective of life.

The uncertain border between the sacred and the profane highlights the gray area in which belief in and belief that uneasily coexist in fictions like the *Lazarillo de Tormes* and suggests that realism, at least in the Spanish tradition, rests on a complicated support system of diverse kinds of belief that at once affirm and destabilize reality. Along with *Don Quijote*, the picaresque genre is considered foundational to Spanish realism, an ill-defined, vexed category for which we have no other name.[148] Realism in general is a broad, inclusive term, ranging from philosophical realism (the reality of universals) to religious realism (belief in the real existence of a divine being), from figural realism (earthly life as the figure of heavenly fulfillment) to literary realism (the faithful representation of everyday life). Realism in fiction can be understood as a mode, a way of seeing, an attitude toward the world, an attribute, or an effect.[149] The mimetic transformation of reality, literary realism can no more be pinned down than the dynamic, fluid nature of the real itself. In a word, realism is a house of many rooms reflecting personal taste, historical change, and continual redesign.

The same is true of Spanish realism in literature. While literary historians conveniently assign the picaresque and *Don Quijote* as foundational texts of Spanish realism (and of European literature generally), realistic effects characterize works as disparate as the *Poema de Mío Cid* and the *Celestina*. Indeed, it is a long-standing topos to define Spanish literature and art as inherently realistic.[150] In this vein, María Zambrano went so far as to proclaim realism a Spanish way of being in the world, spontaneous and immediate, nondogmatic and theory-free. "Spanish realism as [a form of poetic] knowledge," she said, "is nothing less than a being in love with the world, captivated by it, and therefore bound to it."[151] By the time these words appeared in 1939, both José Ortega y Gasset (Zambrano's teacher) and Dámaso Alonso had already argued strenuously against the prevailing view of Spanish literature and culture as realist. Zambrano's essay, along with other pertinent texts from the period like Pedro Salinas's *Reality and the Poet in Spanish Poetry* and Américo Castro's "The Meaning of Spanish Civilization," however, have to be read as the response of Republican exiles to the catastrophe of civil war and Franco's brutal victory. To defend Spanish realism, under these circumstances, was to defend the values of Spanish culture, conceived as a form of realist humanism or humanizing realism.[152] For Castro and Zambrano, moreover, the presumed Spanish failure to follow the Enlightenment model, that is, to fully participate in modernity, can be reread positively as a liberal humanist alternative to the European crisis of rationalism and ensuing dehumanization circa 1939.[153]

For Zambrano the kind of knowledge Spanish realism offers is poetic, the polar opposite of reason, a system of thought that takes possession of its object, whereas poetic knowledge is a form of grace, of revelation. She writes, "Equilibrium between the individual and the community. Through poetic knowledge man never separates himself from the universe, and, preserving intact his private nature, participates in everything, he belongs to the universe, to nature and to the human and even to what exists within the human, and even beyond that."[154] It is easy today to dismiss Zambrano's idealistic, ahistoric approach as reifying the Spanish character and culture, but to do so ignores the history that impelled her to embrace realism. More fundamentally, it ignores the degree to which realism in Spain not only served as an explanatory force in periods of crisis but also was the vehicle for expressing that crisis.

Responses like those of Zambrano and Castro drive home my point that modern literary realism is less a convention than a response itself to the conflicts and dilemmas of a secularizing world. Alas's contention in 1883 that naturalism, a variant of realism, is not an exclusivist doctrine or a set of recipes for writing novels but "a literary opportunism . . . that [is] most appropriate to modern life," can be understood in such terms.[155] Zambrano's own frame of reference to explain the metaphysics of Spanish realism — poetic knowledge as a form of grace or revelation — strikes me as deeply spiritual, indeed inconceivable in the absence of a religious foundation. Her understanding of the relation between individual and community points to a kind of idealized realism of human reality but also draws upon a secularized, Eucharistic notion of spiritual fellowship. Through a form of existential realism, she reimagines the aspiration for communitas that was utterly shattered by civil war.

The world, of course, has never cooperated in substantiating that vision. The novel, above all the realist novel, cries out in the misbegotten wilderness of human frailty and exposes the world's shortcomings, but we do not always notice what the novel builds in place of the world's desolation: an alternative site of community that reattaches us to being in the world with others. The novel creates neighbors, even when neighborhoods themselves are harsh and inhospitable.[156] Don Quijote may be roughed up, the pícaro may starve, a judge's wife may fall from grace, and a peasant may be brutally shot, and we say, that is the way of the world. But there is nothing ordinary about their fictional lives or their relation to us as readers. "There are no *ordinary* people," Lewis wrote, and there are no ordinary characters, for the special sign of the novel is to make us care about them by suggesting that this — this mutual sympathy for the human — is what we should care about.

The Relics of Faith

In sixteenth- and seventeenth-century Spain, the drawing power of Catholicism was palpable. Traces of that fervor show even today in the writings and art of the period. Faith was doubly incarnated as doctrine and as emotional experience. Can a secular age even begin to understand how religious belief imagines itself as sacred embodiment? how the relics of faith are only remains or spiritual residue, if one does not believe in their divine significance? How does one go semantically from one kind of relic to the other, from the sacred to the superfluous? And what effect does such a change have on the secular form of the novel in periods of impending crisis like late eighteenth-century Spain?

What is now often viewed with detachment as a museum piece was once infused with the enthusiasm and passion of popular devotion. I begin with an example, with a figure of beauty as both the backdrop and entryway into the vexed relation between faith and realism and the possible permutations of novel writing produced in circumstances of troubled spirituality. The figure is one of powerful, disturbing beauty derived from violent, protracted death. He is a healthy male in his thirties, lying down, his head on an embroidered pillow, the face somewhat twisted to the right, eyes and mouth partially open. He has various wounds to head, chest, hands, and feet. Except for the covering over his groin, he is unclothed. The blood is coagulated, signs of lividity have set in.

The dead eyes stare with an intensity that defies what has happened. He looks utterly exhausted.

The figure I have described in its barest outlines is one of the most celebrated sculptures of early seventeenth-century Spain: Gregorio Fernández's *Cristo yacente,* or *Reclining Christ,* executed in 1614–15 on commission from King Philip III.[1] Fernández's innovative positioning of the dead Christ — recumbent rather than crucified or in a Pietà — was reproduced with many variations by his disciples and imitators. Like other religious works by Fernández, this sculpture was the object of passionate devotion and reverence, not so much as an art form of inspired religiosity but as constituting a direct line of communication with the divine. Akin to relics, such sculptures were understood to be imbued with special powers and hence to be in a special relationship with the devout, whose intense reception of these works tended to erase the differences between art and experience. For the Church hierarchy, "sculpture was held in higher regard than painting," precisely because the art form spoke more directly to the spectator.[2]

Viewed aesthetically, the polychromed wood of Spanish religious sculpture, along with the dramatic theatricality of glass eyes, horn fingernails, crystal tears, and vividly painted wounds, violates the conventional norms of European high art. Works like Fernández's dead Christ are often profoundly disturbing to the eyes of modern viewers, in part because the artist appears to have reduced the aesthetic distance between object and spectator. The safety zone that protects and delimits art is gone. As Gridley McKim-Smith observes, "The eroticized violence inherent in the naked reclining Jesus has always been there as a repressed subtext of the Passion in Christian art, but the *Cristo yacente* now has allowed it to become unacceptably overt by representing a dead-but-desirable divinity with an inescapable immediacy." In a word, she says, "viewers expect a statue but find a corpse."[3]

A corpse that is remarkably alive, as the powerful gaze and the muscular tension centered upon the head and neck attest. Fernández's sculpture functions as a kind of relic within the theater of resurrection. One cannot divorce such intensely executed and experienced artifacts from the context of seventeenth-century beliefs and practices represented here, beliefs that combined Counter-Reformation Catholic orthodoxies with surviving local cults of near shamanistic veneration. What still stuns viewers today in the figure of the dead Christ is its compelling, inescapable presence, reinforcing the idea that "relics, it seems, of the thing/are always stronger than the thing itself."[4]

The Fernández sculpture, in dramatizing the real signs of physical death, marked visibly and anatomically, goes beyond traditional Christian attitudes toward the material body and suggests a more than ordinary interest in the

Figure 1. Gregorio Fernández, *Cristo yacente* (*Reclining Christ*) (1614–15) (Capuchin Monastery of El Pardo). Courtesy of Arxiu Mas/Institut Amatller d'Art Hispànic.

effects of violent death. Indeed, it distinguishes death as violent. Moreover, the use of artificial eyes, fingernails, and tears in Spanish polychrome sculpture in general draws these objects closer to the uncanny, Freud's *das unheimliche,* which he observes in the automaton and in wax figures, that is, in the unsettling forms of the double and of the desire/dread of the reanimated dead body. Federico García Lorca saw in this art form something of the dark, mysterious qualities of the *duende,* that creative force which he likened to a kind of religious experience circling the edges of death.[5] The exacerbated realism of the dead Christ, the traditional emphasis on his suffering and on the value of martyrdom, were meant to transmit Catholic doctrine and feeling. The corpse lies on a bed of mimesis, anchored like the pillow upon which his head rests, but belief in resurrection brings the Christ figure to life.

Spirit and matter, while distinct, are at the same time compatible in Catholic metaphysics. Relics — parts of saints' bodies, clothing, and other objects that had come into contact with holy persons — partook of the divine. Philip II while he lay dying kissed and adored obsessively large numbers of the more than seven thousand relics he had collected and brought to the Escorial. It is no accident that the relics collection and the royal corpses were stored in the same space. Moreover, popular belief in general ascribed potent, even magical qualities to dead bodies. There was a kind of personality attached to the dead. The uncertain, strange status of the dead body extended to dispute over the actual moment of death, as opposed to apparent death, which has lasted to this day. It is largely true that by the nineteenth century medicine, as a sign of increasing secularization and empiricist, positivistic knowledge, was to abandon belief in the vestiges of life and personality attributed to the dead body. Yet at other levels of experience and perception, among ordinary folk, that belief simply took on another visage or went underground, surfacing in moments of high tension and conflict.[6]

Fernández's dead Christ offers a concrete instance of how representation of the real can function as the doorway or entrance into the transcendent or sacred or into the uncanny. The *Cristo yacente* is both dead and alive. His eyes are glassy with death yet glimmer with unspoken life. His face and torso speak of obscene torture, of flesh profaned and humiliated; but the eyes, half shut and rolled back, suggest an inner vision, and the mouth is agape, drawing the viewer into their openings and intimating the soul that has departed the living eyes and breath.

The sense of the material — the body — as being an inextricable part of the sacred or divine is fundamental to Catholicism. The sacredness of the human body is the centerpiece of Christian faith, primarily understood in the doctrine of Incarnation. More important for my purposes here is its centrality in the emotional experience of practicing Catholics as it is expressed artistically. What happens to this experience in the shift toward a more secular world? Are there moments when the trembling tectonic movements of belief and secular change can be discerned in the stories eighteenth-century writers told themselves? And how would such rumblings look narratively and aesthetically?

This question is what I want to examine here. What direction do fictional writings that are caught up in religious crisis take? Can they be said to be harbingers of narrative change? And what then is the relation between realism and faith in such narratives? How does *belief in* something transcendent reveal itself in the painful struggle with an uncertain outcome, with *belief that* something is true? In singling out the texts I discuss here, in particular one of the most fascinating and challenging of eighteenth-century writings, Cadalso's *Noches lúgubres* (completed ca. 1774–75; published in 1789–90), I propose to reimagine these works as part of the field upon which a freshly embryonic realism is born. The new shape of *Noches lúgubres* issues from a spiritual impasse that turns the protagonist from his subjective imprisonment of self toward humanitarian purposefulness, toward making visible those persons and social classes whose lesser (or in other cases, persecuted) state has rendered them invisible. This humanitarian drive, also discernible in writings like Olavide's *El evangelio en triunfo* (1797–98) and Gutiérrez's *Cornelia Bororquia o la víctima de la Inquisición* (1801), is predicated on a secularized understanding of resurrection that aims to bring back the symbolic dead into the social realm of existence. Along the way, it brings back the novel, in rediscovering the real bodies of the poor and other marginalized figures as a new subject of novelistic inquiry. These bodies are, in essence, the new relics of faith.

For Thomas Laqueur, the humanitarian narrative includes such genres as "the realistic novel, the autopsy, the clinical report, and the social inquiry," all of them "children of the empiricist revolution of the seventeenth century." He studies "how details about the suffering bodies of others engender compassion and how that compassion comes to be understood as a moral imperative to undertake ameliorative action."[7] In such accounts, the body becomes the focus and site of inquiry: dead bodies, diseased bodies, poor bodies, conflicted bodies. This strand of narrative, for which Laqueur finds examples mostly in eighteenth- and nineteenth-century Great Britain, also obtains in Spain. Moreover, a precedent exists in the sixteenth century: Bartolomé de Las Casas's efforts on behalf of the indigenous population's welfare and the impact of the Christian humanist tradition in general upon New World evangelization. If one grants a religious vision at work, one also must question whether details "engender compassion" or whether sympathy for the suffering of others already informs such details. The Spanish humanitarian narrative, I argue, only partly derives from the empiricist side of things, and a Catholic vision of seeing and acting must be considered central to understanding the twists and turns fiction took in Spain following the eighteenth-century decline of genres like the picaresque and the Cervantine narrative. These earlier forms also brought to the fore social distinctions and abjection but lacked the particular focus which we call humanitarian.

That the transition from the sacred to the secular can be detected in the writings of Spanish Enlightenment figures is a largely accepted given in current scholarship, though how to interpret the shift is another question. The continuing strength of religion in the eighteenth century is acknowledged but conceived as an impediment to the triumph of reason. More commonly, key Enlightenment figures like Jovellanos and Feijoo serve in this view as emblems of the problematic reconciliation of faith and reason. Modernity is interpreted as a secular, rational process, void for the most part of religious content or significance. For some critics, the Spanish Enlightenment bears little resemblance to other European progressive movements, given that the country's "cultural life was too steeped in Counter-Reformational traditions to allow these foreign values to be diffused." The extent to which there exists a Spanish Enlightenment thus depends on its vexed relation to the critical perception of a fuller, more "modern" form of Enlightenment experienced in France and elsewhere. Never mind that despite regional and class differences in the reception of faith (much the same could be said of Spain), eighteenth-century prerevolutionary France was still quite Catholic.[8]

Was this the same faith in eighteenth-century Spain? Spanish Catholicism in most of the eighteenth century was at once strong and weak. The spiritual presence of the Church, prosperous if rather complacent, was palpable in all spheres of life. The Inquisition continued to play a visible, if somewhat moderated, role in regulating orthodoxy. At the same time, the Church was poorly organized, with an uneven distribution of ecclesiastical wealth and personnel already showing the classic north–south and urban–rural split so prevalent in the next two centuries.[9] Parish vacancies went unfilled in rural, impoverished areas, while secular clergy preferred living in towns and cities. The Church also provided massive amounts of charity, much needed in a period of agrarian crises and persistent poverty. Its administration, however, was often inefficient, given the uncoordinated, fragmented nature of such assistance. An enlightened monarchy increasingly sought to bring the Church under State control and to make it more useful, but these attempts at reform achieved mixed results at best. The death of the devout and beloved Charles III in 1788 and the French Revolution the following year signaled the start of rocky times for the Church. Decline and a siege mentality were to shape the face of religion in the coming years.

While the practice of religion, in both its institutional and popular venues, could be seen everywhere in eighteenth-century Spain, it is nearly impossible to judge the depth of belief or the quality of faith embedded in such practices. How seriously, for example, should one take the Jesuit Isla's satire of clerical misconduct and ignorance in *Fray Gerundio de Campazas* (1758–70)? Is his book a blanket condemnation of a lukewarm, shallow faith among clergymen? or a more limited, internal critique of ecclesiastical miseducation, in particular the abuse of sacred oratory? Some of his own fellow churchmen could not be certain, accusing him of Lutheranism.[10]

To give another example: in my library there is a small volume (32mo), *Doctrina christiana,* bound together with *Exercicios devotos,* by Juan de Palafox y Mendoza, bishop of Osma (1600–59). While the authorship and year of publication of the *Doctrina christiana* are not known, the edition of Palafox's book bears the date 1711 in one of the *Aprobaciones,* or ecclesiastical approbations. From internal handwriting and a nameplate, the owner of the volume appears as Molloy, along with the year 1729. More interesting than the texts are the marginalia, which are written in English, Spanish, and Latin. I suspect the book user belonged to an Irish (or Anglo-Irish) merchant family who had most likely settled in southern Spain in the early eighteenth century, part of a historical influx of Irish.[11] The handwritten comments, found mostly in the endpapers, range from the devout to the profane. Alongside prayers and blessings in Spanish and once in Latin, in a small, neat hand there are also precise calculations made to reduce the length of time spent in Purgatory through prayers (that is, indulgences for the remission of sins), advice concerning proper conduct in spiritual matters (modesty, silence, obedience), and the physical posture when offering specific prayers. On a more lighthearted, playful note, halfway through *Exercicios devotos* (opposite page 260), evidently someone else has written, date unknown, in English with a loose, sloppy script, that Arnario "is a big black fool" and a "rascal"; then at the bottom, "find me out if you can." How to interpret these comments? On the one hand, the marginalia indicate a serious engagement with religious practice and with salvation. On the other, the use of devotional material for varying purposes offers a glimpse into the secular world of eighteenth-century domestic life. Beyond that, there is no way to generalize from one example.

We lack the means to assess religious feeling adequately. Empirical indexes, like attendance at Sunday Mass or going to confession, afford little insight into the human heart. There were, however, a few small signs of urban de-Christianization in the decline of religious confraternities after 1750 and the avoidance of Easter Communion through the purchase of certificates of compliance in the 1780s.[12] Certainly something had changed or was about to change, something which, combined with the impact of the Napoleonic invasion in 1808, could account for the emerging phenomenon of urban anticlericalism by the 1820s.

While we cannot judge how most ordinary people experienced their faith, there was one sector of the population, a very small one to be sure, that did express in writing a growing sense of spiritual crisis and the awareness that religion did not simply play an oppositional role or second fiddle to modernity: it was intimately bound up with it. Men of the Spanish Enlightenment like Cadalso, Olavide, and Gutiérrez demonstrate in their lives and work how difficult it is to separate religion from other endeavors such as the writing of fiction (see Jean Sarrailh). Their predicament, confined to a minority, also makes clear the distinction between Enlightenment and secularization: "Enlightenment was of the few. Secularization is of the many."[13]

My intention is not to rewrite the history of the novel form in the eighteenth century. This lifetime task is doubtless impossible. Despite the fine scholarship of the past thirty years or so, we still do not have a complete picture of novel production, and we may never have one. Clearly though, the much-trotted-out cliché that there is no eighteenth-century Spanish novel can be safely shelved. There are moral novels, sentimental novels, gothic novels, epistolary novels, satiric-picaresque novels, Cervantine novels, and not a few works that partake of nearly all these categories. Indeed, I am struck by the marked hybrid qualities of much fiction writing in the period, a lack of definition making it difficult to characterize. A novel like Isla's *Fray Gerundio de Campazas* blends the mock sermon with Cervantine and picaresque elements. Moreover, some texts that are not formally novels, like Cadalso's *Noches lúgubres,* nonetheless seem to inhabit a fictional universe in which character and story feel like a narrative embedded in dialogue. The generic blurriness of such writings is hard to interpret. On the one hand, the novel has always been a wild card, its shape-shifting qualities readily cannibalizing other forms. On the other, hybridity can point as much to experimentation as to aesthetic floundering, this last possibly indicating confusion over the direction the novel might take or a stumbling toward new forms of the genre. In either case, in-betweenness suggests something transitional and fluid, like the character of eighteenth-century Spain itself, neither fully Enlightenment nor fully Counter-Reformation, but something else.[14]

I begin my analysis of the relation between religion and the development of narrative with a curious but telling work, Olavide's *El evangelio en triunfo, o historia de un filósofo desengañado.* The text, I suspect, is probably not one most scholars of the period or of the novel would choose in order to highlight the distinctiveness of eighteenth-century Spanish narrative. At least one critic questions the originality of *El evangelio en triunfo,* given its reliance on a French work, the Abbé Antoine Adrien Lamourette's *Les Délices de la religion, ou le Pouvoir de l'Évangile pour nous rendre heureux* (The delights of religion, or the power of the Gospel to make us happy) (1788; Spanish trans. 1796), although I think the differences outweigh the similarities. Twenty-first century readers would find the four volumes heavy sledding. Olavide's work is difficult to read because it is really several works in one, a hybrid product, as Menéndez Pelayo dismissively called it: quasi-autobiography, a confession of sorts, an apology of religion, an Enlightenment project of reform, an epistolary novel, a sentimental novel, maybe even a libertine novel.[15]

However one chooses to categorize the work, *El evangelio en triunfo* was a great publishing success, going through eight editions in Spain alone between 1797 and 1803; fourteen in the years 1797–1848; and fifteen in France from 1805 to 1861. The French translator attributed the book's appeal precisely to its novelesque character. Perhaps, too, the generic variety or the strong devotional component attracted readers.[16] Its popularity may in part also have to do with the main character's initial religious skepticism, his doubts and evident spiritual anguish, for *El evangelio en triunfo* is above all a conversion narrative. There is a built-in appeal to conversion narratives: redemption trumps all for drama. And behind conversion lies the promise of resurrection.

The story line of Olavide's text is simple. The protagonist has led a somewhat dissolute life of pleasure, recalling the much-favored type of the libertine in eighteenth-century literature and culture. Two life-changing events occur: his best friend suddenly dies, and he ends up wounding (mortally, he believes) a stranger in a duel and flees the scene. Taking refuge in a monastery, he meets a clergyman, with whom he has long conversations in which the pros and cons of religion are debated, all very much in an Enlightenment framework. In the meantime, he learns that neither his friend nor the stranger has died.

The first three volumes concentrate on his conversion, while the fourth takes another tack, dwelling on a concrete project of reform that will benefit the impoverished villagers who work on the protagonist's estate. The fourth volume, so strikingly though not exclusively secular in nature, may appear disconnected from the other three of spiritual concern, but in my view the last part needs to be read as the Enlightenment application of Catholic philanthropy, or the consequence of the Philosopher's conversion.[17] Narratively, the parts fit awkwardly; ideologically and emotionally, they are of a piece. What drives the text in quest of itself and of reform (perhaps one and the same thing for Olavide) is a religious crisis. Stated another way, through the spiritual the protagonist and the text wrestle with what represents modernity — Enlightenment reform — in a conflictive age. Reform of the spirit cannot be separated in this text from secular reform of the polis, visualized in the village.

Olavide's presumed literary model, *Les Délices de la religion*, also turns on a case of conversion, but the actual transformation is remarkably quick and painless. Repentance turns to immediate joy. There is almost none of the spiritual anguish or protracted tussle between doubt and faith that torments Olavide's Philosopher and gives him a psychological depth completely absent in Lamourette's main character. Religious disquiet isn't missing from the French work but is muffled by the reconciling of the spiritual notion of happiness with its secular counterpart. Significantly, the use of debate and conversation is minimal. *Les Délices* is much more of a religious meditation, the narrative components taking a back seat. The plot device of two libertine friends, one of whom is mistakenly thought to be dead, which also appears in Olavide's text, occupies very little space and is quickly dispatched. Moreover, Lamourette (1742–94), an enlightened churchman who fell victim to the guillotine, no doubt had reforming instincts, though there is nothing in his text like the specific improvements project painstakingly developed in the last volume of *El evangelio en triunfo*. There are only isolated passages and the occasional short chapter extolling the merits of charity toward the poor and duties regarding one's servants. In his prerevolutionary writings, Lamourette advocated a return to evangelical Christianity, which he expressed in the language of *sensibilité*. Only after 1789 did he modify somewhat his traditional view of poverty, anticipating social Catholicism. A similar rhetoric, which could be likened to evangelical intimacy, suffuses the pages of *El evangelio en triunfo*.[18]

Olavide himself (1725–1803) was a born reformer. He came to Spain after having served (and then been accused of misconduct) as a public official in the cleanup and reconstruction efforts of his native, earthquake-torn Lima. A restless, self-confident man filled with intellectual curiosity and great enthusiasm, he was named director of the new Hospicio San Fernando, a refuge outside Madrid for the indigent and sick, in 1766. Converting a palace for the purpose, he looked after the physical and spiritual well-being of the residents and set up workshops so they could prove themselves socially useful. The 1760s was a great period of reforms under Charles III. By 1767 Olavide had been named royal governor of the province of Sevilla and superintendent of the king's pet project, the Sierra Morena settlement, a scheme to repopulate the region and foment agricultural improvements.

In the meantime, the Inquisition, which had been relatively inactive during this period, took an interest in Olavide's person and activities. A case was secretly building against him. In 1776 he was arrested and for two years remained a prisoner of the Inquisition, his whereabouts unknown. The charges, though largely groundless or exaggerated, were numerous. He was accused of heresy, his enemies claiming that his faith was lukewarm and his morals scandalous. Hostile churchmen attacked his taste in pictures, the contents of his library, his efforts to reform ineffective religious confraternities and the excesses of devotional practices, and a host of other things. Olavide had undoubtedly offended a great many people, in Sevilla especially, among them a very conservative and entrenched clergy and nobility resistant to reform, not to speak of the masses of people steeped in popular expression of the faith.[19] In 1778 he was declared a heretic and condemned to eight years' seclusion in a monastery. Enlightened circles throughout Europe were outraged, and he became known as a "martyr of fanaticism" (see Denis Diderot's account). Olavide's hallmark generosity continued in acts of charity, visiting the sick, and dispensing alms. Eventually he escaped to France, came under suspicion during the French Revolution, was imprisoned, and released a year later. Around this time he began to write *El evangelio en triunfo*. Charles IV rehabilitated him in 1798, and he returned to Spain.

By many accounts and despite the Inquisition's charges, Olavide was a sincere Catholic. He had always had an interest in religion, beginning with his theology studies in Lima. While in the hands of the Inquisition, he wrote in a letter, "I protest . . . from the bottom of my heart, that I have never deviated an inch from the one true and orthodox faith in our sacred mysteries, in the revelation and truths of the Gospel, and that I would sacrifice my life many times over for them."[20]

And yet, reading *El evangelio en triunfo* one senses the passionate *desire to believe* more than belief itself.[21] The tension between belief in and belief that, between trust and verification, between certainty and doubt is mediated through the desire to believe. It is risky to read the book as a literal autobiography. At the same time one cannot separate the book from Olavide's biography: it became his lifeline to Spain and to his eventual rehabilitation, whether it was intended to be or not. More to the point, Olavide inserts himself into the narrative through a prologue that links the book to events in his life: "A destiny as sad as it was inevitable brought me to France. . . . I found myself in Paris in the year 1789, and I saw the birth of that horrific revolution. . . . I was witness to those initial tragic events; and seeing that passions were become more and more inflamed . . . I retired to a place in the country."[22] After this opening paragraph, he reveals how on 16 April 1794 soldiers surrounded his house and conducted him to the local prison.[23]

Unquestionably the French Revolution deeply affected Olavide. The prologue actually represents but a very small part of what he originally wrote about the devastating effects of revolution on religion in France. The material never made it into the original text. The censor's report recommended against publication on three grounds. First, disseminating the material might endanger the life of Olavide, who still resided in France. Second, the material might compromise the political alliance between France and Spain. And finally, it provided an account of such incendiary events as to threaten the tranquility and order of Spain, especially among the popular classes. By this time the effects of civil and ecclesiastical censorship, omnipresent in eighteenth-century

Spain and an additional factor in shaping the content and form of writing, were especially severe. It is ironic, however, that these pages of Olavide, which are so sharply critical of the revolution, should have fallen victim to such an ideological purge.[24]

The prologue contains the bare outlines of his critique, but the fuller account merits reading. Olavide was horrified by the persecution of the clergy, acts of sacrilege, and establishment of a cult of reason, or revolutionary religion. The worst violence and desecrations came in 1793–94. He singles out one episode in which clergy were collectively drowned in boats deliberately scuttled in midstream. These drownings, or *noyades,* ordered by the extreme Jacobin Jean-Baptiste Carrier at Nantes, were inflicted multiple times on both clergy and laypeople. Olavide concludes that "the Catholic religion has not only lost its universality and dignity in France but finds itself poor, beaten down and barely tolerated, wounded by a schism which is destroying it . . . ; the present generation . . . has learned only the bare rudiments of religion . . . [and] learns nothing but impieties and blasphemies."[25]

Olavide thought France had become completely de-Christianized. Certainly if by de-Christianization one means declericalization, secularization, and decline of religious practice, that is most probably the case. But what about loss of religious feeling? Revolution can also foment religious zeal. Olavide was too close to events to judge the relative strength of religious feeling. Like many other observers of the French Revolution, he also saw that religion and its representatives were not afforded the rights guaranteed constitutionally to others.[26]

The cataclysmic loss of religion in France and his own misfortunes there had profoundly shaken Olavide and, one suspects, compelled him to take stock of his life. *El evangelio en triunfo* is not, however, an autobiography, despite the personal references found in the prologue. Indeed, Olavide stresses the fictional qualities of his text, making use of the old Cervantine ploy, the discovery of a manuscript, which is the Philosopher's tale presented here. His aim, he says, is merely to tell a story, a narrative strategy designed to bring readers to a greater understanding of the Catholic faith through the exercise of both Christian and civic virtue.[27]

The first thing the reader notices, however, is the presence not of faith, but of anguish and deep affliction, which even the Philosopher in the initial letter to his friend and confidant, Teodoro, suspects will seem most strange to the recipient.[28] Two nearly simultaneous deaths for which he feels responsible appear to have set off an emotional crisis in the pleasure-loving protagonist. One can understand the guilt he experiences over his duel with a stranger and its unfortunate outcome. But why remorse over the death of his companion, Manuel? Grief, which he also feels, seems more appropriate. Two elements bind together these deaths: their suddenness and unnaturalness. Manuel appears to have mysteriously dropped dead, and the stranger is fatally wounded. Both deaths do violence to the Philosopher's moral and affective universe. It is only much later that readers learn neither man has died. But meanwhile, the protagonist throughout the first three volumes periodically laments the loss of these two men, unable to let go of his feelings of guilt and complicity in their deaths.

In the tenth letter, for example, he writes,

> Amidst so many thoughts that afflicted me, a new one occurred, that made my heart sink, and this was the death I gave the Stranger. Until then this event had presented itself to me as a mishap easily explained away. . . . This misfortune . . . took on a graver character to my eyes and produced in me a bitter feeling in my heart. . . . [R]emorse pierced my soul and filled me with terror.
>
> But what truly shamed me and vexed my very being, was the idea of Manuel. Oh unhappy man, I said, pacing to and fro in my room, now you know, you have seen the truth. If there is a just God, if He loves virtue and punishes vice, how will He have received you? What is to be your fate?[29]

The Philosopher's anguish in the first letter seems to be chronologically misplaced, that is, anticipatory of a later, deeper reaction, here noted. The leitmotif of lamentation is crucial to understanding the narrative realism of the text, its psychological underpinnings in the subjective recesses of the Philosopher's mind and heart. Here, too, as in the instance of expressing remorse over his friend's death, he appears to go overboard in pinning a badge of guilt and shame to his breast for the stranger's death. After all, responsibility for the duel seems to be equally shared. My point is, the Philosopher's anguish cannot be fully explained through his own account of events.

We come closer to the source of his pain when he alludes to feelings of terror in the passage above. Terror over his own fate, which is at least in part the reason for such an intense reaction to the two deaths. It is not so much their deaths as his own — and the possibility of an afterlife that he has hitherto shrugged off — which frightens him. The sudden, unnatural quality of these deaths is a sign of the fragility and uncertainty of all human existence.

Thus when the Philosopher arrives at the monastery, he is predisposed to listen to, if not agree with, the priest's defense of religion. He professes his aversion to the Church and to Christianity itself as mere human invention. Clergymen in his view are useless, uncouth creatures; believers, naïve simpletons. He knows, moreover, that the priest is surely looking to convert him, and yet, despite all his misgivings, he stays.

His staying turns into a drawn-out struggle with doubt. "As for myself," he says, "I have not learned how to believe; what I know better is how to doubt, and I cannot be persuaded by what is repugnant to my reason." Every conversation he has with the priest leaves him filled with admiration for the clergyman yet picking holes in his arguments. The Philosopher's counterarguments often seem more convincing and better constructed than those of the priest.[30] Indeed, the endless and sometimes repetitive exchanges are framed in the classic form of an Enlightenment dialogue. The tension between reason and faith is a kind of crisis, which the protagonist attempts to work out through the dialectic of dialogue. None of this is present in the earlier French text by Lamourette. That the Philosopher's counterarguments are often superior to the priest's position suggests not insincerity on the part of the future convert or a desire to subvert faith. Rather, they betoken a psychological-spiritual impasse, wherein the *will to believe* increasingly replaces belief itself.

The Philosopher has trouble accepting the most basic notions of Christianity. "Who can believe," he asks, "that a God suffers and dies? Who is capable of understanding how the Living Word was eternally engendered by the Father? And what is this Holy Spirit thing?"[31] The mere fact that he feels compelled to pose questions of faith reveals how far incredulity and skepticism had permeated the minds and hearts of at least some Enlightenment figures. What vexes him most is the idea of resurrection: "I struggled with my own thoughts. . . . A dead God! A resurrected God! This is impossible. . . . Eloquence and wit can captivate and give shape to that which has no reality; but when truth is subjected to the crucible of examination, all that which is not solid must of necessity be undone."[32] He goes over and over in his mind Christ's resurrection, which becomes a huge stumbling block he appears at first unable to overcome. Even when he is convinced by the priest's reasoning, his "heart resists." "When I think about a Man who is God, about a dead man coming back to life, and all the consequences this entails, my senses rebel, my blood boils, I forget everything, and I feel great repugnance."[33] Reason appears powerless in the face of such a visceral reaction.

Right after this his emotional state deteriorates even more, as he expresses his terror, anguish, and unease to Teodoro in the tenth letter. He spends a long, restless night of the soul, unable to sleep: "My blood was rushing like a torrent through my veins, and an extraordinary heat was devouring my insides." Finally, he dozes off for a few minutes and has a terrible dream that recalls Saint Teresa de Jesús's experiences and anticipates Ana Ozores's nightmare in *La Regenta*:

> In an instant I saw myself surrounded by baneful images, dreaded ghosts that filled me with terror. . . . I saw only a dark, baleful light, which illuminated so little that I could barely devise the tombs and skeletons which encompassed the scene. . . .
>
> The profound immobility of everything lying about . . . produced in my soul sensations of horror. But how my astonishment grew when I saw that the

tombs were moving, that the sepulchers were opening up and vomiting from their depths animated skeletons, which with a livid, horrible aspect were running in haste, all jumbled together![34]

The Philosopher tries to flee the scene but cannot. Horrifyingly he discovers the threatening presence of both the stranger and his companion-in-pleasure Manuel there. Then a voice issuing from the grave declares that it is not time yet, the ghosts return to their tombs, and a short silence resembling nothingness prevails only to be taken over once more by the terrible cries of the dead in this horrific "theater of anguish."[35] The place no doubt is hell. Like Ana Ozores nearly a hundred years later, the Philosopher has found hell on earth. His Enlightenment mind attempts to dismiss the scene as a thing of the imagination, but the effort leaves him exhausted and depressed.

He further admits to the priest that he has despised Christ and religion as superstition; and the Church as an institution of domination and wealth. By volume two he is preparing for general confession, even while experiencing contradictory feelings and vacillation. Tellingly, for this purpose the priest conducts him to a special chapel deep in the recesses of the monastery, "the place destined for the burial of the dead clergymen, and where their bodies await general resurrection." The Philosopher's feelings spill over in tears, and he nearly faints, a reaction unsurprising in an age when sentiment was treasured as much as reason for their ennobling qualities.[36]

When he finally receives the Host, he is inflamed with rapture and asks himself, "Am I now resurrected?" The priest says to him, "How is Jesus Christ in the Eucharist? He is in the world, as if he were not there; he is in the midst of humankind, but invisible." Communion announces both the death and resurrection of Christ. A torrent of tears flows from Olavide's character. Shortly after, the Philosopher discovers the stranger has not died: "I had imagined so vividly the death of that stranger, that his recovery seemed to me a veritable resurrection." Then some thirty pages later, readers learn Manuel's story, also seen as a resurrection. His friend went into a literal state of catalepsy not once but twice, though the text calls it asphyxia, or apparent death, a subject that obsessed many in the late eighteenth century. The border between life and death was viewed as uncertain, and fear of being buried alive, a thing of horror. Interest in the living dead crested in the 1770s around the time reformers (Olavide was in this camp) began advocating, for hygienic reasons, the creation of new cemeteries outside towns. Manuel falls into a "fatal lethargy" and then slowly awakes in a fog of confusion: "But where was I? Good Lord! In my death bed, shrouded, with my hands and feet bound, four torches surrounding my bier, and a cross upon my breast. This spectacle horrified me."[37]

The "resurrections" of both men fit well symbolically into a conversion narrative. Their return to life not only parallels the Philosopher's spiritual rebirth, but also signals how strongly the narrative is haunted by ghosts, as the apparent deaths of Manuel and the stranger have so long dominated the Philosopher's mind and heart. Indeed, when he unexpectedly encounters Manuel among the living, he says, "I was tempted to see this not as reality, but as a dream, a delirium of fantasy, a phantom of the imagination."[38]

The persistence of these phantoms, which invade his memory and terrorize his dreams, is of a psychological and emotional piece with his drawn-out wrestling between doubt and faith. The inordinate length of the text, in which much of the first three volumes is taken up with the protagonist's spiritual anguish, suggests an impasse, as he goes over and over the same mental and affective territory, sometimes backtracking or unable to proceed. These moments function like phantoms in their stubborn return. A Freudian might call it the return of the repressed, although Olavide's character appears to keep very little beneath his conscious mind. There is psychological realism in the Philosopher's subjectivity, but what drives this realism is couched largely in religious terms.

The struggle over belief can also be connected to the obsession with apparent death, for both things question the ground of reality. Indeed, the fuzzy boundaries between life and death in cases of apparent death suggest this hotly debated subject may have in part stood in for an argument over the truth of spiritual belief, enough to indicate creeping uncertainty at least among the eighteenth-century *lumières*. The Philosopher's difficulty in accepting a dead God who is resurrected turns on the metaphorical figure of the living dead. In some ways the resurrections of Manuel and the stranger offer narrative proof (as opposed to either theological or rational evidence) not just of Christ's return, but of belief itself.

Perhaps the strongest proof for the Philosopher, however, resides in his understanding of faith as personal redemption through the work of the Gospel. The book is called *El evangelio en triunfo,* thus indicating from the start that the message of Christ in the world, not the Church as an institution or its doctrines qua doctrines, is to prevail in the text. Hence the importance of the fourth volume, which focuses on concrete improvements for the poorest of the rural laboring classes. This concern actually begins in the third volume, when the Philosopher includes a long meditation on the poor and his previous aversion to them, which he felt as "a kind of homicidal and ferocious rage against the poor." Conversion transforms his feelings, making him aware of the misery of others. His distaste for almsgiving evaporates, as he sees the necessity for benevolent action, especially since the government seems incapable of providing it. With conversion comes self-examination: "Is it possible that the presence of misery inconvenienced my *amour propre,* so that I wished to remove it from my sight?"[39] Then the philanthropic impulse rushes in, as "the light of the Gospel illuminates [his] soul, and suddenly, without further reflection, these inhuman delusions were dissipated." "My heart changed," he says. "Now a poor man is for me an object of inner respect."[40] In calling the poor "objects of veneration" as well, he alludes to the traditional, sacred figure of the *sanctus pauper,* which is associated with individual salvation, a religious discourse of poverty that persisted in the eighteenth century even as the discourse of labor was slowly replacing it.[41]

He seeks out the local parish priest, whose desire to assist the needy has been thwarted by lack of resources, which the Philosopher is happy to provide. The priest tells him about a particular laborer whose eldest child has broken his leg and whose wife has just given birth to another child, thus necessitating an expenditure the family cannot afford. Later, as the Philosopher inspects his lands and properties, he remarks that for "the first time I reflected that these poor and honest laborers, whom I had until now viewed with such scorn, are the people who are maintaining us at the cost of their own sweat." As Raymond Williams has noted of the propertied in England, here is the eighteenth-century "discovery" that " 'the poor' are not simply a charitable burden, a weight on the economy, but the actual producers of wealth." Most interesting to read in *El evangelio del triunfo* is the genuine surprise of the rural poor in realizing the landowner's sympathy and caring attitude toward them: "But I must tell you," he writes to Teodoro, "to the shame and opprobrium of our century, that these simple people are astonished to see me speaking to them with so much affection and humanity. At every turn they repeat that I am a very good gentleman; and this is no mere expression of courtesy or humility, for I see in their eyes that this is a lively sentiment, which is a consequence of amazement and newness."[42]

Eighteenth-century humanitarianism, with its wellspring of religious feeling, was an attempt to ameliorate the socioeconomic conditions described in Olavide's text.[43] Indisputably Enlightenment ideals mold Olavide's Christian apologetics, but the reverse is equally true in that religion is the fount of civic benevolence. Benevolence extends not only to the rural poor but to servants, with whom the privileged classes have "necessary and domestic relations," which entails both the proper treatment and salvation of servants.[44] Such paternalistic relations suggest a socioeconomic model of reciprocity — one based on mutual, often unspoken dependence — "between the polite and the plebeian cultures of the time."[45] Olavide's social awareness stands out here. The rural poor's astonishment at the Philosopher's concern discloses an unarticulated general disaffection, the beginnings of social resentment that surface in the occasional riot and later in working-class mobilization during the nineteenth and early twentieth centuries.

The fourth and last volume of *El evangelio en triunfo* appropriately focuses right away on its principal subject: "Today . . . is the day of the poor." The Philosopher designs a social-spiritual project of utopian dimensions, which his friend Mariano describes in letters to Antonio. The plan undoubtedly harks back to Olavide's days as a reformer in the 1760s and 1770s and probably draws as well upon philanthropic enterprises in revolutionary and postrevolutionary France, such as La Rochefoucauld-Liancourt's charitable home visits to reduce reliance on hospitals and almsgiving or, closer to home, Charles III's creation of neighborhood associations for relief of the poor in Madrid in 1778 (Diputaciones de Barrio). Olavide had established his own goodwill society in 1792 in Meung-sur-Loire.[46]

Olavide intended a thorough reform of society, from agricultural improvements to good manners, schoolrooms to spiritual reawakening. He proposes a Committee for the Public Good and even spells out its regulations, including the statutes for the inspectors (both men and women) who carry out home visits. Hospitals, he argues, where compassion is in short supply, are less than ideal places for the sick and unfortunate. Home care, in contrast, is more cost-effective and humane. The inspectors are to provide philanthropic assistance while exercising "benevolent, active vigilance." "They should consider themselves as the father and mother of all the poor who reside [in their district], as the guardians of orphaned children and the destitute, and as a neighborhood friend." Olavide urges inspectors to get to know all the families of their district, "inquiring after not only their needs but also their morality and habits."[47] Thus inspectors were to visit the homes of the poor and destitute for both practical and pious reasons. The dual charge of eradicating both dirt and vice, disease and dissipation, may not appeal to us today but in its time conveyed a powerful message of social and spiritual redemption and contributed to the gradual rediscovery of those social classes largely invisible to the privileged members of society. This kind of enlightened behavior eventually spread throughout nineteenth-century Europe, notably with private initiatives like those of the St. Vincent de Paul Society. One cannot reduce humanitarian reform measures like those of Olavide to a veiled form of social control.[48] Such a dismissive response completely ignores how overwhelming the poverty was, how needed the charitable enterprises, and how genuinely distressed people like Olavide felt when contemplating extreme human misery.

I find it especially suggestive that Olavide should present his philanthropic project as part of a narrative of conversion. Significantly, the project allows the Philosopher to bypass the lingering unresolved quality of his spiritual transformation, his continual vacillations and doubts. Like the fictional resurrections of his friend Manuel and the stranger, the village improvement plan, in its material and spiritual dimensions, offers tangible (and narrative) proof of the efficacy and existence of belief. It could be argued that the quintessential Enlightenment, or modern, enterprise, into which he throws himself with great enthusiasm, is realized through a religious crisis; but equally, that religious belief is affirmed through Enlightenment reform. Olavide appears in this way to be working past, if not through, the uncertainties and contradictions of his position, of willing belief into existence through the incarnated experience of the philanthropic embrace.

What does this mean for the form that Olavide chose as his vehicle of expression? If we grant the text the characteristics of a novel, which is the critical consensus, then we need to reach some final considerations on its place in the constellation of eighteenth-century fictional writings. The hybrid nature of *El evangelio en triunfo* suggests a certain narrative awkwardness, a cobbling together of disparate parts. Yet emotionally conversion and reform are linked, as individual conversion leads to class awakening. Indeed, what were once the Philosopher's relics of faith — the vestiges of belief — become embodied in the poor, whose very presence is venerated as mediators of the divine spark. They are the new relics of faith, symbolically akin to the tangible experiencing of faith through contact with literal objects of devotion and sculptures like Fernández's *Cristo yacente*.

Yet these hitherto invisible unfortunates are not simply another version of the traditional *sanctus pauper,* for class differences mark Olavide's poor as humanitarian objects of both sympathy and reform on the part of the privileged: "Fathers work to raise and make their children happy, and young men to smarten themselves up, and appear at gatherings with the adornments and respectability which will make them socially acceptable and esteemed by others . . . this has contributed in great measure to inspiring in all of them a certain veneer of polish, an exterior of urbanity which before was very far from their rustic customs and crude manners."[49]

The novel in the nineteenth century will increasingly be seen as that place where the relation between the individual consciousness, or subjectivity, of the privileged (whether middle or upper class) and the marginalized (such as the poor or women) will play out in all its permutations. In *El evangelio en triunfo* this relation as well as subjectivity itself is couched largely in religious terms, making it difficult to see where experience leaves off and art begins, as Olavide, like Fernández in his sculpture, in seeking the immediacy of the divine feels compelled to turn his narrative into a kind of experience, at once spiritual and secular, truly real but inevitably fictional. Perhaps this helps explain the popularity of Olavide's text, which appealed to readers' emotional and spiritual needs in a period of change and uncertainty following the French Revolution. Here, too, are the beginnings of writings like Ayguals de Izco's *María, la hija de un jornalero* and Galdós's *Fortunata y Jacinta,* writings that increasingly secularize a religiously inspired humanitarian impulse and in the process reestablish the distance between experience and art.

Another text from this period, Luis Gutiérrez's *Cornelia Bororquia o la víctima de la Inquisición,* has been read by one critic as a refutation of Olavide's presumably more orthodox and repentant *El evangelio en triunfo.*[50] Certainly the Inquisition's persecution of Olavide was a cause célèbre and could not have failed to make an impression on Gutiérrez (1771–1809), a former Trinitarian friar whose novel, as noted, would end up on the Holy Office's Index of Prohibited Books. Yet these works have much more in common than not, beyond their use of the epistolary form and consuming interest in the Church. Like Olavide's work, *Cornelia Bororquia* is driven by religious crisis; and religion is the fulcrum moving the novel as genre in another direction. Olavide's deeply felt humanitarian embrace of the poor as the divine Other finds spiritual kinship in Gutiérrez's passionate (and enlightened) advocacy of a more humane religion tolerant of other faiths, even of unbelievers.[51] Both writers imagine a return to Christianity's evangelical origins as redemptive. Resurrection of belief is dependent, however, on something tangible, on a form of embodiment in which the divine spark is experienced. For Olavide's Philosopher, it is the poor; for Gutiérrez's Bartolomé Vargas, his beloved Cornelia. Not coincidentally, the Inquisition's readers strongly objected to the quasi-divine characterization of Cornelia as a form of idolatry.[52] In effect, Vargas has invested her with the aura of a relic, which her martyrdom at the hands of the Inquisition simply magnifies. An anticlerical (though not antireligious) novel, *Cornelia Bororquia* is also a love story, but its romantic elements cannot be read apart from the religious framework into which that story is inserted.

For most of its publishing history, *Cornelia Bororquia* appeared anonymously, beginning in 1801 in Paris. Revised in 1802, it went through twenty-five editions from 1801 until 1881. There were also translations into French, Portuguese, and German as well as popular adaptations in verse. Welcomed under liberal regimes, the novel went underground during more inhospitable times. Despite its popularity and multiple editions, by the mid-twentieth century the book had become so rare that a scholar-collector of first editions like Russell Sebold hunted for it unsuccessfully for more than five decades. Did the novel suffer a massive purge? or did some readers hold on to their copies precisely because it was a banned book, as one critic speculates? Scholarly response to Gutiérrez's novel, especially in the past fifteen years, has turned around its earlier negative critical reception.[53]

The fortunes of the book paralleled those of its author. When the bishop of Pamplona refused to release him from his vows, Gutiérrez fled to France around 1799. There he scrambled to make a living, first as a language teacher, then as a journalist by publishing a commercial enterprise, the *Gaceta de Bayona*. A few years later he set up an elaborate spy scheme, apparently intended to foster a utopian, enlightened Spanish America, during which he forged both documents and his identity. Arrested in Spain, he was accused of being an agent of the French and was garroted on 14 April 1809.[54] It is unclear, however, whether he was a spy for the French or for anti-Napoleonic forces or perhaps even a double agent. He certainly had the makings of a bold con artist. This fascinating figure possessed the gifts of "duplicity, imagination and recklessness," but "his greatest fiction was the one he played out in real life." Gutiérrez — here too he resembles Olavide — appears to have had a penchant for drama.[55] In any event, memory of Gutiérrez, like that of his book, fell into the rabbit hole of history.

To categorize *Cornelia Bororquia* as simply an anticlerical novel does not do it justice. The several voices heard through the epistolary form actually conduct a dialogue on religion as an institution and as a set of beliefs.[56] The story line frames their discussion: Cornelia, the daughter of the governor of Valencia, disappears into the depths of the Inquisition's prison, a victim of the archbishop of Sevilla's lust. Defending her honor, she kills the archbishop, is condemned, and burned at the stake. Her lover, Vargas, after failing to save her, flees with his friend Meneses to a more tolerant Holland.

While Cornelia remains a devout, practicing Catholic, Vargas attacks the Church's inhumanity.[57] In his view the Church has fostered the image of a vengeful, tyrannical God. The Inquisition has betrayed family loyalties, turning fathers and sons, husbands and wives into spies and informers. And an unholy alliance between throne and clergy deceives and exploits the people. Meneses goes further, rejecting religion entirely. Vilified by the Inquisition, even Cornelia envisages her implacable confessor as an executioner and the multitude of priests importuning her as ravenous crows.[58] Though her faith in God never wavers, readers surely are meant to question a Church that allows such terrible suffering. Gutiérrez has left them plenty of signposts in his characters' critiques and in the charge of inquisitorial injustice.

The text, however, also offers an alternative reading of religion in a pastoral interlude Gutiérrez inserted into the second edition (1802). One critic has suggested he made this addition, in which Vargas encounters Casinio, a priest in hiding from the Inquisition, precisely to lessen the antireligious impact of the first edition, demonstrating in the process an "understanding and even sympathy towards religious sentiment notably absent in the 1801 edition."[59] But what about Cornelia's faith or Vargas's insistence on a benevolent God, which comes in letter 15, well before Casinio's appearance in the twenty-eighth letter? Much of the harsh critique can be read as the photographic negative of another, implicitly positive image of religion. Although there is no way of knowing for certain why Gutiérrez introduced the Casinio episode, its effect is to make explicit something that was already there. The interlude, like other passages, carefully distinguishes between the unsatisfactory institutions of religion and the value of faith itself. Only Meneses seems dead set against religion as a vestige of superstition and ignorance. Yet in an evenhanded gesture, his last letter (the penultimate of the novel) observes that religion has produced both good and bad things, consolation and refuge on the one hand, violence and discord on the other.[60]

The pastoral setting in which Vargas meets Casinio, who is disguised as a shepherd, is meaningful, not only for its parallelism with the opening of Olavide's text but for the syncretic view of a natural religion.[61] The ruralism of the scene also fits well into Casinio's vision of an evangelical faith, resonant with the fervor of early Christianity. To Vargas's understandably embittered view of the Church as an institution of terror, intolerance, and criminal behavior, Casinio replies, in the rhetorical cadences of anaphora, "How can you imagine that a God who came into this world to save us . . . a God who . . . continually preached charity, harmony and union, a God who as he was dying prayed . . . for his own enemies, how can you possibly imagine that this God, goodness itself, could authorize *terror, intolerance, and criminal behavior?*"[62]

Casinio elaborates on the evangelical spirit, saying: "If we are to follow Christ, we ought to die as martyrs, not as executioners." The heart of his vision appears a moment later: "*The man of Christ* should be sweet, humble and charitable; there is never any justification for mistreating his brother. When I say brother, don't think that I am excluding those individuals from other creeds, no matter the faith . . . because God tells me that all men are my brothers."[63] This enlightened model of Christianity, a gospel for the here and now, is singularly disengaged from Church institutions and effects a change of heart in Vargas.

Yet his anxiety remains. He has a dream about Cornelia in which his passion for her speaks, but she does not reply. His vision, a form of emotional resurrection, leaves him in despair, knowing he cannot save her from the Inquisition. Indeed, as the novel concludes, Casinio must dissuade him from killing himself, one of several apparent echoes of Cadalso's *Noches lúgubres.*[64] There is little of the consoling spirit of religion that cradles and softens the death of

Olavide's Philosopher. Instead, *Cornelia Bororquia* comes to a close with a brief letter declaring that Vargas, after much struggle, has accepted the ways of Providence. Yet his emotional and spiritual well-being is tenuous at best: "We do not think it a good idea [at present] to give him his beloved's [last] letter, believing it would worsen his unfortunate situation."[65]

Cornelia's death comes in the form of martyrdom: she is at once the secular victim of the Inquisition's cruel persecution and a model of Christian sacrifice, recalling Casinio's evangelical message. Martyrdom is both secular and spiritual, as the novelesque descriptions of Cornelia's final moments reveal. Her celestial appearance at first is veiled in erotic sensibility: "The pallor of her lovely face, her golden hair spread over her back, her eyes sad, yes, but intense and brilliant like a star at midday, her delicate, creamy skin, her rosy lips, her throat half exposed in its alabaster whiteness, the serenity of her soul expressively painted on her face, all this attracted the attention of a people naturally humane and compassionate."[66]

The crowd, however, soon turns ugly, and Cornelia is brought to the stake. Here, the description takes another, far more realistic turn in this fictional reenactment of a sixteenth-century *auto de fe*: "She commences to take trembling steps, her eyes wild and terrified, her hair in disarray, her face twisted in extremis, uttering low moans, badly articulated words with no trace of a human accent. Her hands and feet, her entire body, were shaking uncontrollably with horrible shudders."[67] The image of terror builds on Cornelia's earlier reaction of shame and horror at the thought of being forcibly led in a public procession; and on the picture of Hell with which the clergy torment her.[68] Eighty-five years later, Ana Ozores experiences something painfully similar in *La Regenta*.

The romantic sensibility behind Cornelia's characterization and the love story contains the germ of realism, unsurprising given the generic instability of late eighteenth-century writing and the romantic origins of modern realism itself. In addition, the epistolary form of multiple voices lends itself to a complex fictional reality.[69] Yet the epistolary form alone did not move the novel toward greater realism; indeed, as a subgenre of fiction it faded away in Spain. Moreover, the realist features that Gutiérrez's novel displays have little to do with the earlier picaresque or Cervantine modes. Instead, they have to do with awareness of human suffering. A woman's suffering. Olavide's Philosopher focused on the poor. Here it is a woman, as it will be in many novels of the nineteenth century, outlining a trajectory in which the passive image of feminine virtue under siege eventually turns into fully fleshed characters.[70] The awareness of the pain of others suggests a connection between a different and incipient kind of realism and a reworked spiritual feeling based on compassion.

Thus tender tears and a grim inquisitorial interrogation share the stage in the text because both are intimately bound up in a religious framework. Gutiérrez uses religion and its narrative expression ultimately to promote an antireligious, or perhaps nonreligious, agenda. Those religious elements, however, retain traces of the sacred, notably in the aura of the relic with which Cornelia is imbued (and worshiped by Vargas) and in the message of the Gospel embodied in Casinio's person. The virtue of tolerance, seen today as secular and predicated upon reason, is still divine in Gutiérrez's view: "The right of Tolerance is part and parcel of the Divinity."[71] Indeed, it is part of the Gospel as spelled out by Casinio—another instance of how the pastoral interlude blends with the original material from the edition of 1801. As Cassirer notes about Enlightenment philosophy in general, "The demand for tolerance . . . is completely misunderstood if it is given a purely negative interpretation . . . the principle of the freedom of faith and conscience is the expression of a new and positive religious force."[72]

What motivates Gutiérrez's text is a religious crisis: Cornelia's mistreatment at the hands of the archbishop and the Inquisition is not only the plot device but also the fundamental event that exposes a deeply flawed Church in its relations with society and that in turn begins to work upon Bartolomé Vargas's mind and heart. His encounter with Casinio is crucial as a turning point in his crisis of belief. Yet it will not be sufficient, for, like Cadalso's Tediato, Vargas's belief is bound up in what will soon be a lost love object. His pain is bound up in hers. Unlike Olavide's Philosopher, however, he is unable to direct his more humane reconceptualization of religion (or his romantic love) into humanitarian endeavors, although Casinio has in effect pointed the way. Instead, readers remember his despair, a sentiment and state of being that bring him much closer ultimately to Cadalso's *Noches lúgubres* than to Olavide's work.

The high-born José Cadalso (1741–82) entered the military as a young man, ascending to colonel, and died of wounds sustained during the siege of Gibraltar in February 1782. He received a solid religious upbringing, largely among Jesuit educators, including an uncle, but appears to have fallen away from the faith in later years. It is extremely difficult, however, to pinpoint Cadalso's true feelings, as his statements on religion and belief varied considerably over time. Nigel Glendinning perceives an evolution in his thinking from an orthodox Christian belief toward a kind of stoicism, but the differences between non-Christian and Christian stoicism are not always so clear.[73] At other moments, deist notions unsurprisingly surface in this supreme Enlightenment figure, as the lightly ironic comment in a letter (written possibly in 1775) to Tomás de Iriarte indicates: "One of the things that I as a good Christian praise in divine, ineffable providence is having created the world once and for all and then allowing the stars to turn, the seasons to change, the sea to flow in and out, the animals to perpetuate themselves, and not to have to renew every instant, day, week, month, year, or century, each one of the things that we see and do not see."[74]

In the same letter, he makes note of his lethargic state and complains of being terminally bored in the provincial backwater he finds himself in. His malaise resembles modern-day depression, but Cadalso brushes it off with humor and wit. Thwarted ambition, temporary exile from the court in Madrid, other disappointments at the hands of those he considers inferior to himself in character and intelligence, all these things observed in his memoir and correspondence seemingly shape him as a victim *malgré lui*, molded by ironic detachment. His mindset and beliefs are maddeningly elusive and often impenetrable. Yet whatever Cadalso's beliefs, a moral thrust to his writing prevails.[75]

As with Olavide and Gutiérrez, it is perilous to attribute an unmediated autobiographical link to Cadalso's work. At the same time it is equally important to imagine *Noches lúgubres* within the swirling waters in which Cadalso appears to have experienced things, if we are to understand anything about the complex relation between his writing and belief. A profound sense of crisis that questions the very ground of existence has shaken the affective and social bonds of his protagonist Tediato to the core. The text, completed around 1774–75, undoubtedly contains emotional echoes of Cadalso's intense but short-lived affair with the celebrated actress María Ignacia Ibáñez, who died of typhus at the age of twenty-five in 1771. In a letter to his friend Juan Meléndez Valdés, from April or May 1775, he makes note of the manuscript, referring to its "true part, [as well as] the stylistic [or rhetorical] and fictional parts."[76]

Most critics, however, place the work within a literary tradition associated with, *inter alia*, Edward Young's contemplative *Night Thoughts on Life, Death, and Immortality* (1742–47), despite notable differences in tone, style, and effect.[77] Given Tediato's obsessive focus on his beloved's dead body, one wonders as well whether there are faint allusions to Martín Martínez's *Noches anatómicas, o anatomía compendiosa* (Anatomical nights, or a compendium of anatomy) (1750), a series of dialogues, each followed by a "Lesson," between a physician and a somewhat dimwitted romance surgeon (*cirujano romancista*, that is, trained in Spanish or French texts, not Latin ones) over three nights, in which the anatomist is imagined as a "geographer of the small world which is man."[78] Humanist anatomy, which included dissection, conceived of its work with dead bodies as both scientific and sacred. That said, the texts bear little resemblance to *Noches lúgubres* and do not occupy the same singular emotional territory of suffering and despair; by contrast, in Young the consolation of belief overcomes despair.

In Cadalso's text, the distraught and figuratively named Tediato, whose name alludes symbolically to a state of tedium or weariness, attempts over three nights to disinter his unnamed beloved, spends a night in jail, and in the end presumably intends to go back to her grave, accompanied by his companion, the gravedigger Lorenzo, who, it turns out, is also in mourning over the loss of his father and wife and the disappearance of a daughter. *Noches lúgubres* is actually a good example of the literature of the *revenant,* the ghostly reappearance of the dead.[79] Strictly speaking, there are no phantoms of the departed in the text, but rather the passionate desire to resurrect the dead, the same emotional impulse that lies behind Catholicism and that we have seen in Olavide.

Most suggestive in *Noches lúgubres* is the strong connection established between the return of the dead, or the resurrectional impulse, and humanitarian concern. The spectral presence of the dead is poetically represented in the shadowy figures of *bultos* (vague shapes) and *entes* (entities), which inhabit the dialogic turn of the text. The first Night begins with Tediato's initial monologue, which can be described as a cross between the apocalyptic and the narcissistic. Darkness and violent disorder, signaled by images of night, thunder, and lightning, fill the universe and Tediato's soul. The first thing he sees is the gravedigger Lorenzo, figured as a *bulto.* A few pages later, Lorenzo himself is filled with fear over another vague form, a "human presence," followed by a "phantom."[80] The rationalist Tediato immediately points out that Lorenzo has been spooked by shadows, his and the gravedigger's projected on the walls. Then he says, "If the other world were to abort those prodigious entities, whom nobody's seen and everybody talks about, it would inevitably as always bring us back to good and evil." Tediato judges such phantoms to be "monsters produced by fantasy filled with sadness: human fantasy, fecund only in chimeras, illusions, and objects of terror!"[81]

The word *ente* is a philosophical-metaphysical term referring to that which truly exists, but popular tradition also associates *ente* with monsters, spirits, and fantastical creatures, such as Fray Antonio de Fuentelapeña describes in his *El ente dilucidado: Tratado de monstruos y fantasmas* (The entity unveiled: a treatise on monsters and ghosts) (1676).[82] By using a term imbued with both rationalist and irrationalist connotations, Cadalso leaves the door open to both an enlightened and a popular explanation of events.

Shortly afterward, Tediato relates another episode in which a vague shape provokes fear and uncertainty in him. The creature, which is referred to once again as both an *ente* and a *bulto,* turns out to be a dog. It is perfectly logical — but, I think, inadequate — to see in these scenes an Enlightenment example of the supremacy of human reason. Inadequate, because the existence of rational proof does not do away with the presence of other ghosts, which infuses the text with such intense feeling. "How many objects do I see during the day," says Tediato, "that are, before my eyes, phantoms, visions and at the very least shadows . . . ; some are infernal furies."[83] Tediato's ghosts are the shades of memory, of loss, a leitmotif expressed from the opening monologue onward. It is apparent he cannot let go of the object of loss — his dead love — in a classic case of Freudian mourning, in which melancholia also plays a role. In other words, the unspoken notion of resurrection lies implicitly at the heart of the text.[84]

What haunts Tediato is the body of his beloved in both its material and nonrepresentational aspects. It is impossible for him to reconcile the object of his desire with the physical corruption of a corpse: "Once the object of my delight. . . . Now the object of horror for all to see!" Earlier he speaks in utter misery of her worm-eaten body, but he also says, "In what sad state must the relics of your cadaver be!"[85] Baroque disillusionment (*desengaño*) infuses this Enlightenment text. For Bruce Wardropper, however, Cadalso's faith in reason "denies him any religious explanation of death."[86] Thus, the decomposing body of Tediato's beloved would point only to despair, not to the world beyond.

Yet the key word here, *reliquias,* or relics, is semantically double-edged, just as *bulto* and *ente* are, suggesting both the transcendent (the divine or saintly) and the subjective (remembrance of the enshrined beloved). In this respect, E. C. Graf notes that Cadalso rewrites the Petrarchan "love-object in all her glorious potential as a sacred relic . . . and reduces it to stench, worms, and pus."[87]

Graf's point is well taken, but one cannot ignore the Catholic dimension of relics either. The importation into Spain of large numbers of Roman martyr relics from the Catacombs had been gathering new steam toward the end of the eighteenth century. Tediato's mournful fetishizing of his beloved's corpse, which is evocative of romantic emphasis on personal suffering and the loss of the individual love object, should also be placed in the context of Catholic iconic devotion. The Council of Trent (1545–63) had reaffirmed the value of the senses in the demonstration of faith. Through the viewing and touching of religious relics, the faithful made contact with the divine. Relics and the adored dead body also have in common an inner life born of secret, unseen depth. Enlightened critiques of relics as superstition were numerous but appear to have had little effect on popular religion.[88]

Tediato's ambivalent posture toward otherworldliness in no way negates the presence of this particular belief system, despite such eighteenth-century deist vocabulary as temple (*templo*) rather than church and Creator (*Criador*) and Supreme Being (*Ser Supremo*) rather than God. Are such iconic symbols like relics mere vestiges, in the secular sense? or more deeply entrenched in Cadalso's worldview than previously thought? I think it is impossible to say, since *Noches lúgubres* seems to straddle the fence. The underlying contradictions in the text will simply not go away.[89] Formulated another way, in Cadalso's text and character are signs of a religious crisis of belief.

In this sense, the body of Tediato's lost love object, imagined as a sacred relic, seems to be inhabited or haunted by the vestiges of Catholicism, which in turn have produced another body in Cadalso's text. That is, her body incarnates a very personalized, subjective absorption of religious belief, of transcendent belief made immanent in the imagining of the dead body. Tediato's beloved is both more and less than what it is. On the one hand, it is horrific decay, a state of being that the mind ultimately cannot grasp, can only see, in an exemplary instance of the limitations of vision. On the other hand, the corpse is also remembered, thus enshrining memorialized emotion as a kind of relic. Tediato is unable to move beyond either conception of the dead body. Indeed, there is an abstract, unrealized quality about the beloved's body that points to an absent persona of flesh and blood (we know nothing about her, not even her name) but also hints at some sort of blockage in the imagining self. Here, *Noches lúgubres* marks an important transitional moment in which neither traditional belief systems nor Enlightenment values offer Tediato a way out of his impasse, his inability to let go of the lost love object. The protagonist's attempts to remove the body from the church and die alongside it are frustrated not only by plot events but by what I suspect is Cadalso's own intuition that romantic suicide cannot move beyond the fact of death. The open-ended conclusion of *Noches lúgubres* reinforces the sense of an impasse.

Instead Cadalso turns toward humanitarian concern for others, a move that at once signals the limitations of both romantic love and traditional Catholic belief. The beloved's dead body must be left behind for the text to do its work, work that it is probably safe to say remains incomplete. The driving desire to bring back the dead, in an earlier period satisfied through Catholic belief in the resurrection of the spiritual body, is reinvented in the humanitarian narrative of *Noches lúgubres*. In other words, Cadalso can express humanitarian concern only by filtering it through the specter of Catholicism, a specter that the beloved's dead body incarnates. Tediato's despair is not simply romantic *avant la lettre;* it is deeply spiritual. Only despair of such transcendent proportions can explain the apocalyptic imagery of "darkness [and] terrifying silence broken by laments [and thunder]" noted in the opening monologue and elsewhere, in which "everything trembles. There is no man who does not believe himself mortal in this instant."[90]

The ghost of Catholicism is reproduced through this humanitarian narrative. Appropriately, duplicates and doubling pervade Cadalso's text like specters, starting with the proliferation of shadows and vague forms, even when they generally turn out to be something else. Tediato's loss is echoed in the gravedigger Lorenzo's. Lorenzo's son is also named Lorenzo. The parallels established between the two Lorenzos and Tediato suggest the faint impress of an alter ego or doppelgänger.

The repeated doubling device found in *Noches lúgubres* furthers the impression of a haunted text, haunted above all by the loss of transcendence. Humanitarian concern could be understood in this context not simply as a substitute for Catholic belief but as its reinvented resurrection. The new body that reappears, however, is not dead, simply forgotten and invisible: the bodies of the laboring poor, the orphaned and homeless, the persecuted, all bodies that eventually take on added meaning in the text. Thus "Tediato's initial interest in the body of the beloved is replaced by an interest in the bodies of fellow sufferers."[91]

Humanitarianism, as moral feeling and as a reform movement, begins to flower in the eighteenth century. Cadalso was sympathetic to such reforms. In jail and unjustly accused of murder, Tediato mentally prepares himself for torture (the practice still prevailed in prisons and justice systems nearly everywhere). Cadalso's ironic critique of torture seems to echo the opinions of Cesare Beccaria in his well-known essay *On Crimes and Punishment* (1764), which had circulated in translation throughout Europe. The jailer boasts he will show no compassion toward his prisoner: "Few words, even less food, no pity, much harshness, even more punishment and threats."[92]

In prison, Tediato hears the voice and cries of a man in the cell next to his as well as the man's executioners: "The footsteps of the men leaving the cell . . . the noise of the chains they have no doubt removed from the dead man, the noise of the door make my sensibility tremble in my heart." The experience of the unseen prisoner, who exists only as a disembodied voice emerging out of a dungeon's depths, prepares Tediato for his next encounter with another body after he is released from jail. This time he stumbles across "the vague shape of a man." "It seems as though he comes from a dream," he says to himself. "Who is it?" he asks. "If you are some beggar in need, fallen from weakness, and you are sleeping in the streets with no home for a refuge and no strength to get to a hospital, follow me. My home is yours." Adam Smith would have said that the sympathy he feels "does not arise so much from the view of the passion, as from that of the situation which excites it."[93]

The vague shape turns out to be the gravedigger Lorenzo's young son. Significantly, the term *bulto* reappears here, associated at once with the suggestion of irreality (a dream) and with the crushing social realism of poverty. Tediato has moved from experiencing a haunting invisibility (the prisoner's voice) to the very real and visible presence of human misery. Yet even here, the real is wrapped in dream and in the previous associations of the word *bulto* with irrational elements. The Other for Tediato is first of all a body, a human form. Like the beloved's dead body, this one somehow must be saved.

It is no accident of plot that Tediato's awakened humanitarian impulses center on a gravedigger and his family. There appears to be an obscure linkage between disinterring his beloved's sacralized body and rescuing out of humanitarian concern someone who occasionally digs up unspeakable things for a living. Lorenzo occupies one of the lowest rungs of the social ladder. He works with dead bodies, things that are unclean, that are deeply taboo and therefore fearful. There is an innate "horror of the corpse as a symbol of violence and as a threat of the contagiousness of violence."[94]

We bury dead bodies to keep ourselves safe. In this respect, Randolph Pope argues that Tediato unearths the beloved's dead body out of the "necessity to truly kill it" once and for all, not to resurrect it somehow through romantic obsession with the lost love object. But in seeing the repetitions of the text as instances of a traumatic experience, Pope also inadvertently points to Tediato's inability to kill the corpse. Killing it metaphorically (and repeatedly) is, in other words, the underside of bringing back the dead. A rotting body reveals profound forces of unsettling biological disorder at work. Tediato's disgust over his dead love's worm-ridden corpse is a natural response. Physical death itself produces new bodies out of decomposition, its own life forms of resurrection: "These are the everending days of being dead."[95]

What is perhaps less natural is Tediato's desire to help Lorenzo and his family, given their associations with uncleanness. The lower orders were in general regarded as *viles,* or abject, with a host of other unpleasant meanings attached to the term, leading the *ilustrado* churchman Pedro Antonio Sánchez ("Don Antonio Filántropo") to wonder if such negative views of the laboring classes did not contradict the laws of charity and justice. José Marchena speaks of a certain kind of "sensibility or faculty of identifying myself with another person. In effect, my nerves suffer a violent commotion at the sight of another human being constituted like me and suffering. This impression is disagreeable to me, which is why I attempt either to assuage his pain or to avoid seeing him."[96] Out of self-interest and utilitarian efficiency, Marchena opts for the first solution. Regardless of the motivation behind his response, like Adam Smith, he exalts the moral feeling we call sympathy above all else.

Cadalso's Tediato finds awakened sympathy for another like himself: "I feel as much pity for you as I do for myself." It has been argued that Tediato's interest in the suffering of others simply reflects his own romantic self-involvement, his self-ennobling egotism. But what, then, of Enlightenment belief in the efficacy and beneficence of self-interest? Tediato's humanitarian concern issues first of all out of his sense of self. Smith observes that "as we have no immediate experience of what other men feel, we can form no idea of the manner in which they are affected, but by conceiving what we ourselves should feel in the like situation."[97]

The question is, why? The protagonist's sympathy can in part be explained through the eighteenth-century privileging of friendship, a pivotal concept in Cadalso's personal world. Ironically, Tediato speaks in harsh, despairing terms of family and friends, of all that makes up the social bond, as selfish and corrupt. The last line of the text, however, reinforces the connection between sympathy and friendship: "Let us walk together, my friend, let us walk." (The line ironically echoes the law ordering Tediato to come along to jail, during the second Night: "Andemos, andemos.") This friendship is, however, not among equals but rather one of "brothers" suffering the same destiny. "A higher destiny makes us brothers," Tediato says, "correcting the caprice of chance that divides members of the same species into arbitrary and useless social classes; we all weep . . . we all get sick . . . we all die." One should probably not read too much politically into the statement, given Cadalso's acceptance of social hierarchies elsewhere.[98]

While Enlightenment interest in social equality probably plays a role here, the passage more obviously resonates with traditional Christian notions of spiritual brotherhood in a world of shared human misery, reminiscent of the classic *contemptus mundi*. Cadalso's text is laced with echoes of earlier ascetic and moral writers such as Fray Luis de Granada and Francisco de Quevedo. Moreover, the notion of "spiritual friendship" in the secular world, as advocated by St. Frances de Sales in his *Introduction to the Devout Life* (1608), resonated in both the seventeenth and eighteenth centuries, with translations by Quevedo, Sebastián Fernández de Eyzaguirre, and Francisco de Cubillas Donyague (my edition is from 1764).[99]

But why focus on a gravedigger? Tediato's last words offer another clue and, in the process, return us to the fundamental importance of the dead body: "You [Lorenzo] will contribute more to my happiness with that shovel and pickaxe . . . vile instruments to many . . . venerable in my eyes. . . . Let us walk together, my friend, let us walk."[100] Once again, Cadalso's meaning here seems to point to two apparently antithetical images: the representation of the gravedigger's tools as both vile and venerable. Their vileness reminds us of the body's material corruption. Their venerability brings us back to the realm of the sacred. That which inspires reverence, such as relics, is venerable. Tediato associates Lorenzo's grave-digging tools with the image of his beloved's dead body as a relic. Lorenzo's shameful occupation, indeed his very activity of exhuming unclean things, is dirty but also partakes of the sacred precisely through its close connection with that which is transgressive or taboo.

There may be another association as well to which Cadalso alludes. Beginning with Renaissance culture the notion of unearthing was linked to a particular form of resurrection. Digging up fragments of the classical past brought back a dead era, for "retrieval of antiquity meant resurrecting both buried artifacts and buried texts."[101] Thus disinterring and resurrecting can occupy the same space in the mind's eye and in a text. In attempting to exhume his beloved, Tediato is also plunging into the invisible, into the subterranean, of human existence as terra incognita, akin to Hamlet's "undiscovered country" of death filled with dread and nonreturn. This mysterious underground is, paradoxically, Tediato's lifeline, an inner lifeline that becomes the psychological mapping of the mind in subsequent realist fiction.

Significantly, however, the corpse has receded into the background by now. Tediato's beloved is by no means forgotten, but his relationship with the gravedigger is now in the forefront. The gravedigger falls into the category of the deserving poor, which contemporary social thinkers like Bernardo Ward referred to either as "los verdaderos pobres" (the truly poor) or as "pobres de solemnidad" (the extremely poor). In focusing on the economic and familial woes of a gravedigger, Cadalso was surely well aware just how slippery the line was between poverty and beggary, how quickly the working poor could descend into utter misery and want in a world of economic instability, inflationary prices, and periodic bad harvests. In truth, most of the laboring classes in eighteenth-century Spain showed signs of a generalized pauperization. There were few indications of a nascent capitalism in Cadalso's time, but overwhelming evidence of a stagnant traditional society unable to deal with increasing internal immigration to urban centers, unemployment, and endemic poverty. The laboring classes "were [so close] to the edge that any accident of fortune . . . could push them over that fine line that separated honest poverty from outright indigence."[102] Lorenzo's family misfortunes— the death of his wife in childbirth, the death of his father, two children ill with smallpox, another in hospital, yet another having disappeared—are representative of the physical and emotional sufferings of the poor.

Enlightenment figures like Ward and Meléndez Valdés argued along utilitarian lines that putting the poor, whether deserving or not, to work would reduce the hordes of beggars in urban centers and the countryside. Cadalso's humanitarian concern must be seen against the ideological-economic backdrop of distressing generalized poverty and Enlightenment schemes to benefit the nation by ridding it of the visible signs of social breakdown. Indeed, for the Spanish monarchy it was imperative, given the troubling Esquilache bread riots of 1766 (only a few years before Cadalso composed his text). As Callahan observes, the enlightened count of Aranda "believed that the presence of vagabonds and mendicants in the turbulent crowds . . . had contributed directly to the crisis." The government reacted to such social unrest and to masses of unemployed by periodic sweeps of the streets and countryside. Confinement of beggars in *hospicios,* while viewed popularly as an odious form of imprisonment, grew during the last twenty years of the century.[103]

In general, paternalism, which could be alternately repressive and beneficent, informed the social, religious, and political structure of eighteenth-century Spain. Paternalism also marked Enlightenment discourse, as Olavide's reform project illustrates. Thus Meléndez Valdés (1802) speaks of "a paternal and beneficent hand that would temper with humanity the harshness of law, that would know how to unite the spirit of order with moderation, that would weep over the beggar even in punishing him." Equally, a social reformer like Ward (1750) could speak in the same breath of compassion for the unfortunate — "[knowing] how to be sensitive to such a pitiful spectacle [as poverty]" — and of Spain's "unbearable burden . . . of so many useless mouths."[104] Tediato's exquisite philanthropic gesture toward the gravedigger Lorenzo is inevitably paternalistic, reflecting the deeply marked class distinctions of eighteenth-century Spanish society.

Given the terrible living conditions, low life expectancies, and high mortality rates, especially among children, philanthropic discourse also centered on death. Much of the contemporary literature on the fate of foundlings "focused upon raising public consciousness and leaned heavily upon a vocabulary of 'death,'" with titles such as *Destrucción y conservación de los expósitos* by Antonio Bilbao y Durán, and *Causas prácticas de la muerte de niños expósitos en sus primeros años* by Joaquín Xavier de Uriz."[105] In a telling use of body imagery, Ward complained of the lack of trade, consumption, and credit in Spain: "But what is wanting in all this is the soul, absent the driving force of all this machinery, which is the circulation of money and which performs in the body politic the same function as blood in the human body; and as the difference between a healthy, robust body and a cadaver depends on the circulation of blood, so too with money, which in circulating gives life to the entire Republic and in ceasing to flow, takes the breath out of industry."[106]

Ward would have personal cause to complain of such inactivity. Nothing would come of his *Obra pía* (Good Works) (1750) , a reform project the king himself had supported by funding him to go abroad to investigate how other countries dealt with the problem of the poor. Over fifty years later, Meléndez Valdés was still referring to Ward's philanthropic proposal as unrealized.[107]

More to the point, Ward's secularized resurrectional imagery draws from Catholic discourse in the same way that Cadalso does. While the traditional theological view of the *sanctus pauper,* the poor as a sacred mediating link between this world and Christ, had by no means disappeared in eighteenth-century Spain, as Olavide's text reveals, the masses of beggars in particular were often seen as nuisances. The pitiful spectacle of poverty and of death and disease, however, invoked sympathy and compassion in reform-minded figures like Ward, Olavide, and Cadalso. If in an earlier period helping the poor could save one's soul, now attempts were made to save the poor themselves for their own sake and that of the nation.[108]

But the "vocabulary of death" expressed in the philanthropic gesture — Ward's cadaver — suggests the impasse, the lack of circulation, that also pervades Cadalso's text. In this sense, Tediato's specific love object is ultimately insignificant, since it is the overwhelming presence of death itself, in the rotting body at the heart of the work, that signals how Catholic resurrection, as a humanitarian move, cannot be completed. It is the haunted body of death whose sacredness can no longer be adequately accounted for.

By situating *Noches lúgubres* in the context of religious crisis, my reading goes against the secularist interpretations of most critics. Michael Iarocci concludes that "the text rather eloquently bears witness to the eighteenth-century transition from a religiously inflected conception of compassionate identification to an entirely secular one. In Cadalso's text, ethical critique and sympathetic identification are decidedly secular affairs." His reading, however, ignores how much of the text is haunted by the ghost of religion, as I have endeavored to show in its secularized embodiment of resurrection. My point is that neither a purely secular nor a purely religious interpretation does justice to such an open-ended work that straddles two different worldviews and is unable to resolve its own contradictions. Iarocci is right to single out Tediato "as a 'subject-in-struggle,' a self in conflict with his social milieu." He argues that Cadalso critiques the socially destabilizing influence of money and self-interest on family, friendship, and society in general and that the unnamed beloved represents a superior soul "that has resisted *interés*." He overreaches, however, when he says that Tediato's beloved stands in for "the lost historical possibility of something different. She is the corpse, as it were, of a sociohistorical *it might have been otherwise*." I don't think this can be shown textually. Neither do the sacred qualities attributed to the beloved, qualities which, however one interprets them, nearly all critics acknowledge, fit well into a secularized version of things. If she truly represents the opposite of "exclusionary, self-interested social networks," as Iarocci contends, then she falls into some utopian nonsocial realm of possibility, not of historical possibility, in which case her significance bears the sign of transcendence.[109]

No human society exists or functions without the presence of human interest.[110] Equally, values that transcend mere human interest are intrinsic to human development. The problem that figures like Cadalso, Olavide, and Gutiérrez experienced was how to make those higher values—call them God, call them ethics—work when faced with overwhelming self-interest in the polis and crippling doubt in themselves. Cadalso's Tediato appears to reject all social bonds as being corrupt, yet in the end finds common cause with a lowly gravedigger who literally deals with the material corruption of life. Olavide sets up a similar dilemma with his preconversion Philosopher, whose self-indulgent, socially indifferent persona represents the problem of society in microcosm. Gutiérrez sees the same flawed society, though he lays the blame on the Inquisition's power to distort social ties by converting family and friends into spies and to oppress the most vulnerable members of society, like Cornelia. Yet both Gutiérrez and Olavide reiterate the values of faith as expressed in the Gospel.

It is simplistic to think that the religious framework in which eighteenth-century Spain continued to operate was thrown overboard by the ilustrados in order to embrace a new secular society.[111] If anything, it strikes me that through these texts each of these men was attempting in different ways to reincorporate the religious impulse back into the social body. Cassirer observes of the Enlightenment in general that "all apparent opposition to religion which we meet in this age should not blind us to the fact that all intellectual problems are fused with religious problems, and that the former find their constant and deepest inspiration in the latter."[112]

This religious spirit was deeply humanitarian. It was also traditional. Why should this surprise us, that even the most enlightened figures and texts might bear the mark of continuity as well? Critics sometimes seem to have great difficulty in seeing the modern and the traditional on the same page. Iarocci, for example, says, "One might attempt to reconcile this opposition—'modern' versus 'backward' Spain—by tacking to a middle ground that recognizes 'tradition and change' or 'influence and originality' in both Cadalso's text and its historical moment, but such a splitting of the difference would seem to renounce rather than to resolve the problem of historical discrimination posed by these competing interpretive frames."[113] Eighteenth-century Spain *is*, however, that middle ground, as other historical eras have been. In other words, the assumption may not always pertain that these are necessarily "competing interpretive frames" and, most important, even when they are, may not be something we can or may want to resolve.

The texts I have been looking at are excellent examples of ideological irresolution. Even generically, they occupy a gray area. As fictions, all of them share in the quintessentially eighteenth-century cult of sensibility, with an emphasis on sentiment and suffering, leading some scholars to see in Cadalso and Gutiérrez an early romanticism.[114] *Noches lúgubres,* which went through forty-seven editions in the nineteenth century alone, in this regard has its own history of reception; nineteenth-century adaptations and additions to the text evidently affected some readers, much as Johann Wolfgang von Goethe's *Young Werther* did for the suggestion of suicide and extreme behavior. Sensibility was also, however, a social virtue, secularizing spiritual concern for others through sociability.[115]

These texts cannot be pigeonholed. What interests me more is how such writings begin to move in another direction, a movement prompted in part by religious crisis. Humanitarian concern for others still draws on the evangelical strength of early Christianity, but the emphasis on the poor and other marginalized figures like women is also predicated on a new secular understanding of economic and social privation. In narrative, this growing awareness is sifted through the conflicted individual consciousness of the privileged, usually the protagonist (the Philosopher, Vargas, Tediato), in its relation with those persons and social classes previously neglected as objects of both sympathy and reform. These are the relics of faith in both senses of the word.

Not all novels share such a vision, and there is no single, totalizing explanation for the evolution of the modern novel in Spain or anywhere else. This developing thread, a significant one in my view, is one among several for understanding narrative of the period. My discussion points not so much to a specific form (like the epistolary novel or the picaresque, say) but to a different relation with reality, with the world, as the prime mover for shaping narrative in alternative ways. Humanitarian concern likewise informs the nineteenth-century realist novel but also, tellingly, romantic fiction, thus reaffirming the linkage between the two modes.[116]

2

The Philanthropic Embrace

History has not treated early nineteenth-century Spain well. Invasion, war, empire breakup, political and socioeconomic upheaval, all these things produced deeply unsettling and often chaotic conditions while moving the nation toward greater secularization and social divisiveness. Religion and literature in the period bear the mark of historic trauma. To understand what happened to both requires seeing them together as part of a larger process in which faith and its institutions were to occupy a new space and role in a society made up increasingly of much more sharply (and politically) etched class differences than ever before.

The juncture where religion and the novel converge and clash is precisely the social arena. In this chapter, I want to pursue further the ways in which the philanthropic embrace of once socially invisible classes is the flash point for the creation of a new literary realism of evangelical origin that emerges from radical change and instability, as seen in such texts as Ayguals de Izco's *María, la hija de un jornalero* (1845–46) and culminating in Galdós's *Fortunata y Jacinta* (1886–87). The crisis in which the Catholic Church found itself was not only part of a larger crisis of national proportions; it spilled over into every crevice of the geography of social relations and seeped into the pages of literature. Attacks upon the practices and power of the Church openly appear in satirical pamphlets and polemical writings during the Napoleonic period. By the early 1820s we see the first signs of anticlerical violence. A rupture has begun, cracks in the supposed unity of religious identity appearing as small broken veins or fissures in the social fabric of the country.

These splinters of a fracturing faith were already evident in some Enlightenment figures like Cadalso, Gutiérrez, and Olavide. Following the cataclysms of the French Revolution and Terror of 1793, many Spanish ecclesiastics closed ranks ideologically. A crusade mentality developed, dampening the reform spirit from within the Church. Traditionalists saw danger both in the secular libertinism they thought was undermining the moral foundation of Spanish society and in the policies of regalism undercutting their privileges. As an institution, Catholicism was hurting, though still intact, at the end of the eighteenth century. In 1798 the state, financially strapped, began to sell off church properties, specifically its charitable institutions, a move that seriously compromised the Church's ability to minister poor relief. The Napoleonic invasion of 1808 threw the Church into a full-blown crisis. The government of Joseph Bonaparte suppressed the religious orders and appropriated church resources such as tithes, other monies, and gold and silver ornaments. The popular uprising against the French also exploited church assets. War turned monasteries into stables and barracks, churches fell into ruin. The pastoral relation between parish priests and their congregations suffered markedly. Many churchmen fled the occupied zones and joined the resistance, becoming guerrilla fighters in a new crusade. With little money and fewer ecclesiastics, the Church's charitable work, so necessary in times of generalized poverty and hardship, fell apart.

At the same time internal Church divisions between reformers and traditionalists grew, sparked by the meeting of the constitutional Cortes in Cádiz in 1810. Although Catholicism remained the official religion of Spain, the Inquisition was abolished, the doctrine of national sovereignty was declared, and seigneurial and jurisdictional privileges of the nobility and the Church were done away with. For many churchmen, this initial liberal revolution — secular and less hierarchical — marked the start of Church decline.[1]

A series of regime changes further destabilized the country. A second liberal revolution in 1820 lasting three years arose in reaction to the despotism of Ferdinand VII, with his restoration to the throne in 1814. And again, attempts to reform the Church, to make it into a civic partner of liberal goals, ended up bitterly antagonizing ecclesiastics. At the same time the intransigence of the Church most likely radicalized some of the more progressive elements of liberal opinion. Violent hostility to the Church also surfaced for the first time among the urban underclasses, an indication that the bond between Church and society was weakening under economic and political pressure.[2]

Ten more years of despotic rule under Ferdinand VII followed until his death in 1833, then a civil war erupted. A dynastic quarrel between two branches of the Spanish Bourbons, the first Carlist War (1833–40), like the civil war of 1936–39, was also a religious conflict. Opposing the supporters of María Cristina, the queen regent, were the ultra-Catholic Carlists, whose values were theocratic and absolutist. While friars and monks joined the Carlist cause, many in the religious orders remained passive. At the same time the rivalry between Moderates and Progressives, which shaped liberal politics for the rest of the century, created the conditions for radical liberals to take power in 1835, 1836, and 1840, propelled locally by a provincial urban revolution. Two elements contributed to revolution: "some sharpening of the misery of the urban masses and the fear of Carlist plots and government treason."[3] Here too, as in the war of 1936, revolutionary aims and sentiments complicated a civil conflict.

A central event in precipitating the waves of political turbulence was a rumor. In July 1834, Madrid was in the midst of a heat wave, experiencing a spike in food prices, and fearful of a Carlist offensive, just as a terrible cholera epidemic was raging. A story began to circulate that some pro-Carlist friars and monks had poisoned the city's wells to spread the disease. Bloody mayhem erupted, with riots, looting, church burnings, and the killing of religious (*la matanza de los frailes*). A year later similar violence broke out in places like Zaragoza, Barcelona, and Poblet, as revolutionary juntas arose in Aragon, Catalonia, Andalusia, Galicia, and elsewhere.

While the rest of the century saw little anticlerical violence, these initial outbreaks were signs of a malaise in which religion was seen by some as part of a problem rather than as a reason for being. The politicization of religion took on darker hues for the Church in 1835 and 1836, when Mendizábal suppressed most of the male religious orders and then proceeded to sell off much of the regulars' property. By the 1840s Church politics were decidedly conservative, alternately hostile to the state and on the defensive. Many ecclesiastics were also convinced that Spain was no longer Catholic. Although the traditionalist philosopher Jaume Balmes did not go so far, he believed in 1846 that skepticism, an "emptiness of the soul," was rampant. Nonetheless, there was no evidence of a "massive drift into dechristianization" at this time.[4]

A seven-year civil-religious conflict with revolutionary outbursts had to have been devastating. The first Carlist War and the passions it provoked appear as a very distant event today, but the intensity of feelings and beliefs on both sides remained well into the 1840s, to judge from the two-volume bestseller *María, la hija de un jornalero*.

María, which had gone through seven editions by 1849 and sold well abroad, popularized the Spanish serial novel, inspired by Sue's much-translated *Les Mystères de Paris* (1842–43).[5] Ayguals's work has all the elements of a sensationalist potboiler: a love story between social unequals, a lecherous, scheming friar, bloody mayhem, unjust imprisonment, conspiracies, and betrayals. In the end, María's virtue remains intact, she will wed an aristocrat, her parents are saved from death, and the depraved friar is executed. The importance of the serial novel in the development of the genre and for later realists like Galdós is long established and does not bear repeating here.[6] Many kinds of novels were being written in the first half of the nineteenth century: the epistolary novel persisted, the historical novel was in vogue, and novels of social customs as well as a steady flow of translations catered to a small but growing, largely middle-class readership. As in the eighteenth century, there is also a marked tendency toward the hybrid, in which the very term "novel" is a floating, unstable category.[7] For example, *María* combines elements of, among other things, melodrama, the sentimental novel, the anticlerical novel, and the modern guidebook.

Above all, *María* is a fascinating illustration of the novel as commercial enterprise.[8] But contemporary reviews also stressed the philanthropic, humanitarian character of the work. Ever the promoter, Ayguals inserted at the end of both volumes several very favorable notices of his novel. Thus one review praises the author's "highly humanitarian objective, which is to show how much . . . the working class of Spain endures and suffers."[9] Another publication recommends the novel "to all the classes of society" for its "extremely philanthropic principles."[10]

Most of these reviews, appearing in papers ideologically sympathetic to Ayguals, are mere puffs. A much more hostile commentator read his humanitarian embrace of the laboring classes and critique of the privileged very differently: "His object is to exalt the nation's inferior classes over all others in society and in particular over the throne, flattering the former, often cravenly, and continually wounding the others, especially the monarchy, motivated, it seems, by republican sentiments. But it is the clergy upon whom he has declared all-out war . . . particularly the churchman . . . friar Patricio, a Franciscan, painting him as . . . a monster of lechery, gluttony, treachery, and ferocity."[11]

No less than Ayguals himself, this anonymous reviewer is passionately committed to a Manichean worldview that brooks no opposition. This piece from 1848 appeared in *La Censura*, a monthly published by the Biblioteca Religiosa. Only moral values were of interest to its contributors, whose fanaticism in matters religious defines the tenor of the publication.[12]

La Censura sees Ayguals's novel as fiercely anticlerical. His anticlericalism doubtless grew more intense in response to clerical intransigence during the Carlist War. The action of *María* begins in 1833, at the start of war. Calling it anticlerical, however, does not do full justice to the text. Like Gutiérrez's *Cornelia Bororquia*, Ayguals's novel is conceived within a framework of ideological transcendence and written not only in, but for, a time of crisis. First, Ayguals follows a traditional Catholic critique of Church abuses by singling out priestly corruption in the figure of Fray Patricio. He is quick to point out repeatedly that there are many good priests as well. Second, his own politics, which can loosely be described as republican democrat, possess an evangelical thrust that issues from a liberal-inspired religious feeling, characteristic of an age that was searching for a way to keep religion vital in the social body. If politics is a form of religion for Ayguals, the reverse is probably also true: religion is a form of politics. That the anonymous reviewer of *La Censura* did not see it this way speaks more to the blindness of ideological absolutes, always far more reassuring than doubt and uncertainty in turbulent times.

María is a book about the poor and the rich and about how society and its institutions, including the Church, deal or, more to the point, fail to deal with the growing problem of urban poverty and social inequity. The cover illustration, which depicts the divide between rich and poor, at the same time brings to the fore the significance of the poor while placing the Church in the background but still in a central position. The novel, which is not particularly well written, is filled with digressive material and sermonizing and is loosely and awkwardly constructed. It is significant, however, for literary realism and for its understanding of the novel as the new place of a humanitarian ethic, the place where the pending loss of communitas, the social-spiritual contract connecting the vulnerable with the powerful, might be reestablished.

To understand how the politics of religion can turn into the religion of politics in *María,* one needs to regard the book in context, specifically the conditions under which it was produced and the political-religious landscape that prevailed in the period, especially among the more progressive elements of Spanish society. The classic treatment of Ayguals de Izco's life and works is Rubén Benítez's study from 1979, unsurpassed for its well-balanced, documented rendering of this important literary and cultural figure. Born in the seaport of Vinaròs, province of Castelló de la Plana, Ayguals (1801–73) came from a prosperous mercantile family and was groomed for the commercial life, which he embraced with great enthusiasm and energy, establishing among other things a highly successful publishing house. He was an unrepentant capitalist with reformist opinions. He defended private property and thus was not a socialist, a view Iris Zavala propagated and which has since been effectively dismissed. Indeed, he declared himself unambiguously to be both anti-socialist and anticommunist in his historical novel *El tigre del Maestrazgo* (The tiger of the Maestrazgo) (1846–48).[13]

In stark contrast with Zavala's idealized portrait of the writer as utopian

Figure 2. Cover illustration, *María, la hija de un jornalero* (María, the laborer's daughter), by Wenceslao Ayguals de Izco (1845–46).

socialist, Peter Goldman calls Ayguals a rapacious opportunist, noting, for example, how he made good use of his connections with Sue to further his career and continually promoted his business and himself through endless advertising ploys, including an apparently paid-for-hire biography by Blas María Araque. Ayguals was above all an entrepreneur in an age of great ambitions. But was he also "a wealthy hypocrite of almost limitless opportunism"?[14] The truth, I suspect, lies somewhere in between Zavala's heroic socialist and Goldman's crass opportunist. Dismissing all capitalists as nothing but scheming Pharisees leaves one little to say about the complex and often contradictory relation between entrepreneurial figures like Ayguals and their society. A larger point of view will show how someone like Ayguals, in shaping his small plot of the world, also was shaped by the world. One also needs to see Ayguals not simply as a representative of a specific social order, but in as much of his human richness and imperfection as possible. Otherwise, it will remain obscure how this enterprising, ambitious man could write so passionately about a class to which he did not belong, the laboring poor. Ayguals is not easily understood. The public persona he tirelessly promoted, even going so far as to publicize a phrenology report of his character, gets in the way. A note of sadness that his biographer Araque picks up on, however, suggests beneath his grave exterior hidden depths about which one can only speculate.

By the time the Carlist War began in October 1833 Ayguals was making a name for himself as a writer in Madrid. Two years later his brother Joaquín died fighting the Carlists near Vinaròs. This family tragedy only deepened the hatred he felt toward the Carlists, in particular the military leader Ramón Cabrera, nicknamed the tiger of the Maestrazgo for his brutality and taste for blood, whom he held responsible for his brother's death.[15] Ayguals returned to Vinaròs, eventually assuming command of the National Militia and the mayor's office; he also belonged to the local charity board. In later years he took great pains to recount, on more than one occasion, his role in resisting the Carlist troops. His biographer dwelled at length and in largely hagiographic terms on the same episode, noting, for example, how Ayguals's compassion for a group of shipwrecked Carlist prisoners saved their lives.

Was this a case of self-promotion? Unquestionably. But Ayguals was also very proud of his participation in the war. Vinaròs was not simply the scene of battle. It was also part of the provincial revolutions that were being advanced through the National Militias and democratically elected municipalities in 1836 and furthered by a sergeants' revolt against the throne in Madrid. Conservatives and moderates alike detested these militias, which allowed a working-class membership. According to Raymond Carr, "The militia would become the private army of radical town councils, licensed to terrorize the supporters of a conservative constitution." This was not how Ayguals saw it, needless to say.

He, after all, headed up the militia in Vilaròs and was the town's first constitutionally elected mayor.[16] (Later, he would be elected to the parliament as well.) Tellingly, María's father, Anselmo, a heroic working-class figure in the novel, belongs to the urban militia in Madrid, open to all and established before the national one.

Ayguals's progressive political views cannot be separated from his local experience in war and revolution. As a fervent anti-Carlist, moreover, he understood he was fighting against a theocratic worldview, a point he vehemently stresses more than once, for instance, toward the end of the novel in his over-the-top creation of Fray Patricio, the villain of the piece: "To portray in Fray Patricio the foul inquisitorial gang that still aspires to dominate Spain . . . has been the principal object of my work." In the same chapter he refers to the Carlists as "apostles of absolutism" whose aim is to enthrone "a theocratic despotism in Spain."[17] The fictional world of *María* is as Manichean as the ideological world it opposes, dividing everything into good and evil, black and white, but what has not been sufficiently emphasized is the politicized dimension of his vision. Fray Patricio is not simply evil. He is a Carlist, the equivalent of unredeemable malevolence, for Ayguals.

Indeed, his anti-Carlist rage is as intense in 1846 as it must have been a decade before, as he rails against present-day Carlist machinations to marry off Isabel II to one of their own (and criticizes the temporizing *moderados* as well).[18] (The Carlists would try once again to gain the throne through force in late 1846.) *María* is filled with these temporal dislocations, as Ayguals's real-life time frame, 1845–46, bursts repeatedly by way of authorial commentary and other intromissions into the narrative period of the 1830s. It is easy to dismiss Ayguals's hatred of the Carlists as a personal obsession, but this is to risk underestimating the impact Carlism had on the history and culture of nineteenth-century Spain. Ayguals was not alone in his visceral rejection of Carlism.

More to the point here, anti-Carlism fuels the story line of *María* because everything that Carlism represents for Ayguals doesn't simply go against his liberal social vision; it also catalyzes his humanitarian narrative. The novel begins with a portrait not of María, but of the convent of San Francisco el Grande and Fray Patricio. The initial narrative tack appears to be straightforwardly anticlerical, focusing on what he considers the motivating factors of religious hypocrisy and greed during the convent's rebuilding in the late eighteenth century. Here too we come across the first of Ayguals's many digressions. He observes that the architects of the convent were Pló and Sabatini and then wonders if this last named is related to the Sabatini responsible for garbage pickup in Madrid. The smell, he complains, is really terrible, and something

Figure 3. *El Fraile* (*The Friar*). Lithograph, in *El Motín*.

should be done about it. (Later, he claims his criticisms have brought about improvements in Madrid's sanitation.) What does the stench of refuse have to do with the convent? Nothing apparently, except that Ayguals's value system associates filth with clerical excess, as his subsequent portrayal of Fray Patricio's lechery and voracious appetite suggests. The friar, celebrated for his seductive eloquence in the pulpit, is also partial to teaching the catechism to the young, among whom is María. The narrator says the friar's description "should be sufficient for the reader to understand how repugnant his atten-

Figure 4. *Qué bueno es . . . Dios* (*How Good . . . God Is*). Illustration by
Bordonova, in *El Motín*.

tions to the poor girl [María] were. Fray Patricio was nearly thirty years old. He was short and really fat. The fringe of hair round his tonsure was red. His eyes, exceeding small, were accented by eyebrows that seemed made of hemp, and his pupils were light green, which made his gaze treacherous like a cat's. His face overall was large, round, and extremely fleshy, especially the tip of his nose, which looked like a small ripe tomato . . . this holy personage was as lecherous as a monkey, bold as can be, conceited, hypocritical like most friars."[19]

No doubt this description draws upon the satiric tradition of Quevedo as well as on the gothic novel (Ann Radcliffe's *The Italian* and Matthew Lewis's *The Monk*). Such images became a topos of clerical excess, appearing repeatedly throughout the century, especially in visual forms. I am also struck by how much both the opening and the portrait anticipate Clarín's *La Regenta,* which begins with city debris and later emphasizes similarly marked features in the priest Fermín de Pas, at once seductive and repellent and sharing nearly the same age, green eyes, and fleshy nose, if not the friar's obesity. Indeed, both novels exhibit a continual movement and tension between the eschatological and the scatological.[20] The world in such texts is poised between its dramatic end (things are always coming undone and are at the edge of catastrophe) and its fallen nature (the hidden filth of depravity is everywhere).

Ayguals had also embraced the melodramatic universe of the serial novel, most notably Sue's *The Mysteries of Paris,* a hugely successful commercial enterprise that gave birth to many imitations and adaptations throughout Europe. So popular were these novels that one reviewer envisioned in 1844 a book with the title *Mysteries of the Mysteries of Madrid.* Though the vogue petered out after the 1840s, we find examples even in the 1880s.[21]

Sue's book immediately plunged readers and would-be novelists into a compelling urban netherworld filled with deviant social pathologies. Above all, he exploited, in a highly commercialized genre, the erotic attraction of the sold body, or prostitute, as a figure of that world. Most significantly, with the character Fleur-de-Marie's death, the novelist appears to say that once marked by the filth of the social depths, she can never be fully redeemed.[22]

Ayguals goes in another direction. Although he teases the reader with the possibility of prostitution for María, even allowing her father to mistakenly think she has become one, he preserves her innocence to the end. Indeed, in contrast to Sue's fictional universe, his world contains much less of the social dregs, and by far the most depraved character is not lower class but occupies a respectable position in society: the Franciscan friar Patricio.[23] In effect, Ayguals displaces much of Sue's social deviancy onto a religious figure and the theocratic misuse of religion. Religion weighs far more heavily in *María* than it does in *The Mysteries of Paris,* despite the presence of a kindly abbot.[24] How could it be otherwise, given the specific historic and cultural circumstances within Spain and under which Ayguals's novel was produced?

Sue's humanitarian vision influenced Ayguals (he dedicated *María* to him), but the Spaniard's political and social beliefs had been set well before he read *The Mysteries of Paris*. Indeed, "the term ['democrat,' which Ayguals applied to himself] was used in the first half of the nineteenth century in the same breath as *philanthropist* or *humanitarian,* to indicate the concern of some progressives for social situations contrary to freedom and human dignity."[25] For Ayguals, the Carlists represented a threat to that freedom and human dignity, against which "the people have the unquestionable and sacred right ... we shall not say to rebel against its oppressors, for when nations rise up en masse to punish insolent despots, they exercise an act of sovereign justice."[26]

Two competing systems of salvation inform Ayguals's novel, in which there is a move to convert the politics of religion (Carlism and his reading of it) into the religion of politics (progressive liberalism). This move is a slippery one, prone to contamination, for these are two distinct domains — religion and politics, the sacred and the profane — that most prefer to keep apart. Ayguals himself advocated strict separation of Church and State.[27] The often blurred line between religion and politics in a secular genre like the novel also suggests the effects of growing secularization upon the religious impulse. In these competing systems, we see two different conceptions of religion itself in Ayguals's text: a theocratic despotism hungry for power juxtaposed to an evangelical religion of philanthropy. Anticlerical emotion serves as a necessary prop in this conversion process.

Using anticlericalism as a verbal weapon against Church abuses is, however, tricky. If the aim is to highlight instead a more positive role for socially responsible religious feeling by stressing a redemptive humanitarian vision, as appears the case for Ayguals, the difficulty lies in properly harnessing a worldview that tends to be as polarizing and virulent as the opposing one. How, for example, to justify popular anticlerical violence, which undercuts two of the writer's fundamental positions: belief in the innate goodness of the people (*el pueblo*) and in the socially redemptive power of philanthropic goodwill? Humanitarian tolerance and passionate anticlericalism cannot easily inhabit the same space. The narrator, whose voice is clearly that of Ayguals himself, seems to be dimly aware of the problem when he tries to deal with the killing of religious in July 1834. In narrating the historic episode, he makes two arguments. First, the friars (by this term one assumes he means pro-Carlist religious orders), he says, have converted the pulpit and confessional into a political forum and have committed horrendous acts of violence during the civil war. Enemies of civilization and freedom, they do not deserve the people's sympathy, and in effect there is none to be had, he claims. Second, he distinguishes between the suffering, virtuous people, which include the militiamen, and the bloodthirsty, criminal mob: "A valiant people do not assassinate defenseless men, or profane the fortresses of God."[28]

Ayguals lays on the antimob rhetoric with a thick trowel: "There was among that rabble of soulless beings not a single one whose ferocious visage did not flash furious sparks of frenetic rage. Covered in dust and sweat, those repugnant faces only opened their mouths to vomit blasphemies. The revolting rags that covered their blood-spattered bodies gave an infernal aspect to such a disastrous scene."[29] Later, he describes other acts of profanation, as rowdy women dressed in priestly robes parade through the streets and pause to drink the Communion wine in taverns.[30]

This scene provoked a heated response from the reviewer of *La Censura*. Not true, he says, that the people of Madrid had no sympathy for the religious. They stayed in their homes because they were overwhelmed by the cholera epidemic and fear of the mob, while the government stood by and watched. The regulars were much "esteemed in Madrid for their conduct, their beneficence, and effective discharge of their evangelical mission."[31] Here, the reviewer, whether he knew it or not, indirectly detected a certain ideological vulnerability in the novelist. Ayguals applies the same overheated rhetoric to both the Carlist clergy and the uncontrollable mob, indicating the rhetorical and ideological instability of extreme anticlericalism as both a position and an act. Verbal violence begets a violent world. The single most critical feature that distinguished progressives — though not republican democrats like Ayguals — from other kinds of liberals in Spain during the period was their espousal of revolution as a legitimate course of action.

Ayguals justifies his hatred of the regulars because, in his view, as Carlist supporters they have betrayed the evangelical message of the Gospel. "The enemies of our prosperity . . . ," he says, "under a cloak of evangelical charity, of apostolic meekness and protestations of fraternity, aim to drown us in a lake of blood in order to enthrone themselves upon what remains of us." To hammer home his point, he prints the words of an unnamed clergyman urging the Church to return to its evangelical origins, renounce violence, and embrace one's enemies.[32]

In passages like these, Ayguals attempts to unite the two recurring motifs of *María*: anticlericalism, which is generally merged with anti-Carlism, and humanitarianism. Stressing his philanthropic advocacy on behalf of the poor and laboring classes, he emphasizes elsewhere that his main purpose is to denounce and expose the dangers of Carlism and its supporters. These two concerns do not always make a good narrative fit, but ideologically, together they illuminate the tension between the politics of religion and the religion of politics in the novel. Philanthropy is the secular, or political, expression of religion in *María*. It is for Ayguals, who personally asserted his own faith on more than one occasion, a way of reinserting religion into the social body in an age of upheaval when, for some, belief could no longer be taken for granted and social differences no longer ignored.[33]

The philanthropic turn is not surprising, given an Enlightenment legacy of beneficent reform, renewed private charity efforts in the 1840s, and the appeal of early socialist utopian thinkers, mainly French, to democrats like Ayguals in the 1830s and 1840s. Ayguals belonged to a strand of political thinking called humanitarian democracy. *María* appears to be one of the first Spanish works of fiction to fully embrace the novelist as philanthropist, although there are indications of the model in Olavide's *El evangelio en triunfo*. In another novel that also appeared in 1845–46, *Madrid y nuestro siglo* (Madrid and our century), by Ramón de Navarrete (1818–97), perhaps the most interesting of the secondary characters is a wealthy, middle-aged individual, Don Gil Moralejo. In line with his earnest moral nature (hence the symbolic name), he has decided to become a philanthropist and devote himself to collecting "the statistics of vice and virtue, in all the different social classes," for which project he has conceived a vast, grandiose plan. Rather than rely on official sources or support, "he wanted to see it all with his own eyes, to introduce himself not simply into the gilded salons of the aristocracy but also into the garret of the miserable artisan." In the end, he limits his investigation to the lower classes. He rents a room in the heart of Lavapiés, a working-class neighborhood, and lives the same humble life as his objects of study, which enables him how "best to discover their state of morality or corruption."[34] Navarrete, who appears to treat Don Gil in half-ironic–half-serious terms, characterizes him as a tender-minded, easily duped eccentric.

The narrator takes pains to inform his readers that the story occurs shortly after the Progressive coup of Espartero in 1840, "when the revolutionary doctrines that served to provoke [the *pronunciamiento*, or coup] were still at fever pitch." Even before he introduces Don Gil, the narrator behaves much like an investigative reporter or visiting philanthropist, describing, for example, as "dark and foul-smelling" a humble shop that does double duty as a home and then proceeding to offer many more details about the dwelling and the people who live there Then he makes this point: "If governments were truly paternal and farsighted, they would exercise a beneficial and sacred vigilance over these unfortunate families. . . . Why don't legislators . . . devote themselves to alleviating so much misfortune and prostration, out of humanitarian interest and indeed in their own interest?"[35]

Like Ayguals de Izco's novel, *Madrid y nuestro siglo* stresses class differences, the great divide between rich and poor, attributing to the lower social orders an "instinctive hatred" of the "indifference with which the rich regard the misfortunes and misery of the poor."[36] It is hard to believe this socially aware, progressive text, which is reformist and humanitarian in character, comes from the same pen that later would devote pages and pages to the frivolities and fashions of high society. Navarrete, under the nom de plume Asmodeo, became the foremost chronicler of the privileged classes during the Isabeline and Restoration periods. Starting in 1849, he was closely associated with *La Época*, a conservative daily newspaper read mainly for its society column. Did the waves of revolution that swept through Europe in 1848 (though measurably less so in Spain, which had already gone through a number of revolutionary moments in the 1830s) turn him away from liberalism? [37]

Navarrete's public persona as fashionable society columnist so dominated the rest of his life that none of the few scraps of information I have managed to find discusses his political views or his interest in philanthropy. That he became a reporter of this kind — and continued to write fiction, albeit of a much more lightweight nature than *Madrid y nuestro siglo* — is not so removed in some respects from the philanthropist in search of statistics.[38] The link between journalism and popular forms like the serial novel and the *misterios* is well established. Not only did such novels often appear literally incorporated into newspapers as serial publications (the *folletín*); they also advertised their commercial nature as goods to be sold. The narrator of fictions like those of Ayguals de Izco and Navarrete anticipates the modern reporter in his investigative capacity. In 1851 Henry Mayhew, who happily combined journalism with philanthropy, published *London Labour and the London Poor*. By mid-century it was also common to find medical professionals assuming a philanthropic role. Pere Felip Monlau's *Remedios del pauperismo* (Poor relief) (1846) and *Elementos de higiene pública* (1847), for example, had already appeared.

Philanthropy and humanitarianism were unmistakably in vogue by the 1840s, at least among some political and social circles. The novelist as philanthropist leads readers through the social worlds of texts like *María* and *Madrid y nuestro siglo*. These words and their variants, peppered throughout the reviews of Ayguals's novel, appear to be used interchangeably. In the 1840s the term "philanthropy" was still more common in Spain than "humanitarian," given its Enlightenment pedigree. *Filantropía* as a "Greek word" had already appeared in the celebrated dictionary by Sebastián de Covarrubias (1611) but not, oddly enough, in the first dictionary compiled by the Royal Spanish Academy, the *Diccionario de Autoridades* (1726–39). Only in 1822 do both *filantropía* ("love of humankind") and *filantrópico* appear in a royal academy dictionary; and in 1852, the term *filántropo*, or philanthropist, even though it was being used in print in the late eighteenth century.[39] *Humanitario*, "humanitarian," does not make its first appearance until 1869 in the academy dictionary, but Rafael María Baralt (1810–60), who apparently had been collecting Spanish coinages from the French since the 1840s, had already annotated it as a Gallicism: "Referring to humanity. Used today by some in this sense, from the French. It seems superfluous to me, and sounds wrong to my ears. '*Humanitarian* sentiments, ideas, perspectives, services.' Why not *Human, charitable sentiments; Ideas and perspectives of universal interest and benefit; Services made [to benefit] humankind?*"[40]

In the prologue to Baralt's *Diccionario de galicismos* (1855), Juan Eugenio Hartzenbusch concludes by saying he hopes Spaniards will choose the language of the *Quijote* over that of the *Misterios de París*, suggesting with this last named a link between the popularity of writers like Sue and the adoption of French terms.[41] (The Frenchification of customs was in general a habit much criticized in the 1830s and 1840s, as the *costumbrista* articles of Mariano José de Larra and Ramón de Mesonero Romanos testify.)

"Philanthropy" as well was initially viewed as a French import, its use limited to a reduced group of Spanish intellectuals during the 1780s. In pre-revolutionary France, philanthropy eventually revised the more traditional terms "beneficence" (*bienfaisance*) and "charity" by assuming a plainly utilitarian and temporal social function rather than charity's witness to God's love. At this time, as Catherine Duprat observes, "the meanings of the terms *philanthropist, citizen* and *patriot* now tend to be confused." Freemasons in particular began to disseminate the word "philanthropy." It is not surprising that philanthropy was "elevated to the central value of the Revolution." After 1815 the rivalry and hostility between philanthropic societies and Catholic societies intensified in France.[42]

Thus in early nineteenth-century Spain the term "philanthropy" had acquired, especially among conservative Catholics, a political connotation unfavorably associated with the excesses and secularism of the French Revolution. "Humanitarianism," which may have been additionally tainted by the political tumult of 1848, was also suspect as a French import.[43] Elsewhere, there was uneasiness in adopting such words, whether for the same or other reasons. Although Raymond Williams claims "the use of *humanitarian* was hostile or contemptuous," attitudes toward the concept were more varied than he suggests. In the 1840s, for example, American Catholics, largely working class and lower middle class, saw humanitarianism as a middle- and upper-class pursuit. Moreover, American Catholicism favored poor relief as more in "the spirit of religious giving" than social reform efforts.[44] Class differences along with the immigrant status of many American Catholics in the period shaped charitable giving.

In Spain, I suspect that the poor did not distinguish between church beneficence, or charity, and philanthropy, so desperate were their needs. Such distinctions were more likely to be held among Catholic groups and the more privileged and educated classes. In some cases, irony and ambivalence can be detected in the use of the word "philanthropy." For example, in 1823 an anonymously authored tract accused liberals of identifying words like "virtue," "integrity," "philanthropy" "solely with . . . the desire for blood, horror and extermination." Here, it would appear that philanthropy is valued; but at the same time it is associated with political violence and extremism, which I expect is an allusion to the *exaltados* of the Revolution of 1820.[45] Balmes registers a more nuanced ambivalence toward the idea of philanthropy in 1846, which he links to exaggerated sentimentalism: "Not everything is philanthropy that lies hidden beneath this veil." His comment is embedded in a critique of overly softhearted views toward criminality so that "what gets lost is compassion . . . for the victim."[46] Sentimentalism recalls the eighteenth-century appreciation of sensibility and the cult of tears (which the romantics embraced), while leniency toward crime is placed in the political terrain of liberalism. Like the earlier comment, this one joins philanthropy to what Balmes regards as political and ideological excess; it is not hard to see the violent shadow of the French Revolution behind such critiques.

Fernán Caballero, for whom charity is a central theme, takes a more traditional approach in her story *Lucas García* (1852) when she says, "Charity! Sacred, sublime charity! . . . Why do we not see you in the palaces that philanthropy fashions?" Charity is religiously inspired; philanthropy is not, in this view. She goes on to say that charity is found in the hovels of the poor and in unfortunates like widows "because charity wants to be a queen and not a slave."[47] Here, the traditional idea of the poor as representative of God is reiterated. Giving to the poor is giving to God. It would also appear that Fernán Caballero sees a link between enslaving, secular materialism, and philanthropy, as visualized in its "palaces." Or she may be referring ironically to such public charity institutions as the San Bernardino Asylum in Madrid, chronically underfunded and dismally regimented.[48] In either case, she reveals distrust of bureaucratic, organized beneficence (philanthropy) as contrary to true Christian charity.

The issue of philanthropy versus charity needs to be set as well in the context of crisis and attacks against the faith as perceived in conservative Catholic circles. Writing after the revolutionary year 1848, the traditionalist Juan Donoso Cortés (1809–53) said that "Catholicism, reviled and mocked today by I know not what dark and cruel sectarians in the name of the starving, is the religion of those who suffer hunger. Catholicism, combated today in the name of the proletariat, is the religion of the poor and the needy. Catholicism, combated in the name of liberty, equality, and fraternity, is the religion of human liberty, equality, and fraternity."[49]

In co-opting the language of radicalism, Donoso reveals to what extent religious crisis is viewed through the lens of a social crisis. Also striking is his need to defend the traditional strength of Catholicism and of Christianity in general: its message of compassion and spiritual fellowship. Elsewhere, the crisis is bluntly stated as class warfare: "What has never happened till now in the world is a universal and simultaneous war between the rich and the poor. . . . If the rich had not lost the virtue of charity, God would not have permitted the poor to lose the virtue of patience." He sees a fundamentally flawed distribution of wealth that only charity in the form of giving on a large scale can remedy. An inadequate solution to systemic underemployment and tardy industrialization, nonetheless, Donoso's remarks illuminate to what degree an intractable social problem and the religious question were inseparable as parts of the larger predicament of modernity. Thus the Catholic novelist Francisco Navarro Villoslada felt strongly that the country could not address the one problem without affecting the other. In the last few years of his short life, Donoso not only intensified his devotional practices but made frequent donations and visits to the poor and imprisoned, working with the charitable Society of St. Vincent de Paul.[50]

The traditional distinction between charity and philanthropy, however, is not always clear in practice, as even Donoso's personal example suggests, for what else is the Society of St. Vincent de Paul but a Catholic philanthropic organization? Even those who fully embraced the idea of organized philanthropy often used the vocabulary of Christian charity to promote it, unsurprising given the religious origins and beliefs of both the act of beneficence and its benefactors.[51] Beneficence as an idea is both traditional and modern. *Beneficencia* appears subsumed under the entry *Beneficio*, or "benefice," in Covarrubias. In 1726 the word has a separate entry as "the work [*obra*] of doing good for others, showing oneself to be liberal [generous] and beneficent toward others." The term *obra* is shorthand for the traditional "good works" (*buenas obras*, also in Covarrubias), while "liberal" and "beneficent" gesture toward Enlightenment values. By 1803, the definition now reads, "The virtue of doing good to another." "Virtue" by this time is double-edged semantically, possessing a Christian and an Enlightenment pedigree, recalling Voltaire's secularization of the term. The word *Benefactor* appears in both academy dictionaries but is noted as being infrequently used in 1726; by 1803, it is simply listed as synonymous for *Bienhechor.* Ever the purist, the philologist Baralt, a Venezuelan living in Spain (which may partly explain his lexical reaction), has this to say about "beneficence": "This term has succeeded in supplanting the more appropriate word, CHARITY, in many cases. Thus: *Public Beneficence; Establishments of Beneficence; Branch of Beneficence,* etc. The proper and truly correct [word] is CHARITY, because this term expresses better than the other one the inescapably and essentially Christian obligation of doing good for our fellow man, and the obligation that all governments have to rush to the aid of their neediest subjects. BENEFICENCE has a less inclusive meaning than CHARITY and does not connote, like the latter, the ideas of abnegation and piety that are especially proper to the virtues emanating from religion."[52]

As a replacement for the term "charity," "beneficence" is evidently a secular Gallicism for Baralt, a progressive Catholic who also wrote religious verse.[53] As the century wore on, the lines of distinction between philanthropy, beneficence, and even charity became more blurred and are already discernible in Pere Felip Monlau's *Remedios del pauperismo* from 1846. Monlau (1808–71), an energetic social reformer who established the field of public hygiene in Spain, was also both liberal and Catholic. Like other observers from the late eighteenth century on especially, he faults the misuse of indiscriminate Christian charity as one reason for enabling so much poverty; subsistence wages and insufficient capitalization are other factors he notes. Yet the vision he has of a better society harks back to the *caritas* of early Christianity, tempered by Enlightenment tolerance: "But I conceive of another order of civilization which is *moral,* simple, virtuous, and which is not complicated . . . by the love of luxury and wealth; in which religious beliefs and the wishes of the heart flourish; which establishes, then, and consolidates *true human fraternity,* and not that *artificial cohesion* which turns everything into limited partnerships. A moral civilization does not create poor persons, unlike an industrial society."[54]

Like many contemporary observers, Monlau was profoundly disturbed by the social devastation unbridled industrialization had wrought, already visible in Catalonia. At the same time he believed in unlimited progress and in the ultimate benefits of an industrial society. Poverty, he declared, can never fully be eradicated, but philanthropic efforts can help diminish it under present conditions. In "the age of philanthropy and enlightenment," why are people still destitute and dying?[55]

Following a trend put into practice elsewhere in Europe, Monlau proposes among other things a combination of home relief and reformed charitable establishments to alleviate such human misery, harshly condemning the current "monster-buildings, eternal focal points of infection." Beggars in particular should be housed humanely: they "should not be considered as vile bodies delivered unto professional philanthropists for them to conduct experiments on them, but rather as infirm and delicate, whose speedy and complete recovery society as a whole wishes."[56]

There is a distinction implied here between true philanthropy, which still remains religiously inspired, and the professional philanthropy that Monlau finds so distasteful and inhumane.[57] One encounters the same progressive spirit in Ayguals de Izco's novel. Significantly, philanthropy, for people like Ayguals and Monlau, included not simply conventional charitable activities but also other kinds of enterprises we commonly think of as civic and commercial, such as savings institutions, mercantile societies, and commercial and agricultural improvement associations.

All of these organizations were examples of associationism, or freedom to create associations, including workers' groups in some cases, passionately advocated by more radical thinkers of the 1830s and 1840s in Spain and elsewhere and strongly resisted by others. Thus the republican Mazzini said, "We . . . preach Association as the means of general perfectibility" (1835). These associations were intended to produce a general social and economic prosperity and collective spirit of cooperation, hence their philanthropic character. Years later, Castelar, as noted, an admirer of Mazzini, considered the right to associate, which he saw as freedom in action, sacred; and Galdós cited such endeavors as an opportune "sign of the times." Ayguals lists and describes several of these organizations in the epilogue to *María*. He also proudly claims that his recommendation for more philanthropic enterprises, both public and private, at the start of the novel has resulted in precisely that, citing specific examples. Beneficent groups and persons corresponded with Ayguals, as the installments of the novel were appearing (the same happened with Sue's *Mysteries of Paris*). This interaction between readers and novel, which included influencing the plot, emphasizes, on the one hand, that for Ayguals and Sue the novel was also a vehicle of social action and, on the other, that for some readers it was an ideal medium to publicize their various enterprises.[58]

Ayguals was quick to make clear that those charitable or capitalist undertakings which did not improve the lives of the working classes were not philanthropic but purely speculative, even criminal, in robbing the laboring classes of a living wage. By 1858, however, Monlau was suggesting more bluntly that "Christian charity, that is to say, *philanthropy,* which is an obligation . . . , is also lucrative speculation: let those who disguise their egotism and dry hearts with the mask of caution and prudence, and those thoughtless, miserly souls who stick to a rigid, pitiless official handout, understand and know it thus."[59] At this point the distinctions between charity and philanthropy seem irrelevant. Monlau was more concerned with the general indifference and hypocrisy of the privileged toward the needier classes, as his heavily ironic statement suggests.

Moral apathy, however, is not limited to one social class, according to Monlau. It is, he says, a matter of self-interest for the wealthy to help the poor not simply economically but spiritually, a point of view shared by many in Spain and elsewhere. Yet there is a larger problem, he concludes, "because what is missing in the worker is also missing in practically all the other classes, which is the moral element, that which constitutes the strength of societies and assures the happiness of each and every individual; what is missing is religious conviction, sincere and profound. . . . [A]nd the absence of this faith is the gnawing cancer of modern times. . . . [T]he cause of this universal suffering is found in the custom of daily life: the social heart is damaged."[60]

These comments are not simply a tack-on to Monlau's conclusion, the rehearsal of empty pieties. From the very start of *Higiene industrial,* the social reformer's concern is to situate the plight of the working classes, their "immense martyrdom," within a socially responsible moral framework for the whole of society. Most significant, the moral-religious values he desires for the working classes are the same values applied to *all* social classes. Foucauldian approaches do not do justice to the philanthropic turn of these texts, reductively insisting on the sole rationale of social control of the lower classes as the overriding reason for such moral and practical reforms.[61] That self-interest played a role is evident. Reformers themselves spoke plainly about it. That nearly all of them upheld class hierarchies is also the case.[62] Facing them, they felt, was the chaos of social disintegration. The point of philanthropic reform was not to do away with social classes through economic-moral improvement, a utopian task in any event, but to put back the social in the social body, to reestablish some sense of communitas among all classes and, in particular, a sense of social responsibility among the better off.

Thus, for example, Monlau urges the promotion of the spirit of association in all social classes. Or, to give another instance, he recommends that beggars remain only briefly in asylums and that they be given the tools and training to join the workforce, after which "they should then be incorporated into the ranks of a free society," rejoining their families or even creating one if none exists. The aim is above all "not to break for them all social bonds." Though segregation of undesirables (like prostitutes), the indigent, and vagrant classes certainly occurred on a large scale, charitable institutions were also intimately embedded within local society.[63] This social network connecting all classes is there in embryonic fashion in the texts of Ayguals and Navarrete but is richly realized in fictions like Galdós's *Fortunata y Jacinta.*

In the presence of the unwanted side effects of early industrialization and massive rural immigration to the cities, the separation between the rich and the poor seemed far worse than ever before to many midcentury observers. Writers like Ayguals and Monlau reflect in part the social concerns of a group of progressive thinkers such as Fernando Garrido, Sixto Cámara, and Ramón de la Sagra, who in turn had read Lamennais, Henri de Saint-Simon, François Fourier, and Étienne Cabet.[64]

Before the advent of a coherent working-class movement or press, generally short-lived journals with small readerships like *El Vapor, La Organización del Trabajo,* and *La Fraternidad* took up the cause of a distressed working class. It would be imprecise to call such pre-Marxist writings of the 1830s and 1840s strictly socialist. While ideological platforms varied, a vague humanitarianism of an evangelical, at times even messianic nature inspired many writings, as they did in France. Thus, Saint-Simon (1825) accuses the Church of bad faith for having forgotten "the philanthropic feeling which is the true basis of Christianity." D. G. Charlton suggests that English "honest doubters" attempted "to *adapt and revise* Protestant Christianity," while their French peers wanted "to *replace* Catholic Christianity."[65] Is this the case in Spain? Were they trying to replace Catholicism with new forms of secular religions?

The question is hard to answer. Traditionalists like Donoso and Balmes would call them sectarian, even anti-Catholic. Yet there is genuine religious sentiment in statements like this one from Sixto Cámara: "The principle of fraternity, having emerged from the Christianity of the catacombs, will very soon be the principle of modern societies." Or in this messianic message: "Philanthropists, preach sacrifice; we are going to build the new Jerusalem of the poor and wretched. Preach abnegation, we are going to organize social charity."[66]

The desire for both social harmony and social justice underlies such evangelical appeals and reflects the inadequacy of both traditional religious and political structures to address the economic problem of social misery in times of upheaval. In France, the question was posed, often implicitly, as a debate between charity and justice. Drawing on the Gospel, Lamennais lyrically phrased it this way in 1834, to suggest that one could not exist without the other: "Justice is life; and charity is even more so life, a sweeter and more abundant life." "Justice," he also says, "is the beginnings of charity, and charity . . . is the consummation of justice." Catholic social reformers like Monlau and Concepción Arenal put it more simply: charity is justice.[67]

To what extent, however, was charity more than a palliative, putting off social strife and chaos? This was the question facing all societies in the first stages of industrialization. The question eventually drew social reformers to separate justice from charity, as Frederick Wines does in 1898: "Charity is a fine thing, no doubt; but justice is a finer. Justice is fundamental, charity supplemental." The changing conception of charity marks the transition from philanthropy to social welfare, as another comment from Wines makes evident: "The philanthropist is an accurate observer, a patient collector of facts, the importance of which to science he imperfectly appreciates and for that reason irregularly and fitfully records."[68] (His description of the philanthropist matches Navarrete's from 1845–46.) Not only has Wines marked out his professional territory; he has also made clear that on the eve of the twentieth century philanthropy, or organized charity, was in his view not up to the task of social improvement or justice.

In the 1830s and 1840s, across the entire political spectrum, people saw profound social alienation or, worse, class warfare. The desire for social harmony was paramount. "Individual interest should blend or harmonize with humanitarian interest," remarked de la Sagra in 1849. There is a "hidden war among all classes of society," commented Donoso in 1850. The preface to the English translation of Baron de Gérando's highly influential work on philanthropy, *The Visitor of the Poor,* makes note of the hostility between rich and poor in England in 1833, ascribing "this estrangement, in some cases . . . to that congregating of masses into our large towns . . . [for] the vastness of our towns conceals or destroys all this personal attachment [of the countryside]. . . . There is little contact of benevolence." Here one also reads that the Reverend Joseph Tuckerman, a noted Boston philanthropist, calls for " 'bringing about a *personal knowledge* [between the rich and the poor], and . . . a *personal interest* in each other.' " Tuckerman himself speaks with quiet eloquence of the book's "design [which] is to awaken and give excitement to a sense of human relations, wherever sensibility on this great subject is sluggish and inactive" and "to make the great classes of the rich and the poor . . . known to each other." Thus, in Elizabeth Gaskell's social novel *North and South* (1855), in which the industrialized north is contrasted with the pastoral south of England, the mill owner Thornton concludes that "no mere institutions . . . can attach class to class as they should be attached, unless the working out of such institutions bring the individuals of the different classes into actual personal contact." That social malaise, unquantifiable yet patent, persisted throughout the century can be seen in a comment from the self-made, self-help expert Samuel Smiles (1812–1904) in 1875: "[A] want of sympathy pervades all classes. . . . There are many social gaps between them, which can not yet be crossed. . . . The poor are not dealt with as if they belonged to the same common family of man."[69]

The loss of social connection is everywhere in a novel like Ayguals de Izco's *María,* where the desire to connect, to reestablish the social contract among all classes, is continually enacted through converging plotlines, social alliances, and networks between the working classes and the privileged, and through the symbolic resurrection of characters presumed by others to be dead (María's mother and father, María herself, Don Luis and his father). Above all, Ayguals, merged with his narrator, tirelessly exhorts and recommends the spirit of association in Spanish society. Indeed, he cannot resist saying toward the end of the novel, "The desire to associate . . . has taken root and flourished in an astonishing manner everywhere, [for which] we congratulate ourselves for having been among the first to point out this path as the most favorable for bringing about the happiness of the Spanish people."[70] Afterward follow concrete examples of such philanthropic enterprises, enumerated and described, marking in this way how the number of beneficent (and commercial) organizations were increasing in mid-nineteenth-century Spain.

The fervor with which Ayguals sings the praises of all these undertakings is that of a true believer who has convinced himself of their transcendent social and economic value. Such passionate belief is not unlike the spirit of self-help espoused by Smiles, who extended the idea to preventing social-economic dependence in order that the "poor [should] help themselves." This was the point of the philanthropist. In his scheme of things, the figure of the benefactor, who has through his own self-improvement efforts grown into the very role, assumes a sovereign importance. "Benevolence springs," Smiles, himself a philanthropist, remarked, "from the best qualities of the mind and heart. Its divine spirit elevates the benefactors of the world . . . to the highest pedestals of moral genius and of national worship."[71]

It is not surprising that the supremely self-confident Ayguals should tout the virtues of the benefactor while playing the role of the novelist. The novelist is, in *María*, already a philanthropist, one who investigates the underlying conditions of social distress and lends a helping hand to improving those conditions among his characters. Baron de Gérando, for example, was known for books on philanthropy *and* self-education.[72] Perhaps for this reason Ayguals himself did not see any incongruity between the narrating voice that spoke of charitable juntas and commercial enterprises in real time and the voice that worked on relieving, mending, and even resurrecting the lives of his characters in fictional time. Thus characters dear to other characters (and to readers) are not allowed to die, not simply as plot devices to further the narrative, but as symbols of salvation through philanthropy. María's mother, Luisa, near death, is saved by the beneficent ministrations of a doctor, whose subsequent philanthropic inquiry into the unfortunate circumstances of María's family comes in a chapter titled "Initial Investigation." Characters as philanthropists within this philanthropic narrative abound, mostly among the privileged classes, though in at least one instance a humble black slave, Tomás, saves María, allowing Ayguals to insert an abolitionist subplot as yet another offshoot of humanitarianism.[73]

Significantly, not religious intercession but medicine saves Luisa, as the priest sent to administer last rites terrorizes her with threats of Hell and perdition. By contrast, says Ayguals, there is "nothing more sweet and comforting than to hear the beneficent, paternal voice of a good clergyman, the seed of gratifying hope, in bathing the lacerated heart of the infirm with the salutary words of Jesus Christ."[74] The repeated salvation and resurrection of characters in *María* is so crucial to Ayguals because it makes them visible to readers in ways that that readership could understand, within a secularized framework of transcendence and spirit. These are not the vile bodies Monlau deplored in 1846 but those "infirm and delicate" beings "whose speedy and complete recovery society as a whole wishes." This view is far from Sue's deviant social pathologies, though certainly both novelists write with redemption in mind. Thus Luisa's blindness and ill health are cured; María's temporary madness is overcome; the militiaman Anselmo is spared execution; and so on. No, these are not vile bodies, but they are also not fully realized, with layers and depth, as they are in the later fictions of Galdós, Emilia Pardo Bazán, and Clarín. Ayguals is so eager for readers to love his working-class characters and the well-to-do who care for them (in both senses of the word) that their forms and personas glow in the idealized light enveloping them.[75]

Like the philanthropist, the novelist in Ayguals's world exists to save the vulnerable and in saving them to make them count. He is less generous, however, with the schemers, conspirators, and miscreants of *María* like the Carlist fray Patricio, whose intrigues fuel much of the plot and destroy social relations. Carlism in Ayguals's view incites social disharmony. Carlists themselves, of course, would not have seen it this way. They sought to reaffirm national and social unity through a theocratic monarchy. That liberals like Ayguals thought otherwise and civil war ensued speak not only to a broken social-spiritual contract, but to differing conceptions of what that contract should be.

Despite repeated social, economic, and political upheaval in the first half of nineteenth-century Spain, one particular relationship held that we see reflected in the benefactor-recipient bond of the novel. This bond is in some ways a new variation of clientelism, the paternalistic reciprocity between the privileged and the lesser orders of society that had obtained for centuries throughout Europe. It was a world based on the personal knowledge people had of one another. Thus, when beggars came to new towns or villages in times of economic crisis or unrest, they upset the fragile structures of social relations. Nobody knew them. In such a world of intimate knowledge, family, position, and deference anchored reciprocity.[76] As rural folk immigrated in droves to cities, they were often swallowed up, becoming nameless and socially unmoored. In de la Sagra's morality tale from 1840, *Antonio y Rita ó los niños mendigos* (Antonio and Rita, or the beggar children), the orphaned brother and sister are brought to Madrid, presumably from the provinces, end up begging in the streets, land in jail, and are rescued only when a philanthropic society makes inquiries and a wealthy benefactor from the association takes charge of them.

Urban charity efforts in which the benefactor and the poor met face to face may have reactivated to some small degree the village social network within the threateningly large mysteries of the city. Rural life, which could be just as mean and brutal as city life, was often idealized, especially when it came to social relations: "While living over the face of the land," wrote an English observer, "the poor come into immediate contact with the rich, and the relation of benefactor and beneficiary not only exists, but is felt." Pastoral nostalgia may also explain in part why Monlau recommended placing new factories and workshops in the countryside, to benefit the health and morals of workers.[77]

Early nineteenth-century philanthropists tended to conceive the great social divide as lying between the rich and the poor, a broad-swath categorization with origins in clientelism that did not sufficiently recognize the development of a more specific class consciousness no longer tied to a community to which one belongs.[78] *María* documents this new and urban class difference while clinging to the paternalism of reciprocity. Like the philanthropist, Ayguals evangelizes the city and its inhabitants through a secular conversion process of social reconciliation. This is his "village," the reimagining of Madrid as a place where the rich and the poor converge, where social redemption of the poor is in effect a personal mission. Olavide's Philosopher combined spiritual and secular reform in a model village. And Gutiérrez set Casinio's evangelical faith within a pastoral setting in *Cornelia Bororquia*. Drawing on a long religious tradition, Ayguals, however, gives it a new twist by juxtaposing the evangelical vision with his understanding of the Carlists, whom he sees as having betrayed the message of the Gospel. His frontal attack on Carlism takes on added significance considering that the strongholds of Carlism were precisely in rural areas. *María* thus represents a particular view of community, liberal and humanitarian, in competition with a counterrevolutionary one in defense of a theocratic ancien régime.

This political struggle, which permeates the pages of *María,* is then also about who speaks for religion. Whose views and voice are going to prevail will not only affect the emerging modern state in Spain but the form of the novel as well. In politicizing religion, liberals and Carlists made it a critical issue from which to view change in Spanish society. The humanitarian or philanthropist is the key figure, as narrator and as character, for approaching and uniting the social and the religious in *María*.

Ayguals thought his chief contribution to the novel was the creation of a new genre he called the History-Novel. He notes that he has covered in detail, day by day, hour by hour, the great historical events of the period, "like the most scrupulous historian, making important revelations that we have not read in any of the contemporary chronicles." His biographer claims Ayguals has regenerated the Spanish novel, while one reviewer writes that "*María* is not a historical novel, it is a history inserted into a novel." Ayguals is singularly clumsy, however, in mingling history with fiction; a sense of fiction *as* history fully emerges only with Galdós. The desire to create a new national novel was paramount.[79]

Ayguals excelled not as historian, but as philanthropist in presenting the case for a humanitarian narrative, for the novel as a philanthropic project in which religion in the social and narrative spheres is crucial for shaping both. The model did not bear immediate fruit. It led to the formulaic with the flood of serial and installment novels; it also anticipated the vogue of the thesis novel in the 1870s and early 1880s, all dead ends aesthetically speaking. Yet there is a clear line to be drawn linking fictions like Olavide's *El evangelio en triunfo* and Cadalso's *Noches lúgubres* to Ayguals's *María* and Navarrete's *Madrid y nuestro siglo* and Galdós's culminating achievement in *Fortunata y Jacinta*. The novelist/narrator as philanthropist marks the place where the privileged eye comes into intimate contact with the marginalized in ways that are mutually self-defining. Tierno Galván shrewdly remarked that historically "the mission of the proletariat . . . has been supremely important . . . because it gave the bourgeoisie a class consciousness. In one sense, it created the bourgeoisie."[80] This mission, also present in the novel and in the middle-class writer, cannot be divorced from its evangelical origins, as Ayguals's novel makes clear in the struggle that played out between the religion of politics and the politics of religion. The social body, in Ayguals's world, is both secular and sacred. It comes with sacrifices large and small in which mystery is equally melodramatic plot and transcendent space. And it suggests that the creation of fictional worlds as entertainment also represents high purpose, for it is the real world that must be redeemed.

That Ayguals saw in the novel a quasi-spiritual vehicle of social deliverance suggests that for him religious belief, to be effective, needed to be harnessed to or pressed into the service of a different imaginative structure. That structure was fiction, with its own internal rules of belief which we call verisimilitude. Likewise, to make readers believe in his story and his characters, Ayguals needed them also to believe in their redemption. By directly engaging his readers in this way, he turns them into symbolic activists like himself. Both writing and reading then become a calling. Moreover, the intimate relation between readers and text implies that the border between fiction and the real world is permeable and shifting. Ayguals himself did not always distinguish between the two, suggesting that the humanitarian novel as a writing project was open-ended. It could be used for all manner of purposes,[81] and fulfillment could come in the real world only by being transformed in its image. Such radical reform of the world is a secularized, even civic, version of the coming, the realization of the divine within the material realm. The novel turns into both the sign and the act of such a transformation, rushing toward its own future becoming in the world. Aesthetically, however, it meant that Ayguals felt compelled to throw everything into the novelistic mix, making the outlines of the novel seemingly elastic and all-encompassing for containing all kinds of reform projects, but at the same time diffuse and ungainly, with no sense of how philanthropy could *become* a novel. For that we have Galdós.

As the supreme fictional realization of the philanthropic embrace, Galdós's *Fortunata y Jacinta* portrays a rich and layered world, one filled with human imperfection, with obsessions and desires that have unintended consequences and mysterious, unexpected gifts. *Fortunata y Jacinta* achieves what *María* only hints at: a fully realized world of complex social relations that bridges but does not erase the vast divide between rich and poor, through a powerful philanthropic drive to reestablish the sense of communitas among them. Galdós brilliantly unites the transforming energy behind social-religious philanthropy and the spiritual fellowship of Communion symbolized and performed in the Eucharist into a single, luminous vision of a deeply flawed world electric with fugitive redemption. Philanthropy, which is, symbolically, practically, and spiritually speaking, communion with the other, creates the world of *Fortunata y Jacinta* by suggesting that the good works of charity (*buenas obras*) and the work of writing, or *obra*, are ultimately one and the same. The communitarian embrace of his characters is conveyed through the narrator as philanthropist and epitomized in the Catholic charity activist Guillermina Pacheco. In the classic struggle between individual and society, Galdós offers a third way, which is to adapt the image of Catholic Communion to a secularist vision of an unforgiving, class-conscious world. The religiously grounded perspectives of philanthropy and communion help explain how this Spanish realist novel opens outward to shine upon new urban social classes *and* inward to plumb psychological dilemmas. Thus, in an inward turn of narrative, the wild, misguided working-class Fortunata can feel the beneficent presence of Guillermina "inside [herself], as if she had swallowed her or taken her like a Communion wafer."[82]

Fortunata y Jacinta is structured around the conflictive interweaving between "two stories of married women," as the subtitle reads. One, Fortunata, is of lower-class origins; the other, Jacinta, is upper middle class. Fortunata's adulterous liaison with Jacinta's philandering husband, Juanito, produces the heir that the childless Jacinta so desperately wants. In her final dying act, Fortunata gives the child to Jacinta, a gift that creates a bond of female solidarity in the communion of life that this gesture represents. Philanthropy and plot coincide, connecting philanthropy to progeny. The production of a child is not only the final *obra,* or work, of the novel; it is the ultimate link binding the rich and the poor together, even as it severs the lifeline of Fortunata.

Galdós relies on an imaginative reworking of charity in its two forms: "Affective Charity is the inmost love and preference of the heart. Effective Charity, the love that works outwardly for the benefit of others." They are two aspects of the same thing, found in the same embrace, as Jacinta divines but does not fully understand: "She recalled that the dead woman [Fortunata] had been her archenemy. . . . [But] with death in between, one of them in visible life and the other in invisible life, the two women may quite possibly have looked at each other from opposite banks and wished to embrace." The embrace is, however, an imagined one; it never actually takes place, thus indicating the limits of the philanthropic vision in a world that is profoundly dysfunctional and disordered.[83]

To say that the realm of faith shapes *Fortunata y Jacinta* puts into question other interpretations of Galdós's vision of things. The *galdosista* James Whiston, for one, asserts that narrative irony undermines what little genuine religious influence there is on characters. He argues that "the religious surface" points to "the materialism of life that lies beneath such religious profession."[84] He concludes true religion does not exist in the novel. And he asks, where is God in this novel?

Are these, however, the questions we should be asking? Galdós plainly is not a Catholic novelist in any accepted sense of the word. We should not try to fit him into this mold by seeking the presence of God or sincere religious practice in *Fortunata y Jacinta* (or in any other Galdós text). We know he considered Spanish Catholicism as an institution and as a practice severely deficient. Yet he also thought religious indifference, as he wrote his good friend and devout Catholic Pereda, was a curse nationally and personally. He understood the need for religion as a moral-social force for cohesion. Whiston rightly singles out the pervading presence of irony and materialism in the novel but ignores two critical things shaping both. First, irony is indeed directed at convention and surface but rarely at the deeper, transcendent sense of purpose that drives the text. Religion isn't simply a theme here, but a dimension that permeates and empowers the narrative. Second, the demands of nature and self-interest are never denied, but they are in most cases more than a transparent manifestation of the material world. They are generally so merged with things of the spirit that it is impossible to separate them, hence the Galdosian term "spiritual naturalism." In this respect, I am in complete accord with Teresa Fuentes Peris, who observes that "Galdós conceived the spiritual as an ethical use of the material rather than as the opposite to the material."[85]

I do not share, however, her view of philanthropy in the novel. Heavily influenced by Foucault, she sees the workings of philanthropy as an attribute of the dominant ideology and classes seeking to maintain social control over the supposedly deviant lower orders. Given the religious impulse that inspired nineteenth-century philanthropy, this means in effect that religion too is considered chiefly as an instrument of social regulation.[86] Guillermina's visits to the poor turn into a kind of home invasion peculiar to the Foucauldian obsession with a surveillance society.

This kind of reading presents problems both specific to Galdós's text and to the history of philanthropy. On the one hand, the significance of philanthropy — and, by extension, of religion — in *Fortunata y Jacinta* is double-edged. Certainly Galdós critiques the insufficiencies of philanthropic and religious practice. One has only to think of Doña Guillermina herself, whose charitable feeling is as strong as her sense of class, inciting behavior at times inconsistent with faith and manipulative of more vulnerable characters. He also sees that institutions like the Micaelas convent reformatory are inherently normative (one doesn't need Foucault to grasp this truth). On the other hand, the larger message and loving spirit encircling the novel can only be considered philanthropic. As Douglass Rogers observes, "The whole question of charity in Galdós brings us very near to the secret of the source of [his] monumental energy . . . reminding us that this primary force is in no small measure a kind of humanitarian compulsion, that many of Galdós's novels were the *limosnas* [generosity] born of his own charitable impulses and convictions."[87] If the point of *Fortunata y Jacinta* is merely to demonstrate middle-class control and abuse of the oppressed lower classes through religious and humanitarian manipulation, then how explain the very heart of his narrative, which consists of the same philanthropic sentiment? In seeing the imperfect practices of charity and the self-interested limitations of social class, Galdós is a realist, not a Foucauldian. Recent critics seem to have forgotten a basic truth of his art.

When we enlarge the picture we see more flaws in presenting the philanthropic project in purely dystopian terms.[88] Imprisoned by his own incarcerated vision, Foucault ended up practically denying that the new humanitarianism even existed. Historians have had difficulty in explaining how the sensibility developed, linking it to revived religious feeling, the capitalist mindset, and growing industrialization. The study of humanitarianism has "been achieved only at the expense of a growing ambivalence as we try to acknowledge two things at once: that humanitarian reform not only took courage and brought commendable changes but also served the interests of the reformers. . . . This ambivalence reached painful heights in Michel Foucault's *Discipline and Punish,* in which he questioned whether there really was a new humanitarian sensibility."[89]

A Foucauldian view of Galdós's work is reductive, ultimately impoverishing, undervaluing how the novelist nearly always joins social critique to a humane understanding of his characters' flaws and of the ways of the world. It is not a question of denying or dismissing the indisputable element of social regulation in philanthropy, but of exploring how it was understood within the broader aims and ideals of the philanthropic movement. Moreover, one of the things we learn about *Fortunata y Jacinta* is precisely how ineffective those middle-class social controls really are in dealing with such unruly, vibrant personalities of the lower classes as Fortunata and Mauricia la Dura. The circumstances of their deaths have led some critics to see these characters as having been finally subdued, made to conform, but an alternative reading links the manner of their deaths to the larger philanthropic project informing the novel. For it is the sacred nature of their personas, their embodiment as selves, and their deep expression of the self as part of the other that reveal how Galdós secularized the spiritual notion of Communion, in its equal emphasis on the importance of the individual and fellowship of the whole. Sherman Eoff pointed out years ago, "Almost every character of consequence shows an intense longing for the identification of self with others, and this theme forms the basis of the Fortunata-Jacinta plot." I would extend his observation by saying that the psychological depth of individual characters like Fortunata, Jacinta, and Mauricia arises out of that communitarian sense, of taking Communion with the other, which suggests that Galdós does not necessarily see the full-throated drive to express the individual human personality at the expense of the other as the one aim of life.[90]

My object is to pursue further Eoff's remark, to understand its cultural-historical and structural implications in the novel, keeping in mind the literary-religious back story of the genre that I have recounted up to this point. It is useful to situate *Fortunata y Jacinta* in the contexts of Galdós's personal views of religion, the Catholic Revival, and the role of philanthropy from midcentury on. I am not the first to focus on the question of religion and charity in Galdós, though with a few exceptions many of these studies, often informative and discerning to be sure, have been largely thematic.[91] In examining a religiously based philanthropic origin to the modern novel, I am suggesting that the influence of Cervantes and the European realist novel of Honoré de Balzac, Charles Dickens, and Gustave Flaubert does not fully explain the shape realism takes in Spain. The classic understanding of realism as conflict needs to be seen in dialogue with realism as communion.

It is not at all certain what Galdós believed in, although clearly he distrusted religious institutions and dogmas. The novelist's liberal politics placed him beyond the pale for some Catholic readers like the Jesuit Ladrón de Guevara, who declared his ideas were "revolutionary, irreligious, dominated by a spirit of hatred for priests and monks." (He said something similar about Ayguals de Izco, as noted.) By contrast many others have argued for a spiritual core to Galdós's writings and personality. Was he a "sincere believer"? "A religious, very religious man, [but] . . . not a good Catholic"? Or was Pérez Gutiérrez, to whose commentary I am indebted, closer to the truth in suggesting that Galdós's yearning for faith was a sign of faith?[92]

One thing is certain. Far from despising religion, Galdós felt an ache for it, as these sentiments expressed in a letter from 1877 to Pereda reveal: "In me doubt over certain things is so rooted that nothing can tear it out of me. I lack faith, I lack it absolutely. I have tried to feel it but have been unable. At first this state of affairs bothered me, but now I have gotten used to it." I suspect Galdós never got used to it, to judge from the insistence with which he returned to the subject of religion. From the mid-1860s on, there were two things especially that he found disturbing: the sectarian influence of the ultramontane neo-Catholics and the generalized decay of faith in Spanish society. He disliked the "monstrous coupling" of politics and religion, which he felt killed the evangelical spirit.[93] Religious intransigence, which insisted on a narrowly conceived Catholic unity in Spain, he was convinced, worked against genuine religious feeling. "I sincerely believe," he wrote Pereda in 1877, "that if freedom of worship existed in Spain . . . we would be more religious . . . we would see God with more clarity, we would be less contemptible, less adrift than we are at present."[94] Most significantly, Galdós associated loss of faith with social anomie: "Most of us Spaniards are heedless and indifferent in matters of faith. . . . [O]n the one hand faith is slipping away from us, while no alternative philosophy appears that could give us something with which to substitute that fruitful energy. The elements of unity and general principles are lacking in society. Everything is up in the air, beliefs are undermined, the faith reduced to empty, formulaic practices."[95]

Galdós thought Catholicism a sublime faith, but no religion, he wrote Pereda, "satisfies the intellect or the human *heart* at present." One suspects he found it difficult to distinguish his own crisis of faith from the perceived collapse of the same in society at large. From the start, he rejected a certain kind of belief akin to spiritual absolutism. He thought, for example, the idea of the devil was mere superstition and argued, "We should be good not out of fear of the devil, but out of love for God. . . . Let the empire of terror cease in a religion founded on love."[96] The forward-looking hero-protagonist in *Doña Perfecta* (1876), Pepe Rey, does not believe in the devil, a position that is at once a liberal virtue and a terrible vulnerability exposing him to the evil of absolutism. His liberalism, ironically, makes him ill equipped to deal with those who do believe in the devil — and who may very well represent the devil. An early thesis novel, *Doña Perfecta* reflects Galdós's visceral rejection of the politics of religion ruling Spain during the second major Carlist War of 1872–76, even as the structure and language of the novel duplicate the very authoritarianism he despises. Rhetorical abstractions like Fatherland and Faith loom over the text as absolutes.[97] The religion of love, however, is barely visible.

What did the religion of love look like? As early as 1865, Galdós saw it manifested in very concrete ways. In one example, he takes note of a new antislavery journal, *El Abolicionista,* in which a letter signed by blacks living in Madrid appeared: "The most evangelical humanity, purified by centuries of oppression and martyrdom, breathes in this letter, where not a single word is written in hatred." As a cholera epidemic ravages the country, he finds another example in the selfless, private initiative of home care, the spontaneous outpouring of charity toward the sick and the dying.[98]

Galdós's understanding of religion is plainly humanitarian in its outlines, drawing from Christianity's evangelical origins. An early novel from 1878, *Marianela,* focuses on the difficult relationship between the rich and the poor, which the philanthropic doctor Teodoro Golfín explains to the well-off Sofía: "You see before you, literally in front of your comfortable homes, a multitude of abandoned human beings, bereft of everything that is necessary to childhood, from parents to toys . . . but it never occurs to you to instill in them a little dignity, letting them know that they are human beings, giving them the knowledge they lack."[99]

The novel is about human neglect, incarnated in the underdeveloped, deprived body of Marianela, who has never been told "she had the right . . . to certain attentions . . . which correspond by Christian justice to the disabled, the poor, the orphaned, and the disinherited." Sofía sees the poor as statistics, but Marianela, this tiny, unloved body, defies such abstractions.[100] The poor are visible in *Doña Perfecta* as well. One of the first things Pepe Rey sees in the streets of Orbajosa are hordes of repellent beggars, who inspire in him both pity and the desire to put them to work.

Galdós would return to the realm of the poor, most notably in his late masterpiece *Misericordia (Compassion)* (1897). In 1887, while traveling in England, he was struck by the "truly terrifying aspects [of poverty] in the midst of such wealth."[101] Beggars besiege passersby, the streets teem with gangs of grimy-faced children, their clothes in tatters, and neither the police nor poor relief can cope.

Things were not much better in Spain, to judge from Galdós's depiction of these underworlds in *Marianela, La desheredada (The Disinherited Lady)* (1881), *Nazarín* (1895), and *Misericordia* and from government reports and the pages of newspapers. In 1884 the newly established Commission for Social Reform had begun to collect oral and written testimony on working-class conditions. E. Moreno Nieto spoke of the "colossal proportions" mendicity had assumed. *La Época* complained in 1881 of the same problem, certainly not a new one, as such observations dated from at least the sixteenth century.[102] Visual depictions also abounded, first popularized in lavishly illustrated sketches of customs, such as the collection *Los españoles pintados por sí mismos* (Spaniards on Spaniards) (1843). Only now it was part of "the social question," part of rising class tensions and working-class frustration. The social question, as nineteenth-century commentators understood it, was inherently an economic one.

In *Fortunata y Jacinta,* one of the most memorable secondary characters, the Anglophile Moreno-Isla, has two encounters with beggars shortly before his unexpected death. He feels the same ambivalence of pity and disgust, guilt and impatience toward them that many people do toward the homeless in the early twenty-first century. Indeed, he complains of being harassed by throngs of beggars. Are there no police and charity establishments in Madrid, he fumes? There is a certain irony to these remarks coming from an Anglophile, who surely would have seen worse sights in London. That night, after the first encounter with a deformed, ulcerous beggar, he "envisioned the poor cripple so vividly that he could almost see him in the bedroom."[103] He tells Guillermina that in the dream or vision he asked the beggar if he wanted to trade places with him, envying his supposed freedom and serenity. The next day he runs across a blind beggar girl, whose fetid squalor repulses, though her singing fills him with sweet sadness. Once again he experiences her presence in his bedroom as something real. As with the first vision, he feels compassion for the girl. A rush of thoughts floods his mind: the idea of creating a charitable institution (his Aunt Guillermina's suggestion), unrequited love for Jacinta, the dream of children. And then comes death in the form of an embolism, in waves of blood.

One way to understand the episode is to read it through *Madame Bovary* as a homage-variation of the blind beggar whose hideous appearance and singing symbolically presage Emma Bovary's death by poison. His voice "had something so distant and sad that it filled Emma with dread. It went to the very depths of her soul, like a whirlwind in an abyss." In another encounter, she

Figure 5. *El mendigo* (*The Beggar*). Print by Leonardo Alenza, in *Los españoles pintados por sí mismos* (*Spaniards on Spaniards*) (1843).

gives him a five-franc piece to be rid of him. As she lies dying and the priest prays in haste, Emma hears the beggar once more and raises "herself like a galvanized corpse. . . . A final spasm threw her back upon the mattress. They all drew near. She had ceased to exist."[104] The blind beggar spells not only death but the eclipse of all illusion, revealing the sordid, ugly reality beneath.

Moreno-Isla's death comes suddenly; Emma's is horribly protracted. More important, the narrator and implied authorial presence accompany his death in sympathy: "[Moreno-Isla] rested his forehead on his hands, letting out a stifled moan, and remained like that, motionless, mute. And in that withdrawn, sad posture, the poor man died." His death is followed by one of the single most exquisitely moving paragraphs Galdós ever wrote: "Life ceased in him as a consequence of a ruptured heart. . . . He was torn away from the great tree of humanity, a completely dry leaf whose imperceptible fibers had held him there. The tree felt nothing in its myriad branches. Here and there, at the same moment, leaves and more useless leaves were falling; but the next morning would reveal countless fresh new buds."[105]

What gives this death such poignancy is not simply the indifference of the universe to his passing but the sense of a wasted life.[106] Moreno-Isla's existence lacks purpose. The context in which Galdós places that life in its final days sharply distinguishes the scene from Flaubert's. Before Moreno-Isla's lifeline is severed, it is tied not only to that of other characters but to the promise of philanthropic care, to a vocation he most likely does not have. His phantom, nocturnal encounters with the two beggars are visual reenactments internalizing the presence of the other. It is not clear, however, if Moreno-Isla truly grasps the meaning of his hallucinations. In this double seeing, the literal and the figurative come together, with an intensity that belies the apparent banality of the first encounter on the street. It is as though the vision were necessary for both character and reader to understand not only the beggars' significance but the gap in understanding itself. Ironically, Moreno's philanthropic embrace can occur only in a dream, symbolic of the lacuna between the reality of social difference and the ideal of spiritual fellowship. His offer to trade places cannot be taken seriously, and his motives for turning philanthropic are mixed with the desire to impress and win Jacinta.

Yet Moreno's dream cannot be dismissed simply as ironic futility. His visions metaphorically resurrect in a different light the most miserable specimens of humanity, giving them value and hidden grace. The deepest, most affecting irony of all comes from gathering together in one fold this tenuous resurrection with the finality of Moreno's death, recalling Cadalso's humanitarian inscape of the poor amid the certainty of death in *Noches lúgubres*. By contrast with Galdós's text, in *Madame Bovary* beneath beauty lies horror.

There is no philanthropic embrace, symbolic or otherwise, in Flaubert's novel. These are two radically different visions of the world. Galdós is closer to Dickens, who views with fine irony Mr. Bumble's callous "What have paupers to do with soul or spirit?"[107]

Guillermina's presence is key in the episode, as she encourages Moreno to throw himself into works of charity: "Why don't you dedicate all your money, your activity, and your soul to a vast, holy project [*una obra grande y santa*] . . . a new building, an asylum of one kind or another?" Guillermina represents the literal introjection of beneficence into Galdós's novel. Moreover, she connects the worlds of the rich and the poor, passing through class lines.[108] She is in some ways a figure for the narrator and even the implied author in her ability to do so, suggesting to what degree the narrator himself, not to mention the implied author, is a kind of philanthropist in the novel, offering assistance and investigating the conditions in which his characters live.

The model for Guillermina Pacheco is the historical persona of Doña Ernestina Manuel de Villena (1830–86).[109] Galdós himself praised the charity work and character of Ernestina shortly after her death. He considered her a true saint of the modern world. Fervently Catholic and tenacious of spirit, she built an asylum for orphans in Madrid brick by brick, using up her inheritance and energetically soliciting donations from everyone else. It took her twenty years. She was also committed to other charity projects, including a soup kitchen, workshops and schooling for the asylum orphans, and home relief. An aristocrat by birth, Ernestina was representative of "a new, active type of Christian charity." Choosing not to join a religious order, she remained in the world and shrewdly made the most of modern resources to promote her work. She acquired *La Ilustración Católica*, along with an *Almanaque,* and sought the voice of other journals and newspapers as a platform from which to publicize and seek funding for her projects. José Castro y Serrano, who appears also to have been a good friend of hers, gladly lent a hand, writing about her in the pages of *La Ilustración Española y Americana.* Galdós thought most highly of her financial acumen.[110]

Ernestina understood how to harness the ways of private enterprise to charitable initiatives. It is a misreading of her fictional counterpart to call her a "kleptomaniac almost exclusively interested in money." In a period when state resources were very limited and poverty overwhelming, nineteenth-century philanthropy, like today's, was obsessed with fundraising. The great social reformer Concepción Arenal grasped this fundamental reality: "Without publicity in the sphere of Beneficence, the powerful echo of public opinion is lacking to encourage good works and reprove wrongdoing."[111]

It is important to place Ernestina—and hence Guillermina Pacheco and

DOÑA ERNESTINA MANUEL DE VILLENA,
Fundadora del Asilo de Huérfanos.—Nació en 5 de Setiembre de 1830; † en 27 de Enero de 1886.

Figure 6. Portrait of Ernestina Manuel de Villena, in *La Ilustración Española y Americana* (30 July 1886).

Galdós's novel by extension — within the larger context of the Catholic Revival in relation to the development of philanthropy in Spain and to the larger, more visible role women played in both the revival and philanthropy. Ernestina's personality fascinated her contemporaries. Her motives for dedicating herself to the poor were the subject of endless speculation. With her memorable reincarnation in *Fortunata y Jacinta*, one might be tempted to see her as an isolated figure of Catholic benevolence and religiosity in late nineteenth-century Spain. Consider, however, that Ernestina's youth and early adulthood coincided with a midcentury revival of piety and evangelism and her mature years with yet another wave of devotionalism, centering above all upon the

ARTE CRISTIANO.

MADRID.—PORTADA INTERIOR DE LA IGLESIA DEL «ASILO DE HUÉRFANOS DEL SAGRADO CORAZÓN DE JESÚS», FUNDADO POR DOÑA ERNESTINA MANUEL DE VILLENA
Y CONSTRUÍDO BAJO LA DIRECCIÓN DEL ARQUITECTO EXCMO. SR. D. FRANCISCO DE CUBAS, MARQUÉS DE CUBAS.

Figure 7. Interior façade, Church of the Asilo de Huérfanos del Sagrado Corazón de Jesús
(Orphan Asylum of the Sacred Heart of Jesus), founded by Ernestina Manuel de Villena. In *La
Ilustración Española y Americana* (30 July 1886).

mystery of the Eucharist as well as the Sacred Heart, Mary, and the Holy Family, during the Restoration period. By the 1840s the Church had begun to recuperate institutionally from the turbulence of war and the political and economic upheaval (notably, the sale of Church property) of the first three decades. The Concordat with Rome (1851) regularized the Church's position in Spain, guaranteeing State support. While popular religious practice continued with processions, shrines, and pilgrimages, signs of a more inner-directed, individualized understanding of faith had also appeared, bringing to mind, though with significant differences, the sixteenth-century *devotio moderna* of scriptural reading and meditation, the use of mental prayer, and the Erasmian and late eighteenth-century traditions of a more inward-looking religion. Individual expression of faith often took shape in an emotional outpouring. By midcentury the religious press, spurred on by the phenomenal success of Father Antonio Claret's publishing house, was producing a private devotional literature aimed toward individual salvation. Only the early modern period rivaled the amount of religious literature produced up till then.[112] This devotionalism shows up in *La Regenta*.

In the forties and fifties new female orders dedicated to charity work and education sprang up in Spain. Others, like the Sisters of Charity, who took over the running of many orphanages, hospitals, and asylums, grew significantly and even spilled into the pages of fiction, such as Castelar's much-reprinted romantic, flowery novel *La hermana de la caridad* (The sister of charity) (1857). This now forgotten text is set in an idealized Italian landscape. The heroine Ángela, rejected by her upper-class lover Eduardo, first becomes a celebrated singer and then a Sister of Charity. She ends up saving and converting her rival, Eduardo's mean-spirited, estranged wife, Margarita, who has fallen on hard times. Later, she also saves Eduardo and reconciles husband and wife. The triangular relationship, marked by class and dependency, curiously seems to anticipate *Fortunata y Jacinta* but, more significant, makes explicit the workings of charity in a novel of redemption. Castelar exalts the Sister of Charity's acts as "sublime, truly sublime, to go into hospitals, battlefields, wretched hovels and rooms, to the unfortunate bed of the dying man . . . to guide his soul to grace . . . purified by martyrdom and pain, towards God." He calls Ángela "an artist of charity, for charity, as if it were her creation, shone upon her face."[113] Here too is the Galdosian suggestion of the multiple uses of *obras*, as something both beneficial (good works) and aesthetic (literary work).

There are several orders with the name Sisters of Charity, but Castelar's heroine appears to have joined the Sisters of Charity of St. Vincent de Paul, whose vows are renewed annually. Most, in any event, can trace their origins to the Congregation of the Daughters of Charity, founded in 1633 by Saint

Vincent de Paul. (Galdós makes note of the orders and their work in *Fortunata y Jacinta*.) Castelar's novel speaks of the high visibility this religious community had achieved in the 1850s, as does the philanthropist and Catholic convert Lady Mary Elizabeth Herbert in her travels through Spain.[114]

Moreover, the lay Society of St. Vincent de Paul, established by Frédéric Ozanam in 1833 to assist the Parisian poor, had begun to flourish in Spain by then. Introduced in November 1849 by the musician-composer Santiago Masarnau, the society quickly grew, having established 40 groups, or Conferences, throughout Spain by January 1860; by the end of that year there were 70, and they had made 400,000 visits to the poor in their homes and elsewhere. In October 1868, when the society was dissolved without explanation by government decree, there were 694 Conferences; it continued underground until legally recognized once more in 1875. This lay community attracted such notable personalities as the art critic and poet Pedro de Madrazo, the Catholic thinker Juan Donoso Cortés, the historian and archaeologist José María Quadrado, the acclaimed violinist-composer Jesús Monasterio, the academicians and historians Joaquim Rubió i Ors and Manuel Milá y Fontanals, Concepción Arenal, and Ernestina Manuel de Villena.[115]

The society's insistence on personal visits to the poor in their homes as well as to prisons, asylums, and hospitals was the most significant feature of the organization. To aid members in those visits, Concepción Arenal (1820–93) wrote a manual entitled *El Visitador del pobre* (The visitor of the poor) (1863) sometime in 1860. She had already published another influential work, *La beneficencia, la filantropía y la caridad* (Beneficence, philanthropy, and charity) in 1861. *El Visitador* was dedicated "to the Daughters of Saint Vincent de Paul," with a note appended: "We give this name not only to the Sisters of Charity, but to all persons who endeavor to console the poor, following the sublime spirit of Saint Vincent de Paul, which is the spirit of the Gospels." Arenal's essays can be thought of as speech acts, intended to galvanize social activism. Alas expressed it another way in 1893: as a writer she was an "apostolic spirit" who didn't simply practice charity but made it contagious. She required a committed readership equally interested in social and spiritual advocacy. In this vein, Arenal observed that her manual was not intended merely for readers with leisure time, nor was the book a "literary work."[116] Novels, I expect, were but simple diversions for the philanthropist.

I have referred to the Society of St. Vincent de Paul and Arenal's work not only to place in context Ernestina/Guillermina's Catholic charity activism and to provide concrete examples of such enterprises, but to suggest an even more intimate relation between these visitors of the poor and Galdós's philanthropist narrator/character in *Fortunata y Jacinta*. The most clear-cut example of how the novelist appropriates the figure is found in part 1, chapter 9, "A Visit to the Slums," but she is a diffused presence throughout the text.

Even more intriguing is the quasi-novelistic approach that the visitor of the poor literature sometimes takes. Though less apparent in Arenal's book, it is especially noticeable in the Catholic philanthropist de Gérando's *Visitor of the Poor* from 1820, which I strongly suspect influenced her own manual, starting with the title.[117] His book was translated into Spanish in 1852 and 1854.[118] The 1852 translator notes ruefully that he undertook the task of rendering it into Spanish for his own edification, hoping meanwhile someone else would publish the book in Spain. I think it not coincidental that the translation should appear in Spain precisely when it did, during a revival of piety and the first glimmerings of humanitarian reform.

De Gérando reflects his personal experience working with a newly estab-lished system of home, or outdoor, relief in Paris. The system is based on the understanding that "every thing is bound together by mutual ties and depen-dencies," for which indiscriminate almsgiving is an inadequate expression of charity, "the tie that unites brother to brother." For this relationship, sympa-thy is needed, so that "the poor man sees that you have been moved and affected by his condition, [for] his soul [to enter] into communion with yours." Communion is also mutual: "Let us put ourselves in the place of the poor man, let us speak his language, let us imagine that we have his habits, let us show ourselves seriously occupied with all his interests: especially let us associate ourselves with the interests of his heart!"[119]

For such close identification with the poor to occur, de Gérando recom-mends a specific conduct of respect and kindness for men and women visitors, taking care not to "betray repugnance and disgust" and gaining the confidence of the poor. Above all, the visitor must make personal inquiries. She must learn how to see what is there: "It is in their dwelling-places that you must investigate which is the reality, and which is the phantom. . . . It is not enough that you are open-handed; you must open your eyes too." Look for the reveal-ing detail, he says. What are the internal habits, the history, of the family? Find the "precious facts" in "the childhood and youth of the individual, and en-deavour to ascertain his moral history." How can we know the truth of a person's circumstances if we ourselves do not investigate? De Gérando wasn't interested in poverty as an abstraction but as a concrete reality: "Here is a house near your own. Do you know its inhabitants? It looks poor. Let us enter it. We will ascend the stairs to the garret. What a spectacle! Your presence excites astonishment, perhaps a blush. They seem to be desirous of concealing what you behold. There is a widow extended on the bed of death, and little children about to become orphans. There is a little straw. Everything else—

furniture, linen, clothing, have been sold; and where is food, where medicine, where consolation? Whom can you accuse for your ignorance of this poor neighbour?"[120]

Did he learn from the novel how to observe? or did the novel borrow from philanthropy? What matters is a shared vision between the two, a view of the world whose practical ground is the world itself. In that mode of seeing, de Gérando stresses that "these inquiries should not have been made from a spirit of inquisitorial curiosity, but from benevolent solicitude; so the details should not be obtained by humiliating questioning, but in confidence." In the English translation, Tuckerman sums up the desired qualities for undertaking such an inquiry: "We must therefore carry into the work a teachable mind, and a mind as discriminating and judicious as it is kindly disposed; a mind quick to discern the indications both of good and evil, in the objects of its charity, and at once patient, fair, and firm."[121] He could have been speaking of Benito Pérez Galdós.

Besides physical wretchedness and degradation, de Gérando found virtue among the poor, but by far, he said, "the greatest number . . . is that of the poor who float between vice and virtue; whose thoughts are exclusively absorbed by the necessities of life." His desire was to improve their material circumstances and to resurrect their moral life, for "suffering and privation tend to make man enter into himself." It is easy to judge such moral earnestness as heavy-handed; and the visitor's inquiries as a paternalistic form of invasive social control. Thus one social historian says the book "corresponds — excepting a few details — to the present-day reports of welfare caseworkers."[122] But when *The Visitor of the Poor* is reduced to a technique or a method, philanthropy as it was practiced in the nineteenth century loses its soul.

What I find interesting about a book like *The Visitor of the Poor* is its sacred realism, its spiritual naturalism, to use Galdós's phrase. To begin with, as realists, philanthropists like de Gérando and Arenal were practical-minded people, having no illusions about the debasement and terrible pressures of poverty the poor experienced. "A poor man's lies," wrote the plainspoken Arenal, "is a consequence of the rich man's harshness and of his abandonment." What is a poor person? she asks. "Would the poor be what they are, if we were what we should be?"[123]

De Gérando and Arenal saw with their eyes and with their souls. The poor person in these texts is not so much the traditional *sanctus pauper* embodying the divine spark as one of two sides in the "sacred relations" binding the rich and the poor together. Unsurprisingly, the spiritual aura that envelops the much-desired communion of social classes appears in a period of growing social alienation and uncertainty. Arenal called it the age of the transitory. As used here, the phrase denotes not just impermanence but transition. Everywhere, she says, we "find the skeleton of what *no longer* lives, and the seed of what does not *yet* live. To fill the abyss that separates the society that has ended with that which has begun, believers rush in with their faith, visionaries with their deliriums, thinkers with their systems, all of humanity with their tears, and the abyss seems to swallow up everything thrown into it."[124]

Reading such works as Arenal's *El Visitador del pobre* and *La beneficencia, la filantropía y la caridad,* one senses that the philanthropic embrace of the social body has become in her eyes a metaphor for bringing the pieces of a broken world back together again. In speaking of how public beneficence and private charity do not work well together in Spain, she uses cataclysmic, fragmented images of dissolution and confusion: "Everywhere, remains that are crumbling, unformed embryos, mad hopes of power, cowardly fears of impotence . . . weak direction, doubt, confusion, distrust."[125] The same heightened imagery of disaster serves to characterize both the world and the current, badly run state of beneficence in Spain. A rising bourgeoisie and the gradual proletarianization of the lower classes characterized emerging modernity in nineteenth-century Spanish society. The poor were more visible now insofar as they made it impossible to avoid the reality of social disharmony and economic distress.

The traditional model of clientelism resurfaces as an answer to social disintegration, in the visitor of the poor literature, perhaps in part because clientelism had never really disappeared or because it offered a personal relationship that mutually defined both parties. Stuart Woolf remarks, "[With] a fusion of Christian charity and patronage . . . personal visits to the homes of the poor, as to prisoners, was to characterize *bienfaisance* in the nineteenth century, from De Gérando to Octavia Hill and the Charity Organization Society, in an effort to render philanthropy selectively effective, while encouraging the principle of self-help." In Spain as elsewhere, the same people who organized home relief often worked with charitable establishments, thus creating a complex network of social connections and interests. In *Fortunata y Jacinta,* Guillermina is the link between home visits and institutional beneficence, such as the Micaelas Convent for reforming fallen women (to which Fortunata is sent) and the orphan asylum she founds (in which the counterfeit son of Fortunata is placed). The charity activist's comings and goings crisscross the narration, connecting characters thematically and structurally by shaping the vast scope of Galdós's map of the world into a recognizable urban geography of reciprocal relations; their interdependence, a gently ironic consolation for the anguish and injustices inflicted upon the weak and vulnerable precisely by the same interdependence.[126] Guillermina is certainly not the only character linking disparate social worlds, but her case is paradigmatic.

In the eyes of social reformers like Arenal, the relationship of reciprocity was duty-bound for the privileged. One of the main purposes of *El Visitador del pobre* was to reduce the gap in understanding and knowledge between the rich and the poor. She opens with a series of questions: "What is pain? What is a poor person? What are we?" The three questions are interrelated. By asking these questions, Arenal suggests that the poor and the rich define each other mutually through their very relationship. She observes how often the well-to-do show thinly veiled contempt for the poor, "not so much in what we say, but in the way of saying it, in gesture, the tone of the voice." Disdain comes from not knowing what poverty really is: "We do not know how [utter wretchedness] makes a person suffer and feel, how it modifies morally the unfortunate whom it destroys." All the points de Gérando makes are found in Arenal: respect the dignity and suffering of the poor, gain their confidence, while making discreet but diligent inquiries about their situation. The visitor, or benefactor, is a sharp observer of living conditions, character, and behavior. Both de Gérando and Arenal make use of occasional stories to illustrate their points, thus strengthening the impression of an observed, narrated reality. Their realism, however, is always redemptive, predicated on the idea of bringing back to life the submerged souls of the poor. "For him who after a great misfortune returns to the life of the soul, one can say that a kind of painful resurrection has occurred," writes Arenal. De Gérando asks, "How can you raise the stupefied from their torpor? It is like attempting to resuscitate the dead." But he also says that "to see human beings awake to virtue" is a resurrection.[127]

To do the work of philanthropy one needs, he remarks, "a genius for beneficence as well as for the other arts. This genius requires a certain usefulness of heart, a certain vivacity of imagination, and an enthusiasm whose warmth has not yet been cooled." In a more sober vein, Arenal notes that "there is a great difference between being impressed by the misfortunes of our brothers and feeling distress. For the first, imagination is sufficient, but for the second, a heart is needed." As in the case of Castelar's Sister of Charity, such a rare vocation is likened to an art, one that Moreno-Isla does not possess, nor indeed do many people, as Galdós himself observed. It does, however, bear resemblance to the calling of a certain kind of novelist like Galdós gifted with a large heart and an expansive imagination, both of which far exceeded the narrative capabilities of philanthropic inquiry itself: "There is a specificity about the poor . . . which escapes the historian."[128] It also escaped the philanthropist.

But not the novelist. While all such accounts—historical, philanthropic, or fictional—always come to us through the mind, ideas, and forms of someone else, the novelist has more freedom than most to enter into that special communion between self and other, to see the human body and personality fully clothed or miserably naked. Galdós had learned how to penetrate both the social and psychological realms of life from other masters of the genre, from Cervantes and the picaresque to Balzac and Dickens. Nineteenth-century realist fiction also possessed a humanitarian predisposition that relied "on the personal body, not only as the locus of pain but also as the common bond between those who suffer and those who would help."[129] This kind of humanitarianism surfaces in the late eighteenth century (Olavide, Cadalso) and in romantic texts like Ayguals's *María,* which are linked to an emergent new realism in the early nineteenth century.

As I have been arguing throughout, the development of a secular form like the novel is often still infused with a sacred vision of the social in its collective and individual guises. The emphasis in humanitarian writings can fall in differing degrees on a more secular (the clinical report or the autopsy) or spiritual bent (the visitor of the poor literature), but even in the seemingly most secularized examples the trace of the sacred persists. Thus the physician Emilio Pi y Molist (1824–92), a devout Catholic and medical reformer, defended the practice of autopsy, considered sacrilegious by many, by suggesting in 1852 that offering one's body to science was a kind of religious sacrifice: "Only God knows if my poor remains will one day end up performing a service of so much importance!" He asks, "Why this tenacious hostility toward the opening of a cadaver, if practiced with the reverence owed its previous state?"[130]

One could argue that traditional Catholic views worked negatively in Pi y Molist, in the sense that he felt compelled to write an apologia of autopsy precisely because of Catholic resistance to the practice. But such views also worked in his favor, insofar as humanitarian concern for others — here, for the sacredness of the human body as it serves the calling of science — is religiously inspired. The argument for autopsy's usefulness to modern science is construed through a religious filter because faith and modernity (science) are still tangled together in the period. Pi y Molist's faith, like his science, is part of the modern world, not something separate from it. He hasn't bracketed religious values but trained them upon the contentious issue of autopsy, thereby enlarging the scope of humanitarian concern. The dead body symbolically lives once more, resurrected to science. This argument, needless to say, would not play well with ultramontane Catholics, but it does suggest that liberals and progressives who considered themselves Catholic (and there were still many in nineteenth-century Spain) needed to find ways not simply to accommodate faith to modern life but to illuminate it through faith.

Similarly, Galdós in *Fortunata y Jacinta* does not wall off things of the spirit. Instead, he creates a permeable filter allowing the material and the spiritual to percolate together narratively speaking. The spiritual naturalism of philanthropy is the model vehicle of detailed, critical inquiry and beneficent assistance for a novel that must negotiate privilege and misery in the same breath. It opens up the space of fiction to the intricate social networks and interdependency between the rich and the poor. Galdós does not, however, turn the poor into sacred relics, as Olavide and Cadalso do. He was no believer in the redemptive culture of poverty, which he called a product of an unhealthy spiritualism. Spain needs entrepreneurship, he wrote; claiming poverty as a virtue, as synonymous with honesty, simply encouraged aversion to hard work.[131]

Guillermina Pacheco's blunt-spoken words in response to the protest of the unemployed José Izquierdo that "poverty ain't dishonor" echo the same view: "Certainly it's not, in itself; but it's not honor either, is it? I know very honorable poor people, but there're also some who are fine specimens."[132] Her reply is a wonderful example of Galdós's multiple perspective of things. On the one hand, Guillermina, a practical realist like Arenal or the novelist himself, is spot on to criticize Izquierdo's idleness. She doesn't idealize the poor. On the other hand, the charity activist's own limitations of class and temperament, her restricted field of vision, are apparent.[133] And above these views floats the narrative understanding that the charitable gesture, as a product of flawed characters and imperfect historical being, is of the world and in the world. What grace the gesture possesses in Galdós's universe is infused with an existential, deeply felt irony.[134]

To find such grace, Galdós provides us with a guide or, rather, with a number of guides, such as the narrator and characters like Guillermina, Jacinta, Fortunata, and Mauricia, whose sense of the one and the many, the part and the whole, is held together in the novelist's philanthropic embrace. First, however, he must open the door so that the two worlds, the rich and the poor, can cross the social divide keeping them apart. The spoiled son of a mercantile family, Juanito Santa Cruz, provides the key, as he literally steps into No. 11 Cava Street to pay a visit to Plácido Estupiñá in his sickbed: "And now our attention must shift to the Dauphin's visit to his family's friend and humble servant, for if Juanito Santa Cruz had not paid that visit, this story would not have been written. Another story would surely have been written, because wherever man goes he carries his novel with him; but it would not have been this one."[135]

Strictly speaking, by this point readers have already been introduced to the close relationship between Estupiñá and the Santa Cruz family, whose own history, along with that of other family branches, has also been richly laid out. Juanito's visit, as the narrator conveys, is critical to the story, to his first encounter with the working-class Fortunata. Ironically, in other words, all the heartache and troubles to come emerge from a charitable act. As a visitor of the poor, Juanito, however, leaves much to be desired; his motives are eventually suspect. By the end of part 1, Galdós brilliantly returns to the image of the philanthropist in describing the frantic search of the now-married Santa Cruz for Fortunata, long after he had grown bored with her and abandoned her: "More obsessed every day by his investigative frenzy, Santa Cruz visited various houses, some of worse reputation than others. . . . He knocked on every door he thought might conceal the shameful lost woman as well as the shame of losing himself again. His search seemed like something else, due to his ardor and his endowing it with a humanitarian character. He seemed like a father or brother searching desolately for the loved one who has vanished into the black labyrinth of vice. And he tried to whitewash his uneasiness with philanthropic and even Christian reasoning."[136]

Juanito's phony philanthropy is really social slumming, a form of class exploitation and self-indulgence. Galdós cleverly turns the negative image around during Juanito's and Jacinta's honeymoon, when Jacinta little by little manages to wring from Juanito the story of his love affair with Fortunata. The other woman begins to haunt Jacinta. She grows increasingly sympathetic toward her husband's discarded mistress. In Barcelona the newlyweds visit a textile factory, and Jacinta is utterly enthralled with the inventions of technology. Then the narrator says, "On that instructive excursion through the field of industry, her generous heart overflowed with philanthropic sentiments. . . . 'You have no idea,' she said to her husband . . . 'how sorry I am for those poor girls who come here to earn a measly salary that's not even enough to live on. They don't have any education; they're like machines . . . they let themselves be seduced by the first rascal who comes along. . . . And it's not that they're evil; it's that the time comes when they say, 'It's better to be an evil woman than a good machine.' "[137]

While class prejudices certainly shape the sheltered young woman's vision here, her ability to empathize, to see past the whir and clatter of the looms into social misery, is significant. The episode prepares the terrain for her charity work with Guillermina. The reader also knows the subtext for these observations is the still-unnamed Fortunata, who has been the third wheel during the entire honeymoon. The idea of Fortunata begins to lodge deep inside Jacinta. The thing that links the external social reality of working-class hardship with the internal absorption of another living presence is the philanthropic embrace, the deep sense of shared humanity that Jacinta feels about both the factory girls and her husband's old mistress. At this point in the novel, the link is still not entirely fathomable or visible to readers and characters alike. Moreover, Fortunata's shadowy but continuing presence proves unsettling to Jacinta. Like other ideas that become hard-wired habitations in the minds of several characters, Jacinta's thinking about Fortunata expresses inarticulate anxieties and desires. More generally, through the persistence of such ideas the novelist creates internal pressures for his characters, pressures that take the shape of other characters. This dynamic is partly Cervantes speaking obsessively through Galdós, but there is also an entire world of class relations in *Fortunata y Jacinta* through which individual suffering is made incarnate, a world that exists on the two interconnected levels of conflict and communion.

The communitarian world in turn possesses two features: its accidents, or humanly perceptible appearances, and its substance, or essential reality, terms that I have freely borrowed from the explanation given of the Eucharist. The change of the bread and wine used in Holy Communion into the body and blood of Christ is called transubstantiation. The accidents, or outward appearance of the bread and wine, do not change, but the reality does, emphasizing that Communion is both the re-presentation (and remembering) of Christ's ultimate sacrifice and the participation in that act. Louis Marin remarks that "signs are also forces. They are nowhere more powerful than in the sacramental word of the Eucharist; the proposition that is uttered as part of the ritual of this institution effects the transformation of an existing thing into a produced body."[138]

There is something ultimately mysterious and unexplainable about the notion, which has less to do with theological insufficiencies than with the power of imagining that lies behind the idea. In some ways, the Eucharist is the supreme imaginative act, overriding the willing suspension of disbelief by making the symbol incarnate, that is, more than a symbol or mere representation. In the process, it also creates a community of witnesses who participate in the act.[139]

The Fourth Lateran Council declared the much-debated issue of transubstantiation official Church doctrine in 1215. Arguments over its literalness broke out during the sixteenth-century schism between Protestants and Catholics. As the battle over the meaning of Communion raged, "the eucharist was the hinge on which the symbolic world turned." The Council of Trent settled the matter for Catholics in 1551 by reaffirming the doctrine. By the second half of the nineteenth century, Spain, taking its cue partly from the midcentury Catholic Revival in France, saw a reflowering especially of Eucharistic devotions expressed in frequent Communion, special confraternities, blessings, Corpus Christi processions, and other outward signs of religious practice. Sacred Heart veneration, also extremely popular, was closely associated with that of the Eucharist. The devotions themselves rather than the sacrament's principal meaning of sacrifice took center stage. Congregations like the Handmaids of the Sacred Heart and the Handmaids of the Blessed Sacrament and of

Charity sprang up. This last named was founded by Saint María Micaela del Santísimo Sacramento (María Micaela Desmaisières, 1809–65) and is of interest to readers of *Fortunata y Jacinta*. The Galdosian Micaelas Convent for fallen women is partly modeled on the real one Desmaisières established in 1845. Less noted is the mystical experience of the Eucharist itself that inspired the future saint, often called simply Madre Sacramento in her spiritual and social work.[140]

Galdós does not address or claim transubstantiation as doctrine, but he does extend and enrich the idea by taking the inner reality of the human personality as the underlying substance of his novel, while presenting its accidents in the form of an external social body and bodies. A refashioned Eucharist becomes, once again, the symbolic hinge of the world. Sacred realism cannot be understood without the presence of the one in the many, the inseparability of individual and community. This inevitably secular reading of the sacred is a way of embedding the sacred in the profane. The transformative process that eventually assumes the shape of *Fortunata y Jacinta* becomes more apparent when Jacinta begins to haunt Fortunata in the same manner as Fortunata lodges deep inside Jacinta. To make Fortunata socially and morally acceptable as the future wife of Maxi Rubín, she is placed for reeducation in the Micaelas Convent for fallen women. There she sees from afar Juanito's wife in a charitable Junta de Señoras, one of the characteristic forms of private beneficence in the period. Another inmate, Mauricia, has already told Fortunata about the childless Jacinta's frustrated efforts to adopt a little boy (the *Pituso*) she believes, mistakenly it turns out, is Juanito's son by Fortunata. When Fortunata sees Jacinta,

> the moral impression received was so complex that Fortunata couldn't understand her own feelings . . . [the] feeling [of envy] somehow blended strangely with another very different and sharper one; namely, a burning desire to look like Jacinta, to be like her, to have her air. . . . If the sinner had been offered at that moment to transmigrate into the body of someone else, she would have automatically, unhesitatingly said that she wished to be Jacinta. . . . Thinking so much about [Jacinta] in the solitude of the convent led her to have hallucinatory dreams at night. . . . Now she dreamed . . . that the two of them wondered which of them suffered more; now, finally, that they exchanged identities, Jacinta taking on Fortunata's appearance and Fortunata, Jacinta's.[141]

The wished-for bodily transmigration is in truth a metaphor for the incorporation of one self inside another. In the same way Moreno-Isla conjured up phantom beggars, Fortunata has dreams of Jacinta. Her visions internalize emotionally and psychologically the presence of the other. Like Jacinta, she begins to sympathize with the other woman, in female solidarity, although, this being a realist novel driven by conflict, less attractive feelings also briefly overcome both women later. The transmigration of bodies never occurs, of course, though the idea of exchange and reciprocity will grow, eventually taking shape in the gift of Fortunata's son to Jacinta. Any genuine transformation in *Fortunata y Jacinta* is strictly internal. Outwardly Fortunata remains Fortunata, a working-class girl who has made bad decisions and loved unwisely. Inside she acquires depth and insight, the sense of herself made more meaningful precisely because of her relation to others. This relation Galdós shows to be an indwelling of the human spirit.

In the convent, there are other signs that point to the powerful underground flow of personality as the sacred fount of the world. Another idea comes to Fortunata. This "white idea," as she calls it, arises from the Host inside the monstrance, which speaks to her, urging her to accept life as it is. The voice of the Host speaks like Fortunata herself. Galdós is thus able not only to articulate her thoughts but also to attach them to something of transcendent value, to the dual embodiment of individual worth and fellowship, which is the Host. The deep irony comes from the equivocal source of the message.

Even more marvelous, the alcoholic and occasional prostitute Mauricia has a dream of stealing God from the chapel:

> Pride and happiness filled the daring woman's soul as she saw the tangible representation of God in her own hands. Oh, how the gold rays on the glass pane shone! And what mysterious, placid majesty there was in the pure host's being safely behind the glass — white, divine, and somehow seeming like a person, yet it was really only fine bread! . . . And then she noticed that the holy form not only had profound eyes as luminous as the sky, but also a voice. . . . The material quality of the monstrance had completely vanished; all that remained were the essentials: the representation, the pure symbol; and these are what Mauricia pressed furiously to her breast. "Girl," the voice said, "don't take me. Put me back where I was. Don't do anything crazy. . . . Mauricia, what are you doing, woman? Are you eating me?"[142]

The same irony displayed in the earlier scene with Fortunata and the Host prevails here, leavened, as it were, with Galdós's delicious sense of humor. These scenes are important because they connect Mauricia and Fortunata to the image of the Host but equally to each other in ways that take on added import at the moment of Mauricia's death. The Host is a person; yet there is nothing material left, only the substance or essentials, revealing Galdós's familiarity with Catholic doctrine.[143]

The personalities of Fortunata and Mauricia are associated with the mystery of transformation represented in the Eucharist. A kind of contagious magic envelops many of the character creations in the novel. Fortunata, for example, is enthralled with Mauricia: "If Mauricia said something that appealed to her, she felt it echo in her mind as if it were a truth uttered by a supernatural force. The young woman tried repeatedly to analyze this fascination that she felt, but she was never able to explain it." Guillermina is described as having an "electrifying effect." And the comically unstable José Ido del Sagrario sometimes appears to be "shooting off [electric] sparks."[144] Galdós's characters are not only socially interdependent; they are magically endowed in their profound, transformative effect upon other characters in the novel.

Personality itself appears to be supremely permeable in *Fortunata y Jacinta*, flowing in and out of characters' lives like overlapping waves. Encounters between characters are pivotal moments for such permutations, one of the most meaningful coming in the chapter called "Spiritual Naturalism." Mauricia is dying. Her passage out of the world becomes a conduit bringing together for the first time the two wives of this tale, Fortunata and Jacinta. Mauricia is a hinge character, like Guillermina, who is also very much present in the chapter. They produce encounters between characters. Equally significant, Mauricia's dying illustrates in both literal and symbolic terms Galdós's philanthropic embrace of his characters. They in turn move alternately between convergence and divergence, between community and conflict, in their relations.

The first thing we notice about the episode is precisely its social structure, which is based on the class reciprocity of clientelism. Guillermina oversees everything: she "had taken Mauricia out of the hospital to her sister's house and called in the doctor that the ladies' committee provides for the poor."[145] The destitute Mauricia is a charity case, hence a worthy recipient of home care (*beneficencia domiciliaria*). As a visitor of the poor, Guillermina bathes her and performs the humblest of tasks as she cares for the dying woman; she makes arrangements for last rites, preparing the room and the people for the ceremony. Afterward, she gives Mauricia little kisses; and when she dies, she washes the body and dresses it in a shroud, representative of how much kindness there is in the novel. The scene has been interpreted negatively as a " 'staging' of Mauricia's death for public edification," but such a reading does not take into account the communal force of Catholic ritual; neither can the funeral be seen as a parody of the sacred.[146] Guillermina is at her best here, the embodiment of selfless love, her authoritarian streak and class sensibilities, if not forgotten, tucked away out of sight.

Still, the scene does not allow readers to forget class differences, in both small and large ways. When the uneducated Mauricia, for example, exclaims, "What a pleasure to be saved," she immediately wonders if *gusto* (pleasure) is the proper word for salvation.[147] Above all, Mauricia's deathbed serves as the point of convergence between the rich and the poor. On one level, the scene reinforces the sense of communitas based on shared religious values and the universal understanding of death as the great equalizer. On another level, it underscores social hierarchies as part of the very structure of the philanthropic enterprise.[148] The explosive meeting between Fortunata and Jacinta, which is woven into the episode, heightens these social distinctions.

The chapter ends on a remarkable note, one that pulls together the separateness of class and personality into a single image of communion:

> [Fortunata] couldn't get Guillermina out of her mind. What an extraordinary woman! She could feel her inside, as if she had swallowed her or taken her like a Communion wafer. The saint's eyes and voice stuck to her insides like perfectly assimilated substances. And at night . . . unable to sleep . . . [s]he could see Guillermina as clearly as if she'd been standing before her very eyes, but the odd part wasn't this; it was that she, too, looked like Napoleon, like Mauricia la Dura. And her voice? Her voice was exactly like that of her deceased friend. How could it be, when they were so different? Whatever it was, the mysterious liking she had for Mauricia had transferred to Guillermina. . . . "I don't see how this can be," pondered Fortunata. . . . She racked her brains . . . and it dawned on her that from Mauricia's cold remains a tiny butterfly was emerging and somehow getting into the "ecclesiastical rat" and transforming her. . . . In the darkness . . . the body [of Mauricia] rose, it took a few steps, came toward her, and said, "Fortunata, my dearest friend, don't you recognize me? . . . I'm not dead, kid; I'm still here in this world. . . . I'm Guillermina, Doña Guillermina."[149]

In this richly written passage there is so much going on in Fortunata's vision, so much that is mysterious, that it requires one to enter it delicately. The Eucharistic metaphor dominates and layers the scene, creating a two-tiered effect of internalization. First, Fortunata feels Guillermina's presence inside her, as if she had taken her in Holy Communion. Here again is the magical influence of one personality upon another, seen in the form of assimilation or incorporation. Guillermina's eyes and voice — her very identity — are "substances," which beautifully reflect Galdós's spiritual naturalism: "substance" referring to both material and spiritual qualities, in the sense that the substance of the bread changes into the substance of the body of Christ. These are differing understandings of substance. Empathy creates an intimate bond between Fortunata and Guillermina; the bond is felt materially and spiritually.

Second, the passage goes on to suggest a likeness between Guillermina the charity activist and Mauricia the alcoholic fallen woman. Both in turn bear resemblance to Napoleon.[150] All three possess charisma, a magnetic personality, reminding us as well of the original meaning of *charism:* the free gift of God's grace. Fortunata explains the mysterious similarity between the two women through the traditional metaphor of the butterfly, the soul having transmigrated to another body. The physical resemblance between Mauricia and Guillermina furthers the second internalization. When Fortunata's companion in misfortune says to her, " 'I'm Guillermina,' " she suggests several things at once. First, a bond of empathy links the two women, a shared fellowship that is movingly communicated through association with the initial sacred image of the Host. We also see how permeable personality is in Galdós's novel, how one personality seems to flow into another, its substance melting like a Communion wafer on the tip of the tongue.

Finally, we see that these shared personalities — Fortunata, Guillermina, Mauricia — bring us to the heart of the matter: the persistence of the human, of the individual. When Mauricia's body rises and she says, " 'I'm not dead, kid; I'm still here in this world,' " she is speaking of survival after death. The allusion to resurrection returns us to the transcendent symbolism of the Host, to the body of Christ as the way to salvation. The survival of Mauricia in the physical shape of Guillermina also recalls the *humanitas Christi,* Christ's humanity, his corporal being. It assumes as well a link between bodily continuity and personal identity, with the words " 'Fortunata, my dearest friend, don't you recognize me?' " Theologians in the medieval world argued heatedly over the nature of the resurrected body on Judgment Day. They said it must be the *same* body that rises, leading Caroline Walker Bynum to conclude that the survival of personal identity, then and now, is "the heart of resurrection."[151] Galdós devises an ingenious response to such universal yearning by suggesting that the abiding personality of the one is inextricably tied to that of the other.

Mauricia continues to live through Guillermina because Fortunata's mind has bound them together, having already assimilated the charity activist and, by extension, Mauricia. Symbolically and affectively, Fortunata has taken them in Communion, uniting not only two different personalities but two different social classes, in spiritual fellowship of the one and the many. The philanthropic inclusiveness of this embrace exemplifies the structural reach of Galdós's novel, as he creates analogous, interconnected inner and outer worlds. These worlds illuminate how the mind, like the shimmering Host, is not simply populated with the shape of external reality but refashions and transforms that reality in its own image.[152] The spiritual-social communion inside Fortunata metaphorically links together the worlds of the poor and the rich in an act of love. If the "history of [Christianity's] charity is really the whole history of the inner life of the Church,"[153] then Galdós has done something quite remarkable in *Fortunata y Jacinta:* he has turned that charity, or love, into the very substance of his characters' minds, generating a new inner history of the novel.

Fortunata's death also unites rich and poor, though the irony of her sacrifice is not lost on readers. Fortunata's final speech before she dies represents the ultimate act of generosity, referred to as *el rasgo* in the text, when she gives her son, the fruit of her love affair with Juanito, to his childless wife, Jacinta. Guillermina calls it "a truly Christian gesture." The term *rasgo,* or gesture, brims with rhetorical and historical implications. The historical reference is to Castelar's article from 1865 "El rasgo," in which he criticized Queen Isabel II's pecuniary backhandedness in trying to sell off national property illegally (calling it a donation to the people) while keeping one-fourth of the proceeds for herself. The *rasgo*—the queen's questionable generosity—is also Castelar's written exercise of rhetorical bravura. Both Isabel's and the famed orator's acts take place in what could be called a "market economy." Neither act is gratuitous. Fortunata's, on the other hand, partakes of a "gift economy," when the gift—here, the child—leaves her hands forever, without question, without exchange. The gift of the child arises, as all gifts do, out of Eros. As Lewis Hyde, from whom I take the notion of the two economies, remarks, "We are lightened when our gifts rise from pools we cannot fathom. Then we know they are not a solitary egotism and they are inexhaustible."[154]

How Fortunata gives away her child is crucial, for it allows us to grasp how the plot of philanthropy turns into the plot of progeny, how one kind of good work, the charitable *obra,* has become intimately linked to another kind of *obra,* which is the production of the child and, by extension, the novel itself. Fortunata dictates to Plácido Estupiñá a letter for Jacinta: " 'I don't want to die without doing you a kind deed, and I'm sending you, in care of our friend Don Plácido, the little "angel face" that your husband gave me by mistake.' No, cross out 'by mistake' and put 'that he gave me, stealing him from you.' But no, Don Plácido, not like that . . . because it was me who had him, me, and nobody took anything away from her. What I mean is that I want to give him to her because I know she'll love him and because she's my friend."[155]

Fortunata's search for the right words to express the true meaning of her act reveals an eloquent consciousness of significance. The child, she says, correcting herself, was neither given to her by accident nor stolen from Jacinta. There is no transaction going on here and certainly no restitution. Like giving food over the coffin to ease the journey of the dead, the child is a threshold gift indicating passage or transition. As do all real gifts, this one creates a lasting bond between the giver and the recipient, one that Jacinta too recognizes as a form of "companionship founded on their mutual suffering." In the end, she thinks, "the incredible case of her inheriting the Pituso implicated, even though her intel-

ligence could not decipher the enigma, a reconciliation."[156] That mysterious
nature of the gift has much to do with the inner pools of human personality. In
literally dictating that the child be given away as a gift, the letter is made spirit
and gives life in Fortunata's dying words. By emphasizing the extraordinary
nature of Fortunata's gift, by no means am I suggesting she transcends human
nature. Her imperfections are manifest throughout the novel. Shortly before
this supreme moment, for example, she gives the treacherous Aurora a thorough, well-deserved thrashing for cheating on her with Juanito. Her act of
generosity is made meaningful precisely because she is flawed.

The gift of the son contrasts sharply with the earlier negotiations for the
counterfeit Pituso, during a charity visit to the slums in part 1, chapter 9. In
their roles as visitors of the poor, Jacinta and Guillermina have come not only
to dispense relief but to bargain for Juanito's son by Fortunata, only to discover later he is a figment of Ido del Sagrario's feverish imagination and Izquierdo's deception. It is tempting to read into the episode a damning critique
of philanthropy as exploitative and invasive of the poor.[157] Yet it seems to me
that Galdós presents a far more nuanced picture here. Bargaining for the child
makes explicit the underlying relation of dependency between the rich and the
poor. It does not, however, negate the good work of philanthropy or the value
of compassion. Guillermina, for example, engages the impecunious Ido del
Sagrario in a task of mutual benefit: paying him to deliver bricks to the construction site of her orphans' asylum. A classic case of clientelism, of the
benefactor-beneficiary relation, it is also a good thing.[158] At first, though, Ido,
his head full of enthusiasm for melodramatic potboilers, confuses her allusion
to *obra*, the asylum, with a literary work, or *obra literaria*. Yet he is not
mistaken in seeing, however obscurely, a commonality or relation between the
two: like the Host, they function as "signs [that] are also forces." The asylum
and the literary work alike require forms of the imagination in order to make
them incarnate. Philanthropy is the heart's imagination put to work, the human capacity to see and feel the other as oneself. The novel in Galdós's hands
becomes the written embodiment of that same mysterious act.

The story of the false Pituso reads like one of Ido's sentimental popular
novels and ultimately misfires. Both the narrative and the child are discredited
as spurious, lacking verisimilitude. They are products of a cheap imagination.
For the real son of Fortunata and Juanito to be born, a different kind of
imagination must be present. When Mauricia dreams of the Host, she also
speaks to it: " 'No; I'm not letting you go. You're not going back there. Home
to Mamma, all right?' . . . Saying this, she dared to take the holy form to her
bosom as if it were a baby." The image may appear startling, even funny,
though not to theologians like Frederick William Faber, whose work was

much translated in the 1870s and 1880s and who saw an "analogy between the Blessed Sacrament [the Eucharist] and the Sacred Infancy [of Jesus]." Bynum, moreover, points out that in the medieval period stories of Eucharistic miracles circulated "in which the host or chalice changes into a beautiful baby." Galdós is no advocate of miracles, but he is of metaphors: Mauricia's Host becomes Fortunata's "great idea" when she says to Juanito, "I'm going to offer to make a deal with your wife. . . . I give her your child and she gives me her husband. All it is, is exchanging a little baby for a big baby."[159] Like the false Pituso arrangement, Fortunata's deal will fall through, for a child cannot be negotiated. The real *nene* eventually materializes in a wonderful example of Galdós's spiritual naturalism: the product of passion and spirit.

When Fortunata dies, the work is complete, though the novel continues for several pages more, wrapping up loose ends. The creation of her child is the creation of Galdós's book; her gift of the child to Jacinta, the final philanthropic embrace of female solidarity. As much as passion, philanthropy has plotted the eventual production of this child, from Juanito's first questionable act of charity to Guillermina's visits to the slums, from Jacinta's compassion for the downtrodden to Fortunata's reeducation in the Micaelas Convent. All of these examples of beneficence, however, fall short of their desired effect: Juanito is shallow and self-indulgent; Guillermina runs roughshod over sensibilities and rights and makes mistakes of judgment; Jacinta is limited by her position as Juanito's wife; and Fortunata's untutored heart learns lessons that the convent never intended. Reality is recalcitrant to reform. As J. P. Stern observes, "The human story told here is a worldly story: the world that is presented includes values which are not confined to inwardness but which are moral and religious values at work in, and usually violated by, the world."[160]

The communitas explored here is highly imperfect, as we would expect from a practical realist like Galdós. Neither a religious nor an irreligious novel, *Fortunata y Jacinta* nonetheless stands on sacred ground, for the imagination shaping the text is embodied in metaphors of communion, in which the deepest awareness of the individual self emerges from taking communion with the other.[161] This embrace is more often imagined than real, like Fortunata and Jacinta standing on opposite shores. It is an image that brings to mind de Gérando's biblically infused "principle of mutual succour, by which the rich and the poor meet each other and embrace, as fellow-citizens of the same distant country." [162] The forces connecting people in *Fortunata y Jacinta* — family, class, moral-religious values — do not necessarily always unite them when the world is in such disarray, when "everything is up in the air," as Galdós said. Religion as a solution is absent here.[163] Yet its presence inhabits the text as an indwelling of the spirit. Whatever Galdós believed personally, he felt that spirit do its work in the mysterious effects of human relations; he felt it as an "absorbing, transforming, and deifying" thing, as that love called charity.[164]

Like all philanthropic narratives, this one must ultimately also be concerned with redemption. While *Fortunata y Jacinta* is filled with would-be saviors like Guillermina, there is no messiah. Moreover, even individual redemption is uncertain: the last words Mauricia and Fortunata utter are filled with such ambiguities that it is impossible to disentangle the transcendent from the profane. We do not know if Mauricia was anticipating her personal salvation or asking for more alcohol. Neither can we determine unequivocally what Fortunata, who dies without confession, meant by the phrase, "I'm an angel." And all deaths in the novel are swallowed up in a vast forgetting, as we saw in Moreno-Isla's passing. In their visitor of the poor literature, de Gérando and Arenal practiced a form of redemptive realism. Ayguals de Izco sought social deliverance in the novel, engaging both characters and readers to believe in his redemptive enterprise, which stood in for the world itself. Galdós does not make that leap of faith. Instead, he leaves the last word to Maxi Rubín, Fortunata's mentally unhinged husband, as he is being taken to the madhouse: "These fools think they're deceiving me! This is Leganés, the insane asylum. . . . But they won't be able to confine my thoughts within these walls. I live among the stars. Let them put the man called Maximiliano Rubín in a palace or a dung heap — it's all the same to me."[165]

The stars, of course, reside in Maxi's mind, which has the power to delude but also to believe. In Galdós's hands, belief is especially efficacious in its aesthetic capacity to convince us of the reality not only of Maxi's delusion but of all the things and forces that drive his characters socially and psychologically. We identify this capacity as verisimilitude, the quality of making fictional life appear real to readers. But what makes us believe in Maxi's stars? or in Mauricia's Host? or in Fortunata's and Jacinta's embrace? Is there not something invisible here, a subterranean flow of spirit in realist fiction like *Fortunata y Jacinta* that not only shapes but opens up the social into unsuspected dimensions for characters and readers alike? Reflecting the socially and religiously fractured society in which he lived, Galdós understood that the social question cannot be conceived apart from the religious question, for both were instrumental in forging a new social reality in Spain. Most important, by suggesting a link between the productive force of belief and literary realism, he reimagined what the novel itself would look like and the ground upon which it stood, delirious with stars.

3

The Confessional Body

La Regenta by Leopoldo Alas inhabits a radically different universe from *Fortunata y Jacinta*. Where Galdós creates a flawed world of communitas founded on the Eucharistic model, Clarín works within the frame of confession. Theologically, confession and Holy Communion are coupled. Galdós, however, chose not to emphasize the practice or mindset of confession, while Clarín did. Rosa Chacel commented that "in Galdós there is a conscious intention of not confessing, which is consistent with his unconscious lack of the need to confess."[1] She was referring to the absence of the autobiographical in his work, by way of contrast with the obsessive I of Miguel de Unamuno. Galdós rarely has his characters confessing either, and when they do it is nearly always lightly ironic or regarded with authorial compassion and benevolence. Instead, the novelist embraces them with his all-inclusive generosity of spirit, as a counterpoint to the anguish and injustices of modern life. Forgiveness is built into Galdós's fictional universe.

In choosing confession over Communion, Clarín moves in another direction. The consequences for the kind of fiction produced are profound. The enveloping air of spirit that inhabits and transforms *Fortunata y Jacinta* in *La Regenta* envelops no more but carves wounding gashes into the collective and individual psyches of Vetustan life. On the one hand, Alas sharply criticizes the faults and abuses of churchly power and the shallowness of belief in large

(margin annotation: Chacel p. 135)

portions of Spanish society. This viewpoint was familiar territory for liberal-minded persons like Clarín and Galdós, who saw as clearly as the most intransigent ultramontane observers the clash of religion and modernity, while differing from them on the causes. On the other hand, the question of religious belief is deeply personal to Clarín, even confessional, in the sense that Chacel gives to its absence in Galdós. He struggled with belief most of his life, and that struggle spills over into his writing, which bears the stamp of his inner turmoil. I say nothing new when I insist on the autobiographical character of Alas's writing, but I also do not claim to read the novelist's personality through and in his fiction. For that, there is plenty of testimony in his correspondence, essays, and publicly stated opinions. The confessional nature of a novel like *La Regenta* is more significant for what it says about the genre and the shaping influence of the religious imagination upon the genre of fiction.

The confessional mode has a long, well-known literary tradition in Western culture. Confession is a religious matter, as exemplified in Saint Augustine's redemptive narrative of conversion, but lends itself to more secular aims through introspection, as in Jean Jacques Rousseau. Redemption appeared as an ever-receding horizon for Rousseau, as he struggled with the requirements of revelation: "It isn't a question of saying too much or of saying lies, but of not saying everything, of silencing truths."[2]

His *Confessions,* which are fueled by shame and loss, are not, however, the only available model. The much earlier, picaresque *Lazarillo de Tormes* (1554), produced in an era when confession was linked to a religious politics of persecution through the Inquisition, shows how the fictional I can be both secular and not secular. A profane narrative, the picaresque incorporates not only an entrenched legalistic mindset in the form of a report, or *relación,* but an inquisitorial one as well: "The mere presence of the Inquisition, and the very real possibility that one might be called to account — completely — for the particulars of one's life, made every living soul a potential autobiographer."[3] The continual monitoring of self for sins and heresies created a culture of guilt and encouraged hypocrisy and dissimulation, conditions ripe for the development of fictional fabrications, as Lázaro's *caso,* or case, reveals. In such narrations, self-interest is paramount, hence the protective strategies of choosing one's words and faults well. Yet the same culture also expanded the imaginative reach of writers and artists. Spain's peculiar cultural and historical circumstances must be allowed, in considering the kinds of confessional literature produced even as late as 1884–85, when *La Regenta* appeared in print.

In Clarín's novel, confession retains the power it possessed earlier, despite the visible signs of secularization and religious indifference in the imagined social world of Vetusta. Significantly, the titular protagonist Ana Ozores's examination of conscience, prior to general confession, becomes the catalyst and structuring device setting into motion the apocalyptic unfolding of events that lead to her adulterous downfall and social ostracism as well as to her husband's death in a duel. Nominally a novel of adultery, *La Regenta* is often compared for this reason to *Madame Bovary*. Ana's married life is as unfulfilling and bereft of love as that of Emma Bovary, Anna Karenina, Effi Briest, and a host of other nineteenth-century female characters; her fall into adultery, unexceptional. It would be pointless to deny the impact of Flaubert's novel on Alas's text (or that of *Don Quijote* on *Madame Bovary*), for all national literatures are also international in this respect, especially in the classic period of novel writing. But one of the central differences between Clarín's text and Flaubert's is precisely the crucial significance and role of religion. Religion is largely missing, or ironically trivialized in the two or three scenes in which it appears, in the French novel. This is no small thing. As one critic put it, "Clarín opens the door of the confessional that Flaubert closes to Emma," arguing that "behind the latticed screen lies the true originality of *La Regenta*."[4]

La Regenta is a modern world still full of sin. Galdós allowed for the possibility of redemption because sin was always and already forgiven in his novels. Alas, however, appears to have leeched transgression into the very landscape and psyche of his characters. Flaubert, I strongly suspect, could not have cared less about such things. Indeed, one senses nothingness behind his view of life, the "whirlwind in an abyss" that Emma feels in hearing the repellent blind beggar's voice.[5] By contrast, the world of *La Regenta* is profoundly unredeemed. That failure of redemption discloses a crumbling foundation of moral and spiritual disorder, symbolized in Ana Ozores's tormented soul, divided between the flesh and the spirit, between childhood and adulthood, between a lost paradise and hell.

Early in the novel, Clarín creates a chain of associations linking confession to childhood trauma and thus to the protagonist's body, during her examination of conscience. Ana remembers first her orphaned state and then the psychic wound delivered to her as an accusation of having committed carnal sin with another child. It is as though she had been visited by original sin twice, theologically and narratively. Ana's fall, which most readers place at the end of the novel, in truth has already happened. Narratively, she is born imperfect, reflecting as well the Christian dogma of birth sin, or original sin. The Church during the Restoration placed renewed emphasis on the doctrine of original sin, intensifying thereby the practice of penance. Enlightenment figures like Voltaire and Rousseau had attacked the concept of original sin as an obstacle to the newfound faith in humanity. Fiery preaching on humankind's fallen nature, however, was far more common in Spain, continuing into the early nineteenth century.[6] The Spanish Church boosted the doctrine's high profile through long-standing support of the Immaculate Conception of the Virgin, of having been born free of original sin, which Pius IX pronounced dogma in 1854.

The entire fictional world of Vetusta is as damaged as the protagonist. Elsewhere, I have referred to "Vetustans' tight little islands of self-interest which cause them to shatter their society into knife-like shards and thus rip asunder collective cohesiveness."[7] Ana's dissolving, fragmented psyche is paralleled in the disorder and degeneration of the social body, attributed in my earlier work to a dual naturalist Darwinian and decadent vision. This vision is indisputably present but insufficient as an explanation of the profoundly unredeemed nature of reality in *La Regenta*. Ana's individual trauma, however, also arises out of the particulars of her flawed family origins and childhood. From the consciousness of sin, internalized as an inquisitorial effect, emerge both Ana's need to confess and the authorial desire to write out that confession, to conceive of it as the materialized imagination born from the secret depths of a body and mind in torment.

I cannot think of anything less Flaubertian than Ana's guilt-ridden, fragile persona, rent by infantile repression and imprisoned in a sex-obsessed environment of dissimulation and deceit. There is, after all, practically no childhood in *Madame Bovary,* and it is certainly not traumatic for Emma. (The schoolroom experience of the fifteen-year-old Charles, by contrast, is filled with humiliation, from which he is saved by his mediocrity.) The novel jumps immediately to her adolescence, placidly spent in a convent, where she imbibes a sentimental, vacuous religiosity: "Instead of following mass, she looked at the pious vignettes with their azure borders in her book, and she loved the sick lamb, the sacred heart pierced with sharp arrows, or the poor Jesus sinking beneath the cross he carried." She finds confession, which barely figures in the novel, a pleasant thing, inventing "little sins in order that she might stay there longer." The closest the young Emma comes to real grief is "when her mother died. . . . She had a funeral picture made with the hair of the deceased, and . . . asked to be buried later on in the same grave. . . . Emma was secretly pleased that she had reached at a first attempt the rare ideal of delicate lives, never attained by mediocre hearts." Sorrow, along with any religious vocation, passes, leaving her "with no more sadness at heart than wrinkles on her brow."[8]

Emma tries religion one more time, but the experiment smacks of self-indulgence, marked ironically in the text. Woody Allen was right: Flaubert's character is not all she's cracked up to be. In Allen's "The Kugelmass Episode," a professor of humanities is magically projected into Yonville, makes love to Emma Bovary, and then manages to transport her to New York City. She promptly runs up a huge hotel bill, gets bored, and locks herself in the bathroom. Emma is a brilliantly conceived creature made up of words, not of substance; her banality lies at the very center of Flaubert's novel. "There is no there there," Gertrude Stein said in another context. Allen doesn't lose her in translation; he nails her for the Scarsdale matron she is.

In other words, Emma's spiritual, moral redemption is a nonstarter. *Madame Bovary* is a thoroughly secularized work, as one would expect of a realist novel. But not *La Regenta*. From the biting satire of clerical abuses to the anguish of spiritual dryness, religion is not only taken seriously but thoroughly infuses Alas's worldview. The sacred and the profane are never far apart. Sometimes they are confused, sometimes the sacred is profaned, but at no time does Clarín ever suggest that the sacred is of no consequence, or that sex and religion cancel each other out.[9]

Thus, in chapter 26, Ana's participation as a barefoot penitent in a Good Friday procession is not an exercise in camping it up, as Elizabeth Amann maintains, but a terrible mistake of judgment. The decision to practice self-mortification is in part an attempt to rekindle her faith, shaken by doubts and by the discovery of the priest Fermín's passion for her. Then she begins to see her spiritual brother as beset upon and misunderstood by Vetusta. Her penitential gesture is also intended as spiritual support for Fermín.[10] Significantly, Ana is in church when she makes her vow, "listening to the eloquent silence of an act of manifest transcendence . . . the almost miraculous elevation of an entire people, prosaic and debased by poverty and ignorance, to ideal regions, to the adoration of the Absolute, in an act of prodigious concentration."[11] Passages like this one are often ignored in modern-day readings because they do not fit the iconoclastic image of a ferociously anticlerical Clarín, but, even more important, because they do not fit the academy's dismissal of religion as a vestige of premodern belief.

That Ana feels intense shame during the procession does not cancel out the spiritual potential of the act. The third-person narrator may criticize the superficiality of religious practice and the pedestrian qualities of religious art, but he also observes that the Christ figure, while inferior as sculpture, represents "a sublime sorrow."[12] Ana's act of penitence comes up short because it turns into a profane spectacle, all eyes upon the Regenta, devouring her physical attractions, in particular her beautiful white feet. Her own social class, while hypocritically enjoying it, calls her behavior scandalous, but ordinary religious folk see only her humility. Ana, however, feels sexual and social debasement. There is a strong sadomasochistic component in the scene that has absolutely nothing to do with camp and everything to do with the misuse of spirituality.

That Amann insists on describing the scene as a potentially subversive camp performance of religiosity speaks volumes of how important it is to understand the historical, cultural, and religious contexts of novels like *La Regenta*. Camp as a concept and attitude does not exist in Spain in the 1880s. One glories self-consciously in being and performing camp. What does shame have to do with camp? At heart, religion in Alas's novel is treated as *cursi,* that is, shallow and inconsequential, in Amann's analysis, leading her to confuse the debasement of rituals with religion. Thus she says that Ana "voluntarily embraces the low (religious *cursilería*), walks through the streets, allows herself to become a reproduction and experiences herself as available, as a prostitute of sorts." Fermín's "camp project" for the Regenta, then, is a conscious imitation of cheap religious *cursilería*. This interpretation, besides collapsing camp into *lo cursi,* does not attend to the meaning of *imitatio* in religious practice, which is to follow the way of the cross, participating in the divine, as in Thomas à Kempis's *Imitation of Christ.*[13] "Reproduction," as Amann uses it, refers to copying and is a secular term, much like her reading of the scene. The scene is powerful precisely because it is religious in nature, because religion has been profaned. To reduce it to aesthetic parody, to mere performance, deforms the meaning of the novel. What Amann ignores is the complicated question of belief and its relation to religious-social practices.

In *La Regenta*, Clarín is, first of all, responding to the unsettling, fractious times in which he lived, when the position of the Church and belief itself were being challenged. Having witnessed the liberal Revolution of 1868, its promise and disappointments, he railed against the corruption, conformism, and restrictions of life under the Bourbon Restoration established in 1875, the period in which the novel is set.[14] Church privileges, under assault during the democratic interregnum of 1868–74, were reestablished, and a second Catholic Revival began to flourish. On the surface, the Church enjoyed more stability and support under the Restoration than it had in years. Article 11 of the Constitution of 1876 reaffirmed Catholicism as the official religion of the State, while tolerating the private practice of other creeds. The separation of Church and State, toward which the First Republic was moving in 1873, would not be enacted until the secularization policies of the Second Republic (1931–36).

But the restoration of the Church as an institution masked serious divisions within Spanish society and the Church itself. The Revolution of 1868 had unleashed groups of civilian radicals who were not simply anticlerical but antireligious. Though small in number, they were a sign of growing alienation from the teachings of the Church. Hugh James Rose, chaplain to the English, French, and German mining companies of Linares, entitled a chapter of his *Untrodden Spain* "Decay of Faith in Spain." His thoughtful remarks, made in 1873 in the midst of the First Republic, are drawn from "the tone of conversation in social circles; the statistics of church-going; the observation of various small facts in connexion with this great subject, all of which are small, it is true, but, like the eddying straw of our trite English proverb, 'serve to show the course of the stream'; and, lastly, books and literature." Rose was a Protestant, but he was also critical of the Church of England. While his methods of collecting data may strike us today as somewhat haphazard and partial, his instincts for capturing the feeling of the times are worthy of a novelist. He opens with a comment from a poor Spanish boatman: "My religion has broken down." These despairing words, he believes, are indicative of a larger problem, namely, that "the Church of Spain . . . is an institution which has lost its hold on the masses, both educated and uneducated."[15]

Rose notes the increasing presence in Republican Spain of atheists, the religiously indifferent, and free thinkers; the absence of men at church; and the popularity of unorthodox books like Ernest Renan's *Life of Jesus* (there was also an explosion of periodical literature of all ideological stripes since 1868). What he singles out in educated Spanish men is the sense of spiritual drift, of having come unanchored from their religious moorings. Thus one literary man tells him he is a Roman Catholic and has not "renounced that *credo;* it is more convenient not to have an open rupture," but he no longer believes in "the ceremonies or rites of my Church; I pray to God at home." A student who is a self-described *indiferente* is asked if sermons are of help, to which he replies, "Well, I went into a church the other day to listen to one who was said to be a good preacher . . . with all his flow of language, I only remembered two things . . . : he compared the exceeding purity of the Virgin to a cup of silver and a tower of ivory; and there was no room at all for God or Jesus Christ."[16] Another observer reiterated the same view in 1888: "[The educated classes] have lost their old belief, and have not found a new one."[17]

It was not simply foreigners who spoke of a crisis of faith. Since the eighteenth century, the Church hierarchy had complained of moral decay and of the need for spiritual revival. Spaniards, it seemed, could never be Catholic enough. While there was no question Restoration society as a whole was still religious, what was now being discussed more and more was the nature of religious belief. What did it mean to be Catholic in Spain? Who was a Catholic? Questions like these were extremely troubling to the Church, undermining its authority and very foundations.

In Clarín's time, the issue was enormously politicized, as the most intransigent of churchmen declared that liberals were not Catholics. Taking their cue from Pius IX's *Syllabus of Errors* (1864), which condemned secularism and liberalism, rigid ideologues like Sardá y Salvany excoriated liberalism as a sin and a poisonous sect for espousing "the absolute sovereignty of the individual completely independent of God and of his authority; sovereignty of society absolutely independent of anything beyond itself; . . . freedom of thought with no limitation whatsoever politically, morally, or religiously."[18]

For Integrists and other like-minded traditionalists, liberalism denied "the need for divine revelation." To be a liberal, declared Sardá y Salvany, was worse "than being a blasphemer, thief, adulterer or murderer." The most repugnant thing of all was to be a liberal Catholic or a Catholic liberal, which, no matter how one termed it, was simply monstrous. (The edition of Sardá y Salvany's *El liberalismo es pecado* [1884] I have is, notably, the ninth, published in 1936.)[19]

These views of a distinct, though vocal, minority within the Spanish Church demonstrate how intertwined politics and religion were in the Restoration period. Breakaway groups like the Integrists and other traditionalists objected to the conservative liberalism of Cánovas del Castillo, who had devised power sharing between the two dynastic political parties of conservatives and liberals, and to entities like Alejandro Pidal's Unión Católica, founded in 1881, that agreed to work with government. In particular, the much-debated article 11 of the Constitution of 1876, which favored religious tolerance, was anathema. Such exceptionally strident views not only tended to drown out more moderate voices, which could be found, for example, in Catalonia represented by Manuel Durán i Bas, Josep Coll i Vehí, and Juan Mañé y Flaquer, but also delayed reform of the Church. The internal divisions of the Spanish clergy pointed to a larger problem of the social body: how to reconcile faith with historical change, with modernity. Ostensibly arguing against the intromission of the temporal into things spiritual, the Integrists, Carlists, and other traditionalists ended up politicizing religion. Indeed, they took advantage of mass-marketing techniques and new freedoms of the press and speech to make their points and to that degree participated in the very modernity they found so objectionable.[20]

Most troubling to traditionalists, some religiously inclined progressive spirits like Francisco Giner de los Ríos, molded by the post-Kantian thought of the German philosopher Karl Christian Friedrich Krause, questioned the very foundation of Catholic belief by suggesting that religion could be taught without dogma. "What is not proven," he wrote in 1882, "is whether . . . the development of religious feeling in children requires the aid of specific, historical dogmas drawn from theology . . . rather than an ample and genuinely universal guidance, interested only in awakening in [the child] . . . that common element found deep down in all true creeds." Giner advocated the teaching of religious tolerance.[21]

The Krausist-influenced Clarín harbored persistent doubts about the specific forms of faith, while hungering for the spiritual sustenance he could not live without: "The soul knows for certain only that it is hungry," Simone Weil wrote. "The danger is not lest the soul should doubt whether there is any bread, but lest, by a lie, it should persuade itself that it is not hungry." He found much fault with the Church as an institution at odds with the modern world, but not with the fundamental need for religion. Freud's view that religion is an illusion and religious teachings "neurotic relics" was an alien concept to the Asturian writer, even as his greatest character creation, Ana Ozores, embodies neurotic behavior, which is sometimes expressed, though not equated, with the language of religious feeling. His was an inward-directed religion that focused less on the external practices of faith than on the personal quest for spiritual authenticity, on an "inner God." His unorthodox position placed him in the direct line of fire of the most intransigent elements of Spanish Catholicism, who branded him a rabid anticlericalist. Clarín rejected both extremisms, which he saw as equally fanatical and intolerant. Religious tolerance did not, however, mean neutrality for Alas:

> The extremes are bad, very bad; but the middle way of *social neutrality* is ridiculous, false, unsustainable. That this Spain, which has spilt so much blood . . . for the Catholic religion, should overnight cease to think about Catholicism and in general . . . all religion; that everyone should limit their beliefs to the privacy of the bedroom, as if they were a secret disease, and publicly practice the tolerance of the Belgian school of *neutrality*, which consists in dispensing with Christianity in history, mutilating the spirit itself . . . is absurd. . . . Universal tolerance, true *religious secularization*, should not be negative, or passive, but positive, active. . . . A society is tolerant when all faiths speak and are heard in tranquility; not when there is tranquility because everyone is silent.[22]

In a striking statement, he declared that, rather than sunder violently the intimate and historical association between Church and State, it would be better "to graft liberal Spain onto Catholic Spain." This would be true tolerance, "respecting the old ideas and the sentiments they engender, even participating in those sentiments, for what they have to say about being human and Spanish." Later, at the risk of being misunderstood, he went so far as to recommend not separating the spiritual from the profane but "*secularizing religion* [by] spreading it everywhere." He meant here that walling religion off artificially deprived it of the staff of life, made it unnatural and abstract, a thing unto itself, rather than part of life. The spirit in its human dimensions still speaks to him personally, even as he attempts to express what Otto described as the numinous or sacred quality of religious feeling: "My *natural history* and my *national history* tie me with the chains of reality, sweet chains, to the love of Catholicism . . . as a human endeavor, as a Spanish endeavor. I still consider as *part of me* the cathedral fashioned and built by the faith of my ancestors. . . . I pray in my own way, with what I feel, with what I remember of my childhood . . . with what the music of the organ and the chanting of the choir say to my soul; their words do not reach my ear, though I tremble inside with their melody . . . my spirit speaks within, a kind of glossolalia which must resemble that of the early Christians, still untutored in the concrete affirmations of dogma, but filled with ineffable emotion."[23]

Far from attacking or dismissing religion as inconsequential, Alas yearned to recuperate the certainty and fervor of his childhood faith, which drew sustenance from his mother's devotion to Mary. There is always something mysterious about the loss of faith, something impossible to explain looking from the outside in. His liberal convictions intellectually undermined his religious beliefs, as he himself noted in a fascinating series of articles from 1878. The ultra-Catholics, or *neos,* he wrote, "do not want to believe that the religiosity [of liberals] is real, which is not surprising, given that many liberals think in effect that religion is a thing of the past." Struggling to preserve his faith, he found himself questioning more and more Catholic tenets and the clergy's institutional role. Every day was another heresy committed in his mind. As reason betrayed his faith, reason or, more exactly, the moral philosophy of Krausism, led him back to belief, if not to the Church itself. In a moving passage, he wrote, "Of myself I can say to you that while I believed in God, simply because, because *something ineffable* flowed through my heart, I was religious, sincere . . . but intermittent. Then came those hours of [spiritual] dryness of which a mystic saint speaks in which neither prayer nor faith is enough to make water spring from a rock; . . . if I fixed upon as the substance of this vertigo the idea of God, the torment was horrible. Is there a God? Or isn't there? I asked myself, and as my heart in such agony said nothing to me, and *the proofs of the existence of God* are commonplaces, *topics* of logic . . . [of] a barren intellectualism, there was no way to escape that arid, sterile pain."[24]

Clarín's personal crisis of belief is representative of the nineteenth-century liberal's dilemma with religion. In 1878 he thought he found an intellectual solution in the Krausist scheme of rational harmony. Krausism also inclined him to distrust the effects of the imagination upon belief, specifically the facile romantic imagination of Chateaubriand's *Génie du christianisme* (1802) that feasted on the visual emotion and poetry of Catholicism and that often characterizes the *Regenta*'s spiritual feelings. And yet, everything in these pages and in his subsequent writings indicates the high degree to which sentiment (and by extension, the imagination) infuses Clarín's understanding of faith. Reason alone does not appear to have completely satisfied his spiritual thirst. His deeply felt recollections of childhood faith evidently come from another source that predates any intellectual critique of religion. He never really resolved the contradictions of heart and mind.[25] His was a soul-in-progress.

Within the larger historical context, Clarín regarded the Revolution of 1868, in which the Bourbon monarchy was overthrown, as the crucible for a radical revision of Spanish politics and religion. In 1881, he observed that the effects of 1868 "reached all spheres of social life, penetrated peoples' spirits, and for the first time in Spain raised all the arduous problems that freedom of conscience had already provoked in the free and cultured nations of Europe . . . doubts and negations which before had been food for thought of only a few reached the people, and in the streets, clubs, and meeting rooms the people spoke of theology, free thought, to the shock and dismay of not a small part of society, still orthodox and fanatical or at least intolerant."[26]

The questioning of what had been largely unquestioned, especially religion, points to an underlying dilemma of nineteenth-century liberal Catholics: how reconcile freedom with authority? Indeed little more than a year after the revolution, the first Vatican Council of 1869–70 was convened to deal not so much with theological issues as with "the question of questions, whether liberalism and Catholicism could be reconciled." The Spanish Church certainly brooked no challenge to its authority. For example, the discrediting or rejection of dogma was a serious matter. In Clarín's case, it appears he did not believe in such things as Hell and Purgatory. In a satirical piece from 1882 he mocks the ultra-Catholics' obsession with Hell, recalling with feigned nostalgia his childhood belief in the nether regions. (His powerful portrayal of Ana Ozores's fearful imagining of Hell is thus all the more remarkable.) Elsewhere he humorously disputes a Franciscan's view that belief in Purgatory is a matter not just of faith but of common sense, declaring, "I do not believe in Purgatory and I have as much common sense as [any Franciscan]." The nature of Christ obsessed him cruelly, according to his friend the clergyman Maximiliano Arboleya Martínez, with whom he talked for hours on the subject of religion. "Who was Jesus Christ?" he asked. How can he be both human and divine?[27]

In an earlier period, such doubts could have disastrous consequences. The apostate priest José Blanco White recalled in 1818–19 how in the company of an acquaintance two decades earlier he had carefully broached the subject of his religious predicament:

> I still recollect all the circumstances of fear and trepidation which attended my first utterance of a proposition, which . . . made me guilty of Heresy. . . . I was taking a walk on the Banks of the Guadalquivir, with a Gentleman high in the

Law whom I suspected of unbelief. . . . [W]e gradually, though cautiously came to touch upon religion. Though obliged, as usual, by the fear of the Inquisition to keep a watchful eye upon one another, and to measure and weigh every error and expression, my natural vehemence made me at last declare that *I could not believe the eternity of Hell torments.* . . . The feeling of terror . . . must be inconceivable to any one who has not been brought up in Spain. It was not the fear of the Inquisition which made me tremble: it was the doubt whether I had not incurred the height of Divine anger. The ground seemed to falter under me, and to be ready to swallow me.[28]

Blanco White chose to write about his religious crisis in the form of an "examination," which begins with a question-and-answer session between B. (Blanco) and W. (White), that is, as an inner dialogue modeled on the confessor–confessant exchange typically favored in catechism manuals like those of the much-reprinted Ripalda (1591) and Gaspar Astete (1599). Even after throwing off his priestly garments and forsaking Catholicism, Blanco White retained the structure of authority inherent to confession and to the Church itself through the interrogatory effect. Moreover, while downplaying the power of the Inquisition (much diminished by that time), he cannot avoid expressing fear of an even greater authority, God himself.

Structurally and emotionally, Blanco White has internalized the very authority he seeks to overcome in order to free himself from the forms and beliefs he finds so restrictive and unsatisfactory. In another passage, he explains how much he disliked confession, even as a boy, having "to overcome a very strong reluctance." Elsewhere he is more frank, alluding to the imaginary guilt confession produced in him. Confession became a specter of his imagination. He believed confession damaged children psychologically and morally.[29] Strikingly, the split between B. and W. reveals the extent to which unresolved, inner conflict haunts Blanco White's examination.

Reliance on forms of religious authority that on another, more conscious level have been otherwise rejected is also present in Clarín. The conflict points to both ambivalence and an internalized need for some kind of coherent structure that speaks both emotionally and imaginatively to a mind adrift in uncertainty, as Blanco White and Alas surely were. That structure of authority, whether it is confession or the institution of the Church, creates, however, inner stresses and fault lines that erupt and fissure in the complex narrative turn their writings take. The sense of order that shapes auricular confession produces emotional and moral disorder when it moves to the more secular autobiographical examination of self because it discloses what cannot be spoken of in a methodical manner. Sins that have names and can be absolved and thereby controlled turn out not to have names, or simply cannot be named under the cultural conditions in which they reside.

The structure of confession, which in general permeates *La Regenta* as the pressure to reveal secrets, emerges as a productive, not simply a repressive, force, allowing the imagination to materialize in writing as a body of sin.[30] Much of what makes Alas's novel so compellingly modern and original is precisely its passionate and conflictive engagement with tradition, most tellingly Catholicism. Like Blanco White, Clarín is torn between needing and rejecting the larger spiritual authority upon which confession rests. Similarly, his character Ana Ozores vacillates between longing for religious guidance (in the form of her confessor and devotional practices) and feeling trapped by that very desire, which turns her inner world into a private prison.

Confession does not free her from the psychic wound with which she begins her fictional life, but instead carves out a deeper gash. In his modern reading of Saint Augustine, Jean-François Lyotard observes, "The fissure that zigzags across the confession spreads with all speed over life, over lives." Confession makes clear "the fragmentary character of all life."[31] Ana arrives on the scene as damaged goods, censured as a young girl for a sin she has not committed and cannot name. In remembering the trauma through self-examination prior to confession, she summons forth her own flawed origins. This version of family romance, to use Freud's parlance, is metaphorically linked to the notion of original sin, given the circumstances of carnal knowledge of which Ana is accused. Examination of conscience — a kind of preconfession — gives birth to a modern, secular narrative.

In other words, the religious forms of self-examination and confession provided Alas with the imaginative structures he needed to reconceive realism through the fractured lens of faith under duress. Ana's tormented spirituality, seemingly at times indistinguishable from the sexual drive, with interludes of religious frenzy and despair, is not a residual effect of premodern attitudes. It is an example of religiosity under historical and cultural pressure having produced a modern soul in crisis. Similarly, the novel form, so closely associated with secular modernity, appears as a metaphorical graft of liberal Spain onto Catholic Spain (what Clarín advocated for his country). That graft produces a hybrid fiction in which the confessional State and soul and liberal critique share the same space, shaping though also notably disputing narrative authority. This shared space is the intersection of *belief in* (faith) and *belief that* (liberalism). Confession, as a practice and as a structuring device, is an apt figure for the internalization of a certain kind of authority, at once revelatory and vigilant. This authority is focused on the individual's psychic and social persona and diffused throughout the social body in the prying eyes and busy, gossiping mouths eager to disclose the secret underbelly of Vetustan life. Such disclosures are by their anticipatory nature also sexualized relishments.

Viewed culturally and historically, the intersection of confession and sex is not surprising. Sexual solicitation in the confessional was an enduring topos of the period. Anticlericals and anti-Catholics exploited the theme with great appetite to attack the Church and its representatives. The pages of anticlerical publications like *El Motín* and *Las Dominicales del Libre Pensamiento* and books such as Eduardo López Bago's *El confesonario* (1885) and Arturo Perera's *La confesión de un confesor* (1898) abound with examples. López Bago's novel, the sequel to *El cura* (The priest) (1885), displays a pathology of confessional abuses and was a bestseller.[32] Perera's text is a fictionalized account of a lovesick priest accused of the attempted murder of his penitent's husband and includes excerpts of the prosecution's and defense's cases, presumably presented at criminal trial.

These examples also clearly distinguish themselves from Clarín's novel. They aim for the stereotypical and representative, the case study loosely considered and exploited as scandal, recalling such related meanings of the *caso* as downfall and misfortune, as in the *Lazarillo de Tormes*. In reviewing Alphonse Daudet's *L'Évangéliste* (1883), a novel about a fanatical Protestant fundamentalist and her follower, Clarín is careful to say the book is not a case study of religious hysteria (though modern readers might disagree). He thus differentiates the writing of fiction from lesser or more questionable genres like the medical report or the anticlerical rant.[33]

An even more revealing (and exhaustive) title in the same vein of heightened hysteria found in López Bago and Perera is Constancio Miralta's *Los secretos de la confesión: Revelaciones, misterios, crímenes y monstruosidades; sacrilegios, aberraciones y ridiculeces; miserias, problemas sociales o religiosos y extravagancias humanas; inmoralidades de la moral conservadora y ultramontana, y otros excesos y pecados oídos a los penitentes durante larga práctica del confesionario* (The secrets of confession: revelations, mysteries, crimes, and monstrosities; sacrileges, aberrations, and absurdities; miseries, social and religious problems, and human extravagance; immoralities of conservative, ultramontane morality and other excesses and sins heard from penitents during long practice of the confessional) (1886). Miralta was the pseudonym of the clergyman José Ferrándiz Ruiz (1852–1927), whose off-and-on relationship with the Church coincided with anticlerical outbursts, followed by ecclesiastical persecution. Accused of heresy and concubinage at one point, he was reconciled to the Church in 1915. Among the types of priests he describes is "the pornographic confessor," who "asks imprudent questions, stoops to intimate details, such as the details of matrimonial life; he wants to control and know everything and respects nothing." The book may have been written partly in response to López Bago's novel. Ferrándiz had written abrasive reviews of his work, slamming the novelist for his inaccurate knowledge of the priestly life.[34]

That misuse of the confessional for seduction, masturbation, and other sexual acts was also a real problem is documented in earlier records, such as the denunciations made to the Inquisition. Indeed, the Inquisition may have "eroticized confession" by obsessing over sexual misuse of the confessional. With anticlerical writings like those of López Bago, Ferrándiz Ruiz, and Perera, the sexualized confessional is literally made for scandal. Its ecclesiastical usage refers to the Greek *skandalon,* meaning a "trap" or "obstacle" devised to make someone fall or stumble; and by extension is used to describe persons who are "the source or occasion of scandal, when they lead others into error or sin."[35]

The subject of confession in Clarín's time also lent itself to lighthearted treatment in humorous verse and plays and in paintings. Juan Tomás Salvany wrote a sonnet, "La confesión" (1877), on the basis of a dialogue between a priest and his confessant, whose sin is her love for a man, the remedy for which, declares her confessor, is to marry her off. In a poem by José Estremera, also titled "La confesión" (1883), the confessant, *in extremis,* prefers not to go to heaven if it means forgetting the lover who gave her so much grief in life. By 1896, a one-act comic dialogue, *Confesión general,* by José Feliu y Codina, turns on a completely profane use of the sacrament in which a woman character comes "to confess" a Don Juan type "before the tribunal of penitence."[36] And in an utterly delightful painting, again "La confesión" (1883), Vicente Palmaroli (1834–96) fashions a declaration of love scene on the beach, showing a young man and woman seated in wicker chairs pushed close together. The setting mimics in a secular style the confessional box, the side of the chair being the lattice screen that separates the lovers. The young man is appropriately dressed in black, by contrast with the female figure's light colors, but, more tellingly, recalling the priestly garb of a confessor. The setting and figures hark back to a religious context, which has been gently redrawn.

Whether couched as an anticlerical attack or as an amusement, the perception of confession as eroticized not only says much about the practice, real or imagined, but about sexual expression as dependent upon other cultural frameworks. Stated another way, in late nineteenth-century Spain (and Europe) and in texts like *La Regenta,* sex and the body appear at first glance as though they were forces disengaged or separated from the field of language. The sexual drive, recognized as fundamental and conflictive, came into its own with the pioneering work of researchers like Pierre Janet, Jean-Martin Charcot, Henri Legrand du Saulle, and Havelock Ellis in areas of the hysterical personality and sexology. Sexual dysfunction was attributed either to mental or material causes and at times to both. The sexual, however, was not perceived as a discursive field in itself, in which a complex, shifting play of forces having to do with identity, desire, and power defined and undefined the terms of engagement. Neither was the existence of the sexual always acknowledged in the use of language itself.

Figure 8. *La confesión* (*The Confession*). Painting by Vicente Palmaroli (1883) (Casón del Buen Retiro, Prado Museum). Courtesy of Museo Nacional del Prado.

In the richly textured sociohistorical microcosm of *La Regenta* such non-recognition assumed a number of culturally constituted forms, chief among them traditional Catholic thought, to which vestiges of a Counter-Reformation stripe clung. Foucault popularized the view that the instruments of the confessional, along with the family, school, and medicine, were used to impose and internalize self-control.[37] He rejected the conventional notion of the nineteenth century as synonymous with overwhelming sexual repression. Instead he argued for the uncontainable proliferation of sexual discourses in Western society. In this sense, repression — which by no means disappears under Foucault's thesis — seems to function as its antithesis, by provoking different forms of rupture on the surface of the social order. Disorder — unacceptable desire, passion — comes from deep within, bursting through to visibility in a series of fragmented, distorted shapes of consciousness. Unseen, disorder is also unspoken.

This not speaking — in a direct, conscious fashion — of the sexual discloses, paradoxically, how the body and its sexuality constitute a subterranean obsession that simultaneously incites and deforms revelation of the sexual. Fetishes and other kinds of displacements, such as Ana Ozores's hysterical symptoms, become the outward signs of a permanently disturbed inner life. The body, figuratively and literally, lies at the center of Clarín's narrative. It incites the storytelling drive forward, to reach that almost unspeakable, in part because unbearable, ending incarnated as Ana's inert body lying on the cathedral floor and receiving the material corruption of the world through the sexually perverted kiss of the acolyte Celedonio: "For she thought that she had felt on her lips the cold and slimy belly of a toad."[38]

Something, however, has to initiate the narrative process whereby we end with a symbolically dead body. Most readers point to the heroine's adultery as the primary motivation behind the plot. Ana's fall into sin is thus literalized as punishment in the last scene. I find this explanation inadequate in its neat and reductive disposing of both the body and person of Ana Ozores. For what emerges out of the body is not simply the consciousness of sin, but also the shape of imagination. To see how the sense of the body also leads to the sense of an ending is to grasp how imagination materializes as a metaphorical construct of corporality in Alas's novel.

As the initial nexus between body and imagination, Ana Ozores's examination of conscience in chapter 3 also sets into motion the narrative energy of *La Regenta*. This is an example of that plotting desire traced by Peter Brooks. These introspective moments are in truth also retrospective, as Ana remembers the scene of her childhood. In larger narrative terms, this is the birthing of her predicament, which is that of the novel itself: how to construct being, a self, out of damaged, imperfect parts in a world that is also damaged.

Images of birth — metaphors of bodily origins — inhabit the text. As a product of the nineteenth century, the realist-naturalist novel reflects the mechanistic and biological impulses of its time. Patterns pressed out of underlying concerns for genealogy and fabrication form the narrative and thematic substrata of many nineteenth-century novels. Creating a novelistic world, a totalizing view within a microcosm, has been an essential feature of the genre since *Don Quijote.* The classic form of the novel, however, has never been complete or total, and, as a genre of late-blossoming hybridism, it has never been quite legitimate either. Marthe Robert, in a neo-Freudian analysis, figures the novel form as either an aggressive Bastard (the trope of ambition) or an escapist Foundling (the trope of daydreaming). In either case, proper parentage is lacking. Both figurations are products of what can be called an improper birth.

For all their suggestiveness, Robert's models (devised in 1972) strike one as being based predominantly on male desires and male schemata. Christine van Boheemen enlarges the Freudian frame, proposing that the novel functions "as a confirming mirror of subjectivity" in which the quest for self-identity eventually excludes otherness, denoted symbolically and otherwise as feminine. She also argues that modern narrative, at least since James Joyce, has tended to privilege feminine otherness as the source of fiction's authority, in contradistinction to the traditional Christian view, which "reserved absolute origination and authority to the masculine principle, God the Father."[39]

La Regenta appears here as a conflictive crossing of masculine and feminine principles, in Ana's recreation of the scene of childhood, which can be considered a particular narrative instance of the family romance. Such stories always have a history attached to them. In the absence of a sense of the specific context — of *historia* as both history and story — any discussion of the body in narrative, whether figured as masculine or feminine, tends to strip it down to a reductive essentialism. On the other hand, to deny some universalizing context to this story would hopelessly fracture *La Regenta*'s composition into countless fragments, or unconnected body parts. Neither extreme, it seems to me, does justice to such an extraordinarily complex and innovative novel.

The narrative and thematic axis of Clarín's novel revolves around a woman's body (that of Ana Ozores), as the representatives of secular (Don Álvaro, the local Don Juan) and ecclesiastical (the priest Fermín de Pas) authority compete for her attentions. Girardian triangular or mimetic desire, which is shaped by that of male rivals for the same object of desire, helps us to understand the intense struggle for control over a woman's body. There is, however, something even more fundamental here than Ana Ozores's body: the body *in La Regenta* that is also the body *of La Regenta.* I refer to the body of the text, the text figured as and through the body. Thematization of the narrative *quid* as a body forms part of that complex cluster of meanings called context. Context is above all the text itself, understood as the textual quality of "with-ness" (*con*/with) intimately joined to the religious, the cultural, and the historical. Sex and the body in *La Regenta* are situational, to use Thomas Laqueur's term, meaning "explicable only within the context of battles over gender and power."[40] Power as a gender-marked field of action and of discourse runs through the novel. It is symbolically and narratively positioned at the top in chapter 1, from the viewing heights of the cathedral tower, from which the male eye — of Fermín de Pas and the narrator, collapsed together here — takes possession of all he can see. Ana's body, glimpsed from afar through Fermín's spyglass, becomes another terrain, a t(r)opographical trophy of male conquest. Whoever wins Ana wins power.

Something, however, is lost in this reading of the novel. By interpreting the gender strategies of power through Foucault and Laqueur, one ends up restricting both the terms of understanding and the text itself. The interpretation becomes repressive, relying excessively on the constraints of power. There isn't room enough to maneuver, to move about. When sex and religion are viewed purely as arenas of power struggles, imagination takes a back seat and the kind of narrative mobility that arises from the sexual and the religious is eliminated. Foucault's notion of power is notoriously difficult to pin down, appearing to radiate outward as an expanding series of diffuse points or fields. He did not view power as a monolithic structure of repression. That stated, however, one still comes up against a rather inflexible and limited conception revolving around control. Culture is not only "a system of constraints." It is also "the regulator and guarantor of movement." The culturally imbued and varied capacity for mobility acquires a singularly exquisite and moving shape in the act of narration itself. The narrative act represents imagination in movement. Moving through time, it moves us as well. Plot as a dynamics of desire can also help us to see the narrative imagination as a special form of mobility, an internal counterpoint to the equally compelling restraints operating from within to frame narrative.[41]

The narrative tensions between constraint and mobility, expressed in a knotted web of psychological, religious, social, and other meanings, come into symbolic play in the plot sequence that begins with Ana Ozores's examination of conscience and moves backward in time to her childhood in chapter 3. A more conventional third-person narrative flashback continues her memories in chapter 4. Ana has a new confessor, Don Fermín. To prepare for the next day's general confession with him, that evening she settles into a rocking chair and begins to read from a devotional the pages concerning the sacrament of penance. Her mind refuses to concentrate. Better to do it lying down, she thinks. Ana's bed, along with the overtly decadent touch of a tiger skin, is a richly described sensual space, a surface of skin and touch, cool air and silken sheets enveloping the body.

Such tactile pleasure never enters into the spoken details of Ana's confessions. It is a secret space, a secret pleasure: *and* the space of confession, which cannot be separated from her bodily awareness.[42] " 'General confession!' she was thinking. 'That is the story of a whole life.' " And a paragraph later: "She remembered that she had never known her mother. Maybe her greatest sins sprang from this misfortune." Memory of maternal loss, rubbed into consciousness as her cheek caresses the sheet, is closely linked to the space of origin, the bed as the source of her entry into the world. Ana's permanent state of orphanhood, her mourning for a missing mother, is felt as a kind of nostalgia for her mother's lap.[43]

By now Ana's thoughts have moved from one sort of confessional mode to another, from the penitential to the autobiographical examination of self. She sees herself as split into two personas, the child she once was and the adult she is. With the devotional in front of her again, she stops at the line, "The places where you have been . . ." And remembers: "As a girl—one old enough to confess—she used, whenever the book said, 'Pass your mind over all the places which you have frequented,' to remember, unintentionally, the ferry-boat at Trébol, that great sin which she had committed unawares, the night she had spent in the boat with that boy, Germán, her friend."[44] Ana's penitential self-examination then ceases and memory—autobiography—takes over. This crucial moment, a mental and affective staging of the scene of childhood, marks the transition from one kind of narrative framework to another: a conversion of the confession mode into the family romance.

Freud's family romance focused on the imperfections of birth, symbolized by an unwanted parentage and the invention of a different family history. Our origins haunt us. Ana's orphaned state is symptomatic of an improper birth. When Samuel Beckett heard Carl Jung lecture, "a remark Jung made about a ten-year-old girl who felt she had 'never been born entirely' struck Beckett forcibly: this was the core of his own neurosis! His inability to get out of bed as well as his failure to separate himself from his mother were 'aspects of an improper birth.' "[45] The circumstances of Ana's own improper birth, her state of "never [having] been born entirely," lead one to look more closely at the pairing of confession and childhood in the passage. Confession and childhood both revolve around specific uses of the body in *La Regenta,* uses that also hinge upon the extraordinary functioning of imagination. Confession and childhood are cultural constructs embodying larger social structures and signifying certain forms of behavior, values, and practices. Yet they also possess an enormous symbolic residue that continues to affect readers today.

Keeping this pairing in mind, let me pose a number of interrelated questions about the passage. What is the narrative framework, or form, of the plot sequence? What is its function within the structure and plotting of *La Regenta*? What does it say about certain models of practice of the period that have become incorporated into genres like the novel? Why does Clarín recreate the scene of childhood in his novel? Why is Ana an orphan? What are the connections between kinship and the narrative of confession? How does the remembered scene of childhood illuminate the novel as a whole? In what way is it a reflection of the novel as a genre?

First, the narrative frame. Technically the initial step taken for the sacrament of penance, religious examination of conscience is prior to auricular confession. Both are part of a centuries-long Western tradition of a generalized confessional mode that has seeped into a large variety of structures, institutions, and writings. The examination, like confession itself, reveals deeply ambivalent meanings and elicits conflicting interpretations. Self-examination participates in the Christian Socratic tradition of "Know thyself" as a way of finding the path to God. Thus it is often viewed as the first stage toward beneficial unburdening of the soul, or confession itself. Fray Hernando de Talavera (1428–1507) recommended a general cleansing (*alimpiar*) of both mind and body.[46]

A much-favored image of evacuation found in Origen and other religious writings stresses confession as a form of expulsion: "The more [penitents] put off confessing, the more difficult they find it, and what often happens in these cases of anxiety and remorseful conscience is like what happens to those who have stomach upset. Until they vomit, they find no relief, and everything is dizziness, headache, nausea, lack of appetite, nervousness, and worry." Father Antonio María Claret, the popular religious writer and confessor to Queen Isabel II, says, "Do not permit, Lord, my enemies . . . to make me swallow once again the vomit of my sins that I disgorged at the feet of my confessor." "Sin," comments Lyotard, "must be vomited out in spasms," echoing Saint Augustine: "How I wish that my cries could have been heard by those who still set their hearts on shadows and followed lies! Perhaps they would have been made to feel the error of their ways and would have disgorged it like vomit."[47]

The process of penance, epistemologically and affectively, is one in which the inner is turned outward. Historically, the practice of self-examination and confession in the Church shows the gradual disappearance of public and collective acts of penance and the institutionalization of private, individual acts. These were boosted by making annual confession obligatory in 1215 (Fourth Lateran Council), by the Council of Trent rulings, and by the invention in the sixteenth century of the confessional box. Mandatory annual confession "stimulated a spectacular rise in literature about sin," in an effort to offer guidance. At the same time, confession and examination of conscience encouraged development of the introspective self and individuation. In its historical development, however, confession became institutionalized in an effort to create a larger awareness of community among often isolated groups of Christians. Spiritual communitas is, moreover, an inherent part of the symbolism of confession and Communion. The sense of community and spiritual introspection are bound together through ritual. In each case the inner- becomes outer-directed in acts that establish a public identity among practitioners. In sociological terms, confession is a "ritual of social inclusion."[48]

The psychological need to confess becomes internalized compulsion when confessional practices are increasingly institutionalized. Such compulsion is built into the confessional model, often likened to a tribunal or a criminal court. In the "tribunal of penance," confession "is a judicial process in which the penitent is at once the accuser, the person accused, and the witness, while the priest pronounces judgment and sentence." Early confessors' handbooks were filled with "the judgment of souls" and cases of canon law. The Jesuit Gaspar Druzbicki (1589–1662) tells readers to "place yourself in the presence of God your Judge as a criminal and a sinner," and, as Jeremias bids us, "set up a watch-tower." Brother Philippe (1792–1874) seizes upon the intimate relation of self-examination and confession: "To confess [sins] we must know them, and to know them we must examine ourselves." The belief that sins inhabit us like secret, corrupt bodies within produces an inquisitorial mindset at all levels of the spiritual hierarchy, from God to his spokesman-confessor to the penitent. In a commentary troubling to twenty-first-century minds, Brother Philippe reminds his readers, "Do we consider that our examinations will be examined?"[49]

The sacrament of penance assumed a juridical character when priests were granted "the power of the keys," that is, the power to forgive sins. Church reasoning justifies the necessity of auricular confession by positing the necessity of authority. Edward Hanna writes, "Once it is admitted that the grant [to forgive sins, first bestowed by Christ upon the Apostles] was effectual and consequently that the sacrament is necessary in order to obtain forgiveness, it plainly follows that the penitent must in some way make known his sin to those who exercise the power." The power of priestly authority sets into motion an elaborate process of self-revelation, divulgement of the inner which, again, is a form of expulsion. Evacuation of undesirable thoughts and memories could be seen as produced through a psychoideological act of invasion. In this view, knowledge of self is fashioned to some degree by and through knowledge alien to that self. Jeremy Tambling believes that "the history of confession is that of power at the centre inducing people at the margins to internalise what is said about them."[50]

This account of confession must be situated within the larger context of community acceptance, which brings me to the specific place of confession in Spanish society. Despite a clear move toward modernization in nineteenth-century Spain, many old regime values persisted. Confession during the Counter-Reformation had acquired added legal meaning, as Lázaro's brief account of his father's misdeeds intimates: "He confessed, did not deny, and suffered persecution by justice." A lingering inquisitorial mentality in the nineteenth century, coupled with strong Church influence upon government, education, and the family, encouraged a certain *résistance mentale* to modernity among traditionalists, a conservative peasant class, significant conservative segments of the middle classes, and large numbers of women from all social strata.[51]

The confessional framework continued to mold the thinking of many nineteenth-century Spaniards. An ultramontane condemnation of liberalism, *Casos de conciencia acerca del liberalismo* (Cases of conscience concerning liberalism) (1886), by a certain P.V. (Pablo Villada?), is conceived within the catechistic format of a series of dialogued exchanges between Confessor and Penitent. The title itself is reminiscent of confessors' manuals like Juan de Pedraza's *Summa de casos de consciencia* (1568), which developed out of late twelfth- and thirteenth-century Latin tracts referred to as *summa de casibus* or *summa confessorum*. Recounting one's case, as the *caso* of Lazarillo de Tormes testifies, is, among other things, an act of obedience.[52] Even in acts of disobedience, for example, anticlerical attacks against confessional and other practices of the Church, the same narrative model of confession appears, as in books like Ferrándiz Ruiz's *Los secretos de la confesión* and Perera's *La confesión de un confesor*.

Growing anticlericalism as well as de-Christianization of the working classes toward the end of the century — both present in *La Regenta* — should not blind us to the existence of a Catholic Revival from midcentury on. Renewed popular evangelism, prevalent in the eighteenth century, expanded devotional practices, a publishing avalanche of spiritual writings (especially catechisms and devotionals), the growth of religious orders, and the development of religious lay associations are visible signs of that revival. Father Claret played a key role in promoting both apostolic missions and mass-produced religious publications. Industrialists like Claudio López and Eusebio Güell even attempted through technologically and architecturally innovative projects like the Comillas Seminary and Güell Park to "resacralize" the country.[53]

During the Restoration period especially, the Church initiated a campaign of heavy use of the sacraments. The massive sacramentalization of Catholic society meant that the practices of catechism, Communion, and penance grew enormously, all of which are reflected in the fictional world of Vetusta. Clarín's narrator alludes to the arrival of Jesuit missionaries for the purpose of evangelizing; to the spiritual and charitable activities of the Societies of Saint Vincent de Paul and of the Sacred Heart and the Mission for Catechesis; and to feast days, sermons, spiritual exercises, novenas, and other devotions. The most pious women of Vetusta (*beatas*) and Father Fermín place great emphasis on catechism, reflecting the real-life stimulus that Bishop Benito Sanz y Forés (1868–81) and, later, José María de Cos y Macho gave to catechism in Oviedo in 1869, making religious instruction more appealing to children.[54]

Ana Ozores is encouraged to immerse herself in such outward forms of religiosity: "Ana devoted herself to active piety, to charitable works, to teaching, to propaganda — to all the practices of the complicated, pettifogging devotion which was the predominant kind in Vetusta. All these excesses — as she had previously considered them to be — she now found justifiable, in the way that lovers account for the nonsense they talk when they are alone together." Another passage reads, "[Ana] took refuge in piety and, with ardent charity and apostolic zeal, visited the poor, crowded into hovels and caves, to bring them the consolations of religion for the spirit and alms for the body . . . this was the one [task] she liked best."[55] Such richly observed comments allow us to see at once irony and sincerity, liberal skepticism making room for genuine religious spirit.

The Catholic Revival in Spain also emphasized, along with traditional piety, a more individualized, emotionally charged practice of religion, intended for both men and women. The style of devotional literature was sentimental, suffused with feeling. Thus in *La corte celestial de María* (1855), the beauty of the penitent future Saint Mary of Egypt is "drenched in tears, which are the blood of the soul." In the same devotional text (possibly a translation, as the prints are from a French source), Saint Clare of Assisi's prayers are also bathed in tears, her lips pressed to the crucifix, the "words so inflamed they could not be heard without emotion."[56] With the accent on private prayer and religiosity directed toward personal salvation, the social dimensions of religion took a back seat, although a nascent philanthropic movement was timidly developing at the same time.

It is hard to say whether the Church was trying to be more accommodating to the liberal position by bending to the times, "leading the more conservative elements of liberalism not back to the Church, because they had never left it, but toward more emotional forms of religious practice." In the case of Clarín, Galdós, and many other liberals the tactic did not work. Clarín remained at odds with the institutional stance of Spanish Catholicism. Yet emotionally, like his character Ana Ozores, he was drawn to what we might call the deep structure of faith, to deliverance from uncertainty and mental distress, hence his ambivalent dealings with ecclesiastical authority. Throughout Europe, the "more personal understanding of Christianity" characterized nineteenth-century life, but in Spain obedience to the authority of the Church and its representatives still occupied center stage.[57]

Women of the middle and upper classes therefore sought spiritual direction by frequenting the confessional box. On occasion they gave spiritual direction, as Gertrudis Gómez de Avellaneda did in her *Manual del cristiano* (1847 and 1867). Male family members often looked upon the figure of the confessor as a threat to the family — the thesis, for example, of Jacinto Octavio Picón's ferociously anticlerical novel *El enemigo* (The enemy) (1887). Echoing Jules Michelet, Pardo Bazán observed in 1889, "Looming over the extremely pious woman a father, brother, or husband sees the black shadow of the spiritual director, a rival for his authority."[58] At the same time, a penitent of some social standing conferred worldly prestige upon confessors like Fermín de Pas.

The principal model for Fermín de Pas in *La Regenta* — José María de Cos y Macho (Magistral de Oviedo, 1865–86) — was celebrated as a skillful spiritual director and confessor, catechist, and shrewd courtier. He served as the spiritual director of Mercedes Villaverde Uría, whose "Regla de vida" (Rule of life) has been preserved. Dated 7 June 1886 and approved by Cos y Macho two days later, it briefly describes along monastic lines her daily religious conduct from her first waking hour till bedtime, with the ideal of "walk[ing] in the presence of God." Given the normative nature of the "Rule of life," there is very little to be glimpsed of her inner life, except possibly for one reference: "I will flee with horror from sin and any occasion for it." The sentiment, however, is probably an echo of traditional religiosity found in the sermons of missionary preachers, for example.[59]

Villaverde Uría writes of being obedient and humble. Submission to a spiritual director's guidance, often in the Jesuitical mold of self-examination, as with Cos y Macho, was expected to be total. In revitalizing and stressing the notion of original sin and concupiscence, or the inclination to sin, as part of its spiritual revival, the Church also insisted upon complete obedience to its representatives. As a contemporary reviewer of *La Regenta* says, "The confessional is a throne."[60] Unlike Cos y Macho's real-life penitent, Ana Ozores appears to swing wildly between submission to religious norms and noncompliance, which takes the form of imaginatively rewriting prescriptive literature like the examination of conscience as a continuation of her unsettled inner life.

Much of the renascent spiritual fervor was certainly not new; and it was not confined to Spain. France underwent an earlier similar revival and supplied a number of spiritual models for Spain. Yet a new note was struck in Spain: as Stanley Payne remarks, "For the first time in Spanish history, religious identity and observance were becoming rather sharply divided by region and by social class." The north (where Clarín locates Vetusta) adhered more closely to the faith than the south. Socially, by the early twentieth century one commentator wrote that the poor, fearing the betrayal of confessional secrets, "dread and distrust the confessors" as representing the interests of the rich against the poor.[61] Early signs of the schism surface in *La Regenta*. By century's end, many of the working classes no longer trusted the authority of the Church.

The questioning of authority strikes at the very foundations of the Church as an institution. Massive administration of the sacraments, intended to bolster the faith, became a political and class instrument of power, symbolized in the black confessional box, as Clarín shows in the backstairs scheming of Vetusta's clergy. The critical, often satiric, posture of the third-person narrator in *La Regenta* constitutes a corrosive narrative deauthorizer of religious authority, just as working-class indifference to Catholicism and as Don Pompeyo Guimarán's and Santos Barinaga's atheism on the level of story also undermine the traditional *communitas* of collective belief.

Yet there is profound ambivalence in Clarín's views and use of authority. Carolyn Richmond observes, "Alas fully believed in the function of modern literature as a guide or director of conscience both for fictional and real-life readers."[62] Even as Alas's narrator undermines one form of authority, his own narrative authority is unquestioned. The narrator possesses qualities akin to those of a confessor, or spiritual director, like Fermín de Pas, as we see in the opening scene of *La Regenta* and the subsequent naturalist view of Vetusta in which scrutiny and visual possessiveness disclose the desire to control through knowledge and incorporation. The initial act of examination, as Fermín with his spyglass observes from the cathedral tower everything below him, while couched in the material language of naturalism, derives its imaginative force from a kind of narrative sacramentalization. The narrator, in seeking the revelation of hidden realities, performs his duty as a supradirector of conscience and authorizes himself by making his authority necessary to the text. As noted, once the power of the keys is granted to priests, "it plainly follows that the penitent must in some way make known his sin to those who exercise the power." Once authority is made present, revelation must follow.

This sequence is founded on the unspoken understanding that there is something to be revealed, something hidden and guarded that is kept secret. A sacramentalized view of things converts that undisclosed substance into the prize to be gained, made visible or conscious. So the Capuchin Manuel de Jaén advises that one should review the Ten Commandments during self-examination "the way one searches diligently for a jewel of great value one has lost, looking in every corner." Fermín views the moral and spiritual map of Vetusta as his prize: "Vetusta was his passion and his prey. . . . He knew it inch by inch, inside and out, soul and body; he had examined the corners of consciences and the corners of houses."[63] When he becomes Ana's confessor, her soul is transformed into yet another symbolic guerdon.

In narrative terms, the text itself in being told represents the kind of revelation authority seeks and demands. As a director of conscience, the narrator makes known a larger form of conscience, which is manifested as narrative consciousness. The narrator as director of conscience probes beneath the surface and brings to light a textual conscience that can be expressed only as consciousness, narrative awareness. The relationship between authority and revelation functions within a symbolic topography of inside-outside, depth-surface, skin-soul. Here, the fictional world of *La Regenta* still performs some of the old regime functions of sacramentalization. The Catholic confessional mode in particular, with its necessity for authority, for spiritual direction (unlike most Protestant models), and its compulsion to speak, is an apt instrument for disclosure, for turning the inner outward, by bringing to the surface of narrative the sin of consciousness.

Ana's examination of self recalls Brother Philippe's words, "Do we consider that our examinations will be examined?" The authority implicit in the act of narrating poses inner restraints but also contains and foments its own mobility. The creative tension between restraint and mobility works as a narrative and cultural paradigm in Ana's examination of conscience and confession. Her self-examination is subject to two kinds of external examiners. On the level of story, Fermín de Pas as her confessor questions her words. On the level of discourse, the narrator himself subtly suggests the same examining — that is, controlling — operation through the third-person narration present in this and other plot sequences. Both examiners incorporate symbolically that which has been expelled from the confessant: Ana's consciousness of sin. The creative energy fueling *La Regenta* arises in part out of the complex dialectic between the psychological-spiritual consciousness of sin and the sin of narrative consciousness.

The importance of confession in Alas's novel has not gone unnoticed. The value of confession is more than anecdotal, it is symbolic: "Confession passes from mere anecdote to being a symbol of a city's attitude towards a character." Lou Charnon-Deutsch points out how the confessional "is the tool of ideological power, but also of pleasure." And Beth Bauer explores confession "as a model for communication, as self-revelation for a real or imagined Other."[64] What all previous critics make visible, in different ways, is the significance of confession as a metanarrative of *La Regenta*. Yet the direct presentation of confession is oddly missing. It is the central motive of the first part of the novel, yet while Ana confesses the narrator "takes us somewhere else," as María del Carmen Bobes Naves notes. We can piece together fragments of the confession, indirectly, through the gossip of other characters, the narrator's voice, and Ana's reflections on the act, but the confession itself escapes us. For Bobes Naves, "The significance of the event 'confession' is absolutely textual, not ontological, and proceeds from the form in which the discourse presents it."[65]

Why, though, does confession assume the narrative form that it takes in *La Regenta*? why is it there in the first place? Certainly narrative suspense is well served by postponing revelation of the confessional act. In a larger sense, "confessional practices seem actually to delay the sense of a plot, of a change taking place, introducing instead . . . an endless metonymic displacement, a deferral of narrative."[66]

There are also cultural reasons of a religious-theological stripe for the indirect presentation of confession. The seal of confession normally applies to priests, who vow not to speak of secrets revealed during the act. Strong pressure is also laid against the confessant not to speak of what occurs during confession. Reverence for the sacrament dictates discretion. Moreover, anti-Catholic and anticlerical sentiments exploited the "charnel house" of the confessional box as a place of "unclean talk" in which secrecy promoted seduction and subjection. Protestant pamphlets like one titled *The Confessional Unmasked* (1867), from which I extract these phrases, operated on the same sacramentalized principle of revelation through divine authority as did Catholicism. The very title unmasks the same desire to disclose prized information, in this case a full denunciation of papist practices. *The Confessional Unmasked* is constructed almost entirely out of quotations from Catholic sources: thus it turns the material of moral theology concerning confession against itself. At the same time, the desire to reveal the "degrading and demoralizing office of auricular confession" by alluding in heavily clothed Victorian style to such acts as "morose delight" (*morosa delectatio*) and the dangers of "imperfect pollution" has the unintentional and ironic effect of converting antipapists into Protestant directors of conscience.[67] Anticlericals like López Bago and Ferrándiz Ruiz, immersed in the culture of Catholicism, reveled in crudely spelling out confessions as proof of ecclesiastical abuse.

The Church was acutely aware of anti-Catholic and anticlerical attacks like these that relied on one form of authority, moral rectitude, to fulminate against another form. Thus in *A Narrative of Iniquities and Barbarities Practised at Rome in the Nineteenth Century* (1847), the former monk Raffaele Ciocci structures his conversion to Protestantism as a freedom narrative. His liberation from the inquisitorial, repressive hands of the Church allows him to take the moral high ground. Confession for the young boy is "not to seek for absolution of sins . . . but to listen to insidious questions tending to excite evil passions in my breast." He grows ill when confined to his room during a two-week period for religious exercises. His parents, he said, were unaware that "he was being dragged, an unwilling victim, to the sacrifice."[68] Catholics had to pay attention to such denunciations, if only to demonstrate religious superiority in a moral-ideological debate whose terms and structures the two groups shared.

Avoidance of scandal, therefore, was paramount. For both theological and political reasons concealment of the things that went on during confession had to be maintained. When Huysmans published intimate details of his confession in the quasi-autobiographical conversion narrative *En route* (1895), he was accused of exploiting Catholicism. The confession scene in particular upset quite a few Catholic readers. These cultural strictures against wrongful revelation of confession — still prevalent in some mid-twentieth-century Mediterranean cultures — form part of the ideological restraints operating normatively in *La Regenta*. The same principle of authority that dictates confession also bars us from its complete disclosure. In narrative terms, confession demonstrates both the need for story and the desire to pull back and put off the telling. Confession as narrative also points paradigmatically to the secret senses embedded in all texts.[69]

The narrative and cultural prohibitions against complete disclosure, against full and true confession, paradoxically create a new space of the imagination in *La Regenta*. Repression and compulsion go hand in hand with secrecy. But against compulsion comes resistance. If prohibition discourages revelation, so too does resistance in other ways. The reluctance to speak comes from Ana Ozores, who never tells her confessor de Pas what she really desires.

Even more significant, out of her examination of conscience she creates an entirely different text, an imaginative family romance. When her self-examination swerves from its course, provoking one of those narrative deviations built into a plotted story, Ana subverts one of the levels of authority present in the text by appropriating the instruments of that authority. The techniques and forms of at-home confession — her self-examination — stimulate her memory, which is what they are intended to do. Commenting on the sexualization and vulnerable character of Ana's readerly responses to texts, Benigno Sánchez-Eppler analyzes this passage as the first occasion in which we see the protagonist as a reader. "Reconstructing her own story," he says, "Ana is in fact scanning a self-generated text later characterized as ['a memory in novel form']."[70]

The self-generated text is at the same time a directed narrative. The very form of self-examination is conducive to making narratives. Ana simply uses

orthodox confessional narrative techniques to forge an unexpected story, unexpected because uncalled for. To understand how such a plot transformation
happens, it helps to remember that examination of conscience is normally
conceived within a framework of order and rationality. Penitents are expected
to follow a certain order in scrutinizing their conscience. The conventional
pattern is to go over, one by one, the Decalogue, the five commandments of the
Church, and the seven Deadly Sins. Self-examination as a daily devotional
practice can also take on the varied forms of spiritual exercises. The model
most followed and adapted is Ignatius de Loyola's *Ejercicios espirituales* (*Spiritual Exercises*) (written 1522–24), in which self-examination is reduced to a
system, a result of turning reading itself into a method. At the same time,
Loyola's exercises constitute "the reading of moods [as] the centerpiece of his
discernment method."[71]

All the forms of religious examination rely upon the regulated use of imagination. Out of memory comes imagination. In remembering one's faults or in
concentrating on a certain virtue, the penitent draws forth out of self a spiritual
space propitious for transformation of that self. The imagination is directed
toward salvation. One imagines a new self. For Saint Ignatius, the goal is "to
learn God's will" but always with salvation in mind. The kind of memory called
for, however, is a very special one. As Antonio de Nicolás remarks, Ignatius's
" 'powers of imagining' consist in calling on the sensuous imagination with
great intensity — *exercising* the sensuous powers — in order to reenact, as it
were, in one's own life the symbolic narratives of the past, so as to feel the affects
of one's imagined present participation in the lives and events . . . of the founder
of Christianity and of his disciples." Thus, Ignatius counsels that for the first
(and for every) exercise one should envisage the physical setting of the object of
contemplation: "The first preliminary is a composition for seeing the place . . .
the composition will be to see with the sight of imagination the corporeal place,
where the thing that I wish to contemplate is located." Adapting the rhetorical
art of mnemonics to his purposes, he continues: "I say the corporeal place, for
example a temple or hill, where Jesus Christ or Our Lady may be found,
according to what I wish to contemplate. In what is invisible, as in the case of
sins, the composition will be to see with the imaginative sight and consider my
soul imprisoned within this corruptible body."[72]

The Ignatian *composición viendo el lugar* spread, through the largely Jesuit
control of the confessional and education and the attractiveness of a seemingly
simple model, to nearly all subsequent spiritual exercises and self-examinations.
It functions through image making, a technique possibly inspired in part by
Loyola's interest in illustrations from fifteenth-century Books of Hours. Yet as de
Nicolás observes, "Ignatius provides memory points, describes how to imagine,
but the images to be imagined are absent from the *Exercises*." In a brilliant essay,

Roland Barthes distinguishes between the impoverished Ignatian image reservoir and the powerful imagination cultivated in the text, unlike the mystics' "deprivation of images," or emptying out of the soul. The orderliness of the Ignatian model of imagination comes through clearly in the methodic, incessant classifications, subdivisions, and annotations of the *Exercises*. Point by point, Loyola breaks down everything in scholastic fashion in order that exercitants, in turn, can structure their meditations, articulating and dismembering each of the five senses as the image is composed.[73]

One is encouraged, for example, to imagine Hell by going through five *punctos*, or points, that are the senses separately fixed upon the image of Hell. After a preparatory prayer and two preliminaries, the first of which enjoins that one see "with the sight of the imagination the length, breadth and depth of Hell," one is then to imagine in the first point "the great flames, and souls like bodies ignited," and so on to the next point.[74]

Ana reflects upon the realness of Hell after experiencing a series of horrific nightmares in chapter 19: "Hell was no longer a dogma lumped together with all the other dogmas! she had smelt it, tasted it. . . . Hell existed! And now she knew what it was—the corruption of matter, for souls corrupted by sin. And she had sinned, yes, yes, she had sinned." In this intense moment of *attritio*, or lesser remorse inspired by fear of Hell, Ana's imagination plainly functions according to a sacramentalized view of things. While Saint Teresa and other spiritual and literary sources undoubtedly influence her vision of Hell, the imagery of the senses noted here is also remarkably Ignatian in effect.[75]

Her view of Hell arises from within, from the body itself as an infernal underground dwelling. The same conjunction between body and imagination —aligned textually through self-examination—obtains in Ana's reflections upon her life as an accumulation of sins. Her initial deviation from the text of orthodoxy, in the moment of reading "If you have eaten meat," stresses the body's materiality, its needs and desires in conflict with the prohibition to eat flesh on certain holy days. The more radical turning or swerve of her text comes, however, from her reading of the phrase, "The places where you have been." The context of the phrase refers to the circumstances of a sin—the traditional "quis, quid, ubi, quibus auxiliis, cur, quomodo, quando," which has been rendered into English as "Who, what, where, by what help and whose / Why, how and when do many things disclose." Ignatius writes that the exercitant is to "look at the place and the house where he has lived." Brother Philippe says that we should "recall to our memory the diverse circumstances which might, during the day, cause us to fall again into . . . faults."[76] Even before confession, the penitent must mentally detail through self-examination the exact circumstances of sins.

These circumstances, rooted in classical rhetoric, lend themselves to a specific narrative quality, despite the generic categories emphasized. Through mnemonic mental techniques, one enacts a "positive construction of a narrative in the art of confessing." Ivan Illich suggests that "confession interiorizes the sense of the 'text.' " He believes that "confession . . . produces the subject it wants, and several others too."[77] This view tends to see the confessional process as an inner strait-jacket. Even as a Catholic convert, Huysmans could not bear the *Ejercicios espirituales,* complaining that they "left no initiative to the soul."[78]

To see the confessional process as alienating to the subject and little else, however, ignores the imaginative interplay between the inner text of person-ality and the imposed text of confessional practice. It ignores the way both texts interact to produce a third text that is neither entirely repressive nor entirely liberated. One then sees how psychological consciousness of sin gener-ates the sin of narrative consciousness in an unredeemed world. My point is that awareness of sinfulness also possesses a highly imaginative capacity be-cause it stimulates the self to view itself as a sacramentalized entity, a distinct object to be plumbed and scrutinized. To do this, spiritual exercises like those of Saint Ignatius, Saint Francisco de Borja, and Luis de la Palma encourage the exercitant to set up a scenario of imagining. The position of the body (kneel-ing, prostrate, and so forth), the facial expression (the presence of tears, for example), the physical qualities of the room (shuttered, isolated), the lighting (generally darkened) are all to be carefully chosen so as to exclude any distrac-tions in the penitent's spiritual space.[79] (All of these details are present in the scene from chapter 3 of *La Regenta.*) The penitent can then concentrate on summoning those appropriate images created from the guided use of the senses. In other words, a religious *tableau vivant* is produced that emerges from the human body itself. These are " 'scenes' [that] the exercitant is called upon to live out, as in a psychodrama." It is *this* body — never an abstract one — that "is to occupy [this theater]."[80]

From the symbolic use of the body as a primary text, Ana Ozores moves figuratively to another theater of the mind, the scene of childhood, in which the body once again acquires great significance. She remembers the way Loyola does, through the recall of places, which function not as "mere scenic backdrop for its protagonist; it invents and informs the plot. Setting is structural." Thus Ana's scene of childhood is absolutely fundamental to the plot and meaning of *La Regenta.* Accused at age ten of having carnal knowledge of the boy Germán, Ana only much later grows into an awareness of sinfulness as a thing of bodies. The initial not knowing what her body means culturally and sexually to other people marks her subsequent personal history as deeply divided, irremediably conflictive: "As the judge's wife thought about the girl that she had once been she began to admire her, and to feel that her own life had been divided into two parts. . . . The girl who used to jump out of bed in the dark had been more vigorous than this Anita of the present; she had possessed an extraordinary inner strength for withstanding unhumiliated the demands and the injustices of the curt, cold, capricious people in charge of her."[81]

Ana's consciousness of sin comes "when no one else thought of such matters any longer, Ana still thought of them and, confusing innocent acts with blameworthy ones, took to mistrusting everything." Jacques Lacan would say that Clarín's character has belatedly entered the realm of the Symbolic and been subjected to the inescapable Law of the Father.[82] One could also say that she has fallen into the sin of consciousness, expressed the only way it can be with words: in a narrative of imperfections. Earlier I said that this scene of childhood represents the birthing of her predicament — and that of the novel: how to construct a self out of damaged, imperfect parts. Ana's split in consciousness is a sign of an improper birth, of what we become when we are born into consciousness, flawed in and by knowledge.

The profoundly sacramentalized conception of that consciousness is part of what imbues *La Regenta* with such intense feeling — especially suffering — and images. The authenticity of belief implied here plays a complex role in the genesis of the novel. Belief legitimates authority on the level of story. Without belief, Ana's confession would be meaningless. From the Church's point of view insincere confession constitutes yet another sin. Confession needs preexistent guilt to exist; it is grounded in the notion of the fallen state of humanity, or original sin, "since every personal sin is the fruit of original sin," a doctrine whose pessimism of despair, while offset by the hope of redemption, was largely established by Saint Augustine (and Paul). The historic precedent of the presumption of guilt in the accused during the Inquisition's trials of faith reminds us of how deeply the culture of guilt is embedded in the case of Spain. Guilt is presumed in Ana's escapade with Germán: her ignorance of carnal sin is no excuse in the eyes of her governess and the townspeople of Loreto. Such an attitude is profoundly Augustinian, a view that resulted historically in a "fostering of guilt about religious ignorance . . . [and] a great lack of the distinction between sin and guilt."[83] Thus Ana's examination of conscience stems from an originary scene of culpability. The profound sense of unworthiness would not, however, be so pervasive in *La Regenta* without a substratum of belief. Belief establishes the necessary connections, the mutual dependency of guilt and the functioning of authority. The power to reveal secrets can exist only where hidden realities have become sacramentalized.

The authority to hear revelations, which is both priestly (embodied in story) and authorial (embodied in discourse), carries with it, by implication, the authority to tell. Both readers and the characters of Clarín's novel understand this as an unarticulated given. Otherwise the affective and aesthetic impact of transgression in the work would amount to little more than sexual peccadilloes. Yet we are not reading a text of the Counter-Reformation. Both sin and the authority that makes sin so powerful in *La Regenta* are profoundly problematic, first through third-person narrative irony and co-option of authority itself and, then, through the authority of the subject herself.

By turning self-examination into an autobiographical act, Alas's character subverts the structured, authorized uses of confession. Her mental compositions arise out of an unregulated imagination. "Imagination, left to itself, or badly directed," cautions Brother Philippe, "may become a great obstacle to salvation." Imagination misused, he says, leads to distraction. Or worse: to disorder, as the Jesuit de la Puente (1605) observes "of thoughts and the imagination, which are disordered, whether from injurious or vain things, or inappropriate for the occasion, or overly emphasized."[84] In practicing spiritual exercises one is asked to visualize Hell precisely in order to purge the mind of such images. In other words, Loyola uses the religious imagination to attack another kind of imagination. Sin is provoked through imagined desire, which can be overcome only by a more powerful source of the imagination, faith itself.

Imagination thus enacts a disturbingly equivocal role in *La Regenta*. To understand that role more fully, one needs to see how imagination serves as the hinge connecting the function of confession to the equally critical function of the child. Two conflicting notions of the child are at play in the novel. In one, the traditional Augustinian view of the child as being prone to evil, with original sin a constant reminder of children as transgressors, flourished in writers like Father Claret. Saint Augustine laments, "Who can recall to me the sins I committed as a baby? For in your sight no man is free from sin, not even a child who has lived only one day on earth." "I was a great sinner," he says, "for so small a boy." In the same vein, Claret warns unsuspecting parents that children are naturally corrupt and inclined toward sin, especially sins of the flesh: "As for you fathers and especially you mothers, you should never have your sons and daughters in your bed, particularly if they are more than four or five years old. What damage has come out of this! Nor should little boys and girls, even brothers and sisters, sleep together. Rest assured that I know of much wickedness coming from this." Not only was Claret's own imagination working overtime in his obsession with carnal sin. He apparently had a similar effect upon readers, to judge from the views of unsympathetic contemporaries. The *Llave de oro* (Golden key) (1857), his much-read text, drew sharp attacks from anticlericals and Protestants, who considered the sexually charged yet moralizing work filthy and scandalous, a "vile manual of confession [filled with] systematic moral poisoning [of] the minds of Spanish women." (During his apostolic missions, Claret had long lines of women waiting to be confessed by him.) In another indication of his impact on the imagination, Claret, as the queen's confessor and the author of the *Llave de oro,* figures prominently in the pornosatiric album of watercolors *Los Borbones en pelota* (The Bourbons in the raw) (1868–69), attributed to the Bécquer brothers, Valeriano and Gustavo Adolfo, under the pseudonymous, suggestively obscene name Sem.[85]

In stark contrast, the romantics idealized children as emblems of the soul and of the imagination. The loss of childhood came to be perceived as a terrible loss of self. In Spain, the cult of the child, later welded to the nineteenth-century cult of domesticity in the middle classes, does not seem, however, to have reached the fetish-extremes of worship of little girls found in English cases like Lewis Carroll's. These two highly distinguishable views of children and childhood — both present in *La Regenta* — tend to reinforce Philippe Ariès's thesis that sometime in the eighteenth century parents began to reckon consciously and caringly with the period of childhood as something distinct from adulthood in miniature. Later research suggests, however, that attitudes of concern toward children and awareness of childhood as a special state existed before the eighteenth century.[86] Such roughly established dichotomies — children as monsters, children as angels — should be taken at best as convenient classifications, at worst as reductive stereotypes.

The child in literature is an unreal construct; but with richly layered works like *La Regenta* sometimes what is real in children viewed historically acquires a heightened sense of revelation in an imaginative context. This notion, itself of romantic origin, envisions the child figure as above all a trope of memory. What Dickens creates in *David Copperfield* is remembered childhood. Or as his hero remarks, "I think the memory of most of us can go farther back into such times than many of us suppose. . . . Indeed, I think that most grown men who are remarkable in this respect, may with greater propriety be said not to have lost the faculty, than to have acquired it; the rather, as I generally observe such men to retain a certain freshness, and gentleness, and capacity of being pleased, which are also an inheritance they have preserved from their childhood."[87]

The same inner-directed drive centered on the small and distant figure of childhood fuels key chapters of Alas's novel. Memory, by plumbing backward in acts of disclosure, treats childhood as a sacred object, even when the individual experience described — as in the case of Oliver Twist, Ana Ozores, or Fermín de Pas — is devastatingly ugly. Once sacramentalized, the revealed memory, akin to confession in this respect, comes with a deep sense of loss, which is a modern form of metaphoric, psychic orphanhood. In Clarín's short story "Viaje redondo" (Round trip) (1895), a man who loses his faith and illusions speaks with gentle despair of nature as "an infinite orphanhood" and of the universe as "fatherless."[88]

In privileging the scene of Ana's childhood, Alas exploits a romantic version of the child figure, the orphan. His protagonist is, technically speaking, a half orphan, but early paternal abandonment, by which she is left to the petty tyrannies of a governess and her lover, converts Ana into a full-fledged parent-less being. The circumstances of her upbringing as a female orphan with gov-erness make one think inevitably of texts like Charlotte Brontë's *Jane Eyre* (1847) and the sentimental serial novels popular throughout Europe and the Americas.

In Brontë's novel, orphan and governess are one and the same. In *La Regenta,* they are split into two separate, antithetical, and conflictive identities. The divergent treatment of two stereotypes is significant. Jane Eyre represents a salient example of the "transcendentalizing of the orphan" into a symbol of the soul. Jane Eyre's adult position as governess does not strip her character of spiritual sensibility, but it does complicate her social situation. As paid gentle-woman she suffers from status incongruence.[89] Brontë makes the governess role acceptable for a heroine by converting the stereotype into a symbolic figure of control and self-discipline operating as a counterpoint to Jane's wild heart.

In England, as in Spain and elsewhere in Europe, the governess in real life enjoyed very little esteem and was often perceived as a potential corrupter of youth and seducer of the paterfamilias. In Spain, moreover, a foreign gov-erness or a Spanish lady-employee heavily influenced by foreign customs, while imparting social prestige to the family employing her, could pose a threat to the national and religious identities of her charges.[90] All of these popular images of the governess figure color Alas's characterization of Camila, the "Spanish Englishwoman" who takes over much of Ana's childhood. Given such negative stereotyping, Alas chose not to unite orphan and governess in one character.

There may be other, more cogent reasons for the Ana–Camila dyad. Unlike Jane, Ana Ozores never learns to govern herself; her life lacks control, a sense of order. It is a condition that to a large degree arises from her orphaned or unbonded status. Maternal loss in particular marks her mental and emotional boundaries of self. Alas's novel is as much a narrative of the human mind as it is of a city and a period.[91] In this sense, it is entirely appropriate to speak of a character's life as being the very narrative substance informing the structure of the novel. Here, Camila's role is not maternal. Rather, she functions as a repre-sentative of that external social structure of control that is internalized in the family. She educates Ana into the order of repression, an order that is also the order of carnal knowledge. Ana's governess, along with her lover and the townspeople of Loreto, can be seen as oral sources of an alternative narrative that is constructed for Ana, one in which gossip and verbal abuse reinterpret negatively both the protagonist's family romance and her adventure with Germán.

Their version of the story is a profane reading, as opposed to Ana's inner, sacramentalized "poem" or "novel" of her life that she mentally composes year after year. The narrative of self she first constructs is maternal: "The heroine of the novels which she made up at that time was a mother. At the age of six she composed a poem in her tawny-curled head. The poem was compounded from the tears shed by this ill-treated, motherless girl in her moments of deepest misery, and fragments of stories which she heard from the shepherds of Loreto and the domestics."[92] Later she adds a father-hero (Germán), but the poem, even through progressive modifications in time, consistently raises the mother to a privileged position, seemingly outside the social order.

The mother is inside Ana's head. Camila, mean-spirited and repressive, is no mother substitute. She functions in part to highlight how the maternal is bracketed elsewhere, socially and emotionally, into a protected realm of the sacred, that is, into a secret narrative of loss and longing. To be an orphan is to grieve forever, Eileen Simpson writes.[93] Ana's grief, her mourning over maternal absence, is never stated in those terms, but it is there by implication in the self as a continual fiction in the making. Camila cannot be part of Ana's configuration as a character in the same way that the governess metaphor is incorporated into Jane Eyre's self. Control is viewed externally in *La Regenta*. The mother internalized appears to move beyond questions of control into the realm of the imagination. The self as a reservoir of grief is turned into imagination. Ana's poem shows us how the self is constructed through imagining, furbished through readings — both primary and secondary, in stories and texts — of identity.

One of those readings is Saint Augustine's *Confessions,* a book more properly understood as epideictic, in praise of God, than autobiographical: "Rhetoric invented *from* the self *about* God." Alas's character, however, reads it more personally. Ana remembers especially the saint's harsh opinion of childhood as being sinful in book 1. But another intertext remains unspoken. In book 9, Augustine's mother dies. Distraught, he goes to the baths to rid his "mind of anxiety," addressing God as "O Father of orphans." "Of all this [her devoted love, her tenderness and patience]," he reveals to God, his listener, "I found myself suddenly deprived." A few lines later he says, "And now, O Lord, I make you my confession in this book." Earlier, in book 8, the saint recalls how the epiphanic moment of conversion came to him in "the singsong voice of a child," a child whose sexual identity is left ambiguous, and how he told his mother, "who was overjoyed."[94]

The linkage between conversion, confession, and the maternal is a powerful one in the *Confessions*. Ana has a similar experience, which is highly sexualized (likened to an explosion, or *estallido*) and, as with Lacan's Saint Teresa of Bernini fame, equally unknowing of ecstasy's source: "And she wept over St Augustine's *Confessions*, as over a mother's breast. In that moment her soul grew toward womanhood." Her adventure with Germán is likewise infused with the maternal as she imagines herself in the role of a mother, adrift in the tiny boat of Trébol, itself an archetypal imagining of the mother as protective vessel.[95]

Ana lives in Loreto, a name whose symbolic import seems to have escaped most commentators. Undoubtedly Loreto is meant to suggest a northern or Asturian setting. For nineteenth-century readers, however, Loreto was synonymous with the Holy House of Loreto in Italy and the Litany of Loreto — not to mention the *Madonna of Loreto*, popularly attributed to Raphael — attached to the pilgrimage site since the thirteenth century. This biblically imaged prayer invokes Mary as a sound vessel (thus linking her to the boat of Trébol), such as the Spiritual Vase (Vas spirituale), the Vase of Honor (Vas honorabile), the Tower of David (Turris Davidica), the House of Gold (Domus aurea), and so on. The cult of Our Lady of Loreto was very popular in Spain. In 1581 Philip II founded a Colegio de Nuestra Señora de Loreto for poor and orphaned girls. A French secondary school, or *colegio*, with the same name was established in Madrid in 1843. And on 21 February 1883, a newspaper in Madrid reported that "along the road of the Inn of the Holy Spirit His Majesty the King has acquired a large piece of ground where the School and Church of Loreto will soon be constructed."[96]

The imagery of Marian litanies like that of Loreto also provided motifs for the painterly representation of Mary as *tota pulchra*, all-beautiful. This was a favored depiction of the Immaculate Conception, the notion that the mother of Jesus was herself preserved free from the taint of original sin: *Regina sine labe originali concepta*, a phrase used in the Litany of Loreto by the early nineteenth century. The doctrine, which had been embraced by the Spanish court and clergy since the late Middle Ages and propagated in sixteenth- and seventeenth-century painting and sculpture notably by Diego Velázquez, Bartolomé Esteban Murillo, and Francisco de Zurbarán, became dogma in 1854. (The Virgin Immaculate became the patroness saint of Spain under Charles III.) Four years later, a fourteen-year-old girl named Bernadette Soubirous had repeated visions of Mary in a place called Lourdes. It was not long before news of Lourdes and similar visions seen by other children spread to Spain and elsewhere.[97]

There is a poetic logic to these Marian associations in *La Regenta*, for, like Mary, Ana Ozores's mother is set apart from other women, envisioned in the sacred stories Ana mentally composes. Unlike Mary, however, her mother is not free of original sin, which Clarín unorthodoxly correlates to the impropriety of mixed social origins. Over several centuries, the Immaculate Conception as doctrine had been strongly debated among Catholics and rejected by Protestants. Marina Warner writes, "By her exceptional freedom from original sin, Mary is set apart from the human race in a special and separate transhuman category. . . . Original sin is not an inherited stain, but human weakness, and to deprive Mary of it robs her of her full humanity." In Clarín's time, however, original sin retained its power among the devout, while Catholics, especially in Spain, tended to humanize Mary through the concrete effects of local religion.[98] *La Regenta* imaginatively adapts this rich spiritual culture by enshrining the mother figure as simultaneously pure in memory yet tethered to impurity.

Loreto is intimately connected to the maternal and to the female orphan. Loreto and the little boat of Trébol are fictions of originary loss, sacred memories of maternal absence. This is the Lacanian side of *La Regenta* — the feminine principle that eventually generates an orphaned narrative and an orphaned character. The other side, however, also operates in the text: the Freudian or masculine principle that converts the mother into something "improper." For this narrative we must return to Camila the governess, who reacts to the Trébol episode by exclaiming, " 'Just like her mother!' she would say to acquaintances. 'Improper, improper!' "[99]

Freudian echoes reverberate powerfully in these words. Here are anticipations of Freud's Dora and her governess, without either Freud or Alas ever knowing it. But how does Dora know? How does Ana know? How, in other words, do they come to an awareness of sinfulness, of sexual knowledge? At first, Freud says in a footnote, he thought the governess told Dora what she knew. After all, the governess was in love with Dora's father, which is another way of characterizing the governess as seductress. From perverse creatures like governesses — servants who, disquietingly, resemble their masters — come those "improper words" (*zweideutig* and *unanständig* in the original) Freud refers to later as issuing from "a second and *oral* source of information."[100] Clarín's narrative, which uses the word "improper" in English, is identical: "The governess had tried to seduce Don Carlos [Ana's father]. She knew that his late wife had been a humble dressmaker. . . . She thought that Don Carlos had married out of necessity and that he was the kind of man who marries servants." Camila's efforts at seduction fail, but, as in the Freudian narrative, her social inferiority and status incongruence produce an intolerable situation in which both control (governess as symbolic of the external social structure) and the illusion of control (governess as subordinate) operate.[101]

Camila's malice-ridden allusion to Ana's mother strikes at the very core of the novel. Ana as the issue of an upper-class father and an Italian seamstress mother points to origins saturated with another kind of status incongruence. The occupation of seamstress was frequently associated with prostitution; and female servants in general were viewed as morally suspect throughout nineteenth-century middle-class Europe. Even Ana's father, his passion cooled, eventually reduces his wife to her former position, behaving toward her, "in the end, like a good, gentle, satisfied master." At heart Don Carlos thinks all women are inferior beings. His backhanded disdain for women produces in turn "a neuter education" for his daughter, as though she had no sex.[102] Don Carlos's liberalism in this instance, exposed as spurious through narrative irony, veils a deep reluctance to deal directly with female sexuality. Like his male friends, Ana's father does not know how to talk to women. By neutering his daughter's education, he cushions Ana in ignorance.

Implicit in his tactic is the notion that female children are sexually vulnerable and must be protected from wicked thoughts, as Father Claret suggested. "There is never any danger of corrupting an inexperienced girl," Freud says, who may very well be reflecting indirectly the stereotypical view, commonly held in *fin de siècle* Vienna, that female children and adolescents were sexually precocious. Female orphans in particular seemed to be at greater risk than other children, to judge from commentaries like this one: "Young girls without mothers need to take many more precautions than others, in order to preserve and establish their credit."[103]

By denying the body of his daughter, Don Carlos buries Ana's sexual identity deeper within the body of her mind. Like the governess, he orphans her a second time by implying that a female child is found wanting in a way fundamental to human identity itself. Resembling her mother, Ana is somehow improper, has "never been born entirely." Feeling orphaned, Simpson says, is a universal condition, but when orphanhood is positioned with gender, is a female then ever properly birthed? Is not her engendering in some obscure way a monstrous birth, in which preconceptions about femaleness and female behavior have already molded the female child? Such nineteenth-century preconceptions turn into models of practice, encoded within words like Camila's "improper, improper" and Don Carlos's neutering of his daughter's education.

Ana's transformation of confession into a family romance brings together two kinds of impropriety: sexual knowledge and origins. Both are improper in the social and moral order of Restoration Spain. They occupy secret spaces in nineteenth-century narratives like *La Regenta*, where the maternal and the body infuse a sacramentalized imagination. This form of biological imagination emerges in part out of a naturalist discourse. But it is also deeply rooted within the teleological discourse of Spanish Catholicism, in which the subterranean — the material/maternal, the corporal — is linked to both infernal (sinful) and divine forces.

The two bodies of the novel — those of the text and the heroine — locate these discursive fields within a conflictive, transitional space: the stressful modernizing of Spanish society and the tentative personhood mapped out in a female self. Out of such a body-space is born the condition of being orphaned. The form of the novel itself can be imaged as an orphan, "a faintly disreputable and possibly bastardized offspring of uncertain parentage, always threatening to lose focus and definition, but . . . always managing to survive; a particular product of the modern world."[104] The orphaned state of this particular novel, however, must be placed within the genealogy of the Restoration family, which can also be understood as the familial understructure of Restoration society in general.

Seen as a familial narrative, *La Regenta* suggests a complex relationship governing kinship and textual disclosure. The desire to confess, to remember the scene of childhood, seems to issue out of transgressive impulses and actions that in turn come from presumably improper relationships and behavior. The very telling of these things is improper, underlining the intimate connection between impropriety and language, as Freud intuited in linking ambiguous, inappropriate words with an "*oral* source." Likewise, Clarín stresses Camila's use of "improper" and the pervasiveness of calumny and innuendo in Loreto and Vetusta. Isabel I's confessor, Hernando de Talavera, compares the gossipmonger's throat to the "grave filled with dead bodies, because a great stench comes from both."[105] The power of language to condemn and repress that which should not be openly spoken functions as an analogue to the power of kinship to mutilate origins and deform gender identity. What haunts a text like *La Regenta* is deprivation, the orphaning of words from their proper kinship, the disarticulation of relationship, of feeling related to things and persons around you.

Sacramentalized, narrative consciousness materializes as sinful, as that which should not and does not want to be narrated. The consciousness of telling, of confessing, seems to issue from impropriety itself. Out of the improper, then, comes imagination. Ana's disordered imagination points to the larger functioning and presence of imagination within the narrative as a whole. Gone underground, made visible as it wells upward out of secret spaces, imagination confessed is felt as a bodily power. *La Regenta* attempts to visualize the inner, subterranean life of the body, simultaneously held in contempt and yet pregnant with possibilities, wordless and inchoate (as in Ana's nightmare of Hell) and yet filled with words. The disclosure of imagination as being born from the body is new when viewed as the product of both naturalist and early psychoanalytic and psychological discursive practices. It is, however, deeply embedded within the Catholic tradition of examination of conscience and confession.

La Regenta is unquestionably a novel of disquieting modernity, but with roots profoundly buried within a religious tradition. At the same time, Clarín's novel is also a subversion of that tradition in its splitting of mind and body, making a certain kind of imagination a thing of the body alone and thus dangerous.[106] *La Regenta* shows that split as a terrible wound (Ana's divided psyche) and as a blow to imagination (symbolized in the child as reservoir of imagination and of self), a state of affairs that is institutionalized through the instruments of Church (the confessional and priesthood) and family. Ana's final appearance — as an inert body into which unspeakable sex is to be symbolically poured — is both an inversion of and reversion to suspect Vetustan values.[107] Things confessable — "the cold, viscous belly of a toad" (the acolyte Celedonio's kiss) that she feels on her lips — are a sexual inversion (Celedonio's homosexual urges masked as heterosexual desire), to use late nineteenth-century parlance, that becomes *in-verted,* incorporated into the body rather than expelled, or, in ironic Freudian terms, the repressed returned to its origins.

The image of the toad is, however, a traditional one. P. Náxera in his *Espejo místico* (Mystical mirror) tells the story of a woman confessing while a mass of toads representing sins, some larger than others, flies from her mouth.[108] Only one is left: "a vile, terribly large toad appeared between the lady's lips, attempting to get out." Because one sin is left unexpelled, all the expelled toads return to their place of origin. Later, the woman dies of asphyxiation from "a misfortune occurring in her throat, which suffocated her." That last, powerful image of *La Regenta* can be seen as a modern reversion to an older story, a story in which sin "becomes an almost material substance that 'stains' the soul."[109]

Here is the body become a repository of both divine and infernal forces — the same thing happens during Ana's nightmare of Hell — in which traditional Catholic and modern secularizing notions of the self merge, as they do throughout the narrative. Ana's expulsion from the larger body that is the body of Vetustan society and the Church is accompanied by an inward movement toward incorporation written into the last sentence of the novel. Incorporated is all that is improper — sinful, confessable matter — that in returning to its origins, to its *oral* source, underlines the protagonist's silencing as the ultimate effect of a power play, which is both secular and ecclesiastical. But once authority, narrative, religious or cultural, ceases to perform — has reached closure, or narrative absolution — so too does revelation. The ending to Alas's novel attains closure but no absolution. Narrative consciousness, in emerging out of the psychological consciousness of sin, in being confessed, is constrained in the end to return to that same secret space, that image reservoir, simultaneously banishing language as something unsayable, perhaps untouchable like cold, viscous matter, and reclaiming the imagination as forms of an improper birth.

What Clarín's heroine affirms in the last moment of her fictional life is the hell of her irremediable aloneness. In other words, she has discovered, as Nicolas Berdyaev writes, that "hell belongs entirely to the subjective and not to the objective sphere; it exists in the subject and not in the object, in man and not in God." Berdyaev continues: "In hell the soul is separated from everyone and from everything, completely isolated and at the same time enslaved by everything and everyone. . . . Hell is nothing other than complete separation from God."[110]

It is possible to see in Ana Ozores's tragic passage an inner evolution through which she passes, from a belief in the physical Ignatian reality of Hell to an understanding of Hell as the irreducible state of her own being. Thus, Hell is first dreamed as this: "She thought she could still feel the touch of coarse, salacious apparitions, covered with plague sores; smell the fetid emanations of their putrid flesh; breathe the cold, almost viscous atmosphere of the underground tunnels in which she had been imprisoned in her delirium."[111]

In the end, lying on the cathedral floor, when Ana returns "to life, overcome by nausea and tearing at the mists of delirium," when she completely interiorizes the notion of Hell, when the toad is symbolically *inside* her, she is unable to know God.[112] Some of the same elements — the cold, viscous atmosphere and sense of delirium — are present in both passages, linking them symbolically. In any event, the horrible hell of personality itself condemns the Regenta. Flaubert could accept the possibility that behind human personality there might be nothing; Clarín could not.[113] He did not know what to do with the idea of God. He was unable in his writing either to throw it out or to structure it as the prime mover of human existence.

There is something deeply troubling about this ending. It is as though the ground on which the Regenta and her readers had been standing was simply cut away and revealed in the final moment as fissured through and through, in the same way narrative reliance on the forms of religious authority slides into a quagmire of secular misgivings. A religious imagination profoundly shapes the novel, but it also pulls the world of *La Regenta* apart. There is no sense of communitas such as one sees, however fragile it may be, in Galdós's *Fortunata y Jacinta*. The social and spiritual fracture is down to the bone, the differences too sharp. Clarín's desire to graft liberal Spain onto Catholic Spain, like his character Frígilis's horticultural experiments in hybridity, is a utopian dream. At bottom, neither liberal Spain nor Catholic Spain was capable of understanding the other in the real world. And yet it would have been impossible for Clarín to have written the novel without that religious imagination. It is the sense of flawed being, conceived in sin, mired in the improper, that gives birth to the modern, secular novel that is *La Regenta,* that privileges and redeems the imagination as a sacred object even if the world has fallen apart. Clarín himself probably closely identified with the words expressed by a character in "Viaje redondo," whose "religion was the desire for religion."[114] He could not live without it but did not know how to live with it. Likewise, *La Regenta* embodies the same dilemma in historical, narrative terms: how to reconcile faith with modernity. That question would come up again, most contentiously, in 1936.

4

The Politics of Martyrdom

From 1936 to 1939 Spaniards engaged in a savage conflict over national destiny. They fought for political, socioeconomic, and religious reasons. Their views, ranging from the extreme right to the extreme left, were indicative of a profound ideological splintering of the country. The war has often been reduced to a struggle between fascism and democracy in which each side has a monolithic worldview. Both the Republicans and the Nationalists, however, were made up of diverse groups and mindsets. Franco ultimately merged through forced consensus the Alphonsine monarchists, Carlists, conservatives, and fascist-style Falangists into one National Movement. The Republicans, however, whose base included moderate democrats, socialists, anarchists, communists, and others, had to deal with two major internal difficulties: the rise of anarcho-syndicalist revolution and the growing power of the Spanish Communist Party.[1]

At the same time both sides demonized the enemy. All Republicans were Reds; all Nationalists, Fascists. Well before the war began in July 1936, an exclusionist siege mentality envisaging Armageddon raged in the flaming rhetoric of the press and the political violence of the streets. The center was evaporating as the extremes took over. A tipping point for the spiraling bloodletting and language of apocalypse was the religious question, prompting some historians to see this war as, among other things, a religious conflict or tragedy.[2] Anticlerical legislation during the Second Republic created a rapidly

deteriorating relation between Church and State and galvanized a deeply offended Catholic constituency into political action.

Committed Catholics began to see both the Second Republic and the war as
a battleground between Christianity and the Left or, more commonly, Communism. The conflict was "an armed clash between two totally opposed civil-
isations," according to Cardinal Isidro Gomá y Tomás. Elsewhere, referring to
the two sides, he called the war "infernal and divine." Of all the blunders made
by the Second Republic the worst was probably the direct attack against the
faith. Manuel Azaña, the prime minister and, later, president of the Republic,
and the Left in general seemed "unable to understand how their legislation
affected the devotional lives of ordinary Catholics." It was one thing to reduce
the power of the Church as an institution; it was another to tear at the very
fabric of faith of individual Spaniards. When crucifixes were removed from
the schools, for example, street protests and demonstrations erupted. The
silencing of church bells and prohibition of public processions hit directly at
 the concrete, sensorial way Catholicism was experienced spiritually and culturally. The Left in general badly misread the temper of the times. They under-
estimated the enduring hold of Catholicism on a significant sector of the population and demonstrated a singular insensitivity dismissive of more traditional
views. Popular religiosity and the formal practice of religion alike were deeply
interwoven into the communal life of many Spaniards, especially in villages
and small towns. Nearly 60 percent of the population lived in rural areas in
Spain in the 1930s.[3]

The religious question was thus heavily politicized, given the prevailing
secularizing aims of the Second Republic and the mobilization of the Right.
Clericalism, in turn, spurred on anticlericalism, which had been part of the
cultural-political landscape in Spain since the early nineteenth century. Indeed,
"the radicalization of anticlerical feeling that developed after 1931 was of
such an intensity that it often seems difficult to comprehend." Anticlerical
hatred erupted into a horrific killing field in the first months of the war: 6,832
clergy died, of whom 4,184 were secular clergy, 2,365 male religious, and 283
female religious.[4]

It would be impossible to understand certain kinds of narrative arising from
the Spanish Civil War in the absence of this historical and religious context.
My purpose here is to explore the impact of the religious imagination in
selected civil war writings of Republicans and Nationalists alike, emphasizing
here two texts: the Republican Ramón Sender's masterpiece, *Réquiem por un
campesino español* (1953), in relation to the Nationalist José María Carretero's (El Caballero Audaz) six-volume novelized memoirs *La revolución de
los patibularios* (1940). The writings of the two sides are not normally studied

together. Yet such juxtapositions can be productive in examining the relation between literary realism and belief.

As we have already seen, the bonds of literary realism and faith, or belief, are complex, resistant to arguments of mere influence or adaptation. Mimetic realism in general rests on the notion of verisimilitude. And verisimilitude, which convinces us of the appearance of truth or of the real in fiction, requires the suspension of disbelief. It does not ask one to consider belief in the spiritual sense, except insofar as belief figures into the narrative thematically or ideologically. In the highly secular environment of academia, moreover, most literary critics shy away from questions of belief present in narrative. While indifference and even hostility toward religion may play a role in such neglect, the indisputable difficulty of not knowing *how* to deal with the religious looms even larger.

Fiction as a secular form poses a problem from the very start. Nearly all explanations of the development of the novel rest on the secularization hypothesis: "The novel is the epic of a world that has been abandoned by God." This theory in turn depends on the larger understanding of secularization as an explanatory frame for modernity and modernization. Such a notion "contends that modernization necessarily leads to religion's decline, that the secular and the religious will not coexist in the modern world, that religion represents a premodern vestige of superstition."[5]

Secularization theory does not explain, however, why religion persists in highly modern societies like that of the United States. It does not explain why spiritual thirst continues to be a universal phenomenon. More significantly, this view, rooted in Enlightenment thought, fails to consider the possibility of religion as a point round which questions of modernity, in forms like narrative, might be approached. Faith and modernity, as I have been arguing here, are not unrelated issues, to be treated separately. Rather, part of what makes modernity so complex and vital is precisely the enduring, often conflictive presence of the religious. Nowhere is this more evident than in certain kinds of modern narrative.

The secular nature of modern narrative is not in question. What I have been exploring is precisely how secular literature like novels may open a portal into the realm of the sacred, how literature "is a place where sacred and secular meet."[6] A concrete example can be found in martyr narratives of the Spanish Civil War, in which I include Sender's *Réquiem*. The tradition of martyrdom is associated with the Nationalist side, which depicted its struggle as a holy war and crusade. In contrast, the Franco regime's crusade mentality stigmatized Republicans as an "anti-Spain" that had profaned the sacred territory of the country. Under Franco faith became nationalized. Faith belonged to the winners.

The image of Catholic martyrdom characterizes the heroes and victims of works like Carretero's *La revolución de los patibularios,* which provide insight into the ways political and religious belief systems intersect and permeate one another. Along with the blood of martyrs, the theme of resurrection runs throughout Carretero's narrative, culminating in the last volume, *¡Arriba los espectros!* (Long live our ghosts!), in which he invokes his dead compatriots. But martyrdom and resurrection also haunt Republican narratives like Sender's *Réquiem.* In a deeply ironic twist, the Republican martyrdom of the peasant Paco is remembered, and thus emotionally resurrected, through the guilty conscience of a Nationalist priest, as he prepares for the dead man's requiem mass one year later. The priest's remembrance, like the popular ballad about Paco threaded throughout, is a martyr narrative. It is also a powerful confession of guilt and betrayal, as the priest revealed Paco's hiding place to his eventual executioners.

These narratives are representative of a deeply conflictive crisis of modernity in which the disputed past never dies but is continually replayed. They reenact the political and ideological wars of the dead, brought back through the religious symbolism of martyrdom and resurrection. There is a politics of martyrdom worked out in both texts, though to different ends. Carretero, like Ayguals de Izco, as we saw earlier, continually shifts the emphasis between the religion of politics and the politics of religion. He ends up producing a series of nationalized martyrs. Sender's vision is closer to the transformative politics of martyrdom Anna Peterson sees in progressive Catholicism during the Salvadoran civil war of the late 1970s and 1980s: "Sacred history provides one of the few media through which to link [the] lives [of ordinary people] to larger forces, to conceive of their experiences as having a logic, meaning, and value beyond the immediate. This relationship between sacred and human history is two-way: just as the human becomes divinized, so the divine becomes humanized."[7]

Réquiem is appropriately regarded as an example of symbolic realism, religious imagery providing the poetic frame. Indeed, much commentary on the use of the Gospels and the Christ figure as well as Christian iconography and Church rituals has illuminated how deeply the cultural-spiritual values of Christianity shape the text. The political implications of the text have not escaped readers either. Paco is not, after all, a traditional holy figure but a seeker of social justice in a world of harsh inequities and class stratification, a major theme of the novel. Patricia McDermott observes, "As a revolutionary humanist, Paco is an ironic Christ figure."[8] Like other critics, she contrasts Christian and natural values, this juxtaposition being a constant technique of Sender.

I am not so certain, however, that the secular and the sacred can be that easily untwined in the text, in the same way that Peterson declines to separate the two in the context of El Salvador's civil war. I also wonder whether so much attention paid to religious imagery and rituals in themselves or as poetic artifice has not in effect distracted us from asking larger, more basic questions. Why, for instance, did Sender, a onetime passionate anticlerical and later a spiritual iconoclast, choose to reenact artistically the way of Christ in a secular domain? Is it really possible to talk about *Réquiem* as a religious text, and if so, how is it religious? What role does belief play in writing, especially fiction? Is symbolic realism merely symbolic, or poetic? Or does it possess a world of significance, even transcendence, that points to not only a more layered explanation and genesis of the novel form but also an intricate, uneasy relation between narrative and faith, most particularly faith in crisis?

First, though, we need to see Sender's novel more concretely situated within the context of civil war and the shared values and imaginative structure that both clericalism and anticlericalism demonstrate. Having roots in social romanticism, modern anticlericalists attacked the Church and its representatives precisely for what they regarded as the clergy's "betrayal of the values embodied in the Gospel." Thus one anarchist exile told the historian John Brademas, "'If only a man who professed to be a Christian acted like one — if only we were all genuinely Christian — then we should have no problem.'" Many working-class anticlericalists saw Christ as one of their own: "Jesús era de los nuestros," wrote A. de Lezama in 1931.[9] Much of the anticlerical violence at the start of the war issued from twin political and religious motivations. The killing of priests, the mutilations of sacred objects, the burlesque parodies of Church rites and practices, all these things were performed within a counter-ritualistic framework to destroy the power of the Church as an institution, as a class enemy, and as the bearer of community values.

Anticlericalism was not simply a sign of the growing de-Christianization of Spanish society. Flowing through working-class movements like anarchism, it was also part of a belief system rivaling that of the Church. Like the most recalcitrant elements of Church hierarchy, anticlericalism in its most extreme, violent forms was absolutist and intolerant of dissent.[10] Wartime anticlerical violence happened "because there was a patrimony of culture, values, and persecutory and purging needs, shared by that Church — which was, after all, the Church of the Inquisition, the Church most infamous for its persecution of heretics — and its enemies." During the war Nationalists used a language of purification in identifying and killing Republicans as sources of pollution perceived as threatening to the community. Similarly, the church burnings in May 1931, shortly after the Second Republic was proclaimed, and in 1936 represented a peculiar form of auto de fe, a purging of religious symbols and habitations, purification by fire: "Que el fuego todo lo purifica." Accompanying what the Church called "the martyrdom of things" was the martyrdom of persons, of secular and regular clergy, often so theatrical and ritualized that such acts appear to mimic in cruel irony the faith itself.[11]

While no priest dies in Sender's *Réquiem, El cura de Almuniaced* (The priest of Almuniaced) (1950), a beautifully written and much more neglected novella by Sender's fellow Republican and Aragonese exile José Ramón Arana, ends with the violent death of its central character, a priest, at the hands of a Nationalist Moroccan mercenary. In this regard, the bloody backdrop of atrocities on both sides needs to be taken into account in civil war narratives. If there is something unsayable in *Réquiem,* if betrayal and guilt lie barely repressed beneath the narrative surface, it is because there is something unspeakable about the Spanish Civil War itself. The uncomfortable truth of universal betrayal and mutual brutality is written into texts like *Réquiem* and *El cura de Almuniaced* in the painterly form of a pentimento, in the textual undertow of a palimpsest of impossible atonement. How else is one to interpret the ambiguous ending of Arana's novel, as the priest, a good and decent man, lies dying and his housekeeper cries out that it was his own people who killed him. The priest, in turn, "shakes his head no and, plunging downward, sinks into a wave of silence."[12] It would be easy to read his death as a clear-cut condemnation of Nationalist barbarity. Yet this interpretation begs the question: Who indeed are the priest's own people? who are the people? who is responsible?

These are difficult, perhaps impossible, questions to answer. They speak not only to the extreme aggression of civil wars as *cas-limites,* but also to the ways in which the dreaded aura of violence evokes and becomes bound up in a world of tainted transcendence. In civil war each side is convinced of the rightness, the moral significance, of its cause. Perhaps too for this reason Nationalists and Republicans alike persisted in denying the extent of atrocities their side committed. The fervent Franco supporter and propagandist Luis Bolín is quick to see Republican excesses but is blind to those of his own side. "As war progressed," he remarks in 1967, "I learnt to be surprised at nothing which the Reds could think of or do." And when the war ends, he writes disingenuously, "We were all Spaniards again. No longer did anybody speak of 'Reds' or 'Republicans,'" though he refers continually to the losing side as Reds throughout the book, and Franco certainly didn't hesitate in meting out to the "anti-Spain" harsh punishment in the 1940s. As late as 1996, a pro-Franco American historian denied the well-documented Nationalist massacre of Republicans at Badajoz, calling it "wildly exaggerated by foreign correspondents" and thus proving his point that "there are no neutral histories of the Spanish Civil War."[13]

On the Republican side there are equal claims to historical silence and equivocation. Laurence Fernsworth declared in 1938, "It is not a fact as it is stated to be, that the [Republican] government liquidated the clergy." True enough, yet he does not speak of the militias, principally though not exclusively anarcho-syndicalists, who went on a massive anticlerical killing spree in the Republican zone. In 1954, Claude Bowers, the U.S. ambassador to Spain during the war, said, "The atheistic anarchists . . . killed some priests, though the number was grossly exaggerated in the foreign press."[14] (Both sides attributed misinformation to outside sources; there was both truth and untruth in such allegations.)

An even more telling example of denial is contained in Antonio Bahamonde's *Memoirs of a Nationalist* (1939). Bahamonde was General Gonzalo Queipo de Llano's chief propaganda officer. A devout Catholic, he fled the Nationalist zone to the other side, denouncing the repression he had seen in Andalucía. Chapter 6 of his memoirs, which was reprinted largely intact in Alvah Bessie's well-known anthology *The Heart of Spain,* focuses on the clergy. Taking the standard Republican position, he declared, "The clergy in Spain has rarely been found on the side of the people." As is true of many rhetorical statements coming from both sides, this one needs to be read with caution. On the one hand, it is true that most of the Church sided with the Nationalists during the war. On the other, the speaker makes a far-reaching claim that is not backed up by historical evidence. Nor should one accept unquestioningly the Republican provenance of "the people." The people could also be found on the other side. Thousands of peasants from Navarre, to give but one example, joined Franco's forces. And roughly half the population of Spain supported the Nationalists. In the Popular Front elections of February 1936, "the victorious left totally ignored the fact that they had won only about two percent more of the popular vote than the right and right-center combined."[15]

On the anticlerical violence Bahamonde has this to say: "If the clergy had remained neutral, it would have suffered no harm. But they left their priestly ministrations to convert themselves into belligerents, and must be treated as belligerents. They asked for it." It is disingenuous to suggest that neutrality could protect anyone from reprisals during a civil war. Reporting from the Nationalist zone, Bahamonde probably saw little if any of the anticlerical violence in Republican-held areas and thus could not fairly comment on the motivations behind such acts. He bases his accusations of clerical belligerence on one personal contact with a gun—toting priest, who claimed to have dispatched over a hundred "Marxists," and on hearsay. Most historians now discount the tales of priests firing from bell towers upon the people as popular recollections of nineteenth-century guerrilla priests during the Carlist Wars.[16]

Nor does Bahamonde appear to be aware that the initial killing of clergy occurred either before or at the same time as Nationalist atrocities. Chronologically, the crusade rhetoric of the Church appeared in print *after* the anticlerical killings, leading one historian to suggest that "it might be more realistic to invert the conventionally-accepted sequence of events, from 'first crusade, then persecution' to 'first persecution, then crusade.' "[17] That said, the language of martyrdom and holy war existed well before the outbreak of war.

Significantly, many clergy were killed simply because they were priests. It didn't seem to matter whether individual members of the Church were perceived as having betrayed the message of Christ or not. Indeed, many victims were, in Stanley Payne's words, "simple, poor parish priests of modest background." The bodies of clergy frequently showed signs of mutilation and profane acts, revealing the lethal use of disproportionate force against the corpse itself. When Bahamonde says that "priests, as such, have [not] been assassinated," it is hard to reconcile that statement with the explicit political aims of anarcho-syndicalists and others of ridding Spain entirely of religion and its representatives.[18]

My point in noting this mutual blindness of both sides to atrocities committed by their own and the soft-peddling or justification of clerical deaths in particular is not to single out individual participants, to lay blame. It is not to compare the statistics of culpability but to suggest that civil war leaves a stain of catastrophe and moral waste that few are prepared to face.[19] Hence Bahamonde's rationalizing of priest killings. Or the charge of statistical exaggeration of death. In the discussion that follows the attention paid to left-wing violence against clergy is not at all meant to cut the Nationalists any slack for their own atrocities but issues inevitably from the nature of the subject at hand.

Narratives like Sender's *Réquiem* and Arana's *El cura de Almuniaced* reenact this moral and physical blight, while investing it with an aura of transcendence. In some ways, Sender's text in particular appears to appropriate the religious symbols and traditions that were closely associated with the Nationalists and clothe them in new significance. The question is, why? Part of this has to do with the context of the civil war itself. The Right quickly latched onto a rhetoric of rightness, declaring the conflict a crusade. One Dominican wrote in capitals, "The Spanish national war is a holy war, the holiest recorded in history." Such imagery had a long tradition in medieval Christendom and in nineteenth-century Spain, with the Carlists and Integrists. Thus in 1884, the churchman Sardá y Salvany urged the founding of a Catholic political party as part of a national crusade, referring to Spain as "the land of the eternal crusade." By the 1930s the ultramonarchist, Catholic traditionalist movement, moribund at the turn of the century, was in full revival mode. Carlist *requetés* (militiamen) sprang into action, Sacred Heart badges (*detentes*) and other religious objects pinned to their breast. As one requeté put it, "I never knew so thrilling a joy as seized us. We did not know if we would soon be martyrs or victors. We knew surely that by this we would act above all for God."[20]

Religious fervor was not in evidence, however, in the initial manifestos of the military uprising, which spoke of defeating Communism and disorder and of reestablishing Spain's unity. But as the military coup turned into dreaded civil war, amid persecution of the Church, religious and military rhetoric soon fused. There was also an immediate precedent: the Church could recall the violent deaths of thirty-four priests and religious during the Asturian Revolution in October 1934. Thus we read in one contemporary account that "the blood of martyrs is the seed of Christians." The Tertullian phrase — "Sanguis martyrum, semen christianorum" — shows up over and over in Nationalist martyrdom literature. Pointedly (and improbably), says the author-hagiographer Francisco Martínez, blood continued to flow from the shoe of Brother Juan Arconada sixteen days after his death.[21]

Martyrdom became part of the Nationalist rhetoric of crusade. The fallen, whether lay or clerical, were "Martyrs of the Crusade," a phrase that became a leitmotif of the literature. One of the better-known texts of the period was Father Luis Carreras's *Grandeza cristiana de España: Notas sobre la persecución religiosa* (1938), which was translated as *The Glory of Martyred Spain: Notes on the Religious Persecution* in 1939. A supporter of the Republic in 1931, Carreras could not stomach the explosion of anticlerical bloodletting in July and August 1936 and became a propagandist for the Nationalists. He regarded the violence as "a new kind of sadism the intensity and extent of which had never previously been known." Cardinal Gomá y Tomás's widely distributed pastoral letter "El caso de España" (November 1936) became *The Martyrdom of Spain* in the version published for the pro-Nationalist Irish Christian Front. Elsewhere, he spoke of the "power of blood" in martyrdom. Books like Fray Justo Pérez de Urbel's *Los mártires de la iglesia (Testigos de su fe)* (The martyrs of the Church [Witnesses to faith]) (1956) and Antonio Montero Moreno's *Historia de la persecución religiosa en España 1936–1939* (1961) continued the tradition of martyrology during the Franco dictatorship.[22]

Churchmen also relied on the Augustinian trope of the two cities in making distinctions between the Republicans and the Nationalists. The bishop of Salamanca wrote, "Before so much human degradation of the godless earthly city flourishes the heavenly city of the children of God, whose divine love elevates them to the sublime glories of heroism and martyrdom." The godless city was also a savage "horde," while Catholics represented the "people." Pérez de Urbel, who would later become the abbot of the Benedictine Monastery at the Valley of the Fallen, connected Red aggression to the color red in a simultaneously metaphorical and literal way: " 'Red.' Red is the color of sacrilege; red are the infernal flames destructive of temples and sacred objects; red is the fury of bestial, mad rage; red is the innocent, sacred blood impiously, criminally spilt, out of hatred of God, of virtue and of Spain."[23]

The spilling of blood appears to overflow its own meanings here. Like most churchmen, Pérez de Urbel relies rhetorically and spiritually upon the significance of the blood of martyrs, which is intimately bound to the founding of Christianity and the belief in resurrection.[24] The color of blood has also become hopelessly politicized, as red takes on the hues of the enemy itself: a godless, Marxist anti-Spain enveloped in tainted transcendence. The language is apocalyptic, and this twenty years after the start of war.

The Nationalists had no monopoly on blood or martyrdom, however. Bahamonde writes, "In Spain the 'reds' are with Franco and are Queipo and his group. 'Red' because they are tinted by the blood of thousands for whose deaths they alone are responsible."[25] Here, blood is a stain of culpability, as the color is presumably drained of its political aura, wherein Nationalist rhetoric linked red with the Republicans.

Sharing the same Catholic culture, Republican supporters also used the image of martyrdom. One has only to think of Lorca's allusion to "the spilt blood" or the "thousand little trees of blood" to see the lasting effects of a childhood steeped in Catholic martyrology and rituals. Martyr imagery was reproduced in saints' lives, emblem books, and devotional literature and installed as adornments in Spanish churches. Such imagery was richly favored in Jesuit art of the sixteenth through the eighteenth centuries especially, as a way "to revive the religious fervor of the early Christian period." The Jesuits insisted that "pictures of martyrdom should be bloody and vivid."[26]

Relics of such imagery, now secularized, also appeared in non-Spanish works like Louis Delaprée's passionate dispatches on the relentless Nationalist bombing of Madrid's civilian population. These were collected and published as *The Martyrdom of Madrid* (1937). "I number the ruins," he wrote, "I count the dead, I weigh the blood spilt." One of the more thoughtful accounts of the background to civil war is Alfred Mendizábal's, which was tellingly translated as *The Martyrdom of Spain: Origins of a Civil War* in 1938, with an introduction by the French Catholic philosopher Jacques Maritain. Mendizábal, a law professor at the University of Oviedo, was a conservative Catholic Republican who presided in Paris over the Comité pour la Paix Civile en Espagne. Maritain's introduction has become better known than the book itself for its withering critique of the concept of holy war: "Just or unjust, war against a foreign power or war against fellow-citizens remains . . . , of necessity, what it really is by its own nature, something profane and secular, not sacred. . . . And if sacred values are in question, defended by one side and attacked by the other, this does not make the profane complex either holy or sacred; on the contrary, the sacred values are secularized by this profane complex and dragged down to its temporal ends."[27]

Maritain explicitly attacks the Nationalists for justifying the revolt as holy, but he adds that "the militant Reds are also waging a holy war." He sees repeated acts of profanation among both Republicans and Nationalists: "It is horrible sacrilege to massacre priests—be they 'Fascists,' they are still ministers of Christ—out of hatred for religion; and it is another sacrilege, horrible also, to massacre poor people—be they 'Marxists,' they are still the people of Christ—in the name of religion." At the same time he notes the martyrdom of priests in both zones, in particular that of the Basque clergy, punished by Franco's forces for remaining loyal to the Republican government. (Claude Bowers devotes a chapter to "the martyrdom of the Basques.") For Maritain, the Spanish Civil War is, quite simply, "a war of extermination."[28] Another fervid Catholic, Georges Bernanos, who witnessed the Nationalist terror in Palma de Mallorca, called the war a charnel house and the insurgents' crusade a farce. He went so far as to say that "Christianity has been the making of Europe. Christianity is dead." His son was a lieutenant in the Falange.[29]

Republican supporters of the extreme left also appropriated the imagery of crusade and holy war. Gustav Regler, a Communist and political commissar during the war, spoke of how "[a] holy war must be fought." Serving in an anarchist militia, M. Casanova wrote of "a just and sacred war on the side of the oppressed, of those who are the torchbearers of progress and new human values." *Mundo Obrero* (Workers' world) said that "the struggle between democracy and fascism" had "become transformed into a holy, into a national war, into a defensive war of the people." Ernest Hemingway's Robert Jordan likened the atmosphere at the International Brigade headquarters to that of a crusade: "That was the only word for it although it was a word that had been so worn and abused that it no longer gave its true meaning. . . . [Nevertheless, there] was a feeling of consecration to a duty toward all of the oppressed of the world."[30]

Such rhetoric served an ideological agenda different from that of the Nationalists. Not unexpectedly, on both sides ideology was exclusionist, allowing no room for the enemy and no possibility of compromise or accommodation. In the heat of war and in the fatal clash of belief systems, the notion that some day atonement might be due was scarcely heard (nor expected). Voices like those of Maritain and Bernanos were drowned out in the mutual clamor of revenge and hatred. The imagery of martyrdom and holy war emotionally bolstered people's morale and attitudes; it did not make for clear or impartial thinking.

Part of what is remarkable in postwar texts like those of Sender and Arana is how they enlarge the narrow confines of the martyr narrative by asking the reader to consider within the aesthetic realm the ethical dimensions of faith and conflict, of faith in conflict. Remaining Republican-inspired and secular, such narratives suggest that the religious imagination can not only shape structure and perspective but open them up to the world by focusing on ethical and religious issues of belief and social concern. Whatever the personal credo of the writer, the writing itself, its symbolic realism, issues from a deeper source than poetic artifice and poses questions about the relation between fictional realism and belief. The powerful presence of resurrection in *Réquiem* and the undercurrent of atonement in both these texts should, moreover, prompt two fundamental questions. To what extent do religious values determine how we read secular systems like literary realism? Does realism depend in part on nonsecular values that also make us believe in what we read?

Not all narratives of the Spanish Civil War fit this form. Some civil war narrative makes use of a Catholic imaginary but fails to rise above ideological and political pursuits. While the religious question was undoubtedly politicized by both sides, and fiction cannot fully escape the constraints of worldly ideology, aesthetic achievement lifts narrative into a different dimension. To appreciate more fully the exceptional quality of Sender and Arana and the context in which their novels were produced, one needs to examine lesser works of the period as well. An immensely popular and now almost completely forgotten example of this writing, generally triumphalist and ideologically unrepentant, is Carretero's *La revolución de los patibularios,* a fictionalized account of his experiences while trapped in the besieged capital.

Who was Carretero? Better known as "El Caballero Audaz" (The bold cavalier) (1887–1951), he was a highly successful and early practitioner of that staple of modern life, the celebrity interview. He also made a great deal of money writing erotic novels, some of them close to soft porn. During the dictatorship of Primo de Rivera he moved more and more to the right, producing pamphlets that one historian has called demagogic, libelous, and among "the most polemical and most shoddily written works" of the period. In response to the October Revolution in 1934, he promoted an aggressive Catholicism.[31] The narrative that interests me here has not fallen far from the tree.

In Madrid Carretero lived large and flaunted his success. There is a wonderful if unsympathetic portrait of him in Rafael Cansinos-Asséns's memoirs: "Suddenly the corpulent figure of "The Bold Cavalier" popped up. . . . Tall, practically a giant . . . , arrogant, fat, well dressed with a fantastic waistcoat and buttoned boots . . . the arriviste who owes his fame to those trashy erotic novels . . . and his flashy, vulgar luxury, his fur coat, massive rings and stick pin, his marriage to a menopausal cocotte, "The Bold Carretero," with his loud plebeian voice, like an Andalusian peasant, launches an assault challenging and insulting the speakers who preceded him. . . . But no one dares to make even the least aggressive move. This pornographic novelist has the biceps of a boxer and is an expert bully besides!"[32]

Like Ayguals de Izco, Carretero was a tireless self-promoter. He shamelessly shilled his books through his own publishing house and urged his readers not to lend their copy to anyone else: "Don't forget that a lent book is a book lost for you and for us," he says at the end of each of the first five volumes of his fictionalized memoirs. The first two volumes sold for seven pesetas each; starting with the third volume, he raised the price to eight pesetas. Subscribers to the first five books paid thirty-five pesetas. He added a sixth, as the material seemed to overflow the original plan of five. The series went through at least four printings the first year, with over eight thousand subscribers to the set of six. In volume 1, Carretero claims that before the war his publishing house had more than twenty thousand subscribers.[33] He destroyed the list for fear it would fall into the wrong hands.

The six volumes are as follows: *Declaración de guerra* (Declaration of war); *El cuartel de la Montaña* (The Montaña barracks); *Nosotros los mártires* (We martyrs); *La quinta columna* (The fifth column); *La ciudad inmolada* (The sacrificed city); and *¡Arriba los espectros!* (Long live our ghosts!).

In line with his huge ego, he writes in the prologue to volume 6, "God wanted me to speak, not in His name, but in the name of the thousands and thousands of specters who at night . . . fill its streets, draw close . . . and seem to say to us:

" 'Do you see how there wasn't enough earth to bury us? Our sacrifice will not be in vain; God's designs were to bring us to Glory, closer to Him, so that you could finally enjoy on earth your day of Justice.' " Despite appearing as the protagonist in much of the six volumes, he says his intention was not to make himself out as a "hero, archetype or symbol of the infinite suffering that Madrid experienced during the Red tyranny," only to offer his testimony, "free of partisan passion, free of prejudice, without a trace of hatred or rancor."[34]

Nothing, alas, could be farther from the truth. Carretero's novelized memoirs appear to have been written in a sustained rhetorical frenzy of heightened hysteria, in which the trope of martyrdom bleeds profusely on page after page. It is impossible to ignore his ubiquitous presence as nearly everything is sifted through his own perspective. While there is not a drop of subtlety or nuance in this narrative of Manichean dimensions, Carretero was nonetheless a gifted storyteller. Despite the diatribe and cheap shots at the Republican side, the roughshod narrative, though crude, has a driving force behind it.

That force is above all Carretero himself. The same self-righteous sense of personal identification with collective destiny is stamped into another book I have no doubt he read, Ernesto Giménez Caballero's influential *Genio de España: Exaltaciones a una resurrección nacional. Y del mundo* (The genius of Spain: In exaltation of a national resurrection. And of the world), published in 1932. The edition I have is the fifth, from 1939, with additional material reflecting the wartime period. In the preface to the third edition (1938), he says, "In giving this work to the Combatants of Spain, I give them a sacred deposit which was not mine: a Voice that chose me as the tremulous transmitter, on a long-ago day. The—historic—Voice of the finest dead that the life of Spain had to offer." Like other books produced by the extreme right, this one is filled with self-fulfilling prophecy: "In this book such a firm prophetic spirit beats that its prophecies are now living history. Its faith: a Spanish reality."[35] Carretero's narrative follows a similar vein. Significantly, he shares the same vision: that his voice, like Giménez Caballero's, is joined to the voices of the dead.

The dead are an obsession of Giménez Caballero: "The solution for national life is found always in death, in the dead. The only thing alive, eternally alive, that a nation possesses is its dead. . . . Don't think that in saying this I am thinking about a "cult of the dead," or a "land of forebears." . . . A nation's dead is us . . . the living themselves of this nation, the collective sense of a nation's *living*. For the dead of a nation live in *everything* and in everyone."[36]

Despite his disclaimer, this is indeed a cult of the dead, a shared preoccupation of extreme right-wing ideologies like fascism and *falangismo*. Giménez Caballero identifies the dead with both tradition and the genius, or *genio*, of Spain, but of course *genio* also refers to the peculiar character or temperament of a person or, in this case, of a nation. The dead are, paradoxically, the living past of Spain, incarnated in the nation's people.

This notion is predicated on that of resurrection. When Giménez Caballero explains the significance of the military coup by Primo de Rivera in 1923, he says that the dictator "pacified Morocco," the protectorate having long been a thorn in the political and military life of Spain. But Primo also "pacified life on the peninsula out of uneasiness. He pacified Spain out of corpses. People went back to sleep. That is, to die. And that dream of death dragged the Dictator to death. And right away, the ghosts returned. They returned and were incarnated in the newly dead, in new incitements of life."[37]

The dead not only invade the living but populate an entire city in El Caballero Audaz's narrative from the first to the last volume. Thus in volume 1 as he outlines the series, he says that when Franco's troops entered Madrid in late

Figure 9. Cover illustration, *¡Arriba los espectros!* (Long live our ghosts!), by José María Carretero (El Caballero Audaz) (1940).

March 1939, the city "was like a cadaver that, galvanized by faith, stood up once more. . . . This is the city from whose hiding places emerged processions of specters, like larvae from the sockets of a skeleton, lives racked by suffering, souls collapsed by pain."[38] The imagery of ghostly return, which signals the climax of Carretero's narrative, the liberation of Madrid and, by extension, of Spain by Franco, reveals the structure of his story to be proleptic in the extreme: the anticipation of the future as apocalypse, which signifies the end of the world but also the resurrection of the dead.

The dead are everywhere, in the most literal sense of the killing fields into which the cemeteries, streets, and kangaroo courts, or *chekas,* had turned Madrid. Carretero describes bodies found in all these places. In the streets dead bodies appear with the dawn, anonymous, stripped of all human identity. In the morgue, the bodies become a spectacle, bearing "the red furrow of autopsy, like an enormous seam or the mark of a saw's teeth beneath the breast."[39]

The overwhelming presence of death transforms the capital into a vast cemetery, recalling Larra's image in "Día de difuntos de 1836" ("Day of the Dead, 1836"): "Madrid is an immense cemetery, in which, thanks to a miraculous survival, teem hundreds of thousands of sad, skeletal figures simulating the appearance of life. . . . Madrid doesn't exist. . . . Madrid died: of hunger, cold, and terror. . . . Madrid, like a gigantic pantheon, is filled with shadows and belongs to its ghosts."[40]

At one point, Carretero, in hiding from the Republicans, finds himself literally entombed among the dead. He acquires false papers, assuming a new identity, but is forced to take refuge in a mausoleum in the Cemetery of the East. (How much of his story is true I cannot verify.) There he peruses the tombstones of his uncommunicative neighbors, meditating on the leveling effects of death in "the somber and nauseating kingdom of decay." Recalling Tediato in Cadalso's *Noches lúgubres,* he becomes "obsessed with the idea that I was no longer a stranger, an intruder in this pavilion of the cemetery, but that this place was mine by right and forever. . . . I too was a dead man, one more corpse." He imagines how his death notice in the newspapers will read and eventually scratches on an unmarked gravestone his name and pseudonym. "The man I was has died," he says, "and is buried in this niche."[41] He sees himself as his own double and shortly afterward is liberated from his living entombment. No doubt this episode in the "Mansion of the Dead," as Carretero calls it, is a rite of passage, traversing symbolic death to rebirth.

So much death comes almost exclusively with martyrdom. From the very beginning Carretero is drawn to violent death and sacrifice. When civil war erupted, he was preparing a book on the rightist politician José Calvo Sotelo, whose assassination in July 1936 was the final act of provocation. For El Caballero Audaz, Calvo Sotelo was a protomartyr, a term used to describe the first Christian martyr, Saint Stephen. He describes in great detail the politician's blood-spattered body as it lay in the morgue: "Blood everywhere. Blood from the crime that had changed the color of his suit. The cloth scarcely preserved its original shade of gray. . . . The rest was soaked in great dark stains, of a muddy purplish hue, dried and stiff. Coagulated, even shiny, drops of red invaded his shirt front and dripped in clots to the platform."[42]

Figure 10. Cover illustration, *Nosotros los mártires* (We martyrs), by José María Carretero (El Caballero Audaz) (1940).

The description continues for three more pages. Carretero and the other witnesses cannot take their eyes off "the body of the martyr, with its sunken cheeks, its mouth twisted in a macabre grin, the livid forehead, the nose broken by a brutal contusion." This kind of grotesque realism calls to mind the *tremendismo* style of Camilo José Cela and other novelists in the 1940s with its rhetorical-ideological dimension emerging directly from the war and from writings like Carretero's.[43] The aura of transcendence associated with martyrdom is heavily politicized in the secular figure of Calvo Sotelo and colors our reading of the remaining volumes.

Everyone on the Nationalist side is a martyr, as the title of the third volume, *Nosotros los mártires,* reveals. One of the more memorable — and horrific — scenes of martyrdom comes in the last volume, when two children are blown up as they play with a hand grenade. Carretero focuses (not for the first time) on body parts: "The belly is a shapeless hole, in which one can see his smashed guts, blood, bones sticking through the blackened skin. His face is also a dark mass, swollen and horrible. Not far away is another small child lying in a pool of blood. He is face down. . . . His torso contracts, distends, ripples like that of a reptile. An arm is missing, as if it had been hacked off by the blow of an axe. He twists screaming and howling with a voice that doesn't seem human or childlike."[44]

Someone gives Carretero the bloody, earth-stained arm, "the tiny hand hanging limply, like one of those ex votos of wax that adorn the altars with images made famous for their miracles." His jacket and pants are spattered with the blood from the arm, which he calls a relic. The two children are from a Nationalist family, while the crowd surrounding the class-biased writer is "rabble." He is horrified to see himself momentarily "converted into a specious saint for the unwashed plebes," though he recognizes their genuine warmheartedness. After managing to badger an unwilling driver into taking the children to a clinic, Carretero gives him the child's arm: "Inexplicably . . . I was finding it very difficult to part from that fragile, dead member, as if it were the body of a son or of a dear brother."[45]

Here is a vivid example of how the rhetoric of martyrdom converts bodies into sacred relics, into the bearers of symbolic significance. In speaking of the violent death and cremation of a Carmelite padre, Fray Justo Pérez de Urbel remarks, "We do not possess the relic of his body." In another instance, Father Antonio Montero Moreno relates how, when the Church went underground, nuns wore the host hidden around their necks, like a reliquary: "As there are no tabernacles [*sagrarios*], you yourselves will become one." The bodies of religious are "made holy not only by their moral lives, but also by the sacraments which they have received." A Jesuit supporter of Franco said they were "living temples of God."[46]

Carretero follows a long tradition of sacralizing the human body, as we see in the abundance of medieval and modern hagiographies recounting the lives and martyrdom of saints. Hippolyte Delehaye observes, "The legend is the history that has to be read, *legenda,* on the feast of a saint. It is the passion of the martyr . . . , without reference to its historical value." Like the tales of heroes and warriors, stories of martyrdom single out the special qualities of an individual, which are enhanced with the aura of sacrifice. The generic, repetitive nature of traditional martyrologies seems to work against such singularity. Yet for believers of a different era they excited religious emotion and represented "human creatures lifted up above matter and above the miseries of our little world."[47]

These retellings are also made memorable through their association with specific dates. The fourth volume of Carretero's narrative begins with an impassioned yet elegiac commemoration of the "Day of the Dead, 1936," with obvious reference to Larra's essay of a century earlier. On this particular November 2 the persecuted are the dead, ghosts of what they once were. Later, he says, "The war, which for all decent folk was a school of experience and sacrifice, taught us this imponderable value of the calendar of events, reviving in our souls a personal devotion to special days, like the bonds of faith, of tradition and memory. . . . Christmas Eve 1936. The terrible year. . . . The first, wretched year. The heartfelt, sentimental and religious influence of this day is clear and unavoidable."[48]

Consecrated days like the Victory Parade on April 1 and July 18, the start of the rebellion, were to become fixtures of the Franco regime, but Nationalist commemorations, along with monuments, plaques, and crosses dotting the Spanish urban and rural landscape, were being celebrated and erected even as war raged. Wartime tourism to battlefields further promoted the sacredness of dead bodies and holy sites.[49]

Carretero's emphasis on dates makes explicit the self-conscious creation of a narrative of significance, a *legenda*, its very qualities of fictiveness highlighted not only by the attention to dates but to the physical sites of Nationalist martyrdom, such as the besieged Alcázar of Toledo, the battle at the Montaña barracks, the cemeteries, streets, and houses, indeed, the entire city of Madrid. In hiding, Carretero at one point finds himself literally swinging in midair, hoisted on an improvised hammock of ropes in the inner courtyard of an apartment building. "I became a thing," he writes, "one more shattered object that belonged to the ruins of the martyred city."[50]

Here is a clear instance, one of many, of the intimate bond between city and person, space and body, in the creation of this protracted six-volume martyr narrative. Indeed, Carretero's own body becomes a singular example of how he saw the privations and sufferings of the Nationalists' experience in "red" Madrid, a much-exploited theme in the immediate postwar period: "My thinness was now skeletal. I had eliminated all body fat, which was perhaps the reason for the constant, depressing cold that made me go numb all the time.

My muscles, once powerful, were weak, and the least bit of effort tired me out, causing me to wheeze like a bellows."[51]

Many people, Republicans and Nationalists alike, were at the point of starvation by the time the siege lifted in Madrid. Carretero, however, has little compassion for the other side, which he, like José María Pemán, Agustín de Foxá, and others of the extreme right, sees as inhuman and bestial. And yet he himself feels like a "thing." Elsewhere, he says, "Knowing ourselves to be like a thing, like a wisp in the air, or a coin tossed on a bet, is both demoralizing and distressing."[52]

Here one can see how Carretero has grasped, however myopic his sectarianism, the simultaneously profane and sacred nature of the human body when pressed to its limits. The body is both thing and person. Traditional martyr narratives tend to multiply the number of torments to which a future saint is subjected. A simple account, in its first telling, becomes more elaborate with the passage of time, especially in the number of body parts put to the test.[53] Amplification of such torments is the narrative equivalent of the relic. Like the bones and ashes of heroes in an earlier age, relics not only honor but represent the remains of holy persons and martyrs. They are the metonymical reenactment of personhood. Carretero's drawn-out narrative, as five volumes turn into six, works obsessively on the principle of *amplificatio,* in both thought and speech, as he dwells repeatedly on the metaphorical and literal figure of martyrdom in example after example. His chief preoccupation is dual: to at once extol Nationalist sacrifice at the hands of demonized Republicans and excite the emotions of terror and pity in his readers. The rhetoric of excess, however, turns desire for the sublime into the overkill of amplification.[54]

Amplification operates as a strategy and as an emotional effect in the horrendous descriptions of violent death (those of Calvo Sotelo and the two children, for example) that are strewn across the pages of Carretero's narrative as if they were both sacred sites of flesh and blood and spectacles of horror; hence the odd stylistic fusion of grotesque realism and sacred imagery. In truth, this is El Caballero Audaz's erstwhile pornographic imagination at work, opening a window onto "the pornography of violence," a phrase that the American writer Gamel Woolsey coined in *Malaga Burning* (1939) to describe the atrocity stories told on both sides during the Spanish Civil War. Woolsey, who was living with her husband, Gerald Brenan, in a small village outside Málaga when war erupted, talked of "the dreamy lustful look that accompanies [such stories]." Knowing full well that many horrific acts of violence had occurred, she argued, nonetheless, that most of the atrocity stories were "products of the diseased and perverse imagination."[55]

Catching a lift on a truck on the way to Málaga, Woolsey sees the body of a dead man lying beside the road. It was the body of a large old man dressed in trousers and a white shirt, and it lay on its back with one hand thrown over the head and the other still clasping the torn stomach. The face was glazed with blood and the shirt was almost crimson with it. The thing that was lying there seemed too large and stiff ever to have been a man. It looked like a large dirty doll someone had thrown away.

I only saw the body for a minute. But in that minute I had a very intense and curious impression. I not only knew that what I saw was not alive, I knew that it *never had been alive*. That thing I saw lying beside the road was a cast-away mechanical doll, a broken automaton, nothing more. It never had been anything more.[56]

Woolsey's view of the civil war dead is strikingly different from that of Carretero. The details are certainly vivid, even graphic, as in Carretero, but the overall impression achieved is to deemphasize dramatically the corpse's humanness. By means of this rhetorical strategy, she reveals not insensitivity but the consequences of civil war. It is war that turns the old man into a broken doll, into a thing less than human. There is nothing sacred here. Or pornographic.

Carretero creates a linkage between the sacred and the pornographic, an association that Woolsey does not make. The sacred pornography of violence also characterizes anticlerical killings and acts of profanation on the other side. Anarchists and other groups aimed at desacralizing the Church and its representatives. One of the more shocking episodes — part of the wars of the dead — was the exhumation and display of mummified nuns in front of churches. Bruce Lincoln observes, "It was through their savage violation of sacred objects — a corpse being as much an *object* as it is a *person* — that the exhumers dramatized their rejection of all claims to sacred status." That said, the unearthing of dead religious, ostensibly meant to reveal the dirty secrets and scandals of the Church, also uncovers another layer of the sacred: the residue of power that same faith still exerted over the unbelievers. Had the Church been of little importance in the social fabric of Spanish life, none of these acts would have occurred.[57]

Disproportionate rage mixed with mockery accompanied such acts. Historians and anthropologists alike have speculated why children laughed when they saw the dead bodies of Salesian nuns displayed at La Enseñanza Church in Barcelona. Mary Vincent says that "their laughter was directed at the actual corpses and not, as Lincoln claims, at 'the pretensions of the Church,'" though how can one separate the two motives? The corpses, after all, represented the Church. I suspect the children were amused because, as children, they did not associate actual death with the nuns' bodies but saw humor in incongruity, in the out-of-placeness of the bodies. Believing middle-class adults, however, were shocked at both the exhibit and the children's amusement.[58]

In other cases, an iconoclastic fury prevailed, as it had in the sixteenth- and seventeenth-century European wars of religion and in 1909 during the Tragic Week of Barcelona. Participants in the violence went on a rampage, destroying hundreds of churches and convents and thousands of religious objects. They gouged the eyes out of the images and statues of saints and Christ figures, hacked off the arms and heads, threw the Host on the ground and stamped on it, burned ecclesiastical raiment after wearing it in burlesque parodies of the Mass or religious processions. Cardinal Gomá y Tomás mourned the disfigurement of the celebrated *Custodia,* or monstrance, in the Toledo cathedral, its scattered fragments the result of satanic design; the reunited pieces a symbol of apostolic triumph, he believed. One churchman felt that the wholesale destruction of religious objects was even worse than the killing of the regular and secular clergy because such objects were more "innocent" than people. Another suggested that "the profanation of the idea signified is more terrible even than that of the outward sign. It constitutes an attack upon the divine. . . . [Seeing] those figures of Christ and the Virgin with their eyes brutally put out . . . [one gains] some idea of the force of this explosion of hatred of God. . . . The vandals looked gloatingly at these representations of Divinity and sanctity as though they were living beings for whom they cherished a deadly hatred."[59]

The focus on mutilation extended to the real bodies of priests, whose hands, ears, tongues, eyes, and genitals were subjected to torment either before or after death. For the Church, these priests were martyrs (many have since been beatified). For the anticlericals, this was a parody of martyrdom, and yet by ritualizing violence they also reenacted Church values through inversion. Mary Vincent observes, "Sacerdotal and sacramental practice in the Catholic Church depended on the tactile transmission of grace. Priests used their hands to bless, their ears to hear confession, their tongues to grant absolution, their eyes to survey and, in anticlerical fantasy, to pry and to peek. That they should have been deprived of these in death may be another form of anti-religious catharsis."[60]

Priests themselves noted how closely the anticlericals followed theological forms and liturgical order in carrying out sacrilegious acts. Churchmen also believed the embers of faith smoldered even in the most hardened atheist. Montero Moreno remarked that "the very air of our people, even in the most ignorant social strata, is steeped as it were in theology, so that the incredulous or the anticlerical generally knows precisely how to wound a Catholic or a priest, even if they fail to grasp the deepest meaning of the offense."[61]

A notable feature of anticlerical violence was the presence of blasphemy. Blasphemy "became a sort of anti-fascist identification code" for revolutionaries.[62] Moreover, clergy about to be shot were repeatedly pressured to blaspheme, that is, to betray their faith. Such verbal insults, closely linked to obscenity in the Spanish language and culture, are part of the sacred pornography of violence. Moreover, male clergy were often seen and attacked simultaneously as ecclesiastics and as men, with genital mutilations reported. Popular imagination had long attributed a heightened sexuality to priests, whose proclivity to vices of the flesh was legendary in such accounts. Castrations and the stuffing of genitalia into the mouth could also be read as assaults upon the vow of male chastity.[63] In either case, the special status of the clergy was singled out.

The shared pornography of violence seen in Carretero's narrative and in anticlerical killings and profanations rests on a corporality that is at once literal and metaphoric, sacred and profane. The proliferation of dead bodies and body parts comprises the stories of martyrdom and antimartyrdom alike, although their meanings differ radically. Anticlerical violence ended up sacralizing, that is, treating the bodies of clergy and lay Catholics as though they were relics, by paying such obsessive and repeated attention to them. Millenarian upheaval, in an atmosphere of "no rules," frames such violence, just as a symbolic end of the world characterizes *La revolución de los patibularios*.[64] The kingdom of death reigns supreme but also presages Nationalist-Catholic resurrection for Carretero and hope of a new world for the revolutionaries. Use of religious symbolism to destroy religion meant that both belief and nonbelief, complexly intertwined, played a significant role in the *amplificatio* of bloodletting.

Excessive punishment of the corpses of clerics, such as burnings and mutilations, deliberately dehumanizes the victim in a sign of contempt, but purposeful overkill also speaks of the unacknowledged power of the Church and its representatives over hearts and minds.[65] The complexities of contempt, moreover, provide good cover for underlying, conflictive emotions like resentment and insecurity. Contempt, like outrage, makes it easier to avoid personal guilt or the need for atonement. Deep disrespect of the other side and self-righteousness (which goes with the territory) mark the stories of both Carretero and extreme forms of anticlericalism.

Set within the highly charged context of competing martyr/antimartyr narratives and atrocities, Ramón Sender's *Réquiem* appears before us luminous and haunting, the poetic edifice of his spare text risen from the human condition as inescapably tragic. That *Réquiem* is also a religious tragedy is clear from the outset. Sender's abiding interest in religion is well documented. His father was a devout Catholic, ultraconservative politically, and a strict disciplinarian. Sender (1901–82) lost his faith somewhere around the age of nine or ten, acquiring a social conscience and thirst for justice when he witnessed a man, wretched and bereft of all physical comfort, dying in a cave as a priest administered last rites.[66] The episode figures significantly in *Réquiem*.

Sender veered leftward, first toward anarchism, then communism. By 1929 he was a member of an anarchist group called Spartacus and belonged to the national anarchist union, the Confederación Nacional de Trabajo (CNT), from 1930 to 1932. His novel *Siete domingos rojos* (1932) (*Seven Red Sundays*) reflects this period of his life. By 1933 he had moved away from anarchism while continuing to sympathize, as his account of the brutal repression of an anarchist revolt at Casas Viejas demonstrates. After visiting the Soviet Union in 1933–34, he shifted yet again ideologically, though he was never a card-carrying member. But the civil war broke him; it was "the great divide of the before and after in his life and work."[67] The war was a personal catastrophe for him, as it was for so many: the Nationalists shot both his wife and his brother Manuel. Politically, he became disenchanted with the cynical wartime opportunism of the communists.

As a leftist, Sender was anticlerical and a strong advocate of the separation of Church and State. He regarded the religious conflict in Mexico, which was at its height with the Cristero revolt of the 1920s against the anti-Catholic Constitution of 1917, as "the last episode in the struggle of that country for independence." New anticlerical legislation was also enacted in Spain between 1931 and 1933. Sender thought the Spanish *pueblo* essentially irreligious, though he did concede the aristo-loving middle class was sincerely Catholic. A series of articles he published in *La Libertad* between 22 January and 1 March 1932, which were incorporated into a pamphlet, appeared as government decrees dissolved the Society of Jesus, legalized civil divorce, and secularized the cemeteries.[68]

The 1930s were turbulent times for Catholics in particular. In reaction to the secularizing Republican reforms, Catholics began to mobilize, especially at the local level of devotional life, where the disruptive effects of the legislation were immediately felt. Here are the literal wars of the dead, as the emotional-political struggle over control of the cemeteries was called. Rooted in the nineteenth century, the conflict between ecclesiastical and municipal powers arose over separate burial plots for dissidents, atheists, Protestants, and others, in short, for anyone not considered Catholic. These generally neglected areas (the *corralillo*) were strewn with rubbish and excrement, symbolic of a contaminating moral stain, or pollution (*polución*), which the Church felt had to be contained and segregated from Catholic graves.[69] With the passage of the new laws, the walls between civil and consecrated plots were knocked down. A legal document became necessary to obtain religious burial. The *Marseillaise* and invocations replaced liturgy and prayers in some funerals.

This was also a period of intense religious revival heralded by a wave of missionary propaganda between 1918 and 1930, particularly in northern Spain. In June 1931 visions and prophecies of Christ's reign were being reported in the Basque town of Ezkioga.[70] These visions, which reflected largely agrarian values, eventually took on an air of impending catastrophe attributed to the sins of the Republic (and indeed of the world). Here too the dead played an important role, as they had in the past in rural areas where popular devotion was at least as strong as institutional practice. Seers, many of them children, began to see not only Mary and angelic hosts but also the dead in their visions, meeting in sacred places like rural shrines, semiabandoned chapels, springs, and hillsides, where the dead were thought to congregate.

While the Ezkioga visions were ultimately politically tainted and discredited, the deeply devotional impulse behind them remained a potent force and a sign of the eschatological landscape in which the Second Republic and the war can be situated. The social, political, and cultural conflicts between the Right and the Left can also be seen symbolically as wars of the dead. Certainly for Carretero, Giménez Caballero, and many on the right the dead are not simply sacred. They represent traditional values that must be defended. They are the past that must not die.

For people like Sender, however, this past must die precisely to make room for the living. His wartime novelized memoir, *Counter-Attack in Spain* (1937), provides much insight into the writer's disposition at the time. Here is what he says about the mummified nuns displayed in Barcelona: "I am certain that to put these 'venerable and miraculous relics' in the porch of a church helps to destroy superstition, and cannot really upset the moral equilibrium of the religious authorities who used to invite the public to kiss the relics and tried to get money from that insanitary practice . . . by placing collection-boxes at the feet of the relics."[71] Since the Enlightenment, such commentary has been the standard anticlerical critique of organized religion as superstition. One can't help being astounded, nonetheless, at Sender's complete lack of sensitivity toward believers. How could he have thought that the exhibit would not "upset the moral equilibrium of the religious authorities"?

An episode with a captured priest reveals a more complex response to religion: "The condemned was a Catholic priest who had been arrested a fortnight ago in a house close to the barracks from which a hand machine gun had been fired at our sentinel. . . . Everything was against him. . . . The priest . . . had prejudiced himself greatly by trying to conceal his personality, as the mere fact of his being a priest was nothing against him. His correspondence compromised him, though not by any definite fact." Sender appears ambivalent here as he parses the truth by distinguishing between the priest's personality and his ecclesiastical station. What is the priest's identity if not his "personality," that is, his clerical status? It is unclear where the apparent guilt of the priest lies, although other militiamen believe he took up arms against them. Sender, however, becomes convinced of his innocence: "One had only to look [the priest] in the face to see that he could not lie. He must have been one of those rare examples of the Church, humble and unobtrusive, who believe fervently all its dogmas and who are passed over for that very reason."[72]

In the end, the priest, judged inculpable, joins the militia but is unable to fire his weapon. One senses in Sender, who was probably instrumental in saving the man's life, the need to justify setting him free, as he latches onto the least supportive strand of a defense: the man simply looks innocent. He says, "I was sure of his innocence," even though there appears to be physical evidence against the clergyman. There was a deep moral need in Sender to see this man as blameless, this priest "who really believes in God and in good."[73] The question of guilt comes back to haunt *Réquiem*.

Sender's animus against organized religion notwithstanding, *Counter-Attack* is laden with eschatological signs, with martyrdom and resurrection, albeit secularized. The dead are as important here as they are in Carretero's narrative, but Sender's own symbolic death is expressed in less histrionic and egotistical terms than El Caballero Audaz's: "Looking at the faces of my comrades, I saw that two of them were dead, although they were still upright and advancing. . . . Psychologists of war tell us that in modern war the living are not killed as in the ancient wars, but those who are killed are already dead. Two of my comrades were dead already. Perhaps I was dead too.

"My comrades, soldiers of the people's liberty, how many times have we died! How many times come again to life! . . . My comrades, soldiers of the people, die and be born again!"[74] Sender was already familiar with war, having served in the Moroccan campaign.[75] The hell of modern warfare, so sharply etched in European memory by the Great War, turns into the resurrectional rhetoric of Republican fervor.

Counter-Attack is as much a work of propaganda as Carretero's narrative. Indeed, a similar image of Manichean apocalypse, in which the Beast is now the Fascists, colors Sender's vision of things. Thus it is not surprising that a cult of dead martyred heroes also shows up in Republican narratives: "Close to one of the shelters of branches . . . there was a dead comrade. . . . I sat down at his side . . . and gazed at him. Our dead are not repugnant. He had fallen on his face, and his twitching hands had scraped the ground. With the nails and the fingers he had gathered up earth in his frenzy. His eyes were open, and their last look had been for that soil of Spain which he held in his hands. . . . Take with you the soil of Spain in your clasp, comrade! It is your glory. That soil is for you. You have given it your life, but it, too, is yours forever. It will be yours in the grave, but also in the future and in history. . . . Yours and ours, this soil of Spain, fertilized by your young blood!" The Nationalists had no monopoly on the imagery of blood and sacrifice. Sender's fascination with violence and his aggressive political stance in the 1930s partly explain the rhetoric of writings like *Counter-Attack*.[76]

But some of this rhetoric also comes with the territory: literally, with the land itself. The symbolic import of the land and its relation to the martyred dead is a vision shared by the two sides. Although Carretero's narrative is largely urban, centered on the capital, Nationalist ideology in general privileged rural life as the traditional heartland of Spain, appealing to the *Patria* as the sum of all the local *patrias*. The glorification of Catholicism was, moreover, intimately "tied to the glorification of rural life and the image of rural traditionalism" both before and during Francoism. For the Carlist peasantry from Navarre, in particular, the countryside had a redemptive focus. Extreme rightists like Giménez Caballero conceived of the land as both sacred and imperial. The prophecy of empire, he says, ascends like delirium from the very "depths of this earth, which are also mine."[77] The Ezkioga visionaries had tapped into old beliefs linking the earth with the potent, resurrectionary force of the dead. Men of the right relied on a politicized cult of the dead, drawn from the same well.

On the other side, the Second Republic invested heavily in the symbolism of the land. Land reform and redistribution were essential parts of the government's agenda, but Republicans also had a similar appreciation of rural folk. Artists of the Left and the Right both favored an image of Spain "as an eternal stronghold for peasant traditions, customs, and values." It is one of the paradoxes of twentieth-century Spanish life that "images of Spain's rural traditions and customs became, in turn, the constitutive forms of modernity." Luis Buñuel's documentary *Las Hurdes: Land Without Bread* (1933) dramatized the difficulties the Second Republic had in harmonizing "the modern and the archaic, the urban and the rural." In the wartime pro-Republic film *The Spanish Earth* (1937) the director, Joris Ivens, glosses over the tension between an urban modernizing perspective and the timeless appeal of the countryside by playing down the specifics of Spanish politics and focusing on the land as a unifying "metaphor for the Republican cause." Many civil war posters depicted the redemptive symbolism of the land. "The produce of the peasant is as sacred to everyone as the worker's wages," declares one Republican poster. "Peasants, this land is yours," says another. In the 1930s Spain was still largely agrarian. It is not surprising that the Republican government displayed at the Spanish Pavilion in Paris in 1937 the reverent images of rural traditions taken by the pictorialist photographer José Ortiz-Echagüe, a fervent Franco supporter.[78]

Sender's emphasis in *Counter-Attack* on the sacredness of the land and of the dead who fought for that land fits squarely into a secularized rhetoric of redemption. The soil of Spain is the dead comrade's glory, it is fertilized by his young blood, and it lives forever in the bones and memories of other comrades. The same vision carries over to the much more complex and layered *Réquiem*. By the early 1950s, Sender had moved away from his vehement anticlericalism of the twenties and thirties, though he never had much use for the Church as an institution. "The church," he wrote in 1978, "is always *the body* of a religion. And all bodies are impure." He developed a "poetic theology," in which he denied the historical reality of Jesus, envisioning him instead as the son "of the Holy Spirit — that is, of the creative imagination of mankind." Sender saw Christianity, which he sharply distinguished from clericalism, as a great moral and philosophical repository. He said, "The Logos had to become flesh so that people in anguish over the impossibility of the infinite could conceive of it in images and deeds." As a writer, he also benefited from the religious imagination: "Religious ritual is practical poetry for those willing to seek it. But of course poetic emotion isn't always idyllic. At any rate, such imagery is the appeal, sometimes obvious (like a bell or incense) and sometimes subtle (like the Eucharist), to mystery."[79]

The landscape of *Réquiem* is filled with this practical poetry and with the incarnated mystery of the divine in the peasant Paco and in the *pueblo*, or Aragonese folk themselves. As a narrative of martyrdom, Sender's text re-imagines the way of Christ in the secular figure of Paco, allowing the novelist to focus on issues of social justice at the same time. The revolutionary image of Christ in the world, which is also evangelical, or drawn from the Gospels, may appear, in a post–Vatican II and liberation theology age, anachronistic, but there were precedents in nineteenth-century social Catholicism, which penetrated Spain starting in the 1880s and culminated, if belatedly, in Leo XIII's encyclical letter on the condition of labor, *Rerum Novarum* (1891). While largely ineffective as a movement, with the exception of the Catholic agrarian syndicates, social activism among some notable Spanish clergy like Maximiliano Arboleya Martínez persisted even under the Second Republic. On the eve of civil war, Father Francisco Peiró remarked that the post-Reformation Church had been isolated from the people, "instead of being what it should be: Christ himself inhabiting the world." Peiró was a Jesuit priest of the San Ramón parish in the working-class Vallecas neighborhood of Madrid, with eighty thousand parishioners, "of whom only 7 % attended Sunday Mass."[80]

Most Spanish clergy, however, were content to administer the sacraments, focusing on attendance at Sunday Mass and other outward signs of religious practice. Mosén Millán, the priest in *Réquiem,* is no exception. The message of Christ in the world is put into practice as Paco addresses the question of land use, reminding readers of Lamennais's words from 1834: "What is a poor person? It is he who does not yet have property."[81] The village grazing lands are mostly in the hands of an absentee duke. The Second Republic did away with such feudal rights as the *bienes de señorío,* handing them over to municipalities, but legal loopholes often benefited large landholders. Under Paco's leadership, the village refuses to pay rents to the duke, while the matter remains in the courts.

The specific political-economic issue of land use is set, however, within a sacralized landscape, in which folk practices (the *curandera* Jerónima and the *carasol,* a matriarchal communal space) and religious symbolism (beginning with Paco) seem to work against the flow of history. Thus, sometimes in the *carasol* with the other women, Jerónima, "out of a clear sky, . . . would start dancing all alone, to the rhythm of the church bells." She utters "strange prayers to drive away hailstorms and prevent the river from overflowing its banks." And Paco's baptismal day is "frigid and golden—one of those early mornings on which the river gravel, spread in the square for Corpus Christi, crunched with cold under foot." There is little direct referencing of historical events in the novel. The coming of the Second Republic, the king's abdication, the outbreak of war in July 1936 appear at first almost as throwaway lines in a script. One might conclude that history doesn't count for much in *Réquiem.*[82]

Yet I think such a conclusion is a hasty one. Sender's sense of history may lack precise dates and references but is no less historical for being embedded deep within the fabric of early twentieth-century village life. Social injustices, rigid class hierarchies, and an immobile Church are clearly demarcated historic forces at work.

Of more consequence is the manipulation of history insofar as it radically reshapes the narrative into one of martyrdom. *Réquiem* takes place in an unnamed Aragonese village located on the border with Lérida (Lleida), thus occasioning the sporadic adoption of Catalan words, a distinct linguistic usage the anarchist schoolteacher Víctor Blanco, born in Alcampel, called a *chapurriau.* In Sender's narrative, at the start of war, a group of Falangist *señoritos* crush the village in a brutal killing spree. The villagers are overwhelmed: "The village was frightened and nobody knew what to do."[83]

Historically, however, the northeast part of Aragon remained in the Republican zone until spring 1938. In some cases, Nationalists briefly took over villages but were quickly ousted by the other side. Moreover, about three-fourths of the land in Aragon and more than 70 percent of the population under mostly anarchist control became part of a revolutionary experiment in rural collectivization. An unfriendly observer, José Silva, a member of the Communist Party, said, "It was in Aragón where the most varied and strange experiments in collectivization and socialization were made, where undoubtedly the most violence was used in order to compel the peasants to enter the collective farms, and where a manifestly false policy tore open serious breaches in rural economy."[84]

A more nuanced view suggests that both voluntary and forced collectivization took place. Many Aragonese villages were politically active before the war, which helps explain not only the rapidity with which collectivization occurred but the successful resistance to Nationalist forces. Víctor Blanco's account of his hometown Alcampel is illustrative. In the 1880s there was intense conflict between the town and the local priest over civil burial; in 1914, over remuneration for bearing the religious *pasos* during Holy Week; in 1917, over a civil marriage. In 1933 members of the CNT attempted a revolution in Alcampel, but it was put down. And by 1936 "it was no secret to anyone that the fascists were preparing a coup," he wrote. Rumors, he said, were circulating in the streets; people thirsty for information gathered round the five existing radios in the town: "On everyone's face, anxiety. We had to take the initiative, organize something." They set up a Revolutionary Committee, with guard posts at all entrances and exits, and required safe-conduct passes. The Civil Guard left, and the priest disappeared. Some nine days after the military coup, Alcampel had its own collective.[85]

This is but one example of the level of political awareness and organization that existed (or that was abetted by the arrival of militias from Catalonia and Valencia) in many Aragonese towns and villages. Had Sender's narrative depicted historical reality more closely, *Réquiem* would have been unrecognizable. There would have been no Mosén Millán, for "in none of the Anarchist villages . . . was there any outward sign of religious life." As one anarchist said, "Belief in nature has taken the place of religion, which has been banished."[86] Churches were converted into storehouses and workshops. And there would have been no peasant martyr. Nor would the village have appeared so totally helpless or uninformed, as in Sender's text. The villagers would have prepared themselves to resist.

What happens in the village did happen in many other *pueblos* in Spain, so in this sense the novelist reflects a wider historical reality. My point is not to fault Sender for failing to adhere to the historical facts on the ground, but to ask *why* he did not. I suspect that his old anarchist sympathies may have partly swayed him not to approach a potentially delicate subject, one in which anarchist responsibility for anticlerical violence might very well have to be faced.[87] In this way, too, he avoided the controversial matter of collectivization, imposed or voluntary. The village becomes a scapegoat. Above all, he circumvents many of the thornier complexities and contradictions of the war, in which loyalty to revolutionary goals came into conflict with the aims of the

Republican government and the government itself, struggling to survive, betrayed its own ideals.

History would not have served Sender well here. It would have muddied the ethical thrust fueling the narrative and compromised the symbolic, transcending charge of violence that characterizes the story arc of *Réquiem*. Sender could have chosen an anarchist as his protagonist and still written a martyr narrative. The CNT saw its history as "filled with martyrs who gave their lives fighting oppression."[88] Yet he did not, although he did draw on the anarchist identification with Christ as a symbol of justice. I can only speculate that perhaps he believed an explicitly anarchist figure would have unduly politicized the text, pulling it away from the larger questions he wanted to explore.

Instead, *Réquiem* asks one to consider how a secular work of fiction may depend on nonsecular values whose effects are felt in a world of tainted transcendence. Unquestionably the civil war left a bitter residue of lost illusions and squandered ideals that permeated many narratives after 1939. For Sender, *Réquiem* represented "in its outlines the civil war itself."[89] This is above all war as a religious tragedy in the broadest sense of the term. Moreover, the war as a struggle over belief systems also emblematized the conflictive process of modernity in Spain, a process in which religion, whether defended or excoriated, occupied a central place. Carretero in his wartime narrative wrapped a form of grotesque realism in the heavy cloak of martyrdom. Under the weight of violent sectarianism, however, religious belief reasserted itself as an exclusive national (and nationalist) identity.

Réquiem goes much farther in connecting religion as a crisis of modernity to the narrative genre itself. The symbolic realism of Sender's text is also deeply ethical in suggesting at once the universal tragic condition of humankind as irremediably flawed and the concrete circumstances of unspoken guilt and atonement for the historic betrayal of social justice. Narratively, the priest Mosén Millán serves not only as one of the principal voices of the novel but as the intimate link between the spiritual and the secular. Thematically, it is impossible to understand how the communal desire for justice — as seen in the land issue — attains a sacred dimension if one does not also take into account that the representatives of secular and spiritual power in such communities were joined at the hip. Speaking of Republican-era tensions in the Aragonese village he called Belmonte de los Caballeros, the anthropologist Carmelo Lisón-Tolosana noted that "the most assiduous in the practice of religion . . . were those who in general possessed the greater number of fields, more economic means, greater power and prestige. So in this social upheaval people found themselves involved in a double attack — against property and against their religious ideas. The two objects of attack became identified as the same."[90]

The social-political crisis of modernity in early twentieth-century Spain, which brought changes to the country's social, economic, and cultural structures, was in this sense also a religious crisis. Structurally, the pattern of secular martyrdom illustrates how sacred and profane values cannot be separated in *Réquiem*.

Sender does not eradicate religion from his text, as the anarchists did from so many villages in northeast Aragon. Instead, he makes the spiritual-ethical impulse of religion the motivating imaginative force behind his narrative. Thus the social-economic crisis of modernity is expressed and dramatized as a moral crisis of religious dimensions.

Since 1974, *Réquiem* has carried a dedication to Jesús Vived Mairal, a post–Vatican II priest and Sender's eventual biographer. The novel begins with this passage: "The parish priest, clad in the chasuble of Requiem services, sat in an armchair, head bowed, waiting. An odor of incense hovered in the sacristy. In a corner was a sheaf of olive branches left over from Palm Sunday, its leaves so dry that they looked metallic. Whenever Mosén Millán passed nearby, he avoided brushing against them for they were ready to part from their stems and fall to the floor."[91] From the very start, Sender's text is embedded spatially and temporally in a sacred setting that is communicated through the senses: the smell of incense, the brittle touch of the olive branches, and, in the next two paragraphs, the faint sounds of daily life coming from outside, the furious sweeping of a broom and a voice calling, "María . . . Marieta."

Equally significant is the initial image of a fragile, breakable world, lyrically conveyed in the dry, metallic olive branches ready to crumble, which is reinforced several lines later with that of a frantic grasshopper trapped in a bush. The sacred and the natural worlds come together with fluid grace here, expressing the tiny vulnerabilities of creaturely existence. The initial presentation, however, is deceptive: deceptive because this is a world that has already shattered into a thousand pieces.

Mosén Millán is reciting prayers in preparation for Paco's requiem mass. He hears the dead man's colt whinnying in the distance, which he takes as a "constant reminder of Paco and his tragedy."[92] The artful simplicity with which Sender spins his story is a layered one: "his tragedy" obviously refers to Paco's violent death, but it could just as well be speaking of the priest's misfortune. In little more than a page, Sender's compact narrative reveals that this is a broken world, one in which memory must serve to piece together the fragments. In this sense, *Réquiem* has already been told: the text is a retelling (hence the memorialization) of something that happened before the book was even cracked open.

Memory resurrects the life of a dead man, but it occludes other things, first because the priest as principal narrator cannot recount everything, but more importantly because he *will not*. There is a stain of culpability that cannot be washed away, as permanent as the oily mark on the wall where Mosén Millán rested his head for decades. This stain, which readers eventually recognize as a sign of moral and physical blight, is not told; it is, in narrative and iconic terms, simply shown but bears the symbolic traces attributed, in moral theology, to pollution, originally denoting the emission of semen, and more tellingly to the moral stain of original sin.[93] Sender also alludes to the stain of Nationalist violence committed to cleanse the nation of presumably polluted leftists. The priest himself, in remembering Paco's life and death, traces circles around his own culpability but can never openly admit to it. Instead, he seeks self-justification for betraying Paco's hiding place to the Falangists. Mosén Millán does not appear to understand why he has played the Judas, and Sender is careful not to fully clarify his motivation. Why does the priest trick Paco's father into revealing his son's whereabouts? Is it to test himself? If so, he fails miserably, and once the secret is told he feels horrified yet oddly liberated. He tells himself his love must transcend the human and serve only God: "He loved Paco. He loved him a great deal, but his love was in the name of God, not for the man himself. An affection over and above life and death. And he could not lie."[94] Such self-justification is, however, disingenuous, as he had already lied by omission to Paco's father. More damning is his betrayal of the essential being of Christ in the world.

Sender makes it clear, moreover, that Mosén Millán enjoys having the power of his secret. When Paco is caught, the priest's sense of superiority comes through in another way: Paco's disheveled appearance, limping and with a two-week beard, gives him, he thinks, a guilty air. And after all the blood shed, writes Sender, "Mosén Millán thought of those dead peasants, of the poor women of the *carasol,* and he felt a kind of involuntary scorn which, at the same time, made him feel guilty and ashamed." His contempt is in some ways psychologically similar to the derisive reaction of anticlericals toward their victims, when they burned, mutilated, or simply abandoned the bodies of priests by the roadside.[95] The extreme right, of course, inflicted the same kinds of scornful, brutal offenses on living and dead bodies. The entangled emotions underlying priestly contempt in *Réquiem* suggest that atonement cannot be achieved here. To atone fully, first one must fully confess. It is the priest's involuntary scorn which provokes guilt and shame in him, not his responsibility for Paco's execution. Contempt lingers, bound to resentment and insecurity, making it difficult, if not impossible, to acknowledge openly one's contempt of self.

The complex narrative turn, in which an account of martyrdom (Paco's) is at the same time a botched confession (Mosén Millán's), is brilliantly conveyed through the use of indirect discourse. As a confession, it is, however, an incomplete plot of revelation. The last lines make that clear: "He thought he heard his name on the lips of the dying man. . . . And both terrified and moved to pity, he reflected: 'Now in suffrage of his soul, I say this Requiem Mass, for which his enemies wish to pay.' "[96] Paco's enemies are the *pudientes,* the most prosperous members of the village. There are two forms of irony present here. One hears irony in the priest's words, while a second level of irony infuses the passage in the ghostly shape of the priest's nonconfession. This is the story that cannot be told.[97]

To prevent Paco's martyrdom from being taken over entirely by the priest's guilt-ridden sufferings, Sender introduces another narrative voice, embodied in the acolyte who recalls throughout the narrative snatches of the popular ballad honoring the peasant-martyr. The ballad form, or *romance,* was widely favored especially (though not solely) by Republicans during the Spanish Civil War as poetry in action and as a form of living history. The ballad is "nothing less than the villagers' own secular requiem for Paco." To the popular form of remembrance Jorge Marí adds three other requiems: the mass (institutional), the priest's memories (personal), and the novel itself (authorial), all of which are memorials resurrecting a dead man.[98]

Réquiem can be seen as a thicket of narrative recollection in which each form of requiem crisscrosses another while contributing to the story as a whole. Mosén Millán's memories are personal, but they are also institutional: the priest *is* the Church, and he remembers Paco's life and death as he is preparing for the requiem mass. Moreover, he remembers him principally through the institutional forms and signs of the Church, which are its sacraments (baptism, first communion, marriage, last rites, and so on), and through liturgical time (Holy Week especially). The acolyte, in turn, represents the voice of the people, but he too is part of the Church.

Most significantly, Paco's story is told in fragments, even as different narrative threads weave in and out of the novel, offering snippets of his life. While the fragments still possess linearity, the pieces intrinsically suggest something that is irretrievably broken, as the opening paragraph implies.[99] The point of resurrection is to bring these pieces together.

Sender offers a new rendition of secular martyrdom by capitalizing on the fragmented nature of the modern twentieth-century novel form itself. This he achieves by creating an implicit analogue between narrative fragmentation and the sacrificial body of martyrdom. That Paco's story is roughly modeled as a linear hagiography is evident. From birth to death, his trajectory is marked, like the lives of saints and heroes, with distinctive signs in anticipation of his destiny. At baptism, he sticks "out [his] tongue to lick the salt, and from this [the godmother] concluded that he would have a way with women."[100] Like Jesus among the elders, he shows wisdom at an early age, safeguarding an old revolver so that it won't be misused. And in adulthood he becomes a seeker of social justice.

Burned into his mind is the image of a poor wretch dying in a cave, abandoned by everyone but his wife. These caves on the village outskirts, in which people "hollowed out the earth and built their houses inside," were a feature of some Aragonese communities. Paco's compassion for the dying man is a form of solidarity, of charity. Sender could not have ignored the deeply sacred import of caves as places of worship and refuge from persecution for early Christianity. During the civil war, in response to the socialist Indalecio Prieto's insulting the Navarrese as "cave dwellers," Carlist traditionalists spoke of the cave as "a repository of religious faith, of good customs, of uprightness, of patriotic spirit, of everything decent, healthy and honourable."[101] Sender appropriates both a real social space and a loaded religious (and political) symbol for his own purposes, refiguring the Nationalist monopoly of such imagery in its physical, social, and spiritual properties.

Paco's hagiographical trajectory has its own path, but the straightforwardness with which it is told is repeatedly broken temporally (and spatially) in continually switching back and forth between the remembered past and the narrative present. The insertion of a secondary narrative line, the acolyte's ballad, also works in counterpoint, by offering an alternative version of Paco's life and death. But this story is literally given as fragments interspersed throughout *Réquiem*.

It is Paco's story as meaningful fragment that most closely approximates the narrative of martyrdom and that most profoundly expresses Sender's understanding of the human condition. Memories of Paco come in bits and pieces, like communion wafers individually tendered for consumption. Mosén Millán remembers his voice and then the day of his marriage. He remembers him as a child playing hooky. At one point he lets memory slip for a moment and looks at the acolyte, who with some difficulty picks up another piece recalled in two ballad lines: "*Now they take them, now they take them, / Bound together, arm in arm.*" "The scene," Sender writes, "was present to the acolyte's mind, a bloody scene and full of the crackle of gunfire."[102] This is the scene of Paco's death. In fine ironic counterpoint, the priest remembers at almost the same time the day of his baptism.

Scenes appear like fluid moments of film and disappear in the same manner. But they are remembered in the manner of a much older model: the Loyolan spiritual exercises (already recreated in Clarín's *La Regenta*).[103] Saint Ignatius stressed the use of the five senses to channel and actualize the imagination as a way to access the divine through self-examination. The retreatant was to imagine such things as Hell or the life of Christ, starting with "an imaginative representation of the place." While Ignatius establishes an orderly method based in part on the traditional mnemonic art of seeing memory as a structure or place, he does not generally supply the images themselves. But the method furnishes powerful incentive to produce images and see them as in some sense structural. At the same time, the relentless subdivisions in Loyola's exercises, which create the overarching verbal and ideological edifice and order, also break image making into fragments.[104]

Thus the scene of Paco's death is made present to the acolyte's imagination visually and acoustically, but it is expressed as a narrative scrap. When Mosén Millán closes his eyes and remembers, he too is imagining, seeing the place or person or thing, filling the hole of memory with his senses invaded by the "odors of garlic, of wine-vinegar, and olive oil" at Paco's baptismal feast. At the very moment he betrays Paco's hiding place to the Falangists, he recalls again the same festivities, with "trifling details such as the night owls and the pungent odor of marinated partridge."[105] Sender's temporal dislocations — setting one disparate memory against another or against the narrative present — swerve away from the spiritual aim of the Loyolan imagination, which is to come closer to God's will by participating imaginatively in the founding events of Christianity. Instead, temporal tensions display through incongruity and metonymic detail how far Mosén Millán is from this spiritual ideal.

Paco as martyr-hero is thus remembered not only in narrative fragments but in image-objects as fragments, like the night owls and the marinated partridge. Poetic realism is broken down, its ultimate meaning then reassembled as a necessary narrative of resurrection, necessary because without that meaning *Réquiem* would fall apart as surely as does the fictional world it represents. Objects, natural and man-made, contribute to the simultaneous centrifugal-centripetal vision by being presented as parts of the whole, with the narrative whole understood as something broken, like a body in torment. The language of things invests *Réquiem* in a world of significance, precisely calibrated by Sender's honed prose. The pealing of little bells and the distribution of candies and sugar almonds announce Paco's baptism. The pitch of the bells indicates the baby's sex. The sugar almonds bounce "against doors and windows and occasionally against the heads of the youngsters themselves."[106] In singling out these objects, Sender begins to build the case for the special quality of Paco's life.

A later episode in his childhood also anticipates his fate by focusing on things of iconic significance. During Holy Week, a traditional structure of Eucharistic devotion called the Monument is set up in one of the naves; surrounding it are statues that Paco recognizes from having explored, with another boy, the church attic: "Paco was perturbed, for he had seen those dusty and noseless images in the church attic where rubbish accumulated. Statues of naked and suffering martyrs, legs of Christs separated from their bodies, heads of tearful *ecce homos* were there too, as well as St. Veronica's sudaria hanging from the walls . . .

"When both acolytes were in the attic, the other one exaggerated his familiarity with these figures. He straddled the shoulders of an apostle as if he were on a horse, and knocked on its head with his knuckles to find out, he said, if there were mice inside. In the mouth of another he put a rolled-up piece of paper, as if the statue were smoking."[107]

The passage is narrated in the third person but is sifted through both Paco's and an implied authorial perspective, as though there were a camera alternatively zooming in and moving away from the scene. Sender focuses on body parts, the fragmented imagery of religious martyrdom, recalling what the Church termed the martyrdom of things during the civil war. The other acolyte's irreverent behavior reinforces an anticlerical subtext, which is furthered elsewhere by the village shoemaker's contrarian mockery and criticism of Church representatives. Here, Sender relies on a historic social type known throughout nineteenth- and early twentieth-century Europe as political radicals with an independent turn of mind.[108] After the Falangists appear on the scene, the shoemaker ends up dead by the roadside, his head blown apart.

The other acolyte's specific actions resonate, on the one hand, with long-standing popular anticlericalism and, on the other, with buried memories of civil war violence against the Church. In this respect the passage—and the place (a dusty attic)—functions as a palimpsest, disclosing some of the unspeakable nature of the Spanish Civil War. One can read at least two things into the meaning of the attic rubbish piled up helter-skelter. It can be seen most simply as an anticlerical, demystifying comment on the irrelevance of the Church. But it can also be linked with Paco's future martyrdom, which brings us back to the silent subtext of clerical martyrdom during the war. The associations Sender makes here between Paco and the symbolically mutilated objects in the church attic are weighted with portent. Paco's disturbed feelings reinforce these connections, arising as they do from seeing sacred objects that are presented as at one and the same time neglected, even mocked, and revered. Shortly before, the devotional monument in the nave appears to him as a thing of mystery. When he hears a sad melody issuing from underneath the structure, where two men are playing cane flutes, he has "extremely strong contradictory sensations."[109] The sacred and the profane are side by side, sometimes one and the same, in this complex and not fully understood response to spirit in the world.

The martyrdom of things presages the martyrdom of personhood. Paco, along with two other peasants (paralleling the Christ story) slated for execution, is brought at nightfall to the cemetery. The same car that took Paco and his new bride to the railway station on their honeymoon years ago now serves as a makeshift confessional. When Mosén Millán asks the final question, "Do you repent of your sins?" Paco is stunned. "It was the first of the priest's expressions he did not understand." What sins did he and the other two peasants commit to deserve this? And then Sender writes,

> The headlights of the car in which Mosén Millán was sitting flashed on, and almost simultaneously a volley of shots rang out . . . The other two peasants fell but Paco, covered with blood, ran toward the car.
> "Mosén Millán, you know me!" he cried, demented.
> He tried to climb in but could not. Everything was splattered with his blood. Mosén Millán was silent, his eyes shut, praying. The centurion thrust his revolver behind Paco's ear and somebody said, alarmed, "No! Not there!"
> They dragged Paco away. He kept repeating hoarsely: "Ask Mosén Millán — he knows me."
> Two or three more shots were heard. Then followed a silence in which Paco kept on whispering: "He denounced me . . . , Mosén Millán. Mosén Millán."[110]

This extraordinary scene recalls an earlier description of a botched execution in Bahamonde's *Memoirs of a Spanish Nationalist*: "In Córdoba, confessions were received at first in the cemetery itself. The priest was taken there in an automobile, the little window-door opened to serve as confessional, and there, in the darkness of night, in front of the cemetery walls, in the presence of the executioners, the religious succour was administered. I know a priest who begged insistently . . . to have the executions withheld until his ear was at a distance. . . . This priest fell ill after witnessing a harrowing scene. One of the victims, after receiving the shot, ran badly wounded and took refuge in his car. He was pulled out and killed in the sight of the priest. The impression which this made upon the priest was so great that he was ill for nearly a month."[111]

I do not know if Sender was aware of Bahamonde's book but would not be surprised to learn he had read it. More important, this scene reminds one that fictional deaths like Paco's were historical realities during the civil war. While the priest takes center stage in Bahamonde's narrative, the brutal execution is equally unforgettable, precisely for its horrendously transgressive nature, in which the sacred is savaged through the victim's martyrdom. Sender would not cross that ultimate threshold of having Paco shot in view of the priest: "No! Not there!" somebody says. Mosén Millán does, however, react somewhat like Bahamonde's priest, recoiling in horror and then holing up for two weeks in the abbey except to conduct Mass.

Confession under the circumstances described in *Réquiem* already profanes the sacred, wherever the execution occurs. Both a sacrament (confession, followed by extreme unction) and a consecrated site (the cemetery) are violated. In this sense, there is a double martyrdom, as the Nationalists treat with contempt the integrity of Paco's personhood (not to mention his innocence) as well as that of the Church itself. The intimate link between the two is underscored when Paco says as he confesses, "But you know me, Mosén Millán. You know who I am" and repeats it with his dying breath. Characterized elsewhere as his spiritual father, the priest has personally betrayed Paco. But he has also done so institutionally. The sacredness of personhood is embodied in Christ's sacrifice. That inviolate nature of the individual is denied, as Paco's implicit accusation makes clear: "You know who I am." Mosén Millán has abandoned him. Years later, Sender wrote to a friend, "Catholicism seems to me *divine* if only in the last words of Jesus on the cross: 'Father, why hast thou forsaken me?' If this is what the purest and most perfect of men that humankind has been able to imagine says ([expressing] doubt in agony), what can we mere mortals hope for? For this, Jesus was born with the first man and will continue to die until the last person does. The anguish in which we all find ourselves is not existential but *essential*."[112]

Paco's dying words echo those of Christ. His anguish, however, is that terror, that imperfection "covered with blood" we call a man, which makes Paco's sacrificed life so human a thing. At the same time his agony is prolonged, not in the temporal sense but emotionally, for like saints and martyrs he is hard to kill.[113] Or, as Sender says of Christ, he "will continue to die until the last person does."

Mosén Millán's anguish, however, is filled with guilt. A year later, as he prepares to say the requiem mass, "Paco's death was so recent and fresh that Mosén Millán still thought he had bloodstains on his clothes." As in other martyr narratives, this one bears witness with blood. In recalling the bloodstains, the priest reminds readers of the oily mark his head made where for over fifty years he rested it against the wall. Presaging his own martyrdom is Paco's recollection of painful Holy Week processions of penitents, whose ankles bled from the long chains they were dragging. Urged to do the same so that God might intercede by giving him a high number in the draft lottery, he refuses. When war breaks out, the *señoritos* put the Falangist cult of violence to the test by going on a killing rampage. They murder six peasants, leaving their bodies by the roadside, and the dogs rush to lick their blood. More dead bodies appear, this time the shoemaker and then four town council members. Jerónima—the village midwife and medicine woman whose syncretic religious beliefs mix natural and Christian elements—"in the midst of the catastrophe, sensed something magical and supernatural in the air, and she smelled blood everywhere." This sign of special significance is linked to Paco's fate. Jerónima says he won't easily be caught, noting again "what she had seen when he was an infant and she had changed his diapers," that is, "the size of his masculine attributes."[114]

What Sender also emphasizes in the spilling of blood is the dreadful confusion that Mosén Millán and the villagers feel, which is expressed in a fragmented, incomplete way as "shots in the night, blood, evil passions, gossip, the foul behavior of those strangers [the Falangists] who, nevertheless, appeared to be educated." Having learned through duplicity Paco's hiding place, the priest at first resists the pressure to betray him, saying to one of the influential *pudientes* of the village, " 'Leave him alone. . . . Why shed more blood?' " Shortly after this, he caves in to the Falangists. The horrible confusion Mosén Millán feels is above all a moral fog. The bloodstains he still sees on his clothes will never be washed away. Georges Bernanos, after watching the Nationalist repression in Palma de Mallorca unfold over eight months, wrote, "The atmosphere of Terrorism is not what you think. At first it is like some gigantic misunderstanding, mixing everything up, inextricably entangling good and evil, innocent and guilty, enthusiasm and cruelty."[115] Sender recreates the same atmosphere on a small scale, but one that grows larger with each successive reading of the text.

The bloodstains Mosén Millán cannot forget express moral blight but possess an aura of transcendence as the sign of martyrdom. Paco's spattered blood is one more fragment of this narrative, each piece being treated as a kind of relic. Literal relics also inhabit the text, as the priest continues to hold on to Paco's watch and pocket handkerchief. Given the objects right after the execution, he "wrapped the watch in the handkerchief and held it carefully in his joined hands." The special healing powers of Saint Paul's handkerchiefs come to mind.[116] The watch is a temporal reminder as well. Don Valeriano, one of the *pudientes,* has a relic of Father Claret, beatified in 1934 (and canonized in 1950), along with a lock of his dead wife's hair dangling from his watch chain. These keepsakes, although serving mostly to underline Don Valeriano's religious orthodoxy and conventional attitudes, do, however, figure in the larger narrative frame as memorialized relic.

The rhetoric of martyrdom in Carretero transformed Nationalist bodies into sacred relics. Structurally and emotionally, Sender does something similar from a Republican perspective. Indeed, the aura of the relic was already attached to the poor in Olavide, Cadalso, and Ayguals de Izco, to the beloved in Cadalso and Gutiérrez, to personhood in Galdós, and to childhood in Clarín. Carretero, however, hammers the reiterated technique of amplification as symbolic relics into rhetorical overkill, while Sender manages to bring together two different fragment narratives—the modern novel and the traditional martyr story—into exquisite symbiosis. Every fragment of Paco's life and death—his body, his presence—in being remembered, becomes a relic. These are, literally and figuratively, his remains, or *reliquiae*, from which the word "relic" comes. And they possess the magic or *potentia*, drawn from both supranatural and natural worlds, such objects transmit.[117] Power that not even the irony implied in secular martyrdom can diminish.

Relics are classified by degrees, the most significant being associated with Christ's life or the body of a saint. More significantly, the relics of a martyr are intimately bound up in the idea of resurrection. Early Christian ideas about resurrection were quite literal, emphasizing, as does Tertullian, the rising of the body as the "reassemblage of [its material] bits." The cult of relics fed into this belief; indeed, in the words of Caroline Bynum, "the dead were materialized by being divided up and distributed." Each part was seen as belonging to a whole, the wholeness pointing to resurrection. Bynum further notes, "Resurrection was finally not so much the triumph of martyrs over pain and humiliation as the triumph of martyrs' bodies over fragmentation, scattering, and the loss of a final resting place."[118]

The martyred dead body and its parts as relic also need to be seen in their relation to the divine: "What appears to be almost totally absent from pagan belief about the role of the heroes is the insistence of all Christian writers that the martyrs, precisely because they had died as human beings, enjoyed close intimacy with God."[119] Sender's narration powerfully resurrects through memory fragments the presence of the martyred Paco, but what role does God play in *Réquiem*?[120] Both Carretero and Giménez Caballero were convinced they had a direct line to God, but Sender makes no such claims. Indeed, God exists only as the incarnated human imagination in Sender's poetic theology. And this is what is resurrected every time *Réquiem* is read.

Are God and the modern novel incompatible? Not necessarily. The novel is a secular form, but in the world it represents all things are possible. Novels are secular projects insofar as they are in the world and of the world. But they are also ethically bound up in that world and to that extent beholden to things that are invisible, including the spirit. When a writer like Sender tests the limits of the novel, as he does in practicing a kind of divine materialism, he also tests the limits of faith, even if that faith bears little resemblance to religious orthodoxy. Sender's faith, or whatever one wishes to name it, is ultimately humanistic, even humanitarian, in that he places all hope of redemption in personhood, in human imperfection as embodied in a Spanish peasant who dies in terror and as a human being and is for this reason a martyr. The divine is within. It resides in the individual, whose body becomes for Sender a kind of sacrament.

His novel asks readers to consider religion as part of the crisis of modernity brought about by the Second Republic and the Spanish Civil War. Such historical specificity, while important and formative of the contours of twentieth-century fiction in Spain, is joined to another sense of place and time in these writings, a sense which draws on the sacred topography of the local and of the dead. The sites and graves of martyrs in early Christianity were infused with the particular. *Hic locus est:* "Here is the place," read the inscriptions on shrines and tombs. These places were filled with "*praesentia,* the physical presence of the holy." In analogous if secular fashion, Carretero sacralizes the capital city and its inhabitants; Sender, the land and its people. Both reflect how "local worlds were felt to be threatened," in different ways, by the Second Republic and the war. As religion, scattered topographically and materially throughout the rural and urban landscape in shrines, hermitages, and relics, had been in an earlier period, everything too was local — and hence personal, even intimate, as Sender's narrative discloses — in the Spain of the 1930s.[121]

The long-standing political, religious, and social issues the republic and the war brought to the fore refuse to die in these narratives. In that sense, the writings of Carretero and Sender represent continuing wars of the dead, in which both sides are not only unable to let go of their sufferings, beliefs, and indeed of the dead themselves, but insist on resurrecting what has died. Like Walter Benjamin's angel of history, with "his face . . . turned toward the past," such stories "would like to stay, awaken the dead, and make whole what has been smashed."[122] Thus it is not surprising to see that martyrdom and resurrection especially haunt the writings and art of Republican exiles. The largely forgotten testimonies of Republican inmates in French concentration camps from 1939 to 1945 speak of terrible affliction but also of redemption and new life. Agustí Bartra's autobiographical novel *Cristo de 200.000 brazos (Campo de Argelès)* (1943) (The Christ of 200,000 arms [The Argelès camp]) is infused with the imagery of resurrection, communion, and martyrdom, while envisaging "the massive internment camp as a colossal body of Christ, an anthropomorphic symbol of collective pain and suffering." Narratives written decades later, like Dulce Chacón's *La voz dormida (The Sleeping Voice)* (2002) and Manuel Rivas's *El lápiz del carpintero (The Carpenter's Pencil)* (1998), are as much about repressed Republican memories as about resurrection embodying the very core of narrative.[123]

Putting off death has always been a part of storytelling in general. The narratives explored here strongly suggest that the deaths recorded in them are the offshoot of a sense of crisis, which, though certainly political and cultural, is ultimately of a religious nature in the largest sense of the term. For what was being tested on the ground and with words was faith in humankind. The novel as a modern secular form has always pushed at the boundaries of what was and is human, in what may be loosely called a philanthropic embrace of its subject. This spirit of generosity first emerges, historically and emotionally, from a deeply felt religious impulse of *caritas*. It is what led Cadalso's high-born character in *Noches lúgubres* to turn at last toward the gravedigger in recognition of shared mutuality; and what opened novelists in the nineteenth century to the least privileged classes of society, from Ayguals de Izco's *María, la hija de un jornalero* to Galdós's *Fortunata y Jacinta*.

I think it is no accident that religion should be experienced as a crisis of faith at the same time awareness of social inequities was becoming more acute. Nor is it an accident that the novel form would not simply reflect these circumstances but shape itself accordingly to reveal a strong though not fully understood link between faith and literary realism. The 1930s brought these social and political issues to the boiling point in Spain. The explosion of violence and subsequent resolution were catastrophic.

Do novels like Sender's *Réquiem* signal the end of the complicated association between faith and modern literary realism, at least within the Spanish tradition? That question is difficult to answer. The heavy-handed resacralization of Spain under Francoism ironically appears to have considerably weakened religious feeling since the dictator's death.[124] Moreover, the horrors of civil war brought home the real limits of both belief and fiction, for, unlike the ideal power or *potentia* that saints and relics possessed in an earlier age, there is no cure for death.[125] There is, however, *praesentia*, the presence of the sacred, which leaves its trace in places of fiction like Sender's *Réquiem* and makes us believe at once in something human, something invisible, which may be after all one and the same thing.

Epilogue

In 1940, Ángel Valbuena Prat opened his book on the significance of Catholicism in Spanish literature with these words: "One of the greatest achievements of the twentieth-century Spanish soul is awareness of its Catholicity. . . . While the nineteenth century, essentially prone to mystification and sympathetic with any divisiveness, individualism or anarchy, had an evident attraction for the Protestant forms of religiosity, the new century, tending towards organization, a new classicism, hierarchy and unity, is profoundly characterized by the revalidation of Catholic thought and art. . . . [N]ation and religiosity, Catholicism and empire, have fused into a fasces of unity."[1]

Such sentiments, common in the early years of the Franco regime, drew inspiration from the prevailing Falangist mystique of nation and empire and from the nineteenth-century traditionalist scholar Marcelino Menéndez Pelayo. The latter summed up ultraconservative thinking by declaring that the Spanish character was uniquely Catholic and Catholicism the unifying principle behind Spanish culture.[2] Valbuena's language strikes readers now perhaps as a bit creaky and off-putting, reflecting a mindset that is increasingly foreign to a secular age.

Valbuena saw the nineteenth century as full of contradiction and rebellion, as a period that inflicted damage on the faith and therefore on the nation. He wasn't much kinder to the eighteenth century either, which he considered a terrible precursor to the nineteenth. Where were the militant splendor and religious fervor of the Jesuits, the mystics, and ascetics, he asked? the evangelical energy of Cervantes, the ecclesiastical watchtower of Mateo Alemán? By contrast, romantics in the nineteenth century dressed up religion with pretty ornaments and sentiments. Even Catholic novelists like Fernán Caballero and Pereda struck Valbuena as being emotionally charged and theologically underdeveloped, nostalgic for popular faith in the midst of churchly ruins in the one instance and, in the other, for a child's devotion. He singled out Galdós as "the most typical case of the sign of contradiction in the nineteenth century." Though in his view mostly sectarian, the novelist nonetheless discloses an underlying Catholic vision of things in *Nazarín*. Galdós resembled the orator Castelar, who appeared at times "to approach the Christian faith through a secret and unconscious sympathy."[3]

This conflictive subterranean Catholicism, traces of which Valbuena sees in Unamuno as well, is too weak to staunch the widening floodgates of de-Catholicization. By contrast, Spain's religious exceptionalism expanded under empire. Thus the Society of Jesus, "founded under the imperial sign," and its representatives are emblematic of Spanish Catholicism. Father Pedro de Ribadeneyra, Loyola's biographer, synthesizes the age for Valbuena: "He is essentially Jesuit and essentially Spanish. The [religious] order and the nation fuse in his work." The literary historian consequently associates the loss of empire in the early nineteenth century with the loss of faith: "Just as the American colonial empire is broken up . . . so belief, once firm, fades away and is falsified, and the vigorous outlines of dogma split apart, leaving a sea of errors and ignorance in which the literary creations of the most uneven and contradictory century of our culture are floating."[4]

Valbuena's line of thinking places his book squarely within the Francoist ideology of National Catholicism, which reimagined a supremely Catholic state in the twentieth century. I would not be fair to Valbuena Prat, however, were I to leave the impression that his work and the regime's ideology have a seamless continuity. Valbuena produced a classic history of Spanish literature, originally published in 1937 and reprinted in enlarged editions eight more times. And it was his *Historia de la literatura española* (along with an *Historia de la poesía canaria*) that got him into trouble with the regime, ostensibly for a couple of footnotes in which he mentioned the deaths of the poets Luis Rodríguez de Figueroa and Lorca at the hands of Nationalist rebels.

The consequences for Valbuena were severe: he lost his position at the prestigious Universidad de Barcelona and was transferred to a far lesser institution at that time, the Universidad de Murcia, in 1943. It could have been worse. Many faculty were summarily dismissed in the wholesale ideological purging of suspected Republicans or Republican sympathizers during the 1940s. Indeed, the examining magistrate recommended his dismissal on the basis of not only the offending footnotes but also the allegedly negative portrayal of Philip II and a show of sympathy for the sixteenth-century Erasmians and the presumably defeatist Generation of 1898. The Manichean mindset of the regime was blind to Valbuena's nuanced understanding of literary and cultural complexity, preferring a simplistic narrative of Catholic and national triumphalism.[5]

As part of his defense materials Valbuena included his book *El sentido católico en la literatura española,* from 1940.[6] Whether he wrote it precisely to counter the state's charges of ideological impurity I do not know, but his religious sentiments were genuine. Indeed, he had forged his faith anew in the crucible of war. By the end of his life, however, he considered himself a "prototype of the Unamunian *homo religiosus.*" Valbuena's predicament cannot help but remind one of Olavide's dealings with the Inquisition and his reasons for writing *El evangelio en triunfo.* Was the book an act of contrition, a ploy to return home with the king's blessing? or was it a true spiritual journey? Will we ever know? José Jiménez Lozano observes, "The life of these enlightened men is entirely an enigma and a strange ambiguity and indecision, just as the faith of men today is indecisive and agonizing."[7]

Olavide's spiritual impasse, his will to believe replacing belief itself, seems to occupy an indeterminate space between *belief in* and *belief that,* which I have been exploring throughout the book. Only Carretero makes claims to certainty, but his belief is colored in part by the perception that he is in enemy territory, Republican Madrid, which produces the verbal passive-aggressive reaction of the hostile captive. This kind of defensive belligerence was also very much in evidence among the most intransigent of clergymen like Sardá y Sardany.

Both doubt and certainty in the rough waters of radical social-economic change and secular challenges can be seen as different responses to a religious crisis that came to be associated with an equally profound social crisis. Valbuena Prat's contention that belief in the nineteenth century had come apart, "leaving a sea of errors and ignorance" in which Spanish literature was adrift, resonated not only with the regime's supporters but evidently with literary scholars too. This view came to define the period as largely secular or indifferent to religion, on the one hand, and its literature as inadequate, even deficient, on the other. For Valbuena, as for Menéndez Pelayo, there was a distinct correlation between a fractured faith and an unmoored literature: "Literary decadence coincides with the waves of de-Catholicization."[8] There is also a certain irony that subsequent perceptions, far removed from such views, nonetheless continue to promote, rather unthinkingly, an ideologically blinkered understanding of period and literature alike. In that sense, the modern inherited image of the late eighteenth and nineteenth centuries is still unwittingly filtered and distorted through the decaying remains of Francoism.

I am well aware that the negative reaction to nineteenth-century literature, especially the novel, also arose from a change in aesthetic perception in the early twentieth century. One has only to think of the hostility of modernists and vanguard writers to realism. My point, however, in arguing for an unintended ideological bias toward the period's literary production is precisely to disclose its masking of the complex relation between religion and literature. Such bias fails to see the significance of that relation. It also fails to question critical reliance on outdated, reductive models of the nineteenth century that are historically distorted. The Foucauldianist approach in particular often turns nineteenth-century Spanish novels into Francoist authoritarian fictions, a peculiarly backhand homage to the impact of Francoism on the critical imagination. The nineteenth century is not, however, the twentieth, as such unhistorical renderings regrettably tend to suggest. The effect of this approach is to secularize everything from the late eighteenth century on, ironically feeding into the Francoist critique of the period as religiously disreputable, when both literature and history tell a different story. Indeed, one could argue that not only a reductive Foucauldianism but Francoism itself ultimately secularized the religious sphere. Both blurred the distinctions between the secular and the sacred and cultivated the invasive effects of power relations, theoretically in the one case, practically in the other.

While such studies consider the superior artistic merits of novels like *Fortunata y Jacinta* and *La Regenta* a given, they sometimes narrow critical and artistic understanding of them. They ignore contradictory or ambiguous textual evidence and are too often inattentive to multivalent meanings and irony or difficult-to-grasp but fundamental things like the complex life of the spirit. The thinness of this kind of analysis, which tends to see texts principally as vehicles of thought or ideology, ironically reinforces the mistaken notion that such literature is aesthetically wanting, less original than earlier Spanish or contemporary European works. The vexed relation between religion and fiction is just one example of a woefully neglected area of study that can provide a richer, more layered understanding of the ways in which these texts diverge from other literary-cultural traditions or strikingly reinterpret an older tradition. Hence, the example of *La Regenta,* which is not another *Madame Bovary* but a modern world of sin arising out of a creative and conflictive engagement with religious tradition. We need to take religion of the period seriously, precisely because these writers did.

This is why Valbuena was closer to the mark in dwelling upon what he called "a secret and unconscious sympathy" for the Christian faith in the apparently unlikeliest of writers from the late eighteenth century on. Only I do not think there was anything secret or unconscious about it. That people do not readily see it today speaks more to the limitations of the present age than to those of the recent past. In the three periods I have examined, the fact of faith could no longer be taken for granted, the late eighteenth century marking the beginnings of a religious crisis among enlightenment figures like Cadalso and Olavide. This intimately experienced fractured faith is expressed in fiction through a new embryonic psychological-social realism, which serves to project spiritual feeling onto the page but also to shape it through humanitarian purposefulness. The sufferings of the laboring poor and indigent, made worse by economic and political woes, were the new relics of faith, there for anyone to see, irritating but also distressing the privileged members of society.

What is fascinating about texts like *Noches lúgubres, El evangelio en triunfo,* and *Cornelia Bororquia* is the degree to which their narrating voices internalize such sufferings, regardless of gender or social class, populating their inner lives with the early makings of neighborhoods. The sense of the neighbor as one's lived alternate self—"Let us walk together, my friend," Tediato says—is put to work precisely at the point when a crisis in faith meets up with the impending social-economic crisis of modernity. This is the point when the modern self, infused with the social-affective virtues of sensibility, decides to walk with another, to enter into another home, or into another's inner space through an exchange of letters, and thereby change the world or at least the perception of it.[9]

When fiction takes that step (and not all fiction does), it becomes neither a substitute for religion nor a consolation for its absence, but a piece of shared territory belonging to the imagination of both realms. Durkheim observes generally that although "religious thought is something very different from a system of fictions, still the realities to which it corresponds express themselves religiously only when religion transfigures them. . . . So the world of religious things is a partially imaginary world, though only in its outward form."[10] The transformative uses of the imagination mark both the distinctions and points of contact between religion and fiction as well as the distinctions between different kinds of reality: belief in the reality of the divine and belief in the reality of fictions.

That step toward a humanitarian narrative which issues from the self in its relation with others marks the point at which modern realism departs from *Don Quijote* in both senses of the word. Literary realism is born of a Christian knight whose peculiar reality as a character contradicts his very existence.

Cervantes understood perfectly the dilemma of his particular brand of realism and allowed his character to die. There are no more Christian knights, and maybe there never were. By imagining one who is at once a knight and not a knight, Cervantes brought a form of belief to the fore, both in the creation of his character and in the belief that sustains him and his imagination. This belief is not exclusively religious, though it is certainly infused with Christian values, but emerges from Don Quijote's own fragile, imperfect persona in his relation with the world and in the way he perceives it.

His belief in an imaginary world is contingent on the real world but also belief itself. That belief makes his world real but is also vulnerable to critique, when the two worlds of reality and belief collide, producing uncertainty. Still, he conducts himself with the fervor of true faith, suggesting that different kinds of belief can be instrumental in imagining a fictional universe that is built upon a sliding foundation moving between belief in and belief that.

Modern realism has inherited Cervantine uncertainty but lost the Christian knight. Or perhaps better said, the knight in some cases has become the privileged narrator or character, the philanthropist one sees in Ayguals de Izco's and Galdós's texts, who is still trying to redress injustices and save his neighbors. (Don Quijote's delusions spread throughout Western fiction.) These novelists and their narrative proxies were also, however, responding to a specific social-religious reality of more sharply etched class differences, growing secularization, and political-economic change. Spain remained largely Catholic during much of the period. Signs of spiritual unease and public turmoil, however, such as the killing of religious in 1834, anticlerical attacks in print, and anti-Church measures in parliament, point to a looming religious crisis that finally came to a terrible paroxysm of violence in 1936. That crisis was also social, as I have been arguing throughout this book. Thus, the humanitarian concern reflected here is based not only on evangelical feeling but on a new secular grasp of economic and social privation. The philanthropic embrace of narratives like *María* and *Fortunata y Jacinta* is both religious and social. The central focus moves away from the residual figure of the knight and toward Ayguals's imagined urban village and Galdós's intricate, citywide web of social relations, which strikingly recalls the clientelistic network of benefactor-beneficiary in modern philanthropy. Episodic adventures, which created connections among characters, give way to an emphasis on human relations that produce an urban geography of interdependency. The master–servant bond, notable in *Don Quijote* and the picaresque, doesn't disappear. Instead it becomes part of an extended network of social relations and obligations in which the privileged are encouraged to see the less privileged as humanitarian objects of reform.

The stress on community also becomes the stresses of community, with conflict built into human relations, as Galdós brilliantly shows in large ways and small. His understanding of sacred realism, or spiritual naturalism, as he termed it, is predicated on human imperfection. But he also insists on the transformative nature of the spirit, which binds his characters together as much as economic, familial, and social ties do. In imagining a narrative of philanthropic and Eucharistic design, he does not, however, propose religion as a solution to the ways of the world. Neither is religion divisive or productive of anguish, as it is in Clarín's *La Regenta*. Galdós had explored religious conflict in earlier thesis novels like *Gloria* and *La familia de León Roch* but appears to have recognized in his mature fiction the aesthetic perils of politicizing religion, perils Ayguals de Izco and Carretero overlooked.

Clarín, on the other hand, examines religious divisiveness not only as an image of social decay and rift, but also as opening a window onto secretly fractured individual and collective identities: hence the importance of the confessional model as narrative disclosure that also gives a richly authoritative textual shape. The confessional model allows the novelist, like a director of conscience, to delve into hidden social, religious, and psychological depths and bring them to the narrative surface. The continual play between a politics of religion and a religion of politics structures texts like *María* and *La revolución de los patibularios*. A critique of both, however, informs *La Regenta*, for both are indications of a torn social fabric, as the civil war settings in Ayguals and Carretero suggest.

Perhaps more than any other novel discussed here, *La Regenta* exemplifies what Flannery O'Connor says about fiction in general: "The novelist doesn't write about people in a vacuum; he writes about people in a world where something is obviously lacking, where there is the general mystery of incompleteness and the particular tragedy of our own times to be demonstrated."[11] All these narratives, in different ways, are responding to something that is obviously lacking, to what I have observed as an improper, or flawed, birth. This condition is both singular and familial, spiritual and social, in Clarín's narrative.

The Vetustan world of *La Regenta* is, above all, an unredeemed one, its modern secularism illuminated as in a glass darkly through a powerful religious imagination. Redemption haunts many of these narratives, from Olavide's *Evangelio* to Galdós's *Fortunata y Jacinta* to Sender's *Réquiem*. The peasant who is cruelly sacrificed in Sender's novel has a name but is also nameless. He is the social bond, the empowering moral sense of obligation of one person to another that constitutes society, and he is the individual who is wept over as unique. *Réquiem* enacts a politics of martyrdom. Its political meaning of social justice and reform cannot be fully understood apart from the religious question that sustains Sender's text: what is the meaning of our faith in humankind?

The particular narrative forms that sacred realism assumed — forms like communion, confession, and martyrdom — do not make these novels any less secular. They do suggest, however, a not fully grasped relation between faith and the development of modern literary realism. There are, moreover, no claims to saying all novels share in this special kind of moral-imaginative universe, or even that novels like *La Regenta* and *Fortunata y Jacinta* can be understood only in such terms. Historically, however, religion as an expression of a crisis of modernity appears linked to the appearance of evolving narrative forms focused on ethical-spiritual issues of belief and social concern. More broadly speaking, the kind of belief system we call religion may exercise a role in the kind of belief system we call fiction. Durkheim wrote that "the true justification of religious practices does not lie in the apparent ends which they pursue, but rather in the invisible action which they exercise over the mind and in the way in which they effect our mental status." There is, he said, an "impulse towards believing, [which] is just what constitutes faith." Unamuno went further and declared, "To believe is to create."[12]

Realism as a literary genre has always played a complicated part in convincing readers to believe in its special universe. Whatever the eventual forms of invisible action that motivate belief, they appear as inescapable, constitutive of how we regard what is real, how we distinguish between different kinds of reality, and whether one kind of reality is capable of affecting our perception of another kind. By creating or seeking an alternative secular site of community, the realist novel embodies a specifically imagined neighborliness, belief in the social bonds that make possible belief in ourselves. The practical sense of realism richly observes this being in the world with others, in all the comings and goings, quarrels and chatter of its characters. But such being is also deeply moral, attached to the sacred foundations of sociality. This too has been my focus and object of concern: how that sociality is perceived when a belief system is in crisis, how Spanish Catholicism in periods of destabilizing secularization and religious revival has affected the structures and perspectives of modern narrative in ways that even now continue to reverberate.

Notes

Introduction

1. Alas, "Cartas" 1172: "De mí te puedo decir que mientras creía en Dios, porque sí, porque *algo inefable* me giraba en el corazón, fui religioso, sincero . . . pero intermitente. Llegaban esas horas de sequedad de que habla un santo místico en que ni la oración ni la fe bastan para hacer brotar agua de la peña . . . si escogía por materia de/ese vértigo [espiritual] la idea de Dios, el tormento era horrible. ¿Hay Dios?, ¿no hay Dios?, esto me preguntaba, y como el corazón en tales tormentos nada decía, y como *las pruebas de la existencia de Dios* son lugares comunes, *tópicos* de la lógica . . . [de] un intelectualismo infecundo, no había medio de salir de aquella pena, árida y estéril." I have followed the practice of using "Alas" and "Clarín" interchangeably. Unless otherwise noted, all translations into English are my own; and all emphases, the original author's.

2. C. S. Lewis (1941), "Weight" 15–16.

3. C. S.Lewis, "Weight" 19; Levinas ix, 71. For Levinas's biblical echoes, see *Leviticus* 19: 34 and *Matthew* 25: 35.

4. González Echevarría, Introduction 7; also Valbuena Prat 104. For studies on religion and *Don Quijote,* see: Singleton; Goodwyn; DiSalvo; and Higuera. Modifying his earlier stance (*Pensamiento* 1925) on Don Quijote's alienated hypocritical subterfuge toward religious orthodoxy, Américo Castro calls Cervantes's novel "a secularized form of religious spirituality"(*Cervantes* 90). Other readings see it as "strictly secular literature" (Darst 50), as skeptical or even materialist (Graf, "Martin"). Giles Gunn suggests that "Cervantes's genius, even his religious genius, seems to derive from his ability to hold in tension . . . a desire to valorize the place of religious and moral idealisms even as he

ridicules the lengths to which they can be carried, and a concern to challenge the claims of all vulgar materialism while upholding the sacred integrity of the actual and the ordinary. The result is a novel in which a new and unquestionably unorthodox meaning is given to the Christian understanding of incarnate life" (185).

5. Scarry 205.

6. Borg 20.

7. Borg 20–21.

8. For the historical-cultural study of religion in modern Spain, see: Cuenca Toribio; Drochon; Jiménez Duque; Portero Molina; Vaquero Iglesias; Payne; Longares Alonso; Aubert; Callahan; de la Cueva; Hibbs-Lissorgues; Yetano; J. Sánchez; Lannon; Vincent; and Christian; also J. Varela, who defines early twentieth-century Spanish intellectuals by a struggle between clericalism and anticlericalism. On religion (and anticlericalism) in modern Spanish literature, see: Bécarud; Savaiano; Miranda García; Dendle, *Spanish Novel*; Devlin; García de Cortázar; and Pérez Gutiérrez.

9. See M. S. Fernández; Labanyi, *Gender*; and Fuentes Peris.

10. P. Lewis 673; Cox 208 (decline of religion); also Jakobsen and Pellegrini; G. Smith.

11. Knight and Mason 3, 9.

12. García Montero 28 and Curtius 310 (blood of martyrs); Curtius 319–26 (book of nature); Gossman 27–28, 31 (text as sacred; "ineffable"); Bénichou 57, 93 (theology of sentiment); Chateaubriand 1: 43.

13. Gunn 173.

14. Promey 585.

15. Silverman 34, 13; see also Pecora 179, on evangelical traces in Virginia Woolf.

16. Milbank (in Pecora 2) (*saeculum*); Pecora 2, 13, 205 (secularization; laity); also Jakobsen and Pellegrini 11. Graeme Smith claims that "secularism [is] the latest expression of the Christian religion" (2).

17. See also Berger 24 on the now-widespread antireligious attitudes of the "Enlightened Intelligentsia of Europe."

18. Not all studies follow this model. The nuanced work of Pérez Gutiérrez, Dufour, Lissorgues, and others noted later readily comes to mind. Reductive readings, however, continue to appear. See Timothy Mitchell's 1998 unsubtle psychosocial view of priestly "authoritarian sexuality" and anticlericalism in Alas's *La Regenta* (48–55). Kathy Bacon's earnest attempt to adapt Bourdieu's notion of cultural capital (and my own critique of *cursilería*) to late nineteenth-century notions of saintliness and sainthood in Spanish religious discourse and fiction is ultimately unconvincing, confusing social (namely, *cursilería* and prestige) and religious values indiscriminately and ignoring the real import of religion and religious crisis. No doubt a good deal of Restoration-period religious discourse is riddled with the language of *cursilería* (lachrymose sentimentality especially); and religious behavior in novels like *La Regenta* and Galdós's *La familia de León Roch* appears socially motivated in numerous instances, but that is a far cry from Bacon's claim that religious discourse, or saintliness, was concerned with distinction. This is an imposition of current-day values upon an earlier age.

19. Knight and Mason 3.

20. For this brief historical account, I have profited from the valuable work of Payne, Callahan, Lannon, and others cited in note 8 above.

21. The term "evangelical," as applied to texts by Olavide, Ayguals de Izco, Galdós, and Sender, should not be confused with current-day U.S. conservative fundamentalism. "Evangelical" refers to the Gospel, the good news of Christ. Though Olavide, for example, stresses the significance of religious conversion, conversion leads to humanitarian activism in *El evangelio en triunfo*. Thus conversionism by and in itself (*sola fide*) is not the point, nor does biblicism (*sola scriptura*), basic to U.S. fundamentalism, figure in any of these narratives, almost all of which lean variously leftward.

22. Galdós, *Fortunata* 594: "Sentíala dentro de sí, como si se la hubiera tragado, cual si la hubiera tomado en comunión" (2: 236).

23. Alas, "Revista literaria" 1635: "injertar en la España católica la España liberal."

24. For a lucid study of the conflict between religion and politics in the West, see Burleigh.

25. A. Peterson xix, 13–14, 89.

26. Thrower 9, 44.

27. James (mystical states); Otto, 5–7, 12–13, 94 (numinous in Catholicism).

28. See Voltaire 358.

29. Feuerbach 2; Nietzsche, *Portable* 95, 634; Freud (1927), *Future* 31, 44, 28, 48, 49; Marx 12, 11; Durkheim 466.

30. Thrower 202; Runzo xiii (religious realism).

31. Hick 11 (universe), 13.

32. Geertz 124 (template); Eliade 22–23 (sacred world); C. S. Lewis, "Membership" 106 (way of life).

33. Chadwick 6.

34. See C. S. Lewis, "Transposition" (glossolalia); Alas, "Revista literaria" 1634–35: "Rezo a mi modo, con lo que siento, con lo que recuerdo de la niñez de mi vida . . . con lo que le dicen al alma la música del órgano y los cantos del coro, cuya letra no llega a mi oído, pero cuyas melodías me estremecen . . . ; mi espíritu habla allí para sus adentros una especie de glosolalia que debe de parecerse a la de aquellos cristianos de la primera Iglesia, poco aleccionados todavía en las afirmaciones concretas de sus dogmas, pero llenos de inefables emociones."

35. C. S. Lewis, "Theology" 78.

36. C. S. Lewis, "Theology" 78; Geertz 112 ("really real") (also Eliade 27, 41, 83); Gunn 181.

37. Gunn 181; also Nussbaum's utilitarian view of the literary imagination.

38. Scarry 197 ("sustained imagining"); Unamuno, "Prólogo" 18: "Creer es crear."

39. Greeley 1 (also Tracy 413); S. Fitzgerald xxi (Flannery O'Connor's view of the invisible); see also Weil 169.

40. See Greeley 6, on metaphor; also Weil 171. Greeley and Heartney acknowledge their debt to David Tracy, who argues that "the classic works of Catholic theologians and artists tend to emphasize the presence of God in the world, while the classic works of Protestant theologians tend to emphasize the absence of God from the world" (Greeley 5); see Tracy 383, 387.

41. Promey 598 (critique of Heartney).

42. Greeley 4, 31; Minnis 242–43 (imagination as troubling); della Mirandola (qtd in Minnis 243); de la Puente (1605), *Sentimientos* 322: "desorden es en pensamientos e

imaginaciones, los cuales son desordenados, o por ser de cosas dañosas, o vanas, o impertinentes para el tiempo, o con demasiado ahinco"; de la Puente (1605), *Meditaciones* 333: "imaginar a su alma dentro deste cuerpo, como está un reo en la cárcel, con una cadena al cuello, con grillos en los pies y esposas en las manos."

43. See Forcione 14, 30–33, 92–104, on the canon of Toledo; Plato 339 (also Ife 17–21); Vives (1524), *Education* 74–75; Castro, *Pensamiento* 60–61 n20, Bataillon 615–23 and Ife 11, 14–15 (hostility to romances of chivalry); Ife 15, 12, 14 (anxiety).

44. See Ilie, "¿Luces?" (Enlightenment critiques of imagination); Forner 69: "¿Dónde está aquella fecundidad de imaginación tan pródiga, que, pasando los términos de lo conveniente, a modo de río que sale de madre por la abundancia del caudal, hacía a la poesía más poética de lo que debía ser?" (*Exequias,* composed 1786–88); Isla 1:9–10: "¿qué razón habrá divina ni humana para que mi imaginativa no se divierta en fabricarse un padrecito rechoncho, atusado y vivaracho . . . ? ¿Por ventura la imaginación [de ellos] tuvo algún privilegio que no tenga también la mía, aunque pobre y pecadora?"; Cadalso, *Noches* 69: "monstruos producidos por una fantasía llena de tristeza. ¡Fantasía humana!, ¡fecunda sólo en quimeras, ilusiones y objetos de terror!"; Feijoo 99: "No son pocos los que de noche juzguen ver espectros, o fantasmas, aunque a los más dicta la razón que no son más que apariencias engañosas." Ilie, "¿Luces?," also cites these sources.

45. Feijoo 98–99: "¿Pero los que leen, u oyen estas fabulosas narraciones, no saben que lo son? . . . ¿No saben también, que sólo los acontecimientos reales, y en ninguna manera los fingidos merecen mover nuestros afectos? . . . ¿Qué es esto sino un ejercicio de potencia tiránica, un declarado *Despotismo de la Imaginativa,* una violenta intrusión de ésta en los derechos del entendimiento, una usurpación, que ejerce la facultad inferior sobre los fueros de la superior?" Such criticisms could be found in many places. See, for example, Gérard's *Le Comte de Valmont, ou les égaremens de la raison* (The count of Valmont, or the errancy of reason) (1774–76): "Novels seduce and carry one away. . . . They inspire in a young heart a vague and uncertain sensibility. . . . A sweet and seductive reverie attaches [the reader] to imaginary objects. . . . The imagination heats up; all the passions are on fire; the senses too acquire a dangerous and precocious activity; and one feels guilty" (1: 291).

46. Feijoo 99; Pascual de Sanjuan and Viñas y Cusí 105–06 (training manual).

47. López Peláez 150: "La lectura de novelas puede concluir por alterar violentamente la regularidad del funcionamiento de los nervios, produciendo trastornos cerebrales muy profundos. . . . No es raro que las mujeres entregadas á estas perturbadoras lecturas padezcan de histerismo, tengan pesadillas, y prorrumpan por el menor motivo en llanto nervioso"; 151: "los terrores nocturnos, las alucinaciones, los vértigos, los desvanecimientos, los presentimientos vanos y los temores pueriles"; "el abuso de la imaginación produce el desgaste de las células del cerebro."

48. Ladrón de Guevara 49–50; Ugarte (qtd in Ladrón de Guevara 676).

49. Coloma, "Prólogo" vii; viii: "La novela . . . exalta . . . la imaginación del lector bisoño . . . y forja en su fantasía un bello mundo ideal . . . : de aquí nace el desengaño prematuro, el descontento de la vida práctica." See also Mainer, *Escritura* 26–32.

50. Coloma, "Prólogo" viii: "esta cosa árida es la prosa de la vida, que despoetiza todos los sueños"; ix.

51. Sardá y Salvany 24: "que ser blasfemo, ladrón, adúltero u homicida."

52. See Durkheim 52.

53. Sardá y Salvany 18: "libertad de pensamiento sin limitación alguna en política, en moral o en religión."

54. Alas, "Libre" 159: "la influencia liberal, expansiva, noble, profunda, espontánea"; 161: "la novela de Galdós no ha influido sólo en estudiantes libre-pensadores y en socios de ateneos y clubes, sino que ha penetrado en el santuario del hogar, allí donde solían ser alimento del espíritu libros devotos y libros profanos de hipócrita o estúpida moralidad casera, sin grandeza y hermosura"; Ladrón de Guevara 438.

55. Durkheim 475.

56. A. Baker ("religion of uncertainty"); Unamuno, "Mi religión" 10: "Mi religión es buscar la verdad en la vida y la vida en la verdad, aun a sabiendas de que no he de encontrarlas mientras viva; mi religión es luchar incesante e incansablemente con el misterio; mi religión es luchar con Dios desde el romper del alba hasta el caer de la noche."

57. See Fernández Sebastián and Fuentes, for use of the word "crisis" in Spain; Rawlings, Bataillon, Higuera, A. D. Wright, and Homza, for religion in early modern Spain; Rawlings 120–27, 143.

58. Payne, *Spanish Catholicism* 44, 53, 69–70 (religion in eighteenth-century Spain); Noel 867 (preachers).

59. Liguori 254–55.

60. See Lannon 21.

61. Callahan, *Church, Politics* 48–49.

62. See Herr 31, 33–34 (condition of the laboring classes); Callahan, "Confinement" 3–5 and Martz 7–13 (Vives and social reforms).

63. Vives, *Assistance* 35 (poor folk as threat), 44–45.

64. Vives, *Assistance* 45. Amar y Borbón 152 echoes the emphasis on inner faith (1790). Years later, Ayguals writes that "sublime religion does not consist in trifling externals" (*El tigre del Maestrazgo* 413) (1846–48).

65. Sarrailh 4, 8. Sarrailh (6–7) questions the sincerity of conversion in *El evangelio en triunfo*. Interestingly, the traditionalist Menéndez Pelayo felt that *El evangelio* was filled with "conviction and faith" (2: 847; and 693), as does Alonso Seoane, "Obra" 38.

66. Meléndez Valdés 278: "las máximas de que *el pobre es una imagen viva del Redentor; la pobreza, Dios la amó; pobre de Jesucristo; pobre, pero honrado,* aplicadas a la mendiguez por la ignorancia o una caridad irreflexiva, la fomentan, la canonizan y producen en la sociedad las consecuencias más fatales . . . Sépase que [el cristianismo] no sólo recomienda el trabajo como un remedio contra las tentaciones compañeras del ocio, sino que lo manda rigurosamente como una pena de nuestra corrupción; sépase que la mendiguez es una plaga de la sociedad que la degrada y la destruye . . . sépase que estamos obligados a distribuirlas con discreción y conocimiento, si las queremos dar según la razón y el Evangelio." By contrast, the traditional view of the poor as the image of Christ (and of poverty as a Christian ideal) persists in the nineteenth-century pronouncements of clerics, who sought a resacralized, archaic view of society; see Portero Molina 182–83 and Yetano 138.

67. Cassirer 136.

68. See Marchena's advocacy of religious liberty in "A la nación española" (To the

Spanish nation) (1792) (*Obras* 159–64) and Herr 273–77; Gutiérrez 171: "*el hombre de Cristo* debe ser dulce, humilde y caritativo, y jamás puede lícitamente maltratar a su hermano. Cuando digo hermano, no creáis que excluyo a los individuos de otra secta cualquiera que sea . . . porque Dios me dice que todos los hombres son mis hermanos."

69. Callahan, *Church, Politics* 78.

70. Herr 444.

71. Among the translations of French religious apologists was that of Gérard's popular *Le comte de Valmont, ou les égaremens de la raison* (1774–76). The Spanish title became *Triunfos de la verdadera religion, contra los extravios de la razon, en el Conde de Valmont* (The triumph of true religion, against the errancy of reason, in the count of Valmont) (1792–93). See also Herrero 24, 35–45, 48–50; and Y. Fuentes, for the impact of French anti-Enlightenment thought and the French Revolution on ultraconservative Spanish Catholics.

72. Such reformers, often characterized as Jansenists, challenged the authority of the Inquisition and Rome and advocated an inner-directed religion and religious tolerance. See Herr 398–434; 442 (struggle over church reform); also Callahan, *Church, Politics* 70–72, 79–85.

73. See Herrero 373–83; and Álvarez Junco, *Mater Dolorosa* 344.

74. *Semanario Patriótico* (qtd in Fernández Sebastián and Fuentes, "Crisis" 201) (Annals); Larra (qtd in Tarr 11): "hay crisis para rato."

75. Jiménez Lozano, *Meditación* 45–46 (long war); see also G. Smith 190–205, on the vexed relation between liberalism and Christianity.

76. Jiménez Lozano maintains that nineteenth-century Spain was "in sum a sacralized universe," meaning that "all the institutions and even the smallest gesture possess a religious meaning" (*Meditación* 55, 128 n62).

77. Naharro, *Método* 78: "hacedme la gracia de recibir este estudio en parte de mi penitencia, á fin de que mis conocimientos estén libres de error y vanidad." I have maintained original orthography and punctuation when citing original sources not available in modern editions.

78. Naharro, *Arte* vi. For Naharro, see Cotarelo y Mori 2: 105; Castañeda y Alcover 397–99; and Valis, *Culture* 78.

79. Larra 261: "blasfeman contra la Providencia . . . porque suponen que ha puesto en lucha en nuestro corazón la creencia y la realidad. Criarnos para eso hubiera sido un sarcasmo." For the Larra-Lamennais relationship, see J. L.Varela; and La Parra López ("Eco"). Larra was apparently translating Lamennais by spring 1836; the translation appeared in print on September 4 (see J. L.Varela 301; and Tarr 20). Lamennais's influence among the left-wing of Spanish liberalism — from Larra and Espronceda to Monlau, Ribot i Fontseré, and Ayguals — in the 1830s and 1840s was enormous (R. M. González 90).

80. Larra 268: "Religión pura, fuente de toda moral, y religión . . . acompañada de la tolerancia y de la libertad de conciencia; libertad civil; igualdad completa ante la ley, e igualdad [de oportunidades] . . . y libertad absoluta del pensamiento escrito. He aquí la profesión de fe del traductor." See also Portero Molina 127–32, for the Church's critique of liberty as undermining Catholic teachings.

81. Alas, *Juan Ruiz* 135–36: "Acabo de leerlo y mi ánimo se ha afectado profundamente . . . Religión y justicia, he ahí en lo que se funda la felicidad terrena . . . Buscar la

felicidad temporal de nuestros semejantes es el más bello mérito que podemos presentar a nuestro Hacedor para lograr la nuestra eterna. . . . [¿Q]uién me negará que el progreso es amado de Dios, porque se esfuerza en presentarle hijos dignos de su amor divino? . . . ¿es Dios el autor de la felicidad o es el progreso? Dios, respondo, es el autor. Él nos la ha presentado asequible, y a nosotros nos toca el alcanzarla." I have merged the one-sentence paragraphs for the sake of readability.

82. Lissorgues, *Leopoldo Alas* 93 n28. While it has been suggested Larra lacked faith or was indifferent to it, La Parra López ("Eco") inclines toward calling him a troubled liberal Catholic, as do I. He also properly notes that neither doubts nor liberal attacks on the ultra-Catholic Carlists in the 1830s are a clear indication of lack of belief (324–28).

83. Callahan, *Church, Politics* 131, 134 (violent anticlericalism).

84. Galdós, *Un faccioso* 237 (*matanza*); Callahan, *Church, Politics* 153; see also Menéndez Pelayo 2: 1136–43, for the conspiratorial view, and Fray Francisco García's eyewitness account (rptd in Revuelta González, *Anticlericalismo* 39–45), orig. in *Archivo Iberoamericano*, 2ª época, 2 (1914): 493–98. The participation of urban militiamen in the clergy killings is of particular interest, since its membership was largely open to all and included a good number of middle- and upper middle-class liberals, among them writers like Larra, Espronceda, Gil de Zárate, and Ventura de la Vega, although there is no evidence they took part in the violence (see J. L. Varela 298). García calls the militiamen *nacionales*, not *urbanos* (39, 42). There is a fascinating reference to this period from Gil de Zárate (1843), who regrets having been carried away by his anticlerical passions (357–59).

85. See Cuenca Toribio, *Iglesia* 57 and Longares Alonso 187, on the religious crisis; Wiseman 121, 135–36. The Anglo-Irish Cardinal Wiseman (1802–65), author of the popular historical novel *Fabiola* (1854), was born and lived his first three years in Seville, where his father, a merchant, had settled in 1771. See Valis, "Huella."

86. Wiseman 143. See also Gil de Zárate 364–65, for examples of private charity toward ex-clergy whose religious orders Mendizábal had dissolved.

87. See also Baulo, "Novela popular" 68.

88. Aranguren 60, 177; Artola 348. Although I disagree with Aranguren here, his is a pioneering study, indispensable to understanding nineteenth-century Spain. See Dufour ("Diffusion"; and "*Crónica*"), on a small group of liberal Catholics, including the clergyman Juan Antonio Llorente, in the period 1820–23. Their history has been largely eradicated from mainstream accounts. See also Ginger's enlightening reappraisal of the period 1830–50 (350); and La Parra López, "Anticlericalismo." In the wake of the Revolution of 1868, some clergy who veered toward liberalism were further influenced by Protestant missions active in post-1868 Spain (Drochon, "Un curé' " 284–86, 288; also Hughey 53–68).

89. Cuenca Toribio, "Catholicisme" 107 n11 (Larra); Longares Alonso (Barcelona newspapers); Ayguals de Izco, *El tigre del Maestrazgo* 341 (also *La marquesa de Bellaflor* 1:39); *El Guardia Nacional* (1 January 1840) (qtd in Longares Alonso 194): "La religión cristiana, aun prescindiendo de su carácter divino, y políticamente mirada, es la más libre y la primera constitución del mundo"; and *El Guardia Nacional* (29 November 1838) (qtd in Longares Alonso 195): "la religión cristiana . . . es la religión del hombre y hermana con la libertad."

90. *El Constitucional* (20 August 1837) (qtd in Longares Alonso 222): "la fraternidad

universal, la fraternidad de Cristo . . . la *humanidad* anunciada por Cristo, que comprende a todo el género humano"; *El Constitucional* (20 August 1837) (qtd in Longares Alonso 221): "Cristo vino para todos . . . antes de su venida había dos naturalezas para los hombres: la naturaleza de amo y la naturaleza de esclavo. El las hizo desaparecer"; *El Constitucional* (5 March 1840) (qtd in Longares Alonso 222): "todas las clases están confundidas, . . . el rico y el pobre, el sabio y el ignorante, el progresista y el retrógrado, el demócrata y el aristócrata." See R. M. González's useful study of nineteenth-century humanitarian democracy ("democracia humanitaria").

91. Mazzini, "Faith" 168.

92. Mazzini, "Faith" 174.

93. Mazzini, "Faith" 183; "Patriots" (1835) 214, 207, 206 (also 197–98, 207–08). Mazzinian ideas permeated the thinking and actions of "Young Spain," founded by Fernando Garrido in 1848, and influenced insurrectionists in southern Spain during the 1850s and 1860s (Thomson 354, 361, 373–74). Mazzini maintained contact with Garrido, Castelar, Nicolás Díaz-Pérez, and other Spanish democrats.

94. Mazzini, "Faith" 179; "Patriots" 210; "Faith" 150.

95. See Longares Alonso 208 (perilous ground); Castelar, *Fórmula* 97, 77: "La Democracia no es contraria al Cristianismo, es la realización social del Cristianismo"; "El progreso es nuestra creencia, nuestra fé. El progreso es . . . la fé del siglo XIX." See also Toscano Liria 84–91, for Castelar's religiously inspired rhetoric. Most churchmen, however, considered Castelar an enemy of religion. The Jesuits in Pérez de Ayala's novel *A.M.D.G.* derisively name a burro "Castelar" (130–31).

96. Valera, "Doctrina" 83, 88, 91: "considerar el cristianismo como un progreso vale tanto como tenerle por una invención humana"; "[caer] en las tinieblas"; "Estos han dicho que el cristianismo es liberal para que los liberales sean cristianos: aquellos que es absolutista para que los absolutistas lo sean."

97. Valera, "Doctrina" 104, 115: "sea una doctrina política y social"; "que el Sr. Castelar sea demócrata, liberal, progresista y católico ferviente, todo a la vez. . . . Lo que sí repugno es que haga . . . una síntesis o combinación peligrosa de todas estas doctrinas, sosteniéndolas todas, o haciéndolas dimanar de la santa doctrina de Nuestro Señor Jesucristo." See also the similar opinion of the Republican Manuel Azaña in 1931 ("Política" 52).

98. See Pérez Gutiérrez 28 (Valera's theory of secularization).

99. Valera, *Correspondencia* 2: 169 (letter dated 27 April 1864): "Yo creo que los artículos más *impíos* del tomo son los que te chocan por demasiado teológicos: los artículos contra Castelar. Todos aquellos misticismos y teologías no son más que para despojar a la religión católica de toda influencia en la civilización y en los destinos humanos positivos, reduciéndola a una cosa excelente para los que quieran irse al cielo por el camino derecho. Esto es achicar la religión y convertirla en una inutilidad para todo lo grande, activo y enérgico de la vida de las naciones, del arte, de la política, de la ciencia y de la economía social. ¿Cómo quieres tú que en España, sin inutilizarme para todo y para siempre, hubiera yo podido decir tales cosas sin velarlas con reticencia e ironía?"

100. See also Garagorri 68–73, who brings together Valera's view of *Don Quijote* and his letter of 1864 as proof of a kind of "heroic hypocrisy," akin to how Ortega y Gasset and Castro saw Cervantes.

101. Azaña, *Ensayos* 40. See also Tierno Galván, on Valera as both a pícaro and an "idealist-pragmatist" ("Valera").

102. Pérez Gutiérrez 96.

103. Valera, "Doctrina" 93; Palacio Valdés 466. See also Dendle, *Spanish Novel* 15.

104. Canalejas 294, 295: "el hambre de lo sobrenatural"; "Hemos arrancado la ortodoxia del seno de la sociedad actual . . . en religion, como en política, romper con lo tradicional equivale á imponerse una peregrinacion dolorosa, agitadísima, al traves del verdadero laberinto que la febril actividad espiritual de nuestro siglo crea y enmaraña incesantemente. Es necesario tomar viril y noblemente una resolucion en esta crisis espiritual."

105. Canalejas 329: "Es la negacion de Dios, que el hombre tiene la terrible facultad de formular, negacion que va creciendo como testimonio de la libertad humana, al compás que la religion obra y actúa y engrandece al espíritu de los hombres . . . El ateismo aparecerá siempre con mayor intensidad en los períodos más religiosos, expresando la relacion lógica que enlaza la afirmacion con las negaciones."

106. Fernández Sebastián and Fuentes, "Crisis" 204.

107. D.J.M.L. ix, vi: "el siglo de las luces está rodeado de tinieblas. Se titula humanitario, é inventa todos los medios para matar . . . Se titula filántropo, amante del pueblo, y destruye todos los elementos que dieron vida á las clases proletarias." Menéndez Pelayo called this period of civil war and cantonalism "times of apocalyptic desolation" (2: 1353). See also Christian, *Visionaries* 348–72, for the apocalyptic tradition and its relation to the Ezkioga apparitions and prophecies of the early 1930s.

108. See Christian, *Visionaries* 4–5, 352.

109. See Clark 25; Herrero 23–24 refers to a similar pan-Europeanism for the eighteenth and early nineteenth centuries.

110. Jonas 90 (Sacred Heart), 176.

111. Payne, *Spanish Catholicism* 106 (Sacred Heart cult); Lannon 30 (*Messenger*).

112. See J. Sánchez 1.

113. See Christian, *Visionaries* 394.

114. Qtd in Lannon 31.

115. See Boyd 51; qtd in Boyd 48.

116. See Boyd 59.

117. See Bosco Sanromán 183–85; Carr, *Spain* 466–67; and González Martín 359.

118. For an example of the romantic, emotional style of the Catholic Revival, see the account of Saint Teresa's religious experience in *La corte celestial de María* (1855), in which Teresa "read [Augustine's] *Confessions* with indescribable eagerness, and upon reaching the point when Saint Augustine describes his conversion, a torrent of tears gushed from her eyes . . . she felt in her soul a certain sensation analogous to that which one experiences on the peaks of tall mountains, where the pure, thin air invigorates the body, dissipates the clouds of imagination and carries thought to infinite spaces" (204).

119. See Alas's "El Centenario de Santa Teresa," from *El Progreso* (15 October 1882). For more on Saint Teresa's status in Spain in the 1870s and 1880s, see my *Reading* 63–64, from which I have taken this discussion.

120. See Clark; Hibbs-Lissorgues; and Botrel.

121. Qtd in Montero 170.

122. Tierno Galván, *Leyes* 158; Cánovas 285: "en el artículo que es objeto del debate ... no se interrumpe la unidad religiosa, no se interrumpe la intolerancia religiosa; porque esta unidad, porque esta intolerancia, sean un bien o sean un mal, están rotas, están interrumpidas bastante tiempo hace; el Gobierno sostiene que no es posible considerar esta cuestión aisladamente y separándola del examen y del juicio imparcial de la situación intelectual y de la situación moral del mundo moderno." See also Tierno Galván, *Leyes,* for the articles; Hughey 37–49, 76–84 for useful summaries of the debates; and Menéndez Pelayo 2: 1339–44, for a traditionalist's view of the Constitution of 1869.

123. Bonnie Smith stresses this point in her study of nineteenth-century charitable bourgeois women in the French Nord (136).

124. See Alas, *El hambre* (Andalusia); and Anon., "Huelga."

125. See Galdós's political speeches in V. Fuentes; also Berkowitz, *Pérez Galdós* 393.

126. See Ullman; and Casanova, "Terror."

127. R. Shaw 16–17.

128. R. Shaw 93. Shaw's hostility toward the Church and ultramontanism and his sympathy for the working classes of Spain incline him to accept anecdotal evidence and hearsay as fact, such as the undocumented charge that Carlists were responsible for bomb attacks in 1909. Nonetheless, the book is invaluable for its reportage of working-class attitudes and fascinating detail of life during a turbulent period of Spanish history.

129. See Payne, *Spanish Catholicism* 133. Not all the working class was hostile to religion. See the life histories and writings of Sor Ángela de la Cruz (1846–1932) and Francisca Javiera del Valle (1856–1930), women of humble social origins; also M. González; M. Sánchez; and Javierre.

130. R. Shaw 19, 52, 55; Granoff 87 ("likenesses").

131. Azaña, "Política religiosa" 50, 52.

132. Azaña's novel, *El jardín de los frailes* (The friars' garden) (1927), provides a fictional recreation of his religious education during adolescence. For other critical, quasi-autobiographical accounts, see Dionisio Pérez's *Jesús (Memorias de un jesuita novicio)* (Jesus [Memoirs of a novice Jesuit]) (1898), opportunely reprinted in 1932; and Ramón Pérez de Ayala's novel *A.M.D.G.* (To the greater glory of God) (1910). The theatrical adaptation of *A.M.D.G.,* which debuted on 7 November 1931 precisely as the religious question was being debated in parliament, occasioned riots and protests. See Aubert, "Luchar contra los poderes fácticos" 247–48; and the rightist de Foxá's fictionalized account (1938) (93–95).

133. Azaña, "Política religiosa" 52.

134. See Carretero, "La ofensiva contra la España católica" (1933) (*Farsa* 147–53).

135. See Payne, *Spanish Civil War* 57, 117–18, on the apocalyptic atmosphere of Spain in the 1930s; and Bunk, on the polarizing propaganda triggered by the October Revolution of 1934. Carretero's prewar writings of the 1930s are representative. "[It's] politics, the politicians," he says, "who have made of governance . . . a battle of sectarianism. . . . And the result of this political tragedy [is]. . . : half of Spain the enemy or distrustful of the other half, the ties of solidarity broken, and . . . a country convulsed, alarmed, in continual violent tension, boiling over with resentment, marching desperately towards catastrophe" (*Secretos* 126–27).

136. The anarchists favored the martyr trope of "proletarian blood"; see Casanova,

"Terror" 90, 92. An earlier rhetorical precedent emerged from the violence of the Barcelona Tragic Week in 1909 and the execution of Francisco Ferrer, the founder of the rationalist Modern School (Casanova, "Terror" 86). See, for example, McCabe, *Martyrdom;* and J. Lewis, *Spain* (1933) (90).

137. Lukács 88, 92.

138. M. Weber 30.

139. See M. Weber 28.

140. See Roberts, "Notas," and Sobejano, *Clarín.*

141. E. Auerbach 555.

142. See Eliade 172.

143. M. Brown 227; also Mainer 127 and Martin 62.

144. See A. Cruz 11–12, 30. The Inquisition placed the irreverent *Lazarillo* on the Index in 1559; an expurgated edition appeared in 1573 (see Close 15).

145. Dunn 39. Dunn also notes that "the name Lázaro proverbially signified poverty ('Por Lázaro laceramos' [old Castilian *lazrar, lacerar* = to suffer poverty]; 'más pobre que Lázaro' [poorer than Lázaro]; 'más pobre que Lázaro y que Job' [poorer than Lázaro and Job]" (33).

146. As Dunn aptly remarks, "Readers in 1554 were not serious about fiction in the same way that we often are; the readerly codes that command sustained emotional sympathy for and identification with fictional characters are an invention of the nineteenth-century masters" (134).

147. For the profane–sacred distinction, see Durkheim 53–54; Eliade; and Bandera 15–19. For the view of religion as residual, see Anne Cruz: "The residual religious element that viewed charity as part of the Christian ritual of salvation . . . weighed too heavily on the social fabric to yield to revisionary methods of social welfare that sought resolution not through conventional moral means, but by rational procedures" (73). If religion was so residual in Spain, how then did it persist until well into the early twentieth century? How can it be residual and at the same time weigh too heavily? Similarly, Kathy Bacon maintains that Restoration-era religious texts "appear to represent a *cursi* survival of religious ways of thinking which many contemporaries regarded as already outmoded in the increasingly secularized nineteenth century" (24).

148. See González Echevarría, "Cervantes" 268.

149. See M. Brown 225–26. I am indebted to a long critical tradition on realism, including (but not limited to) E. Auerbach, G. Becker, Bacarisse, Wellek, Barthes ("Reality Effect"), Medina, M. Brown, Martin, Furst, H. Turner ("Toward a Poetics"), and P. Brooks (*Realist Vision*).

150. See Gómez Blesa 53–54.

151. Zambrano, *Pensamiento* 130–31, 135: "El realismo español no es otra cosa como conocimiento que un estar enamorado del mundo, prendido de él, sin poderse desligar, por tanto."

152. The essays by Zambrano (1939), Salinas (1940), and Castro (1940) were first delivered as talks: at the Palacio de Bellas Artes in Mexico City (12, 14, and 16 June 1939), the Johns Hopkins University (26–30 April 1937), and Princeton University (11 December 1940), respectively. Although Salinas's essay does not dwell expressly on Spanish realism, "some of the inferences to be drawn . . . may apply to [realism]" (Salinas 3).

His book begins with "the reproduction of reality" (the Cid) and ends with "the revolt against reality" (Espronceda), suggesting that realism lies at the heart of his discussion. Castro refers explicitly to realism only once in his talk, noting "the seed of integral realism" in the *Poem of the Cid* (35). Instead, he emphasizes a kind of humanizing realism essential to Spanish culture. See also Pereira Muro's thoughtful discussion of "humanizing realism" in Zambrano and Castro.

153. See Pereira Muro 130; also Bernardete, on Spain as an alternative to the West's crisis. The Republican defeat of 1939 motivated Zambrano to think about the subject of her essay (see her opening chapter, "La crisis del racionalismo europeo," and "Propósito"); also Gómez Blesa's first-rate introduction (41–44, 91 n10); and Castro, "Meaning" 28. "The Meaning of Spanish Civilization" would prove crucial to Castro's later work (see Rubia Barcia 12).

154. Zambrano, *Pensamiento* 155, 158, 159: "Equilibrio individual y comunidad. Por el conocimiento poético el hombre no se separa jamás del universo y conservando intacta su intimidad, participa de todo, es miembro del universo, de la naturaleza y de lo humano y aun de lo que hay entre lo humano, y aun más allá de él"; also Castro, "Meaning" 31.

155. Alas, "Prólogo" 1040: "un oportunismo literario . . . que [es] más adecuada a la vida moderna."

156. As Anthony Close observes of the *Lazarillo de Tormes*, "Its author found a convincing means of representing fictionally a fundamental truth about human experience: the individual's awareness, beginning in childhood, of his or her isolation in a hostile world, where adults are potential adversaries from whom insubordinate thoughts need to be concealed behind a polite face, and stratagems of survival must continually be improvised" (18).

Chapter 1. The Relics of Faith

1. Fernández's sculpture is in the Capuchin monastery of El Pardo. See McKim-Smith; and Gómez Moreno.

2. McKim-Smith 23 (passionate devotion); Stoichita 70 (Church hierarchy).

3. McKim-Smith 22.

4. C. Wright 58 (relics); see also McKim-Smith 22; Christian, *Local Religion;* Eire; Stoichita; and García Lorca, "Teoría" 116.

5. García Lorca, "Teoría" 113, 116, 118.

6. Eire 323 (spirit/matter); also 266–68, 333, on relics; Ariès, *Hour,* 358, 360, on the uncertain status of the dead body; and Ferreres.

7. Laqueur, "Bodies" 177, 176.

8. Ilie, "Cultural Norms" 11 (Counter-Reformational traditions); Ozouf, "De-Christianization" 24 (France).

9. Callahan, *Church, Politics* chap. 1.

10. See Callahan, *Church, Politics* 52 (quality of faith); Sebold, Introducción, *Fray Gerundio* xii–xiii (Isla).

11. See O'Donnell, chap. 15; Fitzgerald; and Valis, "Huella." Different handwriting may also come from different periods.

12. Callahan, *Church, Politics* 53–54.

13. Chadwick 9.

14. See Carnero 30; also Rodríguez, Sebold, "Continuidad," and Rueda 28, 33, for the eighteenth-century novel's generic fluidity.

15. Carnero 34 (originality); Menéndez Pelayo 2: 849 (also Dufour, "Elementos" 107). See also Défourneaux, Dufour, "Elementos," Alonso Seoane, Ferraz Martínez, Valle 149 n3, and Rueda 414–15. Ferraz Martínez convincingly argues that *El evangelio* also influenced nineteenth-century conservative Catholic novelists, who combined Christian apologetics, historical trauma (like the first Carlist War), martyrdom, and fiction in one venue. See also Herrero 136.

16. Dufour, Introducción, *Cartas* 13, 29–30 (French translator [Buynand des Échelles]); Aguilar Piñal, *Bibliografía* 6:120–22, 126 (editions); Dufour, "Elementos" 107–08, 114; also Dufour, "Historia de . . . la fabricación," for the successful marketing campaign. Subsequent works of Olavide were presented as written "by the author of *El evangelio en triunfo*" (Alonso Seoane, "Últimas obras" 49).

17. See Rueda 417–18, for a contrary view.

18. See Alonso Seoane, "Obra" 38–40, 46 on the question of Olavide's originality; Ravitch 363, 366, 381, 383, and Blanc, for Lamourette.

19. See Défourneaux's indispensable book (291–305); Aguilar Piñal, *Sevilla* 208–19.

20. Olavide (qtd in Aguilar Piñal, *Sevilla* 218): "Yo protesto . . . con toda la verdad de mi corazón que jamás me he desviado un ápice de la pura y verdadera creencia ortodoxa hacia nuestros sagrados misterios, las verdades del Evangelio y las reveladas, y que por ellas sacrificaría muchas veces mi vida"; también Alonso Seoane, "Último sueño" and "Dos principios" (288–92), for Olavide's renewed faith in his final years. For a modern fictionalization of Olavide's Inquisition experience, see Jiménez Lozano's *El sambenito* (The sackcloth).

21. See Défourneaux 464.

22. Olavide, *Evangelio* 1:iii: "Un destino tan triste como inevitable me conduxo á Francia. . . . Yo me hallaba en París el año de 1789, y vi nacer la espantosa revolucion. . . . Yo fuí testigo de sus primeros tragicos sucesos; y viendo que cada dia se encrespaban mas las pasiones . . . me retiré á un lugar de corta poblacion."

23. Olavide, *Evangelio* 1:viii.

24. See "Informe" 649–50; also Aguilar Piñal, "Mundo."

25. Olavide, "Historia" 469–70, 480: "la religion católica no solo ha perdido en Francia su universalidad y decoro, sino que esta pobre, abatida y apénas tolerada, que se halla herida por un cisma que la destroza . . . ; que la generacion actual . . . apénas aprehendió los simples rudimentos de la Religion . . . no aprende mas que las impiedades y blasfemias." Also Ozouf, "De-Christianization" and "Revolutionary Religion."

26. Ozouf, "De-Christianization" 30–31 (religious feeling; rights); Olavide, "Historia" 456.

27. Olavide, *Evangelio* 1: viii, ix–x.

28. Olavide, *Evangelio* 1: 1.

29. Olavide, *Evangelio* 1: 322–23: "Entre tantas reflexiones que me acongojaban, me ocurrió una nueva, que me hizo dar un vuelco al corazon, y esta fué la muerte que dí al Extrangero. Hasta entónces este suceso no se me habia presentado sino como una desgracia de que me consolaba facilmente. . . . Esta desgracia . . . tomó á mis ojos un carácter

mas grave, y me produxo un sentimiento amargo en el corazon. . . . [El] remordimiento me atravesó el alma, y me llenó de terror.

Pero lo que acabó de confundirme, y apuró mi constancia, fué la idea de Manuel. ¡Ay infeliz! decia yo corriendo por mi quarto, tú sabes ahora, tú has visto ya la verdad. Si hay un Dios justo, si ama la virtud, si castiga los vicios, ¿cómo puede haberte recibido? ¿quál será tu suerte?"

30. Olavide, *Evangelio* 1: 44: "En quanto á mí yo no he aprendido á creer; lo que mas he sabido es dudar, y es imposible persuadirme lo que repugna á mi razon"; Défourneaux (Philosopher's counterarguments).

31. Olavide, *Evangelio* 1: 189: "¿quién puede creer que un Dios padece y muere? ¿quién es capaz de entender como el Verbo fué eternamente engendrado por el Padre? ¿y qué cosa es el Espíritu Santo . . . ?"

32. Olavide, *Evangelio* 1: 271: "Luchaba con mis propios pensamientos. . . . ¡Un Dios muerto! ¡Un Dios resucitado! esto es imposible. . . . La eloqüencia y el ingenio pueden fascinar, y dar bulto á lo que no tiene realidad; pero quando se apura la verdad en el crisol del exámen, es preciso que se deshaga todo lo que no es sólido."

33. Olavide, *Evangelio* 1: 320: "mi corazon se resiste: Quando pienso en un Hombre Dios, en un muerto que se resucita, y en todas las conseqüencias que esto trae, mis sentidos se amotinan, la sangre me bulle, todo se me olvida, y experimento una gran repugnancia."

34. Olavide, *Evangelio* 1: 326: "La sangre me circulaba como un torrente por las venas, y un calor extraordinario me devoraba las entrañas"; 1: 327: "Al instante me ví rodeado de imágenes funestas, de espantosos fantasmas, que me llenáron de terror . . . no veia mas que una luz funesta y denegrida, que apénas alumbraba, para poder divisar las tumbas y esqueletos de que estaba cubierta. . . . La profunda inmobilidad de quanto allí yacía . . . produxéron en mi alma sensaciones de horror. ¡Pero quánto creció mi sobresalto, quando ví que las tumbas se movian! ¡qué se abrian los sepulcros, y vomitaban de su seno esqueletos animados que con semblante cárdeno y horrible corrian presurosos, y se mezclaban los unos con los otros! "

35. Olavide, *Evangelio* 1: 328.

36. Olavide, *Evangelio* 2: 354: "el lugar destinado á enterrar los muertos de esta casa, y donde sus cuerpos esperan la resurreccion general"; see also Alonso Seoane, "Obra" 14–15, on the narrative value of emotion.

37. Olavide, *Evangelio* 3: 161, 171: "¿Cómo está Jesu Christo en la Eucaristía? Está en el mundo, como si no estuviera; está en medio de los hombres, pero invisible"; 3: 210: "Yo habia imaginado con tanta viveza la muerte de aquel Extrangero, que su recobro me pareció una resurreccion verdadera"; 3: 343–44: "¿Pero cómo me ví? ¡gran Dios! En un lecho fúnebre, amortajado, con las manos y pies atados, con quatro luces que rodeaban mi féretro, y una cruz sobre el pecho. Este espectáculo me horrorizó." See also Ariès, *Hour* 396–404, 479–94, on the living dead and the relocation of cemeteries.

38. Olavide, *Evangelio* 3: 340: "Queria persuadirme, que aquello no era realidad, y que era un sueño, un delirio de la fantasia, un fantasma de la imaginacion."

39. Olavide, *Evangelio* 3: 314: "una especie de rabia homicida y feroz contra los pobres"; 3: 315: "¿Será que el aspecto de la miseria importunaba á mi amor propio, y queria alejarla de mi vista?" By contrast, Lamourette simply sermonizes the need to care for the poor; and Philemon has no feelings of aversion or inner conflict.

40. Olavide, *Evangelio* 3: 315–16: "la luz del Evangelio brilló en mi alma, de repente, y sin ninguna nueva reflexion se disipáron estas inhumanas ilusiones"; 3: 316: "mi corazon se ha mudado. Ya un pobre para mí es un objeto de respeto interior."

41. See Olavide, *Evangelio* 3: 325; Múzquiz 33 (discourse of labor).

42. Olavide, *Evangelio* 3: 324: "la primera vez que reflexioné, que aquellos pobres y honrados labradores, que habia visto hasta allí con tanto desden, son los que nos mantienen á costa de su propio sudor"; 3: 325: "Pero debo decirte para oprobrio y vergüenza de nuestro siglo, que estas gentes sencillas estan asombradas de verme hablar con ellas con tanta aficion y humanidad. Á cada instante me repiten que soy un Señor muy bueno; y no es esta una expresion de cortesía ó de humildad, pues veo en sus ojos que es un sentimiento vivo, que nace de la sorpresa y de la novedad"; Williams, *Country* 70.

43. Raymond Williams suggests the word "humanitarian" appeared "in the [early nineteenth-century] context of arguments about religion: it described the position from which Christ was affirmed as a man and not a god" (*Keywords* 150). But modern humanitarianism, if not the term, already existed in the eighteenth century, as he himself notes elsewhere (*Country* 93).

44. See Dufour, "Elementos" 110; Olavide, *Evangelio* 3: 382, 3: 393.

45. Thompson 152.

46. See Olavide, *Evangelio* 4: 3; Callahan, "Confinement" 11–12; Dufour, Introducción, *Cartas* 23–24; Soubeyroux, *Paupérisme* 2: 649; and Duprat.

47. Olavide, *Evangelio* 4: 198–99 (home care); 4: 218: "Deben considerarse como el padre y la madre de todos los pobres que le habitan, como tutores de los niños huérfanos, y demas desvalidos que le pueblan; y como amigos de todos los vecinos"; 4: 256: "enterándose no solo de sus necesidades, sino tambien de su moralidad y costumbres."

48. See Prochaska 52.

49. Olavide, *Evangelio* 4: 262: "Los padres trabajan para criar y hacer felices á sus hijos, y los mozos para asearse, y parecer en las asambleas con el aliño y la decencia que puede hacerlos bien vistos y estimados de los otros . . . esto ha contribuido mucho á inspirar á todos un cierto barniz de policia, un exterior de urbanidad que estaba ántes muy léjos de sus costumbres rústicas, y de sus modales groseros."

50. Dufour, Introducción *Cornelia* 57–61.

51. By contrast, John Locke had no tolerance for atheists; see *Letter* 172.

52. Dufour, Introducción *Cornelia* 17.

53. Sebold, "Sadismo" 56, 57 (readers' copies); Dufour, Introducción *Cornelia* 30 (massive purge). The novel was attacked either for its presumed immorality or poor composition. See Menéndez Pelayo 2: 946n; and Dufour, Introducción, *Cornelia* 31–33, 61–62, for a brief summary of authorship and reception. Also Ferreras, "Novela anticlerical," who brought this novel to scholars' attention in 1973; Malin; Rueda 301–12; and Dale, "Luis Gutiérrez."

54. Murphy 245–46; Larriba; Dufour.

55. Murphy 251 ("greatest fiction"). Sebold calls Olavide a role-player of picaresque tendencies ("Novelas" 174).

56. See also Rueda 310.

57. Gutiérrez, *Cornelia* 140: "Un hereje, un incrédulo, cesan de ser hombres a los ojos de un supersticioso" (A heretic, an unbeliever, cease to be men in the eyes of the superstitious).

58. Gutiérrez, *Cornelia* 184.

59. Dufour, Introducción *Cornelia* 54.

60. See Gutiérrez, *Cornelia* 163–64, 197.

61. See Dufour, *Cornelia* 167, n161.

62. Gutiérrez, *Cornelia* 170: "¿Cómo podéis imaginaros que un Dios que vino al mundo para salvar a los hombres . . . un Dios que . . . predicó constantemente la caridad, la concordia y la unión, un Dios . . . que en el cadalso mismo rogaba . . . por sus propios enemigos, cómo podéis pues imaginaros que este Dios, la bondad misma, pueda autorizar *el terror, la intolerancia y los crímenes?*" Ayguals de Izco makes a similar argument in *El tigre del Maestrazgo* 413.

63. Gutiérrez, *Cornelia* 170: "Si hemos de parecernos a Jesucristo, debemos morir antes mártires que verdugos"; 171: "*el hombre de Cristo* debe ser dulce, humilde y caritativo, y jamás puede lícitamente maltratar a su hermano. Cuando digo hermano, no creáis que excluyo a los individuos de otra secta cualquiera que sea . . . porque Dios me dice que todos los hombres son mis hermanos."

64. See Sebold, "Sadismo" 65–66.

65. Gutiérrez, *Cornelia* 199: "No hemos tenido a bien comunicarle la carta de su querida, creyendo empeorar con ella su triste situación."

66. Gutiérrez, *Cornelia* 194: "La palidez de su bello rostro, sus dorados cabellos tendidos sobre la espalda, sus ojos tristes, sí, pero vivos y brillantes como el astro del mediodía, su blanca y delicada tez, sus labios de rosa, su garganta medio desnuda en donde sobresalía la blancura del alabastro, la serenidad de su alma pintada al vivo en su rostro, todo coadyuvó a fijar la atención de un pueblo naturalmente humano y compasivo."

67. Gutiérrez, *Cornelia* 196: "Comienza a marchar con paso trémulo, los ojos desencajados, los cabellos dispersos, el rostro extremamente desfigurado, lanzando sordos gemidos, mal articuladas palabras que nada tenían del humano acento. Las manos y pies, todo el cuerpo, lo agitaba un horrible temblor."

68. See Gutiérrez, *Cornelia* 184–85.

69. Sebold, "Sadismo" 64 (romantic origins of realism); Gold, "Sensibility" 134 (epistolary novel) (also Rueda 47–48, 310–12).

70. See also Rueda 309.

71. Gutiérrez, *Cornelia* 77: "El derecho de Tolerancia es propio y peculiar de la Divinidad." The secularization of virtue was ongoing in the eighteenth-century Enlightenment. See Voltaire, "Vertu" (*Dictionnaire*); and Hafter's excellent observations on the ability of eighteenth-century intellectuals to compartmentalize secular and religious concerns ("Secularization").

72. Cassirer 164; also Locke 151–52.

73. Glendinning, "Ideas" 247–48, 257–58; Glendinning, *Vida* 161.

74. Cadalso, *Escritos* 117: "Una de las cosas que, como buen cristiano, alabo en la divina e inefable providencia, es haber criado el mundo de una vez y dejar luego que los astros den su giro, las estaciones se sucedan, el mar fluya y refluya, los animales se perpetúen &c., y no tener que renovar cada instante, día, semana, mes, año y siglo, cada una de las cosas que vemos, y de las que no vemos."

75. Deacon 328 (mindset); Glendinning, "Ideas" 261; also Glendinning, *Vida* 224–25, n46 (moral thrust).

76. Cadalso, *Escritos* 102: "la parte verdadera, la de adorno y la de ficción." See also Glendinning, Introducción (1993) 20–22.

77. See Helman; Wardropper; Sebold, *Cadalso* and Introducción, *Noches;* and Arce.

78. M. Martínez, *Noches anatómicas* 155: "Geographo del Mundo pequeño, que es el Hombre."

79. Nigel Glendinning connects Cadalso's work to the folk tradition of the *difunta pleiteada,* which centers on the dead lover brought back to life ("Traditional Story"). In this vein, magic lantern shows called *fantasmagorías* of the *Noches lúgubres* were popular entertainments in the 1840s; see Glendinning, Introducción (1969) viii and Introducción (1993) 14. Phantasmagorias specialized in "spectral" illusions.

80. Cadalso, *Noches* 69. All citations are from Nigel Glendinning's 1993 edition. My thanks to David Gies and Philip Deacon for their invaluable bibliographic help and expertise in the eighteenth century.

81. Cadalso, *Noches* 69: "Si el otro mundo abortase esos prodigiosos entes a quienes nadie ha visto, y de quienes todos hablan, sería el bien o mal que nos traerían siempre inevitable"; "monstruos producidos por una fantasía llena de tristeza. ¡Fantasía humana!, ¡fecunda sólo en quimeras, ilusiones y objetos de terror!" See also Feijoo 99; and Haidt, "Gothic Larra" 54.

82. See Arce's edition of *Noches lúgubres* 314 n12; and Isla's *Fray Gerundio de Campazas* (1758–70), for a satire of theological ineptitude revolving around the metaphysical properties of *ente* (2:27–28).The *Diccionario de Autoridades* cites *ente* as synonymous with God.

83. Cadalso, *Noches* 80: "Cuantos objetos veo en lo que llaman día, son a mi vista fantasmas, visiones y sombras, cuando menos . . . algunos son furias infernales."

84. See Glendinning, Introducción (1993) 44–45; also Iarocci, *Properties* 62.

85. Cadalso, *Noches* 80: "Objeto antiguo de mis delicias . . . ¡hoy objeto de horror para cuantos te vean!"; 79: "¡En qué estado estarán las tristes reliquias de tu cadáver!" This vision of human decay has a long tradition, especially in *contemptus mundi* writings, of which at least three hundred prose works, produced from the end of the eleventh through the sixteenth century, are known (Howard xxiv–xxv). See "On the Putrefaction of the Dead Body," in dei Segni's influential *On the Misery of the Human Condition (De miseria humane conditionis)* (1195?) (70–71).

86. Wardropper 626, 627; see also Sebold, Introducción, *Noches* 89, 168–69 n18; Martínez Mata lix; and Goldin 131.

87. Graf, "Necrophilia" 218; also Iarocci, *Properties* 67–72.

88. Bouza Álvarez 169; Sarrailh 14–15; Callahan, *Church, Politics* 71.

89. Glendinning, Introducción (1993) 36 (contradictions).

90. Cadalso, *Noches* 65: "oscuridad [y] el silencio pavoroso interrumpido por los lamentos [y truenos]"; "todo tiembla. No hay hombre que no se crea mortal en este instante."

91. Graf, "Necrophilia" 220.

92. Helman 47 (Beccaria); Cadalso, *Noches* 86: "Pocas palabras, menos alimento, ninguna lástima, mucha dureza, mayor castigo y mucha amenaza." Unlike Helman (and Sebold, in *Cadalso* 132, 161–62), Glendinning does not see the influence of Beccaria in the text (see his 1969 Introducción liv–lv). The Spanish translation of *On Crimes and*

Punishment, which appeared in 1774, landed on the Inquisition's Index of Prohibited Books in 1777 (see Herr 60; 205–06).

93. Cadalso, *Noches* 89: "Las pisadas de los que salen de su calabozo . . . el ruido de las cadenas que sin duda han quitado del cadáver, el ruido de la puerta, estremecen lo sensible de mi corazón"; 91: "Parece como que sale de un sueño"; "¿Quién es? Si eres algún mendigo necesitado, que de flaquezas has caído, y duermes en la calle por faltarte casa en que recogerte, y fuerzas para llegarte a un hospital, sígueme. Mi casa será tuya"; Adam Smith 6.

94. Bataille 45 ("horror of the corpse"); also La Rubia Prado. The grave diggers (fossors) of the Roman catacombs, however, were respected figures in the early Church.

95. Pope 24; Bataille 46 (rotting body); Crace 196 ("everending days").

96. Moliner 2:1529 (*viles*); P. A. Sánchez, "Discurso LX" *Censor* 115 (also Williams, *Keywords* 55); Marchena, *Obras* 30: "sensibilidad ó la facultad de identificarme con él [otra persona]. En efecto mis nervios sufren una violenta conmocion á la vida de un ser que organizado del mismo modo que yo padece, y esta impresion me es desagradable; ve aquí por qué procuro sustraerle al dolor ó apartar mi vista de él" (*Discurso tercero,* from Marchena's journal, *El Observador* 1787–90).

97. Cadalso, *Noches* 93: "Te compadezco tanto como a mí mismo"; Sebold, Introducción, *Noches* 105–06 (Tediato's self-involvement); Adam Smith 3. Cadalso and Smith continue to draw on traditional Christianity; see also Alemán 2: 203, on neighborly compassion as "a true sign of our predestination."

98. See Gies; Sánchez-Blanco; Haidt, *Embodying* 160–71, on eighteenth-century friendship; Cadalso, *Noches* 98: "Andemos, amigo, andemos"; 97: "Hermanos nos hace un superior destino, corrigiendo los caprichos de la suerte, que divide en arbitrarias e inútiles clases a los que somos de una misma especie. Todos lloramos . . . todos enfermamos . . . todos morimos"; Glendinning, "Ideas" 256–57 (social hierarchies).

99. See Glendinning, Introducción (1969); Sebold, Introducción, *Noches;* dei Segni, for the *contemptus mundi* tradition (also Howard); Martínez Mata, for the influence of ascetic and moral writers in Cadalso; de Sales 146–48 (also Darst 48–49); Montaigne 63 and Alemán 3:225, in praise of a similarly conceived friendship notable for its absence in the picaresque world of Guzmán de Alfarache.

100. Cadalso, *Noches* 98: "Más contribuirás a mi dicha con ese pico, ese azadón. . . viles instrumentos a otros ojos . . . venerables a los míos . . . Andemos, amigo, andemos."

101. Lowenthal 252.

102. Sherwood 71, 72 ("accident of fortune"); also Soubeyroux, *Paupérisme* 1:91.

103. See Pérez Estévez; Trinidad Fernández; Callahan, "Confinement" 6, 12, 15, 17.

104. Meléndez Valdés 294: "una mano paternal y benéfica que temple con la humanidad lo duro de la ley, y sepa unir el espíritu de orden con la moderación, que llore sobre el mendigo aun cuando le castigue"; B. Ward 322: "ser sensibles a tan lastimoso espectáculo"; 399: "carga insoportable . . . [del] número de bocas inútiles." Ward's *Obra pía,* originally published in 1750, was appended to his *Proyecto económico* (1762).

105. Sherwood xiii.

106. B. Ward 358: "Pero a todo esto le falta el alma, faltando el mobil de toda esta máquina, que es la circulacion del dinero, que hace en el cuerpo político el mismo oficio, que la sangre en el humano; y como la diferencia de un cuerpo sano y robusto a un

cadáver, depende de la circulacion de ésta, lo mismo sucede con el dinero, que girando anima toda la República, y en cesando su circulacion, queda sin aliento la industria."

107. Meléndez Valdés 286.

108. See Soubeyroux, *Paupérisme* 1:248–49, 252–53; Sebold, Introducción, *Noches* 103; Callahan, "Confinement" 24.

109. Iarocci, *Properties* 95, 71, 83 (see also Graf, "Necrophilia"), 86; Valis, Rev. 112.

110. A view found in the Stoics, with whom Cadalso was familiar; see Epictetus 156.

111. See Carl Becker's classic statement on the new religion of humanity.

112. Cassirer 136.

113. Iarocci, *Properties* 55.

114. Notably Sebold; see his *Cadalso* and "Sadismo."

115. See Dowling (reception); Bredvold, and Haidt, "Enlightenment" 40–41 (sensibility).

116. Galdós owned a copy of Olavide's *Evangelio en triunfo* (see Berkowitz, *Biblioteca* 65, under "anonymous," as it was originally published).

Chapter 2. The Philanthropic Embrace

1. See Callahan, *Church, Politics* 95.

2. Jutglar, *Ideología* 68, 76 (radicalization); Callahan, *Church, Politics* 134 (bond).

3. Delgado 83 (friars); Carr, *Spain* 165 (revolution).

4. Balmes 20; Callahan, *Church, Politics* 181 (dechristianization).

5. See Montesinos 115, 296–301.

6. See Goldman; also R. Brown; Ferreras, *Novela por entregas;* Marco; Carrillo, "Marketing"; Romero Tobar; Ouimette; Ynduráin; Andreu; Sieburth; Martí-López, *Borrowed Words* and "*Folletín*"; and Ríos-Font. For the Ayguals de Izco–Galdós connection, see Dendle ("Galdós") and Rodríguez-Puértolas. Menéndez Pelayo remarked, "Today in the novel the heterodox figure par excellence, the implacable, cold enemy of Catholicism, is no longer a national militiaman [Ayguals], but a narrator of great talent . . . Pérez Galdós" (2: 1396).

7. See Montesinos; García; Goldman; Sebold, *Novela;* Rueda; and Giménez Caro.

8. See Martí-López; and Ríos-Font.

9. *María* 1:440. See Romero Tobar, "Forma" 65–66, on Ayguals's social activism; also Baulo, "Amparo." Ayguals poked gentle fun at the humanitarian figure in his journal, *La Linterna Mágica* (1849–50); see Pomares 92; Puch and Roger; and the anonymous "Letrilla humanitaria" (probably by Ayguals himself). See also Barriobero y Herrán's version of *María* (1922). Barriobero (1875–1939), a republican federalist sympathetic to anarchism, presided over a People's Tribunal in Barcelona during the civil war and was executed by the Nationalists (see Ruiz Pérez).

10. *María* 2: 391 (reviews from *El Nuevo Defensor del Pueblo* and *La Aurora*). The sequel to *María, La marquesa de Bellaflor* (1846–47) also stresses philanthropic ideals in the working-class María, now titled, who devotes her time to visiting asylums, hospitals, and the homes of the poor. By contrast, in 1845 Sabino de Armada disparaged such writings as the work of "pseudo-philanthropists" more interested in promoting social revolution (see Zavala, *Ideología* 89). See also Catalina 214–15, for charity as sacred and

philanthropy as secular (1858); and the clergyman Martínez Izquierdo's similar opinion from 1889 (in Portero Molina 228). In 1936, the Nationalist colonel Marcelino Gavilán said, "all that crap about the rights of man, humanitarianism, and philanthropy [can] go to hell" (qtd in Casanova, "Rebelión" 60).

11. *"María"* (in Zavala, *Ideología* 270): "Su objeto es ensalzar a las clases inferiores del pueblo sobre todas las demás de la sociedad y sobre los reyes, adulando a las primeras, no muy noblemente las más veces, y zahiriendo de continuo a las otras y en especial a los príncipes, impelido de sentimientos quizá republicanos. Pero a quien declara guerra sin tregua . . . es al clero, particularmente al regular . . . fray Patricio, religioso franciscano, pintándole . . . [como] un monstruo de lujuria, glotonería, perfidia y ferocidad." Orig. *La Censura* 12 (1848): 435–38.

12. García 190 (*La Censura*); also E. Hartzenbusch 90 and Romero Tobar, *Novela popular* 81–82.

13. See Carrillo, "Marketing" and *"Guindilla"*; Zavala, *Ideología* 106, 110, and "Socialismo"; Ayguals, *Tigre* 399–400. Also Goldman 204–09; Elorza, *Socialismo* 93; Benítez 75–76, 91; Martínez-Gallego; and Romero Tobar, "Forma" 68.

14. Goldman 209.

15. See *El tigre del Maestrazgo,* which is dedicated to Joaquín.

16. Carr, *Spain* 159; also Fuentes, "Milicia" 443–48; and Martínez Gallego 54.

17. Ayguals, *María* 2: 237: "Retratar en fray Patricio á la inmunda pandilla inquisitorial que aun aspira al dominio de España . . . he aquí el objeto primordial de nuestro trabajo"; 2: 237, 340. Ayguals's equally diabolical portrait of Carlism in the historical guerrilla figure Ramón Cabrera, in *El tigre del Maestrazgo,* provoked a heated response from Carlist writers (see Benítez 140–41; Chant 124–26).

18. See Baulo and Hibbs 276; also Baulo, "Novela popular."

19. Ayguals, *María* 1: 14: "será bastante para que conciba el lector cuán repugnantes debían ser sus halagos á la pobre muchacha. Fray Patricio rayaba en la edad de los 30 años. Era bajo de estatura y estúpidamente gordo. El pelo que formaba su cerquillo era rojo. Los ojos, sumamente pequeños, estaban acentuados por sendas cejas que parecian de cáñamo, y la pupila era de un verde tan claro que hacía su mirada traidora como la de los gatos. El conjunto de su rostro era grande, redondo y estremadamente encarnado, particularmente la punta de la nariz que parecia un pequeño tomate maduro . . . era el santo varon lujurioso como un mico, osado si los hay, presumido, hipócrita como los mas de los frailes." See Baulo, "Novela popular" 63–64, 66–67 for Fray Patricio as a connecting link between history and fiction.

20. Ayguals also observes that Fray Patricio "sniffed yellow tobacco incessantly" (1: 14). Fermín's green eyes are snuff-flecked (Alas, *La Regenta* 1: 102). Fray Patricio is a rival to the highborn Don Luis de Mendoza for María's affections; a similar triangle appears in Clarín's novel. See Valis, *Decadent Vision* 33–40 and *Reading* 29–40.

21. "Revista literaria"; Zavala, *Ideología* 252–53. Orig. *Revista de Madrid* 4 (1844): 402–13. For the *misterios* vogue, see Zavala, *Ideología* 90–95; Brooks, *Reading* 143–70; Martí-López, *Borrowed Words* 17–24; Martí-López, "Folletín" 73–78; Gies 294; Solá; also Muñoz Molina.

22. See Brooks, *Reading* 159, 150.

23. See Wiseman 131 (social status of ecclesiastics); also Gil de Zárate 360–61, for the

example of an ex-friar of humble origins whose entry into the Church meant increased social respect at the turn of the century.

24. In contrast, Sue goes after the Jesuits in *The Wandering Jew.* Ayguals, who translated Sue's novel (*El judío errante*), also published the six-volume *Los jesuitas,* no doubt for both commercial and ideological reasons (see Carrillo, "Radiografía" 163). In reply to Sue's book, the ultra-Catholic novelist Navarro Villoslada wrote *El Ante-Cristo* (The antichrist) (1845) (see also Baulo and Hibbs).

25. Benítez 76; see also Jutglar, *Ideologías* 119–22, Longares Alonso 218–25, and R. M. González's illuminating account of humanitarian democracy in Spain; and Romero Tobar, "Forma" 65–68.

26. Ayguals, *María* 1: 11: "el incuestionable y santo derecho que tienen los pueblos . . . no diremos de rebelarse contra sus opresores, porque cuando las naciones se alzan en masa para castigar á insolentes déspotas, egercen un acto de su justicia soberana."

27. Ayguals, *María* 2: 273.

28. Ayguals, *María* 1: 59: "un pueblo valiente no asesina á hombres indefensos, ni profana los alcázares de Dios"; also 1: 56–57; Rodríguez-Puértolas. See Rabaté, "Familia" 212–13, on the ambivalent use of *pueblo* in Ayguals; and Ayguals, *La maravilla del siglo* (The marvel of the century; 1852) 2: 204, where *pueblo* includes "all the social classes." In the 1830s, liberal rhetoric in the Barcelona press distinguished between an urban, liberal proletariat (*pueblo*) and a rural, fanaticized peasantry (*campesino*) (Longares Alonso 237). ✳

29. Ayguals, *María* 1: 58: "No habia entre aquella turba de entes desalmados uno solo cuyo semblante feroz no arrojase destellos iracundos de frenética rabia. Cubiertos de polvo y de sudor aquellos rostros repugnantes, solo abrian la boca para vomitar blasfemias. Los asquerosos andrajos que cubrian sus cuerpos salpicados de sangre, daban un aspecto infernal á tan desastrosa escena." See also Rodríguez-Puértolas; Galdós, *Un faccioso* 219–32 (1879); Baroja, *La Isabelina* 1101–04 (1919); Gil de Zárate 362; Menéndez Pelayo (2: 1136–43); and a cleric's firsthand account, Francisco García 39–45.

30. Ayguals, *María* 1: 59.

31. *"María"* (in Zavala, *Ideología* 271).

32. Ayguals, *María* 2: 340: "los enemigos de nuestra prosperidad, . . . so capa de caridad evangélica, de mansedumbre apostólica, y de anhelos de fraternidad, pretenden ahogarnos en un lago de sangre para entronizarse sobre nuestros restos"; 2: 344.

33. See Ayguals, *María* 2: 274 and *Tigre* 400, 408–09. Among the works Ayguals's Sociedad Literaria published were *Los santos evangelios* (The holy gospels), Ripalda's catechism, Chateaubriand's *Memorias de ultra-tumba* (Memoirs), and *La joya de la niñez* (The jewel of childhood), this last containing a compendium of religion. See also Carrillo, "Marketing" 16, 40, and Romero Tobar, "Forma" 61–65, 88–90, for the Sociedad Literaria.

34. Navarrete, *Madrid* 4: 134: "estadística del vicio y de la virtud, en todas las diferentes clases sociales"; "queria él verlo todo por sus propios ojos, é introducirse lo mismo en los dorados salones aristocráticos, que en la guardilla del miserable artesano"; 4: 138: "para descubrir mejor su estado de moralidad ó de corrupcion."

35. Navarrete, *Madrid* 2: 193: "cuando aun estaban en todo su fervor las doctrinas revolucionarias que sirvieron para provocarle"; 2: 69; 2: 91–92: "Si los gobiernos fuesen

de veras paternales y previsores, ejercerian una vigilancia provechosa y santa sobre esas familias infelices ... ¿Por qué los legisladores ... no se dedican á aliviar tanto infortunio y tanto desvalimiento, en un interés humanitario, y en un interés de conveniencia propia?" See also Navarrete's "Novela española" (1847), which praises Sue's humanitarian fiction as the ideal narrative model (262).

36. Navarrete, *Madrid* 1: 60: "la indiferencia con que contemplan las clases ricas las desventuras y las miserias de las pobres."

37. Edward Baker calls him a moderate (102). For more on Navarrete, see Araujo-Costa 106–11; Zavala, *Ideología* 96–97; E. Baker 102, 104; and Valis, *Culture* 111–14, for Asmodeo and the society chronicler.

38. For examples of his later fiction, see *Verdades y ficciones* (1874) and *Sueños y realidades* (1878).

39. Soubeyroux, "Figura" (723), cites 1843 for the first entry of *filantropía* in a nineteenth-century dictionary, and 1884, for *filántropo,* but clearly these words appear earlier, in 1822 and 1852, respectively.

40. *Humanitario:* "regarding or referring to the good of humankind." Baralt, *Diccionario* 299.

41. J. E. Hartzenbusch xxi.

42. Soubeyroux, "Figura" 723 (French import); Duprat xxx, xxxiv, 477.

43. Zavala, *Románticos* 63.

44. Williams, *Keywords* 151; Oates 119, 50 (American Catholics).

45. Qtd in Molina Martínez 129 (from Anon., *El amante de la razón y de su patria.* Murcia: Bellido, 1823). The tract takes aim at the anticlerical, revolutionary *El Zurriago* (The whiplashing) (1821–23).

46. Balmes 39: "que no es todo filantropía lo que bajo este velo se oculta"; "que se olvida de la compasión que ... es debida a la víctima"; also D. Shaw 607.

47. Fernán Caballero, *Lucas, Obras* 4: 205: "¡Caridad! ¡Santa, sublime caridad! ... ¿Por qué no se te ve en los palacios que te labra la filantropía?"; "porque la caridad quiere ser reina y no esclava." (See also Miranda García, *Religión* 127; Catalina 215.) In Clarín's *La Regenta* (1884–85), a philanthropic circle called the Free Fraternity languishes until its atheist president resigns, realizing "that the time was not yet ripe for the secularization of charity [that is, philanthropy]" (264) (1: 456; see also Coffey; and Vaquero Iglesias 367–75 for the charity/philanthropy issue in Asturias specifically. The catechistical association of the bishop of Oviedo Sanz y Forés disseminated a pamphlet (1878) intended to combat the secularizing and therefore un-Christian implications of philanthropy (Vaquero Iglesias 371).

48. See Shubert, " 'Charity' " 45; Mesonero Romanos, "Visita"; and Ayguals, *María* 1: 232–33, 266.

49. Donoso Cortés, "Caridad" 261: "El catolicismo, escarnecido y vilipendiado hoy por no sé qué sectarios oscuros y feroces en nombre de los hambrientos, es la religión de los que padecen hambre. El catolicismo, combatido hoy en nombre de los proletarios, es la religión de los pobres y los menesterosos. El catolicismo, combatido en nombre de la libertad, de la igualdad y de la fraternidad, es la religión de la libertad, de la igualdad y de la fraternidad humanas."

50. Donoso Cortés, "Carta" 724: "lo que no ha habido en el mundo hasta ahora es

guerra universal y simultánea entre los ricos y los pobres. . . . Si los ricos no hubieran perdido la virtud de la caridad, Dios no hubiera permitido que los pobres hubieran perdido la virtud de la paciencia"; "Carta" 726; see also his "Discurso" and the Carlist Navarro Villoslada's *El Ante-Cristo* (1845) 19,171; Herrera 105 (Donoso's charity).

51. See Arenal; Prochaska.

52. Baralt, *Diccionario* 81.

53. See Baralt, *Obras;* Díaz Plaja, xxx, lvii; and Ginger 71–73.

54. Monlau, *Remedios* 12: "Pero yo concibo otro órden de civilizacion que se llama *moral,* y que es sencilla, virtuosa, que no está complicada . . . con el amor del lujo y de las riquezas; en la cual florecen las creencias religiosas y las inspiraciones del corazon; que establece, en fin, y consolida la *verdadera fraternidad humana,* y no esa *cohesion facticia* que toda se resuelve en sociedades en comandita. La civilizacion moral no crea pobres, como los crea la industrial." Fuentes ("Utopía" 686) says Monlau was a Saintsimonian in the 1830s; Longares Alonso calls him a *demócrata,* ideologically close to French "Catholic liberalism" (219). Proliferating political labels suggest how confusing and overlapping the ideologies of liberalism were in the period.

55. Monlau, *Remedios* 20; also 27. See also Cervera, whose "Memoria sobre el pauperismo" (1846), like Monlau's *Remedios,* was submitted to a competition of the Sociedad Económica Matritense in 1845.

56. Monlau, *Remedios* 34: "edificios-monstruos, focos eternos de infeccion"; 41: "los mendigos no han de ser considerados como cuerpos viles entregados á los filántropos de profesion para que hagan experimentos en ellos; sino como enfermos delicados, y por cuyo pronto y cabal restablecimiento se interesa la sociedad entera." For a satiric view of mendicity, see Tenorio's sketch of the professional beggar.

57. In *Elementos* 2: 873, Monlau says, "Christianity is hygiene canonized by God."

58. Mazzini, "Patriots" 204; Castelar, *Fórmula* 161; Pérez Galdós, "Solidaridad" 127; Ayguals, *María* 1: 226–29, 2: 371–73; Benítez 176 and Brooks, *Reading* 164 (vehicle of social action and publicity). See also Cervera; and Monlau, "Asociación" (in Elorza, "Pauperismo" 341) (orig. *El Popular* [Barcelona] 20, 21, 23 April 1841).

59. Ayguals, *María* 2: 382; Monlau, *Higiene industrial* 112–13: "La caridad cristiana, o llámese la *filantropía,* sobre ser una obligación . . . , es una especulación lucrativa: ténganlo así entendido los que disfrazan su egoísmo y sequedad de corazón con la máscara de previsión y prudencia, y sépanlo los inconsiderados avarientos que se ciñen a una estricta e inmisericordiosa reciprocidad de oficios."

60. Monlau, *Higiene industrial* 117–18: "porque lo que hoy falta al obrero, como a casi todas las demás clases, es el elemento moral, que constituye la fuerza de las sociedades y asegura la felicidad de cada uno de sus individuos; lo que le falta es una convicción religiosa, sincera y profunda . . . y la falta de esa fe es el cáncer roedor de los tiempos modernos. . . . Y la causa de ese dolor universal se encuentra en las costumbres: el corazón social está dañado."

61. See Monlau's spirited defense of Christianity in *Elementos* 2: 872–82; Monlau, *Higiene industrial* 66; also Haskell 116, on Foucault and humanitarianism.

62. See Monlau, *Higiene industrial* 117.

63. Monlau, *Remedios* 31; 42; Woolf 28 (charities).

64. See Elorza, *Socialismo;* also J. L.Varela; and Longares Alonso 219–22.

65. R. M. González (evangelical humanitarianism); Bowman 12; Saint-Simon 163; Charlton 12.

66. Cámara, "Muere" (in Elorza, *Socialismo* 169) (orig. *La Organización del Trabajo*, no. 5 [15 March 1848]); "A los icarianos" (in Elorza, *Socialismo* 107) (orig. *La Fraternidad*, no. 10 [9 January 1848]); see also "Los jornaleros" (in Elorza, *Socialismo* 113) (orig. *El Padre de Familia* [11 November 1849]).

67. Bowman 15 (France) (see also Aynard); Lamennais 23, 37: "La justice, c'est la vie; et la charité, c'est encore la vie, et une plus douce et plus abondante vie"; "la justice qui est le commencement de la charité, et la charité qui est la consummation de la justice"; Monlau, *Remedios* 9; Arenal, *Beneficencia* 99; see also Donoso Cortés, "Carta" 726.

68. Wines 55, 54.

69. De la Sagra, "Aforismos" (in Elorza, *Socialismo* 88) (see also Garrido, "Reinado" 196; and de la Sagra, "Lecciones" 78); Donoso Cortés, "Discurso" 494; J. R. B., Preface xxii, xxxvi; Tuckerman, Introduction 2–3; Gaskell 421; Smiles, *Thrift* 197–98. Leo XIII in his encyclical letter *Rerum Novarum* (1891) considered it a "great mistake . . . to take up with the notion that class is naturally hostile to class" (174). See also Ayguals, *La marquesa de Bellaflor* (2: 726).

70. Ayguals, *María* 2: 372: "el afán de asociarse . . . de un modo asombroso germina y se desarrolla por todas partes, [por el cual] nos congratulamos de haber sido de los primeros que han señalado esta senda como la más a propósito para labrar la felicidad del pueblo español."

71. Smiles, *Thrift* 325, 306; also *Self-Help* 174–78, 315.

72. See Anon., "De Gérando."

73. See Surwillo's commentary on the antislavery issue in Spain and Ayguals de Izco's role as translator and promoter of *Uncle Tom's Cabin* (769, 771). For the religious and humanitarian origins of the antislavery movement, see Bender, Haskell, and Davis.

74. Ayguals, *María* 1: 259: "Nada mas dulce y consolador que oir la voz benéfica y paternal de un buen religioso, gérmen de halagüeñas esperanzas, al verter sobre el lacerado corazon de un enfermo las saludables máximas de Jesucristo." The evangelical strain is especially noticeable in Aygual's later fiction (see Calvo Carillo 308–09).

75. See also Rabaté, "Familia."

76. See Thompson; Woolf 21.

77. Preface, *Visitor* xxii (see also Wach 544); Monlau, *Higiene industrial* 70. Monlau coined a word — *rurizar,* to ruralize — in making the case for decentralizing industrial development (*Higiene industrial* 70–71).

78. See Tierno Galván, "Formas" 43; also Thompson; and Fuentes, "Clase" 157.

79. Ayguals, *María* 2: 384; Araque 41; Ribot i Fontseré 395. The radical progressive Ribot i Fontseré was a close friend of Ayguals (Carrillo, "Marketing" 14; Ginger 187–89). For the new national novel, see Martí-López, Ríos-Font, Rabaté, and Giménez Caro; also Sebold, for the importance of Ayguals's fiction in the development of modern Spanish realism (*Credo*).

80. Tierno Galván, "Formas" 49.

81. See Benítez 157.

82. Galdós, *Fortunata* 594: "Sentíala dentro de sí, como si se la hubiera tragado, cual si la hubiera tomado en comunión" (2: 236). Quotations are from Agnes Moncy Gullón's transla-

tion. See also Sieber's discussion of how the sacrament of communion is incorporated into the picaresque *Lazarillo de Tormes* linguistically and semiotically (*Language* 30).

83. Buckler 101 (charity); Galdós, *Fortunata* 810: "Recordaba, sí, que la muerta había sido su mayor enemiga. . . . Con la muerte de por medio, la una en la vida visible y la otra en la invisible, bien podría ser que las dos mujeres se miraran de orilla a orilla, con intención y deseos de darse un abrazo" (2: 531–32).

84. Whiston, "Materialism" 65, 79–80.

85. Bravo Villasante 15 (letter to Pereda); Rodgers 76 ("force for cohesion"); Pérez Gutiérrez 231 ("dimension"); Fuentes Peris 142.

86. See Fuentes Peris 90. The relatively small attention paid to religion in Fuentes Peris's book is surprising, given her interest in philanthropy.

87. Rogers 172.

88. Although Fuentes Peris notes that it is "difficult to subscribe to the simplistic idea of philanthropy as the successful imposition of control" (13), she essentially reads philanthropy this way in the novel. See also Labanyi, *Gender,* 193–94 for similar views, which fail to get at the heart of *Fortunata y Jacinta*. Indeed, Labanyi interprets the realist novel of the 1880s as "a surveillance exercise," or form of social control, arguing that "the key to social control is to make society describable" (*Gender* 65, 87). Foucauldian reductionism turns novelists into meddling bureaucrats. Organizing words into a coherent, ordered pattern of fictional events and characters is not an act of social control but of aesthetic suasiveness, empowering a liberated imagination. See Clarín's essay "Del naturalismo" (1882) for a spirited defense of the novel as "the genre of freedom in literature" (132). In "El libre examen y nuestra literatura presente" (1881), he singled out Galdós's novels precisely for their liberating effect on readers (161).

89. See Foucault, *Power* 166–82, *Discipline* 78, 82; Haskell 108 ("growing ambivalence").

90. Eoff, *Novels* 136–37; also C. S. Lewis, "Membership" 119.

91. For religion and Galdós, see Scatori; Saenz; Savaiano; Alfieri; Correa; Eoff, *Novels;* Parker; Rodgers; Russell; Cardona; Pérez Gutiérrez; Shoemaker; Urbina; Whiston; López-Sanz; Estébanez Calderón; González Povedano; Mora García; Nos Muro; also Alan Smith, on the relation between religion and the mythological imagination in Galdós. For the study of charity and Galdós, see: Fedorchek; Paolini; Penuel; Rogers; Bly; Varey; and Hoff. Interest in religion and charity can also be found in *Marianela, Misericordia, Nazarín, Halma,* and *Ángel Guerra.* A detailed analysis of a corpus of his novels is beyond the scope of this book.

92. Ladrón de Guevara 438, 49–50 (Ayguals); Scatori 118 ("sincere believer"); Shoemaker, *God's Role* 11 ("religious man"); Pérez Gutiérrez 266.

93. Galdós (in Bravo Villasante 23): "En mí está tan arraigada la duda de ciertas cosas que nada me la puede arrancar. Carezco de fe, carezco de ella en absoluto. He procurado poseerme de ella y no lo he podido conseguir. Al principio no me agradaba semejante estado; pero hoy, vamos viviendo" (6 June 1877). For Galdós on sectarianism and the decay of faith, see "Revista de la semana" (16 July 1865) and "Revista de la semana" (15 October 1865), *Artículos* 93; 169–70; Carta 18 May 1884 and Carta 5 May 1885, *Cartas* 86–93; 145–53.

94. Galdós (in Bravo Villasante 19): "Creo sinceramente que si en España existiera la

libertad de cultos . . . seríamos más religiosos . . . veríamos a Dios con más claridad, seríamos menos canallas, menos perdidos de lo que somos" (10 March 1877). In a celebrated speech advocating freedom of religion, the Republican statesman Emilio Castelar concluded, "Great is the religion of power, but greater still is the religion of love; great is the religion of implacable justice, but greater still is the religion of compassionate forgiveness; and I, in the name of the Gospels, stand here, to ask that you write into your fundamental Law religious freedom, that is, liberty, fraternity, equality among all men" ("Libertad" 17 [12 April 1869]; see also Jarnés 23–24, on "the religion of liberty"; and Hughey). This image of Christianity coincides with Galdós's.

95. Galdós, *Cartas* 152: "la gran mayoría de los españoles no creemos ni pensamos . . . si por un lado la fe se nos va, no aparece la filosofía que nos ha de dar algo con que sustituir aquella eficaz energía. Faltan en la sociedad principios de unidad y generalización. Todo está en el aire, las creencias minadas, el culto reducido a puras prácticas de fórmula" (Carta 5 May 1885).

96. Galdós (in Bravo Villasante 25): "satisface el pensamiento ni el *corazón* del hombre en nuestros días" (June 1877); *Artículos* 173–74: "No seamos buenos por miedo al demonio, sino por amor á Dios. . . . Cese el imperio del terror en una religion fundada en el amor." ("Revista de la semana" [22 October 1865]).

97. See Valis, *Reading* 177–80.

98. Galdós, *Artículos* 129: "La humanidad más evangélica, purificada por siglos de opresión y martirio, respira en esta carta, donde el odio no ha escrito una palabra" ("Revista de la semana" 27 August 1865); Galdós, "Revista de la semana" 15 October 1865, *Artículos* 170.

99. Galdós, *Marianela* 732–33: "Estáis viendo delante de vosotros, al pie mismo de vuestras cómodas casas, a una multitud de seres abandonados, faltos de todo lo que es necesario a la niñez, desde los padres hasta los juguetes . . . nunca se os ocurre infundirles un poco de dignidad, haciéndoles saber que son seres humanos, dándoles las ideas de que carecen." See also Giner de los Ríos, "Prohibición" 49, who questioned the sincerity of indiscriminate almsgiving practices.

100. Galdós, *Marianela* 716: "tenía derecho, . . . a ciertas atenciones . . . que corresponden por jurisprudencia cristiana al inválido, al pobre, al huérfano y al desheredado." See also Dendle, "Galdós" 11; Bly 50.

101. Galdós, *Cartas* 287: "El pauperismo ofrece aspectos verdaderamente terroríficos en medio de tanta riqueza"; and 288. See also Ayguals de Izco's travel text of 1852, *La maravilla del siglo* 2: 82, for a similar view of the London poor; and 1: 221–22, 232–45, for his impressions of Parisian poverty and beneficence (1: 221, 246).

102. See Elorza and Iglesias (Comisión de Reformas Sociales); Moreno Nieto, "Beneficencia" 187; Anon., "Mendicidad" 367 (25 March 1881); also *Vagrancy* 368–75.

103. Galdós, *Fortunata* 674: "se le representó el pobre paralítico con tanta viveza, que casi casi creía verle en su alcoba" (2: 344).

104. Flaubert 193: "elle avait quelque chose de lointain qui bouleversait Emma. Cela lui descendait au fond de l'âme comme un tourbillon dans un abîme" (312); 238: "comme un cadavre que l'on galvanise . . . Une convulsion la rabattit sur le matelas. Tous s'approchèrent. Elle n'existait plus" (372–73). The translation is Paul de Man's.

105. Galdós, *Fortunata* 688–89: "apoyó la frente en ellas exhalando un sordo gemido."

Dejóse estar así, inmóvil, mudo. Y en aquella actitud de recogimiento y tristeza, expiró aquel infeliz hombre" (2: 363); "La vida cesó en él, a consecuencia del estallido y desbordamiento vascular. . . . Se desprendió de la humanidad, cayó del gran árbol la hoja completamente seca, sólo sostenida por fibra imperceptible. El árbol no sintió nada en sus inmensas ramas. Por aquí y por allí caían en el mismo instante hojas y más hojas inútiles; pero la mañana próxima había de alumbrar innumerables pimpollos, frescos y nuevos" (2: 363).

106. Caudet reads the scene as a harsh attack bordering on sarcasm against Moreno-Isla's character (*Fortunata* 2: 363, n53).

107. Dickens, *Oliver Twist* 43.

108. Galdós, *Fortunata* 680: "¿Por qué no dedicas tu dinero, tu actividad y todo tu espíritu a una obra grande y santa . . . un buen edificio, un asilo para este o el otro fin . . . ?" (2: 353); Braun 50–51 (class lines).

109. For Ernestina Manuel de Villena, see Castro y Serrano; Galdós, "Santos"; Vales Failde; Braun; and Lamet. Guillermina Pacheco's character and role have produced multiple interpretations: see J. L. Brooks; Braun; Lida; Estébanez Calderón; Nadal Colón; Rodríguez and García Sprackling; and Dale. On philanthropy in Spain: Arenal; Hernández Iglesias; Giner de los Ríos, "Prohibición"; Bahamonde Magro; Gutiérrez Sánchez; Shubert, "Charity"; Lacalzada de Mateo; Maza; Thion Soriano-Mollá, for an example of late nineteenth-century private charity, an artistic-literary album called *Limosna* (Alms), organized by the statesman Antonio Maura; and Hoff.

110. Galdós, "Santos" 256; Braun 35 (new, active charity); Castro y Serrano, "Limosna" and "Ernestina"; Galdós, "Santos" 258; Vales Failde 50.

111. Dale, "Dialéctica" 288 (kleptomaniac); Prochaska 16 (also 13, 59) (fundraising); Arenal, *Beneficencia* 132: "Sin publicidad en el ramo de Beneficencia, falta el poderoso eco de la opinión pública para alentar el bien y reprobar el mal."

112. See Jiménez Duque 145–60 (wave of devotionalism); Cuenca Toribio, *Iglesia* 128–42 (Concordat); A. Weber 150, 152 (inner religion); Callahan, *Church, Politics* 235 (emotion), Payne, *Spanish Catholicism* 104–05, Botrel, C. Fernández 437–38 (religious press); A. Weber 149 (early modern period).

113. Castelar, *Hermana* 2: 107: "sublime, verdaderamente sublime, bajar á los tristes hospitales, á los campos de batalla, á las negras chozas, á las casas miserables, al lecho infeliz del moribundo . . . á guiar su alma á la bienaventuranza . . . purificada por el martirio y el dolor, hacia Dios"; 2: 137: "una artista de la caridad; pues la caridad, como si fuera su creación, resplandecía sobre su frente." See also Catalina (213–18).

114. See Galdós, *Fortunata* 330–31 (1: 590–91); Herbert 29–31; also Aranguren 115–16; Callahan, *Church, Politics* 194, 212.

115. See Suárez 160, 191, 196; Lamet 132; Campo Alange 121–25; J. Varela 30; Vales Failde 39. The father of the traditionalist Menéndez Pelayo was a *progresista* but also a devout Catholic and vice president of the Society of St. Vincent de Paul in Santander (Madariaga de la Campa 22–23).

116. Arenal, *Visitador* 5: "Damos este nombre, no sólo a las Hermanas de la Caridad, sino a todas las personas que procuran el consuelo de los pobres, siguiendo el sublime espíritu de San Vicente de Paúl, que es el espíritu del Evangelio"; Irizarry 13 (speech acts); Alas, "Como gustéis" 514; Arenal, *Visitador* 5.

117. See Lacalzada de Mateo 240–41, for the Arenal–de Gérando relation. Elsewhere, she suggests, without comment, however, that Arenal's *El Visitador del pobre* was not inspired by his *Visitor of the Poor* (256–57, n235).

118. Palau y Dulcet 6: 167 lists an anonymous translation of the fourth edition (Valladolid: Imprenta D. M. Aparicio, 1852) and another by Luis Bordas (Barcelona: Imprenta Hispana de V. Castaños, 1854); as well as other de Gérando works (*La moral en acción* [1823; 1857]; and *De la perfección moral y de la educación de sí mismo* [1841]). I have consulted the *Visitador* of 1852. The English version (1833), translated by either Elizabeth Peabody or Susan D. Nickerson, is quite lovely though abridged, but for my purposes includes the most important chapters of the original, omitting sections of specific interest to Paris.

119. De Gérando, *Visitor* 38, 40, 75, 106.

120. De Gérando, *Visitor* 45, 105, 42, 49, 43.

121. De Gérando, *Visitor* 45; Tuckerman, Introduction 7–8. Joseph Tuckerman (1778–1840) was a Unitarian minister and philanthropist from Boston. Like de Gérando, he advocated "making the rich and the poor advantageously known to each other," especially through home visits (*Elevation* 28); see also Wach 544, on Tuckerman's belief that city life eroded social cohesion.

122. De Gérando, *Visitor* 96, 85; Donzelot 69 (welfare case workers).

123. Arenal, *Visitador* 10: "La mentira del pobre es una consecuencia de la dureza del rico y de su abandono"; "¿Los pobres serían lo que son, si nosotros fuéramos lo que debíamos ser?"

124. De Gérando, *Visitor* 105 ("sacred relations"); Arenal, *Beneficencia* 97: "hallan el esqueleto de lo que no vive *ya*, el germen de lo que no vive *todavía*. Para llenar el abismo que separa la sociedad que se acabó de la sociedad que empieza, los creyentes acuden con su fe, los visionarios con sus delirios, los pensadores con sus sistemas, la humanidad entera con sus lágrimas, y el abismo parece tragar todo lo que se le arroja." Castelar, in 1858, speaks of a "general uneasiness" and a "most profound malaise," in which "the transition in which we find ourselves wastes and erodes great qualities" (*Fórmula* 171). Balmes, however, commonsensically says that things are always in transition (*Cartas* 65). See also Fernández Sebastián and Fuentes, "Crisis" 201–02, for the link between the notion of "transition" and "crisis" in the period.

125. Arenal, *Beneficencia* 98: "Por donde quiera, restos que se desmoronan, embriones informes, locas esperanzas de poderlo todo, cobardes temores de impotencia . . . dirección sin fuerza, duda, confusión, desconfianza." For an overview of the vexed relation between public and private beneficence in Spain, see Shubert, "Charity"; also Monlau, *Elementos* 2: 838–39.

126. Woolf 36; Woolf 32 and Cavallo 52 (social network); Earle (Galdosian interdependence) (also Ribbans).

127. Arenal, *Visitador* 7: "¿Qué es el dolor? ¿Qué es el pobre? ¿Qué somos nosotros?"; 10: "no está en lo que decimos, sino en el modo de decirlo, en la mímica, en la inflexión de la voz"; 11: "ignoramos cómo hace sufrir y sentir, cómo modifica moralmente al desdichado que inmola"; 65: "Para el que después de una gran desgracia vuelve a la vida del alma, puede decirse que hay como una especie de resurrección dolorosa"; de Gérando, *Visitor* 49, 111.

128. De Gérando, *Visitor* 176–77; Arenal, *Visitador* 21: "Hay gran diferencia entre impresionarse con los males de nuestros hermanos y afligirse. Para lo primero basta imaginación y se necesita corazón para lo segundo"; Galdós, "Santos" 260 (vocation); Woolf 38 (specificity).

129. Laqueur, "Bodies" 77.

130. Pi y Molist 38, 9. See also Valis, *Reading* 260–61.

131. Galdós, "Moral" 300–01 (14 April 1887); also Galdós, "El 1° de mayo" 273 (15 April 1885), and Bahamonde Magro.

132. Galdós, *Fortunata* 168: "La probeza no es deshonra"; "No lo es, cierto, por sí; pero tampoco es honra, ¿estamos? Conozco pobres muy honrados; pero también los hay que son buenos pájaros" (1: 369).

133. See also Fuentes Peris 14–15.

134. See also Ribbans 279.

135. Galdós, *Fortunata* 42: "Y sale a relucir aquí la visita del Delfín al anciano servidor y amigo de su casa, porque si Juanito Santa Cruz no hubiera hecho aquella visita, esta historia no se habría escrito. Se hubiera escrito otra, eso sí, porque por do quiera que el hombre vaya lleva consigo su novela; pero ésta no" (1: 181).

136. Galdós, *Fortunata* 222–23: "Cada día más dominado por su frenesí investigador, visitó Santa Cruz diferentes casas, unas de peor fama que otras. . . . No dejó de tocar a ninguna puerta tras de la cual pudieran esconderse la vergüenza perdida o la perdición vergonzosa. Sus exploraciones parecían lo que no eran por el ardor con que las practicaba y el carácter humanitario de que las revestía. Parecía un padre, un hermano que desalado busca a la prenda querida que ha caído en los dédalos tenebrosos del vicio. Y quería cohonestar su inquietud con razones filantrópicas y aun cristianas que sacaba de su entendimiento rico en sofisterías" (1: 442).

137. Galdós, *Fortunata* 63: "En aquella excursión por el campo instructivo de la industria, su generoso corazón se desbordaba en sentimientos filantrópicos . . . — No puedes figurarte — decía a su marido . . . cuánta lástima me dan esas infelices muchachas que están aquí ganando un triste jornal, con el cual no sacan ni para vestirse. No tienen educación, son como máquinas . . . en cuanto se les presenta un pillo cualquiera se dejan seducir. . . . Y no es maldad; es que llega un momento en que dicen: 'Vale más ser mujer mala que máquina buena'" (1: 214).

138. Marin xvii; see also Schillebeeckx 64, 73; Doueihi 624.

139. See Doueihi 623.

140. Rubin 353 (Eucharist as hinge); Black 31–35 and Sieber, *"Don Quixote"* 4–5 (Trent); Jiménez Duque 147 (devotions center stage); Jiménez Duque 151 and Lamet 133 (Madre Sacramento). The Micaelas convent occupies a special place in Galdosian criticism. Current views tend to see it in heavily Foucauldian terms; see Fuentes Peris, Tsuchiya, and Ewald's well-documented study.

141. Galdós, *Fortunata* 355: "La impresión moral que recibió la samaritana era tan compleja, que ella misma no se daba cuenta de lo que sentía . . . a este sentimiento [de la envidia] mezclábase con extraña amalgama otro muy distinto y más acentuado. Era un deseo ardentísimo de parecerse a Jacinta, de ser como ella, de tener su aire. . . . De modo que si le propusieran a la prójima, en aquel momento, transmigrar al cuerpo de otra persona, sin vacilar y a ojos cerrados habría dicho que quería ser Jacinta. . . . El mucho

pensar en [Jacinta] la llevó, al amparo de la soledad del convento, a tener por las noches ensueños. . . . Ya soñaba . . . que las dos cuestionaban sobre cuál era más víctima; ya, en fin, que transmigraban recíprocamente, tomando Jacinta el exterior de Fortunata y Fortunata el exterior de Jacinta" (1: 625–26).

142. Galdós, *Fortunata* 372: "Orgullo y alegría inundaron el alma de la atrevida mujer al mirar en su propia mano la representación visible de Dios. . . . ¡Cómo brillaban los rayos de oro que circundan el viril, y qué misteriosa y plácida majestad la de la hostia purísima, guardada tras el cristal, blanca, divina y con todo el aquel de persona, sin ser más que una sustancia de delicado pan! . . . Entonces notó que la sagrada forma no sólo tenía ya ojos profundos tan luminosos como el cielo, sino también voz. . . . Había desaparecido toda sensación de la materialidad de la custodia; no quedaba más que lo esencial, la representación, el símbolo puro, y eso era lo que Mauricia apretaba furiosamente contra sí. — Chica — le decía la voz —, no me saques, vuelve a ponerme donde estaba. No hagas locuras. . . . Mauricia, chica, ¿qué haces . . . ? ¿Me comes, me comes . . . ?" (1: 647).

143. On the Eucharist, see de la Palma (1662) (*Meditaciones* 217); Matthew 26: 26–28; Mark 14: 22–24; Luke 22: 19–20; Faber; and Schillebeeckx. On Galdós's knowledge of religion, see Berkowitz, *Biblioteca* 65–70; also de la Nuez 56–60, for books on religion found in the novelist's personal library. He was extremely familiar with the Bible. There are over four hundred biblical quotations in his work, according to Nos Muro (164, 170).

144. Galdós, *Fortunata* 549: "Ejercía sobre ella una atracción querenciosa, y como le dijera algún concepto lisonjero a su corazón, sentíalo retumbar en su mente cual si fuera verdad pronunciada por sobrenatural labio. Mil veces analizó la joven este poder fascinador de su amiga, sin lograr encontrarle nunca el sentido" (2: 179); 550: "es una mujer esa que electriza" (2: 180); 120: "como echando chispas . . . me pongo eléctrico" (1: 298).

145. Galdós, *Fortunata* 544: "Doña Guillermina había sacado del Hospital a Mauricia, trasladándola a casa de la hermana de ésta, y la asistía el médico de la Beneficiencia Domiciliaria y de la Junta de señoras" (2: 171).

146. Labanyi, *Gender* 199 (staging); Rodero 81–82 (parody).

147. Galdós, *Fortunata* 555 (2: 187).

148. See Williams, *Keywords* 55.

149. Galdós, *Fortunata* 594–95: "[Fortunata] no la pudo apartar de su mente. ¡Qué extraordinaria mujer aquella! Sentíala dentro de sí, como si se la hubiera tragado, cual si la hubiera tomado en comunión. Las miradas y la voz de la santa se le agarraban a su interior como sustancias perfectamente asimiladas. Y por la noche . . . sin poder coger el sueño . . . [c]on tal claridad veía a Guillermina como si la tuviera delante; pero lo raro no era esto, sino que se le parecía también a Napoleón, como Mauricia la Dura. ¿Y la voz? . . . La voz era enteramente igual a la de su difunta amiga. ¿Cómo así, siendo una y otra personas tan distintas? Fuera lo que fuese, la simpatía misteriosa que le había inspirado Mauricia, se pasaba a Guillermina. . . . 'Yo no sé cómo es esto — discurría Fortunata . . . Se devanaba los sesos . . . y llegó a figurarse que de los restos fríos de Mauricia salía volando una mariposita, la cual mariposita se metía dentro de la *rata eclesiástica* y la transformaba. . . . En la oscuridad . . . el cuerpo [de Mauricia] se levantaba, daba algunos pasos, iba hacia ella y le decía: 'Fortunata, querida amiga de mi alma, ¿no me conoces? . . . Si no me he muerto, chica, si estoy en el mundo. . . . Soy Guillermina, doña Guillermina'" (2: 236–37).

150. See also Galdós, *Fortunata* 341; 1: 607.

151. Bynum, *Fragmentation* 258.

152. I am indebted here to Stephen Gilman's indispensable "The Art of Consciousness" (*Galdós* 320–55) and to Harriet Turner's analysis of "metaphors of mind" (*Galdós* 97–100).

153. O'Grady 100.

154. S. Gilman 287–88 (act of generosity); Galdós, *Fortunata* 806 (2: 526); Hyde, 22, 20. This paragraph and the next two are an expanded revision of an earlier interpretation (*Reading* 172–73).

155. Galdós, *Fortunata* 802: " 'No quiero morirme sin hacerle a usted una fineza y le mando a usted, por mano del amigo D. Plácido, ese *mono del Cielo* que su esposo de usted me dio a mí, equivocadamente' . . . No, no, borre usted el *equivocadamente;* ponga: 'Que me lo dio a mí robándoselo a usted . . . ' No, D. Plácido, así no . . . porque yo lo tuve . . . yo, y a ella no se le ha quitado nada. Lo que hay es que yo se lo quiero dar, porque sé que ha de quererle, y porque es mi amiga' " (2: 521).

156. Hyde 40–41 (threshold gift); Galdós, *Fortunata* 810: "compañerismo, frater-nidad fundada en desgracias comunes" (2: 531); 810: "el caso increíble de la herencia del *Pituso,* envolví[a], sin que la inteligencia pudiera desentrañar este enigma, una reconcilia-ción" (2: 531–32).

157. Thus Labanyi declares that "[Guillermina's] invasion of privacy is total" (*Gender* 197), a statement that needs to be qualified by a more historical and nuanced understand-ing of poverty, philanthropy, and the complex relations between the rich and the poor. Fortunately, we have Galdós for that. Of interest is a contemporary outsider's view of philanthropy in Spain: "Galdós in some of his popular novels does not fail to hold up — not exactly for admiration — the fashionable ladies who think it 'smart' . . . to join these boards and societies, while neglecting the poor and the needy at their own doors, or trying to send into 'Homes' those who have no desire or need to go there if a little Christian charity were only shown them by their neighbours. Nevertheless, there is a large amount of organised philanthropy in Spain to-day, and it appears to be of a wise and efficient kind" (Higgin 228–29).

158. Bahamonde Magro would call the episode an example of the deleterious "culture of poverty" created through paternalistic dependency (see also Jutglar, "Estudio pre-liminar" 43–44; and the anticlerical Anon., "Caridad" [orig. *El Motín* 7 January 1886]). Galdós's view is more nuanced. While manual labor does not necessarily appeal to Ido, he also experiences happiness in contributing to Guillermina's charitable project. Projects like Sor Ángela de la Cruz's Sisters of the Cross, founded in 1875 and dedicated to caring for the poor and the sick, built bridges between the social classes but were obliged to work within the existing social-economic structures (see Javierre 151). This set of circum-stances was as true for aristocrats like Ernestina Manuel de Villena (Guillermina's histor-ical counterpart) as for the working-class Angelita Guerrero (Sor Ángela de la Cruz, 1846–1932). Charity was not, moreover, solely a middle- or upper-class practice; see R. Shaw 118–20, for examples of working-class generosity.

159. Galdós, *Fortunata* 372: " — No, no te suelto, ya no vuelves allí . . . ¡A casa con tu mamá . . . ! ¿sí? . . . Diciendo esto, atrevíase a agasajar contra su pecho la sagrada forma" (1: 647); Faber 155 (see Palau y Dulcet 5: 238); Bynum, *Fragmentation* 123; Galdós, *Fortunata* 410: "Le voy a proponer un trato a tu mujer. . . . Yo le cedo a ella un hijo tuyo y ella me cede a mí su marido. Total, cambiar un nene chico por el nene grande" (1: 695).

160. Stern 30.

161. Whiston notes that "all the substantial characters of the novel, except Juanito and Guillermina, are endowed with a significantly richer interior life from the early to the later versions" (*Practice* 247); also Ribbans.

162. De Gérando, *Visitor* 33.

163. Galdós owned several books by the Chilean Juan Enrique Lagarrigue, among them *La religión de la humanidad* (1884) (Berkowitz, *Biblioteca* 67–68). A Comtian, Lagarrigue argued that the social question was not just an economic but a moral-religious question. Catholicism, he said, was a precursor to the new redemptive religion of humanity based on altruism. See also Gold, "Galdós and Lamennais," for the Lagarrigue–Galdós connection (48, n19); and Alas, "Palique" (orig. *Madrid Cómico* 2 October 1897), for a skeptical view of Lagarrigue as a second-rate, outdated positivist.

164. Buckler 207. In a much-cited article on *Fortunata y Jacinta*, Sherman Eoff links the transformative nature of personality and its relation to others to the development of social psychology, in which personality was studied "as a process of becoming," and to Hegel ("Deification"125; 139).

165. See Urbina (messiah); Galdós, *Fortunata* 818: "¡Si creerán estos tontos que me engañan! Esto es Leganés. . . . No encerrarán entre murallas mi pensamiento. Resido en las estrellas. Pongan al llamado Maximiliano Rubín en un palacio o en un muladar . . . lo mismo da" (2: 541–42). While Galdós establishes a link between stars and madness, Castelar (1858; 1870) associates the stars with the sacred image of poverty (*Fórmula* 217).

Chapter 3. The Confessional Body

1. Chacel 135: "Hay en Galdós un propósito consciente de no confesar, que condice muy bien con su inconsciente falta de necesidad de confesar."

2. Rousseau 1:276.

3. González Echevarría, *Myth* 56 (*relación*); Gitlitz 59 (potential autobiographer), also 70–71. The Augustinian confessional mode is especially compelling in Mateo Alemán; see Dunn 166–68, 176–80.

4. Cerrón Puga 169.

5. Flaubert 193 (312).

6. See García de Cortázar 42 and Noel 890, for the eighteenth- and nineteenth-century emphasis on original sin. In his story "El pecado original" (1894), Clarín uses the notion to condemn "egotism, indifference, envy" (776).

7. Valis, *Decadent* 104.

8. Flaubert 25, 27, 28: "Au lieu de suivre la messe, elle regardait dans son livre les vignettes pieuses bordées d'azur, et elle aimait la brebis malade, le sacré coeur percé de flèches aiguës, ou le pauvre Jésus qui tombe en marchant sur sa croix" (67); "elle inventait de petits péchés, afin de rester là plus longtemps" (67); "Quand sa mère mourut . . . Elle se fit faire un tableau funèbre avec les cheveux de la défunte, et . . . elle demandait qu'on l'ensevelît plus tard dans le même tombeau . . . Emma fut intérieurement satisfaite de se sentir arrivée du premier coup à ce rare idéal des existences pâles, où ne parviennent jamais les coeurs médiocres" (70–71); "sans plus de tristesse au coeur que de rides sur son front" (71).

9. See Coffey 596 (religion in *La Regenta*); Nimetz 243 (sex and religion). See also Valis, *Reading* 29–40 (significance of eschatology) and 55–81 (politicization of Saint Teresa's tricentenary in 1882). Resina incisively argues that "the novel's modernity does not lie in its anticlerical stance but in the overlay of the clerical world-view with the language of nervous disorder" (248).

10. Amann misreads the traditional religious term *hermano del alma* as politically subversive here ("Forma" 18). Fermín may be her spiritual brother, but he does not belong to the community of "oppressed brothers."

11. Alas, *La Regenta* 572: "oía la elocuencia silenciosa de aquel hecho patente . . . aquella elevación casi milagrosa de un pueblo entero prosaico, empequeñecido por la pobreza y la ignorancia, a las regiones de lo ideal, a la adoración de lo Absoluto por abstracción prodigiosa" (2: 334). I am using Gonzalo Sobejano's edition and John Rutherford's translation. The belief that *La Regenta* offers only a bleak and crushing view of religion persists in literary criticism. See, for example, T. Mitchell 48–55 and Deaver 91.

12. Alas, *La Regenta* 594 (2: 366).

13. See Amann, "Forma" 15, 17; also Bacon 18, 27–28 in a similar vein (and misunderstanding).

14. Amann argues for the mediating importance of the revolution of 1848 and the manipulative discourses of Bonapartism in Clarín's novel, thus moving away from the historical realities of Spain (the September Revolution of 1868 and the Restoration) (*Importing*). Spanish, not French, history and politics, however, obsessed Clarín over the course of twenty-five years (see his *Obras completas* vols. 4–10). He did not need to rely on the "manipulation and misapplication of discourses" of Louis Napoléon (Amann 12). The Spanish Restoration period teems with duplicity and misrepresentation, based as it was on the complicit sharing of power between the two dynastic political parties and the system of *caciquismo*, or local bosses.

15. See Payne, *Spanish Catholicism* 93 and Fuentes, "Juntas" 393, for civilian radicals; Rose 1: 229, 224–25.

16. Rose 1: 235, 236. The imagery attributed to the Virgin is drawn from traditional Marian litanies. Regarding religious belief, Rose declares that "an *Indiferente* often becomes indifferent from long continuance in sin or prayerlessness; still more often, from utter indecision of character" (1: 230–31). Indifferentism is one of the errors singled out in Pius IX's *Syllabus*: "Every man is free to embrace and profess the religion he thinks true, according to the light of reason"(Error 15). Error 16 claims that the "road to eternal salvation [can be found and embraced] in any faith"(4–5). In *Casos de conciencia*, by P.V., liberalism "is nothing less than . . . the political system of religious indifference" (245). P.V. is probably Pablo Villada (1845–1921), the first director of the Jesuit journal *Razón y Fe* (1901–06) (see Aranguren 179; and Segura 167–68).

17. Field 255.

18. Sardá y Salvany 17–18: "la absoluta soberanía del individuo con entera independencia de Dios y de su autoridad; soberanía de la sociedad con absoluta independencia de lo que no nazca de ella misma . . . libertad de pensamiento sin limitación alguna en política, en moral o en religión."

19. Sardá y Salvany 20: "la necesidad de la divina revelación"; 24: "que ser blasfemo, ladrón, adúltero u homicida"; 28 (liberal as monstrous). See Palau y Dulcet 20: 127; also

Schumacher 358–59; and Hibbs-Lissorgues 261–88 for an excellent account of Sardá y Salvany's impact. During the Spanish Civil War, in a propaganda pamphlet, the Republican supporter Langdon-Davies pointed out to English Catholics that the same sentiment (liberalism is a sin) could be found in a popular catechism by Ángel María de Arcos (4).

20. See Hibbs-Lissorgues 14–15, 26, 355–402 (modernity); also Botrel; and Barnes.

21. Giner de los Ríos, "Enseñanza" 172–73. Javier Varela considers Spanish Krausism "a movement of religious reform; a dissident movement of Spanish Catholicism" (78). They were Christians without a church (Varela 77).

22. Weil 210; Freud, *Future* 44 (also Valis, *Reading* 61, 80); Pérez Gutiérrez 284 ("inner God"); Alas, "Revista literaria [November 1889]" 1632–33: "Malos, sí, muy malos son los extremos; pero el término medio de la *neutralidad social* es ridículo, falso, insostenible. Que en esta España, que ha vertido tanta sangre . . . por la religión católica, de la noche a la mañana dejemos de pensar en el catolicismo, y en general . . . en toda religión; que cada cual guarde sus creencias para el retiro de su alcoba, como si fuesen enfermedades secretas, y ante el mundo practiquemos la tolerancia de la *neutralidad* de la escuela belga, que consiste en prescindir del cristianismo en la historia, mutilando el espíritu propio . . . es absurdo. . . . La tolerancia universal, la verdadera *secularización religiosa,* no ha de ser negativa, pasiva, sino positiva, activa. . . . Una sociedad es tolerante cuando todas las creencias hablan y se las oye en calma; no cuando hay esta calma porque callan todas." Clarín refers to a Belgian bill of 1879 to approve the secularization of primary education, unleashing several years of "school war" between progressive liberals and Catholics (1879–84) (see Witte 118–26).

23. Alas, "Revista literaria" 1635: "injertar en la España católica la España liberal"; 1635: "de respetar las antiguas ideas y los sentimientos que engendran, y hasta de participar de esos sentimientos, por lo que tienen de humanos y por lo que tienen de españoles"; "Revista mínima [April 1893]" 521: "*secularizar la religión,* es decir . . . llevar la religión a todas partes"; "Revista literaria" 1634–35: "Mi *historia natural* y mi *historia nacional* me atan con cadenas de realidad, dulces cadenas, al amor del catolicismo . . . como obra humana y como obra española. Yo todavía considero como *cosa mía* la catedral labrada y erigida por la fe de mis mayores. . . . Rezo a mi modo, con lo que siento, con lo que recuerdo de la niñez de mi vida . . . con lo que le dicen al alma la música del órgano y los cantos del coro, cuya letra no llega a mi oído, pero cuyas melodías me estremecen . . .; mi espíritu habla allí para sus adentros una especie de glosolalia que debe de parecerse a la de aquellos cristianos de la primera Iglesia, poco aleccionados todavía en las afirmaciones concretas de sus dogmas, pero llenos de inefables emociones." The liberal politician Emilio Castelar also linked his faith to memories of childhood y to the maternal (*Fórmula* 210–11; 219).

24. See García Sarriá 62–66 and Sobejano, "Clarín" 133–34 (mother's devotion). Alas, "Cartas" 1170: "No quieren creer . . . que nuestra religiosidad sea real; y no es extraño que ellos lo duden, cuando muchos liberales piensan que efectivamente la religión se queda en el pasado"; "Cartas" 1172 (see Introduction, n1, for orig.). For spiritual dryness as observed by Thomas à Kempis and others, see Madeleva 23–37. Spiritual dryness afflicts Alas's character Ana Ozores. See also the seamstress Francisca Javiera del Valle (1856–1930), a contemporary mystic, who spoke of her spiritual aridity and loss of faith at the age of eighteen (67; 71). Enrique de Ossó wrote that the affliction came from several sources, among them, the imagination itself (23).

25. Alas, "Cartas" 1171 (romantic imagination). For the theme of religion in Alas's life and works, see, in addition to Lissorgues's indispensable *Pensée:* Arboleya Martínez; Savaiano; Bécarud; F. W. Weber, "Ideology"; Nimetz; Pérez Gutiérrez 269–338; Gil de Muro; Lissorgues, "Autenticidad"; Laso Prieto; García de Cortázar; Elizalde; Diederich; Coffey; and Sobejano, "Clarín."

26. Alas, "Libre" 156: "llegó a todas las esferas de la vida social, penetró en los espíritus y planteó por vez primera en España todos los arduos problemas que la libertad de conciencia había ido suscitando en los pueblos libres y cultos de Europa . . . las dudas y las negaciones que habían sido antes alimento de escasos espíritus llegaron al pueblo, y se habló en calles, clubes y congresos, de teología, de libre-examen, con escándalo de no pequeña parte del público, ortodoxo todavía y fanático, o, por lo menos, intolerante."

27. Chadwick 113 (Vatican Council I); Alas, "De profundis" 620 (Hell); Alas, "Palique" (1882) 891: "yo no creo en el purgatorio y tengo tanto sentido común como [cualquier fraile franciscano]"; Arboleya Martínez 50. In a moving letter to Giner de los Ríos, Clarín wrote, "In the midst of my paltry literary endeavors, at every moment I think I hear voices. . . . Can it be the Lord? Can it be the Lord, Don Francisco? Or is it vanity, *useless* rhetoric, an unconscious desire for originality, or the literary mirage of believing myself to be like a character of a certain novel I am devising?" ("a cada momento, en medio de mis humildes faenas literarias, creo oír voces . . . ¿Será el Señor? ¿Será el Señor, don Francisco? O ¿será vanidad, o *vana* retórica, o inconsciente afán de originalidad, o el espejismo literario de creerme yo como un personaje de cierta novela que estoy fraguando?") (20 October 1887; in Gómez-Tabanera and Rodríguez Arrieta 478).

28. Blanco White, "Examination" 20.

29. Blanco White, "Examination" 9; *Cartas* (1822) 85, 86.

30. Bettina Diederich analyzes, along Bakhtinian and intertextual lines, Clarín's novel as a parodic discourse drawn from Catholic moral theology, in which the seven deadly sins are reconstituted in the characters considered as literary artifacts.

31. Lyotard 57; Zambrano (1943), *Confesión* 22: "el carácter fragmentario de toda vida."

32. See P. Fernández 126, for López Bago's *El cura* as a bestseller.

33. Nepaulsingh 421 (*Lazarillo*); Alas, "Evangelista" 291.

34. Ferrándiz Ruiz, *Secretos* 241–42; "Bibliografía" and "La segunda parte de *El cura*" (reviews of López Bago's work). Haliczer refers to Michel Morphy's *Les mystères de la pornographie cléricale* (1884) (187), which I have been unable to see. Could Ferrándiz have been familiar with it? For more on López Bago, Ferrándiz, and Perera, see P. Fernández; Molina Martínez 295–345; and Cejador Frauca 9: 250, respectively.

35. For confessional abuses, consult Haliczer, and Dufour, *Clero;* Haliczer 207 ("eroticized confession"); Steinmueller and Sullivan 576 (*skandalon*). See also Leiva and Montoya, on the discovery in 1977 of the priest Francisco González Vázquez's written confession recounting his sexual transgressions, mostly with adolescent boys, between 1788 and 1824; he had placed it inside a reed, which he then hid in the ceiling of his convent cell.

36. Feliu y Codina 7.

37. Foucault, *History* 1.

38. Alas, *La Regenta* 715: "[Ana] había creído sentir sobre la boca el vientre viscoso y frío de un sapo" (2: 537).

39. Van Boheemen ix, 6–7, 2.

40. See Mandrell (Girardian desire); Laqueur, *Making Sex* 11.

41. Foucault, *Power* 188; Greenblatt 227–28 (system of constraints); Brooks, *Reading* (dynamics of desire).

42. Peter Brooks observes the similarities of the confessional and the *alcôve* as secret spaces (*Troubling* 89–90).

43. Alas, *La Regenta* 65–66: "— ¡Confesión general! — estaba pensando —. Eso es la historia de toda la vida"; "Se acordó de que no había conocido a su madre. Tal vez de esta desgracia nacían sus mayores pecados" (1: 165); 66; 1:166 (nostalgia).

44. Alas, *La Regenta* 67: "Cuando era niña, pero ya confesaba, siempre que el libro de examen decía 'pase la memoria por los lugares que ha recorrido,' se acordaba sin querer de la barca de Trébol, de aquel gran pecado que había cometido, sin saberlo ella, la noche que pasó dentro de la barca con aquel Germán, su amigo" (1: 167).

45. Simpson 216–17.

46. Richard 64 and Morris 66 ("Know thyself"); Talavera, *Comulgar* 36.

47. De Jaén 33: "mientras mas dilatan [los penitentes] el desahogarse, mas se van endureciendo, y suele sucederles en estas inquietudes y remordimientos de conciencia lo que sucede a los que tienen algun asiento ó acedo al estómago, que mientras no lo vomitan no hallan alivio, todo es vahidos y dolores de cabeza, bascas, desganas de comer, zozobra y desasosiego"; Claret (1860–61), *Colegial* 1: 361–62: "No permitáis, Señor, que mis enemigos . . . de nuevo me hagan tragar el vómito de mis pecados que arrojé a los pies del confesor"; Lyotard 92; Saint Augustine 187; also, dei Segni's bleak vision, in the classic statement of *contemptus mundi* (68).

48. See Lea 1: 225, 394–95, Orsy 27–51, and Tambling 8, for the evolution of penance; Delumeau 198 (sin literature); Morris 70–75 (introspective self); Doody 21 (individuation); Hepworth and Turner 14 ("social inclusion").

49. Berggren part I, chap. 1 (need to confess); Hanna, "Penance" ("tribunal of penance"); Delumeau 199–200 (confessors' handbooks); Druzbicki 45; Brother Philippe 204, 205.

50. Hanna, "Penance" (also M. Boyle 87–88); Tambling 6.

51. *Lazarillo* 92: "confesó, y no negó, y padeció persecución por justicia" (also Guillén 269); see also Témime; Dedieu; and J. Pérez (*résistance mentale*).

52. Homza 153 (confessors' manuals); Guillén 268 (Lazarillo's *caso*).

53. See Payne, *Spanish Catholicism* chap. 4; Jiménez Duque; Botrel; and Morales Muñoz, for the Catholic Revival in Spain; Kent 113, 119 ("resacralize").

54. García de Cortázar 41 (sacramentalization); Alas, *La Regenta* 569 (2: 329), 440 (2: 139), 407 (2: 91–92); Uría 62 and García de Cortázar 43 (catechism in Oviedo). Sanz y Forés initiated the practice of giving "to first communion that festive air which it had never before enjoyed in Asturias" (Uría 78). The new sensibility was anticipated in the evangelizing missions Father Claret popularized in the 1840s and 1850s, in which he preached consolation and hope and downplayed the more terrifying aspects of hell (Viñas 32).

55. Alas, *La Regenta* 495–96: "Ana se consagró a la piedad activa, a las obras de caridad, a la enseñanza, a la propaganda, a las prácticas de la devoción complicada y bizantina, que era la que predominaba en Vetusta. Aquellas exageraciones, que tal le habían parecido en otro tiempo, ahora las encontraba justificables, como los amantes se

explican las mil tonterías ridículas que se dicen a solas" (2: 223); 499–500: "[Ana] acogíase a la piedad, y visitaba con celo apostólico y ardiente caridad las moradas miserables de los pobres hacinados en pocilgas y cuevas; llevaba el consuelo de la religión para el espíritu y la limosna para el cuerpo . . .ésta [ocupación] era la que más le agradaba" (2: 228–29). Clarín, nonetheless, continued to have little use for certain excesses of piety, as his story "Para vicios" (1894) demonstrates. Here, a *beata*, Doña Indalecia, loves "charitable organizations much more than charity" and persecutes vice with the zeal of a Grand Inquisitor. For Doña Indalecia, "charity properly understood" is organized and highly regulated (565).

56. See Payne, *Spanish Catholicism* 105 (devotional style); *Corte* 90, 151.

57. Callahan, *Church, Politics* 235 ("conservative elements"); Rowell 16 ("personal understanding") (also P. Lewis 674–75).

58. Pardo Bazán 36; also Zeldin 14. Pardo Bazán goes on to say that husbands and confessors as authority figures are natural allies. Nonetheless, husbands, in Spain at least, look askance at frequent confession and excessive devotion in wives (37). Catalina (1858), on the other hand, thought that religious skepticism in women was not only repugnant but implausible (115).

59. González López 28–31 (Cos y Macho); "Regla" 17; Noel 870 (sermons). For more on Cos y Macho and his penitent Mercedes Villaverde Uría, see González López, who also reproduces her "Regla de vida" (17–18). Her religious routine duplicates that recommended in manuals like Claret's *Catecismo de la doctrina cristiana* (1864), de Ossó's *El cuarto de hora de oración* (1874), and Sayol y Echevarría's *Eucologio romano: Devocionario completo* (1877).

60. See de Ossó 26 (submission to one's spiritual director); Vicenti 134 ("throne").

61. See Payne, *Spanish Catholicism* 106 and B. Smith, chap. 5, for the French spiritual model; Payne, *Spanish Catholicism* 110; R. Shaw, 42, 74 (distrust of confessors).

62. Richmond, "En torno" 349. The Krausist Giner de los Ríos, whose thinking and presence heavily influenced Clarín, was also regarded as a kind of spiritual director (J. Varela 82).

63. De Jaén 281; Alas, *La Regenta* 28: "Vetusta era su pasión y su presa. . . . La conocía palmo a palmo, por dentro y por fuera, por el alma y por el cuerpo, había escudriñado los rincones de las conciencias y los rincones de las casas" (1: 105).

64. See Nimetz; F. W. Weber; Bobes Naves; Charnon-Deutsch; Bauer; and Cerrón Puga. Bobes Naves 229 (confession as symbolic); Charnon-Deutsch 111; Bauer 313.

65. Bobes Naves 347–48, 352.

66. Tambling 19–20.

67. See Hanna (confessant's silence); Zeldin 16–17 ("charnel house"); *Confessional* 37.

68. See Zeldin 36 and Drochon, "L'Église"(anti-Church attacks); Ciocci 11, 47.

69. See Dumesnil 119 (Huysmans's confession); Valentini and di Meglio 7 (cultural strictures); Barthes, *S/Z* 75 and Brooks, *Reading* 58, 92 (need for story); Kermode x–xi, 47 (secret senses).

70. Brooks, *Reading* 85 (narrative deviations); Sánchez-Eppler 205, 207. See also Jaffe on this passage (10).

71. Eickhoff 17 (reading as method); Meissner 347 (reading of moods).

72. A. de Nicolás x; Loyola 39–40: "el primer preámbulo es composición viendo el

lugar . . . la composición será ver con la vista de la imaginación el lugar corpóreo, donde se halla la cosa que quiero contemplar"; "Digo el lugar corpóreo, así como un templo o monte, donde se halla Jesu Christo o Nuestra Señora, según lo que quiero contemplar. En la invisible, como es aquí de los pecados, la composición será ver con la vista imaginativa y considerar mi ánima ser encarcerada en este cuerpo corruptible." The "composición viendo el lugar" is called "the materialization of the spirit" in Pérez de Ayala's novel *A.M.D.G.* (83).

73. Donnelly 11 and Leturia (Books of Hours); A. de Nicolás 41, 42; Barthes, "Loyola" 50–51, 66, 4.

74. Loyola 47: "con la vista de la imaginación la longura, anchura y profundidad del infierno"; "los grandes fuegos, y las ánimas como en cuerpos ígneos."

75. Alas, *La Regenta* 430 : "el Infierno ya no era un dogma englobado en otros; ella había sentido su olor, su sabor. . . . ¡Había infierno! Era así . . . la podredumbre de la materia para los espíritus podridos . . . y ella había pecado, sí, sí, había pecado" (2: 126–27); Pohle 157 (*attritio*); also dei Segni, for related imagery of Hell, from the *contemptus mundi* tradition (74–77). Educated in part by the Jesuits, Clarín was familiar with Ignatius's image-making techniques. See his article "La pedagogía de los jesuitas" (1878), in which he cites directly from Loyola (1156–57). For the importance of the visual in Alas's work, see Richmond, "*La Regenta*"; and Martínez Carazo.

76. Valis, *Reading* 41–54 (Hell in *La Regenta*); Tambling 40 (circumstances of sin); Loyola 44: "mirar el lugar y la casa adonde [h]a habitado"; Brother Philippe 78, also 206.

77. Tambling 41 ("positive construction") (also M. Boyle 9); Illich 94, 96. Illich's view is typical of modern scholars. "Imagining penance as an exercise in power is nearly a cliché of current scholarship," as Lu Ann Homza notes (114). See also Homza 150–75 for a more nuanced view of the relation between clergy and laity during the process of confession and absolution in the early modern period.

78. Huysmans, *En route* 331: "[Ils] ne laissaient aucune initiative à l'âme."

79. More generally, a discreet physical deportment in sacred settings and for acts like confession and communion was important. In her etiquette manual for women, Felipa Máxima de Cabeza stresses circumspection and modesty of movement, looking neither to the left nor right, in such circumstances (154–55). The edition I have consulted is the seventh, from 1859. Her advice recalls similar admonitions from Counter-Reformation works like the Jesuit de la Palma's *Práctica y breve declaración del camino espiritual* (1629) (390), which was reprinted in 1859 and 1887 (xxix). See also Stoichita 162, 174–75 for the importance of bodily posture in sixteenth- and seventeenth-century Spanish art as a figural code of spiritual experience.

80. Barthes, "Loyola" 61, 63; see also A. de Nicolás 36–37.

81. A. de Nicolás xxi (body as primary text); M. Boyle 10 (Loyolan setting); Alas, *La Regenta* 67: "Pensando la Regenta en aquella niña que había sido ella, la admiraba, y le parecía que su vida se había partido en dos. . . . La niña que saltaba del lecho a oscuras era más enérgica que esta Anita de ahora, tenía una fuerza interior pasmosa para resistir sin humillarse las exigencias y las injusticias de las personas frías, secas y caprichosas que la criaban" (1: 167).

82. Alas, *La Regenta* 82: "cuando ya nadie pensaba en tal cosa, [pero] pensaba ella todavía y confundiendo actos inocentes con verdaderas culpas, de todo iba desconfiando" (1: 195); Lacan 1–7, 281–91 (also Mitchell 23 and Rose 30).

83. Rahner 313 (original sin); Delumeau 247–49 (Saint Augustine); Kagan 136–37 (Inquisition's trials); Delumeau 261 (guilt). See also Romans 5: 12, for Paul's words: "Wherefore, as by one man sin entered into the world, and death by sin; and so death passed upon all men, for that all have sinned."

84. Brother Philippe 351; de la Puente, *Sentimientos* 322: "desorden es en pensamientos e imaginaciones, los cuales son desordenados, o por ser de cosas dañosas, o vanas, o impertinentes para el tiempo, o con demasiado ahinco."

85. Saint Augustine 27, 33; Claret, *Llave* 46: "Por lo que, padres, y especialmente Vds las madres, no tendrán Vds. jamás a sus hijos e hijas en su cama, mayormente si son mayores de cuatro o cinco años. ¡Qué daños se han seguido de esto! Tampoco hará V. dormir juntos los niños y niñas aunque sean hermanos. Mire V. que yo sé muchas maldades que de esto se han seguido"; *Llave* 45; Ferrándiz Ruiz, *Secretos* 303 (*Llave*); Hay 38 (1871) ("vile manual"); La Fuente y Zamalloa 2:121 (Claret's apostolic missions). See also C. Fernández 26, for Claret's "black legend."

86. Jordan 65 (Carroll); Ariès, *Centuries*; Boswell 36–38 and Larque 381 (pre-eighteenth century childhood).

87. Dickens, *David Copperfield* 13.

88. Simpson 220–21 (orphanhood); Alas, "Viaje redondo" 653.

89. N. Auerbach 72 ("trascendentalizing"); M. J. Peterson 10–11 (status incongruence).

90. For Spanish examples see Tamayo y Baus; Blasco; Palacio; and Sepúlveda.

91. On the narrative of mind, see Van Buren 24.

92. Alas, *La Regenta* 83: "La heroína de sus novelas de entonces era una madre. A los seis años había hecho un poema en su cabecita rizada de un rubio oscuro. Aquel poema estaba compuesto de las lágrimas de sus tristezas de huérfana maltratada y de fragmentos de cuentos que oía a los criados y a los pastores de Loreto" (1: 190).

93. Simpson 15, 153.

94. M. Boyle 1 (rhetoric); Sobejano, in *La Regenta* 1:203 n27 (saint's harsh opinion); Saint Augustine 202, 177.

95. Alas, *La Regenta* 92: "Y lloró sobre las *Confesiones* de San Agustín, como sobre el seno de una madre. Su alma se hacía mujer en aquel momento" (1: 204); see also Sobejano, "Clarín" 128–29; Alas, *La Regenta* 68; 1: 168. Saint Augustine was moved to convert through reading, as was Loyola, whose transformation was that of a "conversion of a reader through reading" (Eickhoff 15). By contrast, Ana's metamorphosis is sexually charged. Ana's reaction can also be compared to the emotional account of Saint Teresa's experience in devotional literature like *La corte celestial de María* (1855), in which the future saint "read [Augustine's] *Confessions* with indescribable eagerness, and upon reaching the point when Saint Augustine describes his conversion, a torrent of tears gushed from her eyes . . . she felt mystical inspiration and the sublime delirium of divine love born in her . . . from her soul came ardent sighs and inconsolable moans, her words possessing a sweetness and power impossible to resist" (205).

96. Sobejano, in *La Regenta* 1: 168–69 n8 (Loreto); Warner, *Monuments* 254 and de Santi (Litany of Loreto); Sánchez Pérez 235–36 (Loreto cult in Spain); D.L.F.M. 236 (Colegio); Jiménez Duque 62 (French *colegio*); Agulló y Cobo 4: 4 (School and Church of Loreto).

97. Stratton 40 (*tota pulchra*); O'Connor xiii (*Regina sine labe*); Warner, *Alone* 249–50 (Bernadette); Christian, *Visionaries* 4–6 (Lourdes and Spain).

98. Warner, *Alone* 252. See R. Shaw 55–57, for the domestic, local feelings attached to the different images of Mary. As one informant said, "It is that we feel towards her [Mary] as one of the family, and talk to her as we should to one of ourselves" (56).

99. Alas, *La Regenta* 85: "—¡Como su madre!—decía a las personas de confianza.—¡*Improper! ¡improper!*"(1: 193).

100. Freud, *Dora* 52, 126 (English translation emphasis) (also Gallop 143). See also Alas's article from 1882 "*El Siglo Futuro*" 946, where he recalls the mordant and repeated use of the word "improper" to satirize stuffy English manners in Balzac's *La Maison Nucingen*. Appropriately, the novella, from 1837, is an extended gossipy conversation, a quasi-oral source from which the leitmotif of "improper" emerges (see esp. 410–14).

101. Alas, *La Regenta* 82: "El aya había procurado seducir a don Carlos; sabía que su difunta esposa era una humilde modista. . . . Creyó que don Carlos se había casado por compromiso, que era un hombre que se casaba con la servidumbre" (1: 189); see also Sprengnether 54 (governess).

102. Capel Martínez 274 (prostitution); Alas, *La Regenta* 90: "al fin como un buen amo, suave y contento" (1: 200).

103. See Claret (1854), *Instrucción* 18–19; Freud, *Dora* 66; Sander Gilman 39–58 (Vienna); Le Prince de Beaumont 356 ("young girls"). *Almacén de las señoritas adolescentes* is a translation from 1804 of Le Prince's *Magasin des adolescentes* (1760). Josefa Amar y Borbón (1790) singled out her work for praise (265).

104. N. Auerbach 57–58.

105. Talavera, *De murmurar* 49: "al sepulcro lleno de cuerpos muertos, porque de ambos sale grand hedor."

106. As Homza notes, "Whether in the sixth or the sixteenth century, Catholicism was not a dualistic religion, split between the spirit and the flesh" (165).

107. Hernando de Talavera issues the traditional warning against receiving the Host if the mind or body has been contaminated by impure thoughts or actions, even in dreams: "the pollution that happens in dreams, especially with some fantasies" (1496) (*Breve forma* 12).

108. For a related, if less expressive image, see also de la Palma, *Práctica*, who advises the penitent "to know the *inner root* of one's faults in order to cut it out" during an examination of conscience (353).

109. Náxera (qtd in de Jaén 39–41): "un escuerzo o sapo de extraña grandeza y muy horrible asomaba por los labios de aquella señora, intentando salir fuera"; "un accidente en la garganta [que] la ahogó"; Delumeau 298 ("material substance").

110. Berdyaev 268, 277. This and the following paragraph are taken, with modifications, from my *Reading* 38.

111. Alas, *La Regenta* 429–30: "Parecía sentir todavía el roce de los fantasmas groseros y cínicos, cubiertos de peste; oler hediondas emanaciones de sus podredumbres, respirar en la atmósfera fría, casi viscosa, de los subterráneos en que el delirio la aprisionaba" (2: 125). The passage, of which I have given only a fragment, is a marvelous example of what Delumeau calls "the excessive materialization of sin [which] causes physical impurity to bring about religious and moral impurity" (298). The vivid descriptions of Hell in *La Regenta*, recalling those of Teresa de Jesús, may also be an echo of a similar emphasis in Enrique de Ossó's *El cuarto de hora de oración* (1874). De Ossó in effect ventriloquizes Saint Teresa on the subject of Hell (409–18; also 419–24).

112. Alas, *La Regenta* 715: "Ana volvió a la vida rasgando las nieblas de un delirio que le causaba náuseas" (2: 537). One cannot help thinking of Sartre's use of nausea as something viscous in *La nausée* (1938). Mary Warnock explains the horror and fascination of Sartre's imagery of viscosity "as a threat which is built into the nature of the world — the threat that we conscious beings might be taken over, annihilated, our powers of consciousness sucked away from us by things. We hate the viscous because of our precarious position as conscious beings in an alien world" (333).

113. See Morse Peckham for a penetrating analysis of the loss of transcendence in the nineteenth-century mindset of writers like Flaubert, Baudelaire, and others.

114. Alas, "Viaje redondo" 652. See also Maresca's comments on Clarín's need to believe (326).

Chapter 4. The Politics of Martyrdom

1. See Ealham and Richards; Bolloten; and Payne, *Spanish Civil War*.

2. See J. Sánchez; also Vincent, "Spanish Civil War."

3. Gomá y Tomás, "Martyrdom" 7; Gomá y Tomás, "Guerra" 368; Vincent, *Catholicism* 257–58 (Azaña) (also Robinson; Carr; and Payne); Fraser 522–23 (rural population).

4. Payne, *Spanish Catholicism* 149 (radicalization). Absent an accurate accounting of the total number of clergy deaths, historians generally accept Montero Moreno's figures (762). There was much uncertainty over the fate of religious, as in the case of the Jesuit Demetrio Zurbitu, director of *Razón y Fe* (1928–29): "Starting in 1937 an anguished silence settled over his person. In the 1937 Catalogue of his province, he appears as 'separated' with an unknown destination. In that of 1938 his name is marked with the sign ! (meaning 'very probably assassinated'). . . . Finally in the 1940 Catalogue his name appears on the list of those who died for Christ, 'pro Christo occisi,' with two question marks (? ?) because no details or the exact date of his death are known" (Segura 171). Vincent notes the Church's monopoly of source material on anticlerical violence (" 'Keys' " 75). Much material comes from the Francoist archive of the *Causa General* (Vincent, "Spanish Civil War" 60).

5. P. Lewis 673 (hypothesis); Lukács 88 (epic); Promey 584 (decline). Moreover, secularism and religious faith "may well exist side by side"(G. Smith 61).

6. N. Boyle 7.

7. A. Peterson 130.

8. See McDermott, Introduction 39, 35; also Busette, Pennington, King, Uceda, Alcalá, and Rufat, for Sender's religious imagination and spirit. McDermott (Introduction 36–38) summarizes the religious elements in *Réquiem*.

9. De la Cueva 366 ("betrayal"); Brademas, "Anarchists" 38; Lezama (qtd in Álvarez Junco, "Anticlericalismo" 293).

10. The range of anticlerical thought and behavior is considerable, depending on social class, ideology, and circumstance. Modern anticlericalism has an Enlightenment pedigree crossed with social-political movements as diverse as republicanism, socialism, and anarchism. The first significant anticlerical violence in Spain took place in July 1834, during the first Carlist War, also a civil conflict, in which profanations similar to those in 1936–39 occurred. See Revuelta González, "Anticlericalismo"; Pérez Ledesma; and Kaiser, for

the pan-European context. Here, I focus on the specific actions and rhetoric of violent anticlericalism during the war.

11. Ranzato 101 (also Delgado 94–95) (patrimony); Graham 29, 31 (language of purification) (also Casanova, "Rebelión" 127); *La Traca* (1931) (qtd in Álvarez Junco, "Anticlericalismo" 299) (fuego); see also Lincoln; de la Cueva; and Vincent, " 'Keys' " (martyrdom).

12. Arana, *El cura* 93.

13. Bolín 252, 331; Carroll 2, 102.

14. Fernsworth 265 (orig. *New York Times* 10 April 1938); Delgado 79 (militias); Bowers 305.

15. Bahamonde, *Memoirs* 56 (orig. *Un año con Queipo* [1938]); Payne, *Spanish Civil War* 82 (elections).

16. Bahamonde, *Memoirs* 67, 68–69; also Vincent, " 'Keys' " 68; J. Sánchez 107–08 and Vincent, "Spanish Civil War" 58 (fighting clerics). The anticlerical phrase, "They asked for it" ("Ellos se lo buscaron"), was a mantra in the anarchist and socialist press (Casanova, "Rebelión" 156).

17. De la Cueva 359–60.

18. Payne, *Spanish Catholicism* 168 (also Delgado 82); Bahamonde, *Memoirs* 71; and Vincent, " 'Keys' " 69 (purge of religion).

19. Dispute over which side committed the greatest number of atrocities has occasionally reached lamentable proportions. See Armengou and Belis 111–15; also Corbin, for the ways atrocity stories get told. On the vexed question of Republican violence, see Ledesma ("1936"); also Casanova, "Rebelión 117–57).

20. Menéndez-Reigada 15 (holy war); Sardá y Salvany 164, 178; Urra Lusarreta (qtd in Carroll 68) (*requeté*).

21. Núñez Seixas 58–59 (manifestos); Montero Moreno 44 (also Salm 21) (Asturian Revolution); F. Martínez 4 (also Anon., *Mártires* 76; and S. Sánchez 202–12) (blood); F. Martínez 59 (Arconada).

22. Barrios Masera 107 ("Martyrs"); Carreras 107, 151; Gomá y Tomás, "Riego de sangre" (July 1937) 338. See "Fuentes y bibliografía" (Montero Moreno xvii–xl) for the extensive martyrology literature of the war. Brian Bunk discusses martyrdom imagery in both conservative and revolutionary propagandistic commemorations of the revolution of October 1934 in Asturias. He argues that such remembrances contributed to the resulting polarization of Spain and eventually led to the war itself. The imagery of martyrdom is also found in popular stories of tragic love (see Fernández y González and Guardón Gallardo). Even here, the sacred and the profane are linked, by creating a sacred aura around love as a form of suffering and sacrifice and by plotting devices for those unfortunate in love to turn to religion. Nor is this surprising, given the religious import of the phrase "martyrdom of love," found in Aquinas, Saint Teresa, Jeanne de Chantal, and many other sources.

23. Pla y Deniel 689; Carreras, *Grandeza* x ("hordes"); Pérez de Urbel 85.

24. See Balmes 66 (blood of martyrs).

25. Bahamonde, *Memoirs* 126.

26. García Lorca, "Llanto por Ignacio Sánchez Mejías" 289 and "Martirio de Santa Olalla" (*Romancero gitano*) 135; Barea 56–57 (Lorca's childhood); ten Brink Goldsmith 16 (Jesuit art); Donnelly 11–12 (pictures of martyrdom).

27. Delaprée 21; Maritain 2–3 and Raguer 96–97, 120 (Mendizábal); Maritain 31 (also J. Sánchez 155).

28. Maritain 40–41, 34–35, 12 n1, 19, 42. Maritain said, "It is no business of a foreigner to take sides in this civil war" (42; see also Llaurado 468). His introduction, however, appears in a book written by a Catholic Republican supporter.

29. Bernanos 118, 122, 120.

30. Stradling 107–22 (Republican imagery); Regler 22; M. Casanova (pseud. for Mieczyslaw Bortenstein) (qtd in Revuelta González, *Anticlericalismo* 152); *Mundo Obrero* (18 August 1936) (qtd in Payne, *Spanish Civil War* 121); Hemingway 235.

31. See López Hidalgo and Cruz Casado (Carretero); González Calleja 29 (pamphlets); Bunk 55–56 (response to October Revolution).

32. Cansinos Asséns 2: 308–09: "De pronto salta al escenario la corpulenta figura del 'Caballero Audaz'. . . . Alto, hasta parecer un gigante . . . , arrogante, gordo, bien vestido con su chaleco de fantasía y sus botitos . . . el arribista que debe su fama a esas noveluchas eróticas . . . y su lujo llamativo y vulgar, su abrigo de pieles, sus sortijones y su alfiler, a su casamiento con una *cocotte* menopáusica, 'El Carretero Audaz,' con su vocejón plebeyo, de labriego andaluz, arremete despectivo y retador con los oradores que lo han precedido. . . . Pero ninguno se atreve a iniciar el menor gesto agresivo. ¡Ese novelista pornográfico tiene unos biceps de boxeador y además es un espadachín!"

33. Carretero, *Declaración* 295.

34. Carretero, *¡Arriba!* 7: "Dios quiso que yo hablara, no en nombre de Él, sino en nombre de los miles y miles de espectros que de noche . . . pueblan sus calles, se acercan . . . y parecen decirnos: '¿Veis cómo no hubo bastante tierra para enterrarnos? Nuestro sacrificio no será estéril; los designios de Dios fueron llevarnos a la Gloria para, desde allí, más cerca de Él, pedirle que vosotros, al fin, gozaseis en la tierra de un día de Justicia' "; 5: "héroe, arquetipo o símbolo de los infinitos sufrimientos soportados por Madrid durante el despotismo rojo"; 8: "limpio de pasiones partidistas, libre de apasionamientos, sin huella de odio ni de rencor."

35. Giménez Caballero xiii, xv.

36. Giménez Caballero 106.

37. Giménez Caballero 139.

38. Carretero, *Declaración* 10: "era como un cadáver que, galvanizado por la fe, se ponía en pie. . . . Es la ciudad de cuyos escondites, como larvas por los alveolos de un esqueleto, salían teorías de espectros, vidas extenuadas por el sufrimiento, almas colapsadas por el dolor." Carretero's imagery appears drawn in part from Matthew 27: 52–53: "And the graves were opened; and many bodies of the saints which slept arose, And came out of the graves after his resurrection, and went into the holy city, and appeared unto many."

39. Carretero, *Nosotros* 72–73, 81: "el surco rojo de la autopsia, que era un enorme costurón, como la huella de los dientes de una sierra bajo el pecho."

40. Carretero, *¡Arriba!* 12–13: "Madrid es un inmenso cementerio, por el que, gracias a un milagro de supervivencia, pululan centenares de miles de figuras tristes, esqueléticas, que simulan una apariencia de vida. . . . Madrid no existe. . . . Madrid murió: de hambre, de frío, de terror. . . . Madrid, como un gigantesco panteón, está poblado de sombras y pertenece a sus espectros."

41. Carretero, *Ciudad* 103: "el reino sombrío y nauseabundo de la putrefacción"; 110:

"Había empezado a obsesionarme la idea de que no era ya un extraño, un intruso en este pabellón del cementerio, sino que aquél era mi sitio propio, por derecho y para siempre . . . yo era también un muerto, un cadáver más"; 114: "el hombre que yo era ha muerto y está encerrado en ese nicho."

42. Carretero, *Declaración* 69: "Sangre por todas partes. Sangre del crimen que había cambiado el colorido del traje. . . . El resto lo empapaban grandes manchas oscuras de un cárdeno terroso, seco y rígido. Coágulos rojos, aún brillantes, invadían la pechera y resbalaban en cuajarones hasta la plataforma."

43. Carretero, *Declaración* 72: "[el] cuerpo del mártir, de sus mejillas maceradas, de su boca torcida en un rictus macabro, de su frente lívida, de su nariz rota por la contusión brutal"; Albert (*tremendismo*).

44. Carretero, *¡Arriba!* 127: "Su vientre es un boquete informe, en el que se ven vísceras destrozadas, sangre, huesos que asoman por la piel ennegrecida. Su rostro es también una masa negra, tumefacta, horripilante. No lejos de él se revuelca, en un charco de sangre, otro pequeñuelo. Está de cara al suelo. . . . Su torso se contrae, se distiende, palpita como el de un reptil. Le falta un brazo, como si se le hubieran cortado en un golpe de hacha. Se retuerce gritando, aullando con voz que no parece humana ni infantil."

45. Carretero, *¡Arriba!* 131: "La manecita colgaba exangüe, como uno de esos ex votos de cera que exhornan los altares de las imágenes famosas por sus milagros"; 133: "convertido en una especie de santón de aquella plebe sucia"; 134: "inexplicablemente . . . me costaba trabajo desprenderme de aquel miembro débil y muerto, como si fuera del cuerpo de un hijo, de un hermanillo."

46. Pérez de Urbel 209; Montero Moreno 116 (attributed to Father Remigio de Papiol); Lincoln 256 (bodies of religious); qtd in Lincoln 256 (temples).

47. Delehaye 10, 230.

48. Delehaye 178 (specific dates); Carretero, *Quinta* 12 (ghosts); 187: "La guerra, que para todos los biennacidos fue escuela de experiencia y sacrificio, nos enseñó este valor imponderable de las efemérides, reavivó en nuestras almas la devoción entrañable a los días señalados, como jalones de fe, de tradición, de recuerdos. . . . Día de Nochebuena de 1936. El año terrible. . . . El primer año maldito. Es exacta, ineludible, la influencia cordial, sentimental y religiosa de este día."

49. See Bahamonde, *Memoirs* 56–58; Richards, "Doctrine" 91–93; and Aguilar 71–92 (Nationalist commemorations); Holguín, and Bolín 302–06 (wartime tourism).

50. Carretero, *Quinta* 72: "yo me convertía en una cosa, en un destrozo más que pertenecía a las ruinas de la ciudad martirizada."

51. Carretero, *¡Arriba!* 16: "Mi delgadez era ya esquelética. Había eliminado mis grasas, lo que tal vez era la causa del frío constante, irreparable, que me entumecía en todo momento. Mis músculos, antaño potentes, estaban laxos, y el más mínimo esfuerzo me fatigaba, haciéndome exhalar un ronquido anhelante de fuelle." See also Mainer, "De Madrid" 189–90, for the Nationalist image of the besieged capital as a site of privileged suffering. Imagery of "red" violence inflicted upon Madrid and the entire country was already appearing in Carretero's books attacking the Second Republic. In *La agonía de España* (1936), he includes the daily accounts of church burnings, assaults, political assassinations, and public disorder, from 16 February to 4 May 1936, taken from the Cortes' *Diario de Sesiones* (201–02; 265–304).

52. Carretero, *Nosotros* 193: "Sabernos así, como una 'cosa,' como una brizna al aire, como una moneda arriesgada en un albur, nos desmoraliza y nos angustia."

53. See Delehaye for the method of amplification in martyrdom stories (95–97); also Hernández 322. Saint Clement of Ancyra's torments, for example, continue for some twenty-eight years (Delehaye 96).

54. See Longinus 116–18 for the relation between the sublime and amplification.

55. Woolsey 138–39.

56. Woolsey 134.

57. Lincoln 256. With the diminishment of faith since Franco's death, virulent anticlericalism appears to be a thing of the past in Spain. See Richburg; and Pérez Ledesma 248–49.

58. Fraser 152 and Lincoln 258 (children's amusement); Vincent, " 'Keys' " 8.

59. Ullman 268 (Tragic Week); Montero Moreno chap. 25 and Pérez de Urbel 197, 291 (anticlerical destruction); Gomá y Tomás, "Discurso" (May 1938) 518–19; Montero Moreno 627 (innocent objects); Carreras 100 (profanation).

60. See "Los obispos" and Bedoya (beatifications); Vincent, " 'Keys' " 78–79.

61. Pérez de Urbel 196 (liturgical order); Menéndez-Reigada 4 (embers of faith); Montero Moreno 599.

62. De la Cueva 363 (code). Blasphemy as a sign of revolutionary fervor appears prominently in Hemingway's *For Whom the Bell Tolls* (1940). Conducting a quixotic antiprofanity campaign in Mataró, Father Claret founded a "Spiritual Society of the Most Holy Mary Against Blasphemy" in 1845 (La Fuente y Zamalloa 2:120).

63. Vincent, " 'Keys' " 78 (genital mutilations); Pérez Ledesma 233–37 (sexuality of priests); Vincent, " 'Keys' " 87 (male chastity).

64. See Lincoln 251.

65. Vincent, " 'Keys' " 77.

66. See Vived Mairal 30, 61.

67. See Sender, *Casas* (1933); Vived Mairal 201, 268 and McDermott, Introduction 1 (Sender and Communism) and 5 (great divide).

68. Sender, *Problema* 18 (Mexico); Sender, *República* 13, 20 (social classes' religiosity); Vived Mairal 228 (articles). The pamphlet was *La república y la cuestión religiosa* (1932).

69. See Graham 10–11 (Catholic mobilization); Callahan, *Catholic Church* 293 and Jiménez Lozano, *Cementerios* 222 (wars of the dead); Jiménez Lozano, *Cementerio* 228.

70. See Christian, *Moving*, on missionary propaganda. I have also relied upon Christian's rich account of Ezkioga (*Visionaries*).

71. Sender, *Counter-Attack* 87–88.

72. Sender, *Counter-Attack* 281.

73. Sender, *Counter-Attack* 281, 282.

74. Sender, *Counter-Attack* 53.

75. See Sender's *Imán;* and Santiáñez.

76. McDermott, Introduction 9 (Manichean apocalypse); McDermott, Introduction 11 and Bunk 11 (martyred heroes); Sender, *Counter-Attack* 134; Santiáñez 50 (fascination with violence).

77. Núñez Seixas 49 (*patria*); Behar 88 (also Vincent, *Catholicism* 8) (glorification); Caspistegui 188 (Carlist peasantry); Giménez Caballero 234.

78. Mendelson 128, xxxv, 68 (stronghold; rural traditions; Buñuel); Shubert, "Documentary" 105 (*Spanish Earth*); Tisa 40 and Carr, *Spanish Civil War* 66 (Republican posters); Mendelson 180–81 (Ortiz-Echagüe).

79. Sender, *Counter-Attack* 134 (bones); Sender (qtd in Vived Mairal 632): "La iglesia es siempre el *cuerpo* de una religión. Y todos los cuerpos son impuros"; King (poetic theology); Sender, *Ensayos* 64: "del espíritu santo — es decir de la imaginación creadora del hombre"; *Ensayos* 131: "Era necesario que el Logos se hiciera carne para que las gentes angustiadas por la imposibilidad del infinito pudieran concebirlo en imágenes y hechos"; Sender (qtd in Vived Mairal 632): "El ritual religioso es poesía práctica para quien sabe buscar esas cosas. Pero, naturalmente, la emoción poética no es siempre idílica. En todo caso, esa imaginería es la apelación tosca (campana o incienso) o sutil (eucaristía) al misterio."

80. Callahan, *Catholic Church* chap. 5, 142–43 (social Catholicism in Spain); Peiró 57 n4; Lannon 16–17 (Vallecas).

81. Lamennais 38: "Qu'est-ce qu'un pauvre? C'est celui qui n'a point encore de propriété."

82. Sender, *Requiem* 43: "a veces, sin más ni más . . . se ponía ella a bailar sola, siguiendo el compás de las campanas de la iglesia" (41); 15: "extrañas oraciones para ahuyentar el pedrisco y evitar las inundaciones" (19); 7: "fría y dorada, una de esas mañanitas en que la grava del río que habían puesto en la plaza durante el *Corpus*, crujía de frío bajo los pies" (13); see Ressot 88, 91 (history in *Réquiem*). I am citing from the most accessible edition in Spanish (Destino 1991); and from Elinor Randall's English version.

83. Blanco 95; Sender, *Requiem* 95: "El pueblo estaba asustado, y nadie sabía qué hacer" (81).

84. Leval 1:76 and Souchy Bauer 12 (Nationalist takeovers); Fraser 348; Bolloten 71; and Brademas, "Note" 127–28 (collectivization); Silva (qtd in Bolloten 200). McDermott in her introduction to *Réquiem* notes the historical manipulation but does not pursue its implications (22). To my knowledge, there is no evidence to indicate that Sender fudged historical details to make the book acceptable to a potential Spanish publisher. *Réquiem*, which appeared under the Aquelarre imprint in Mexico, was originally written for a projected volume of novellas to be edited by Edward R. Mulvihill and Roberto Sánchez of the University of Wisconsin and published in the United States (Carrasquer xliv; and Vived Mairal 450).

85. Blanco 112, 114. Blanco's account, based on notes compiled in 1972, is included as an appendix in the 1977 Spanish edition of Souchy (1937), but not in the English version.

86. Souchy Bauer, and Leval (political organization); Bolloten 68 (religious life); Souchy Bauer 50 (belief in nature).

87. The single worst killing of secular clergy took place in Barbastro, an Aragonese town of approximately 10,000 inhabitants and the headquarters of "one of the largest [anarcho-syndicalist] Regional Federations" in 1936 (Souchy Bauer 58): 123 of the town's 140 clergymen, or 87.8 percent, died (Montero Moreno 763; and chap. 9). Souchy Bauer makes no mention of it. Municipal governance in Alcolea de Cinca, where Sender spent several years of his childhood, appeared to be entirely made up of CNT members after July 1936 (Lorenzo 154–55; see also Carrasquer lvii–lviii; Casanova, "Rebelión" 136–40; and Ledesma, *Días* 250–59, for anticlerical violence in Zaragoza province).

Casanova maintains that "despite the presence of republicans and anarchists, [poor farmers in this part of Aragón] never lost confidence in the Church, in Catholicism and in the ruling class" ("Rebelión" 136).

88. Souchy Bauer 6 (CNT); also González Calleja 39; and Casanova, "Terror" 90, 92.

89. Sender (qtd in Peñuelas 131): "el esquema de toda la guerra civil nuestra."

90. Lisón-Tolosana 50–51.

91. Sender, *Requiem* 3: "El cura esperaba sentado en un sillón con la cabeza inclinada sobre la casulla de los oficios de *réquiem*. La sacristía olía a incienso. En un rincón había un fajo de ramitas de olivo de las que habían sobrado el Domingo de Ramos. Las hojas estaban muy secas, y parecían de metal. Al pasar cerca, Mosén Millán evitaba rozarlas porque se desprendían y caían al suelo" (9).

92. Sender, *Requiem* 3: "una alusión constante a Paco y al recuerdo de su desdicha" (10).

93. See M..-J. Nicolas 333.

94. Sender, *Requiem* 105: "Lo quería mucho, pero sus afectos no eran por el hombre en sí mismo, sino *por Dios*. Era el suyo un cariño por encima de la muerte y la vida. Y no podía mentir" (89).

95. Sender, *Requiem* 98: "le encontraba un aire culpable"; 121: "Pensando Mosén Millán en los campesinos muertos, en las pobres mujeres del carasol, sentía una especie de desdén involuntario, que al mismo tiempo le hacía avergonzarse y sentirse culpable" (103); Vincent, " 'Keys' " 77 (anticlerical contempt).

96. Marí 259 and Chatman 48 (plot of revelation); Sender, *Requiem* 123: "Creía oír su nombre en los labios del agonizante. . . . Y pensaba aterrado y enternecido al mismo tiempo: Ahora yo digo en sufragio de su alma esa misa de *réquiem,* que sus enemigos quieren pagar" (105). Requiem masses held "in memory of neighbors 'vilely assassinated by the Marxist hordes' " abounded well into the 1950s (Ledesma, *Días* 300–01).

97. See also Iglesias Ovejero 217.

98. See Iarocci's perceptive comments on the wartime ballad ("War" 186); Havard, " 'Romance' " 90 (ballad in *Réquiem*); Marí 271.

99. See also Marí 258.

100. Criado Miguel 340 and Iglesias Ovejero 221 (hagiographical linearity); Sender, *Requiem* 11: "el niño había sacado la lengua para recoger la sal, y de eso deducía [la madrina] que tendría gracia y atractivo con las mujeres" (16).

101. Lisón-Tolosana 2, 4 (caves); qtd in Caspistegui 182 (Carlist traditionalists).

102. Sender, *Requiem* 13: ". . . *ya los llevan, ya los llevan/atados brazo con brazo*" (18); 13: "el monaguillo tenía presente la escena, que fue sangrienta y llena de estampidos" (18).

103. Havard (*Crucified* 22–28) and McDermott ("Songlines" 6) also see the Loyolan imagination in the poets Rafael Alberti and Antonio Machado, respectively. Pérez de Ayala inserts a deliberate rip-off of the *Spiritual Exercises* in his anti-Jesuitical novel of 1910, *A.M.D.G.* (135–48).

104. M.Boyle 40 (access the divine); Loyola 30; A. de Nicolás 41 and Barthes, "Loyola" 44, 54 (Loyolan method and image making).

105. Sender, *Requiem* 13: "los olores de ajo, vinagrillo y aceite de oliva" (17); 105: "detalles nimios, como los buhos nocturnos y el olor de las perdices en adobo" (89).

106. Sender, *Requiem* 9: "contra las puertas y las ventanas y a veces contra las cabezas de los mismos chicos" (14).

107. Sender, *Requiem* 31: "La turbación de Paco procedía del hecho de haber visto aquellas imágenes polvorientas y desnarigadas en un desván del templo donde amontonaban los trastos viejos. Había también allí piernas de cristos desprendidas de los cuerpos, estatuas de mártires desnudos y sufrientes. Cabezas de *ecce homos* lacrimosos, paños de verónicas colgados del muro. . . . El otro monaguillo — cuando estaban los dos en el desván — exageraba su familiaridad con aquellas figuras. Se ponía a caballo en uno de los apóstoles, en cuya cabeza golpeaba con los nudillos para ver — decía — si había ratones; le ponía a otro un papelito arrollado en la boca como si estuviera fumando" (32).

108. See Hobsbawm and Scott 86 and 112, who make note of the shoemaker Francisco Mora (1842–1924), a founding member of the Spanish Socialist Party, later its secretary and historian. M. Sensfelder observed that shoemakers have "a restless, sometimes aggressive spirit and . . . an enormous tendency to loquacity" (qtd in Hobsbawm and Scott 86), qualities Sender's character shares. Samuel Smiles said, "Shoemakers are proverbially political characters"(*Self-Help* 71). In the 1980s, a sixty-nine-year-old shoe repairman proved a helpful informant for Candace Slater's ethnographic research in Granada (13).

109. Sender, *Requiem* 29: "sensaciones contradictorias muy fuertes" (31).

110. Sender, *Requiem* 119: "Era la primera expresión del cura que no entendía" (101); 121: "Los faros del coche — del mismo coche donde estaba Mosén Millán — se encendieron, y la descarga sonó casi al mismo tiempo. . . . Los otros dos campesinos cayeron, pero Paco, cubierto de sangre, corrió hacia el coche.

'Mosén Millán, usted me conoce' — gritaba enloquecido.

Quiso entrar, no podía. Todo lo manchaba de sangre. Mosén Millán callaba, con los ojos cerrados y rezando. El centurión puso su revólver detrás de la oreja de Paco, y alguien dijo alarmado:

'No. ¡Ahí no!'

Se llevaron a Paco arrastrando. Iba repitiendo en voz ronca:

'Pregunten a Mosén Millán; él me conoce.'

Se oyeron dos o tres tiros más. Luego siguió un silencio en el cual todavía susurraba Paco: 'El me denunció. . ., Mosén Millán. Mosén Millán. . ." (102–03).

The image of the centurion neatly combines Falangist and Christian meanings: "The centurion is the commanding officer of a *centuria* (100 men) in the Spanish Fascist Falange, whose organisation was modeled on the Roman legions . . . the Synoptic Gospels record the centurion recognising His divinity after the crucifixion at Golgotha" (McDermott, in her edition of *Réquiem* 99). The term may also refer to the Jesuit teaching practice of dividing pupils into Romans and Carthaginians, in which the centurions served "to inspect the application of their respective armies and to keep the schoolmaster constantly apprised, by way of frequent denunciations, of the pupils' conduct" (Pérez de Ayala 118).

111. Bahamonde, *Memoirs* 59–60.

112. Sender, *Requiem* 117: "Pero usted me conoce, Mosén Millán. Usted sabe quién soy" (99); Sender (qtd in Vived Mairal 597; Sender's emphasis): "El catolicismo me parece *divino* sólo por las últimas palabras de Jesús en la cruz: 'Padre, ¿por qué me has abandonado?' Si eso dice el hombre más puro y perfecto que ha podido imaginar la humanidad (dudar en la agonía), ¿qué podemos esperar los demás? Por eso Jesús nació con el primer hombre y no acabará de morir hasta que muera el último. Es la angustia no existencial sino *esencial* en la que estamos todos." See also his correspondence with

Carmen Laforet 92. In 1971 he wrote, "Nonetheless I am very Christian in my own way, and would perhaps be capable of facing martyrdom for that Christianity of mine if I had to. Or maybe I'm deceiving myself and I wouldn't be so brave" (Laforet/Sender 146).

113. See Delehaye 132.

114. Sender, *Requiem* 123: "La muerte de Paco estaba tan fresca, que Mosén Millán creía tener todavía manchas de sangre en sus vestidos" (104); 97, 99: "en medio de la catástrofe, percibía algo mágico y sobrenatural, y sentía en todas partes el olor de sangre" (84); 99: "las cosas que había visto cuando de niño le cambiaba los pañales" (84); 11: "[el] volumen de sus atributos masculinos" (16). See also Carrasquer lxiv–lxvii, on Sender's realism as "magical."

115. Sender, *Requiem* 99: "Disparos por la noche, sangre, malas pasiones, habladuría, procacidades de aquella gente forastera, que, sin embargo, parecía educada" (84); 103: "Déjelo en paz. ¿Para qué derramar más sangre?" (87); Bernanos 107.

116. Sender, *Requiem* 121: "envolvía el reloj en el pañuelo, y lo conservaba cuidadosamente con las dos manos juntas" (103); *Acts* 19: 11–12 (Saint Paul's handkerchiefs).

117. See P. Brown 107, 120. Carlos Eire observes that the "relics of the saints, then, did more than cure when they worked miracles, they served as a denial of death itself, as evidence of the Resurrection to come, and as a negation of 'the full horror of the dissolving body'" (471).

118. Bynum, *Resurrection* xviii, 35, 105, 50.

119. P. Brown 5–6.

120. See also Sender's moving poem on his brother Manuel's death during the civil war, in which he likens him to a martyr and, above all, to Christ ("Al hermano Manuel" 136).

121. P. Brown 86, 88 (*praesentia*); Graham 11 ("threatened"); Ledesma, *Días* 29 and Christian, *Local Religion* (the local in Spain). Take, for example, the conflict-laden circumstances surrounding the martyrdom of eight De La Salle Brothers and a Passionist priest in the mining town of Turón during the Asturian revolution in 1934. The Brothers' school was "located directly across the street from the Masonic lodge" (Salm 23). Political tensions and violence were never abstract but embodied in individual personalities and places. See also the contemporary account, Anon., *Mártires*.

122. Benjamin 257. By stark contrast with the continuing Spanish wars of the dead, the American Civil War dead had become, by the early twentieth century, "the vehicle for a unifying national project of memorialization" (Faust 269).

123. See Cate-Arries 189 (camp literature; camp as body of Christ); also Labanyi's excellent discussion of the past as a memorialized haunting ("Teaching" 436–47). The recent exhumations of Republican mass grave sites are also enveloped in resurrecting the dead and investing them in a secularized aura of the relic.

124. The decline of Christianity in late twentieth- and twenty-first-century Western Europe is now a commonplace, along with a perceived Eurosecularity (see McLeod; Callum Brown; and Berger 24). Church attendance has dipped precipitously in both Protestant and Catholic faiths, and suspicion of religious institutions remains high. Yet spiritual hunger has not diminished, as the growth of Catholic lay movements suggests (see Shorto). Many Spaniards continue to identify themselves as culturally Catholic but do not attend Mass. The legacy of Francoism and the civil war still colors perceptions of the Church. Thus, as Rome was preparing the beatification of 498 martyrs of the war in fall 2007, an article in *El País* called them both victims and executioners, failing to

distinguish between the hierarchy's lamentable support of Franco (and politicization of the martyrs) and the victims of anticlerical violence (see Bedoya).

125. Civil wars in general test belief. See Faust, for the crisis of belief that emerged from the American Civil War (210).

Epilogue

1. Valbuena Prat 3: "Una de las más grandes adquisiciones para el alma española del siglo XX es la conciencia de su catolicidad. . . . Así como el siglo XIX, esencialmente confusionista, simpatizante con toda escisión, individualismo o anarquía, tuvo una evidente atracción por las formas protestantes de religiosidad, la nueva centuria, tendiente a la organización, a un nuevo clasicismo, a la jerarquía y a la unión, se caracteriza profundamente por la revalorización del pensamiento y el arte católico. . . . [N]ación y religiosidad, catolicismo e imperio se unen en estrecho haz de unidad."

2. Menéndez Pelayo 1: 61–62; on the impact of Menéndez Pelayo's ideas, see J. Varela 27–76.

3. Valbuena Prat 162: "el caso más típico del signo de contradicción de nuestro XIX"; 166: "aproximarse a la fe cristiana, por secreta y subconsciente simpatía."

4. Valbuena Prat 79: "se fundó bajo un signo imperial"; 81: "Es esencialmente jesuita y esencialmente español. La Orden y la nación se funden en su obra"; 147: "Como se nos rompe . . . el imperio colonial americano, así las creencias, antes firmes, se esfuman y falsean, y las vigorosas líneas del dogma se parten, dejando un mar de errores o de ignorancias, en el que sobrenadan las creaciones literarias del siglo más desigual y contradictorio de nuestra cultura."

5. See Serrano Asenjo's reconstruction of the episode; Serrano Asenjo 254 ("Manichean mindset").

6. In his dossier were letters on Valbuena's behalf from Allison Peers and Alexander A. Parker as well as other works of his, including his poetry, editions of Calderón's *autos,* and an *Antología de la poesía sacra española* (Serrano Asenjo 255). Valbuena may also have been persecuted for his Catalanist activities during the war (see Díez de Revenga).

7. Serrano Asenjo 255–56 (prototype); Jiménez Lozano, *El sambenito* 193: "así la vida de estos ilustrados es enigma y extraña ambigüedad e indecisión y así la fe de los hombres de hoy es indecisa y agonizante." Palomo and Prieto likewise note the "deep religious anxiety" and inner disquiet in Valbuena (23).

8. Valbuena Prat 4: "la decadencia de las letras coincide con las oleadas de descatolización."

9. Guzmán de Alfarache also privileges friendship, though ironically there are almost no true friends in the world of the pícaro: "The twain are as much alike as two peas in a pod, for my friend is otherwise myself" ("Hanse de avenir los dos como cada uno consigo mismo, por ser otro yo mi amigo") (Alemán 3:225).

10. Durkheim 426.

11. F. O'Connor 167.

12. Durkheim 403. Here is the larger Unamunian context: "And faith is the source of reality, because it is life. To believe is to create" ("Y la fe es la fuente de la realidad, porque es la vida. Creer es crear") ("Prólogo" 18).

Bibliography

Aguilar, Paloma. *Memory and Amnesia: The Role of the Spanish Civil War in the Transition to Democracy.* Translated by Mark Oakley. New York: Bregan Books, 2002.

Aguilar Piñal, Francisco. *Bibliografía de autores españoles del siglo XVIII.* 6. Madrid: Consejo Superior de Investigaciones Científicas, 1991.

———. "El mundo del libro en el siglo XVIII." *Varia bibliographica: Homenaje a José Simón Díaz,* 25–33. Kassel: Edition Reichenberger, 1988.

———. *La Sevilla de Olavide 1767–1778.* Sevilla: Excmo. Ayuntamiento de Sevilla, 1966.

Agulló y Cobo, Mercedes, ed. *Madrid en sus diarios. IV (1876–1890).* Madrid: Instituto de Estudios Madrileños, 1971.

Alas, Leopoldo (Clarín). "Cartas de un estudiante." *Obras completas* 5: 1140–50, 1169–73. Edited by Jean-François Botrel and Yvan Lissorgues.

———. "El Centenario de Santa Teresa." *Obras completas* 7: 149–51. Edited by Jean-François Botrel and Yvan Lissorgues.

———. "Como gustéis." *Obras completas* 8: 509–14. Edited by Jean-François Botrel and Yvan Lissorgues.

———. "De profundis." *Sermón perdido. Obras completas* 4: 620–22 (Primera parte). Edited by Laureano Bonet.

———. "*La Evangelista.* Novela de Alfonso Daudet." *Obras completas* 7: 288–97. Edited by Jean-François Botrel and Yvan Lissorgues.

———. *El hambre en Andalucía.* Edited by Simone Saillard. Toulouse: Presses Universitaires du Mirail, 2001.

———. *Juan Ruiz. Obras completas* 11: 13–495. Edited by Leonardo Romero Tobar, with the collaboration of Sofía Martín-Gamero, Luis García San Miguel, Yvan Lissorgues, and José María Martínez Cachero.

——. "El libre examen y nuestra literatura presente." *Solos de Clarín. Obras completas* 4: 154–65 (Primera parte). Edited by Laureano Bonet.

——. "Del naturalismo." *Leopoldo Alas: Teoría y crítica de la novela española,* 108–49. Edited by Sergio Beser. Barcelona: Laia, 1972.

——. *Obras completas.* 1–11. Oviedo: Nobel, 2002–06.

——. "Palique" [28 February 1882]. *Obras completas* 6: 889–91. Edited by Jean-François Botrel and Yvan Lissorgues.

——. "Palique" [2 October 1897]. *Obras completas* 9: 1120–22. Edited by Jean-François Botrel and Yvan Lissorgues.

——. "Para vicios." *Obras completas* 3: 565–68. Edited by Carolyn Richmond.

——. "El pecado original." *Obras completas* 3: 772–76. Edited by Carolyn Richmond.

——. "La pedagogía de los jesuitas." *Obras completas* 5: 1150–57. Edited by Jean-François Botrel and Yvan Lissorgues.

——. "Prólogo." *La cuestión palpitante* by Emilia Pardo Bazán. *Obras completas* 11: 1037–45. Edited by Leonardo Romero Tobar, with the collaboration of Sofía Martín-Gamero, Luis García San Miguel, Yvan Lissorgues, and José María Martínez Cachero.

——. *La Regenta.* 2 vols. Edited by Gonzalo Sobejano. Madrid: Castalia, 1981.

——. *La Regenta.* Translated by John Rutherford. Athens: University of Georgia Press, 1984.

——. "Revista literaria (Noviembre, 1889)." *Ensayos y revistas. Obras completas* 4: 1628–45. (Segunda parte). Edited by Laureano Bonet.

——. "Revista mínima." *Obras completas* 8: 519–24. Edited by Jean-François Botrel and Yvan Lissorgues.

——. "El Siglo Futuro naturalista." *Obras completas* 6: 945–47. Edited by Jean-François Botrel and Yvan Lissorgues.

——. "Viaje redondo." *Obras completas* 3: 650–56. Edited by Carolyn Richmond.

Albert, Mechthild. "El tremendismo en la novela fascista." *Vencer no es convencer: Literatura e ideología del fascismo español,* ed. M. Albert, 101–18. Frankfurt am Main/Madrid: Vervuert/Iberoamericana, 1998.

Alcalá, Ángel. "El fondo filosófico-religioso de la obra madura de Sender." *Sender y su tiempo: Crónica de un siglo. Actas del II Congreso sobre Ramón J. Sender.* Huesca, 27–31 marzo 2001, ed. José Domingo Dueñas Lorente, 165–93. Huesca: Instituto de Estudios Altoaragoneses/Diputación de Huesca, 2001.

Alemán, Mateo. *Guzmán de Alfarache.* 5 vols. Edited by Samuel Gili Gaya. Madrid: Espasa-Calpe, 1942–53.

Alfieri, J. J. "Images of the *Sacra Familia* in Galdós' Novels." *Hispanófila,* no. 74 (1982): 25–40.

Allen, Woody. *Side Effects.* 1975. Reprint, New York: Ballantine Books, 1981.

Alonso, Dámaso. "Escila y Caribdis de la literatura española." *Estudios y ensayos gongorinos,* 3d ed., 11–28. Madrid: Gredos, 1970.

Alonso Seoane, María José. "Dos principios ilustrados en las últimas obras literarias de Olavide." *Carlos III y las 'Nuevas Poblaciones,'* ed. Miguel Avilés Fernández and Guillermo Sena Medina, 3: 281–98. Córdoba: Servicio de Publicaciones, Universidad de Córdoba, 1988.

——. "La obra narrativa de Pablo de Olavide: Nuevo planteamiento para su estudio." *Axerquía*, no. 11 (1984): 11–49.

——. "Las últimas obras de Olavide a través de los expedientes de censura." *El siglo que llaman ilustrado: Homenaje a Francisco Aguilar Piñal*, ed. Joaquín Álvarez Barrientos and José Checa Beltrán, 47–54. Madrid: Consejo Superior de Investigaciones Científicas, 1996.

——. "El último sueño de Pablo de Olavide." *Cuadernos Dieciochistas*, no. 4 (2003): 47–65.

Álvarez Junco, José. "El anticlericalismo en el movimiento obrero." *Octubre 1934: Cincuenta años para la reflexión*, Gabriel Jackson et al., 283–300. Madrid: Siglo XXI, 1985.

——. *Mater Dolorosa: La idea de España en el siglo XIX*. 7th ed. Madrid: Taurus, 2003.

Amann, Elizabeth. " 'La forma es fondo': The Politics of Camp in *La Regenta*." *Journal of Spanish Cultural Studies* 5.1 (2004): 11–23.

——. *Importing "Madame Bovary": The Politics of Adultery*. New York: Palgrave Macmillan, 2006.

Amar y Borbón, Josefa. *Discurso sobre la educación física y moral de las mujeres*. Edited by María Victoria López-Cordón. Madrid: Cátedra/Universitat de Valencia/Instituto de la Mujer, 1994.

Andreu, Alicia. *Galdós y la literatura popular*. Madrid: Sociedad General Española de Librería, 1982.

Anon. "La caridad católica." Revuelta González, *El anticlericalismo español*, 95–96.

——. *The Confessional Unmasked*. London: Protestant Electoral Union and Protestant Evangelical Mission, 1867.

——. "De Gérando." *North American Review* 92, no. 191 (April 1861): 391–415.

——. *Doctrina christiana*. Granada: Imprenta de Andrés Sánchez, n.d.

——. "La huelga de Gijón." *Nuestro Tiempo* 1 (1901): 423–29.

——. "A los icarianos, socialistas, demócratas y filántropos de España." Elorza, *Socialismo utópico español*, 106–07.

——. "Los jornaleros." Elorza, *Socialismo utópico español*, 109–15.

——. "Letrilla humanitaria." *La Linterna Mágica* 20ª Función (1 August 1850): 153–54.

——. "*María, la hija de un jornalero*." Zavala, *Ideología*, 269–74.

——. *Los mártires de Turón. Notas biográficas y reseña del martirio de los religiosos bárbaramente asesinados por los revolucionarios en Turón (Asturias), el 9 de octubre de 1934*. Madrid and Barcelona: La Instrucción Popular, 1935.

——. "La mendicidad en Madrid." Bahamonde Magro and Toro Mérida 367.

——. "Los obispos preparan una peregrinación a Roma para la beatificación de 498 'mártires' de la guerra civil." *El País Digital* (27 April 2007).

——. "Revista literaria." Zavala, *Ideología*, 247–54.

——. *La vida de Lazarillo de Tormes y de sus fortunas y adversidades*. Edited by Alberto Blecua. 3d ed. Madrid: Castalia, 1982.

Arana, José Ramón. *El cura de Almuniaced*. Prologue by Manuel Andújar. Madrid: Turner, 1979.

Aranguren, José Luis L. *Moral y sociedad: Introducción a la moral social española en el siglo XIX*. 1966. Reprint, Madrid: Cuadernos Para el Diálogo/Edicusa, 1974.

Araque, Blas María. *Biografía del señor D. Wenceslao Ayguals de Izco*. Madrid: Imprenta de la Sociedad Literaria, 1851.

Araujo-Costa, Luis. *Biografía de "La Época."* Madrid: Libros y Revistas, 1946.

Arboleya Martínez, Maximiliano. "Alma religiosa de 'Clarín' (Datos íntimos e inéditos)." *Leopoldo Alas "Clarín,"* ed. José María Martínez Cachero, 43–59. Madrid: Taurus, 1978.

Arce, Joaquín. "Introducción." *Noches lúgubres* (with *Cartas marruecas*), by José Cadalso. Madrid: Cátedra, 1983.

Arenal, Concepción. *La Beneficencia, la Filantropía, la Caridad. Obras completas* I. Edited by Carmen Díaz Castañón. 1861. Reprint, Madrid: Atlas, 1993.

——. *El Visitador del pobre. Obras completas* I. Edited by Carmen Díaz Castañón. 1863. Reprint, Madrid: Atlas, 1993.

Ariès, Philippe. *Centuries of Childhood*. Translated by Robert Baldick. 1960. Reprint, New York: Vintage, 1962.

——. *The Hour of Our Death*. Translated by Helen Weaver. New York: Oxford University Press, 1981.

Armengou, Montse, and Ricard Belis. *Las fosas del silencio. ¿Hay un Holocausto español?* Prologue by Santiago Carrillo. Barcelona: Plaza y Janés/Televisió de Catalunya, 2004.

Artola, Miguel. *La burguesía revolucionaria (1808–1874)*. 9th ed. 1973. Reprint, Madrid: Alianza, 1983.

Astete, Gaspar. *Catecismo de la doctrina cristiana*. 1599. www.mercaba.org/FICHAS/CEC/catecismo_astete.htm

Aubert, Paul. "Luchar contra los poderes fácticos." Aubert 219–53.

——, ed. *Religión y sociedad en España (siglos XIX y XX)*. Madrid: Casa de Velázquez, 2002.

Auerbach, Erich. *Mimesis: The Representation of Reality in Western Literature*. Translated by Willard R. Trask. Princeton: Princeton University Press, 1968.

Auerbach, Nina. *Romantic Imprisonment: Women and Other Glorified Outcasts*. New York: Columbia University Press, 1986.

Augustine, Saint. *Confessions*. Translated by R. S. Pine-Coffin. 1961. Reprint, Harmondsworth: Penguin, 1971.

Ayguals de Izco, Wenceslao. *La maravilla del siglo, Cartas á María Enriqueta, ó sea una visita á París y Londres durante la famosa Exhibición de la Industria Universal de 1851*. 2 vols. Madrid: Imprenta de D. Wenceslao Ayguals de Izco, 1852.

——. *María, la hija de un jornalero*. 2 vols. Madrid: Imprenta de D. Wenceslao Ayguals de Izco, 1845–46.

——. *La marquesa de Bellaflor ó el niño de la Inclusa*. 2 vols. 9th ed. Madrid: Imprenta y Librería de M. Guijarro, 1869.

——. *El tigre del Maestrazgo, ó sea de grumete á general*. 2d ed. Madrid: Imprenta de D. Wenceslao Ayguals de Izco, 1849.

Aymes, Jean-René, Eve-Marie Fell, and Jean-Louis Guereña, eds. *École et église en Espagne et en Amérique Latine — Aspects idéologiques et institutionnels*. Tours: Université de Tours, 1988.

Aynard, Joseph. *Justice ou charité? Le drame social et ses témoins de 1825 à 1845*. Paris: Librairie Plon, 1945.

Azaña, Manuel. *Ensayos sobre Valera*. Prologue by Juan Marichal. Madrid: Alianza, 1971.

———. *El jardín de los frailes*. Madrid: Alianza, 1982.

———. "Política religiosa: El artículo 26 de la Constitución." *Obras completas* 2: 49–58. Edited by Juan Marichal. Mexico City: Ediciones Oasis, 1966.

Bacarisse, S[alvador]. "The Realism of Galdós: Some Reflections on Language and the Perception of Reality." *Bulletin of Hispanic Studies* (Liverpool) 42 (1965): 239–50.

Bacon, Kathy. *Negotiating Sainthood: Distinction,* Cursilería *and Saintliness in Spanish Novels*. London: Modern Humanities Research Association and Maney Publishing, 2007.

Bahamonde, Antonio. "The Ancient Christian Traditions." Bessie 403–13.

———. *Memoirs of a Spanish Nationalist*. London: United Editorial Limited, 1939.

Bahamonde Magro, Ángel. "Cultura de la pobreza y mendicidad involuntaria en el Madrid del siglo XIX." *Madrid en Galdós/Galdós en Madrid,* 163–82. Madrid: Comunidad de Madrid, 1988.

Bahamonde Magro, Ángel, and Julián Toro Mérida. "Mendicidad y paro en el Madrid de la Restauración." *Estudios de Historia Social,* no. 7 (1978): 353–84.

Baker, Armand F. "Unamuno and the Religion of Uncertainty." *Hispanic Review* 58 (1990): 37–56.

Baker, Edward. *Materiales para escribir Madrid: Literatura y espacio urbano de Moratín a Galdós*. Madrid: Siglo XXI, 1991.

Balmes, Jaume. *Cartas a un escéptico en materia de religión*. 4th ed. 1846. Reprint, Madrid: Espasa-Calpe, 1959.

Balzac, Honoré de. *César Birotteau. La Maison Nucingen*. Edited by Félicien Marceau. Paris: Livre de Poche, 1966.

Bandera, Cesáreo. *The Sacred Game: The Role of the Sacred in the Genesis of Modern Literary Fiction*. University Park: Pennsylvania State University Press, 1994.

Baralt, Rafael María. *Diccionario de galicismos (Voces, locuciones y frases)*. Prologue by Juan Eugenio Hartzenbusch. 1855. Reprint, Madrid: Visor, 1995.

———. *Obras literarias*. Edited by Guillermo Díaz-Plaja. Madrid: Atlas, 1967.

Barea, Arturo. *Lorca: The Poet and His People*. Translated by Ilsa Barea. New York: Grove Press, 1949.

Barnes, Gwendolyn. "The Power of the Word: Religious Oratory in Nineteenth-Century Spain." *The Crisis of Institutionalized Literature in Spain,* ed. Wlad Godzich and Nicholas Spadaccini, 123–47. Minneapolis: Prisma Institute, 1988.

Baroja, Pío. *La Isabelina: Memorias de un hombre de acción. Obras completas* 3. Madrid: Biblioteca Nueva, 1947.

Barriobero y Herrán, Eduardo. *María, ó la hija de otro jornalero. La Novela Semanal,* no. 35 (25 February 1922).

Barrios Masero, M. *Poemas de la nueva España: Motivos líricos de la Santa Cruzada*. Prologue by José María Pemán. Sevilla: Tipografía de Manuel Carmona de los Ríos, November 1937.

Barthes, Roland. "Loyola." *Sade/Fourier/Loyola,* trans. Richard Miller, 38–75. 1971. Reprint, Berkeley: University of California Press, 1989.

———. "The Reality Effect." *French Literary Theory Today,* trans. R. Carter, ed. Tzvetan Todorov, 11–17. Cambridge: Cambridge University Press, 1982.

———. *S/Z.* Translated by Richard Miller. New York: Hill and Wang, 1974.

Bartra, Agustí. *Cristo de 200.000 brazos (Campo de Argelès).* Barcelona: Plaza y Janés, 1970.

Bataille, Georges. *Erotism: Death and Sensuality.* Translated by Mary Dalwood. San Francisco: City Lights Books, 1986.

Bauer, Beth Wietelmann. "Confession in *La Regenta:* The Secular Sacrament." *Bulletin of Hispanic Studies* (Liverpool) 70 (1993): 313–23.

Baulo, Sylvie. "Ayguals de Izco y el amparo de pobres." *Pensamiento y literatura en España en el siglo XIX: Idealismo, positivismo, espiritualismo,* ed. Yvan Lissorgues and Gonzalo Sobejano, 45–58. Toulouse: Presses Universitaires du Mirail, 1998.

———. "Novela popular y carlismo: Ayguals de Izco y la historia-novela." *Príncipe de Viana.* Anejo 17. *Congreso Internacional Novela Histórica: Homenaje a Navarro Villoslada,* ed. Ignacio Arellano and Carlos Mata Indurain, 59–68. Pamplona: Institución Príncipe de Viana, 1996.

Baulo, Sylvie, and Solange Hibbs. "Parti pris idéologique et perversion de l'histoire dans le roman clérical et anti-clérical du XIXe siècle." *Moenia* 8 (2002): 263–78.

Bécarud, Jean. *"La Regenta" de Clarín y la Restauración.* Madrid: Taurus, 1964.

Beccaria, Cesare. *On Crimes and Punishments.* Translated by David Young. Indianapolis: Hackett, 1986.

Becker, Carl L. *The Heavenly City of the Eighteenth-Century Philosophers.* 1932. Reprint, New Haven: Yale University Press, 1978.

Becker, George, ed. *Documents of Modern Literary Realism.* Princeton: Princeton University Press, 1963.

Bécquer, Valeriano, and Gustavo Adolfo Bécquer (Sem). *Los Borbones en pelota.* Madrid: Ediciones El Museo Universal, 1991.

Bedoya, Juan G. "Los obispos quieren llenar el Vaticano para reivindicar su visión de la Guerra Civil." *El País* (5 October 2007). www.elpais.com

Behar, Ruth. "The Struggle for the Church: Popular Anticlericalism and Religiosity in Post-Franco Spain." *Religious Orthodoxy and Popular Faith in European Society,* ed. Ellen Badone, 76–112. Princeton: Princeton University Press, 1990.

Benardete, M[air].J[osé]. "España y la crisis espiritual de nuestro tiempo." *Boletín del Instituto de las Españas en los Estados Unidos,* no. 7 (February 1933): 1–4.

Bender, Thomas, ed. *The Antislavery Debate: Capitalism and Abolitionism as a Problem in Historical Interpretation.* Berkeley: University of California Press, 1992.

———. "Introduction." Bender 1–13.

Bénichou, Paul. *The Consecration of the Writer, 1750–1830.* Translated by Mark K. Jensen. Lincoln: University of Nebraska Press, 1999.

Benítez, Rubén. *Ideología del folletín español: Wenceslao Ayguals de Izco.* Madrid: José Porrúa Turanzas, 1979.

Benjamin, Walter. "Theses on the Philosophy of History." *Illuminations,* trans. Harry Zohn, ed. Hannah Arendt, 253–64. New York: Schocken Books, 1985.

Berdyaev, Nicolas. *The Destiny of Man.* Translated by Natalie Duddington. 1937. Reprint London: Geoffrey Bles, 1954.

Berger, Peter L. "Secularization Falsified." *First Things,* no. 180 (February 2008): 23–27.

Berggren, Erik. *The Psychology of Confession.* Leiden: E. J. Brill, 1975.

Berkowitz, H. Chonon. *La biblioteca de Benito Pérez Galdós*. Las Palmas de Gran Canaria: Ediciones El Museo Canario, 1951.

——. *Pérez Galdós: Spanish Liberal Crusader*. Madison: University of Wisconsin Press, 1948.

Bernanos, Georges. *A Diary of My Times*. Translated by Pamela Morris. London: Boriswood, 1938.

Bessie, Alvah, ed. *The Heart of Spain*. Introduction by Dorothy Parker. New York: Veterans of the Abraham Lincoln Brigade, 1952.

The Bible. Authorized King James Version with Apocrypha. Introduction and notes by Robert Carroll and Stephen Prickett. Oxford: Oxford University Press, 1997.

Black, Georgina Dopico. *Perfect Wives, Other Women: Adultery and Inquisition in Early Modern Spain*. Durham: Duke University Press, 2001.

Blanc, Caroline. "Adrien Lamourette: une apologétique du bonheur." *Chrétiens et Sociétés, XVIe–XXe siècles*, no. 10 (2003): 47–68.

Blanco, Víctor. "Alcampel." *Entre los campesinos de Aragón* by Agustín Souchy Bauer, 93–125. Barcelona: Tusquets, 1977.

Blanco White, José. *Cartas de España*. Translated by Antonio Garnica. Introduction by Vicente Llorens. Madrid: Alianza, 1972.

——. "The Examination of Blanco by White, Concerning His Religious Notions and Other Subjects Connected with Them." Loureiro 8–40.

Blasco, Eusebio. "La educación a la inglesa." *Día de Moda*, año I, no. 40 (8 November 1880): 4, 6.

Bly, Peter A. "Egotism and Charity in *Marianela*." *Anales Galdosianos* 7 (1972): 49–66.

Bobes Naves, María del Carmen. *Teoría general de la novela: Semiología de "La Regenta."* Madrid: Gredos, 1985.

Boheemen, Christine van. *The Novel as Family Romance: Language, Gender, and Authority from Fielding to Joyce*. Ithaca: Cornell University Press, 1987.

Bolín, Luis. *Spain: The Vital Years*. Philadelphia: J. B. Lippincott, 1967.

Bolloten, Burnett. *The Grand Camouflage: The Spanish Civil War and Revolution 1936–39*. Introduction by H. R. Trevor-Roper. New York: Frederick A. Praeger, 1968.

Borg, Marcus J. *Jesus: Uncovering the Life, Teachings, and Relevance of a Religious Revolutionary*. San Francisco: HarperSanFrancisco, 2006.

Borja, Saint Francisco de. *Tratados espirituales*. Edited by Cándido de Dalmases. Barcelona: Juan Flors, 1964.

Bosco Sanromán, Juan. "Anteriores centenarios de la muerte de Santa Teresa." *Perfil histórico de Santa Teresa*, Teófanes Egido et al., 173–95. 2d ed. Madrid: Editorial de Espiritualidad, 1981.

Boswell, John. *The Kindness of Strangers: The Abandonment of Children in Western Europe from Late Antiquity to the Renaissance*. New York: Pantheon Books, 1988.

Botrel, Jean-François. "La iglesia católica y los medios de comunicación impresos en España de 1847 a 1917: Doctrina y prácticas." *Metodología de la historia de la prensa española*, 119–76. Madrid: Siglo XXI, 1982.

Bouza Álvarez, José Luis. *Religiosidad contrarreformista y cultura simbólica del barroco*. Prologue by Julio Caro Baroja and Antonio Domínguez Ortiz. Madrid: CSIC, 1990.

Bowers, Claude G. *My Mission to Spain: Watching the Rehearsal for World War II*. New York: Simon and Schuster, 1954.

Bowman, Frank Paul. "The Pleasures and Pitfalls of Reading Literature in a Historical Context." *Le siècle de George Sand,* ed. David A. Powell, 3–16. Amsterdam: Rodopi, 1998.

Boyd, Carolyn P. "The Second Battle of Covadonga: The Politics of Commemoration in Modern Spain." *History and Memory* 14.1–2 (2002): 37–64.

Boyle, Marjorie O'Rourke. *Loyola's Acts: The Rhetoric of the Self.* Berkeley: University of California Press, 1997.

Boyle, Nicholas. *Sacred and Secular Scriptures: A Catholic Approach to Literature.* Notre Dame: University of Notre Dame Press, 2005.

Brademas, John. "A Note on the Anarcho-Syndicalists and the Spanish Civil War." *Occidente* anno 11, no. 2 (1955): 121–35.

———. "The Spanish Anarchists." *Oxford Angle* 1.3 (1952): 35–40.

Braun, Lucille V. "Galdós' Re-creation of Ernestina Manuel de Villena as Guillermina Pacheco." *Hispanic Review* 38 (1970): 32–55.

Bravo Villasante, Carmen. "Veintiocho cartas de Galdós a Pereda." *Cuadernos Hispanoamericanos,* nos. 250–52 (1970–71): 9–51.

Bredvold, Louis I. *The Natural History of Sensibility.* Detroit: Wayne State University Press, 1962.

Brontë, Charlotte. *Jane Eyre.* New York: Dell, 1968.

Brooks, J. L. "The Character of Doña Guillermina Pacheco in Galdós' *Fortunata y Jacinta.*" *Bulletin of Hispanic Studies* (Liverpool) 38 (1961): 86–94.

Brooks, Peter. *Reading for the Plot: Design and Intention in Narrative.* New York: Vintage Books, 1985.

———. *Realist Vision.* New Haven: Yale University Press, 2005.

———. *Troubling Confessions.* Chicago: University of Chicago Press, 2000.

Brother Philippe (Bransiet, Philippe). *Subjects for Particular Examen.* New York: P. O. O'Shea, 1869.

Brown, Callum. "The Secularisation Decade: What the 1960s Have Done to the Study of Religious History." McLeod and Ustorf 29–46.

Brown, Marshall. "The Logic of Realism: A Hegelian Approach." *PMLA* 96 (1981): 224–41.

Brown, Peter. *The Cult of the Saints: Its Rise and Function in Latin Christianity.* Chicago: University of Chicago Press, 1981.

Brown, Reginald. *La novela española 1700–1850.* Madrid: Bibliografías de Archivos y Bibliotecas, Dirección General de Archivos y Bibliotecas, Servicio de Publicaciones del Ministerio de Educación Nacional, 1953.

Buckler, Reginald. *The Perfection of Man by Charity.* 1889. Reprint London: Blackfriars Publications, 1954.

Bunk, Brian D. *Ghosts of Passion: Martyrdom, Gender, and the Origins of the Spanish Civil War.* Durham: Duke University Press, 2007.

Burleigh, Michael. *Sacred Causes: The Clash of Religion and Politics, from the Great War to the War on Terror.* New York: HarperCollins, 2007.

Busette, Cedric. "Religious Symbolism in Sender's *Mosén Millán.*" *Romance Notes* 11.3 (1970): 482–86.

Bynum, Caroline Walker. *Fragmentation and Redemption: Essays on Gender and the Human Body in Medieval Religion.* New York: Zone Books, 1992.

——. *The Resurrection of the Body in Western Christianity, 200–1336.* New York: Columbia University Press, 1995.

Cabeza, Felipa Máxima de. *La señorita instruida o sea manual del bello sexo.* Aumentado notablemente por Doña María Paula de Cabeza. 7th ed. Madrid: Imp. de las Escuelas Pías, 1859.

Cadalso, José. *Escritos autobiográficos y epistolario.* Edited by Nigel Glendinning and Nicole Harrison. London: Tamesis, 1979.

——. *Noches lúgubres.* Edited by Nigel Glendinning. Madrid: Espasa Calpe, 1993.

Callahan, William. *The Catholic Church in Spain 1875–1998.* Washington D.C.: Catholic University of America Press, 2000.

——. *Church, Politics, and Society in Spain, 1750–1874.* Cambridge: Harvard University Press, 1984.

——. "The Problem of Confinement: An Aspect of Poor Relief in Eighteenth-Century Spain." *Hispanic American Historical Review* 51.1 (1971): 1–24.

Calvo Carilla, José Luis. "Utopía y novela en el siglo XIX: Wenceslao Ayguals de Izco (1801–1873)." *Utopías, quimeras y desencantos: El universo utópico en la España liberal,* ed. Manuel Suárez Cortina, 283–318. Santander: Ediciones de la Universidad de Cantabria / Sociedad Menéndez Pelayo, 2008.

Cámara, Sixto. "Muere, muere sin remedio." Elorza, *Socialismo utópico español,* 165–70.

Campo Alange, María. *Concepción Arenal 1820–1893: Estudio biográfico documental.* Madrid: Revista de Occidente, 1973.

Canalejas, Francisco de P. "La historia de las religiones." *Revista Europea,* año 1, 3.10 (3 May 1874): 294–301; no. 11 (10 May 1874): 321–30.

Cánovas del Castillo, Antonio. "Proyecto de Constitución: Artículo 11, cuestión religiosa." *Discursos parlamentarios,* ed. Diego López Garrido, 263–86. Madrid: Centro de Estudios Constitucionales, 1987.

Cansinos-Asséns, Rafael. *La novela de un literato.* 2. 1914–1923. Edited by Rafael M. Cansinos. Madrid: Alianza, 1985.

Capel Martínez, Rosa María. "La prostitución en España: Notas para un estudio sociohistórico." *Mujer y sociedad en España (1700–1975),* ed. R. M. Capel Martínez, 269–98. 1982. Reprint Madrid: Ministerio de Cultura, Instituto de la Mujer, 1986.

Cardona, Rodolfo. "Galdós and Liberation Theology." *Ideologies and Literature* 3.2 (1988): 9–22.

Carnero, Guillermo. "La novela española del siglo XVIII: Estado de la cuestión (1985–1994)." *Razón, tradición y modernidad: Re-visión de la Ilustración hispánica,* ed. Francisco La Rubia Prado and Jesús Torrecilla, 15–52. Madrid: Tecnos, 1996.

Carr, Raymond. *Spain 1808–1939.* Oxford: Oxford at the Clarendon Press, 1966.

——. *The Spanish Civil War: A History in Pictures.* New York: W. W. Norton, 1986.

Carrasquer, Francisco. "Introducción." *Réquiem por un campesino español* by R. J. Sender. Barcelona: Destino, 1998.

Carreras, Luis. *The Glory of Martyred Spain: Notes on the Religious Persecution.* London: Burns Oates and Washbourne, 1939.

——. *Grandeza cristiana de España: Notas sobre la persecución religiosa.* Toulouse: Les Frères Douladoure, 1938.

Carretero, José María (El Caballero Audaz). *La agonía de España: Los culpables.* Madrid: Ediciones Caballero Audaz, 1936.

——. *La farsa de la crisis ó España hacia el fascismo (Opiniones de un hombre de la calle).* Madrid: Ediciones Caballero Audaz, 1933.

——. *La revolución de los patibularios.* 6 vols. Madrid: Ediciones Caballero Audaz, 1940.

——. *Secretos y misterios del terrorismo en España (Opiniones de un hombre de la calle).* Madrid: Ediciones Caballero Audaz, 1933.

Carrillo, Víctor. "Marketing et édition au XIXè siècle: La Sociedad Literaria de Madrid." *L'Infra-littérature en Espagne aux XIXe et XXe siècles: Du roman feuilleton au romancero de la guerre d'Espagne (Étude d'approche),* 7–101. Grenoble: Presses Universitaires de Grenoble, 1977.

——. "El periódico *Guindilla* (1842–1843) de W. Ayguals de Izco y la evolución de las ideas republicano-federalistas en España." *La prensa en la revolución liberal: España, Portugal y América Latina,* ed. Alberto Gil Novales, 37–55. Actas del Coloquio Internacional (1, 2 y 3 de abril de 1982). Madrid: Universidad Complutense de Madrid, 1983.

——. "Radiografía de una colección de novelas a mediados del siglo XIX." *Movimiento obrero, política y literatura en la España contemporánea,* ed. Manuel Tuñón de Lara and Jean-François Botrel, 159–77. Madrid: Cuadernos para el Diálogo/Edicusa, 1974.

Carroll, Warren. *The Last Crusade: Spain, 1936.* Front Royal, Va.: Christendom Press, 1996.

Casanova, Julián. "Rebelión y revolución." *Víctimas de la guerra civil,* ed. Santos Juliá, 57–177. Madrid: Temas de Hoy, 1999.

——. "Terror and Violence: The Dark Face of Spanish Anarchism." *International Labor and Working-Class History* 67 (2005): 79–99.

Caspistegui, Francisco Javier. " 'Spain's Vendée': Carlist Identity in Navarre as a Mobilising Model." Ealham and Richards 177–95.

Cassirer, Ernst. *The Philosophy of the Enlightenment.* 8th printing. Translated by Fritz C. A. Koelln and James P. Pettegrove. Boston: Beacon Press, 1966.

Castañeda y Alcover, Vicente. *Ensayo de una bibliografía comentada de manuales de artes, ciencias, oficios, costumbres públicas y privadas de España (Siglos XVI al XIX).* Madrid: Imprenta y Editorial Maestre, 1955.

Castelar, Emilio. *La fórmula del progreso.* 1858. Reprint Madrid: Saenz de Jubera Hermanos/Ángel de San Martín, 1870.

——. *La hermana de la caridad.* 2 vols. 5th ed. 1857. Reprint Madrid: Antonio de San Martín/Sáenz de Jubera, Hermanos, n.d.

——. "El rasgo." Jarnés 96–102.

——. "Sobre la libertad religiosa." *Discursos. Recuerdos de Italia. Ensayos,* ed. Arturo Souto Alabarce, 7–17. Mexico City: Porrúa, 1980.

Castro, Américo. *Cervantes y los casticismos españoles.* 2d ed. Madrid: Alianza, 1974.

——. *El pensamiento de Cervantes.* 2d ed. Barcelona: Noguer, 1972.

——. "The Meaning of Spanish Civilization." *Américo Castro and the Meaning of Spanish Civilization,* ed. José Rubia Barcia, 23–40. Berkeley: University of California Press, 1976.

Castro y Serrano, José de. "Ernestina Manuel de Villena." *La Ilustración Española y Americana,* no. 28 (30 July 1886): 51–55.

———. "Una limosna por Dios." *La Ilustración Española y Americana,* no. 37 (8 October 1882): 198–99.

Catalina, Severo. *La mujer: Apuntes para un libro.* 18th ed. Madrid: Librería y Casa Editorial Hernando, 1946.

Cate-Arries, Francie. *Spanish Culture behind Barbed Wire: Memory and Representation of the French Concentration Camps, 1939–1945.* Lewisburg, Pa.: Bucknell University Press, 2004.

The Catholic Encyclopedia. New York: Robert Appleton, 1907–14. www.newadvent .org/cathen/index.html

Cavallo, Sandra. "The Motivations of Benefactors: An Overview of Approaches to the Study of Charity." *Medicine and Charity Before the Welfare State,* ed. Jonathan Barry and Colin Jones, 46–61. London: Routledge, 1994.

Cejador y Frauca, Julio. *Historia de la lengua y literatura castellana.* 9. 1918. Reprint Madrid: Gredos, 1973.

"El Censor" (1781–1787): Antología. Prologue by José F. Montesinos. Edited by Elsa García Pandavenes. Barcelona: Labor, 1972.

Cerrón Puga, María Luisa. "Las confesiones de Ana: Modelos de introspección en *La Regenta* de Clarín." *Cervantes,* no. 1 (October 2001): 143–69.

Cervantes, Miguel de. *El ingenioso hidalgo don Quijote de la Mancha.* 3 vols. Edited by Luis Murillo. Madrid: Castalia, 1978.

Cervera, Antonio Ignacio. "Memoria sobre el pauperismo." Elorza, "El pauperismo," 386–402.

Chacel, Rosa. *La confesión.* 1971. Reprint Barcelona: Edhasa, 1980.

Chacón, Dulce. *The Sleeping Voice.* Translated by Nick Caistor. London: Harvill Secker, 2006.

———. *La voz dormida.* Madrid: Alfaguara, 2002.

Chadwick, Owen. *The Secularization of the European Mind in the 19th Century.* 1975. Reprint Cambridge: Cambridge University Press, 1990.

Chant, Roy Heman. *Spanish Tiger: The Life and Times of Ramón Cabrera.* New York: Midas Books/Hippocrene Books, 1983.

Charlton, D. G. *Secular Religions in France 1815–1870.* London: Oxford University Press, for the University of Hull, 1963.

Charnon-Deutsch, Lou. *Gender and Representation: Women in Spanish Realist Fiction.* Amsterdam: John Benjamins, 1990.

Chateaubriand, François-René, vicomte de. *Génie du christianisme.* 2 vols. Edited by Pierre Reboul. Paris: Garnier-Flammarion, 1966.

———. *Mémoires d'outre-tombe.* 1. Edited by Edmond Biré. Paris: Librairie Garnier Frères, 1910.

Chatman, Seymour. *Story and Discourse: Narrative Structure in Fiction and Film.* Ithaca: Cornell University Press, 1980.

Christian, William A., Jr. *Local Religion in Sixteenth-Century Spain.* Princeton: Princeton University Press, 1981.

———. *Moving Crucifixes in Modern Spain.* Princeton: Princeton University Press, 1992.

———. *Visionaries: The Spanish Republic and the Reign of Christ.* Berkeley: University of California Press, 1996.

Ciocci, Raffaele. *A Narrative of Iniquities and Barbarities Practised at Rome in the Nineteenth Century.* New York: American Protestant Society, 1847.

Claret, Antonio María. *Catecismo de la doctrina cristiana explicado y adoptado a la capacidad de los niños y niñas.* 1848. Reprint Barcelona: Imprenta de los Herederos de la Viuda Pla, 1864.

———. *El colegial o seminarista teórica y prácticamente instruido.* 2 vols. 13th ed. 1860–61. Reprint Madrid: Coculsa, 1951.

———. *Instrucción que debe tener la mujer para desempeñar bien la misión que el Todopoderoso le ha confiado.* 1854. Reprint Barcelona: Librería Religiosa, 1862.

———. *Llave de oro, o serie de reflexiones que, para abrir el corazón cerrado de los pobres pecadores ofrece a los confesores nuevos . . . Seguida del Apparatus et praxis formae pro doctrina sacra in concione proponenda,* auctore R. P. Richardo Arsdekin. Barcelona: Librería Religiosa, 1857.

Clark, Christopher. "The New Catholicism and the European Culture Wars." Clark and Kaiser 11–46.

Clark, Christopher, and Wolfram Kaiser, ed. *Culture Wars: Secular-Catholic Conflict in Nineteenth-Century Europe.* Cambridge: Cambridge University Press, 2003.

Close, Anthony J. "The Legacy of *Don Quijote* and the Picaresque Novel." Turner and López de Martínez 15–30.

Coffey, Mary L. "*Un teólogo patas arriba:* Subplots and Short-circuits in *La Regenta.*" *Bulletin of Hispanic Studies* (Glasgow) 78 (2001): 577–96.

Coloma, Luis. *Pequeñeces* (with *Jeromín*). Prologue by Joaquín Antonio Peñalosa. Mexico City: Porrúa, 1968.

———. "Prólogo." *Colección de lecturas recreativas. 1884–1885–1886.* 6th ed. Bilbao: Imprenta del Corazón de Jesús, 1902.

Corbin, John. "Truth and Myth in History: An Example from the Spanish Civil War." *Journal of Interdisciplinary History* 25 (1995): 609–25.

Correa, Gustavo. *El simbolismo religioso en las novelas de Pérez Galdós.* Madrid: Gredos, 1974.

La corte celestial de María. Revisada por Mariano Costa. Madrid: Librería Española, 1855.

Cotarelo y Mori, Emilio. *Diccionario biográfico y bibliográfico de calígrafos españoles.* 2 vols. Madrid: Tip. de la "Revista de Archivos, Bibliotecas y Museos," 1913–16.

Covarrubias, Sebastián de. *Tesoro de la lengua castellana o española.* Edited by Martín de Riquer. Barcelona: Alta Fulla, 1993.

Cox, Jeffrey. "Master Narratives of Long-Term Religious Change." McLeod and Ustorf 201–17.

Crace, Jim. *Being Dead.* New York: Picador, 2001.

Criado Miguel, Isabel. "Mito y desmitificación de la guerra en dos novelas de posguerra." *Estudios sobre literatura y arte dedicados al profesor Emilio Orozco Díaz,* 333–56. Granada: Universidad de Granada, 1979.

Cruz, Sor Ángela de la. *Escritos íntimos.* Edited by José María Javierre. Madrid: Biblioteca de Autores Cristianos, 1992.

Cruz, Anne J. *Discourses of Poverty: Social Reform and the Picaresque Novel in Early Modern Spain.* Toronto: University of Toronto Press, 1999.

Cruz Casado, Antonio. "'El Caballero Audaz' entre el erotismo y la pornografía." *Cuadernos Hispanoamericanos* 463 (January 1989): 97–112.

Cuenca Toribio, José Manuel. "Le Catholicisme libéral espagnol: Les raisons d'une absence." *Les Catholiques libéraux au XIXe siècle,* 103–12. Actes du Colloque international d'histoire religieuse de Grenoble des 30 septembre–3 octobre 1971. Grenoble: Presses Universitaires de Grenoble, 1974.

——. *Iglesia y burguesía en la España liberal.* Madrid: Pegaso, 1979.

Cueva, Julio de la. "Religious Persecution, Anticlerical Tradition and Revolution: On Atrocities against the Clergy during the Spanish Civil War." *Journal of Contemporary History* 33.3 (1998): 355–69.

Curtius, Ernst Robert. *European Literature and the Latin Middle Ages.* Translated by Willard R. Trask. 1948. Reprint New York: Harper and Row, 1953.

D.J.M.L. *El fin del mundo: Los tres días de tinieblas y la gran crisis social seguida del triunfo de la Iglesia.* Mexico City: Tip. Religiosa de M. Torner y Compañía, 1874.

D.L.F.M. *Madrid en la mano o el amigo del forastero.* Madrid: Imprenta de Gaspar y Roig, 1850.

Dale, Scott. "La dialéctica Guillermina de *Fortunata y Jacinta,* o la primera 'rata eclesiástica' de la Restauración." *Lexis* 24.2 (2000): 283–301.

——. "Luis Gutiérrez y la epistolaridad escandalosa en *Cornelia Bororquia." Salina,* no. 18 (2004): 127–32.

Darst, David H. *Converting Fiction: Counter Reformational Closure in the Secular Literature of Golden Age Spain.* Chapel Hill: North Carolina Studies in the Romance Languages and Literatures, 1998.

Daudet, Alphonse. *L'Évangéliste.* 1883. Reprint Paris: Ernest Flammarion, 1892.

Davis, David Brion. "The Perils of Doing History by Ahistorical Abstraction: A Reply to Thomas L. Haskell's *AHR Forum* Reply." Bender 290–309.

——. "The Problem of Slavery in the Age of Revolution, 1770–1823." Bender 17–103.

Deacon, Philip. "José de Cadalso, una personalidad esquiva." *Cuadernos Hispanoamericanos,* no. 389 (1982): 327–30.

Deaver, William O. "Lo religioso en un cuento de Clarín." *Romance Notes* 43.1 (2002): 91–98.

Dedieu, Jean-Pierre. "Responsabilité de l'Inquisition dans le retard économique de l'Espagne? Éléments de réponse." *Aux origines du retard économique de l'Espagne XVIe–XIXe siècles,* 143–53. Paris: Éditions du CNRS, 1983.

Défourneaux, Marcelin. *Pablo de Olavide ou l'afrancesado (1725–1803).* Paris: Presses Universitaires de France, 1959.

De la beneficencia al bienestar social: Cuatro siglos de acción social. Madrid: Siglo XXI de España, 1985.

Delaprée, Louis. *The Martyrdom of Madrid.* Madrid, 1937.

Delehaye, Hippolyte, S.J. *The Legends of the Saints: An Introduction to Hagiography.* Translated by V. M. Crawford. Introduction by Richard J. Schoeck. 1907. Reprint Notre Dame: University of Notre Dame Press, 1961.

Delgado, Manuel. "Violencia anticlerical e iconoclasta en la España contemporánea."

Culturas y políticas de la violencia: España siglo XX, ed. Javier Muñoz Soro, José Luis Ledesma, and Javier Rodrigo, 75–99. Madrid: Siete Mares, 2005.

Delumeau, Jean. *Sin and Fear: The Emergence of a Western Guilt Culture 13th–18th Centuries.* Translated by Eric Nicholson. New York: St. Martin's Press, 1990.

Dendle, Brian J. "Galdós, Ayguals de Izco, and the Hellenic Inspiration of *Marianela.*" *Galdós Studies II,* ed. Robert J. Weber, 1–11. London: Tamesis Books, 1974.

——. *The Spanish Novel of Religious Thesis 1876–1936.* Princeton and Madrid: Princeton University/Castalia, 1968.

Devlin, John. *Spanish Anticlericalism: A Study in Modern Alienation.* New York: Las Américas, 1966.

Díaz-Plaja, Guillermo. "Estudio crítico." Baralt, *Obras literarias* vii–c.

Diccionario de la Real Academia Española. Madrid: Real Academia Española, 1822, 1852, 1869. www.rae.es

Diccionario de Autoridades. Madrid: Real Academia Española, 1726–39. www.rae.es

Dickens, Charles. *David Copperfield. Works* 1. New York: Books, n.d.

——. *Oliver Twist. Works* 5. New York: Books, n.d.

Diderot, Denis. "Don Pablo Olavidès: Précis historique." Défourneaux 472–75.

Diederich, Bettina. *Clarín: "La Regenta" — Ein Babel der Sieben Todsunden.* Bonn: Romanistischeer Verlag, 1997.

Díez de Revenga, Francisco Javier. "Ángel Valbuena Prat y los estudios literarios: Fecundidad y originalidad." *Tonos: Revista Electrónica de Estudios Filológicos,* no. 8 (December 2004).

DiSalvo, Angelo J. *Cervantes and the Augustinian Religious Tradition.* York, S.C.: Spanish Literature Publications, 1989.

Donnelly, J. Patrick. "Art and the Early Jesuits: The Historical Context." *Jesuit Art in North American Collections* by Jane ten Brink Goldsmith et al., 10–15. Milwaukee: Patrick and Beatrice Haggerty Museum of Art, Marquette University, 1991.

Donoso Cortés, Juan. "Carta a María Cristina." *Obras completas* 2: 722–29.

——. "De la caridad." *Estudios sobre la historia. Obras completas* 2: 261–65.

——. "Discurso sobre la situación de España." *Obras completas* 2: 479–97.

——. *Obras completas.* 2 vols. Edited by Carlos Valverde. Madrid: Biblioteca de Autores Cristianos, 1970.

Donzelot, Jacques. *The Policing of Families.* Translated by Robert Hurley. Foreword by Gilles Deleuze. Baltimore: Johns Hopkins University Press, 1997.

Doody, Terrence. *Confession and Community in the Novel.* Baton Rouge: Louisiana State University Press, 1980.

Doueihi, Milad. "*Hoc est sacramentum:* Painting Blasphemy." *MLN* 109 (1994): 617–31.

Dowling, John. "Las *Noches lúgubres* de Cadalso y la juventud romántica del Ochocientos." *Coloquio Internacional sobre José Cadalso,* 105–24. Bologna, 26–29 October 1982. Abano Terme: Piovan Editore, 1985.

Drochon, Paul. "Un curé 'libéral' sous la Révolution de 1868: Don José García Mora." *La revolución de 1868: Historia, pensamiento, literatura,* ed. Clara E. Lida and Iris M. Zavala, 273–92. New York: Las Américas, 1970.

——. "L'Église catholique vue par la presse protestante espagnole sous la Révolution de

1868." *La revolución de 1868: Historia, pensamiento, literatura,* ed. Clara E. Lida and Iris M. Zavala, 316–47. New York: Las Américas, 1970.

Druzbicki, Gaspar, S.J. *The Tribunal of Conscience.* London: Burns and Oates, 1884.

Dufour, Gérard. *Clero y sexto mandamiento: La confesión en la España del siglo XVIII.* Valladolid: Ámbito, 1996.

———. "La *Crónica Religiosa:* Un intento de liberalismo cristiano, ¿español o francés?" *La prensa en la revolución liberal: España, Portugal y América Latina,* ed. Alberto Gil Novales, 57–65. Actas del Coloquio Internacional (1, 2 y 3 de abril de 1982). Madrid: Universidad Complutense de Madrid, 1983.

———. "La diffusion en France et en Espagne du libéralisme chrétien dans les années 1820." *Libéralisme chrétien et catholicisme libéral en Espagne, France et Italie dans la première moitié du XIXe siècle,* 267–74. Colloque International, 12–14 novembre 1987. Aix-en-Provence: Université de Provence, 1989.

———. "Elementos novelescos de *El evangelio en triunfo* de Olavide." *Anales de Literatura Española,* no. 11 (1995): 107–15.

———. "*El evangelio en triunfo* o la historia de . . . la fabricación de un éxito editorial." *Cuadernos Dieciochistas,* no. 4 (2003): 67–77.

———. "Introducción." *Cartas de Mariano a Antonio: "El programa ilustrado de 'El evangelio en triunfo.'"* By Pablo de Olavide. Aix-en-Provence: Publications de l'Université de Provence, 1997.

———. "Introducción." *Cornelia Bororquia o la víctima de la Inquisición.* By Luis Gutiérrez. Madrid: Cátedra, 2005.

Dumesnil, René. *La Publication d'"En route" de J.-K. Huysmans.* Paris: Société Française d'Éditions Littéraires et Techniques, 1931.

Dunn, Peter N. *Spanish Picaresque Fiction: A New Literary History.* Ithaca: Cornell University Press, 1993.

Duprat, Catherine. *Le temps des philanthropes: La philanthropie parisienne des Lumières à la monarchie de Juillet 1.* Paris: Éditions du C.T.H.S., 1993.

Durkheim, Émile. *The Elementary Forms of the Religious Life.* Translated by Joseph Ward Swain. New York: Free Press, 1965.

Ealham, Chris, and Michael Richards, eds. *The Splintering of Spain: Cultural History and the Spanish Civil War, 1936–1939.* Cambridge: Cambridge University Press, 2005.

Earle, Peter G. "La interdependencia de los personajes galdosianos." *Cuadernos Hispanoamericanos,* nos. 250–52 (1970–71): 117–34.

Eickhoff, Georg. "Ignacio de Loyola entre *armas y letras*: Los preceptos de lectura del humanismo castellano y los *Ejercicios espirituales* como arte de leer." *Iberoromania,* no. 36 (1992): 1–20.

Eire, Carlos M. N. *From Madrid to Purgatory: The Art and Craft of Dying in Sixteenth-Century Spain.* Cambridge: Cambridge University Press, 1995.

Eliade, Mircea. *Le sacré et le profane.* Paris: Gallimard, 1965.

Elizalde, Ignacio. "Ideología religiosa de 'Clarín.'" *Letras de Deusto* 15.32 (1985): 45–68.

Elorza, Antonio, ed. "El pauperismo y las asociaciones obreras en España (1833–1868)." *Estudios de Historia Social,* nos. 10–11 (July–December 1979).

———, ed. *Socialismo utópico español.* Madrid: Alianza, 1970.

Elorza, Antonio, and María del Carmen Iglesias. *Burgueses y proletarios: Clase obrera y reforma social en la Restauración.* Barcelona: Laia, 1973.

Eoff, Sherman H. "The Deification of Conscious Process." *The Modern Spanish Novel: Comparative Essays Examining the Philosophical Impact of Science on Fiction,* 120–47. New York: New York University Press, 1961.

———. *The Novels of Pérez Galdós: The Concept of Life as Dynamic Process.* St. Louis: Washington University Studies, 1954.

Epictetus. "Of Friendship." *Discourses and Enchiridion,* trans. Thomas Wentworth Higginson, introduction by Irwin Edman, 154–59. Roslyn, N.Y.: Walter J. Black, 1944.

Estébanez Calderón, Demetrio. *Lenguaje moral y sociedad en "Fortunata y Jacinta" de Galdós.* 2 vols. Tesis doctoral. Madrid: Departamento de Filología Hispánica, Universidad Complutense de Madrid, 1984.

Estremera, José. "La confesión." *Madrid Cómico,* año 3, no. 43 (16 December 1883): 3.

Ewald, Liana J. "Imagining the *Asilo:* Institutions of Social Reform in the Works of Benito Pérez Galdós." Diss., Boston University, 2007.

Faber, Frederick William. *The Blessed Sacrament or, the Works and Ways of God.* 3d ed. 1854. Reprint London: Burns Oates and Washbourne, 1861.

Faust, Drew Gilpin. *This Republic of Suffering: Death and the American Civil War.* New York: Alfred A. Knopf, 2008.

Fedorchek, Robert M. "The Idea of Christian Poverty in Galdós' Novels." *Romance Notes* 11.1 (1969): 76–81.

Feijoo, Benito Jerónimo. "Carta VIII: Despotismo, o dominio tiránico de la Imaginación." *Cartas eruditas y curiosas,* 1742–60, 2: 93–102. Madrid: Imprenta Real de la Gazeta, a costa de la Real Compañía de Impresores y Libreros, 1774.

Feliu y Codina, José. *Confesión general: Diálogo en prosa.* Madrid: R. Velasco, 1896.

Fernán Caballero (Cecilia Böhl de Faber). *Lucas García. Obras* 4: 195–226. Edited by José María Castro Calvo. Madrid: Atlas, 1961.

Fernández, Cristóbal. *El Confesor de Isabel II y sus actividades en Madrid.* Madrid: Editorial Co. Cul., 1964.

Fernández, María Soledad. "Estrategias de poder en el discurso realista: *La Regenta* y *Fortunata y Jacinta*." *Hispania* 75 (1992): 266–74.

Fernández, Pura. *Eduardo López Bago y el naturalismo radical: La novela y el mercado literario en el siglo XIX.* Amsterdam: Rodopi, 1995.

Fernández y González, Manuel. *El martirio del alma.* 2 vols. 2d ed. 1860–61. Reprint Madrid: Miguel Prats, 1864–65.

Fernández Sebastián, Javier, and Juan Francisco Fuentes. "Crisis." Fernández Sebastián and Fuentes 199–205.

———, ed. *Diccionario político y social del siglo XIX español.* Madrid: Alianza, 2002.

Fernsworth, Lawrence A. "It Is Not a Fact." Bessie 264–66.

Ferrándiz Ruiz, José (pseud. Constancio Miralta). "Bibliografía." *Las Dominicales del Libre Pensamiento,* año 3, no. 148 (7 November 1885): 4.

———. *Los secretos de la confesión.* Madrid: Tipografía de Alfredo Alonso, 1886.

———. "La segunda parte de *El cura* por López Bago." *Las Dominicales del Libre Pensamiento,* no. 159 (17 January 1886): [3].

Ferraz Martínez, Antonio. "De la apologética a la novela: Lamourette, Olavide, D.J.O.F.M.

y F., Siñériz y Trelles, Balmes, Patxot." *El siglo que llaman ilustrado: Homenaje a Francisco Aguilar Piñal,* ed. Joaquín Álvarez Barrientos and José Checa Beltrán, 347–57. Madrid: Consejo Superior de Investigaciones Científicas, 1996.

Ferreras, Juan Ignacio. *Catálogo de novelas y novelistas españoles del siglo XIX.* Madrid: Cátedra, 1979.

———. "La novela anticlerical." *Los orígenes de la novela decimonónica (1800–1830),* 265–87. Madrid: Taurus, 1973.

———. *La novela por entregas: 1840–1900.* Madrid: Taurus, 1972.

Ferreres, Juan B., S.J. *Death, Real and Apparent in Relation to the Sacraments: A Physiologico-Theological Study.* Freiburg (Baden): B. Herder, 1906.

Feuerbach, Ludwig. *The Essence of Christianity.* Translated by George Eliot. Amherst, N.Y.: Prometheus Books, 1989.

Field, Henry M. *Old Spain and New Spain.* New York: Charles Scribner's Sons, 1888.

Fitzgerald, Sister Marie Christine. "The Irish in Spain." Diss., Western Reserve University, 1955.

Fitzgerald, Sally. "Introduction." *Three by Flannery O'Connor.* New York: Penguin, 1983.

Flaubert, Gustave. *Madame Bovary.* Edited by Iris Friederich. New York: Dell, 1964.

———. *Madame Bovary.* Edited and translated by Paul de Man. New York: W. W. Norton, 1965.

Forcione, Alban K. *Cervantes, Aristotle, and the "Persiles."* Princeton: Princeton University Press, 1970.

Forner, Juan Pablo. *Exequias de la lengua castellana.* Madrid: Espasa-Calpe, 1952.

Foucault, Michel. *Discipline and Punish: The Birth of the Prison.* Translated by Alan Sheridan. New York: Vintage, 1979.

———. *The History of Sexuality* 1. Translated by Robert Hurley. 1976. New York: Vintage Books, 1980.

———. *Power/Knowledge.* Edited by Colin Gordon. Translated by C. Gordon, Leo Marshall, John Mepham, and Kate Soper. New York: Pantheon Books, 1980.

Fouilloux, Étienne. "Iglesia Católica y 'mundo moderno' (siglos XIX y XX)." Aubert 77–89.

Foxá, Agustín de. *Madrid, de corte a checa.* 3d ed. Madrid: Editorial Prensa Española, 1962.

Fraser, Ronald. *Blood of Spain: An Oral History of the Spanish Civil War.* New York: Pantheon Books, 1979.

Freud, Sigmund. *Dora: An Analysis of a Case of Hysteria.* Edited by Philip Rieff. 1963. Reprint New York: Collier Books, 1969.

———. "Family Romances (1908)." *The Sexual Enlightenment of Children,* ed. Philip Rieff, 41–45. New York: Collier Books, 1963.

———. *The Future of an Illusion.* Translated and edited by James Strachey. New York: W. W. Norton, 1961.

———. "Mourning and Melancholia (1917)." *Collected Papers* 4: 152:70. Translated by Joan Riviere. 7th impression. London: Hogarth Press, 1953.

———. "The 'Uncanny' (1919)." *Collected Papers* 4: 368–407. Translated by Joan Riviere. 7th impression. London: Hogarth Press, 1953.

Fuentelapeña, Fray Antonio de. *El ente dilucidado: Tratado de monstruos y fantasmas.* Edited by Javier Ruiz. Madrid: Editora Nacional, 1978.

Fuentes, Juan Francisco. "Clase." Fernández Sebastián and Fuentes 156–61.

———. "Juntas." Fernández Sebastián and Fuentes 390–94.

———. "Milicia nacional." Fernández Sebastián and Fuentes 443–48.

———. "Utopía." Fernández Sebastián and Fuentes 685–88.

Fuentes, Víctor, ed. *Galdós demócrata y republicano (escritos y discursos 1907–1913).* Santa Cruz de Tenerife: Cabildo Insular de Gran Canaria/Universidad de La Laguna, 1982.

Fuentes, Yvonne. *Mártires y Anticristos: Análisis bibliográfico sobre la Revolución francesa en España.* Madrid/Frankfurt am Main: Iberoamericana/Vervuert, 2006.

Fuentes Peris, Teresa. *Visions of Filth: Deviancy and Social Control in the Novels of Galdós.* Liverpool: Liverpool University Press, 2003.

Furet, François, and Mona Ozouf, eds. *A Critical Dictionary of the French Revolution.* Translated by Arthur Goldhammer. Cambridge: Belknap Press of Harvard University Press, 1989.

Furst, Lilian R. *"All Is True": The Claims and Strategies of Realist Fiction.* Durham: Duke University Press, 1995.

Gallop, Jane. *The Daughter's Seduction: Feminism and Psychoanalysis.* Ithaca: Cornell University Press, 1982.

Garagorri, Paulino. *Introducción a Américo Castro: El estilo vital hispánico.* Madrid: Alianza, 1984.

García, Francisco. "17 de Julio de 1834. En el Convento de San Francisco el Grande de Madrid. Por un testigo ocular. Sin comentarios." Revuelta González, *El anticlericalismo español,* 39–45.

García, Salvador. *Las ideas literarias en España entre 1840 y 1850.* Berkeley: University of California Press, 1971.

García de Cortázar Ruiz de Aguirre, Fernando. "Iglesia y religión en la España de *La Regenta." Letras de Deusto* 15.32 (1985): 25–44.

García Lorca, Federico. *Diván del Tamarit. Seis poemas galegos. Llanto por Ignacio Sánchez Mejías. Poemas sueltos.* Edited by Andrew A. Anderson. Madrid: Espasa-Calpe, 1988.

———. "Teoría y juego del duende." *Obras completas,* ed. Arturo del Hoyo 109–21. Madrid: Aguilar, 1971.

———. *Romancero gitano.* Edited by Derek Harris. London: Grant and Cutler, 1991.

García Montero, Luis. "¿Por qué no sirve para nada la poesía? (Observaciones en defensa de una poesía para los seres normales)." *¿Por qué no es útil la literatura?* by L. García Montero and Antonio Muñoz Molina, 9–41. Madrid: Hiperión, 1993.

García Sarriá, Francisco. *Clarín o la herejía amorosa.* Madrid: Gredos, 1975.

Garmendia de Otaola, A[ntonio]. *Lecturas buenas y malas a la luz del dogma y de la moral.* Bilbao: El Mensajero del Corazón de Jesús, 1949.

Garrido, Fernando. "El reinado de Dios" (Soneto). Elorza, *Socialismo utópico español,* 195–96.

Gaskell, Elizabeth. *North and South.* Edited by Patricia Ingham. London: Penguin, 2003.

Geertz, Clifford. "Religion as a Cultural System." *The Interpretation of Cultures: Selected Essays,* 87–125. New York: Basic Books, 1973.

Gérando, Joseph-Marie de (Baron). *El Visitador del pobre.* Valladolid: Imprenta de D. M. Aparicio, 1852.

——. *Le Visiteur du pauvre.* Paris: Chez Louis Colas; Treuttel et Wurtz, 1820.

——. *The Visitor of the Poor.* Introduction by Rev. J[oseph] Tuckerman. London: Simpkin and Marshall, 1833.

Gérard, Philippe-Louis. *Le Comte de Valmont, ou les égaremens de la raison.* 5 vols. 1774–76; Avignon: Jean-Albert Joly, Imprimeur-Libraire, 1792–93.

Gies, David T. " 'Ars amicitiae,' poesía y vida: El ejemplo de Cadalso." *Coloquio Internacional sobre José Cadalso,* 155–71. Bologna, 26–29 October 1982. Abano Terme: Piovan Editore, 1985.

——. *The Theatre in Nineteenth-Century Spain.* Cambridge: Cambridge University Press, 1994.

Gil de Muro, Eduardo T. "Clarín, un cristiano en la balanza." *Los Cuadernos del Norte,* año 2, no. 7 (1981): 114–19.

Gil de Zárate, Antonio. "El exclaustrado." *Los españoles pintados por sí mismos* 1: 357–65. Madrid: I[gnacio] Boix Editor, 1843.

Gilman, Sander L. "Male Stereotypes of Female Sexuality in Fin-de-Siècle Vienna." *Difference and Pathology: Stereotypes of Sexuality, Race, and Madness,* 39–58. Ithaca: Cornell University Press, 1985.

Gilman, Stephen. *Galdós and the Art of the European Novel, 1867–1887.* Princeton: Princeton University Press, 1981.

Giménez Caballero, Ernesto. *Genio de España: Exaltaciones a una resurrección nacional. Y del mundo.* 5th ed. Barcelona: Ediciones Jerarquía, 1939.

Giménez Caro, María Isabel. *Ideas acerca de la novela española a mediados del siglo XIX.* Almería: Universidad de Almería, 2003.

Giner de los Ríos, Francisco. "La enseñanza confesional y la escuela." *Ensayos,* ed. Juan López-Morillas, 172–75. Madrid: Alianza, 1969.

——. "La prohibición de la mendicidad y las Hermanitas de los Pobres." *Boletín de la Institución Libre de Enseñanza* 5 (20 April 1881): 49–50.

Ginger, Andrew. *Political Revolution and Literary Experiment in the Spanish Romantic Period (1830–1850).* Lewiston, N.Y.: Edwin Mellen Press, 1999.

Gitlitz, David. "Inquisition Confessions and *Lazarillo de Tormes.*" *Hispanic Review* 68 (2000): 53–74.

Glendinning, Nigel. "Ideas políticas y religiosas de Cadalso." *Cuadernos Hispanoamericanos,* no. 389 (1982): 247–62.

——. "Introducción." *Noches lúgubres* by José Cadalso. 2d ed. Clásicos Castellanos. 1961. Reprint Madrid: Espasa Calpe, 1969.

——. "Introducción." *Noches lúgubres* by José Cadalso. Madrid: Espasa Calpe, 1993.

——. "The Traditional Story of 'La difunta pleiteada,' Cadalso's *Noches lúgubres,* and the Romantics." *Bulletin of Hispanic Studies* (Liverpool) 38 (1961): 206–15.

——. *Vida y obra de Cadalso.* Madrid: Gredos, 1962.

Gold, Hazel. "From Sensibility to Intelligibility: Transformations in the Spanish Epistolary Novel from Romanticism to Realism." *La Chispa '85: Selected Proceedings,* ed. Gilbert Paolini, 133–43. New Orleans: Tulane University, 1985.

——. "Galdós and Lamennais: *Torquemada en la hoguera,* or the Prophet Deposed." *Revista Canadiense de Estudios Hispánicos* 13.1 (1988): 29–48.

Goldin, David. "Cadalso's *Noches lúgubres:* Autobiography and Fiction." *Hispanic Journal* 5.2 (1984): 127–36.

Goldman, Peter M. "Toward a Sociology of the Modern Spanish Novel: The Early Years." *MLN* 89 (1974): 173–90; 90 (1975): 183–211.

Gomá y Tomás, Isidro. "El caso de España." *Por Dios y por España,* 17–45.

———. "Discurso pronunciado en Budapest. El tema doctrinal del Congreso Eucarístico de Budapest y el actual momento de España." *Por Dios y por España,* 489–520.

———. "La guerra: Providencia y Satanismo." *Por Dios y por España,* 360–71.

———. *The Martyrdom of Spain.* Pastoral Letter. Foreword by Rev. Richard Devane, S.J. Dublin: Published for the Irish Christian Front by James Duffy, 1936.

———. *Por Dios y por España.* Barcelona: Rafael Casulleras Librero-Editor, 1940.

———. "Riego de sangre." *Por Dios y por España,* 334–39.

Gómez de Avellaneda, Gertrudis. *Manual del cristiano: Nuevo y completo devocionario.* Edited by Carmen Bravo-Villasante. Madrid: Fundación Universitaria Española, 1975.

Gómez Blesa, Mercedes. "Introducción." *Pensamiento y poesía en la vida española* by M. Zambrano. Madrid: Biblioteca Nueva, 2004.

Gómez Moreno, Manuel. *The Golden Age of Spanish Sculpture.* Greenwich, Conn.: New York Graphic Society, 1964.

Gómez-Tabanera, José M., and Esteban Rodríguez Arrieta. "La 'conversión' de Leopoldo Alas, 'Clarín': Ante una carta inédita de 'Clarín' a Don Francisco Giner (20-X-1887)." *Boletín del Instituto de Estudios Asturianos,* año 39, no. 115 (1985): 467–82.

González, Marcelino. *Vida de la Sierva de Dios Francisca Javiera del Valle 1856–1930.* 2d ed. Valladolid: Editorial Casa Martín, 1942.

González, Román Miguel. *La pasión revolucionaria: Culturas políticas republicanas y movilización popular en la España del siglo XIX.* Madrid: Centro de Estudios Políticos y Constitucionales, 2007.

González Calleja, Eduardo. "The Symbolism of Violence during the Second Republic in Spain, 1931–1936." Ealham and Richards 23–44.

González Echevarría, Roberto. "Cervantes en *Cecilia Valdés:* Realismo y ciencias sociales." *Revista Canadiense de Estudios Hispánicos* 31.2 (2007): 267–83.

———. "Introduction." *Cervantes' "Don Quixote": A Casebook,* ed. R. González Echevarría. Oxford: Oxford University Press, 2005.

———. *Myth and Archive: A Theory of Latin American Narrative.* Cambridge: Cambridge University Press, 1990.

González López, Etelvino. *Un Magistral para "La Regenta."* Villaviciosa: Cuadernos Cubera, 1985.

González Martín, Marcelo. *Enrique de Ossó: La fuerza del sacerdocio.* 1953. Reprint Madrid: Biblioteca de Autores Cristianos, 1983.

González Povedano, Francisco. "La fe cristiana en Galdós y en sus novelas." *Actas del Tercer Congreso Internacional de Estudios Galdosianos* 1: 179–88. Las Palmas de Gran Canaria: Excmo Cabildo Insular de Gran Canaria, 1989.

Goodwyn, Frank. "The Religious Aspect of the *Quijote.*" *Estudios literarios de hispanistas norteamericanos dedicados a Helmut Hatzfeld con motivo de su 80 aniversario,* ed. Josep M. Sola-Solé, Alessandro Crisafulli, and Bruno Damiani, 109–17. Barcelona: Ediciones Hispam, 1974.

Gossman, Lionel. "History and the Study of Literature." *Profession 94,* 26–33. New York: Modern Language Association, 1994.

Graf, E[ric] C[lifford]. "Martin and the Ghosts of the Papacy: *Don Quijote* 1.19 between Sulpicius Severus and Thomas Hobbes." *MLN* 119 (2004): 949–78.

———. "Necrophilia and Materialist Thoughts in José Cadalso's *Noches lúgubres:* Romanticism's Anxious Adornment of Political Economy." *Journal of Spanish Cultural Studies* 2.2 (2001): 211–30.

Graham, Helen. *The Spanish Civil War: A Very Short Introduction.* Oxford: Oxford University Press, 2005.

Granoff, Phyllis. "Divine Delicacies: Monks, Images, and Miracles in the Contest between Jainism and Buddhism." *Images, Miracles and Authority in Asian Religious Traditions,* ed. Richard Davis, 55–97. Boulder: Westview Press, 1998.

Greeley, Andrew. *The Catholic Imagination.* Berkeley: University of California Press, 2000.

Greenblatt, Stephen. "Culture." *Critical Terms for Literary Study,* ed. Frank Lentricchia and Thomas McLaughlin, 225–32. Chicago: University of Chicago Press, 1990.

Guardón Gallardo, Federico. *El martirio del amor.* Novela de costumbres original. Madrid: Administración de la Galería Literaria, 1884.

Guillén, Claudio. "La disposición temporal del *Lazarillo de Tormes.*" *Hispanic Review* 25 (1957): 264–79.

Gunn, Giles. "Recent Criticism and the Sediments of the Sacred." *The Culture of Criticism and the Criticism of Culture,* 173–96. New York: Oxford University Press, 1987.

Gutiérrez, Luis. *Cornelia Bororquia o la víctima de la Inquisición.* Edited by Gérard Dufour. Madrid: Cátedra, 2005.

Gutiérrez Sánchez, María Mercedes. "La beneficencia pública en Madrid durante el último tercio del s. XIX." *La sociedad madrileña durante la Restauración 1876–1931,* ed. Ángel Bahamonde Magro and Luis Enrique Otero Carvajal, 2: 425–34. Madrid: Comunidad de Madrid, 1989.

Hafter, Monroe Z. "Secularization in Eighteenth-Century Spain." *Modern Language Studies* ("Ideas and Letters in Eighteenth-Century Spain," ed. Peter B. Goldman) 14.2 (1984): 36–52.

Haidt, Rebecca. *Embodying Enlightenment: Knowing the Body in Eighteenth-Century Spanish Literature and Culture.* New York: St. Martin's Press, 1998.

———. "The Enlightenment and Fictional Form." Turner and López de Martínez 31–46.

———. "Gothic Larra."*Decimonónica* 1.1 (2004): 52–66.

Haliczer, Stephen. *Sexuality in the Confessional: A Sacrament Profaned.* Oxford: Oxford University Press, 1996.

Hanna, Edward J. "Penance." *Catholic Encyclopedia.*

Hartzenbusch, Eugenio. *Apuntes para un catálogo de periódicos madrileños desde el año 1661 al 1870.* 1894. Reprint Madrid: Biblioteca Nacional/Ollero y Ramos, 1993.

Hartzenbusch, Juan Eugenio. "Prólogo." Baralt, *Diccionario de galicismos,* v–xxi.

Haskell, Thomas L. "Capitalism and the Origins of the Humanitarian Sensibility, Part 1." Bender 107–35.

Havard, Robert G. *The Crucified Mind: Rafael Alberti and the Surrealist Ethos in Spain.* London: Tamesis, 2001.

———. "The 'Romance' in Sender's *Réquiem por un campesino español.*" *Modern Language Review* 79 (January 1984): 88–96.

Hay, John. *Castilian Days.* 1871. Reprint Boston: Houghton, Mifflin [1899?].

Heartney, Eleanor. *Postmodern Heretics: The Catholic Imagination in Contemporary Art.* New York: Midmarch Arts Press, 2004.

Helman, Edith F. "Introducción." *Noches lúgubres* by José Cadalso. Madrid: Taurus, 1968.

Hemingway, Ernest. *For Whom the Bell Tolls.* 1940. Reprint New York: Scribner, 1995.

Hepworth, Mike, and Bryan S. Turner. *Confession: Studies in Deviance and Religion.* London: Routledge and Kegan Paul, 1982.

Herbert, Mary Elizabeth (Lady). *Impressions of Spain in 1866.* London: Richard Bentley, 1867.

Hernández, Vanesa. "Las vidas de los mártires: Modelos para imitar." *Archivum* 54–55 (2004–05): 315–30.

Hernández Iglesias, Fermín. *La beneficencia en España.* 2 vols. Madrid: Establecimientos Tipográficos de Manuel Minuesa, 1876.

Herr, Richard. *The Eighteenth-Century Revolution in Spain.* 1958. Reprint Princeton: Princeton University Press, 1973.

Herrera, R. A. *Donoso Cortés: Cassandra of the Age.* Grand Rapids: William B. Eerdmans, 1995.

Herrero, Javier. *Orígenes del pensamiento reaccionario español.* Madrid: Editorial Cuadernos para el Diálogo, 1971.

Hibbs-Lissorgues, Solange. *Iglesia, prensa y sociedad en España (1868–1904).* Alicante: Instituto de Cultura "Juan Gil-Albert"/Diputación de Alicante, 1995.

Hick, John. "Religious Realism and Non-Realism: Defining the Issue." Runzo 3–16.

Higgin, L[etitia]. *Spanish Life in Town and Country.* New York: G. P. Putnam's Sons, 1902.

Higuera, Henry. *Eros and Empire: Politics and Christianity in "Don Quixote."* London: Rowman and Littlefield, 1995.

Hitchens, Christopher. *God Is Not Great: How Religion Poisons Everything.* New York: Twelve, 2007.

Hobsbawm, E. J., and Joan Wallach Scott. "Political Shoemakers." *Past and Present,* no. 89 (November 1980): 86–114.

Hoff, Ruth J. "Questions of Gender and Religious Foundation in *Halma.*" *Bulletin of Spanish Studies* 83 (2006): 1059–83.

Holguín, Sandie. " 'National Spain Invites You': Battlefield Tourism during the Spanish Civil War." *American Historical Review* 110 (2005): 1399–1426.

Homza, Lu Ann. *Religious Authority in the Spanish Renaissance.* Baltimore: Johns Hopkins University Press, 2000.

Howard, Donald R. "Introduction." *On the Misery of the Human Condition* by Lothario dei Segni. Indianapolis: Bobbs-Merrill, 1969.

Hughey, John David. *Religious Freedom in Spain: Its Ebb and Flow.* Nashville: Broadman Press, 1955.

Las Hurdes: Land Without Bread. Directed by Luis Buñuel, 1933.

Huysmans, J[oris]-K[arl]. *Against Nature.* Translated by Margaret Mauldon. Edited by Nicholas White. Oxford: Oxford University Press, 1998.

———. *À rebours.* 1884. Reprint Paris: Fasquelles, 1970.

———. *En route.* 1895. Reprint Paris: Plon, 1947.

Hyde, Lewis. *The Gift: Imagination and the Erotic Life of Property.* New York: Vintage, 1983.

Iarocci, Michael. *Properties of Modernity: Romantic Spain, Modern Europe, and the Legacies of Empire.* Nashville: Vanderbilt University Press, 2006.

———. "War and the Work of Poetry: Issues in Teaching Spanish Poetry of the Civil War." Valis, *Teaching Representations,* 184–95.

Ife, B[arry] W. *Reading and Fiction in Golden-Age Spain: A Platonic Critique and Some Picaresque Replies.* Cambridge: Cambridge University Press, 1985.

Iglesias Ovejero, Ángel. "Estructuras mítico-narrativas de *Réquiem por un campesino español.*" *Anales de la Literatura Española Contemporánea* 7.2 (1982): 215–36.

Ilie, Paul. "Cultural Norms in the Spain of Soler (1729–1783)." *Modern Language Studies* ("Ideas and Letters in Eighteenth-Century Spain," ed. Peter B. Goldman) 14.2 (1984): 10–35.

———. "¿Luces sin ilustración? Las voces 'imaginación/fantasía' como testigos léxicos." *Razón, tradición y modernidad: Re-visión de la Ilustración hispánica,* ed. Francisco La Rubia Prado and Jesús Torrecilla, 133–92. Madrid: Tecnos, 1996.

Illich, Ivan. "La alfabetización de la mentalidad: Un llamamiento a investigarla." *La Torre,* Nueva época, año 2, no. 5 (January–March 1988): 79–102.

"Informe de la Censura sobre la primera edición española de *El evangelio en triunfo.*" Olavide, *Obras selectas,* 649–50.

Irizarry, Estelle. "Concepción Arenal and the Essay of Advocacy: 'The Medium Is the Message.'" *Spanish Women Writers and the Essay: Gender, Politics, and the Self,* ed. Kathleen M. Glenn and Mercedes Mazquiarán de Rodríguez, 6–24. Columbia: University of Missouri Press, 1998.

Isla, José Francisco de. *Fray Gerundio de Campazas.* 4 vols. Edited by Russell P. Sebold. Madrid: Espasa-Calpe, 1960–64.

J.R.B. "Preface." De Gérando i–xxxviii.

Jaén, Manuel de. *Instrucción utilísima y fácil para confesar particular y generalmente.* 13th ed. Madrid: Viuda de Barco López, 1813.

Jaffe, Catherine. "In Her Father's Library: Women's Reading in *La Regenta.*" *Revista de Estudios Hispánicos* 39.1 (2005): 3–25.

Jakobsen, Janet R., and Ann Pellegrini. "Introduction: Times Like These." *Secularisms,* ed. Jakobsen and Pellegrini, 1–35. Durham: Duke University Press, 2008.

James, William. *The Varieties of Religious Experience.* 1902. Reprint New York: Mentor, 1958.

Jarnés, Benjamín. *Castelar: Hombre del Sinaí.* 1935. Reprint Madrid: Espasa-Calpe, 1971.

Javierre, José María. "Introducción biográfica" and "Introducción." *Escritos íntimos* by Sor Ángela de la Cruz, 3–144, 146–64. Madrid: Biblioteca de Autores Cristianos, 1992.

Jiménez Duque, Baldomero. *La espiritualidad en el siglo XIX español.* Salamanca and Madrid: Universidad Pontificia de Salamanca/Fundación Universitaria Española, 1974.

Jiménez Lozano, José. *Los cementerios civiles y la heterodoxia española.* Madrid: Taurus, 1978.

——. *Meditación española sobre la libertad religiosa.* Barcelona: Destino, 1966.

——. *El sambenito.* Barcelona: Destino, 1972.

Jonas, Raymond. *France and the Cult of the Sacred Heart: An Epic Tale for Modern Times.* Berkeley: University of California Press, 2000.

Jordan, Thomas E. *Victorian Childhood: Themes and Variations.* Albany: State University of New York Press, 1987.

Jutglar, Antoni. "Estudio preliminar." *Condiciones de vida y trabajo obrero en España a mediados del siglo XIX,* 9–55. Barcelona: Anthropos, 1984.

——. *Ideologías y clases en la España contemporánea (1808–1874)* 1. Madrid: Cuadernos Para el Diálogo, 1973.

Kagan, Richard L. *Lucrecia's Dreams: Politics and Prophecy in Sixteenth-Century Spain.* Berkeley: University of California Press, 1990.

Kaiser, Wolfram. " 'Clericalism—That Is Our Enemy!': European Anticlericalism and the Culture Wars." Clark and Kaiser 47–76.

Kent, Conrad. "Claudio López y Eusebio Güell: Industriales como forjadores de cultura." *La voluntad de humanismo: Homenaje a Juan Marichal,* ed. Biruté Ciplijauskaité and Christopher Maurer, 107–20. Barcelona: Anthropos, 1990.

Kermode, Frank. *The Genesis of Secrecy: On the Interpretation of Narrative.* Cambridge: Harvard University Press, 1979.

King, Charles L. "Sender's Poetic Theology." *Homenaje a Ramón J. Sender,* ed. Mary S. Vásquez, 101–09. Newark, Del.: Juan de la Cuesta, 1987.

Knight, Mark, and Emma Mason. *Nineteenth-Century Religion and Literature: An Introduction.* Oxford: Oxford University Press, 2006.

Labanyi, Jo. *Gender and Modernization in the Spanish Realist Novel.* Oxford: Oxford University Press, 2000.

——. "Teaching History through Memory Work." Valis, *Teaching Representations,* 436–47.

Lacalzada de Mateo, María José. *Mentalidad y proyección social de Concepción Arenal.* Ferrol: Cámara Oficial de Comercio, Industria e Navegación/Concello de Ferrol, 1994.

Lacan, Jacques. *Écrits: A Selection.* Translated by Alan Sheridan. New York: W. W. Norton, 1977. 1–7; 281–91.

Ladrón de Guevara, Pablo. *Novelistas malos y buenos.* 4th ed. 1910. Reprint Bilbao: El Mensajero del Corazón de Jesús, 1933.

Laforet, Carmen, and Ramón J. Sender. *Puedo contar contigo: Correspondencia.* Edited by Israel Rolón Barada. Barcelona: Destino, 2003.

La Fuente y Zamalloa, Modesto (Fray Gerundio). *Teatro social del siglo XIX.* 2. Madrid: Est. tip. de D. F. de P. Mellado, 1846.

Lagarrigue, Juan Enrique. *La religión de la humanidad.* 4th ed. 1884. Reprint Santiago de Chile: Imprenta Blanco y Negro, 1917.

Lamennais, Félicité de. *Paroles d'un croyant.* Preface by André Derval. Paris: Pocket, 1996.

Lamet, Pedro Miguel. *La santa de Galdós: Ernestina Manuel de Villena (1830–1886), Un personaje histórico de "Fortunata y Jacinta."* Madrid: Trotta, 2000.

Lamourette, Antoine Adrien. *Las delicias de la religion christiana, ó el poder del evangelio para hacernos felices.* Barcelona: Librería Religiosa, 1861.

Langdon-Davies, John. *The Spanish Church and Politics.* London: Watts, 1937.

Lannon, Frances. *Privilege, Persecution, and Prophecy: The Catholic Church in Spain 1875–1975.* Oxford: Oxford University Press, 1987.

La Parra López, Emilio. "Anticlericalismo y secularización en España (1808–1850)." *Pensamiento y literatura en España en el siglo XIX. Idealismo, positivismo, espiritualismo,* ed. Yvan Lissorgues and Gonzalo Sobejano, 59–70. Toulouse: Presses Universitaires du Mirail, 1998.

———. "El eco de Lamennais en el progresismo español: Larra y Joaquín María López." *Libéralisme chrétien et catholicisme libéral en Espagne, France et Italie dans la première moitié du XIXe siècle,* 323–42. Colloque International 12–14 novembre 1987. Études Hispano-Italiennes no. 3. Aix-en-Provence: Université de Provence, 1989.

Laqueur, Thomas. "Bodies, Details, and the Humanitarian Narrative." *The New Cultural History,* ed. Lynn Hunt, 176–204. Berkeley: University of California Press, 1989.

———. *Making Sex: Body and Gender from the Greeks to Freud.* Cambridge: Harvard University Press, 1990.

Larque, Claude. "La crianza de los niños madrileños abandonados en el siglo XVII." *Anales del Instituto de Estudios Madrileños* 23 (1986): 363–84.

Larra, Mariano José de. "El dogma de los hombres libres: *Palabras de un creyente,* por M. F. Lammenais. Cuatro palabras del traductor." *Artículos políticos y sociales,* ed. José R. Lomba y Pedraja, 3: 258–68. Madrid: Espasa-Calpe, 1966.

Larriba, Elisabel. "La prensa, verdadera vocación de tres eclesiásticos a finales del antiguo régimen." *Hispania Nova,* no. 4 (2004): [1–15]. http://hispanianova.rediris.es.

La Rubia Prado, Francisco. "Historia desde la cripta: Terror y fascinación del cadáver en *Noches lúgubres* de José de Cadalso." *Dieciocho: Hispanic Enlightenment* 25.1 (2002): 65–74.

Laso Prieto, José María. "La religión en la obra cumbre de Leopoldo Alas." *Argumentos,* nos. 63–64 (1984): 38–43.

Lea, Henry Charles. *A History of Auricular Confession and Indulgences in the Latin Church* 1–2. 1896. Reprint New York: Greenwood Press, 1968.

Ledesma, José Luis. *Los días de llamas de la revolución: Violencia y política en la retaguardia republicana de Zaragoza durante la guerra civil.* Zaragoza: Institución Fernando el Católico, 2003.

———. "El 1936 más opaco: Las violencias en la zona republicana durante la guerra civil y sus narrativas." *Historia Social,* no. 58 (2007): 151–68.

Leiva, Juan, and Nicolás Montoya. *La caña rota: La confesión de un confesor del siglo XVIII.* [Jerez de la Frontera?]: Azagaya, 1995.

Leo XIII. *Rerum Novarum. The Papal Encyclicals in Their Historical Context,* ed. Anne Fremantle, 166–95. 4th printing. New York: New American Library, 1960.

Leturia, Pedro. "Libros de Horas, Anima Christi y Ejercicios espirituales de S. Ignacio." *Archivum Historicum Societatis Iesu* (Rome) 17 (1948): 3–50.

Leval, Gastón. *Colectividades libertarias en España.* 2 vols. Buenos Aires: Proyección, 1972, 1974.

Levinas, Emmanuel. *Of God Who Comes to Mind.* Translated by Bettina Bergo. Stanford: Stanford University Press, 1998.

Lewis, C. S. "Is Theology Poetry?" Lewis 74–92.

———. "Membership." Lewis 106–20.

———. "Transposition." Lewis 54–73.

———. "The Weight of Glory." Lewis 3–19.

✳ ———. *"The Weight of Glory" and Other Addresses*. Edited by Walter Hooper. Rev. ed. New York: Macmillan, 1980.

Lewis, Joseph. *Spain: A Land Blighted by Religion*. New York: Freethought Press Association, 1933.

Lewis, Matthew G. *The Monk*. Introduction by John Berryman. New York: Grove, 1959.

Lewis, Pericles. "Churchgoing in the Modern Novel." *Modernism/Modernity* 11.4 (2004): 669–94.

Lida, Denah. "Galdós y sus santas modernas." *Anales Galdosianos* 10 (1975): 19–31.

Liguori, Alphonsus de. *The Great Means of Salvation and of Perfection*. 3. *Complete Works*, ed. Eugene Grimm. Brooklyn: Redemptorist Fathers, 1927.

Lincoln, Bruce. "Revolutionary Exhumations in Spain, July 1936." *Comparative Studies in Society and History* 27.2 (1985): 241–60.

Lisón-Tolosana, Carmelo. *Belmonte de los Caballeros: Anthropology and History in an Aragonese Community*. Introduction by James W. Fernandez. Princeton: Princeton University Press, 1983.

Lissorgues, Yvan. "La autenticidad religiosa de Leopoldo Alas." *Ínsula*, no. 451 (June 1984): 3.

———. *Leopoldo Alas, "Clarín," en sus palabras (1852–1901): Biografía*. Oviedo: Nobel, 2007.

———. *La Pensée philosophique et religieuse de Leopoldo Alas (Clarín)—1875–1901*. Paris: Éditions du CNRS, 1983.

Llaurado, Joseph G. "Jacques Maritain on the Spanish Civil War." *Letras Peninsulares* 11.1 (1998): 455–69.

Locke, John. *Two Treatises of Government and A Letter Concerning Toleration*. Stilwell, Kan.: Digireads, 2005.

Longares Alonso, Jesús. *Política y religión en Barcelona (1833–1843)*. Madrid: Editora Nacional, 1976.

Longinus. *On the Sublime. Classical Literary Criticism* (Aristotle. Horace. Longinus). Edited and translated by T. S. Dorsch. Baltimore: Penguin, 1967.

López Bago, Eduardo. *El confesonario (Satiriasis) (Segunda parte de "El cura")*. Madrid: Administración, Juan Muñoz y Compañía, Editores, n.d. [1885].

———. *El cura (Caso de incesto): Novela médico-social*. Madrid: Juan Muñoz, n.d. [1885].

López Hidalgo, Antonio. *Las entrevistas periodísticas de José María Carretero*. Córdoba: Diputación de Córdoba, 1999.

López Peláez, Antolín. *Los daños del libro*. Barcelona: Gustavo Gili, 1905.

López-Sanz, Mariano. *Naturalismo y espiritualismo en la novelística de Galdós y Pardo Bazán*. Madrid: Pliegos, 1985.

Lorenzo, César M. *Les anarchistes espagnols et le pouvoir 1868–1969*. Paris: Editions du Seuil, 1969.

Loureiro, Ángel G. "The Examination of Blanco by White." *Revista de Estudios Hispánicos* 33 (1999): 3–40.

Lowenthal, David. *The Past Is a Foreign Country.* Cambridge: Cambridge University Press, 1985.

Loyola, Ignacio de. *Ejercicios espirituales.* Barcelona: Editorial Librería Religiosa, [1958].

Lukács, Georg. *The Theory of the Novel.* Translated by Anna Bostock. Cambridge: MIT Press, 1971.

Lyotard, Jean-François. *The Confession of Augustine.* Translated by Richard Beardsworth. Stanford: Stanford University Press, 2000.

McCabe, Joseph. *The Martyrdom of Ferrer, Being a True Account of his Life and Work.* London: Watts, 1909.

McDermott, Patricia. "Introduction." *Réquiem por un campesino español* by Ramón J. Sender. Manchester: Manchester University Press, 1991.

——. "Songlines of the Dreamtime on a Map of Misreading (An Unscientific Meditation on the *Soledades* of Antonio Machado for the Evening of Palm Sunday 1989)." *Estelas en la Mar: Essays on the Poetry of Antonio Machado (1875–1939),* ed. D. Gareth Walters, 1–17. Glasgow: Department of Hispanic Studies, 1992.

McKim-Smith, Gridley. "Spanish Polychrome Sculpture and Its Critical Misfortunes." *Spanish Polychrome Sculpture 1500–1800 in United States Collections,* ed. Suzanne L. Stratton, 13–31. New York: Spanish Institute, 1994.

McLeod, Hugo. "Introduction." McLeod and Ustorf 1–26.

McLeod, Hugo, and Werner Ustorf, eds. *The Decline of Christendom in Western Europe, 1750–2000.* Cambridge: Cambridge University Press, 2003.

Madariaga de la Campa, Benito. "Bosquejo biográfico de un humanista." *Tres estudios bio-bibliográficos sobre Marcelino Menéndez Pelayo,* by B. Madariaga de la Campa, Ciriaco Morón Arroyo, and Adolfo Bonilla y San Martín, 13–124. Santander: Real Sociedad Menéndez Pelayo, 2008.

Madeleva, M[ary]. *Pearl: A Study in Spiritual Dryness.* New York: D. Appleton, 1925.

Mainer, José-Carlos. "De Madrid a Madridgrado (1936–1939): La capital vista por sus sitiadores." *Vencer no es convencer: Literatura e ideología del fascismo español,* ed. Mechthild Albert, 181–98. Frankfurt am Main/Madrid: Vervuert/Iberoamericana, 1998.

——. *La escritura desatada: El mundo de las novelas.* Madrid: Temas de Hoy, 2000.

Malin, Mark R. "The Truth of Power and the Power of Truth: Luis Gutiérrez's *Cornelia Bororquia." Dieciocho: Hispanic Enlightenment* 25 (2002): 7–24.

Mandrell, James. "Malevolent Insemination: *Don Juan Tenorio* in *La Regenta.*" *"Malevolent Insemination" and Other Essays on Clarín,* ed. Noël Valis, 1–28. Ann Arbor: Michigan Romance Studies, 10, 1990.

Marchena, José (Abate). *Obras en prosa.* Edited by Fernando Díaz Plaja. Madrid: Alianza, 1985.

Marco, Joaquín. *Literatura popular en España en los siglos XVIII y XIX.* Madrid: Taurus, 1977.

Marcus, Steven. "Freud and Dora: Story, History, Case History." *In Dora's Case: Freud-Hysteria-Feminism,* ed. Charles Bernheimer and Claire Kahane, 56–91. 2d ed. 1985. Reprint New York: Columbia University Press, 1990.

Maresca, Mariano. *Hipótesis sobre Clarín: El pensamiento crítico del reformismo español.* Granada: Diputación Provincial de Granada, 1985.

Marí, Jorge. "Ironía, relectura y suspense: La estructura narrativa del *Réquiem* de Sender." *Letras Peninsulares* 9.2 (1996): 257–74.

Marin, Louis. *Food for Thought.* Translated by Mette Hjort. Baltimore: Johns Hopkins University Press, 1989.

Maritain, Jacques. "Introduction." Mendizábal, *The Martyrdom of Spain.*

Martí-López, Elisa. *Borrowed Words: Translation, Imitation, and the Making of the Nineteenth-Century Novel in Spain.* Lewisburg, Pa.: Bucknell University Press, 2002.

——. "The *folletín*: Spain Looks to Europe." Turner and López de Martínez 65–80.

Martin, Wallace. *Recent Theories of Narrative.* Ithaca: Cornell University Press, 1986.

Martínez, Francisco. *Dos jesuitas mártires en Asturias: El P. Emilio Martínez y H. Juan B. Arconada.* Prologue by Enrique Herrera Oria. Burgos: Imprenta Aldecoa, 1936.

Martínez, Martín. *Noches anatómicas, o anatomía compendiosa.* 2d printing. Madrid: M. F. [Miguel Francisco] Rodríguez, 1750.

Martínez Carazo, Cristina. *De la visualidad literaria a la visualidad fílmica: "La Regenta" de Leopoldo Alas "Clarín."* Gijón: Llibros del Pexe, 2006.

Martínez-Gallego, Francesc A. "Democracia y república en la España isabelina: El caso de Ayguals de Izco." *Federalismo y cuestión federal en España,* ed. Manuel Chust, 45–90. Castelló de la Plana: Publicacions de la Universitat Jaime I, 2004.

Martínez Mata, Emilio. "Prólogo." *Cartas marruecas. Noches lúgubres* by José Cadalso. Barcelona: Crítica, 2000.

Martz, Linda. *Poverty and Welfare in Habsburg Spain: The Example of Toledo.* Cambridge: Cambridge University Press, 1983.

Marx, Karl. "A Criticism of the Hegelian Philosophy of Right." *Selected Essays,* trans. H. J. Stenning, 11–39. New York: International Publishers, 1926.

Mayhew, Henry. *Mayhew's London.* Edited by Peter Quennell. London: Bracken Books, 1987.

Maza, Elena. *Pobreza y beneficencia en la España contemporánea (1808–1936).* Barcelona: Ariel, 1999.

Mazzini, Joseph. *"The Duties of Man" and Other Essays.* Introduction by Thomas Jones. London: J. M. Dent and Sons, 1961.

——. "Faith and the Future." Translated by Thomas Okey. *"Duties"* 141–94.

——. "The Patriots and the Clergy." Translated by Thomas Okey. *"Duties"* 197–217.

Medina, Jeremy T. *Spanish Realism: The Theory and Practice of a Concept in the Nineteenth Century.* Prologue by Ciriaco Morón Arroyo. Potomac, Md.: José Porrúa Turanzas, 1979.

Meissner, W. W. *Ignatius of Loyola: The Psychology of a Saint.* New Haven: Yale University Press, 1992.

Meléndez Valdés, Juan. "Fragmentos de un discurso sobre la mendiguez." *Obras completas* 3: 273–94. Madrid: Biblioteca Castro, 1997.

Mendelson, Jordana. *Documenting Spain: Artists, Exhibition Culture, and the Modern Nation, 1929–1939.* University Park: Pennsylvania State University Press, 2005.

Mendizábal, Alfred. *Aux origines d'une tragédie: La politique espagnole de 1923 à 1936.* 2d ed. Introduction by Jacques Maritain. Paris: Desclée de Brouwer, [1937].

——. *The Martyrdom of Spain: Origins of a Civil War.* Introduction by Jacques Maritain. Translated by Charles Hope Lumley. London: Geoffrey Bles/The Centenary Press, 1938.

Menéndez Pelayo, Marcelino. *Historia de los heterodoxos españoles.* 3 vols. Facsimile ed. Madrid: CSIC, 1992.

Menéndez-Reigada, P. Ignacio G. *La guerra nacional española ante la moral y el derecho.* Bilbao: Editora Nacional, n.d. [1937].

Mesonero Romanos, Ramón de. "Una visita a San Bernardino." *Obras,* ed. Carlos Seco Serrano, 2: 38–43. Madrid: Atlas, 1967.

Minnis, Alastair. "Medieval Imagination and Memory." *The Cambridge History of Literary Criticism. 2. The Middle Ages,* ed. A. Minnis and Ian Johnson, 239–74. Cambridge: Cambridge University Press, 2005.

Mir, Miguel, ed. *Escritores místicos españoles* 1. Nueva Biblioteca de Autores Españoles 16. Madrid: Casa Editorial Bailly Baillière, 1911.

Miranda García, Soledad. *Pluma y altar en el XIX: De Galdós al cura Sta. Cruz.* Madrid: Pegaso, 1983.

———. *Religión y clero en la gran novela española del siglo XIX.* Madrid: Pegaso, 1982.

Mitchell, Timothy. *Betrayal of the Innocents: Desire, Power, and the Catholic Church in Spain.* Philadelphia: University of Pennsylvania Press, 1998.

Mitchell, Juliet, and Jacqueline Rose, eds. *Feminine Sexuality: Jacques Lacan and the "école freudienne,"* trans. Jacqueline Rose, 1–26, 27–57. New York: W. W. Norton, 1985.

Molina Martínez, José Luis. *Anticlericalismo y literatura en el siglo XIX.* Murcia: Universidad de Murcia, 1998.

Moliner, María. *Diccionario de uso del español.* 2 vols. Madrid: Gredos, 1986.

Monlau, Pere Felip. "De la asociación." Elorza, "El pauperismo," 341–44.

———. *Elementos de higiene pública.* 2 vols. 2d ed. 1847. Madrid: Imprenta y Estereotipia de M. Rivadeneyra, 1862.

———. *Higiene del matrimonio o el libro de los casados.* 1853. 13th ed. rev. Paris: Garnier Hermanos [1865].

———. *Higiene industrial.* 1856. *Condiciones de vida y trabajo obrero en España a mediados del siglo XIX,* ed. Antoni Jutglar. Barcelona: Anthropos, 1984.

———. *Remedios del pauperismo.* Valencia: Imprenta de D. Mariano de Cabrerizo, 1846.

Montaigne, Michel de. "Of Friendship." *Selected Essays,* trans. Donald M. Frame, 56–72. Roslyn, N.Y.: Walter J. Black, 1943.

Montero, Feliciano. "Catolicismo y reforma social en España en el tránsito del siglo XIX al XX." *De la beneficencia,* 167–76.

Montero Moreno, Antonio. *Historia de la persecución religiosa en España 1936–1939.* Madrid: Biblioteca de Autores Cristianos, 1961.

Montesinos, José F. *Introducción a una historia de la novela en España en el siglo XIX.* Madrid: Castalia, 1955.

Mora García, José Luis. *Hombre, sociedad y religión en la novelística galdosiana (1888–1905).* Salamanca: Ediciones Universidad de Salamanca/Excmo. Cabildo Insular de Gran Canaria, 1981.

Morales Muñoz, Manuel. "Los catecismos y la instrucción popular en la España del siglo XIX." Aymes et al. 33–46.

Moreno Nieto, E. "Beneficencia." Elorza and Iglesias 182–95.

Morris, Colin. *The Discovery of the Individual 1050–1200.* 1972. Reprint New York: Harper and Row, 1973.

Muñoz Molina, Antonio. *Los misterios de Madrid.* Barcelona: Seix Barral, 1992.

Murphy, Martin. "Luis Gutiérrez, Novelist and Impostor." *Spain and Its Literature: Essays in Memory of E. Allison Peers,* ed. Ann L. Mackenzie, 235–52. Liverpool: Liverpool University Press/Modern Humanities Research Association, 1997.

Múzquiz, Marlene. "Charity, Punishment, and Labor: The Textualization of Poverty in XVII and XVIII Century Spain." Diss., University of California-San Diego, 1994.

Nadal Colón, Mayra. "Guillermina y Mauricio: Dos personajes, una misma función estructural." *La Torre,* Nueva época, año 2, no. 6 (April–June 1988): 363–74.

Naharro, Vicente. *Arte de enseñar á escribir cursivo y liberal.* Madrid: Imprenta de Vega y Compañía, 1820.

———. *Método práctico de enseñar á leer.* 1815? Reprint Madrid: Imprenta y Librería de la Viuda de Vázquez e Hijos, 1856.

Navarrete, Ramón de. *Madrid y nuestro siglo.* 4 vols. Madrid: Imprenta de la V. de Jordan e Hijos, 1845–46.

———. "La novela española. Artículo II & III." Zavala, *Ideología,* 258–66.

———. *Sueños y realidades.* Prologue by Carlos Coello. Madrid: Oficinas de la Ilustración Española y Americana, 1878.

———. *Verdades y ficciones.* Prologue by Luis Mariano de Larra. Madrid: A. de Carlos e hijo, Editores, 1874.

Navarro Villoslada, Francisco. *El Ante-Cristo. La princesa de Viana. Obras completas* 5. Edited by Segundo Otatzu Jaurrieta. Iruña: Mintzoa, 1992.

Nepaulsingh, Colbert I. "Lázaro's Fortune." *Romance Notes* 20.3 (1980): 1–7.

Nicolás, Antonio T. de. *Powers of Imagining: Ignatius de Loyola.* Albany: State University of New York Press, 1986.

Nicolas, Marie-Joseph. "The Meaning of the Immaculate Conception in the Perspectives of St. Thomas." O'Connor 327–45.

Nietzsche, Friedrich. *The Antichrist. The Portable Nietzsche,* trans. and ed. Walter Kaufmann. New York: Viking Press, 1972.

Nimetz, Michael. "Eros and Ecclesia in Clarín's Vetusta." *MLN* 86 (1971): 242–53.

Noel, Charles C. "Missionary Preachers in Spain: Teaching Social Virtue in the Eighteenth Century." *American Historical Review* 90 (1985): 866–92.

Nos Muro, Luis. "Aproximación a la persona y obra de don Benito Pérez Galdós: Para un intento de reconciliación con el gran novelista de nuestro siglo XIX." *Letras de Deusto* 30, no. 88 (2000): 161–77.

Nuez, Sebastián de la. *Biblioteca y archivo de la Casa Museo Pérez Galdós.* (With Marcos G. Martínez). Gran Canaria: Ediciones del Cabildo Insular de Gran Canaria, 1990.

Núñez Seixas, Xosé-Manoel. "Nations in Arms against the Invader: On Nationalist Discourses during the Spanish Civil War." Ealham and Richards 45–67.

Nussbaum, Martha C. *Poetic Justice: The Literary Imagination and Public Life.* Boston: Beacon Press, 1995.

Oates, Mary J. *The Catholic Philanthropic Tradition in America.* Bloomington: Indiana University Press, 1995.

O'Connor, Edward Dennis, ed. *The Dogma of the Immaculate Conception: History and Significance.* Notre Dame: University of Notre Dame Press, 1958.

———. "Preface." O'Connor v–xvi.

O'Connor, Flannery. *Mystery and Manners: Occasional Prose.* 17th printing. Edited by Sally and Robert Fitzgerald. New York: Farrar, Straus and Giroux, 1989.

O'Donnell, Elliot. *The Irish Abroad.* London: Sir Isaac Pitman and Sons, 1915.

O'Grady, John. *The Catholic Church and the Destitute.* New York: Macmillan, 1929.

Olavide y Jáuregui, Pablo de. *Cartas de Mariano a Antonio: "El programa ilustrado de 'El evangelio en triunfo.'"* Edited by Gérard Dufour. Aix-en-Provence: Publications de l'Université de Provence, 1997.

———. *El evangelio en triunfo, o historia de un filósofo desengañado.* 4 vols. 8th ed. Madrid: Imprenta de Don Josef Doblado, 1803–08.

———. "La historia religiosa de la revolución francesa." *Obras selectas,* ed. Estuardo Núñez, 439–81. Lima: Banco de Crédito del Perú, 1987.

Orsy, Ladislas. *The Evolving Church and the Sacrament of Penance.* Denville, N.J.: Dimension Books, 1978.

Ortega y Gasset, José. *Meditaciones del Quijote.* Edited by Julián Marías. Madrid: Cátedra, 1984.

———. "Del realismo en pintura." *Obras completas* 1: 565–69. Madrid: Alianza/Revista de Occidente, 1983.

Ossó, Enrique de. *El cuarto de hora de oración según las enseñanzas de la seráfica virgen y doctora Santa Teresa de Jesús.* 38th ed. Barcelona: Ramón Casals, Editor, 1950.

Otto, Rudolf. *The Idea of the Holy: An Inquiry into the Non-Rational Factor in the Idea of the Divine and Its Relation to the Rational.* Translated by John W. Harvey. 1917. Reprint London: Oxford University Press, 1958.

Ouimette, Victor. "'Monstrous Fecundity': The Popular Novel in Nineteenth-Century Spain." *Canadian Review of Comparative Literature* 9.3 (1982): 383–405.

Ozouf, Mona. "De-Christianization." Furet and Ozouf 20–32.

———. "Revolutionary Religion." Furet and Ozouf 560–70.

P.V. (Pablo Villada?). *Casos de conciencia acerca del liberalismo, sacados de la obra escrita en latín.* Translated by Jerónimo Seisdedos y Sanz. Prologue by J. M. Ortí y Lara. Madrid: Biblioteca de la Ciencia Cristiana, 1886.

Palacio, Eduardo de. "La institutriz." *Álbum poético,* 194. Barcelona: Establecimiento Editorial de Ramón Molinas, 1885.

Palacio Valdés, Armando. "El problema religioso. *Doctrinas religiosas del racionalismo contemporáneo,* por Don Francisco de Paula Canalejas." *Revista Europea,* año 2, 4.65 (23 May 1875): 466–71.

Palafox y Mendoza, Juan de. *Exercicios devotos en que se pide a la Virgen Santíssima su amparo, para la hora de la muerte.* Sevilla: Herederos de Thomás López de Haro, [1711?].

Palau y Dulcet, Antonio. *Manual del librero hispano-americano.* 28 vols. 2d ed. Barcelona: Palau y Dulcet, 1948–77.

Palma, Luis de la. *Meditaciones para prepararse a la sagrada comunión. Obras completas* 3. Edited by Camilo María Abad. Madrid: Atlas, 1963.

———. *Práctica y breve declaración del camino espiritual como lo enseña el bienaventurado padre san Ignacio fundador de la Compañía de Jesús, en las cuatro semanas de su Libro de los ejercicios. Obras completas.* Biblioteca de Autores Españoles 144. Edited by Camilo María Abad. Madrid: Atlas, 1961.

Palomo, María del, and Antonio Prieto. "Historia de una *Historia* y evocación de Ángel Valbuena Prat." *Monteagudo* 3ª época, no. 5 (2000): 13–27.

Paolini, Gilberto. *An Aspect of Spiritualistic Naturalism in the Novels of B. P. Galdós: Charity.* New York: Las Américas, 1969.

——. "The Benefactor in the Novels of Galdós." *Revista de Estudios Hispánicos* 2.2 (1968): 241–49.

Pardo Bazán, Emilia. "La mujer española." *La mujer española,* 1889, ed. Leda Schiavo, 25–70. 1976. Reprint Madrid: Editora Nacional, 1981.

Parker, Alexander A. "*Nazarín,* or the Passion of Our Lord Jesus Christ According to Galdós." *Anales Galdosianos* 2 (1967): 83–101.

Pascual de Sanjuan, Pilar, and Jaime Viñas y Cusí. *La educación de la mujer: Tratado de pedagogía para las maestras de primera enseñanza y aspirantes al magisterio.* Prologue by the Censor, Eduardo María Vilarrasa. Barcelona: Antonio J. Bastinos, 1896.

Payne, Stanley. *Spanish Catholicism: An Historical Overview.* Madison: University of Wisconsin Press, 1984.

——. *The Spanish Civil War, the Soviet Union, and Communism.* New Haven: Yale University Press, 2004.

Peckham, Morse. *Beyond the Tragic Vision.* 2d printing. New York: George Braziller, 1962.

Pecora, Vincent P. *Secularization and Cultural Criticism: Religion, Nation, and Modernity.* Chicago: University of Chicago Press, 2006.

Pedraza, Juan de. *Summa de casos de consciencia.* 1568. Reprint Bilbao: Mathias Mares, 1579.

Peiró, P. Francisco. *El problema religioso-social de España.* Madrid: Razón y Fe, 1936.

Pennington, Eric. "*Mosén Millán,* Christ Figure vs. Christianity." *USF Language Quarterly* 26.3–4 (1988): 22–24.

Penuel, Arnold. *Charity in the Novels of Galdós.* Athens: University of Georgia Press, 1972.

Peñuelas, Marcelino C. *Conversaciones con Ramón J. Sender.* Madrid: Emesa, 1970.

Pereira Muro, Carmen. "De la crisis del pensamiento liberal al pensamiento poético: Subirats, Zambrano y la figura del Padre Feijoo en la modernidad española." *Journal of Spanish Cultural Studies* 8.3 (2007): 317–40.

Perera, Arturo. *La confesión de un confesor (De una causa célebre).* Carta-prólogo de José Canalejas. Madrid: R. Velasco, Imp., n.d. [1898; 1908].

Pérez, Dionisio. *Jesús (Memorias de un jesuita novicio).* 1898. Reprint Madrid: Editorial Pueyo, 1932.

Pérez, Joseph. "L'Espagne et la modernité." *Aux origines du retard économique de l'Espagne XVIe–XIXe siècles,* 155–69. Paris: Éditions du CNRS, 1983.

Pérez de Ayala, Ramón. *A.M.D.G.* Madrid: Mundo Latino, 1923.

Pérez Estévez, Rosa María. *El problema de los vagos en la España del siglo XVIII.* Madrid: Confederación Española de Cajas de Ahorros, 1976.

Pérez Galdós, Benito. *Ángel Guerra. Obras completas* 5. Edited by Federico Carlos Sáinz de Robles. Madrid: Aguilar, 1970.

——. *Los artículos de Galdós en "La Nación" 1865–1866, 1868.* Edited by William H. Shoemaker. Madrid: Ínsula, 1972.

———. *Las cartas desconocidas de Galdós en "La Prensa" de Buenos Aires.* Edited by William H. Shoemaker. Madrid: Ediciones Cultura Hispánica, 1973.

———. *La desheredada.* Edited by Germán Gullón. Madrid: Cátedra, 2000.

———. *Doña Perfecta.* 2d ed. Edited by Rodolfo Cardona. Madrid: Cátedra, 1984.

———. *Un faccioso más y algunos frailes menos.* Madrid: Alianza, 2005.

———. *Fortunata and Jacinta: Two Stories of Married Women.* Translated by Agnes Moncy Gullón. Athens: University of Georgia Press, 1986.

———. *Fortunata y Jacinta: Dos historias de casadas.* 2 vols. Edited by Francisco Caudet. Madrid: Cátedra, 1983.

———. *Halma. Obras completas* 5. Edited by Federico Carlos Sáinz de Robles. Madrid: Aguilar, 1970.

———. *Marianela. Obras completas* 4. 7th ed. Edited by Federico Carlos Sáinz de Robles. Madrid: Aguilar, 1969.

———. *Misericordia.* Edited by Luciano García Lorenzo. Madrid: Cátedra, 1982.

———. "La moral y los negocios de estado." *Política española. Obras inéditas,* ed. Alberto Ghiraldo, 3: 299–310. Madrid: Renacimiento, 1923.

———. *Nazarín. Obras completas* 5. Edited by Federico Carlos Sáinz de Robles. Madrid: Aguilar, 1970.

———. "El 1º de Mayo." *Política española. Obras inéditas,* ed. Alberto Ghiraldo, 4: 267–77. Madrid: Renacimiento, 1923.

———. "Santos modernos." Lamet 255–60.

———. "Solidaridad." *Fisonomías sociales. Obras inéditas,* ed. Alberto Ghiraldo, 1: 127–31. Madrid: Renacimiento, 1923.

Pérez Gutiérrez, Francisco. *El problema religioso en la generación de 1868: "La leyenda de Dios."* Madrid: Taurus, 1975.

Pérez Ledesma, Manuel. "Studies on Anticlericalism in Contemporary Spain." *International Review of Social History* 46 (2001): 227–55.

Pérez de Urbel, Fray Justo. *Los mártires de la iglesia (Testigos de su fe).* Barcelona: AHR, 1956.

Peters, Edward. *Torture.* Expanded ed. Philadelphia: University of Pennsylvania Press, 1996.

Peterson, Anna L. *Martyrdom and the Politics of Religion: Progressive Catholicism in El Salvador's Civil War.* Albany: State University of New York Press, 1997.

Peterson, M. Jeanne. "The Victorian Governess: Status Incongruence in Family and Society." *Suffer and Be Still: Women in the Victorian Age,* ed. Martha Vicinus, 3–19. Bloomington: Indiana University Press, 1972.

Pi y Molist, Emilio. *Examen médico del siguiente pasage de Chateaubriand en sus "Mémoires d'outre-tombe"; 'Lejos de mi cadáver la sacrílega autopsia . . .'; o sea Consideraciones sobre el impulso y carácter comunicados por la anatomía a la medicina moderna. Memoria.* Barcelona: Imprenta y Librería Politécnica de Tomás Gorchs, 1852.

Picón, Jacinto Octavio. *El enemigo.* Madrid: Est. Tip. de El Correo, 1887.

Pius IX. *Syllabus.* Buenos Aires: Cursos de Cultura Católica, 1934.

Pla y Deniel, Enrique (Bishop of Salamanca). "Las dos ciudades." Carta pastoral, 30 September 1936. Montero Moreno 688–708.

Plato. *The Republic.* Translated and introduction by R. E. Allen. New Haven: Yale University Press, 2006.

Pohle, Joseph. *The Sacraments: A Dogmatic Treatise* 3. Adapted and edited by Arthur Preuss. 1917. Reprint St. Louis: B. Herder, 1956.

Pomares, Laureano. "Mula 13 de noviembre de 1849." *La Linterna Mágica,* 12ª función (1 December 1849): 92–93.

Pope, Randolph. "Intrusos en el templo: Profanando tumbas en las *Noches lúgubres.*" *Dieciocho: Hispanic Enlightenment* 21.1 (1998): 21–36.

Portero Molina, José Antonio. *Púlpito e ideología en la España del siglo XIX.* Zaragoza: Libros Pórtico, 1978.

Le Prince de Beaumont, Jeanne-Marie. *Almacén de las señoritas adolescentes, o diálogos de una sabia directora con sus nobles discípulas.* Para servir de continuación al *Almacén de los niños.* Translated by Plácido Barco López. Madrid: Por la Viuda de Barco López, 1804.

Prochaska, Frank. *The Voluntary Impulse: Philanthropy in Modern Britain.* London: Faber and Faber, 1988.

Promey, Sally M. "The 'Return' of Religion in the Scholarship of American Art." *Art Bulletin* 85 (2003): 581–603.

Puche, Federico, and José Roger. "Solicitud." *La Linterna Mágica,* 12ª función (1 December 1849): 91–92.

Puente, Luis de la. *Meditaciones breves sobre temas de los ejercicios de san Ignacio. Obras escogidas.* Biblioteca de Autores Españoles 111. Edited by Camilo María Abad. Madrid: Atlas, 1958.

———. *Sentimientos y avisos espirituales. Obras escogidas.* Biblioteca de Autores Españoles 111. Edited by Camilo María Abad. Madrid: Atlas, 1958.

Rabaté, Colette. "La familia popular en la trilogía de Wenceslao Ayguals de Izco." *Historia social y literatura: Familia y clases populares en España (siglos XVIII–XIX),* ed. Roberto Fernández and Jacques Soubeyroux, 209–29. Lleida and Saint-Étienne: Milenio/Université Jean Monnet, 2001.

———. "Wenceslao Ayguals de Izco: De 'l'Eugène Sue espagnol' au 'regénérateur' du roman national." *Le métissage culturel en Espagne,* ed. Jean-René Aymes and Serge Salaün, 119–35. Paris: Presses de la Sorbonne Nouvelle, 2001.

Radcliffe, Ann. *The Italian or, the Confessional of the Black Penitents.* Edited by Frederick Garber. London: Oxford University Press, 1970.

Raguer, Hilari. *La espada y la cruz (La Iglesia 1936–1939).* Barcelona: Bruguera, 1977.

Rahner, Hugo. "Notes on the Spiritual Exercises." *Woodstock Letters* 85 (1956): 281–336.

Ranzato, Gabriele. *The Spanish Civil War.* Translated by Janet Sethre Paxia. New York: Interlink Books, 1999.

Ravitch, Norman. "Catholicism in Crisis: The Impact of the French Revolution on the Thought of the Abbé Adrien Lamourette." *Cahiers internationaux d'histoire économique et sociale* 9 (1978): 354–85.

Rawlings, Helen. *Church, Religion and Society in Early Modern Spain.* New York: Palgrave, 2002.

Regler, Gustav. *The Great Crusade.* Preface by Ernest Hemingway. Translated by Whittaker Chambers and Barrows Mussey. New York: Longmans, Green, 1940.

Resina, Joan Ramon. "Ana Ozores's Nerves." *Hispanic Review* 71 (2003): 229–52.

Ressot, Jean-Pierre. "Les espagnols face à leur guerre: La solution négativiste de Ramón J. Sender." *Imprévue* 2 (1986): 87–98.

Revuelta González, Manuel. "El anticlericalismo español en el siglo XIX." Aubert 155–78.

———, ed. *El anticlericalismo español en sus documentos.* Barcelona: Ariel, 1999.

Ribbans, Geoffrey. *Conflicts and Conciliations: The Evolution of Galdós's "Fortunata y Jacinta."* West Lafayette: Purdue University Press, 1997.

Ribot i Fontseré, Antonio. "Juicio crítico." Ayguals de Izco, *María,* 2: 393–95.

Ricard, Robert. "Notas y materiales para el estudio del 'socratismo cristiano' en Santa Teresa y en los espirituales españoles." *Estudios de literatura religiosa española,* 22–147. Madrid: Gredos, 1964.

Richards, Michael. "Doctrine and Politics in Nationalist Spain." Valis, *Teaching Representations,* 88–98.

———. *A Time of Silence: Civil War and the Culture of Repression in Franco's Spain, 1936–1945.* Cambridge: Cambridge University Press, 1998.

Richburg, Keith B. "Church's Influence Waning in Once Fervently Catholic Spain." *Washington Post* (11 April 2005): A15.

Richmond, Carolyn. "En torno al vacío: La mujer, idea hecha carne de ficción, en *La Regenta* de Clarín." *Realismo y naturalismo en España en la segunda mitad del siglo XIX,* ed. Yvan Lissorgues, 341–67. Barcelona: Anthropos, 1988.

———. "*La Regenta,* mirada y vista." *Ínsula,* no. 451 (June 1984): 4.

Ríos-Font, Wadda C. *The Canon and the Archive: Configuring Literature in Modern Spain.* Lewisburg, Pa.: Bucknell University Press, 2004.

Ripalda, Jerónimo de. *Catecismo y exposicion breve de la doctrina christiana.* 1591. Reprint Madrid: Antonio de Sancha, 1783.

Rivas, Manuel. *The Carpenter's Pencil.* Translated by Jonathan Dunne. Woodstock, N.Y.: Overlook Press, 2001.

———. *El lápiz del carpintero.* Madrid: Alfaguara, 1998.

Robert, Marthe. *Origins of the Novel.* Translated by Sacha Rabinovitch. 1972. Reprint Bloomington: Indiana University Press, 1980.

Roberts, Gemma. "Notas sobre el realismo psicológico de *La Regenta.*" *Archivum* 18 (1968): 189–202.

Robinson, Richard A. H. *The Origins of Franco's Spain: The Right, the Republic and Revolution, 1931–1936.* Newton Abbot, U.K.: David and Charles, 1970.

Rodero, Jesús. "*Fortunata y Jacinta:* Heteroglosia y polifonía en el discurso del narrador." *Anales Galdosianos* 29–30 (1994–95): 75–85.

Rodgers, Eamonn. "Religion in a Liberal Polity: Galdós Revisited." *Belief and Unbelief in Hispanic Literature,* ed. Helen Wing and John Jones, 72–76. Papers from a Conference at the University of Hull, 12–13 December 1994. Warminster: Aris and Phillips, 1995.

Rodríguez, Rodney. "Continuity and Innovation in the Spanish Novel: 1700–1833." *Studies in Eighteenth-Century Spanish Literature and Romanticism in Honor of John Clarkson Dowling,* ed. Douglas and Linda Jane Barnette, 49–63. Newark, Del.: Juan de la Cuesta, 1985.

Rodríguez, Alfred, and Soledad García Sprackling. "Mauricia *La Dura* y Guillermina Pacheco: Su función simbólica." *Iris* (Montpellier) (1994): 239–48.

Rodríguez-Puértolas, Julio. "La degollina de frailes en el Madrid de 1834. Tres puntos de vista: Ayguals de Izco, Galdós, Baroja." *Galdós: Burguesía y revolución, 177–202.* Madrid: Turner, 1975.

Rogers, Douglass. "Charity in Galdós." *Anales Galdosianos* 9 (1974): 169–73.

Román Gutiérrez, Isabel. *Persona y forma: Una historia interna de la novela española del siglo XIX. 2. La novela realista.* Sevilla: Alfar, 1988.

Romero Tobar, Leonardo. "Forma y contenido en la novela popular: Ayguals de Izco." *Prohemio* 3 (April 1972): 45–90.

———. *La novela popular española del siglo XIX.* Madrid: Ariel, 1976.

Rose, Hugh James. *Untrodden Spain, and Her Black Country; Being Sketches of the Life and Character of the Spaniard of the Interior.* 2 vols. 2d ed. London: Samuel Tinsley, 1875.

Rousseau, Jean-Jacques. *Les confessions.* 2 vols. Edited by Jean Guéhenno. Paris: Gallimard, 1969.

Rowell, Geoffrey. *Hell and the Victorians.* Oxford: Clarendon Press, 1974.

Rubia Barcia, José. "What's in a Name: Américo Castro (y Quesada)." *Américo Castro and the Meaning of Spanish Civilization,* ed. J. Rubia Barcia, 3–22. Berkeley: University of California Press, 1976.

Rubin, Miri. *Corpus Christi: The Eucharist in Late Medieval Culture.* Cambridge: Cambridge University Press, 1991.

Rueda, Ana. *Cartas sin lacrar: La novela epistolar y la España Ilustrada 1789–1840.* Madrid/Frankfurt am Main: Iberoamericana/Vervuert, 2001.

Rufat, Ramón. "El sentimiento religioso en Ramón J. Sender." *Alazet* 4 (1992): 181–86.

Ruiz Pérez, Jesús. "República y anarquía: El pensamiento político de Eduardo Barriobero (1875–1939)." *Berceo* (Logroño) 144 (2003): 177–202.

Runzo, Joseph, ed. *Is God Real?* Houndmills, Basingstoke: Macmillan, 1993.

———. "Introduction." Runzo xiii–xxiii.

Russell, Robert A. "The Christ Figure in *Misericordia.*" *Anales Galdosianos* 2 (1967): 103–30.

Saenz, Hilario S. "Visión galdosiana de la religiosidad de los españoles." *Hispania* 20.3 (1937): 235–42.

Sagra, Ramón de la. "Aforismos sociales (1849)." Elorza, *Socialismo utópico español,* 78–91.

———. *Antonio y Rita ó los niños mendigos.* Madrid: Imprenta del Colegio de Sordomudos, 1840.

———. "Lecciones de economía social, dadas en el Ateneo literario y científico de Madrid (1840)." Elorza, *Socialismo utópico español,* 70–78.

Saint-Simon, Henri de. *"Le nouveau christianisme" et les écrits sur la religion.* Edited by H[enri] Desroche. Paris: Éditions du Seuil, 1969.

Sales, Saint Francis de. *Introducción a la vida devota.* Translated by Francisco de Cubillas Donyague. Madrid: Imprenta Real de la Gazeta, 1764.

Salm, Luke. *The Martyrs of Turón and Tarragona: The De La Salle Brothers in Spain 1934–1939.* Romeoville, Ill.: Christian Brothers, 1990.

Salvany, Juan Tomás. "La confesión." *Poesías,* 9. Madrid: Librería de D. Francisco Yravedra, 1877.

Sánchez, José. *The Spanish Civil War as a Religious Tragedy.* Notre Dame: University of Notre Dame Press, 1987.

Sánchez, Manuel Diego. "Castilla mística: Fisonomía espiritual de Francisca del Valle." *Revista de Espiritualidad* 45 (1986): 605–29.

Sánchez, Sarah. *Fact and Fiction: Representations of the Asturian Revolution (1934–1938).* Leeds: Maney Publishing for the Modern Humanities Research Association, 2003.

Sánchez-Blanco Parody, Francisco. "Una ética secular: La amistad entre los ilustrados." *Cuadernos de Estudio del Siglo XVIII,* no. 2 (1992): 97–116.

Sánchez-Eppler, Benigno. "Stakes: The Sexual Vulnerability of the Reader in *La Regenta.*" *Romanic Review* 78 (1987): 202–17.

Sánchez Pérez, José Augusto. *El culto mariano en España.* Madrid: Consejo Superior de Investigaciones Científicas, 1943.

Santi, Angelo de. *Les litanies de la Sainte Vierge: Étude historique et critique.* Translated by A. Boudinhon. 1897. Reprint Paris: P. Lethielleux, Libraire-Éditeur, 1900.

———. "Litany of Loreto." *Catholic Encyclopedia.*

Santiáñez, Nil. "Prologue" ("*Imán* y la escritura de guerra"). *Imán* by Ramón J. Sender.

Sardá y Salvany, Félix. *El liberalismo es pecado: Cuestiones candentes.* 9th ed. 1884. Reprint Madrid: E.P.C., 1936.

Sarrailh, Jean. *La crise religieuse en Espagne à la fin du XVIIIe siècle.* Taylorian Lecture 1951. Oxford: Oxford at the Clarendon Press, 1951.

Sartre, Jean-Paul. *La nausée.* 1938. Reprint Paris: Livre de Poche, 1962.

Savaiano, Eugene. *An Historical Justification of the Anticlericalism of Galdós and Alas.* Wichita, Kan.: Wichita State University Studies 24, 1952.

Sayol y Echevarría, José. *Eucologio romano: Devocionario completo.* 6th ed. Barcelona: Llorens Hermanos, 1877.

Scarry, Elaine. *The Body in Pain: The Making and Unmaking of the World.* New York: Oxford University Press, 1985.

Scatori, Stephen. *La idea religiosa en la obra de Benito Pérez Galdós.* Thèse de doctorat d'université. Toulouse: Imprimerie et Librairie Édouard Privat, 1926.

Schillebeeckx, E[dward]. *Christ the Sacrament of the Encounter with God.* Foreword by Cornelius Ernst. 1960. Reprint Kansas City: Sheed and Ward, 1963.

Schumacher, John N. "Integrism: A Study in Nineteenth-Century Spanish Politico-Religious Thought." *Catholic Historical Review* 48 (1962–63): 343–64.

Sebold, Russell P. *Cadalso: El primer romántico 'europeo' de España.* Madrid: Gredos, 1974.

———. "La continuidad de la novela española." *De ilustrados y románticos,* 121–25. Madrid: Ediciones El Museo Universal, 1992.

———. *En el principio del movimiento realista: Credo y novelística de Ayguals de Izco.* Madrid: Cátedra, 2007.

———. "Introducción." *Fray Gerundio de Campazas* 1 by José Francisco de Isla. Madrid: Espasa-Calpe, 1960–64.

———. "Introducción." *Noches lúgubres* by José Cadalso. Madrid: Taurus, 1993.

———. *La novela romántica en España: Entre libro de caballerías y novela moderna.* Salamanca: Ediciones Universidad de Salamanca, 2002.

——. "Novelas de 'muchos Cervantes': Olavide y el realismo." *Anales de Literatura Española,* no. 11 (1995): 173–91.

——. "Sadismo y sensibilidad en *Cornelia Bororquia o la víctima de la Inquisición* (1801), de Luis Gutiérrez." *La novela romántica en España,* 55–70.

Segni, Lothario dei (Innocent III). *On the Misery of the Human Condition.* Translated by Margaret Mary Dietz. Edited by Donald R. Howard. Indianapolis: Bobbs-Merrill Company, 1969.

Segura, Florencio. "Los directores de *Razón y Fe.*" *Razón y Fe* 204 (September 1981): 167–75.

Sender, Ramón J. "Al hermano Manuel." *Rimas compulsivas (Antología poética),* 135–38. Edited by Francisco Carrasquer Launed. Ferrol: Esquío, 1998.

——. *Casas Viejas.* Edited by José Domingo Dueñas and Antonio Pérez Lasheras. Estudio preliminar by Ignacio Martínez de Pisón. Zaragoza: Prensas Universitarias/Instituto de Estudios Altoaragoneses, 2004.

——. *Counter-Attack in Spain.* Translated by Peter Chalmers Mitchell. Boston: Houghton Mifflin, 1937.

——. *Ensayos sobre el infringimiento cristiano.* Madrid: Editora Nacional, 1975.

——. *Imán.* Edited by Nil Santiáñez. Barcelona: Crítica, 2006.

——. *El problema religioso en Méjico: Católicos y cristianos.* Madrid: Cenit, 1928.

——. *La república y la cuestión religiosa.* Barcelona: Tipografía Cosmos, 1932.

——. *Requiem for a Spanish Peasant.* Translated by Elinor Randall. Preface by Mair José Benardete. New York: Las Américas, 1960.

——. *Réquiem por un campesino español.* Barcelona: Destino, 1991.

——. *Seven Red Sundays.* Translated by Peter Chalmers Mitchell. Chicago: Ivan R. Dee, 1990.

——. *Siete domingos rojos.* Buenos Aires: Proyección, 1970.

Sepúlveda, Enrique. "La vida moderna. La institutriz (Ins-te-too-tore)." *La vida en Madrid en 1888* (año cuarto), 209–16. 6th ed. Madrid: Est. Tip. de Ricardo Fe, 1889.

Serrano Asenjo, Enrique. "Historia y punición: Ángel Valbuena Prat, depurado." *Revista de Literatura* 68, no. 135 (2006): 249–59.

Shaw, D. L. "The Anti-Romantic Reaction in Spain." *Modern Language Review* 63.3 (1968): 606–11.

Shaw, Rafael. *Spain from Within.* New York: Frederick A. Stokes, 1910.

Sherwood, Joan. *Poverty in Eighteenth-Century Spain: The Women and Children of the Inclusa.* Toronto: University of Toronto Press, 1988.

Shoemaker, William H. *God's Role and His Religion in Galdós' Novels: 1876–1888.* Valencia: Albatrós Ediciones/Hispanófila, 1988.

Shorto, Russell. "Keeping the Faith." *New York Times* (8 April 2007). www.nytimes.com

Shubert, Adrian. "Between Documentary and Propaganda: Teaching *The Spanish Earth.*" Valis, *Teaching Representations,* 99–107.

——. " 'Charity Properly Understood': Changing Ideas about Poor Relief in Liberal Spain." *Comparative Studies in Society and History* 33.1 (1991): 36–55.

Sieber, Harry. "*Don Quixote* and the Art of Reading." Beall-Russell Lectures in the Humanities, 15 September 1997. Waco: Baylor University, [1998].

——. *Language and Society in "La vida de Lazarillo de Tormes."* Baltimore: Johns Hopkins University Press, 1978.

Sieburth, Stephanie. *Inventing High and Low: Literature, Mass Culture, and Uneven Modernity in Spain.* Durham: Duke University Press, 1994.

Silverman, Debora. *Van Gogh and Gauguin: The Search for Sacred Art.* New York: Farrar, Straus and Giroux, 2000.

Simpson, Eileen. *Orphans: Real and Imaginary.* New York: New American Library, 1987.

Singleton, Mack. "*Don Quixote:* Sin, Grace, and Redemption." *Estudios literarios de hispanistas norteamericanos dedicados a Helmut Hatzfeld con motivo de su 80 aniversario,* ed. Josep M. Sola-Solé, Alessandro Crisafulli and Bruno Damiani, 197–207. Barcelona: Ediciones Hispam, 1974.

Slater, Candace. *City Steeple, City Streets: Saints' Tales from Granada and a Changing Spain.* Berkeley: University of California Press, 1990.

Smiles, Samuel. *Self-Help.* 1859. Reprint New York: Lovell, Coryell, n.d.

——. *Thrift.* Chicago: M. A. Donohue, [1875].

Smith, Adam. *The Theory of Moral Sentiments.* Amherst, N.Y.: Prometheus Books, 2000.

Smith, Alan E. *Galdós y la imaginación mitológica.* Madrid: Cátedra, 2005.

Smith, Bonnie G. *Ladies of the Leisure Class: The Bourgeoises of Northern France in the Nineteenth Century.* Princeton: Princeton University Press, 1981.

Smith, Graeme. *A Short History of Secularism.* London: I. B. Tauris, 2008.

Sobejano, Gonzalo. *Clarín en su obra ejemplar.* Madrid: Castalia, 1985.

——. "Clarín y el sentimiento de la Virgen." *Clarín crítico, Alas novelador (Catorce estudios),* 109–36. Murcia: Real Academia Alfonso X el Sabio, 2007.

Solá, Emilio (pseud.). *Misterios del hospital.* Barcelona: Guillermo Parera, Librero, n.d. [1883].

Soubeyroux, Jacques. "Una figura clave de la Ilustración española: Pedro Antonio Sánchez (Don Antonio Filántropo)." *Actas del VI Congreso Internacional de Hispanistas.* ed. Alan M. Gordon and Evelyn Rugg, 723–26. Toronto: Department of Spanish and Portuguese, University of Toronto, 1980.

——. *Paupérisme et rapports sociaux à Madrid au XVIIIème siècle.* 2 vols. Paris and Lille: Librairie Honoré Champion/Université de Lille III, 1978.

Souchy Bauer, Agustín. *Entre los campesinos de Aragón: El comunismo libertario en las comarcas liberadas.* Prologue by Sam Dolgoff. Barcelona: Tusquets, 1977.

——. *With the Peasants of Aragon: Libertarian Communism in a Liberated Area of Spain.* Translated by Abe Bluestein. Minor revisions by Ed Stamm. Lawrence, Kan.: Ed Stamm, 1996.

The Spanish Earth. Directed by Joris Ivens, 1937.

Sprengnether, Madelon. "Enforcing Oedipus: Freud and Dora." *The (M)other Tongue: Essays in Feminist Psychoanalytic Interpretation,* ed. Shirley Nelson Garner, Claire Kahane, and Madelon Sprengnether, 51–71. Ithaca: Cornell University Press, 1985.

Steinmueller, John E., and Kathryn Sullivan. *Catholic Biblical Encyclopedia: New Testament.* New York: Joseph F. Wagner, 1950.

Stern, J. P. "*Fortunata y Jacinta* in the Context of European Realism." *Textos y contextos de Galdós,* ed. John W. Kronik and Harriet S. Turner, 17–36. Madrid: Castalia, 1994.

Stoichita, Victor I. *Visionary Experience in the Golden Age of Spanish Art.* London: Reaktion Books, 1995.

Stradling, Robert. *History and Legend: Writing the International Brigades.* Cardiff: University of Wales Press, 2003.

Stratton, Suzanne L. *The Immaculate Conception in Spanish Art.* Cambridge: Cambridge University Press, 1994.

Suárez, Federico. *Santiago Masarnau y las Conferencias de San Vicente de Paúl.* Madrid: Rialp, 1994.

Sue, Eugène. *The Mysteries of Paris.* New York: Walter J. Black, n.d.

———. *The Wandering Jew.* New York: Modern Library, n.d.

Surwillo, Lisa. "Representing the Slave Trader: *Haley* and the Slave Ship; or, Spain's *Uncle Tom's Cabin.*" *PMLA* 120 (2005): 768–82.

Talavera, Hernando de. *Breve forma de confesar reduciendo todos los pecados mortales y veniales a los diez mandamientos.* Mir 3–35.

———. *De murmurar ó mal decir.* Mir 47–56.

———. *En qué manera se deve haver la persona que ha de comulgar.* Mir 36–46.

Tamayo y Baus, Manuel. *Los hombres de bien.* 1870. *Obras completas* 4. Madrid: Est. Tip. "Sucesores de Rivadeneyra," 1900.

Tambling, Jeremy. *Confession: Sexuality, Sin, the Subject.* Manchester: Manchester University Press, 1990.

Tarr, F. Courtney. "Reconstruction of a Decisive Period in Larra's Life (May–November, 1836)." *Hispanic Review* 5.1 (1937): 1–24.

Témime, Émile. "Études des résistances mentales à l'évolution économique libérale et à la transformation vers une société industrielle." *Permanences, émergences et résurgences culturelles dans le monde ibérique et ibéro-américain,* 39–56. Actes du XVIe Congrès National de la Société des Hispanistes Français (Aix-en-Provence 15–17 mars 1980). Aix-en-Provence: Université de Provence, 1981.

ten Brink Goldsmith, Jane. "Jesuit Iconography: The Evolution of a Visual Idiom." *Jesuit Art in North American Collections* by ten Brink Goldsmith et al., 16–21. Milwaukee: Patrick and Beatrice Hagerty Museum of Art, Marquette University, 1991.

Tenorio, José María. "El mendigo." *Los españoles pintados por sí mismos* 1: 301–09. Madrid: I[gnacio] Boix Editor, 1843.

Teresa de Jesús, Saint. *Libro de su vida.* Garden City: Doubleday, 1961.

Thion Soriano-Mollá, Dolores. "*Limosna,* l'album littéraire et artistique d'Antonio Maura." *Hommage à Carlos Serrano,* ed. Annie Molinié, Marie-Claire Zimmermann, and Michel Ralle, 2: 349–61. Paris: Éditions Hispaniques, Université Paris-Sorbonne (Paris IV), 2005.

Thompson, E. P. "Eighteenth-Century English Society: Class Struggle without Class?" *Social History* 3.2 (1978): 133–65.

Thomson, Guy. "Garibaldi and the Legacy of the Revolutions of 1848 in Southern Spain." *European History Quarterly* 31 (2001): 353–95.

Thrower, James. *Religion: The Classical Theories.* Washington: Georgetown University Press, 1999.

Tierno Galván, Enrique. "Don Juan Valera, o el buen sentido." *Idealismo y pragmatismo en el siglo XIX español,* 95–129. Madrid: Tecnos, 1977.

———. "Formas y modos de vida en torno a la revolución de 1848." *Revista de Estudios Políticos* 26, no. 46 (1949): 15–64.

———, ed. *Leyes políticas españolas fundamentales (1808–1936)*. Madrid: Tecnos, 1968.

Tisa, John, ed. *The Palette and the Flame: Posters of the Spanish Civil War*. New York: International Publishers, 1979.

Toscano Liria, Teresa. *Retórica e ideología de la Generación de 1868 en la obra de Galdós*. Madrid: Pliegos, 1993.

Tracy, David. *The Analogical Imagination: Christian Theology and the Culture of Pluralism*. New York: Crossroad, 1981.

Trinidad Fernández, Pedro. "Asistencia y previsión social en el siglo XVIII." *De la beneficencia*, 89–115.

Tsuchiya, Akiko. " 'Las Micaelas por fuera y por dentro': Discipline and Resistance in *Fortunata y Jacinta*." *A Sesquicentennial Tribute to Galdós 1843–1993*, ed. Linda M. Willem, 56–71. Newark, Del.: Juan de la Cuesta, 1993.

Tuckerman, Joseph. "Introduction." De Gérando, *Visitor* 1–30.

———. *On the Elevation of the Poor: A Selection from His Reports as Minister at Large in Boston*. Introduction by Edward E. Hale. 1874. Reprint New York: Arno P and The New York Times, 1971.

Turner, Harriet S. *Benito Pérez Galdós: "Fortunata and Jacinta."* Cambridge: Cambridge University Press, 1992.

———. "Toward a Poetics of Realism." *Letras Peninsulares* 13.1 (spring 2000): 11–23.

———, and Adelaida López de Martínez, ed. *The Cambridge Companion to the Spanish Novel from 1600 to the Present*. Cambridge: Cambridge University Press, 2003.

Uceda, Julia. "Realismo y esencias en Ramón J. Sender." *Ramón J. Sender: In Memoriam*, ed. José-Carlos Mainer, 113–25. Zaragoza: Diputación General de Aragón/Ayuntamiento de Zaragoza/Institución "Fernando el Católico," 1983.

Ullman, Joan Connelly. *The Tragic Week: A Study of Anticlericalism in Spain, 1875–1912*. Cambridge: Harvard University Press, 1968.

Unamuno, Miguel de. *"Mi religión" y otros ensayos breves*, 9–15. 5th ed. Madrid: Espasa-Calpe, 1968.

———. "Prólogo." *Tres novelas ejemplares y un prólogo*, 9–28. Madrid: Calpe, 1920.

———. *San Manuel Bueno, mártir*. Edited by Mario Valdés. Madrid: Cátedra, 1985.

Urbina, Eduardo. "Mesías y redentores: Constante estructural y motivo temático en *Fortunata y Jacinta*." *Bulletin Hispanique* 83, nos. 3–4 (1981): 379–98.

Uría, Jorge. "La enseñanza del catecismo en Asturias en los inicios del siglo XX." Aymes et al. 61–88.

Vagrancy and Public Charities in Foreign Countries. Special Consular Reports. Washington: Government Printing Office, 1893.

Valbuena Prat, Ángel. *El sentido católico en la literatura española*. Zaragoza: Ediciones Partenón, 1940.

Valentini, Norberto, and Clara di Meglio. *Sex and the Confessional*. Translated by Melton S. Davis. London: Hutchinson, 1974.

Valera, Juan. *Correspondencia. 2 (Años 1862–1875)*. Edited by Leonardo Romero Tobar, María Ángeles Ezama Gil, and Enrique Serrano Asenjo. Madrid: Castalia, 2003.

———. "De la doctrina del progreso con relación a la doctrina cristiana." *Estudios críticos sobre literatura, política y costumbres de nuestros días* 1: 63–118. Madrid: Librerías de A. Durán, 1864.

Vales Failde, Javier. *Ernestina Manuel de Villena.* Madrid: Imp. del Asilo de Huérfanos del Sagrado Corazón de Jesús, 1908.

Valis, Noël. "Aspects of an Improper Birth: Clarín's *La Regenta.*" *New Hispanisms: Literature, Culture, Theory,* ed. Mark I. Millington and Paul Julian Smith, 96–126. Ottawa: Dovehouse, 1994.

——. *The Culture of Cursilería: Bad Taste, Kitsch, and Class in Modern Spain.* Durham: Duke University Press, 2002.

——. *The Decadent Vision in Leopoldo Alas: A Study of "La Regenta" and "Su único hijo."* Baton Rouge: Louisiana State University Press, 1981.

——. "La huella del cardenal Wiseman en España." *Boletín de la Real Academia Española* 64 (September–December 1984): 423–49.

——. *Reading the Nineteenth-Century Spanish Novel: Selected Essays.* Newark, Del.: Juan de la Cuesta, 2005.

——. Review of *Properties of Modernity: Romantic Spain, Modern Europe, and the Legacies of Empire* by Michael Iarocci. *Revista Hispánica Moderna* 60.1 (2007): 111–13.

——, ed. *Teaching Representations of the Spanish Civil War.* New York: Modern Language Association, 2007.

Valle, Enid M. "La estructura narrativa de *El evangelio en triunfo* de Pablo de Olavide y Jáuregui." *Pen and Peruke: Spanish Literature of the Eighteenth Century,* ed. Monroe Z. Hafter, 135–51. Ann Arbor: Michigan Romance Studies 12, 1992.

Valle, Francisca Javiera del. *About the Holy Spirit.* Princeton: Scepter, 1998.

Van Buren, Jane Silverman. *The Modernist Madonna: Semiotics of the Maternal Metaphor.* Bloomington and London: Indiana University Press/Karnac Books, 1989.

Vaquero Iglesias, Julio Antonio. *Muerte e ideología en la Asturias del siglo XIX.* Madrid: Siglo XXI de España, 1991.

Varela, Javier. *La novela de España: Los intelectuales y el problema español.* Madrid: Taurus, 1999.

Varela, José Luis. "Lamennais en la evolución ideológica de Larra." *Hispanic Review* 48 (1980): 287–306.

Varey, J. E. "Charity in *Misericordia.*" *Galdós Studies,* ed. J. E. Varey, 164–94. London: Tamesis Books, 1970.

Verheyden, Jack. "Ludwig Feuerbach's Philosophy of God." Runzo 19–39.

Vicenti, Alfredo. "Una novela: *La Regenta.*" 1885. *"La Regenta" de Clarín y la crítica de su tiempo* by María José Tintoré, 128–37. Barcelona: Lumen, 1987.

Viñas, José María. "Introducción general." *Escritos autobiográficos* by Antonio María Claret. 2d ed. Edited by J. M. Viñas and Jesús Bermejo. Madrid: Biblioteca de Autores Cristianos, 1981.

Vincent, Mary. *Catholicism in the Second Spanish Republic: Religion and Politics in Salamanca, 1930–1936.* Oxford: Clarendon Press, 1996.

——. "The 'Keys of the Kingdom': Religious Violence in the Spanish Civil War, July–August 1936." Ealham and Richards 68–89.

——. "The Spanish Civil War as a Religious Conflict." Valis, *Teaching Representations,* 54–62.

Vives, Juan Luis. *The Education of a Christian Woman: A Sixteenth-Century Manual.* Edited and translated by Charles Fantazzi. Chicago: University of Chicago Press, 2000.

——. *On Assistance to the Poor.* Edited and translated by Alice Tobriner. Toronto: University of Toronto Press, 1999.

Voltaire. *Dictionnaire philosophique.* Edited by René Pomeau. Paris: Garnier-Flammarion, 1964.

Wach, Howard M. "Unitarian Philanthropy and Cultural Hegemony in Comparative Perspective: Manchester and Boston, 1827–1848." *Journal of Social History* 26.3 (1993): 539–57.

Ward, Bernardo. *Obra pía.* In *Proyecto económico: en que se proponen varias providencias, dirigidas a promover los intereses de España, con los medios y fondos necesarios para su plantificación,* 320–400. 2d impression. Madrid: D. Joachin Ibarra, Impresor de Cámara de S.M., 1779.

Ward, Keith. *Religion and Revelation: A Theology of Revelation in the World's Religions.* Oxford: Clarendon Press, 1994.

Wardropper, Bruce W. "Cadalso's *Noches lúgubres* and Literary Tradition." *Studies in Philology* 49 (1952): 619–30.

Warner, Marina. *Alone of All Her Sex: The Myth and the Cult of the Virgin Mary.* New York: Pocket Books, 1976.

——. *Monuments and Maidens: The Allegory of the Female Form.* London: Weidenfeld and Nicolson, 1985.

Warnock, Mary. "Imagination in Sartre." *British Journal of Aesthetics* 10 (1970): 323–36.

Weber, Alison P. "Religious Literature in Early Modern Spain." *Cambridge History of Spanish Literature,* ed. David T. Gies, 149–58. Cambridge: Cambridge University Press, 2004.

Weber, Frances Wyers. "The Dynamics of Motif in Leopoldo Alas' *La Regenta.*" *Romanic Review* 57 (1966): 188–99.

——. "Ideology and Religious Parody in the Novels of Leopoldo Alas." *Bulletin of Hispanic Studies* (Liverpool) 43 (1966): 197–208.

Weber, Max. "Science as a Vocation." *The Vocation Lectures. "Science as a Vocation." "Politics as a Vocation,"* ed. David Owen and Tracy B. Strong, 1–31. Translated by Rodney Livingstone. Indianapolis: Hackett, 2004.

Weil, Simone. *Waiting for God.* Translated by Emma Craufurd. Introduction by Leslie A. Fiedler. New York: Harper and Row, 1973.

Wellek, René. "The Concept of Realism in Literary Scholarship." *Concepts of Criticism,* 222–33. New Haven: Yale University Press, 1963.

Whiston, James. "The Materialism of Life: Religion in *Fortunata y Jacinta.*" *Anales Galdosianos* 14 (1979): 65–81.

——. *The Practice of Realism: Change and Creativity in the Manuscript of Galdós's "Fortunata y Jacinta."* Lewisburg, Pa.: Bucknell University Press, 2004.

Williams, Raymond. *The Country and the City.* New York: Oxford University Press, 1973.

——. *Keywords: A Vocabulary of Culture and Society.* Rev. ed. New York: Oxford University Press, 1985.

Wines, Frederick Howard. "Sociology and Philanthropy." *Annals of the American Academy of Political and Social Science* 12 (July 1898): 49–57.

Wiseman, Nicholas. "Spain." *Essays on Various Subjects* 3: 3–158. London: Charles Dolman, 1853.

Witte, Els. "The Battle for Monasteries, Cemeteries and Schools: Belgium." Clark and Kaiser 102–28.

Woolf, Stuart. *The Poor in Western Europe in the Eighteenth and Nineteenth Centuries.* London: Methuen, 1986.

Woolsey, Gamel. *Malaga Burning: An American Woman's Eyewitness Account of the Spanish Civil War.* Introduction by Zalin Grant. Paris: Pythia Press, 1998.

Wright, A. D. *Catholicism and Spanish Society under the Reign of Philip II, 1555–1598, and Philip III, 1598–1621.* Lewiston, N.Y.: Edwin Mellen Press, 1991.

Wright, Charles. "Relics." *New Yorker* (7 August 2000): 58–59.

Yetano, Ana. *La enseñanza religiosa en la España de la Restauración (1900–1920).* Barcelona: Anthropos, 1988.

Ynduráin, Francisco. *Galdós entre la novela y el folletín.* Madrid: Taurus, 1970.

Young, Edward. *The Complaint, or Night Thoughts.* Philadelphia: Jesper Harding, 1847.

Zambrano, María. *La confesión: Género literario.* 1943. Reprint Madrid: Mondadori, 1988.

———. *Pensamiento y poesía en la vida española.* Edited by Mercedes Gómez Blesa. Madrid: Biblioteca Nueva, 2004.

Zavala, Iris M. *Ideología y política en la novela española del siglo XIX.* Salamanca: Anaya, 1971.

———. *Románticos y socialistas: Prensa española del XIX.* Madrid: Siglo XXI de España, 1972.

———. "Socialismo y literatura: Ayguals de Izco y la novela española." *Revista de Occidente* 80 (1969): 167–88.

Zeldin, Theodore. "The Conflict of Moralities: Confession, Sin and Pleasure in the Nineteenth Century." *Conflicts in French Society: Anticlericalism, Education and Morals in the Nineteenth Century,* ed. Theodore Zeldin, 13–50. London: George Allen and Unwin, 1970.

Index

Abolicionista, El, 125

Alas, Leopoldo (Clarín) (chap. 3), 1–3, 6,
15, 19, 20, 245; authority and, 13, 47,
161, 162, 176; belief and, 1, 15, 152,
158–61, 281n27; Bonapartism and,
279n14; characters and, 117; Church/
State, view of, 159, 163; "Del naturalismo" and, 271n88; dogma, attitude
toward, 161; Flaubert and, 153, 154,
155, 193, 241; Gijón strike and, 48;
glossolalia and, 18, 160; history, use
of, 279n14; "inner God" and, 159;
Krausism, influence of, 158–59, 160,
283n62; labor unrest and, 48; Lagarrigue, view of, 278n163; Lamennais
and, 34; Larra and, 34; liberalism and,
1, 9, 13, 160, 161; "El libre examen y
nuestra literatura presente" and, 25,
271n88; Loyolan imagination and, 21,
284n75; *María, la hija de un jornalero*
and, 103; naturalism and, 55; "Para
vicios" and, 283n55; parodic discourse

and, 281n30; "El pecado original"
and, 278n6; "La pedagogía de los
jesuitas" and, 284n75; politics of religion and, 44; redemption and, 47, 153,
244; *La Regenta* and, 1–2, 13, 24, 44–
45, 51, 52, 70–71, 151–56, 163, 167–
71, 176–79, 181–94, 248n18,
279n11; religious crisis, 1, 34, 44; religious tolerance and, 159; social reform and, 47–48; Teresa de Jesús and,
45, 285n95; Valera and, 40; "Viaje redondo" and, 185, 194; visual element
in, 284n75

Alcampel, 223, 224

Alemán, Mateo, 239, 264n97, 264n99,
278n3, 296n9

Allen, Woody, 154–55

Alonso, Dámaso, 54

Alonso Seoane, María José, 251n65

Alphonse XIII, 43

Álvarez Mendizábal, Juan, 35, 95,
253n86

Amann, Elizabeth, 155–56, 279n10, 279n14

Amar y Borbón, Josefa, 251n64

amplificatio, 214, 217, 291n53–54

anticlericalism, 2, 8, 10, 11, 34, 173, 243, 287n10, 288n16; Alas and, 155, 159; blasphemy and, 216–17; clergy deaths and, 196, 243; clericalism and, 11, 196, 248n8; contempt and, 217, 227; *matanza de los frailes* and, 35; pornography of violence and, 217; post-Franco period and, 291n57; Second Republic and, 196; sexual solicitation in confessional and, 164, 165, 178; Spanish Civil War and, 196, 199, 203, 231; Tragic Week and, 48; violence and, 215–17, 231

Arana, José Ramón, 206; *El cura de Almuniaced* and, 200

Aranda, conde de (Pedro Pablo Abarca de Bolea), 88

Aranguren, José Luis L., 37, 253n88

Araque, Blas María, 99, 119

Arboleya Martínez, Maximiliano, 161, 222

Arconada, Juan, 203

Arenal, Concepción, 12, 47, 136–37; as practical realist, 135, 139; *La beneficencia, la filantropía y la caridad* and, 133, 136; de Gérando and, 274n117; justice and, 114; novelistic approach, use of, 137; public opinion and, 129; Society of St. Vincent de Paul and, 133; *El Visitador del pobre* and, 133, 134, 136, 137

Ariès, Philippe, 185

Armada, Sabino de, 265n10

Artola, Miguel, 37

Astete, Gaspar, 162

Asturian Revolution of 1934, 203, 206, 256n135; clergy deaths in Turón and, 295n121

attritio, 181

Auerbach, Erich, 52

Augustine, Saint, 152, 163, 171, 183,
255n118, 285n95; *La Regenta* and, 183, 184, 187–88

authority, 13; belief and, 183; Blanco White and, 162; Church and, 46; confession and, 177, 179; narrative and, 176, 193; priest and, 172, 175, 183–84, 283n58; *La Regenta* and, 13, 163, 176, 192; revelation and, 177, 179, 192

Ayguals de Izco, Wenceslao (chap. 2), 12, 14, 35, 53, 150; anti-Carlism and, 100, 117; anticlericalism and, 96, 101, 104–5, 124; antislavery and, 117, 270n73; as progressive, 114, 252n79; as promoter/translator of *Uncle Tom's Cabin*, 270n73; associationism and, 112, 116; belief and, 119, 251n64; benefactor and, 116; brother Joaquín, death of, 99, 266n15; Catholicism and, 37; *Cornelia Bororquia* and, 97; History-Novel, creation of, 119–20; life of, 97–100; *La maravilla del siglo* and, 267n28, 272n101; *María, la hija de un jornalero* and, 12, 23, 51, 76, 95–98, 115–20, 266n19; *La marquesa de Bellaflor* and, 265n10; *matanza de los frailes*, literary use of, 35, 104–5; national novel and, 119, 270n79; philanthropic embrace and, 36, 96–97, 104, 112, 119–20, 243; politics of religion and, 12, 14, 97, 104, 119, 244; poor of London and Paris and, 272n101; *pueblo* and, 267n28; readership and, 112, 119–20; redemption and, 118, 120; *La Regenta* and, 266n20; religion of politics and, 12, 14, 97, 104, 119, 244; satire of humanitarian and, 265n9; social network and, 113, 116, 118; Sociedad Literaria and, 267n33; *El tigre del Maestrazgo* and, 97, 262n62, 266n17. *See also* Carlist Wars

Azaña, Manuel, 40, 51, 254n97; *El jardín de los frailes* and, 256n132; Second Republic and, 49–50, 196; view of Valera, 40

Bacon, Kathy, 248n18, 257n147
Bahamonde, Antonio, 201–2, 204, 232
Bahamonde Magro, Ángel, 277n158
Balmes, Jaume, 95, 114; philanthropy, attitude toward, 109; transition and, 274n124
Balzac, Honoré de, 123, 138; "improper," use of, 286n100; *La Maison Nucingen* and, 286n100
Baralt, Rafael María, 108, 111
Barbastro, 292n87
Baroja, Pío, 35; *matanza de los frailes,* literary use of, 35
Barriobero y Herrán, Eduardo, 265n9
Barthes, Roland, 181
Bartra, Agustí, 236
Bauer, Beth Wietelmann, 177
Beccaria, Cesare, 85, 263n92
Becker, Carl, 265n111
Beckett, Samuel, 170
Bécquer, Gustavo Adolfo, 185; *Los Borbones en pelota* and, 185
Bécquer, Valeriano, 185; *Los Borbones en pelota* and, 185
Belgian school war, 280n22
belief, 3–5, 19, 48, 237, 245, 253n82; Alas and, 1, 15, 152, 158–61; American Civil War and, 296n125; anarchists and, 199, 224; apparent death and, 72; Cervantes and, 4, 243; crisis and, 30, 41, 50, 52, 84, 157, 242; early modern Spain and, 27; Enlightenment and, 62; *El evangelio en triunfo* and, 67, 70, 240; identity and, 15; imagination and, 3–4, 206; in First Republic, 157; nineteenth century and, 240; novel and, 5–6, 18, 24, 26, 61; realism and, 5, 16, 54, 57, 60–61, 72, 150, 163, 197, 206, 237, 243, 245; *La Regenta* and, 183; relics and, 57–60, 75; religious realism and, 17; religious-social practices and, 156
benefactor: dictionary, appearance in, 110–11
beneficencia: dictionary, appearance in, 110

Bénichou, Paul, 7
Benítez, Rubén, 97
Benjamin, Walter, 236
Berdyaev, Nicolas, 193
Berger, Peter L., 248n17
Bernanos, Georges, 17, 205, 234
Bessie, Alvah, 201
Bilbao y Durán, Antonio, 89
Bismarck, Otto von, 8
Blanco, Víctor, 223, 224, 292n85
Blanco White, José, 161–62, 163
blasphemy, 216–17, 291n62; Claret campaign against, 291n62; Hemingway's use of, 291n62
Bobes Naves, María del Carmen, 178
Boheemen, Christine van, 168
Bolín, Luis, 200
Bonaparte, Joseph, 94
Bordas, Luis, 274n118
Borg, Marcus, 4
Borja, Francisco de, 182
Bourbon Restoration, 10, 42, 45; Alas and, 156; politics of religion, 46; *La Regenta* and 47, 190–91; religion and, 46
Bowers, Claude, 201, 205
Brademas, John, 199
Brenan, Gerald, 214
Brontë, Charlotte, 186; governess and, 186; *Jane Eyre* and, 186; orphan and, 186; *La Regenta* and, 186
Brooks, Peter, 167, 282n42
Brother Philippe (Philippe Bransiet), 172, 177, 181, 184
Brown, Marshall, 53
bulto, 82, 83, 85
Bunk, Brian D., 256n135, 288n22
Buñuel, Luis, 221; *Las Hurdes* and, 221
Bynum, Caroline Walker, 146, 235

Caballero Audaz, El. *See* Carretero, José María
Cabet, Étienne, 114
Cabeza, Felipa Máxima de, 284n79
Cabrera, Ramón, 99, 266n17

Cadalso, José (chap. 1), 10, 11, 15, 53, 80–81, 264n99; belief and, 11, 30, 80–81, 91, 242, 264n97; deism and, 80, 83; friendship and, 87, 264n99; humanitarianism and, 84–88, 90, 119, 128; imagination and, 22; *Noches lúgubres* and, 10, 51, 61, 64, 80–88, 90; secularist interpretation and, 90; stoicism and, 80, 265n110

Cádiz, Diego José de, 27

Calatayud, Pedro de, 27

Callahan, William, 28, 34, 35, 88

Calvo Sotelo, José, 50, 51, 210, 214

Cámara, Sixto, 114

Canalejas, Francisco de P., 41

Cánovas del Castillo, Antonio, 46, 158; Article 11 (Constitution) and, 46

Cansinos-Asséns, Rafael, 206

Cárcel de amor, 21

Carlist Wars, 11, 32, 34, 38, 41, 95; Ayguals de Izco and, 12, 36, 96, 99–100; Spanish Civil War and, 201

Carr, Raymond, 99

Carrera, Luis, 203

Carretero, José María (El Caballero Audaz) (chap. 4), 14, 15, 235, 240, 256n135; *amplificatio* and, 214; Ayguals de Izco and, 207; Biblical imagery and, 289n38; Cadalso and, 210; dead, obsession with, 208, 219; *Declaración de guerra* and, 50–51; imagery of "red" violence and, 290n51; life, 206–7; Nationalist ideology and, 221; *Nosotros los mártires* and, 212; politics of religion and, 198, 244; pornography of violence and, 214–15, 217; religion of politics and, 198, 244; *La revolución de los patibularios* and, 14, 51, 207; self-promoter, 207; Spanish Civil War and, 196; symbolic death and, 210, 220

Carrier, Jean-Baptiste, 68

Carroll, Lewis, 185

Casanova, M., 205

Casas, Bartolomé de las, 61

Cassirer, Ernst, 30, 80, 91

Castelar, Emilio, 38, 41, 50, 51, 239; associationism and, 112; belief in progress, 39; clerical hostility toward, 254n95; faith and, 280n23; Galdós and, 132, 272n94, 278n165; *La hermana de la caridad* and, 132–33, 137; Mazzini and, 254n93; *el rasgo* and, 147; redemption and, 132; rhetoric and, 254n95; transition and, 274n124; Valera and, 39–40

Castro, Américo, 54–55, 247n4, 254n100, 257n152, 258n153

Castro y Serrano, José, 129

Catalina, Severo, 265n10, 283n58

Catholic Church (Spanish), 5, 10–11, 19; disamortization and, 95; French anti-Enlightenment thought and, 252n71; French Revolution and, 31, 62, 252n71; hostility against, 34, 49, 93; in early modern Spain, 27; in eighteenth century, 27–28, 62, 94; modernity and, 158; Second Republic and, 49–50, 196, 199; social-economic crisis and, 28, 31, 33, 42, 45–46; Spanish Civil War and, 199; State and, 8, 31, 34, 35, 41, 42, 46; use of sacraments and, 173, 176, 228; war and, 32

Catholicism (American), 108–09

Catholicism (French), 43; apocalyptic tradition and, 43; de-Christianization, 68; revival and, 43

Catholicism (Spanish), 2, 5, 9–11; apocalyptic tradition and, 42–43, 50, 255n107; class and, 13, 48, 176, 256n128, 256n129; de-Christianization, 2, 63, 95, 173, 176, 199; devotional practices and, 27, 58, 63, 132, 173, 175; gender and, 13; glorification of, 221; humanitarianism and, 61; legacy of Francoism and, 295n124; liberals and, 33, 36–37, 39–40, 157–58, 174, 252n75, 252n80, 253n88; literature and, 238, 241; National Catholicism, 14, 23, 239; politicization and, 9, 13, 14, 36, 39, 46, 50; prophecies and, 42, 50; Protestant missions and, 253n88; regional differences and, 176; Spanish character and, 238

Catholic Revival (French), 141

Catholic Revival (Spanish), 11, 12, 43, 44–46, 47; Bourbon Restoration and, 156, 173, 175; catechism and, 173, 174; confessor and, 175; devotional literature and, 132; during Second Republic, 218, 219; emotionalism of, 45, 132, 174, 255n118; Eucharistic devotions and, 141, 173; Ezkioga visions and, 219, 221, 255n107; *Fortunata y Jacinta* and, 123; individualized devotionalism and, 132, 174, 175; missionary propaganda (1930s) and, 219; *La Regenta* and, 173–74; resacralization of Spain and, 48; women and, 47, 130, 132, 175, 256n123, 256n129

Caudet, Francisco, 273n106

Cela, Camilo José, 211

Celestina, 21, 54

Censura, La, 96, 97, 105

centurión, 294n110

Cervantes, Miguel de, 61, 64, 138, 239; Flaubert and, 153; Galdós and, 141; *El ingenioso hidalgo don Quijote de la Mancha* and, 3, 4, 21, 52, 54, 108, 247n4, 254n100; novel and, 168, 243; realism and, 3, 53, 123, 242, 243

Cervera, Antonio Ignacio, 269n55

Chacel, Rosa, 151

Chacón, Dulce, 236

Charcot, Jean-Martin, 165

charism, 146

charity, 28–29, 253n86, 265n10, 268n47, 272n99; beneficence and, 111; Bourbon Restoration and, 47; Church and, 28–29, 31, 36, 62, 94; as domestic virtue, 47; early Christianity and, 111; eighteenth century and, 28–29, 31; in *Fortunata y Jacinta,* 121; justice, relation to, 114; *Limosna* and,

273n109; Monlau and, 112–13; rural setting and, 118; urban setting and, 118

Charles III, 62, 66, 74, 188

Charles IV, 67

Charlton, D.G., 114

Charnon-Deutsch, Lou, 177

Chateaubriand, François-René de, 7; Augustine (St.) and, 184; Claret and, 184; *Génie du christianisme* and, 160; imagination and, 182, 184, 185; *Mémoires* and, 267n33; child, 170; orphan and, 186; philanthropy and, 147, 148–49; *La Regenta* and, 185–87; romantics and, 185; soul and, 185; stereotypes of, 185

Christian, William A., Jr., 255n107

Ciocci, Raffaele, 178–79

Clare of Assisi, Saint, 174

Claret, Antonio María, 132, 171, 173, 184, 190, 282n54; anti-blasphemy campaign and, 291n62; *Catecismo de la doctrina cristiana* and, 283n59; *Llave de oro* and, 184–85; *Réquiem por un campesino español* and, 234

Clarín. *See* Alas, Leopoldo

Clement of Ancyra, Saint, 291n53

clericalism. *See* anticlericalism

clientelism, 47, 136, 243; Ayguals de Izco and, 118; *Fortunata y Jacinta* and, 144, 148; novel and, 117, 118

Close, Anthony, 258n156

Coll i Vehí, Josep, 158

Coloma, Luis, 9, 15, 23; *Pequeñeces* and, 23

Communion (chap. 2), 3, 141, 230, 244; Alas and, 151; Arenal and, 135–36; in Asturias, 282n54; *El evangelio en triunfo* and, 71; *Fortunata y Jacinta* and, 12, 120, 123, 142–46, 149, 244; Galdós and, 151; de Gérando and, 134; *Lazarillo de Tormes* and, 53, 271n82; novel and, 3, 15; realism and, 124; Zambrano and, 55

community, 3–4, 18, 244, 245; confession and, 172; *Cornelia Bororquia*

community (*cont.*)
    and, 242; *El evangelio en triunfo* and,
    242; *Fortunata y Jacinta* and, 47, 120,
    145, 149, 151, 244; *María, la hija de
    un jornalero* and, 97, 115–16, 118;
    Noches lúgubres and, 242; novel and,
    3–4, 118; philanthropy and, 113, 135;
    La Regenta and, 13, 151, 193; *Ré-
    quiem por un campesino español* and,
    229; socially marginalized and, 53
Confederación Nacional de Trabajo
    (CNT), 218, 224, 225
confession (chap. 3), 13, 15, 244; anti-
    clerical attacks and, 173; Augustine
    (St.) and, 152; Blanco White and, 162;
    body and, 182; Ciocci and, 179; con-
    fessional box and, 171, 178, 282n42;
    confessors' handbooks and, 172; cul-
    tural strictures and, 179; as eroticized,
    165; as expulsion, 171, 172; family ro-
    mance and, 163, 170, 179, 190; Galdós
    and, 151; historical development, 172–
    73; image of toad and, 192; imagina-
    tion and, 182; juridical character, 172,
    173; *Lazarillo de Tormes* and, 152; as
    mandatory, 171; as metanarrative,
    177–78; narrative consciousness and,
    182–83; power and, 172, 284n77;
    power of the keys and, 172; *La Re-
    genta* and, 13, 151–53, 163, 170, 176–
    78, 183–84, 192, 244; *Réquiem por
    un campesino español* and, 227, 228,
    233; Rousseau and, 152; seal of, 178;
    sex and, 163, 164; as tribunal of pen-
    ance, 172. *See also* authority
Confessional Unmasked, The, 178
Constitution of 1869, 42, 46, 256n122
Constitution of 1876, 42, 46, 156; re-
    ligious tolerance and, 158
contemptus mundi, 87, 263n85
corte celestial de María, La, 174,
    255n118, 285n95
Cortes de Cádiz, 10, 32, 33, 94
Cos y Macho, José María de, 174; model
    for Fermín de Pas, 175

Council of Trent, 83, 141, 171
Covadonga, 44
Covarrubias, Sebastián de, 107, 110
crusade, 14; imagery of, 14; mentality of,
    94; Nationalists and, 205; Republicans
    and, 205; Spanish Civil War and, 202,
    205
Cruz, Ángela de la (Angelita Guerrero),
    256n129, 277n158
Cruz, Anne, 257n147
Cruz, Juan de la, 27
Cubillas Donyague, Francisco de, 87
cult of the dead, 208, 219
cursilería, 156, 248n18, 257n147

Dante, 17
Darst, David H., 247n4
Daudet, Alphonse, 164; Alas and, 164;
    L'Évangéliste and, 164
dead body, 58–60, 85, 86, 88; autopsy
    and, 138; baroque disillusionment and,
    83; belief and, 84; pornography of vio-
    lence and, 215, 217; *La Regenta* and,
    167, 192; relics and, 60, 83; resurrec-
    tion and, 60, 61, 86; Second Republic
    and, 222; Spanish Civil War and, 210,
    215
Delaprée, Louis, 204
Delehaye, Hippolyte, 212–13, 291n53
Delumeau, Jean, 286n111
Descartes, René, 22
Desmaisières, María Micaela (St. María
    Micaela del Santísimo Sacramento), 142
Díaz-Pérez, Nicólas, 254n93
Diccionario de Autoridades, 107,
    263n82
Diccionario de galicismos, 108
Dickens, Charles, 123, 129, 185; *David
    Copperfield* and, 185
Diderot, Denis, 67, 138
Diederich, Bettina, 281n30
difunta pleiteada, 263n79
Doctrina christiana, 63
Dominicales del Libre Pensamiento, Las,
    164

Donoso Cortés, Juan, 109–10, 114; class warfare and, 110, 115; defender of Catholicism, 110; St. Vincent de Paul Society and, 110, 133
double, 59; *Noches lúgubres* and, 84–85; *das unheimliche* and, 59
Druzbicki, Gaspar, 172
duende, 59
Dufour, Gérard, 248n18, 253n88, 261n53
Dunn, Peter N., 257nn145–46
Dupanloup, Félix-Antoine-Philibert, 8
Duprat, Catherine, 108
Durán i Bas, Manuel, 158
Durkheim, Émile, 17, 26, 50, 242, 245

Eire, Carlos, 295n117
Ellis, Havelock, 165
Enlightenment (chap. 1), 4, 7, 10, 11, 16; France and, 62; imagination and, 24; paternalism and, 89; religion and, 28, 91, 94; religious tolerance and, 30, 111, 252n72; secularization and, 64, 90–91, 262n71; social equality and, 87; Spain and, 55, 64
ente, 82, 83, 263n82
Eoff, Sherman, 123, 278n164
Época, La, 126
Erasmianism, 10, 21, 24, 27, 240
españoles pintados por sí mismos, Los, 126
Espartero, Baldomero, 106
Espronceda, José de, 252n79, 253n84
Esquilache riots, 88
Estremera, José, 165
Eucharist. *See* Communion
evangelical. *See* Gospel
examination of conscience, 163, 180–82; autobiographical act and, 184; family romance and, 179; imagination and, 180; *La Regenta* and, 167, 169, 171–72, 175, 177, 179, 181, 183; spiritual exercises and, 180
Ezkioga, 219, 221

Faber, Frederick William, 148–49
fantasmagorías, 263n79
Feijoo, Benito Jerónimo, 22, 62
Feliu y Codina, José, 165
Ferdinand VII, 10, 32, 34, 94, 95
Fernán Caballero, 9, 239; charity and, 109; *Lucas García* and, 109
Fernández, Gregorio, 58–60, 75, 258n1
Fernández de Eyzaguirre, Sebastián, 87
Fernández y González, Manuel, 28n22
Fernsworth, Laurence, 201
Ferrándiz Ruiz, José. *See* Miralta, Constancio
Ferraz Martínez, Antonio, 259n15
Ferrer, Francisco, 257n136
Ferreras, Juan Ignacio, 261n53
Feuerbach, Ludwig, 3, 16, 17
filantropía: dictionary, appearance in, 268n39
fin del mundo, El, 42
First Republic, 156–57
Flaubert, Gustave, 123, 153, 154, 193; *Madame Bovary* and, 126, 128–29, 153, 155, 241; redemption and, 155
Fontenelle, Bernard de, 22
Forner, Juan Pablo, 21
fossors, 264n94
Foucauldianism, 5, 6, 45, 113, 122, 123, 241, 271n88, 275n140
Foucault, Michel, 5–6, 122–23, 169; *Discipline and Punish* and, 123; sexual discourses and, 167
Fouilloux, Étienne, 8
Fourier, François, 114
Fourth Lateran Council, 141, 171
Foxá, Agustín de, 214, 256n132
Franco, Francisco, 33, 55, 204, 237; "anti-Spain" and, 200; Covadonga and, 44; dictatorship and, 8, 238, 241; faith and, 197; National Catholicism and, 14, 23; National Movement and, 195; Nationalist commemorations and, 213; Spanish Civil War and, 44, 50, 205, 208–9; supporters of, 14, 201, 212

Fraternidad, La, 114
Frazer, James, 16
Freud, Sigmund, 17, 72, 83; family romance and, 163, 170; female children, view of, 190; governess and, 189; neurotic relics and, 17, 159; novel and, 168; *La Regenta* and, 168, 189, 191; *das unheimliche* and, 59
Fuentelapeña, Antonio de, 82
Fuentes Peris, Teresa, 122, 271n86, 271n88

Garagorri, Paulino, 254n100
Garcés, Antonio, 27
García, Francisco, 253n84
García Lorca, Federico, 59, 204, 239
Garmendia de Otaola, Antonio, 23
Garrido, Fernando, 114, 254n93
Gaskell, Elizabeth, 26; *North and South* and, 26, 115
Gauguin, Paul, 8
Gavilán, Marcelino, 266n10
Geertz, Clifford, 54
Generation of 1898, 240
Gérando, Joseph-Marie de, 12, 136, 137, 149; Galdós and, 135; novelistic approach, use of, 134–35, 137; self-education books, author of, 116; translations and, 274n118; *The Visitor of the Poor* and, 115, 134–35
Gérard, Philippe-Louis, 250n45, 252n71
Gil de Zárate, Antonio, 253n84, 253n86, 266n23
Giménez Caballero, Ernesto, 208, 235; dead, obsession with, 208, 219; *Genio de España* and, 208
Giner de los Ríos, Francisco, 158, 272n99; as spiritual director, 283n62
Ginger, Andrew, 253n88
Glendinning, Nigel, 80, 263n79, 263n92
Godoy, Manuel de, 31
Goethe, Johann Wolfgang von, 91
Goldman, Peter, 99
Gomá y Tomás, Isidro, 196, 203, 216
Gómez de Avellaneda, Gertrudis, 175

González, Román Miguel, 254n90
González Vázquez, Francisco, 281n35
Gospel, 29, 30, 38, 50, 249n21; anticlericals and, 199; Arenal and, 133; Carlists and, 118; *Cornelia Bororquia* and, 76, 78, 80, 91; *El evangelio en triunfo* and, 66, 67, 72–73, 91; *Fortunata y Jacinta* and, 93; Galdós and, 125; Lamennais and, 114; *María, la hija de un jornalero* and, 93, 105, 118, 119; *Réquiem por un campesino español* and, 198, 222
Graf, E.C., 83, 247n4
Granada, Luis de, 7, 87
Greeley, Andrew, 19–20, 52, 249n40
Greene, Graham, 17
Guardón Gallardo, Federico, 288n22
Güell, Eusebio, 173
Gunn, Giles, 18–19, 247n4
Gutiérrez, Luis (chap. 1), 11, 29, 64, 76–77; belief and, 30–31, 91; Cadalso and, 78, 80, 81; *Cornelia Bororquia o la víctima de la Inquisición* and, 11, 76–80, 118, 261n53; humanitarianism and, 61; Olavide and, 80; *La Regenta* and, 79; tolerance, advocate of, 76, 78, 80

Hafter, Monroe Z., 262n71
Haliczer, Stephen, 281n34
Hanna, Edward, 172
Hartzenbusch, Juan Eugenio, 108
Heartney, Eleanor, 20, 249n40
Hegel, G. W. F., 16
Hemingway, Ernest, 205, 291n62
Herbert, Mary Elizabeth, 133
Herrero, Javier, 255n109
Hick, John, 17
Higgin, L[etitia], 277n157
Hill, Octavia, 136
Hitchens, Christopher, 17
holy war. *See* crusade
Homza, Lu Ann, 284n77
Hughey, John David, 256n122
Hugo, Victor, 12

humanitarian, 261n43

humanitarian democracy, 37–38, 106, 254n90, 267n25

humanitarianism. *See* philanthropy

humanitarian narrative, 61, 119, 138, 242, 268n35

humanitario: dictionary, appearance in, 108. *See* philanthropy

humanitas Christi, 146

Huysmans, Joris-Karl, 26, 179, 182; *À rebours* and, 26; *En route* and, 179

Hyde, Lewis, 147

Iarocci, Michael, 90, 293n98

Ibáñez, María Ignacia, 81

Ife, Barry, 21

Illich, Ivan, 182

Ilustración Católica, La, 129

Ilustración Española y Americana, La, 129

imagination, 5; art and, 8; as body of sin, 163, 167; body and, 181, 182, 191–92; Catholicism and, 19–20, 25, 52; childhood and, 170, 182, 185–87, 192; confession and, 163, 170, 184; Eucharist and, 141; fantasy and, 21; gender and, 22; improper birth and, 170, 193; Loyola and, 20; maternal and, 187; narrative movement and, 169; novel and, 5, 15, 22, 23, 24–25, 242, 245, 271n88; philanthropy and, 6, 148; religion and, 8, 13, 242; Revolution of 1868 and, 25; romances of chivalry and, 21; sacred and, 194; self-examination and, 163

imitatio, 156

indifferentism, 279n16

Inquisition, 10, 30, 31, 32, 62, 252n72; Beccaria and, 264n92; Blanco White and, 162; confession and, 152; *Cornelia Bororquia* and, 77, 79; Cortes and, 94; culture of guilt and, 183; denunciations made to, 165; *Lazarillo de Tormes* and, 257n144; Olavide and, 66–67, 76, 240

Iriarte, Tomás de, 80

Isabel I, 191

Isabel II, 32, 41, 100, 147, 171

Isla, José Francisco de, 21–22, 28, 62, 64, 263n82

Ivens, Joris, 221; *The Spanish Earth* and, 221

Jaén, Manuel de, 176–77

James, Henry, 6

Janet, Pierre, 165

Jansenists, 252n72

Jeremias, 172

Jiménez Lozano, José, 240, 252nn75–76; *El sambenito* and, 259n20

Jovellanos, Gaspar Melchor de, 29, 62

joya de la niñez, La, 267n33

Joyce, James, 168

Jung, Carl, 170

Kant, Immanuel, 16, 41

Kempis, Thomas à, 156, 280n24

Krause, Karl Christian Friedrich, 158

Krausism, 158–59, 160, 280n21

Kulturkampf, 8

Labanyi, Jo, 271n88, 277n157, 295n123

Lacalzada de Mateo, María José, 274n117

Lacan, Jacques, 183, 188, 189; Teresa de Jesús and, 188

Ladrón de Guevara, Pablo, 23, 25, 124

Lagarrigue, Juan Enrique, 278n163

Lamennais, Félicité de, 33, 34, 37, 114; influence on Spanish liberals, 252n79; liberal Catholicism and, 38; *Paroles d'un croyant* and, 33, 35, 223

Lamourette, Antoine Adrien, 64, 260n39; *Les Délices de la religion* and, 64, 65–66, 70

Langdon-Davies, John, 280n19

La Parra López, Emilio, 253n82, 253n88

Laqueur, Thomas, 61, 169

La Rochefoucauld-Liancourt, François-Alexandre-Frédéric, 74

Larra, Mariano José de, 32, 33–34, 253n84; as *costumbrista* writer, 108; Carretero and, 210, 213; crisis and, 32; "Día de difuntos de 1836" and, 210; Lamennais and, 33, 35, 252n79; as liberal Catholic, 37, 253n82

Lazarillo de Tormes, 53–54, 152, 173, 257nn144–46, 258n156; *caso* and, 152, 164, 173

Lazarus, 53, 257n145

Legrand du Saulle, Henri, 165

Leiva, Juan, 281n35

Leo XIII, 47, 222; *Rerum Novarum* and, 47, 222, 270n69

Levinas, Emmanuel, 3

Lewis, C.S., 2, 3, 17, 18, 56

Lewis, Matthew, 103

Lewis, Pericles, 6

Lezama, A. de, 199

liberalism, 24; novel and, 24–25; religion and, 32, 33

Liguori, Alphonsus, 27

Lincoln, Bruce, 215

Lisón-Tolosana, Carmelo, 225

Lissorgues, Yvan, 34, 248n18

living dead, 71, 260n37

Llorente, Juan Antonio, 253n88

Locke, John, 261n51

Longares Alonso, Jesús, 269n54

Longinus, 291n54

López, Claudio, 173

López Bago, Eduardo, 164, 165, 178; *El confesonario* and, 164; *El cura* and, 164

López Peláez, Antolín, 22, 24, 25

Lorenzana, Francisco Antonio, 31

Loreto, 187–89

Louis XVI, 31

Loyola, Ignacio de, 20, 27, 180, 239; Alberti and, 293n103; *composición viendo el lugar* and, 180; *Ejercicios espirituales* and, 180–81, 182; imagination and, 180–81, 184, 229–30; Machado and, 293n103; Pérez de Ayala and, 293n103; *La Regenta* and,

181, 229; *Réquiem por un campesino español* and, 229–30

Lukács, Georg, 52

Lyotard, Jean-François, 163, 171

Madrazo, Pedro de, 133

Malón de Chaide, Pedro, 21

Mañé y Flaquer, Juan, 158

Manuel de Villena, Ernestina, 47, 129, 277n158; charity activism and, 133; model for Guillermina Pacheco, 47, 129; relation to religious revival, 130, 132; St. Vincent de Paul Society and, 133

Mapplethorpe, Robert, 20

Marchena, José, 32, 86, 251n68

Maresca, Mariano, 287n114

Marí, Jorge, 228

María Cristina, 95

Marin, Louis, 141

Maritain, Jacques, 17, 204–5, 289n28; on just war, 204–5

Martínez, Francisco, 203

Martínez, Martín, 81

Martínez Izquierdo, Narciso, 266n10

Martínez Vigil, Ramón, 44

Martyrdom (chap. 4), 14, 15; amplification and, 291n53; anarchists and, 51, 225, 256n136; Asturian Revolution of 1934 and, 288n22; Calvo Sotelo and, 210; Catholic culture and, 204; CNT and, 225; *Cornelia Bororquia* and, 79; *Counter-Attack in Spain* and, 220; *El cura de Almuniaced* and, 206; Jesuit art and, 204; martyrology literature, 288n22; narrative and, 197; Nationalists and, 197, 203, 213; places of, 236; politics of, 14, 198; *praesentia* and, 236; protomartyr and, 210; Republicans and, 204, 236; *Réquiem por un campesino español* and, 198, 206, 222, 223, 226, 227–35; *La revolución de los patibularios* and, 198, 207, 210–13, 234; saints and, 212–14; Spanish Civil War and, 202–3; symbolism of land and, 221; of things, 200, 216, 231, 232; tragic love and, 288n22. *See also* crusade

Marx, Karl, 17

Mary (Virgin), 42, 44, 132, 160, 174, 188; as sound vessel, 188; Immaculate Conception and, 188; litanies and, 188, 279n16; local feelings toward, 286n98; Loreto and, 188; visions of, 219

Masarnau, Santiago, 133

matanza de los frailes, 35, 38, 95, 253n84; urban militiamen and, 253n84

Maura, Antonio, 273n109

Maximin of La Salette, 42

Mayhew, Henry, 107

Mazzini, Joseph, 38, 39; associationism and, 112; influence on "Young Spain," 254n93

McDermott, Patricia, 198

McKim-Smith, Gridley, 58

Mélanie of La Salette, 42

Meléndez Valdés, Juan, 29, 81, 88–89

Mendizábal, Alfred, 204

Menéndez Pelayo, Marcelino, 37, 65, 238, 240, 251n65, 253n84, 256n122, 261n53; father of, 273n115

Mesonero Romanos, Ramón de, 108

Michelet, Jules, 50, 51, 175

Milá y Fontanals, Manuel, 133

Miralta, Constancio (José Ferrándiz Ruiz), 164, 165, 178, 281n34; *Los secretos de la confesión* and, 164, 173; *misterios,* 107

Mitchell, Timothy, 248n18

Monasterio, Jesús, 133

Monlau, Pere Felip: associationism and, 113; as democrat, 269n43; *Elementos de higiene pública* and, 107; *Higiene industrial* and, 113; as humanitarian, 107, 111–13, 117; as liberal Catholic, 111, 252n79, 269n61; as progressive, 114; *Remedios del pauperismo* and, 107, 111; *rurizar* and, 270n77; social

network and, 113; working classes and, 113, 118

Montaigne, Michel de, 264n99

Montero Moreno, Antonio, 203, 212, 216, 287n4

Montoya, Nicolás, 281n35

Mora, Francisco, 294n108

Moreno Nieto, E., 126

Morphy, Michel, 281n34

Mos y Rosa, Manuel, 42

Motín, El, 164

Mundo Obrero, 205

Murillo, Bartolomé Esteban, 188

Naharro, Vicente, 33

National Militia, 99, 253n84; Ayguals de Izco and, 99

Nationalist Irish Christian Front, 203

Navarrete, Ramón de (Asmodeo), 106–7, 115, 119, 268nn35–36; as society columnist, 107; *La Época* and, 107; social network and, 113

Navarro Villoslada, Francisco, 110; *El Ante-Cristo* and, 267n24

Náxera, P., 192

Nickerson, Susan D., 274n118

Nicolás, Antonio de, 180

Nietzsche, Friedrich, 16–17

numinous, 16, 18, 159

Núñez de Arce, Gaspar, 45

Nussbaum, Martha C., 249n37

O'Connor, Flannery, 244

Olavide, Pablo de (chap. 1), 11, 12, 29, 53, 240, 261n55; belief and, 30, 67, 70, 91, 240, 242, 259n20; Cadalso and, 81; *El evangelio en triunfo* and, 11, 30, 64–76, 79, 251n65, 259n16, 259n18; French Revolution, impact of, 67–68, 76; Galdós and, 265n116; Gutiérrez and, 77; influence on Catholic novelists and, 259n15; Inquisition and, 66–67, 76, 259n20; Lamourette and, 64; model village, use of, 118; philanthropy and, 30, 61, 64–76, 119;

Olavide, Pablo de (chap. 1) (*cont.*)
  redemption and, 65, 72, 74, 117, 244;
  reform projects and, 65, 66, 74, 89, 90
Organización del Trabajo, La, 114
Origen, 171
original sin, 13, 153, 175, 188, 278n6;
  Immaculate Conception of the Virgin
  and, 154, 188–89; *La Regenta* and,
  13, 153, 163, 183, 189; *Réquiem por
  un campesino español* and, 227
orphan, 2, 129, 136; novel and, 168,
  189, 191; *La Regenta* and, 153, 170,
  171, 185–87, 189–91; Restoration
  family and, 191
Ortega y Gasset, José, 54, 254n100
Ortiz-Echagüe, José, 221
Ossó, Enrique de, 45, 280n24; *El cuarto
  de hora de oración* and, 283n59; *La
  Regenta* and, 286n111; Teresa de Jesús
  and, 45, 286n111
Otto, Rudolf, 16, 159
Ozanam, Frédéric, 133

P.V. (Pablo Villada?), 173, 279n16
Palacio Valdés, Armando, 40–41
Palafox y Mendoza, Juan, 63
Palma, Luis de la, 182, 284n79, 286n108
Palmaroli, Vicente, 165
Pardo Bazán, Emilia, 117, 175, 283n58
Paris Commune, 42, 43
Parker, Alexander A., 296n6
Paul, Saint, 29, 183, 234
Payne, Stanley, 176, 202, 256n135
Peabody, Elizabeth, 274n118
Peckham, Morse, 287n113
Pedraza, Juan de, 173
Peers, Allison, 296n6
Peiró, Francisco, 222
Pemán, José María, 214
Pereda, José María de, 9, 15, 239;
  Galdós, friend of, 121, 124
Pereira Muro, Carmen, 258n152
Perera, Arturo, 164, 165; *La confesión
  de un confesor* and, 164, 173
Pérez, Dionisio, 256n132

Pérez de Ayala, Ramón: *A.M.D.G.* and,
  254n95, 256n132, 284n72
Pérez Galdós, Benito (chap. 2), 3, 6, 9,
  15, 19, 25, 53, 245; Alas and, 271n88;
  Ángel Guerra and, 271n91; associationism and, 112; Ayguals de Izco and,
  265n6; beggars and, 125–26; belief
  and, 124, 239; Castelar and, 132,
  272n94; character development and,
  117; charity in, 271n91; Christianity
  and, 125; *La desheredada* and, 126;
  Doña Perfecta and, 125; *Electra* and,
  48; *La familia de León Roch* and, 244;
  Fortunata y Jacinta and, 3, 12–13, 23,
  24, 47, 76, 120–21, 139–50; *Gloria*
  and, 244; *Halma* and, 271n91; imagination and, 137, 271n91; knowledge
  of Bible and, 276n143; Lagarrigue
  and, 278n163; *Marianela* and, 125,
  126, 271n91; *matanza de los frailes,*
  literary use of, 35; *Misericordia* and,
  125, 126, 271n91; *Nazarín* and, 126,
  239, 271n91; Olavide and, 265n116;
  philanthropy and, 119, 120, 122, 128,
  243, 277n157; poverty and, 125; redemption and, 13, 120, 132, 150, 153,
  244; serial novel, importance of, 96;
  social network and, 113; social reform
  and, 47–48
Pérez Gutiérrez, Francisco, 40, 124,
  248n18
Pérez de Urbel, Justo, 203–4, 212
Peterson, Anna, 14, 198
philanthropy, 6, 10, 11, 85, 237, 243,
  249n21, 265n10, 268n47, 274n125;
  antislavery and, 117, 270n73; Arenal
  and, 135–36; in Asturias, 268n47; attitude toward, 109; child and, 147, 148–
  49; class warfare and, 115; clientelism
  and, 47; culture of poverty and,
  277n158; death and, 89, 90; democrat,
  relation to, 104; dictionary, appearance in, 107–8; Enlightenment
  and, 61, 73–74, 84–85, 88, 91–92; *El
  evangelio en triunfo* and, 72–75, 106,

138; female solidarity and, 149; *Fortunata y Jacinta* and, 12, 47, 122, 136, 139–40, 144, 147–50, 237; Foucault and, 113, 122–23; French Revolution, association with, 108; fundraising and, 129; de Gérando and, 135; history and, 119; imagination and, 148; in pre-revolutionary France, 108; justice, relation to, 115; *Madrid y nuestro siglo* and, 106–7; *María, la hija de un jornalero* and, 105, 106, 138, 237; *Noches lúgubres* and, 84, 138, 237; poor and, 72–76, 79, 85, 88–89, 90, 92, 118, 133–37, 139; *La Regenta* and, 268n47; religion and, 114; resurrection and, 90; socialist utopian thinkers and, 106. *See also* charity

Philip II, 60, 188, 240

Philip III, 58

picaresque, 53–54, 61, 64, 138; inquisitorial mindset and, 152. *See also* *Lazarillo de Tormes*

Pico della Mirandola, Giovan Francesco, 20

Picón, Jacinto Octavio, 175

Pidal, Alejandro, 158

Pius IX, 24, 154; *Syllabus of Errors* and, 24, 157

Pi y Molist, Emilio, 138

Plato, 21, 22

pobres de solemnidad, 88

Poema de Mío Cid, 54, 258n152

Pope, Randolph, 86

Portero Molina, José Antonio, 252n80

Prieto, Indalecio, 229

Primo de Rivera, Miguel, 49, 206, 208

Promey, Sally, 7

Proust, Marcel, 6

pueblo, 267n28

Puente, Luis de la, 20, 184

Quadrado, José María, 133

Queipo de Llano, Gonzalo, 201, 204

Quevedo, Francisco de, 87, 103

Radcliffe, Ann, 103

rasgo, 147

Rawlings, Helen, 27

realism, 3, 16, 52–56, 245, 257n152; Arenal and, 135, 137, 150; Carretero and, 225; Cervantine uncertainty and, 243; crisis of modernity and, 16, 19, 55, 198, 225–26, 236, 242, 245; eighteenth century and, 61; Foucauldianism and, 241, 271n88; de Gérando and, 135, 137, 150; hostility toward, 241; images of birth and, 168; neighborliness and, 3, 242, 245; non-secular values and, 206; philosophy of religion and, 17; redemption and, 137, 150, 244; romanticism and, 79; sacred and, 5, 51, 52, 53, 135, 142, 242; Sender and, 225. *See also* belief

Regler, Gustav, 205

relic (chap. 1), 11; *amplificatio* and, 214; anticlerical violence and, 217; *Cornelia Bororquia* and, 76, 80, 92, 234; dead body and, 235; *El evangelio en triunfo* and, 75, 92, 139, 234; *Fortunata y Jacinta* and, 49, 234; land and, 221; *María, la hija de un jornalero* and, 234; martyr and, 235; mummified nuns and, 219; neurosis and, 17; *Noches lúgubres* and, 11, 83, 87, 92, 139, 234; *potentia* and, 235, 237; *La Regenta* and, 234; *Réquiem por un campesino español* and, 49, 234, 235; resurrection and, 235, 295n117; *La revolución de los patibularios* and, 234. *See also* sacred

religion, 6–7; as cultural system, 18; as feeling, 16; as residual, 54, 163, 257n147; camp and, 155–56; conversion and, 249n21; decline of Christianity, 295n124; Foucauldianism and, 5; imagination and, 15, 18–20, 163, 245; in Great Britain, 6, 10; in Mexico, 218; modernity and, 2, 8–10, 11, 16, 19, 64, 65, 198, 225–26, 236, 242, 245; religion of humanity, 278n163;

religion (*cont.*)

La revolución de los patibularios and, 212; saintliness and, 248n18; theories of, 16–17, 26

Renan, Ernest, 157

Resina, Joan Ramon, 279n9

resurrection, 14; Arenal and, 137; civil war and, 51, 204; *Cornelia Bororquia* and, 76; dead body and, 138, 146, 235; early Christian ideas of, 235; *El evangelio en triunfo* and, 65, 70, 71–72, 82; exhumations of Republican mass graves and, 295n123; Ezkioga visions and, 221; *Fortunata y Jacinta* and, 146; *Genio de España* and, 208; de Gérando and, 137; human body and, 235; humanitarianism and, 61, 85, 89, 90; land and, 221; *María, la hija de un jornalero* and, 116, 117; *Noches lúgubres* and, 82, 83, 85; past and, 88; Republican exiles and, 236; *Réquiem por un campesino español* and, 198, 206, 220, 226, 228, 230; *La revolución de los patibularios* and, 198, 208–9, 210, 217; storytelling and, 236; theme of, 14, 15

revenant, 82

Revolution of 1868, 25, 41; Alas and, 156, 161

Ribadeneyra, Pedro de, 239

Ribot i Fontseré, Antonio, 252n79, 270n79

Richmond, Carolyn, 176

Ripalda, Jerónimo de, 33, 162, 267n33

Rivas, Manuel, 236

Robert, Marthe, 168

Rodríguez de Figueroa, Luis, 239

Rogers, Douglass, 122

Rose, Hugh James, 156–57

Rousseau, Jean Jacques, 152, 153

Rubió i Ors, Joaquim, 133

sacrament of sensibility, 19–20

sacred, 7, 16, 87, 244; childhood and, 185–86; Church and, 215–16; deport-ment and, 284n79; *Fortunata y Jacinta* and, 149; Francoist resacralization and, 237; history and, 198; human body and, 60, 138, 190, 192, 212–14; human personality, relation to, 123, 143, 233; imagination and, 194; land and, 221; *Lazarillo de Tormes* and, 53–54; literature and, 7; *María, la hija de un jornalero* and, 104; maternal and, 189, 190; narrative consciousness and, 177, 182, 191; nineteenth-century Spain and, 252n76; *Noches lúgubres* and, 90; novel and, 138, 142, 176, 197, 245; places and, 219, 236; poor and, 53, 73, 75–76, 89, 92, 135, 251n66, 278n165; pornography and, 215, 217; *praesentia* and, 236, 237; *La Regenta* and, 155, 176, 177, 182–83; *Réquiem por un campesino español* and, 222, 223, 225, 226, 231, 236; revelation and, 176; *La revolución de los patibularios* and, 214, 236; romantics and, 7. *See also* relic

Sacred Heart, 27, 174; France and, 43; Spain and, 43–44, 141

Sagasta, Práxedes, 45

Sagra, Ramón de la, 114, 115; *Antonio y Rita* and, 118

Saint-Simon, Henri de, 114

Sales, Francis de, 27, 87

Salinas, Pedro, 54, 257n152

Salvany, Juan Tomás, 165

Sánchez, Pedro Antonio, 86

Sánchez-Eppler, Benigno, 179

sanctus pauper, 53, 73, 75, 89, 135

Sand, George, 12

santos evangelios, Los, 267n33

Sanz y Forés, Benito, 44, 174, 268n47, 282n54

Sardá y Salvany, Félix, 24, 157–58, 202, 240, 280n19; *El liberalismo es pecado* and, 24, 158

Sarrailh, Jean, 29, 64, 251n65

Sartre, Jean-Paul, 287n112; *La Regenta* and, 287n112

Sayol y Echevarría, José: *Eucologio romano* and, 283n59

Scarry, Elaine, 3

sculpture (polychrome), 57–60

Sebold, Russell, 76, 261n55

Second Republic, 2, 8, 10; anticlerical measures and, 49, 156, 218, 256n132; apocalyptic atmosphere of, 50, 195, 256n135; *bienes de señorío* and, 223; Catholics and, 196; local and, 236

secularization, 5, 8, 64; clash with religion, 9; land reform and, 221; modernity and, 10, 197, 221; Popular Front, 201; process of, 33; realism and, 55, 197; theory of, 6, 197

Segni, Lothario dei (Innocent III), 263n85

self-examination. *See* examination of conscience

Sender, Ramón J. (chap. 4), 6, 9, 14, 15, 19, 20, 245; Alcolea de Cinca and, 292n87; as anarchist, 218, 224; as anticlerical, 199, 218–19, 222; belief and, 217–18, 235; brother's death, 218, 295n120; Casas Viejas, account of, 218; Church, attitude toward, 222; *Counter-Attack in Spain* and, 219–22; history, use of, 223–25; life, 217–18; Loyolan imagination, 21; martyr narrative and, 197, 220; poetic theology and, 222, 235; political beliefs and, 218; redemption and, 222, 235, 244; *Réquiem por un campesino español* and, 14, 51, 200, 217–18, 222–37; 292n84; shoemaker figure, use of, 294n108; *Siete domingos rojos* and, 218; Spanish Civil War and, 196, 202, 218; symbolic death and, 220; symbolism of land and, 220–21; trip to Soviet Union, 218; wife's death, 218

Sensfelder, M., 294n108

Serrano, Andrés, 20

Shaw, Rafael, 48–49, 256n128

Sieber, Harry, 271n82

Silva, José, 223–24

Silvela, Francisco, 45

Silverman, Debora, 8

Simpson, Eileen, 187, 190

Sisters of Charity, 28, 132–33; Arenal and, 133

skandalon, 165

Slater, Candace, 294n108

Smiles, Samuel, 115, 116, 294n108; benefactor and, 116

Smith, Adam, 85, 86, 264n97

Smith, Alan, 271n91

Smith, Bonnie, 256n123

Smith, Graeme, 248n16

Society of Jesus, 41, 218, 239

Soubirous, Bernadette, 188

Souchy Bauer, Agustín, 292n87

Spain, 2; anarchists in, 48, 51, 199, 201, 205, 215, 218, 223–24, 226; as alternative to West's crisis, 258n153; confessional state, 2, 35, 243; Franco regime, 239–40, 241; Irish in, 63; pan-Europeanism and, 255n109; pauperization and, 88; political-social crisis, 41, 89, 226, 237, 242, 251n57, 256n128, 274n124; religious crisis, 5, 41, 114, 243; requiem masses for Nationalists, 293n96

Spanish Civil War (chap. 4), 10, 11, 55, 195–237; American Civil War and, 295n122; apocalyptic atmosphere of, 50, 195, 256n135; as religious conflict, 195–96, 225; atrocities and, 200–2, 214–17, 234, 288n19; Basque clergy and, 205; Carlists and, 202–3; clergy deaths and, 196, 201–2, 216, 243, 287n4, 292n87; collectivization and, 223–24; demonization and, 195, 200; Nationalist repression and, 234

spiritual dryness, 280n24

St. Vincent de Paul Society, 74, 133, 174; Donoso Cortés and, 110; Menéndez Pelayo's father and, 273n115; in Spain, 133

Stein, Gertrude, 155

Stern, J.P., 149

Stoichita, Victor I., 284n79
Sue, Eugène: Ayguals de Izco and, 12, 117, 267n24; Jesuits and, 267n24; *Les Mystères de Paris* and, 36, 96, 103–4, 108; Navarrete and, 268n35; readership and, 112
summa de casibus, 173
Surwillo, Lisa, 270n73
sympathy, 86–87, 90

Talavera, Hernando de, 171, 191, 286n107
Tambling, Jeremy, 172
Tenorio, José María, 269n56
Teresa de Jesús, Saint, 27, 70; Bernini and, 188; Catholic Revival and, 45, 255n119; Lacan and, 188; *La Regenta* and, 45, 181
Tertullian, 203, 235
Thrower, James, 16, 17
Tierno Galván, Enrique, 119, 255n101, 256n122
Tracy, David, 249n40
Tragic Week (Barcelona), 48, 216, 257n136
transubstantiation, 142
Tuckerman, Joseph, 115, 135; de Gérando and, 274n121
Tylor, Edward, 16

Ugarte, R.V., 23, 24
Unamuno, Miguel de, 19, 151, 239, 245, 296n12; *homo religiosus* and, 240; "Mi religión" and, 26; *San Manuel Bueno, mártir* and, 26
Uriz, Joaquín de, 89

Valbuena Prat, Ángel, 238–40, 242, 296n6; dossier and, 296n6; faith and, 240, 296n7; Olavide and, 240
Valera, Juan, 39–41, 50, 254n100, 255n101; Castelar and, 39; faith and, 40–41; rejection of social Catholicism, 39

Valle, Francisca Javiera del, 256n129, 280n24
van Gogh, Vincent, 8
Vapor, El, 114
Varela, Javier, 248n8, 280n21
Vatican Council of 1869–70, 161
Vega, Ventura de la, 253n84
Velázquez, Diego, 188
verdaderos pobres, 88
Verheyden, Jack, 17
Villaverde Uría, Mercedes, 175, 283n59
Vincent, Mary, 215, 216, 287n4
Vived Mairel, Jesús, 226
Vives, Juan Luis, 21, 28–29
Voltaire, 7, 110, 153

Ward, Bernardo, 88, 89, 90, 264n104
Wardropper, Bruce, 83
Warhol, Andy, 20
Warner, Marina, 189
Warnock, Mary, 287n112
wars of the dead, 15, 51, 198, 215, 218, 219, 236, 295n122
Weber, Max, 52
Weil, Simone, 159
Whiston, James, 121
Williams, Raymond, 73, 108, 261n43
Wines, Frederick, 114–15
Wiseman, Nicholas, 35–36, 253n85
Woolf, Stuart, 136
Woolsey, Gamel, 214–15; Carretero and, 215; pornography of violence and, 214

Young, Edward, 81

Zambrano, María, 54–55, 257n152, 258n153
Zavala, Iris, 97, 99
Zola, Émile, 26
Zurbarán, Francisco de, 188
Zurbitu, Demetrio, 287n4
Zurriago, El, 268n45

pp. 2: Spain, a confessional state (until advent of Second Republic)

Guillermina Pacheco: pp. 12-13

p. 196

pp. 150, 151

p. 181

p. 243. Cervantine uncertainty